THE PAPERS OF ULYSSES S. GRANT

THE PAPERS OF

ULYSSES S. GRANT

Volume 6:

September 1 – December 8, 1862

Edited by John Y. Simon

SOUTHERN ILLINOIS UNIVERSITY PRESS

CARBONDALE AND EDWARDSVILLE

FEFFER & SIMONS, INC.

LONDON AND AMSTERDAM

Library of Congress Cataloging in Publication Data

Grant, Ulysses Simpson, Pres. U.S., 1822–1885.
   The papers of Ulysses S. Grant.

   Prepared under the auspices of the Ulysses S. Grant Association.
Includes bibliographical references and index.
   CONTENTS: v. 1. 1837–1861.—v. 2. April–September 1861.
—v. 3. October 1, 1861–January 7, 1862.—v. 4. January 8–March 31,
1862.—v. 5. April 1–August 31, 1862.—v. 6. September 1–December 8, 1862.
   1. Grant, Ulysses, Simpson, Pres. U.S., 1822–1885. I. Simon,
John Y., ed. II. Ulysses S. Grant Association.
E660.G75   973.8'2'0924   67–10725
ISBN 0-8093-0694-8 (v. 6)

93784

To E. B. Long

Contents

―――

List of Maps and Illustrations   xii

Introduction   xiii

Editorial Procedure   xvi

Chronology   xxi

The Papers of Ulysses S. Grant, September 1–
     December 8, 1862   3

Calendar   415

Index   461

Maps and Illustrations

MAP

Major Operations of Grant's Command in late 1862   14–15

ILLUSTRATIONS

Frontispiece

Maj. Gen. Ulysses S. Grant

between pages 32–33

U. S. Grant. Portrait by S. B. Waugh
U. S. Grant. Portrait by James Reid Lambdin
Henry W. Halleck. Portrait by James Reid Lambdin
William T. Sherman. Portrait by James Reid Lambdin

Introduction

In the closing months of 1862, Major General Ulysses S. Grant regained the initiative in military operations which he had lost after the battle of Shiloh in April when Major General Henry W. Halleck had taken personal command of the army. After Halleck was called to Washington in July, Grant inherited independence of command, accompanied by responsibility for maintaining U.S. control over rebellious territory between the Tennessee and Mississippi rivers from northern Mississippi to the Ohio River. He had to protect miles of river, railroad, and telegraph with a force steadily diminished by demands to send troops eastward in anticipation of Confederate General Braxton Bragg's drive into Kentucky.

In fact, Grant was so effectively immobilized by circumstance that only his opponents could free him. This they obligingly did. General Sterling Price had the good fortune to occupy the eastern end of Grant's defensive line at Iuka, Mississippi, with large quantities of valuable supplies, just as Grant was pulling back toward Corinth, Mississippi, to consolidate. Price could easily have crossed the Tennessee River to join Bragg, but instead remained pointlessly in Iuka. Grant planned an elaborate pincers attack, with Brigadier General William S. Rosecrans approaching by the two roads which ran south of Iuka, while Major General Edward O. C. Ord launched the major attack from the northwest. U.S. plans disintegrated: Rosecrans attacked from the south while Ord waited, and Rosecrans covered only one of the two roads. Yet, even though he let Price's army escape, Rosecrans did so much damage that it no longer posed an offensive threat. While Price had awaited attack at Iuka, President Jefferson Davis telegraphed to Bragg: "Telegrams from Tennessee and Mississippi indicate a want of co-intelligence and co-operation among the generals of the several columns. . . . disaster to all must be the probable result." The Confederate solution was to appoint Major General Earl Van Dorn to overall command of the troops in Mississippi. Not to be outdone by Price in miscalculating risks, Van Dorn threw his army against the fortifications at Corinth early in October, with equally disastrous results. Grant was now free to set his sights on Vicksburg.

Late in October, Grant assumed command of the Department of the Tennessee, gaining belated recognition that he was something more than Halleck's caretaker, and also receiving assurances of reinforcements. Although Grant had requested reinforcements on the basis of a threat by the Confederates to the vital railroad center of Corinth, he planned to use his increased force for a major offensive southward on the line of the Mississippi Central Railroad from Grand Junction, Tennessee, halfway through Mississippi to compel the evacuation of Vicksburg. On November 2, the army moved, and within five weeks had advanced nearly to Grenada, halfway to Vicksburg, where Grant's offensive halted.

Two outside factors stopped the offensive. First, Grant had expected major assistance from Brigadier General Frederick Steele's army in Arkansas, but the small cavalry force which had easily advanced close to Grenada had then withdrawn. Second, Halleck's original willingness to send reinforcements had been connected with his hope of forestalling the ambitious plans of Major General John A. McClernand, who had received permission from President Abraham Lincoln to recruit an army in the Midwest to lead down the Mississippi River to Vicksburg; Halleck preferred to send the new regiments to Grant, forestalling McClernand. Once Grant learned of McClernand's impending arrival at Memphis to assume command, he hurried Major General William T. Sherman back to Memphis, with some of the troops he had brought with him, to launch the expedition before McClernand arrived.

Once Grant lost his momentum, the tide turned. Van Dorn launched a cavalry raid which captured and ravaged the major supply base at Holly Springs, Mississippi, while Brigadier General Nathan B. Forrest crossed the Tennessee River to cut lines even farther north. At the end of December, Sherman's force launched a premature attack on Vicksburg at Chickasaw Bayou which was repelled with heavy losses. The Confederate cavalry forced Grant to withdraw his army northward, while Sherman's failure to capture Vicksburg eventually forced Grant to take personal command of the Mississippi River expedition, which otherwise would have been commanded by McClernand.

As the U.S. Army penetrated deeper into the plantation South in late 1862, two problems encountered earlier increased in intensity. Thousands of slaves fled to the Union lines with immediate needs for food and shelter. Grant responded with a relief program tied to the labor needs of his army, administered by Chaplain John Eaton. Grant was less successful in coping with ambitious fortune-hunters who followed his army to purchase cotton, and the result was General Orders No. 11, December 17, 1862, his notorious expulsion of Jews, which will be discussed at length in the note to the document.

At the same time, Grant encountered important problems with his commanders. In addition to the obvious threat of the ambitious McClernand, Grant quarrelled with Rosecrans, whose victories at Iuka and Corinth made him a rival, and only the timely transfer of Rosecrans to independent command averted a major confrontation. Through late 1862, Grant placed heavy reliance on Sherman, but Sherman had written privately on September 25 that Halleck was "the only real Great man thus far. McClellan is next.—All others are Mediocre." If elements of Grant's eventual success can now be discerned in 1862 through hindsight, even contemporaries who knew him best still had doubts.

We are indebted to W. Neil Franklin and Karl L. Trever for searching the National Archives; to Barbara Long for maps; to M. Elaine Cook, Harriet Simon, and Susan Stover for typing; to Janet Bridges, David W. Smith, and Karine Tyrrell, graduate students at Southern Illinois University, for research assistance; and to David L. Wilson, graduate student at the University of Tennessee, for research assistance.

Financial support for the Ulysses S. Grant Association for the period during which this volume was prepared came from Southern Illinois University and the National Historical Publications Commission.

JOHN Y. SIMON

January 28, 1974

Editorial Procedure

===

1. Editorial Insertions

A. Words or letters in roman type within brackets represent editorial reconstruction of parts of manuscripts torn, mutilated, or illegible.

B. [. . .] or [— — —] within brackets represent lost material which cannot be reconstructed. The number of dots represents the approximate number of lost letters; dashes represent lost words.

C. Words in *italic* type within brackets represent material such as dates which were not part of the original manuscript.

D. Other material crossed out is indicated by ~~cancelled type~~.

E. Material raised in manuscript, as "4th," has been brought in line, as "4th."

2. Symbols Used to Describe Manuscripts

AD	Autograph Document
ADS	Autograph Document Signed
ADf	Autograph Draft
ADfS	Autograph Draft Signed
AES	Autograph Endorsement Signed
AL	Autograph Letter
ALS	Autograph Letter Signed
ANS	Autograph Note Signed
D	Document
DS	Document Signed

Df	Draft
DfS	Draft Signed
ES	Endorsement Signed
LS	Letter Signed

3. Military Terms and Abbreviations

Act.	Acting
Adjt.	Adjutant
AG	Adjutant General
AGO	Adjutant General's Office
Art.	Artillery
Asst.	Assistant
Bvt.	Brevet
Brig.	Brigadier
Capt.	Captain
Cav.	Cavalry
Col.	Colonel
Co.	Company
C.S.A.	Confederate States of America
Dept.	Department
Gen.	General
Hd. Qrs.	Headquarters
Inf.	Infantry
Lt.	Lieutenant
Maj.	Major
Q. M.	Quartermaster
Regt.	Regiment or regimental
Sgt.	Sergeant
USMA	United States Military Academy, West Point, N.Y.
Vols.	Volunteers

4. Short Titles and Abbreviations

ABPC	*American Book-Prices Current* (New York, 1895–)
CG	*Congressional Globe* Numbers following represent the Congress, session, and page.

J. G. Cramer	Jesse Grant Cramer, ed., *Letters of Ulysses S. Grant to his Father and his Youngest Sister, 1857–78* (New York and London, 1912)
DAB	*Dictionary of American Biography* (New York, 1928–36)
Garland	Hamlin Garland, *Ulysses S. Grant: His Life and Character* (New York, 1898)
HED	*House Executive Documents*
HMD	*House Miscellaneous Documents*
HRC	*House Reports of Committees* Numbers following *HED, HMD,* or *HRC* represent the number of the Congress, the session, and the document.
Ill. AG Report	J. N. Reece, ed., *Report of the Adjutant General of the State of Illinois* (Springfield, 1900)
Lewis	Lloyd Lewis, *Captain Sam Grant* (Boston, 1950)
Lincoln, Works	Roy P. Basler, Marion Dolores Pratt, and Lloyd A. Dunlap, eds., *The Collected Works of Abraham Lincoln* (New Brunswick, 1953–55)
Memoirs	*Personal Memoirs of U. S. Grant* (New York, 1885–86)
O.R.	*The War of the Rebellion: A Compilation of the Official Records of the Union and Confederate Armies* (Washington, 1880–1901)
O.R. (Navy)	*Official Records of the Union and Confederate Navies in the War of the Rebellion* (Washington, 1894–1927) Roman numerals following *O.R.* or *O.R.* (Navy) represent the series and the volume.
PUSG	John Y. Simon, ed., *The Papers of Ulysses S. Grant* (Carbondale and Edwardsville, 1967–)
Richardson	Albert D. Richardson, *A Personal History of Ulysses S. Grant* (Hartford, Conn., 1868)
SED	*Senate Executive Documents*
SMD	*Senate Miscellaneous Documents*
SRC	*Senate Reports of Committees* Numbers following *SED, SMD,* or *SRC* represent the number of the Congress, the session, and the document.
USGA Newsletter	*Ulysses S. Grant Association Newsletter*
Young	John Russell Young, *Around the World with General Grant* (New York, 1879)

5. *Location Symbols*

CLU	University of California at Los Angeles, Los Angeles, Calif.
CoHi	Colorado State Historical Society, Denver, Colo.
CSmH	Henry E. Huntington Library, San Marino, Calif.
CU-B	Bancroft Library, University of California, Berkeley, Calif.
DLC	Library of Congress, Washington, D.C. Numbers following DLC-USG represent the series and volume of military records in the USG papers.
DNA	National Archives, Washington, D.C. Additional numbers identify record groups.
IaHA	Iowa State Department of History and Archives, Des Moines, Iowa
I-ar	Illinois State Archives, Springfield, Ill.
IC	Chicago Public Library, Chicago, Ill.
ICarbS	Southern Illinois University, Carbondale, Ill.
ICHi	Chicago Historical Society, Chicago, Ill.
ICN	Newberry Library, Chicago, Ill.
IHi	Illinois State Historical Library, Springfield, Ill.
In	Indiana State Library, Indianapolis, Ind.
InHi	Indiana Historical Society, Indianapolis, Ind.
InNd	University of Notre Dame, Notre Dame, Ind.
InU	Indiana University, Bloomington, Ind.
KHi	Kansas State Historical Society, Topeka, Kan.
MH	Harvard University, Cambridge, Mass.
MHi	Massachusetts Historical Society, Boston, Mass.
MiD	Detroit Public Library, Detroit, Mich.
MiU-C	William L. Clements Library, University of Michigan, Ann Arbor, Mich.
MoSHi	Missouri Historical Society, St. Louis, Mo.
NHi	New-York Historical Society, New York, N.Y.
NIC	Cornell University, Ithaca, N.Y.
NjP	Princeton University, Princeton, N.J.
NjR	Rutgers University, New Brunswick, N.J.
NN	New York Public Library, New York, N.Y.
NNP	Pierpont Morgan Library, New York, N.Y.

OClWHi	Western Reserve Historical Society, Cleveland, Ohio.
OFH	Rutherford B. Hayes Library, Fremont, Ohio.
OHi	Ohio Historical Society, Columbus, Ohio.
OrHi	Oregon Historical Society, Portland, Ore.
PHi	Historical Society of Pennsylvania, Philadelphia, Pa.
PPRF	Rosenbach Foundation, Philadelphia, Pa.
RPB	Brown University, Providence, R.I.
TxHR	Rice University, Houston, Tex.
USG 3	Maj. Gen. Ulysses S. Grant 3rd, Clinton, N.Y.
USMA	United States Military Academy Library, West Point, N.Y.
ViU	University of Virginia, Charlottesville, Va.
WHi	State Historical Society of Wisconsin, Madison, Wis.

Chronology

SEPTEMBER 1–DECEMBER 8, 1862

SEPT. 1. C.S.A. Act. Brig. Gen. Frank C. Armstrong concluded his cav. raid on USG's forces with a skirmish at Britton's Lane, near Denmark, Tenn.

SEPT. 2. Maj. Gen. Henry W. Halleck ordered USG to send the division of Brig. Gen. Gordon Granger to Louisville, Ky.

SEPT. 2. USG ordered the division of Brig. Gen. Stephen A. Hurlbut to move from Memphis, Tenn., to Bolivar, Tenn.

SEPT. 2. Maj. Gen. George B. McClellan was restored to command of the Army of the Potomac.

SEPT. 13. Col. Robert C. Murphy retreated from Iuka, Miss., abandoning extensive supplies to Maj. Gen. Sterling Price.

SEPT. 15. Following the battle at South Mountain the previous day, C.S.A. forces captured Harper's Ferry, Va.

SEPT. 16. USG began to move his troops toward Iuka.

SEPT. 17. Battle of Antietam, Md.

SEPT. 18. USG moved to Burnsville, Miss., to coordinate the attack on Iuka.

SEPT. 19. Brig. Gen. William S. Rosecrans attacked Iuka from the south. U.S. forces were successful despite the failure of Maj. Gen. Edward O. C. Ord to carry through a coordinated attack from the north.

SEPT. 20. Price evacuated Iuka, escaping on an uncovered road leading south.

SEPT. 22. President Abraham Lincoln issued the preliminary Emancipation Proclamation.

SEPT. 24. USG left for St. Louis, Mo., to confer with Maj. Gen. Samuel R. Curtis.

SEPT. 26. USG's hd. qrs. were moved to Jackson, Tenn.

SEPT. 27. USG in Columbus, Ky.

SEPT. 30. USG returned to Corinth, Miss.

OCT. 1. USG learned that C.S.A. Maj. Gen. Earl Van Dorn had moved to threaten either Bolivar or Corinth.

OCT. 3–4. Van Dorn attacked Rosecrans at Corinth, and was repulsed with heavy losses on both days.

OCT. 3. USG ordered Hurlbut to advance from Bolivar to block Van Dorn's retreat. Maj. Gen. James B. McPherson reinforced Corinth from Bethel, Tenn.

OCT. 5. Van Dorn's army, in retreat from Corinth, was mauled at Hatchie (Davis's) Bridge, Tenn., by Hurlbut's forces commanded by Ord.

OCT. 7. USG ordered Rosecrans to cease his pursuit of Van Dorn. Rosecrans's resentment of the order marked the onset of steadily deteriorating relations with USG.

OCT. 8. Lincoln congratulated USG on his recent victories.

OCT. 8. Maj. Gen. Don Carlos Buell fought C.S.A. Gen. Braxton Bragg at Perryville, Ky. After an inconclusive battle, Bragg withdrew, ending his invasion of Ky.

OCT. 14. C.S.A. Lt. Gen. John C. Pemberton assumed command of the Dept. of Miss. and East La., coordinating the forces opposed to USG.

OCT. 16. USG was assigned command of the Dept. of the Tenn., which extended from Cairo, Ill., to northern Miss., bounded by the Tennessee and Mississippi rivers.

OCT. 20. Lincoln authorized Maj. Gen. John A. McClernand to organize troops for an expedition against Vicksburg, Miss.

OCT. 23. Halleck ordered Rosecrans to Cincinnati, Ohio, where he received further orders to relieve Buell.

OCT. 25. USG assumed command of the Dept. of the Tenn.

OCT. 25. USG alerted his forces for another C.S.A. move on Bolivar or Corinth.

OCT. 26. USG asked Halleck for reinforcements, and proposed an advance down the Mississippi Central Railroad. Halleck promised the reinforcements on Oct. 27.

NOV. 4. USG occupied La Grange and Grand Junction, Tenn.

NOV. 4. Democrats gained in congressional and state elections.

NOV. 5. Halleck promised USG 20,000 additional men.

NOV. 5. Lincoln prepared orders relieving McClellan.

NOV. 10. USG asked Halleck whether he could command forces at Memphis assembled for McClernand. Halleck replied the next day that USG commanded all troops in his dept. and could "fight the enemy when you please."

NOV. 10. Maj. Gen. Ambrose E. Burnside replaced McClellan in command of the Army of the Potomac.

NOV. 12. USG prepared to order Hurlbut to Memphis.

NOV. 13. USG's cav. occupied Holly Springs, Miss.

NOV. 13. USG appointed Chaplain John Eaton, 27th Ohio, to take charge of fugitive slaves.

NOV. 14. USG ordered Maj. Gen. William T. Sherman to march from Memphis to join forces in Miss.

NOV. 19. USG sent cav. to Ripley, Miss.

NOV. 19. USG issued orders regulating trade in cotton.

NOV. 21. USG conferred with Sherman at Memphis.

NOV. 24. C.S.A. Gen. Joseph E. Johnston was assigned overall command in the West.

NOV. 28. USG left La Grange and spent the night at Lamar, Miss.

NOV. 29. USG advanced toward the Tallahatchie River, and established hd. qrs. at Holly Springs.

NOV. 30. USG arrested John C. Van Duzer, telegraph superintendent in his dept. On Dec. 5, under orders from Washington, he released Van Duzer and ordered him out of his dept.

DEC. 1. USG's cav. crossed the Tallahatchie River, and reached Oxford, Miss., the next day.

DEC. 1. USG's forces occupied Abbeville, Miss.

DEC. 4. USG occupied Oxford.

DEC. 5. USG's cav., under Col. T. Lyle Dickey, engaged C.S.A. forces at Coffeeville, Miss.

DEC. 8. USG decided to send Sherman to Memphis to launch an attack on Vicksburg on the Mississippi River.

The Papers of Ulysses S. Grant
September 1–December 8, 1862

To Brig. Gen. Lorenzo Thomas

Grants Hd Qrs [*Sept.*] 1st 10. a m [*1862*]

GENL THOMAS
A. GEL.
GENL.

Can I give Genl Oglesby leave of absence   he has recd an injury from the fall of his horse rendering him unfit to take the field

U. S. GRANT
Maj Genl

Telegram received, DNA, RG 94, Generals' Papers and Books, Telegrams Received by Gen. Halleck; *ibid.*, RG 107, Telegrams Received (Bound, Press). On Sept. 6, 1862, Maj. Gen. Henry W. Halleck telegraphed to USG. "If Genl Ogelsby is so injured as to unable to do duty you are authorised to send him home to assist in organizing new troops"   ALS (telegram sent), *ibid.*, Telegrams Collected (Bound); telegram received, *ibid.*, RG 393, Dept. of the Tenn., Telegrams Received. On Sept. 4, 1st Lt. Theodore S. Bowers had issued Special Orders No. 184 granting Brig. Gen. Richard J. Oglesby fifteen days absence owing to his disability. DS, *ibid.*, RG 94, Special Orders, District of West Tenn.; copies, *ibid.*, RG 393, USG Special Orders, DLC-USG, V, 15, 16, 82, 87.

On July 30, Oglesby had written to Maj. John A. Rawlins asking for a leave of absence for twenty days. ALS, Oglesby Papers, IHi. On July 31, Rawlins had disapproved the request. ES, *ibid.* On Aug. 1, Rawlins issued Special Orders No. 150. "Brig. Gen. R. J. Oglesby having been relieved from the command of the 2nd Division, Gen. Daviess having returned, will resume command of the Brigade formerly commanded by him." DS, DNA, RG 94, Special Orders, District of West Tenn.; copies, *ibid.*, RG 393, USG Special Orders; DLC-USG, V, 15, 16, 82, 87.

To Maj. Gen. Henry W. Halleck

Gen Grants Hd Qrs
[*Sept. 1, 1862*]

MAJ GEN H W. HALLECK
GEN IN CHIEF

Rebel Cavalry attacked our Bridge guard at Medon[1] yesterday—Guard held them at bay until reinforced when the Guerillas were repulsed leaving about fifty of their number on the field dead & wounded   Our loss two killed fifteen wounded   Much trouble may be expected on Rail road for next few days   We will be ready for them at all points

U. S. GRANT
Maj Genl

Telegram received, DNA, RG 94, Generals' Papers and Books, Telegrams Received by Gen. Halleck; copies, *ibid.*, RG 107, Telegrams Received in Cipher; *ibid.*, RG 393, USG Hd. Qrs. Correspondence; DLC-USG, V, 4, 5, 8, 9, 88. On Aug. 31, 1862, Brig. Gen. Leonard F. Ross, Jackson, telegraphed to USG. "About 15 min'ts after our train passed up this morning there was a force of (500) guerrillas attacked the road   telegraph wires are cut   I am sending out force to attack them & repair the road   a large force of cavalry is reported just crossing the hatchee at Brownsville & infantry is said to be following but this is doubtful"   Telegram received, DNA, RG 393, Dept. of the Mo., Telegrams Received. On the same day, Ross telegraphed to USG. "I sent out six companies of Infantry to clear the RR of guerrillas & on my return they found the guard at Medon surrounded by a force of cavalry & find it four 4 regts. There is sharp fighting going on now. I am sending reinforcements & expect a force which left Estorola this A M to come in upon their rear of the Attacking force"   Telegram received, *ibid.* Also on Aug. 31, Ross telegraphed to USG. "A scout just from Brownsville reports that rebels cavalry two thousand (2000) strong crossed the Hatchee at that point about sunrise this morning probably making for some point north of here   I have telegraphed Gen Dodge   It would be next to impossible to get a courier through to Bolivar tonight—"   Telegram received, *ibid.* On Sept. 1, Ross telegraphed to USG. "My R R guards at Medon held out though entirely surrounded by overwhelming numbers till reinforcements reached them & the rebels have been routed. We have lost 2 killed & 15 wounded   The Rebels have left about 50 killed & wounded on the field—"   Telegram received, *ibid.*

1. Medon, Tenn., about twelve miles south of Jackson, Tenn. After leaving Bolivar, C. S. A. Act. Brig. Gen. Frank C. Armstrong moved northward along the line of the Mississippi Central Railroad toward Medon.

To Maj. Gen. Henry W. Halleck

Gen Grant's Hd Qrs
5 30 P m [*Sept.*] 1 [*1862*]

GENL H W HALLECK
GENL IN CHF—

I am weak & threatened with present forces from Humboldt to Bolivar & at this point¹ would deem it very unsafe to spare any more troops except by abandoning Railroad east of Bear Creek²   In that case could send one Division from Tuscumbia or any point from there to Decatur. Would send Stanley's³ Division.

U. S. GRANT
M G C

Telegram received, DNA, RG 94, Generals' Papers and Books, Telegrams Received by Gen. Halleck; copies, *ibid.*, RG 107, Telegrams Received in Cipher; *ibid.*, RG 393, USG Hd. Qrs. Correspondence; DLC-USG, V, 4, 5, 7, 8, 9, 88. *O.R.*, I, xvii, part 2, 194.

1. At the same time that C. S. A. Act. Brig. Gen. Frank C. Armstrong was pushing northward into Tenn., he ordered Col. William C. Falkner and units of partisan rangers numbering about four hundred men to move in the direction of Chewalla, Tenn., about ten miles northwest of Corinth. *Ibid.*, p. 682. See telegram to Maj. Gen. Henry W. Halleck, Aug. 31, 1862. On Aug. 29, 1862, Brig. Gen. William S. Rosecrans telegraphed to Maj. John A. Rawlins. "I have the honor to state for the information of the comdg Gen that Gen Granger reports that faulkner with 11 companies left Ripley on the 24th went north through the woods in vicinity of Corinth spied about took 7 or 8 of our men straggling from there passed down by Kossuth & danville avoiding roads attempted to surprise cavalry camp at Rienzi which they supposed to be small & vacated   they however found their mistake & were pursued by our cavalry within five 5 miles of Ripley When night put an End to the chase they scattered in every direction   were treated as guerrillas wi[th] the exception of elven (11) who were brought in prisoners   we took 200 shot guns many pistols an indefinate number of hats one of which belonged to Col Wm C Faulkner & containd the muster roll of 2nd Regt 3d Brigade Miss Vols—The affair altogether appears to have been creditable to our troops   our scouts from the south report prices people moving southward except an Infantry force with four (4) pieces of Artillery at Guntown—one says those forces were going to Vicksburg intelligence having reached Jackson where our spy was a prisoner that the yankees with a fleet of eight (8) Gun boats & forty transports had landed at The mouth of the Yazoo   this is worthy of notice —scouts from northern alabama report the corn crop south of the russellville

valley as a failure for want of rain   two (2) suggestions are respectifully made
based upon information rec'd within the last few days   Kossuth ought to be
occupied as a look out by Cavalry from Corinth—Every rebel coming within our
lines with discharges from Price ought to be sent to alton or hung as as spy   in-
dubitable evidence shows this is one of Prices ways of getting information   warn
our cavalry and Infantry pickets that rebel cavalry now seldom travel roads except
perhaps a short distance in the wrong direction—"   Telegram received, DNA,
RG 393, Dept. of the Mo., Telegrams Received; copy, *ibid.*, Army of the Miss.,
Telegrams Sent. On Aug. 31, Brig. Gen. Gordon Granger telegraphed to USG.
"I have news from the Enemies lines   up to 8 oclock this A M no genaral
movemt is on foot   so far as I can learn armstrong is expected back at the end
of 10 days when his rations expire after which it is there   among the soldiers
there is to be a movement up this way   it is reported that timbers have been
brought up to repair the bridge over twenty mile creek—that armstrong started
with a heavy force of cavalry—strong pickets are extended out to 20 mile creek—
it is also reported that Buell is retreating towards Nashville & that all the troops
from chattanooga are going out after him under Bragg that heavey fighting is
going on at Richmond—That Price has from twenty five thousand (25000) to
thirty thousand 30000) men that the troops who attacked this camp are coming
in in sqads of three (3) & four 4 who reports ~~an~~ one (1) capt killed & a Great
many of their men missing   two deserters from the 2d Mich cavalry had arrived
there safely—"   Telegram received, *ibid.*, Dept. of the Mo., Telegrams Received. On the same day, Granger telegraphed to Rosecrans. "Two battallions
of my Cavalry found Enemies pickets on tear breeches creek 3½ oclock P M
today   are following them up   Citizens report a large rebel force 11 oclock A M
today—I suppose Cavalry—"   Telegram received, *ibid.* Later the same day,
Granger telegraphed to USG. "My last telegram should have read clear creek 7
miles east of Ripley instead of tear breeches creek north west of Kossuth—"
Telegram received, *ibid.* On Aug. 31, Granger telegraphed to USG. "From all
I could ascertain from prisoners & deserters I dont think bolivar was the real
point of their attack but some point north—Humboldt was the place mentioned
—I am disposed to think the move on Bolivar only a feint—"   Telegram received,
ibid. On Sept. 1, Brig. Gen. Grenville M. Dodge, Trenton, Tenn., about twelve
miles northwest of Humboldt, telegraphed to USG. "We are prepared at all
points for them & will do all in our power." Telegram received, *ibid.* On the
same day, Dodge telegraphed to USG. "The Rebel force that crossed the Hatchee
at Brownsville camped at Poplar corners on forked deer river last night   this is
about 12 miles from Humboldt southwest   I have no surplus force only enough
to guard road & hardly that effectively   all important bridges I have good block
houses & beleive my forces guarding them can hold their positions against any
Cavalry"   Telegram received, *ibid.*; copy, *ibid.*, Hd. Qrs., Central Division of
the Miss., Letters and Telegrams Sent. *O.R.*, I, xvii, part 2, 194. On Sept. 1,
Brig. Gen. Isaac F. Quinby telegraphed to USG. "I have given Col Webster all
of the 13th Wisconsin except one Co which is at Hickman   I have here 3 Co's
of regulars & six (6) co's of the 71st Ills 3 months all much reduced & the 76 Ills
raw with but 200 muskets altered Springfield. The 3 months men will not be
worth the expense of sending down. The 76th is good material but as yet would
be worthless in the field. Troops at this end of the road except those at Columbus
at the disposal of Gen Dodge can & will be ready to enable him to concentrate
should it be necessary   The country back of New Madrid is in a bad condition

overun with Guerrillas   I have been trying to send out an expedition to capture & dispose but am too weak. Shall I send forward the 76th. I would like to have an interview with you   will come down tomorrow or next day with your consent"   Telegram received, DNA, RG 393, Dept. of the Mo., Telegrams Received. On Sept. 2, Quinby telegraphed to USG. "Will you aid me in getting arms promptly for the 76th Ills   a cotton buyer says the rebels are moving up from Grand Junction towards Jackson along the R R repairing bridges on the R R. Thereby leaving out the unarmed men   my effective force after the 71st Ills leaves tomorrow morning does not exceed (300)   I wish to be prepared for any emergency—"   Telegram received, *ibid.* On the same day, Quinby telegraphed to USG. "I send company of the 71st to relieve those of 54 Ills Vols now at the little obion bridge & Moscow intending the latter to reinforce Gen Dodge—"   Telegram received, *ibid.*

On Sept. 2, Granger telegraphed to Rosecrans and USG. "Shall I make a grand raid to ripley salem Ruckersville—& C—"   Telegram received, *ibid.* On the same day, Rosecrans telegraphed to USG. "Rec'd your good news   Cant we manage to smash those fellows up or is Van Dorn there—I think we can work them into confidence and catch them—"   Telegram received, *ibid.*

On Sept. 1, Brig. Gen. Leonard F. Ross, Jackson, telegraphed to USG. "Bolivar is reported invested by Infantry from below so that I can draw no forces from there for pursuit   I can spare none from here   can you assist me—"   Telegram received, *ibid.* On Sept. 2, Ross telegraphed to USG. "Was my dispatch of yesterday Evening received asking for aid"   Telegram received, *ibid.* On Sept. 3, Ross telegraphed to USG. "one of genl Armstrong body guard a Pennsylvania boy by birth is just in. he reports that he left the rebel force five thousand strong at Estinola on the hatchie River early yesterday morning crossing south   men & horses wore out by their late marches exposure & want of food—They lost heavily in their few different engaagemts with our troops— he thinks they are going to Holly springs to recruit it & states that when they left guntown Ten days ago Price was expected to move from Tupello in bolivar with thirty thousand (30000) infantry. & attack it on one side while Armstrongs force made demonstrations on the other & that their last fight south of Bolivar was unexpected to them as they merely intended to drive in our pickets & pass around the place & come in north of it   he seems intelligent & honest—"   Telegram received, *ibid.* On Sept. 2, Brig. Gen. James B. McPherson telegraphed to USG. "Can I get guns to arm my employees in the machine shop at Jackson   I have about 80 men   capt McCormick fifty second (52d Ind vols will command the men & be responsible for the arms   the engine goes back this afternoon & I would like to send them up—"   Telegram received, *ibid.*

2. On Aug. 31, Maj. Gen. Henry W. Halleck telegraphed to USG. "Could you send any more troops into Tenn or Ky east of the Cumberland, if so without risking your own positions? If so, from what points can you best spare them." ALS (telegram sent), *ibid.*, RG 107, Telegrams Collected (Bound); telegram received, *ibid.*, RG 393, Dept. of the Tenn., Telegrams Received. *O.R.*, I, xvii, part 2, 194. On Sept. 2, Halleck telegraphed to USG. "R Road east of Corinth may be abandoned & Grander's Division sent to Louisville, Ky. with all possible dispatch"   ALS (telegram sent), DNA, RG 107, Telegrams Collected (Bound); telegrams received (all garbled), *ibid.*, RG 393, Dept. of the Tenn., Telegrams Received. *O.R.*, I, xvii, part 2, 194. See telegram to Maj. Gen. Henry W. Halleck, Sept. 3, 1862.

On Sept. 1, Rosecrans telegraphed to USG. "That regt is merely a hospital guard it may go to Danville but that will only releive the mackeriel brigade leaving those two reg'ts still at Rienzi. I will order Gen Hamilton to releive the onion brigade by the 56th Ills I must think it would be better to let the Rebels involve themselves if they will in Tennessee & hold what forces we can spare to throw on their rear. Is the Telegraph correct about 2 regts or is it 2 Co's." Telegram received, DNA, RG 393, Dept. of the Mo., Telegrams Received. On Sept. 2, Rosecrans telegraphed to USG. "Brand Stout detailed from the 25th Ills & serving here in same capacity has deserted & the circumstances show a bad case for him he can & will probably will tell everything he knows about our lines—We must change them right away you will not send Grangers cavalry will you—Your dispatch rec'd I have ordered Stanly to prepare at once with secrecy & dispatch to remove his troops to this place & instructed not to loose a pound of anything to cover the movement by an apparent advance south westwards towards Fulton—similar directions have been given the cavalry under Misner it will require 4 or 5 days to perfect this—Please tell me when the Kentucky affair took place—" Telegram received, *ibid.*; copy, *ibid.*, Army of the Miss., Telegrams Sent. *O.R.*, I, xvii, part 2, 196–97. Rosecrans's copy says "Brand scout" instead of "Brand Stout." On the same day, Rosecrans telegraphed to USG. "Your dispatches & rec'd orders given accordingly one brigade will cover Iuka & points east—Tuscumbia must be held till the Team of two divisions & other public property are taken away—Iuka covers Eastport & is the surest way of our getting provisions it must be well held—Have ordered the Troops at Iuka to get ready to move & will move them as soon as they can be replaced—if that is a real attack on bolivar it will be good for us we must watch the front—Leave by hand car to get train at Barton—" Telegram received, DNA, RG 393, Dept. of the Mo., Telegrams Received. *O.R.*, I, xvii, part 2, 196. On Sept. 3, Rosecrans telegraphed to USG. "If we abandon this line it must be done with great deliberation we have a large Hospital here commissary stores both here & at Eastport Every thing on the front must appear if possible exceedingly stong & have an offensive look dont let Granger move till we are all right & our stores & sick cared for—Will be down to see you by cars this morning—" Telegram received, DNA, RG 393, Dept. of the Mo., Telegrams Received; copy, *ibid.*, Army of the Miss., Telegrams Sent. *O.R.*, I, xvii, part 2, 198.

3. David S. Stanley of Ohio, USMA 1852, reached the rank of capt. before the Civil War. He refused a C. S. A. command; was nominated Dec. 21, 1861, to be U.S. brig. gen. of vols.; and served in Mo. On April 24, 1862, he was assigned to command the 2nd Division, Army of the Miss., and served in the battles of New Madrid and Island No. 10 and in the siege of Corinth. *Ibid.*, I, x, part 2, 121.

To Maj. Gen. Henry W. Halleck

Gen Grants Hd Q'rs
Sept 2nd 1. P.M. [*1862*]

MAJ GEN H. W. HALLECK

GEN IN CHIEF—

Col Dennis[1] with from four 4 to five 5 Hundred (500) met Rebel Cavalry yesterday few miles west of Medon in superior force driving them & whipping them badly. The Enemy left one hundred & ten (110) dead on the field—wounded estimated at over two hundred & fifty (250). Our loss five (5) killed & forty (40) wounded—

U S GRANT
Maj Genl

Telegram received, DNA, RG 94, Generals' Papers and Books, Telegrams Received by Gen. Halleck; copies, *ibid.*, RG 393, USG Hd. Qrs. Correspondence; DLC-USG, V, 5, 7, 8, 9, 88. On Sept. 1, 1862, Brig. Gen. Leonard F. Ross, Jackson, telegraphed to USG. "Col Dennis' command while moving from Estinola to Medon this Moring as it seems misled by their guide drawn into an ambuscade & most of them captured after a short fight I have ordered (700) seven hundred men under Col Stevinson now at Medon to hasten to Tooks station united with forces from Bolivar there & pursue the Rebels force—is reported at 7 regts—" Telegram received, DNA, RG 393, Dept. of the Mo., Telegrams Received. On Sept. 2, Ross telegraphed to USG. "Col Dennis command all right hard fight yesterday & rebels completly routed. Dennis loosing 5 killed 40 wounded 110 Rebels left dead on the field & their wounded estimated 250 to 300—We are pursuing—" Telegram received, *ibid.*

After leaving Medon, Tenn., Act. Brig. Gen. Frank C. Armstrong marched his troops northwestward toward Denmark instead of northward on the railroad toward Jackson. Col. Elias S. Dennis, Estenaula, Tenn., had been ordered to Jackson, but upon hearing news of the attack on Medon, Col. Michael K. Lawler ordered him to Medon. By the evening of Aug. 31, Dennis's force had returned to Denmark, Tenn.; and on the morning of Sept. 1, began moving toward Medon. Upon contacting Armstrong's superior force on a road between Denmark and Medon called Britton Lane, Dennis assumed a defensive position on a small ridge, and through effective use of his art. was able to repulse Armstrong's force. Immediately thereafter, Armstrong retreated south toward the Hatchie River and returned to Miss. Harbert L. Rice Alexander, "The Armstrong Raid Including the Battles of Bolivar, Medon Station and Britton Lane," *Tennessee Historical Quarterly*, XXI, 1 (March, 1962), 39–44. *O.R.*, I, xvii, part 1, 49–52.

1. Elias S. Dennis of Ill. operated a gristmill, served in the Ill. legislature and as marshal in Kan. Territory before the war. He was mustered in on Aug. 28,

1861, as lt. col., 30th Ill. Commended for service in the battle of Fort Donelson, he was promoted to col. on April 22, 1862, and assumed command of the 30th Ill. on May 1.

To Brig. Gen. Leonard F. Ross

Headquarters, District of West T.
Corinth, September 2d, 1862.

Gen. L. F. Ross,
Com. U. S. Forces, Sub-District of Jackson.
General:—

Your dispatch by telegraph must have been sent subsequent to that by express. It puts a much more favorable aspect upon affairs and induced me to withhold the reinforcements I was attempting to send you from here.

This point, besides its importance, is very weak and should be reinforced rather than drawn from.

The rumors you have cannot all be true. It cannot be that Villapigue[1] has crossed at Brownsville,[2] and that from 6,000 to 8,000, or an investing force, is around Bolivar. Besides, if Villapigue should attempt a move, Sherman, who is watching him, would be in his rear in short order.

The last I heard of Villapigue his entire force only amounted to 6,000, all arms, besides some conscripts, who were being held by force of arms.

Sherman is instructed to send a division to Brownsville to co-operate with the Bolivar or Jackson forces, as circumstances may require.

My opinion is, that no large force threatens the line from Bolivar north, but it needs watching.

I have instructed Gen. Tuttle to reinforce you as soon as possible.[3]

Very respectfully,
Your obedient servant,
U. S. Grant, Major General.

"A Chapter of War History," *Iowa Historical Record*, I, 3 (July, 1886), 187–88. On Sept. 2, 1862, Brig. Gen. Leonard F. Ross wrote to USG. "I telegraphed you yesterday that Col Dennis command moving in from Estinola were surrounded by superior force of rebels. I sent him all the reinforcements I could spare & have not heard yet from the expedition. Bolivar is reported invested by a large force under Price—I can spare no force to assist them being threatened here by largely superior numbers. Col Crockers reports heavy force of enemy at Van Buren and Middleburg & rebel pickets within 4 miles of Bolivar—And has moved all his supplies within the fortifications—A force of rebels reported 6000 to 8000 strong encamped seven miles from here last night—Gen Villepigue is reported to have crossed the Hatchie near Brownsville night before last with infantry and artillery. Can you send me assistance. I send a locomotive with this dispatch being satisfied that telegrams between here and Corinth are intercepted by the enemy. Being doubtful of this reaching you I telegraph to Gen Tuttle to assist us if possible but have little expectation of help from there" ALS, DNA, RG 94, Letters Received. *O.R.*, I, xvii, part 2, 197. USG forwarded the letter to hd. qrs. of the army. ES, DNA, RG 94, Letters Received. On Sept. 2, Ross telegraphed to USG. "I have just heard from Crocker at Bolivar there are large bodies of the enemy at Middlebury & Van Buren reported under Price an attack on the place is expected Crocker feels confident of being able to repulse them our stores there are removed to the fortifications I have thrown up works with cotton for our defence here I would like much an addition to my force the enemy encamped within 7 miles of us last night reported six 6 to eight 8 thousand ~~strong~~ men—" Telegram received, *ibid.*, RG 393, Dept. of the Mo., Telegrams Received. On Sept. 3, Ross telegraphed to USG. "What time may we expect the reinforcements spoke of in your dispatch of last evening—" Telegram received, *ibid.*

1. John B. Villepigue of S. C., USMA 1854, served principally with the 2nd Dragoons and reached the rank of 1st lt. before resigning on March 31, 1861. Appointed C. S. A. capt. of art. and shortly thereafter col., 36th Ga., he was wounded in the defense of Fort McRee at Pensacola, Fla. Confirmed as brig. gen. on March 18, 1862, he served in the siege of Corinth, in the defense of Fort Pillow, and on June 24 was assigned to command along the line of the Mississippi Central Railroad from the Tallahatchie River southward to the thirty-third parallel. *O.R.*, I, xvii, part 2, 622.

2. Brownsville, Tenn., about twenty-two miles west of Jackson, Tenn.

3. On Sept. 2, Brig. Gen. James M. Tuttle, Cairo, telegraphed to USG. "Have Telegrams from Governors of Iowa & Ills that they are sending troops to StLouis how can they be got from there I have no more troops here that I can send Genl Ross I send one Reg't to Col Lowe this Evening—" Telegram received, DNA, RG 393, Dept. of the Mo., Telegrams Received. On Sept. 2, Tuttle telegraphed to USG. "Col Lowe is at Donelson waiting reinforcements I have one regt ready to move this evening—Shall I sent it to Lowe or Ross at Jackson." Telegram received, *ibid.* On Aug. 28, Col. William W. Lowe reported an attack on Fort Donelson. DLC-USG, V, 10; DNA, RG 393, USG Register of Letters Received. On Aug. 31, Tuttle telegraphed to USG. "Hon Washburn and Party not arrived yet. will convey your message. I this morning rec'd a dispatch from Col Lowe at Fort Henry that Morgan is advancing on donelson & he is forced to leave henry much weakened I could send him troops but they

have no arms   maj callender promised arms but was ordered by seccy of war to hold them. I will get them of Gov Yates tomorrow—" Telegram received, *ibid.*, Dept. of the Mo., Telegrams Received. On Sept. 2, Tuttle telegraphed to USG. "Steamer DesMoines City is here   nothing on board   am going to send her to Fort Henry this Evening with part of 83d Ills regt   balance of regt on another boat   Col Lowe telegraphs that he needs help—arms receved this morning for 3 regts   will have more here soon   have telegraphed to Governors of Ills & Iowa to send troops as soon as possible" Telegram received, *ibid.* On Sept. 3, Brig. Gen. John M. Schofield telegraphed to USG. "none of the new Regts yet arrived at St Louis or equipped for the field   may be possible to send you two regts next week." Telegram received, *ibid.* On Sept. 7, Tuttle telegraphed to USG. "I have sent seventy second 72d Reg't Col Starring to Paducah [&] smithland   those points are threatened—Regt 81 arrived here this a m   I need one regt here   gov Yates has promised to send another soon say a day or two will send to Gen Quinby as soon as they arrive—" Telegram received, *ibid.* On Sept. 8, Schofield telegraphed to USG. "I will dispose of the twenty first 21st mo as you request   hope it will come soon—" Telegram received, *ibid.*

To Maj. Gen. Henry W. Halleck

Gen Grants Had Qrs 12m
Sept 3rd [1862]

MAJ GEN H. W. HALLECK
GEN IN CHIEF.

Your dispatch for troops to go to Kentucky was received at 12. last night—Arrangements were immediately made to send some troops but your dispatch could not be made out where they were to go nor what route.[1] They will be sent as promptly as possible[2]   Bolivar has been surrounded [for] several days but I think can hold out.[3] Jackson was threatened [with] strong force of cavalry estimated at 4.000. I think however [only] four (4) Regiments. They were [badly] handled in our front again. [In] front of Bolivar three at Medon & at last four miles West from there where I reported over one hundred dead were left on the field. Reports now show that we buried 179 of the Enemy's dead. I understood that the whole country around the Scene of battle is a hospital for Rebel wounded. I have ordered one Division from Memphis to Brownsville & by concentrating the troops west of us at this place I can hold if that is important   I will do it at all hazards or be very badly beaten   I immediately telegraphed back for correction of your dispatch

U S GRANT
Maj Genl

Telegram received, DNA, RG 107, Telegrams Collected (Bound); copies, *ibid.*, RG 393, USG Hd. Qrs. Correspondence; DLC-USG, V, 4, 5, 7, 8, 9, 88. *O.R.*, I, xvii, part 2, 197.

1. USG's copies read "or what Division." See telegram to Maj. Gen. Henry W. Halleck, Sept. 1, 1862. On Sept. 4, 1862, Maj. Gen. Henry W. Halleck telegraphed to USG. "My telegram was to send Grangers division to Louisville, Ky. to form the basis for the new troops organizing there. Inform Genl Wright at Cincinnati of the progress of the movement & when they will reach him." ALS (telegram sent), DNA, RG 107, Telegrams Collected (Bound); copies, *ibid.*, RG 393, Dept. of the Tenn., Telegrams Received; *ibid.*, USG Hd. Qrs. Correspondence; DLC-USG, V, 4, 5, 7, 8, 9, 88. *O.R.*, I, xvii, part 2, 198. The decision to send Brig. Gen. Gordon Granger to Louisville, Ky., was apparently made following representations by Maj. Gen. Horatio G. Wright of the inability of raw recruits to defend northern Ky., and the disastrous defeat of troops under Maj. Gen. William Nelson near Richmond, Ky., about twenty miles southeast of Lexington. *Ibid.*, I, xvi, part 2, 447–48, 464–65, 469, 471–72. The movement into Ky. was part of a coordinated advance by Gen. Braxton Bragg from Chattanooga, Tenn., and by Maj. Gen. Edmund Kirby Smith from the Cumberland Gap region. Grady McWhiney, *Braxton Bragg and Confederate Defeat: Volume I, Field Command* (New York and London, 1969), pp. 272–83.

2. On Sept. 2, Brig. Gen. James B. McPherson, Corinth, telegraphed to USG. "Will have engine & 11 cars ready in 2 hours   can carry about 600 men—" Telegram received, DNA, RG 393, Dept. of the Mo., Telegrams Received.

3. On Sept. 4, Brig. Gen. Leonard F. Ross telegraphed to USG. "All is quiet at Bolivar   a force infantry & cavalry reported at Salisbury waiting arrival of Genl Price force   was looked for on Monday last   I am now waiting information   Genl Logan has prepared a force to take to Bolivar with me if needed Telegraph communication is now open to Bolivar & the RR will be repaired in 2 or 3 days—" Telegram received, *ibid.*

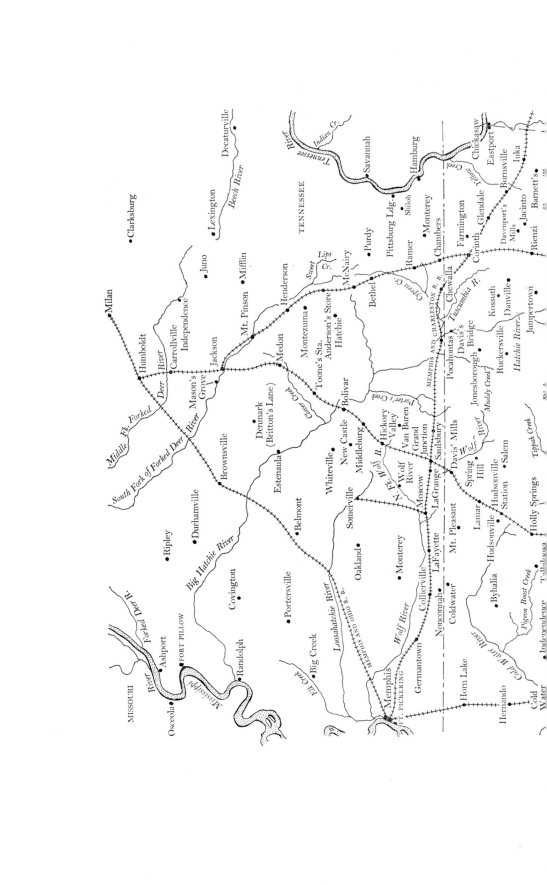

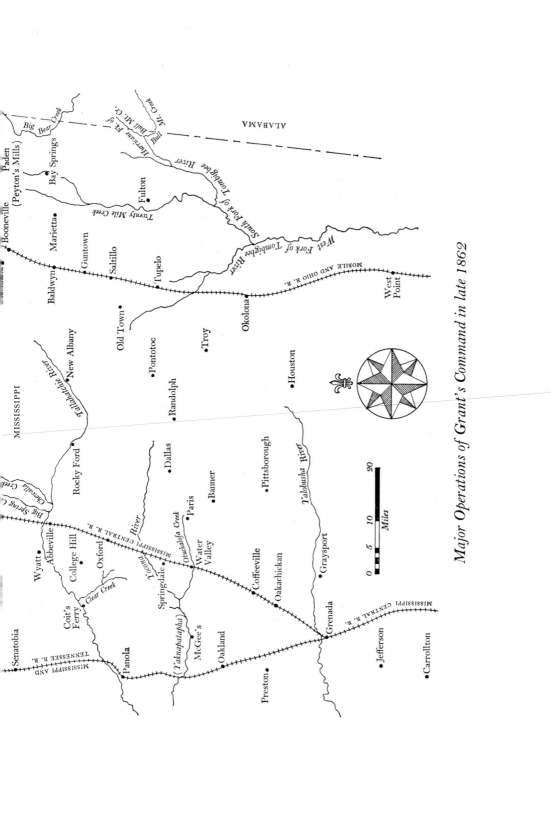

Major Operations of Grant's Command in late 1862

To Brig. Gen. Leonard F. Ross

Head Qrs. Dist of West. Tenn
Corinth Miss. Sept. 3d 1862

GENL. L. F. ROSS

The 5th Missouri left this morning at 4 O'clock for Jackson. Your telegram about Genl. Logan is correctly understood. You will detail a mustering officer & muster in the Tennesseans at once. If you lack blanks they can be had here

U S GRANT.
Maj. Genl.

Telegram, copies, DNA, RG 393, Post of Jackson, Telegrams Received; *ibid.*, 17th Army Corps, 3rd Division, Telegrams Received. On Sept. 3, 1862, Brig. Gen. Leonard F. Ross sent two telegrams to USG. "I fear my language last evening in relation to Gen Logan might be misconstrued—The reason for not taking command seemed to be that he did not wish to depri[ve] me the privelege of closing a work commenced under my admistration that I should go through with it & he would help me—" "There are some Tenn troops here that I wish mustered into service at once   will you send a mustering officer" Telegrams received, *ibid.*, Dept. of the Mo., Telegrams Received.

On Sept. 4, Ross sent five telegrams to USG. "Col Crocker telegraphs me from Bolivar that the enemy fell back from Middleburg last night   his cavalry are pursuing & reconnoitering the country south—" "I have rec'd the following from Col Crocker—The rebels have left middleburg & all of them are taking their way as fast as they can in the direction of holly springs   they left past night   unless I recive information that they have made a stand I shall not attempt to follow them—" "Have you any information of the whereabouts of Genl Price or of the movemt of any part of his command" "The Enemy has retreated from before Bolivar   quiet is restored again in this part of the command now— Have you any objections to my making a short visit to some relations at Decatur Ala—" "Gen Logan haven taken command of the troops in this dept I will rejoin my command at Bolivar as soon as Rail Road is repaired wh[ich] will be some time tomorrow" Telegrams received, *ibid.*

On Sept. 8, Ross, Bolivar, telegraphed to USG. "I arrived at 12 m   all quiet   our forts and rifle pits about completed & the works a good state for defense   was my application for leave of absence rec'd—Can it be granted" Telegram received, *ibid.*

To Maj. Gen. Henry W. Halleck

——————

Gen Grants H'd Q'rs
Sept. 4th 3.15 P.M. 1862

MAJ GEN H. W. HALLECK
GEN IN CHIEF.

I am hurrying Granger all practicable. Your dispatch was explained by one from Genl Boyle[1]

U S GRANT
Maj Genl

Telegram received, DNA, RG 94, Generals' Papers and Books, Telegrams Received by Gen. Halleck; copies, *ibid.*, RG 107, Telegrams Collected (Bound); *ibid.*, Telegrams Received in Cipher; *ibid.*, RG 393, USG Hd. Qrs. Correspondence; DLC-USG, V, 4, 5, 7, 8, 9, 88. *O.R.*, I, xvii, part 2, 199. On Sept. 4, 1862, Brig. Gen. William S. Rosecrans, Rienzi, Tenn., telegraphed to USG. "Granger thinks it means the cavalry division   had we not better have it ~~thoug~~ thoroughly understood—at least you must decide before I give orders—" Telegram received, DNA, RG 393, Dept. of the Mo., Telegrams Received. On Sept. 4, Rosecrans telegraphed again to USG. "Granger has orders to move taking sheridans regt & 2 two batteries leaving his transportation   1st The sick & baggage 2nd the troops 3d the cavalry which is too much worn down to march—We will take Great care to cover the movement—Hamilton will remain at Jacinto for the present   the (2) two Regts of cavalry will occupy Kossuth on the big spring this side of Boonville to cover all and when over will encamp on the north side of the tuscumbia two 2 miles from Danville—What about that boat captured   We have stores coming   Will they be expired" Telegram received, *ibid.* On Sept. 5, Rosecrans telegraphed to USG. "Your dispatches rec'd   Granger moves one (1) brigade tomorrow. Hamilton occupies this with 2 Reg'ts which comes in tomorrow. I am told old Buford learned & blabbed our movements to Maj Alger. this is so!" Telegram received, *ibid. O.R.*, I, xvii, part 2, 203. On Sept. 6, Rosecrans telegraphed to USG. "Does the union brigade go—" Telegram received, DNA, RG 393, Dept. of the Mo., Telegrams Received; copy, *ibid.*, Army of the Miss., Telegrams Sent. On Sept. 7, Brig. Gen. James B. McPherson, Corinth, telegraphed to USG. "I have arraged to send a train of 10 cars to Renzi in three quarters of an hour   Gen Granger is here having left Renzi at 11 oclock—" Telegram received, *ibid.*, Dept. of the Mo., Telegrams Received. On Sept. 10, L. N. Duff, Columbus, Ky., telegraphed to USG. "Two 2 small boat here for Grangers command—one of his division that have arrived here have gone forward except the battery which will leave here in an hour." Telegram received, *ibid.*

1. Jeremiah T. Boyle of Ky. studied at Princeton, and practiced law at Danville, Ky., until the outbreak of the Civil War. Active in securing recruits for the U.S. Army, he was confirmed as brig. gen. on April 28, 1862. On June 4, Boyle assumed command of U.S. forces in Ky. *O.R.*, I, x, part 2, 631. For the telegram to which USG refers, see following telegram.

To Maj. Gen. Horatio G. Wright

———

By Telegraph from Grants Head Quarters
Sept. 4, 3 30 P M *1862*

To H G Wright
Maj Gen

I am hurrying Granger all possible—Artillery & Cavalry will march to Paducah. Infantry will go by rail to Columbus Ky —*my old* regiments are very much reduced from the number of engagements they have been in. I will spare them however if organized   I will send troops as fast as the capacity of our railroad will permit—Send light draft boats to Columbus Ky—

U S Grant
Maj Gen Comdg

Telegram received, DNA, RG 393, Dept. of the Ohio (Cincinnati), Telegrams Received; copies, *ibid.*, USG Letters Sent; DLC-USG, V, 1, 2, 3, 9, 88. *O.R.*, I, xvi, part 2, 482–83. Horatio G. Wright of Conn., USMA 1841, served as asst. professor of engineering at USMA, and as army engineer, and reached the rank of maj., corps of engineers, on Aug. 6, 1861. Confirmed as brig. gen. on Feb. 3, 1862, Wright commanded a brigade in various expeditions on the southeastern Atlantic coast. He was appointed maj. gen. on July 18, though the U.S. Senate rejected the appointment on Feb. 12, 1863. On Aug. 23, 1862, pursuant to AGO General Orders No. 112, Aug. 19, Wright issued General Orders No. 1, assuming command of the Dept. of the Ohio, composed of the states of Ohio, Mich., Ind., Ill. (except the District of Cairo), Wis., and Ky. (east of the Tennessee River). *O.R.*, I, xvi, part 2, 404; *ibid.*, I, xvii, part 2, 190.

On Sept. 3, Brig. Gen. Jeremiah T. Boyle, Louisville, Ky., telegraphed to USG. "The Genl in Chief informs Maj Genl Wright that he had ordered Genl Grangers division to Louisville   when did it leave   how will it come   shall I send light draft boats down the Ohio to Bring them up—" Telegram received, DNA, RG 393, Dept. of the Mo., Telegrams Received. On Sept. 4, Wright, Cincinnati, telegraphed to USG. "Hurry up Grangers division & keep me advised of its movements   we want it at the earliest possible moment   cant you spare a larger force of old troops if replaced by new ones—" Telegram received, *ibid*. On Sept. 5, Boyle telegraphed to USG. "Please hurry forward Genl Grangers division let no time be lost much depends on it" Telegram received, *ibid*. On Sept. 6, Wright telegraphed to USG. "I am in great want of artillery at Memphis there are two light field batteries of Wallaces old Divission Capt Wood & Capt Chesny's chicago companies Cant you order them off to me Rebels 30 miles off." Telegram received (misdated Sept. 10), *ibid*.; copy, *ibid*., Dept. of the Ohio (Cincinnati), Telegrams Sent. Capt. Peter P. Wood, Chicago, commanded Battery A, 1st Ill. Light Art.; Capt. John T. Cheney, Dixon, commanded Battery F, 1st Ill. Light Art.

To Brig. Gen. John A. Logan

Head Quarters Dist of West. Tenn
Corinth Miss. Sept. 4, 1862

Genl Jno. A Logan

If not already you will soon have a force from Sherman's command in supporting distance of you—be as quiet as possible with your men to give them all the rest possible. Price has not moved toward Salsbury.[1]

U S Grant
Maj Genl, comdg.

Telegram, copies, DNA, RG 393, Post of Jackson, Telegrams Received; *ibid*., 17th Army Corps, 3rd Division, Telegrams Received. *O.R.*, I, xvii, part 2, 199.

On Sept. 5, 1862, Brig. Gen. John A. Logan telegraphed to USG. "Rebels attacked & burned the bridge this side of Humboldt this morning as I am informed" Telegram received, DNA, RG 393, Dept. of the Mo., Telegrams Received. On the same day, USG telegraphed to Logan. "Send particulars of the engagement to day. Your dispatch is not fully understood" Copies, *ibid*., Post of Jackson, Telegrams Received; *ibid*., 17th Army Corps, 3rd Division, Telegrams Received. On the same day, Logan wrote to USG. "At 4 o'clock this A.M. a force of 200 Cavalry attacked the guard at the Barnes bridge this side of Humboldt, drove off the guard, and set fire to the bridge The guard renewed the fight repulsing the Enemy and saved the bridge. Our force consisted of 28 men under a Lieut. our loss, 1 killed and 8 wounded. The enemy's loss not known. Lieut. com'dg the Enemy's force is here a prisoner, not seriously wounded. Our Cavalry are in pursuit." Copy, *ibid*., RG 94, War Records Office, Union Battle Reports. *O.R.*, I, xvii, part 1, 54. Also on Sept. 5, Logan wrote to USG. "All damage repaired on the road to Humboldt. We have Lt. Col. Borup prisoner, wounded. We have eighty 80 wounded and one 1 killed. No credit claimed on our side for the difference against us." Copy, DNA, RG 94, War Records Office, Union Battle Reports. *O.R.*, I, xvii, part 1, 54. Also on the same day, Logan wrote to USG. "I am induced to believe that my information this A.M. about the bridge is not wholly correct. I got my information from Col. Bryant, Humboldt. I have, however, sent reinforcements to the guard, also sent cavalry and infantry to try to intercept the rebels in their retreat—" Copy, DNA, RG 94, War Records Office, Union Battle Reports. *O.R.*, I, xvii, part 1, 54.

1. Saulsbury, Tenn., about eighteen miles south of Bolivar.

To Brig. Gen. James M. Tuttle

[*Thursday Sept. 4, 1862*]

I see my dispatch to Gen. Halleck sent in Cypher and without authority to have them published, appear in the Papers over my signature. Inform the Operator at Cairo that this is not to occur again.

U. S. GRANT

Copy, Gross Papers, OClWHi. On Sept. 4, 1862, John C. Van Duzer, superintendent of the military telegraph, Cairo, telegraphed to USG. "Gen Tuttle desires a reply to your message relating to the publication of your dispatch to Gen Halleck. that dispatch was rec'd at this office & transmitted to Washington on the Evening of the 31st aug was there made public & returned by telegraph dated Sept 1st & appeared in Chicago & St Louis papers of 2d not having been made public at Cairo until arrival of papers on the 3d—" Telegram received, DNA, RG 393, Dept. of the Mo., Telegrams Received.
On July 8, Maj. Gen. Henry W. Halleck telegraphed to USG. "The cincinati Gazette contains the substance of your demanding reinforcements & my refusing them. You either have a newspaper correspondent on your staff, or your staff is very leaky. This publication of our correspondence did not come from these Head Qrs." ALS (telegram sent), *ibid.*, RG 108, Telegrams Sent; telegram received, *ibid.*, RG 393, Dept. of the Mo., Telegrams Received. *O.R.*, I, xvii, part 2, 83. On July 13, the *Memphis Bulletin* reprinted a dispatch of the *Cincinnati Gazette*. "It is known that Gen. GRANT has called for reenforcements from HALLECK and has been refused. HALLECK will not or cannot see the use of sending them and thinks it 'all right.' "

To Maj. Gen. Henry W. Halleck

Grants Head Quarters
Sept 5th [*1862*]

MAJOR GENL HALLECK
GENERAL:

I now am convinced that Steamers Skylark & Calie burned on the Tenn. River about 2 weeks ago by Rebels was done with the connivance of the Captains or Trasy agents.[1] The Steamer Terry just captured on the Same River[2] was probably done with the connivance of her commander Capt Klinck.[3] I had just ordered the Expulsion of Klinck from our lines on the Strength of a letter rec'd sent through Washn Exposing his secession proclivities. The very morning his Brother the Q.M.[4] sent him in command of the Terry   Klinck is now in Cairo under arrest.[5]

U. S. GRANT
Maj Genl

Telegram received, DNA, RG 94, Generals' Papers and Books, Telegrams Received by Gen. Halleck; copies, *ibid.*, RG 393, USG Hd. Qrs. Correspondence; DLC–USG, V, 4, 5, 7, 8, 9, 88. *O.R.*, I, xvii, part 2, 202.

1. See telegram to Maj. Gen. Henry W. Halleck, Aug. 21, 1862.
2. On Sept. 4, 1862, Col. Thomas Morton, Hamburg, Tenn., telegraphed to USG. "The information has reached me of the capture of the steam boat Terry with two pieces of artillery aboard.   by this the rebels have control of the river & from what I learn are moving up the river—for the protection of the stores here I need one battery & an additional force of infantry or cavalry   could not the steamer Baton Rouge be sent down   if possible I will clear the river"   Telegram received, DNA, RG 393, Dept. of the Mo., Telegrams Received. On the same day, L. D. Allen, Hamburg, telegraphed to USG. "Two (2) men residents of savannah have just arrived from Rockport Tenn river & report they were on the W B. Terry & captured on monday by a rebel force one thousand (1000) strong   at That place one woman shot all citizens robbed & seized   clipp's battery has fallen into their hands   they further report that the band will keep the boat & use her on the river—"   Telegram received, *ibid.*
3. Leonard G. Klinck, master of the U.S. transport steamer *W. B. Terry,* filed a report in which he said that he had left Paducah, loaded with coal, on Aug. 30, bound for Hamburg. Unable to proceed beyond Duck River Sucks because of low water, the steamer was captured by a group of about 200 guerrillas, who used it to ferry some troops across the river, then burned it. *O.R.,*

I, xvii, part 1, 52–53. USG transmitted the report to hd. qrs. of the army. DNA, RG 94, Register of Letters Received.

On Sept. 5, USG telegraphed to Maj. Gen. Horatio G. Wright. "Cotton has been shipped to Cincinnati from Tenn. by L. Klinck. Requests that it be seized, Klinck being in Government service has violated orders & may be liable to more serious charges." *Ibid.*, RG 393, Dept. of the Ohio (Cincinnati), Register of Letters Received. On Sept. 8, Capt. John H. Dickerson, Cincinnati, telegraphed to USG. "On what boat did Leonard Klinck ship his cotton" Telegram received, *ibid.*, Dept. of the Mo., Telegrams Received.

4. John G. Klinck of Ohio was commissioned capt. and asst. q.m. of vols. to rank from Aug. 3, 1861. On Sept. 5, 1862, Morton telegraphed to USG. "Capt J G Klinck left for cornett at 4 oclock this morning—" Telegram received, *ibid.*

5. On Sept. 5, Brig. Gen. James M. Tuttle telegraphed to USG. "Officers of Terry are here   have just placed capt Klinck in arrest   who is to investigate the matter   none of the soldiers come down   they were not paroled   have you sent me an A Q M   am terribly annoyed by cannon" Telegram received, *ibid.* On the same day, Capt. John G. Klinck, Corinth, telegraphed to USG. "Gen Tuttle says the Officers of the W B Terry are there paroled & wants to know what shall be done with them—" Telegram received, *ibid.*

To Maj. Gen. Henry W. Halleck

Head Qrs Disct of West Tenn
Corinth Sept 7, 1862

MAJ GENL H W. HALLECK
GENL IN CHIEF
WASHINGTON D. C.
GENL

Your letter of the 29 of Augt enclosing copy of a permit purporting to have been by your order and signed by Maj G. M. Van Hosen, granting authority to the proprietors of the Tishomingo Hotel to bring certain articles to Corinth, is received, and the matter has been investigated.

Maj Van Hosen was relieved from duty about the date of the permit alluded to, and sent to his Regiment at Bolivar. ~~Finding~~   If it is found that the permit was given and signed as charged I will order the arrest of Maj Van Hosen

It is perhaps proper to remark that the proprietors of the Hotel say the articles embraced within this authority were never

brough to Corinth they being unable to get authority to do so
from the Treasury Dept.

> I am Genl
> Very Respcty
> U. S. Grant

Copies, DLC-USG, V, 4, 5, 7, 8, 9, 88; DNA, RG 108, Letters Received; *ibid.*,
RG 393, USG Hd. Qrs. Correspondence. On Aug. 29, 1862, Maj. Gen. Henry
W. Halleck wrote to USG. "It appears from enclosed copy of a paper received
from the Treasury Dept that Major G. M. Van Hosen has used my name without
authority for the purpose of evading the Regulations of the Secretary of the
Treasury & my general orders relating to trade. You will ascertain wether the
paper is genuine, & if so will arrest Major Van Hosen & report the facts of the
case to these Head Qrs." LS, *ibid.*, RG 108, Letters Sent (Press); copies, *ibid.*,
RG 393, USG Hd. Qrs. Correspondence; DLC-USG, V, 7. George M. Van
Hosen of Davenport, Iowa, was mustered into U.S. service on Oct. 28, 1861, as
capt., 13th Iowa, and was promoted to maj. on April 17, 1862. On Aug. 17,
Maj. John A. Rawlins issued Special Orders No. 166 relieving Van Hosen from
duty as provost marshal and ordering him to return to his regt. DS, DNA, RG 94,
Special Orders, District of West Tenn.; copies, *ibid.*, RG 393, USG Special
Orders; DLC-USG, V, 15, 16, 82, 87.

The document in question, dated Aug. 16, authorized Spencer & Wells of
the Tishomingo House to bring to Corinth "hotel stores," 250 boxes of wine,
and 5,000 cigars. Copy, DNA, RG 109, Union Provost Marshals' Files of Papers
Relating to Two or More Civilians. On Sept. 5, Col. George P. Ihrie endorsed
the document. "No record of the Permit, of which this purports to be a copy, is
on file in the office of the Provost Marshal of Corinth, Miss." AES, *ibid.*

To Col. John C. Kelton

> Head Quarters Dist of West. Tenn.
> Corinth Sept 7th 1862.

Col J. C. Kelton,
A. A. Genl.
Washington City.
Sir.

For the information of the Genl. in chief I have the honor to
report the following changes being made in the disposition of
the forces in this District.

The two remaining Div. of the Army of the Miss. under Gen Rosecrans, are being collected at this place and will form the garrison of Corinth. Rienzi, Jacinto[1] & Danville will be held for the present. Besides these two Divisions, there will be here Genl Davies Division, two Brigades of McArthurs and the Cavalry & artillery, with the exception of one Battery, of the entire Div. The whole will be under the command of Gen Rosecrans.

The Jackson command which guards the road from Bethel to Humboldt, and from Jackson to Bolivar, will be under Maj Genl Ord, the forces remaining as now, that is, the former command of Genl McClernand has been increased by one Brigade from Genl McArthurs Div. and one Battery.

Two Brigades from Memphis will occupy Brownsville probably commanded by Brig Genl M. L. Smith—This arrangement gives me Maj Genl Sherman commanding on the right, Maj Genl Ord in the center, and Brig Genl Rosecrans on the left. With the force at Brownsville, the line of the Hatchee will be well guarded, and that force will be in readiness to reinforce Bolivar in case of an attack there, or to occupy that place and leave the present garrison loose to reinforce Corinth should it become necessary.

When this arrangement is entirely completed I will probably move Head Quarters to Jackson. From that place with a garrison at Brownsville I will always be able to communicate with Memphis by means of Courier in seven or eight hours in case of necessity.

> Very respectfully
> Your Obt Servt
> U. S. GRANT
> Maj Genl.

Copies, DNA, RG 108, Letters Received; *ibid.*, RG 393, USG Hd. Qrs. Correspondence; DLC-USG, V, 4, 5, 7, 8, 9, 88. *O.R.*, I, xvii, part 2, 206.

1. Jacinto, Miss., about twelve miles west of Iuka, and about twelve miles southeast of Corinth.

To Col. Robert C. Wood

———

Head Quarters, Dist. of West Ten.
Corinth, Sept. 7th 1862

Asst. Surg. Gen. R. C. Wood
St. Louis Mo.
Sir:

Surgeon L. H. Stone, U.S.A. reported to me for duty in this Military District on the morning of the 31st Ult. Before orders were issued assigning him to duty he became so much intoxicated that I defered publishing them for a day or two hoping by that time he would be in a condition to receive them. Finding however that he continued drinking to excess I caused him to be admonished that his course would not be tolerated, and that he had better apply for another field for his services. After waiting some two days more, until the 5th inst. and finding that his condition grew no better, I made an order for him to report to you. A copy of that order was sent by mail to St. Louis.

When the Dr. will be able to comply with that order is hard to judge from the course he has pursued while here.

I am sir, very respectfully
your obt. svt.
U. S. Grant
Maj. Gen. Com

ALS, DNA, RG 94, Personal Papers, Medical Officers and Physicians. Robert C. Wood of R. I. entered the U.S. Army as asst. surgeon in 1825 and was promoted to maj. and surgeon in 1836. He served as act. U.S. surgeon gen. from shortly after the outbreak of the Civil War until April 25, 1862, when the office of the surgeon gen. was reorganized. Wood was confirmed as col. and asst. surgeon gen. on June 14, 1862. George W. Adams, *Doctors in Blue: The Medical History of the Union Army in the Civil War* (New York, 1952), pp. 6, 8, 30.

On Sept. 5, Maj. John A. Rawlins issued Special Orders No. 185. "Surgeon L. H. Stone, U. S. Army on his own application, is relieved from duty in the District of West. Tenn, and will report in person to Asst. Surgeon General Wood, U. S. Army in St Louis, Mo." Copies, DLC-USG, V, 15, 16, 82, 87; DNA, RG 393, USG Special Orders. On Sept. 11, Wood wrote to Brig. Gen. William A. Hammond, surgeon gen., sustaining USG's estimate of Asst. Surgeon Lyman H. Stone and stating that "the services of Surgeon Stone are perfectly valueless in this department, and his presence an embaressment." LS, *ibid.*, RG 94, Personal Papers, Medical Officers and Physicians.

Stone, born in Vt., entered the army as asst. surgeon in 1847. He was convicted of misconduct and drunkenness in 1852 and 1859, and arrested by order of Brig. Gen. William S. Harney in 1861, only to be released owing to the great need for surgeons during the war. After being captured in the battle of Bull Run, he was paroled and sent to St. Louis in July, 1862. On Sept. 16, Hammond wrote to Secretary of War Edwin M. Stanton recommending Stone's dismissal. ALS, *ibid.*, Letters Received. He was dismissed the same day. ES (by Peter H. Watson), *ibid.*

To Maj. Gen. Henry W. Halleck

Grants Hd Qrs
Sept 9th 11 A M [*1862*]

MAJ GEN HALLECK
GEN IN CHIEF

For two days now I have been advised of the advance of Price and VanDorn on this place   I presume there is no doubt of the advance of a large force   One Division will arrive from Memphis to Bolivar this Evening or tomorrow which will enable me to use all the force now at the latter place whenever required   should the Enemy come I will be as ready as possible with the means at hand   I do not believe that a force can be brought against us at present that cannot be successfully resisted

U S GRANT
Maj Genl

Telegram received, DNA, RG 94, Generals' Papers and Books, Telegrams Received by Gen. Halleck; copies, *ibid.*, RG 107, Telegrams Received in Cipher; *ibid.*, Telegrams Collected (Bound); *ibid.*, RG 393, USG Hd. Qrs. Correspondence; DLC-USG, V, 4, 5, 7, 8, 9, 88. *O.R.*, I, xvii, part 2, 209–10.

On Sept. 7, 1862, Brig. Gen. William S. Rosecrans, Iuka, Miss., telegraphed to USG. "Report from Hamilton says that information leads him to belive that reports are errionious & that no immediate attack is intended but that Price & VanDorn have united   cavalry are out on that route to gather futher news" Telegram received, DNA, RG 393, Dept. of the Mo., Telegrams Received; copy, *ibid.*, Army of the Miss., Telegrams Sent. *O.R.*, I, xvii, part 2, 207. On the same day, Brig. Gen. Charles S. Hamilton, Rienzi, telegraphed to USG. "Citizen scouts sent out yesterday report Price at 20 mile creek with 36,000 men moving north to attack   I have given instructions to move things to the rear & to be in readiness to move or fight—I should like to have an experienced officer sent Rienzi   a train of cars ought to be sent thru for surplus stores—"   Telegram received, DNA, RG 393, Dept. of the Mo., Telegrams Received. On the same day, Hamilton telegraphed again to USG. "Your dispatches rec'd   further investigation lead me to belive that Price & VanDorn have been uniting their forces—But there is no danger of immediate attack   the advance is at 20 mile creek   I have sent out cavalry & shall know of further advance if any before Morng—supplies at Rienzi except 10 day rations will be sent to Corinth tomorrow"   Telegram received, *ibid*. On the same day, Brig. Gen. Gordon Granger, Corinth, telegraphed to USG. "I think the reports about Price's advancing are premature as I have a regt in front of 20 mile creek & no report from it since morning"   Telegram received, *ibid*.

Also on Sept. 7, Rosecrans telegraphed to USG. "I have no advices from the cavalry to corroborate the statements of the citizen scouts of Hamilton   have telegraphed for them. Can you detail Col Dubois force few days to command at Rienzi I and handle those troops & bring them off if necessary—"   Telegram received, *ibid*.; copy, *ibid*., Army of the Miss., Telegrams Sent. On the same day, Rosecrans telegraphed again to USG. "I would like to have dubois ordered to Report to me by telegraph—I will send him down to Danville & Rinzi if there should be anything confirmatory of this move—"   Telegram received, *ibid*., Dept. of the Mo., Telegrams Received; copy, *ibid*., Army of the Miss., Telegrams Sent.

On Sept. 8, Rosecrans telegraphed to USG. "Col merry telegraphed that col Hatch cavalry reports the enemy in force at twenty 20 mile creek—What force I do not know—"   Telegram received, *ibid*., Dept. of the Mo., Telegrams Received; copy, *ibid*., Army of the Miss., Telegrams Sent. *O.R.*, I, xvii, part 2, 208. On the same day, Rosecrans telegraphed to USG. "The information I sent you is all I have at present—all things considered it would seem probably that vanDorn Breckenridge & Price should combine & if we withdraw from the east should hold us in check & move on buell or make an attempt to disloge us if they think they have the power   the best result for them all things considered is via Ripley & chewalla if they have transportation   the railroad by Rienzi is the next best   if we have our troops in hand so as to meet this attack we shall be able to whip them & crush them out   if they move east we shall be able to counteract them   if they should try to penetrate between us & Memphis & cross the hatchie it would be the best for us of all   they would never return—"   Telegram received, DNA, RG 393, Dept. of the Mo., Telegrams Received; copy, *ibid*., Army of the Miss., Telegrams Sent. *O.R.*, I, xvii, part 2, 208. On the same day, Rosecrans telegraphed to USG. "Hamilton telegraphs news from a Deserter that Price & VanDorn have united for a move into Kentucky but he thinks they are moving on corinth   they are working on the rail road—Would it be well for us to take up the rails & haul them off for a mile or two & break up the track bed down towards Boonville—"   Telegram received, DNA, RG 393, Dept. of the Mo., Telegrams Received; copy, *ibid*., Army of the Miss., Telegrams Sent. *O.R.*, I, xvii, part 2, 208.

On Sept. 9, Rosecrans telegraphed to USG. "Reports from the front show that it is probably four (4) or five (5) regts of infantry & that they are in their camp at Baldwin with no particular signs of movement   I begin very strongly to suspect they are practicing a move on us & in tind to cover up a movement on Buells right & rear via Bluntsville gunters landing Huntsville & C—is it possible they want to push themselves in a position to foil an attack on vicksburg"   Telegram received, DNA, RG 393, Dept. of the Mo., Telegrams Received; copy, *ibid.*, Army of the Miss., Telegrams Sent. *O.R.*, I, xvii, part 2, 210. On the same day, Rosecrans telegraphed to USG. "A private of 39th Ohio captured while straggling from their camp just returned from Tupelo paroled & with a pass to bay springs dated Tupello Sept 6th—signed Brig Genl Cabell—says he was taken to Baldwin thence to Guntown thence to Saltillo & Tupello where he saw Genl Price—heard two 2 citizens tell him damed yankees were coming close burning ravishing & destroying Price advised them to go home mind their business not shoot any one as that only made matters worse he would rectify matters in a week or two—he was told by soldiers he could not leave till after the fight—his remarks to the soldiers that he wanted to know how many engines we had on the M & O RR as he wished them all that the soldiers could not leave till after the fight. Then giving him a pass to go by himslf to bay springs alone to manns company of rebel cavalry—all combined in induces me to belive the rebels are playing a game of bluff & are very weak say 12000 effectives—" Telegram received, DNA, RG 393, Dept. of the Mo., Telegrams Received; copy, *ibid.*, Army of the Miss., Telegrams Sent. *O.R.*, I, xvii, part 2, 210. See telegrams to Maj. Gen. Henry W. Halleck, Sept. 10, 11, 15, 1862, to Brig. Gen. John A. Logan, Sept. 9, 1862, and letter to Brig. Gen. William S. Rosecrans, Sept. 14, 1862.

To Brig. Gen. John A. Logan

Head Quarters Dist of W Tenn
Corinth Miss. Sept. 9 1862

BRIG GENL. J. A. LOGAN

Hurlbuts division left Memphis on Saturday last.[1] I want him to come to Bolivar immediately, and all the forces at the latter place to hold themselves in readiness to move here at a moments warning—either by rail or march as ordered.[2] We are prepared for moving Four Thousand (4000) at one Time if necessary the enemy are at Twenty mile Creek[3] to a certainty I do not believe they are going to attack us because it would be so much against military principles to do so just here the drought in front of us is at against it. We must be ready for any emergency however, & should they move on Bolivar instead of this place—we must be equally so

U S GRANT
Maj. Genl. comdg.

Telegram, copy, DNA, RG 393, 17th Army Corps, 3rd Division, Telegrams Received.

1. On Sept. 18, 1862, Brig. Gen. Stephen A. Hurlbut wrote to Maj. John A. Rawlins reporting the details of his move from Memphis to Brownsville and thence to Bolivar, Tenn., which began on Sept. 6. *O.R.*, I, xvii, part 2, 226. On Sept. 7, Maj. Gen. William T. Sherman, Memphis, telegraphed to USG. "Lagow arrived   Hurlburts division will move in the morning   The force which is about & above Bolivar is four 4 reg'ts of cavalry and two 2 batallions   no infantry has passed north of the tallahathie—Villiput is still at abbeville—" Telegram received, DNA, RG 393, Dept. of the Mo., Telegrams Received. On Sept. 6, Sherman had written to Rawlins stating that Col. Clark B. Lagow had delivered a letter from USG dated Sept. 2. In response, Hurlbut was ordered to Brownsville. *O.R.*, I, xvii, part 2, 204–5. On Sept. 9, Sherman wrote again to Rawlins reporting the movement of Hurlbut and discussing other military matters. *Ibid.*, pp. 210–11.

On Sept. 8, USG telegraphed to Brig. Gen. John A. Logan. "Under existing Rumors a[nd] information it will be more prudent for the force ordered to Brownsville to come to Bolivar and the force at the latter place, hold itself in readiness to come here at short notice if ordered" Copies, DNA, RG 393, 17th Army Corps, 3rd Division, Telegrams Received; *ibid.*, District of West Tenn., 4th Division, Letters and Telegrams Received. On the same day, USG telegraphed to Logan. "Send, a cavalry Force to Brownsville to ascertain if the troops have arrived from Memphis   if so direct them to march to Bolivar without delay." Copy, *ibid.*, 17th Army Corps, 3rd Division, Telegrams Received. On the same day, Logan telegraphed to USG. "I am starting a co of cavalry with orders to forces at Brownsville if there or where they may be if heard from   when the company get there to proceed to Bolivar with all possible despatch" Telegram received, *ibid.*, Dept. of the Mo., Telegrams Received. Also on Sept. 8, USG telegraphed to Logan. "A, Division has arrived at Brownsville or is on its way there. I have heard from them to day & they left on Saturday last." Copy, *ibid.*, 17th Army Corps, 3rd Division, Telegrams Received. On the same day, Logan telegraphed to USG. "I have heard nothing of force ordered to Brownsville as yet nor have they at Bolivar—do you desire me to send a messenger ordering to Bolivar at once—" Telegram received, *ibid.*, Dept. of the Mo., Telegrams Received. On the same day, USG telegraphed to Logan. "Have you sent a Messenger to Brownsville—The Force there need not move to Bolivar until further orders." Copy, *ibid.*, 17th Army Corps, 3rd Division, Telegrams Received. On the same day, Logan telegraphed to USG. "I am just starting a messenger to Brownsville   have not heard of the force arriving there as yet" Telegram received, *ibid.*, Dept. of the Mo., Telegrams Received.

On Sept. 9, Logan telegraphed to USG. "The messenger I sent to Brownsville on yesterday with your first order for our forces to remain there has returned back this A M at 3 o'clock   forces had not arrived & nothing of them—The cavalry sent there later in the Evening with orders to forces to move at once to Bolivar have returned & have taken a different road to the one the messenger came back   did not meet them   I ordered the cavalry to move on beyond Brownsville until they ascertained something of them   I look for their return tonight   I will inform you at once when I get the report from Cavalry—" Telegram received, *ibid.* On the same day, Logan telegraphed to USG. "Messenger just arrived from Brownsville left there at 11 oclock a[nd] no forces had

arrived nor did he hear of them—" Telegram received, *ibid*. On Sept. 10, USG
telegraphed to Logan. "Genl Hurlbut left Memphis last Saturday for Brownsville ought to reach there today." Copy, *ibid*., 17th Army Corps, 3rd Division,
Telegrams Received. On the same day, Logan telegraphed to USG. "Hurlburt
had not arrived at six (6) oclock yesterday evening—what route was he to
come I can hear nothing of him if I know the road he is on I will dispatch in
that direction—" Telegram received, *ibid*., Dept. of the Mo., Telegrams
Received. On Sept. 12, USG telegraphed to Logan. "Has anything been heard
from Hurlbut, yet." Telegram received, *ibid*., 17th Army Corps, 3rd Division,
Telegrams Received. On the same day, Logan telegraphed to USG. "I have not
heard from Hurlbut as yet—Genl Ross sent south yesterday & I have sent all
direction to'ght I have again sent to Brownsville will telegraph you in the
morning" Telegram received, *ibid*., Dept. of the Mo., Telegrams Received.

2. On Sept. 12, Hurlbut wrote to Rawlins that he had received USG's orders
on Sept. 11 to move to Bolivar. *O.R.*, I, xvii, part 2, 215. On Sept. 13, Logan
telegraphed to USG. "Genl Ross has just dispatched me that Gen Hurlbut &
staff are in Bolivar his troops will arrive this Evening" Telegram received,
DNA, RG 393, Dept. of the Mo., Telegrams Received. On the same day, USG
telegraphed to Hurlbut. "notify all the Infantry at Bolivar Except any that belongs to your Division to Prepare to Hold themselves in Readiness to be Brought
to this Place by Rail Road at the Shortest notice" Telegram received, *ibid*.,
District of West Tenn., 4th Division, Letters and Telegrams Received. On
Sept. 14, USG telegraphed to Hurlbut. "if Ross infantry is sent for his transportation can be left for use of your Division & the Genl shipped out of a train
Probably about ten (10) days ago to send—I will Probably Know tonight
whether Genl Ross will have to be sent for." Telegram received, *ibid*. On Sept. 13,
Brig. Gen. James B. McPherson, Corinth, had telegraphed to USG. "Road open
to Bolivar train went through this morning all right from Jackson—" Telegram received, *ibid*., Dept. of the Mo., Telegrams Received. On the same day,
McPherson telegraphed to USG. "Do you wish me to make arrangements to
have troops brought from Bolivar if so how many thousand men" Telegram
received, *ibid*. On Sept. 14, USG telegraphed to Hurlbut. "cars will be at Bolivar
tomorrow morning to Bring ~~Rosses~~ Rosses command Let them come with out
Delay" Telegram received, *ibid*., District of West Tenn., 4th Division, Letters
and Telegrams Received. On Sept. 14, Hurlbut telegraphed to Rawlins. "Orders
to have Ross Ify ready are recd & Extended They are now ready whenever
orderd." Telegram received, *ibid*., Dept. of the Mo., Telegrams Received. On
Sept. 15, McPherson telegraphed to USG. "I have no engine or train here—All
were sent north to Bring troops from Bolivar Will have no engine until train
arrives from Columbus." Telegram received, *ibid*. On Sept. 15, Brig. Gen.
Leonard F. Ross, Jackson, telegraphed to USG. "I am here with about two
thousand men a down train run off the track one mile below and the track will
not be cleared before four oclock this afternoon if you think best we can march
across to the M C R R and go down at once shall I do so or wait For the track
to be cleard off" Telegram received, *ibid*. On Sept. 14, McPherson had telegraphed to USG. "Two (2) trains are just ready to start for Jackson 9 P M & 2
more will start tomorrow morning at 4 oclock in all (42) passenger & freight
I shall not send a train through to Columbus tomorrow—" Telegram received,
ibid. On Sept. 15, Ross telegraphed to USG. "The R R Track is clear & we will
be under way in less than half hour—" Telegram received, *ibid*.

In his letter to Rawlins of Sept. 12, Hurlbut had written that one of his units, the 52nd Ind., was at Fort Pillow. On Sept. 15, USG telegraphed to Logan. "Send orders to Com'dg officer of the fifty second Ind. at Brownsville to join his Comd. at Bolivar." Copy, *ibid.*, 17th Army Corps, 3rd Division, Telegrams Received. On Sept. 16, Logan telegraphed to Rawlins. "My messager has just returned from Brownsville & reports that the commanding officer of the 52d Ind is not there   he also report a body of 250 secesh cavalry within 2 miles & half of that place" Telegram received, *ibid.*, Dept. of the Mo., Telegrams Received.

3. Twenty Mile Creek flows southward from about five miles south of Jacinto, Miss., to the East Fork of the Tombigbee River about forty miles south of Jacinto.

To Maj. Gen. Henry W. Halleck

Corinth 10th Sep. 9 45 PM [*1862*]

GENL H. W. HALLECK
GENL-IN-CHF-USA

With all the vigilance I can bring to bear I cannot determine the objects of the Enemy. Everything threatens an attack here but my fear is that it is to cover some other movement   It may have been instituted to prevent sending reinforcements to Wright or to cover a movement on New Orleans by Van Dorn or to the East on Genl Buell.

Should there be an attack I will be ready.

U. S. GRANT.
M G C

Telegram received, DNA, RG 94, Generals' Papers and Books, Telegrams Received by Gen. Halleck; copies, *ibid.*, RG 107, Telegrams Collected (Bound); *ibid.*, Telegrams Received in Cipher; *ibid.*, RG 393, USG Hd. Qrs. Correspondence; DLC-USG, V, 4, 5, 7, 8, 9, 88. *O.R.*, I, xvii, part 2, 213.

On Sept. 9, 1862, Brig. Gen. William S. Rosecrans, Iuka, transmitted a telegram of Col. John V. D. Du Bois, Rienzi, by telegraph to USG. "I have only been here 8 hours & have not formed an opinion but seen no reason to expect an attack in force—8 companies can go in sqads to boonville & Jumpertown   will visit all the pickets tomorrow   the line of communication between the secesh army & vicksburg & Bragg is too far south to to examine by scouts—I want secret service money for this purpose   would it not be well to keep the corinth telegraph office open all night for a few days" Telegram received, DNA, RG 393,

Dept. of the Mo., Telegrams Received. On the same day, John C. Van Duzer, asst. superintendent of the military telegraph, Corinth, telegraphed to USG. "What telegraph offices will you want open nights & days   please answer that I may supply operators—"   Telegram received, *ibid.*

On Sept. 10, Rosecrans telegraphed to USG. "No movement on the Rienzi front reported. Scouts to Booneville and Dick Smiths road. Drums of a Regiment in the direction between Spains and Crockets on the road from Booneville to Blackland. DuBois wishes you to order a scout from Kossuth to Hatchie to meet one of his at Dr. Wills tomorrow evening. A perfect stampede of contrabands east has filled us with men women & children carts waggons bedding &c. I shall start them towards Farmington to secure them from Guerrillas. But when a burden what shall be done with them then." Copy, *ibid.*, Army of the Miss., Telegrams Sent. On the same day, Rosecrans telegraphed to USG. "Dubois says a negro escaped from Ripley confirms the movement of some cavalry North West   Scouts on the front report a column moving from Blackland towards Boonville at 6 P M tonight size not stated   We have a reg't at Pienes mill who probably went to Bay Springs last night. A Regt of Infantry & 2 pieces of Artillery at Barnetts on the Tuscumbia & Jacinto Road." Telegram received, *ibid.*, Dept. of the Mo., Telegrams Received; copy, *ibid.*, Army of the Miss., Telegrams Sent. Also on Sept. 10, Rosecrans telegraphed to Maj. John A. Rawlins. "Col Dubois wishes the cavalry scouts from Kossuth to leave there at day break by the Ruckersville road to Hatchie, thence south & back [*to*] Dr Wells house to meet Col Lee's south there an hour before sun down"   Telegram received, *ibid.*, Dept. of the Mo., Telegrams Received; copy, *ibid.*, Army of the Miss., Telegrams Sent. On the same day, Rosecrans telegraphed to USG. "DuBois finds nothing east of the Hatchie. Where are these troops? I dont believe a large force in motion for our reports put them all near old positions on the 8th inst. Your order will be promptly obeyed. We must use teams." Copy, *ibid.* Dated Sept. 11 in *O.R.*, I, xvii, part 2, 214.

On Sept. 10, Brig. Gen. Charles S. Hamilton, Jacinto, telegraphed to USG. "No firing in front   our own muskets are discharged every Wednesday morning —Enemy finished rail road bridge over 20 mile creek yesterday   He is concentrating between Baldwin Boonville—Breckinridge is reported as having joined Price   Col DuBois reports column of Cavalry moving from Blackland towards Boonvil[le]" Telegram received, DNA, RG 393, Dept. of the Mo., Telegrams Received. On the same day, Du Bois telegraphed to USG. "a column of cavalry reported by cavalry south moving from Blackland towards Boonville about 6 oclock P M—"   Telegram received, *ibid.* On the same day, Du Bois telegraphed again to USG. "a few stray shots fired south east of here   I have sent out to investigate   no report from the pickets—shall I send your message to Genl Hamilton—"   Telegram received, *ibid.* On the same day or the next, Rosecrans telegraphed to USG. "Have at Jacinto 8 Regts and two batteries—Rienzi 3 infantry one battery—two cavalry at Burnsville. two infantry one infantry at Barnetts east of Jacinto three at this place & three (3) east which can be called in tonight   these troops here can leave tonight   those behind can cover the depots   news from towards Bay sprigs & marietta shows no troops on fulton road—News from Tuscumbia shows only Price promises to recover the negroes —front only Dubois—dispatch this morning—slaves still coming in—"   Telegram received (dated Sept. 11), *ibid.*; copy (dated Sept. 10), *ibid.*, Army of the Miss., Telegrams Sent. A copy of this telegram in cipher is *ibid.*

Gen. U. S. Grant. Portrait by S. B. Waugh, 1869.
Courtesy Art Collection of The Union League of Philadelphia.

Gen. U. S. Grant. Portrait by James Reid Lambdin.
Courtesy Art Collection of The Union League of Philadelphia.

Maj. Gen. Henry W. Halleck. Portrait by James Reid Lambdin.
Courtesy Art Collection of The Union League of Philadelphia.

Maj. Gen. William T. Sherman. Portrait by James Reid Lambdin.
Courtesy Art Collection of The Union League of Philadelphia.

To Maj. Gen. Henry W. Halleck

Corinth Miss
Sept 11th 1862

MAJ GEN HALLECK
GEN IN CHIEF

Grangers Division was moved as rapidly as possible after the receipt of your order   Some of the Division must now be in Louisville

U. S GRANT
Maj Gen.

Telegram received, DNA, RG 107, Telegrams Received in Cipher; copies, *ibid.*, RG 393, USG Hd. Qrs. Correspondence; DLC-USG, V, 4, 5, 7, 8, 88. On Sept. 11, 1862, Maj. Gen. Henry W. Halleck telegraphed to USG. "Where are the troops sent to Genl Wright? They should be pushed forward with all possible dispatch to save Louisville & Cincinnati. There can be no very large force to attack you. Attack the enemy, if you can reach him with advantage." ALS (telegram sent), DNA, RG 107, Telegrams Collected (Bound); copies, *ibid.*, RG 393, USG Hd. Qrs. Correspondence; DLC-USG, V, 4, 5, 7, 8, 9, 88. *O.R.*, I, xvii, part 2, 214. On Sept. 11, Brig. Gen. Isaac F. Quinby, Columbus, Ky., telegraphed to USG. "There are now here five 5 light draft boats sent to transport Grangers Div to Louisville   all of the troops which have arrived up to this hour have been forwarded to Cairo to proceed from there by rail road as the boats were not here   a master of transportation did not know that boats were expected   what shall be done with the boats   shall they be ordered back to the place at which chartered—"   Telegram received, DNA, RG 393, Dept. of the Mo., Telegrams Received.

On Sept. 13, Brig. Gen. William S. Rosecrans, Corinth, telegraphed to USG. "I forgot to ask you about sending off the convalescent & sick ones of the first 1st & 4th Division to Columbus—I intend to form a battallion of them but found orders reported to have been given yesterday morning—under which a Train load have gone to Columbus   I am sending off the others this morning but unless strict orders are given the government will not only lose their services here but elsewhere   they ought to be obliged to go into camp at Columbus & do duty till they can be sent to their command   will you please give orders—"   Telegram received, *ibid.* On Sept. 13, Brig. Gen. James B. McPherson, Corinth, telegraphed to USG. "Shall I retain all the well men & convalescents here who belong to the Divisions which have gone to Kentucky & Tennessee   there are a hundred or more waiting transportation"   Telegram received, *ibid.* On Sept. 14, Quinby telegraphed to USG. "Your Telegraphic order regarding convalescents complied with   others are constantly arriving in search of Buells army   shall they also be detained until further orders"   Telegram received, *ibid.*

To Maj. Gen. Henry W. Halleck

Corinth Miss.
"Grant's Hd Qrs." 7 30 P m [*Sept.*] 11, [*1862*]

GEN H W HALLECK
GENL IN CHF—

Everything indicates that we will be attacked here in the next 48 hours   At present the route indicated is by the South West. I will be ready at all points. Gen Rosecrans is not yet in with all his forces but will be by tomorrow night   Price's forces are estimated at from thirty six (36) to forty (40) thousand (40.000). I cannot believe he has half that number of good Troops[1]   He may have conscripts to a large number.

U. S. GRANT M G

Telegram received, DNA, RG 94, Generals' Papers and Books, Telegrams Received by Gen. Halleck; copies, *ibid.*, RG 107, Telegrams Collected (Bound); *ibid.*, Telegrams Received in Cipher; *ibid.*, RG 393, USG Hd. Qrs. Correspondence; DLC-USG, V, 4, 5, 7, 8, 9, 88. *O.R.*, I, xvii, part 2, 214. On Sept. 9, 1862, Brig. Gen. John A. Logan, Jackson, telegraphed to USG. "I have just rec'd the following dispatch from Genl Dodge—A rebel force three hundred (300) strong with one (1) piece of artillery took Huntington yesterday about four (4) oclock p m—they captured a few Tenn' troops"   Telegram received, DNA, RG 393, Dept. of the Mo., Telegrams Received. On Sept. 11, Logan telegraphed to USG. "I have rec'd a dispatch from Genl Dodge with information as follows—Substantialy that his scouts had just brought in 2 men from Villipigues Command saying that he Jackson & Armstrong had fallen back from in front of Bolivar & were expecting Price and Breckenridge to join them there very soon—I give it you as I got it   you are better advised of course than Genl Dodge or myself—there is a force east from here but it is not large and I can manage them if they make a move—"   Telegram received, *ibid.*

On Sept. 11, Brig. Gen. William S. Rosecrans, Iuka, telegraphed to USG. "I must think the movement a demonstration to cover a move on Buell   first they ordered up a large Quantity of rolling stock not needed for a move on us. second—they have been making a great noise about this move   warning us not usual   3rd they see us closing in and have known it for many days & yet delayed the move—4th They tried have it as a part of their plan that Price should cross the Tennessee in Buells rear   this I am sure was a plan of Bragg & Beuregard. 5th it is their interest to do this & Roddy has taken post at Courtland—"   Telegram received, *ibid.*; copy, *ibid.*, Army of the Miss., Telegrams Sent. *O.R.*, I, xvii, part 2, 213. On Sept. 11, Col. John V. D. Du Bois, Rienzi, telegraphed to USG. "scouts report tracks of a company of Infantry moving north on the Boonville & Jacinto road about five (5) miles south east of Rienzi   I dont beleive it

—I wish to send all surplus wagons to the rear not that I feel any alarm but we have too much transportation for an outpost—" Telegram received, DNA, RG 393, Dept. of the Mo., Telegrams Received. On the same day, Du Bois telegraphed to USG. "Col Lee reports the force coming into Boonville at Sundown yesterday consisting of 2 Regts of Cavalry said to belong to Armstrongs Divn They remained not more than half hour & returned as they came by the Blackland road a scout East of the Rail Road discloses no force—there is no force at Ripley & I am confident none on that flank very near—There is at or near Crocketts three (3) miles below Dick Smiths—a force in camp which I estimate at two (2) regts of Cavalry & about the same amount of infantry—I think there has been and possibly is now a design to move on us but my men were in boonville two (2) hours ago & below dick Smiths the same time & all is quiet—The above statement you can rely on—all quiet west I shall feel the force south today far enough to drive in or pass their pickets—" Telegram received, *ibid.*

Also on Sept. 11, Maj. Gen. Edward O. C. Ord, Corinth, telegraphed to USG. "I have just rec'd this report from Col Moore at Kossuth—Col Lee commanding 2d cavalry being at Rienzi sent us word yesterday that it was reported a large cavalry force has left Guntown moving in direction of Ripley—I have had our Cavalry scouting since early this morning west of here and not yet returned —Can learn nothing of the enemy—will this report of Col Moores make any difference in my orders for the force at Chewalla and Kossuth—if the orders to those places are changed please notify Genl McArthur at once." Telegram received, *ibid.* On the same day, Brig. Gen. Charles S. Hamilton, Jacinto, telegraphed to USG. "Everything indicates that Price will move on this line within the next 48 hours—His cavalry force is so large that prudence dictates an early removal of our things if he comes in on the west of Rienzi he threatens our communication with Corinth we have now about (4) days rations—my Instructions are such that I cannot move unless attacked If the trains are out of the way we can take care of ourselves—I await orders" Telegram received, *ibid.* On the same day, Rosecrans telegraphed to USG. "The following is a copy sent to Brig Genl. C. S. Hamilton Jacinto—Telegraphed you that mower was at Barnetts 14 companies of cavalry will be on that same front this evening a little west & south on the bay springs road Two Regts have gone to Burnesville two more will follow tonight 2 more tomorrow—our maps show three roads from Jacinto to Corinth Glendale road Road by Mrs Taylors & campbells mill & the two (2) crossings hurricane at Van Derferds & Rongs mills mitchells mill commands both & hurricane has a bad stream to cross—Should the rebels advance on you in force feel & let them in front & stop their advance Guard & quietly and firmly withdraw by these routes obstructing their passage at advantageous points break down the brides on hurricane—Fell trees & fight them but not to entagle yourself falling back towards your old camp at clear creek where I think we can find a good battle ground—Your baggage should take the glendale road covered by a regiment & section of artillery—Establish at once and maintain an efficient line of communication to head quarters—" Telegram received, *ibid.* O.R., I, xvii, part 2, 214. Also on Sept. 11, Hamilton telegraphed to USG. "I have just received your dispatch. With regard to holding this line (Jacinto to Rienzi), it is & will be a difficult matter without a larger force. Both positions can be turned on either flank. A deserter from Price army at Tupello, came in this morning. He says Price has 40,000 men & has promised his army to take Corinth. A much stronger position for a battle will be our old Camp at Clear

Creek, and I shall be compelled to fall back in that direction if attacked. Deserter says preparations were all complete for a movement forward when he left, 4 days since. A strong rebel cavalry force apparently a covering force, is now within eleven miles of this place. It will be neessary to concentrate my force either at Rienzi or this place in order to make any show of success   Part of my force is now at Rienzi, 6 miles distant—but there is not force enough in either place to hold the ground two hours, if attacked by superior forces, owing to the ease the positions can be turned. I hold everything in readiness to move the trains, & to make as big a fight as any body can make with my force. If I may be permitted, I would suggest the occupation of the clear creek camp as the place to give battle. The position is a strong one, I have had the track torn up & the bridges burned between Rienzi & Boonville. Price's whole force yesterday was between Baldwin & Boonville." Telegram received, DNA, RG 393, Dept. of the Mo., Telegrams Received. On the same day, Rosecrans telegraphed to USG. "all our troops have orders to have their 3 days cooked rations & all spare regiments move west tonight those east of bear creek to it—these here to Burnsville—I will order those tents to be dumped & wagons to move only with ammunition & provisions   please let me know if the move is on the pocahontas road for Dubois says the ripley front is clear   it is important for me to know all so as to give orders to Hamilton" Telegram received, *ibid.*; copy, *ibid.*, Army of the Miss., Telegrams Sent. *O.R.*, I, xvii, part 2, 215. Also on Sept. 11, Rosecrans telegraphed to USG. "That force has been at crocketts for two (2) days & seems probably to be two reg'ts of cavalry with a support of 2 of Infantry   considering all things I see nothing in this to alarm us—" Telegram received, DNA, RG 393, Dept. of the Mo., Telegrams Received; copy, *ibid.*, Army of the Miss., Telegrams Sent. *O.R.*, I, xvii, part 2, 215. On the same day, Du Bois telegraphed to USG. "Battallion has just come in which went west to the hatchie then off the hatchie at Dr Wells   scout from Kossuth had left 2 Hours before their arrival   all quiet   no enemy on the flank of any account—" Telegram received, DNA, RG 393, Dept. of the Mo., Telegrams Received.

1. On Sept. 4, Maj. Gen. Sterling Price, Tupelo, Miss., wrote to Maj. Gen. Earl Van Dorn that he could "put in the field 13,000 infantry, 3,000 cavalry, and 800 artillery, effective total." *O.R.*, I, xvii, part 2, 692. On Sept. 9, Price, Guntown, Miss., wrote to Van Dorn, who had suggested driving USG's forces out of west Tenn., that Gen. Braxton Bragg had ordered him to move to Nashville, and that he planned to move toward Iuka on Sept. 11. *Ibid.*, p. 698.

To Col. Jesse Hildebrand

Head Quarters Dist of West Tenn
Corinth Sept 11th 1862

COMD.G OFFICER ALTON ILL
SIR

There were two Citizens of Boliver arrested and sent to Alton by the Names of R P Neely (Col) and J R Fentress who I would wish to have released on their Parole   Their cases' never came before me but from the Commanding officer at Boliver I understand they are persons for discharge

Respectfully Your Obt Svt
U. S GRANT
Maj Genl

Copy, DNA, RG 249, Letters Received. Jesse Hildebrand was appointed col., 77th Ohio, on Oct. 5, 1861. Late in Aug., 1862, his regt. was sent to Alton, Ill. See telegram to Maj. Nathaniel McLean, Aug. 21, 1862.

Soon after assuming command at Bolivar, Tenn., Brig. Gen. Leonard F. Ross arrested seventeen citizens who had not taken an oath of allegiance and asked them whether they preferred to be sent south to their friends or north to prison. Sixteen, including R. P. Neely and John R. Fentress, who chose to go south were immediately sent to the military prison at Alton. Letter of "Illinoian," Bolivar, Aug. 13, 1862, in *Missouri Democrat*, Aug. 20, 1862. Copies of the order for their arrest on Aug. 11 are in DNA, RG 109, Union Provost Marshals' File of Papers Relating to Two or More Civilians. See letter to Col. Jesse Hildebrand, Sept. 21, 1862.

On Aug. 11, USG endorsed a "List of prisoners in custody of Major Van Hosen, acting Provost Marshal at Corinth and ordered to be sent to and confined in the Military Prison at Alton, Ills. August 11th 1862." "List of prisoners and charges upon which they are sent to Alton Penitentiary to be confined until the close of the present war unless sooner discharged by competant authority." AES, DNA, RG 249, Records of Prisoners Confined at Alton. The fourteen names on this list do not include three which appear in a letter of Aug. 23 from Capt. William R. Rowley to Hildebrand. "By direction of Maj Gen Grant, I am desired to request you to release from confinement (upon their entering into the necessary obligation) the following named persons. To wit R L Lightford, Joseph H Neilson and James P Dancer. These persons were sent up from this Military district and delivered at Alton on the 14th inst but their cases did not come under the immediate notice of the Gen Commanding until quite recently." ALS, *ibid.*

On Aug. 10, Maj. John A. Rawlins telegraphed to Brig. Gen. William S. Rosecrans. "If you have any prisoners sentenced to be sent to Alton have them in readiness to go on Tuesday as a number will be forwarded from here on that

day. If you prefer, they may be sent to the Provost Marshal here to be forwarded
by him to others" Copy, *ibid.*, RG 393, Army of the Miss., Telegrams Received.

To Brig. Gen. William S. Rosecrans

Head Quarters, Dist. of W. Ten
Corinth, Sept. 14th 1862.

GEN. ROSECRANS
COMD.G ARMY OF THE MISS.
GEN.

Your dispatch just received.[1] I was disgusted when news
came of Col. Murphy having retreated to Farmington[2] or near
there.[3] Gave orders at once for Ord to watch well in that direction.[4] Col. Crocker has arrived with his Brigade about 2500
effective.[5] Gen. Ross will be here to-morrow evening with about
4000 more. I gave orders this afternoon for the cars to go after
them and McPherson says they will be at Bolivar in the morning.—The troops were duly notified before to be in readiness
to move at a moments notice if called for. This afternoon a reply
came, before the cars were ordered, that they were all ready.[6]

This will give us a force that I think we can push the enemy
if ~~they~~ he does not push us.

The testimony of young Jake I do not take as throwing much
light upon the enemies movements altho' reliable as far as he
could obtain information.[7]

Murphy's command should push out as far towards Iuka as
possible without delay. The enemy should be made to abandon
that place befor geting benefit from the stores left there Since
writing the above the enclosed dispatch has been received from
Hamilton.[8] I have no map that shows Barnetts[9] or Peytons
Mills,[10] but judge from the general tenor of the dispatch that
the former is about East from Jacinto and the latter Southeast.

I do not see that the whole should change the plan for sending Murphy's forces back towards Iuka.

Respectfully &c.

U. S. GRANT

Maj. Gen.

ALS, DNA, RG 393, Army of the Miss., Letters Received.

1. On Sept. 13, 1862, Brig. Gen. William S. Rosecrans, Corinth, telegraphed to USG. "The Little fight at Iuka was a cavlry attack the rebels supposing we had evacuated—they were much surprised & badly scared   a Tennessee capt taken says Price with his staff was at Bay Sprigs but the infantry were two 2 days behind. The scout from Ripley went all the way down to Four 4 miles off Guntown   There was no force or movement in that direction   Report at Guntown Baldwin & up to Booneville water so scarce that it seems though to me if they have a large force—I go up to Ords to consult with Prince about cavalry defense work here" Telegram received, *ibid.*, Dept. of the Mo., Telegrams Received. *O.R.*, I, xvii, part 2, 217. On Sept. 14, Brig. Gen. James B. McPherson, Corinth, telegraphed to USG. "Is it true our troops have left Iuka   I am just starting a train with men to repair the road & open communication   shall I send it beyond Bursville   answer quick" Telegram received, DNA, RG 393, Dept. of the Mo., Telegrams Received. On the same day, McPherson telegraphed to USG. "Gen Roscrans not here   left for his old Camp at Clear Creek this morning" Telegram received, *ibid.* On the same day, Rosecrans, Clear Creek, Miss., telegraphed to USG. "Your dispatch recieved. Iuka office not open   no news from there to day—Scouts in from Bay springs says no rebel force on the Bay spring & Jacinto road yesterday—Dubois has cavalry four miles below Booneville   no rebel force there 10 a m   two regiments left at the old camps at sunrise yesterday going East—Secret agent in from Orizaba. small camp there another four miles sout west of Ripley—Falkner reported to be Prices body guard—says Hamilton reports this a m. our cavalry going to Bay Iuka springs   reports falling in with rebel cavalry near Barnetts—Suppose it was the armstrong cavalry—that tried Iuka yesterday a. m.—Hamilton says our cavalry was to attack them at day light this morning & he would pitch in with ring   no news yet from Jacinto—. . . Sharpshooters seant out of Burnsvill by a few Rebel pickets—stray scalywags from the armstrong command" Telegram received, *ibid. O.R.*, I, xvii, part 2, 218.

2. Farmington, Miss., about four miles east of Corinth.

3. As Brig. Gen. Gordon Granger began to remove his command from Rienzi, Miss., Rosecrans began to withdraw troops from posts at Iuka, Miss., and eastward toward Corinth. See letter to Col. John C. Kelton, Sept. 7, 1862. On Sept. 11, in the midst of this move, Rosecrans, Iuka, telegraphed to USG. "We have here fifty car loads of subsistance & five car loads of Sick   three (3) regts will arrive from the east by day light & will need rest   should there need be cars might bring them down. What orders about these stores & sick—Where is the rebel force said to be—" Telegram received, DNA, RG 393, Dept. of the Mo., Telegrams Received; copy, *ibid.*, Army of the Miss., Telegrams Sent.

On the same day, McPherson, Corinth, telegraphed to USG. "In case trains do not go to Iuka tonight had I not better detain them here & not send them to Columbus in the morning—" Telegram received, *ibid.*, Dept. of the Mo., Telegrams Received. On the same day, McPherson telegraphed to USG. "Will it be necessary to send train tonight—I can send a large train if required" Telegram received, *ibid.* Later on Sept. 11, McPherson telegraphed to USG. "Two trains thirty 30 cars will leave for Iuka in one hour—" Telegram received, *ibid.* On Sept. 12, McPherson telegraphed to USG. "I sent 2 trains to Iuka last night one of them has returned   the other is loaaded with commissary stores & will be in soon—shall I send mail train to Columbus this morning   through frt with battery for Gangers division left at four a m   please answer quickly—" Telegram received, *ibid.*

The movement of Maj. Gen. Sterling Price toward Iuka disrupted the orderly withdrawal of Rosecrans's forces. On Sept. 12, Brig. Gen. Charles S. Hamilton, Jacinto, telegraphed to USG. "Pickets on maratta road attacked this morning at day light—have sent out a battallion of infantry to sound the enemy preparations all complete   I dont think enemy in force in immediate front" Telegram received, *ibid.* On the same day, Hamilton telegraphed to USG. "Since the attack on my pickets this morning the rebel cavalry has retreated & there is no force within 6 miles—The roads from the south have been obstructed & we are ready for the fray   at present all quiet here & at Rienzi" Telegram received, *ibid.* On the same day, Col. John V. D. Du Bois, Rienzi, telegraphed to USG. "Two (2) companies of Infantry on special duty three (3) miles on the Boonville road driven in by about 300 cavalry & 200 Infantry. They reformed on the Cavalry grand guard—drove the Rebels back—The Rebel Infantry threw away some clothing in their retreat. I have been beyond all the pickets on our front & just returned. The people show no alarm—I will keep you informed of everything. The enemy are very bold—" Telegram received, *ibid.* On Sept. 14, Du Bois telegraphed to USG. "My cavalry four hundred (400) strong are all around Boonvill & are moving west   They are well supported by four hunded (400) Infy moving paralell with them & about Three miles south of here   friday a column of Rebels moved from Crockett Eastward & returned to Big Spring   this was the Cavalry which drove in our pickets yesterday morning earley   this Column was joined by another & the two about Twelve Hundred strong moved across the R R towards Iuka   the Column I am looking after slemmer [*Slemons*] Comds the Cavalry   price is believed to be at Iuka by the people   no news from Jacinto   I cant find any body west   I sent this Report to Genls Hamilton & Rosecrans at 9 15 a m" Telegram received, *ibid.* On the same day, Du Bois telegraphed to USG. "Col Lee reports 10 a m from Four miles below Boonville having thoroughly examined the old camps there—two (2) Regts left at sunrise yesterday going east   Col Clinton ~~and~~ 2 Ark & Col Adams Miss Reg both Cavalry with four small Iron field guns   Col Lee will now move west & on the trail of the Rebels & prhaps return by Jacinto   man just in from a trip secretly as far west as Orizaba   a small Camp three (3) miles south west   another four miles west of Ripley   Col Falkners Reg is Genl Prices Body Guard   Price has kept his men at work for two weeks getting out timber for trestle work to repair the bridge over the Tuscumbia which he expects us to burn   my cavalry are nearly exhausted" Telegram received, *ibid.*

On Sept. 13, only a small rear guard under the command of Col. Robert C. Murphy had been left to guard a rather large quantity of supplies. Murphy was attacked by cav. under Act. Brig. Gen. Frank C. Armstrong, which he repulsed, but when faced with Price's large force, he retired.

4. On Sept. 13, USG wrote to Maj. Gen. Edward O. C. Ord. "Watch & be ready to guard the Road well towards Farmington   report says that Iuka & Burnsville are taken & Enemy now within eight (8) or nine miles East of us" Copy, Ord Papers, CU-B. On Sept. 14, Ord, Corinth, telegraphed to USG. "I send you copy of dispatch Col Buke recd this a m 9 oclock   Burnsville 14   Col Burke —Brigade from Iuka just passed here   skirmishers were fired upon two miles back   also rearguard of Col Murphys Command   I am waiting orders   signed CAPT PIGGOTT   I head of it in my absence & on return sent for it   have sent copy to Gen Rosecrans—"   Telegram received, DNA, RG 393, Dept. of the Mo., Telegrams Received. On the same day, Ord telegraphed to USG. "The Eighty first O. is in & stationed between here & Farmington   nothing heard of or from Col Crockers command   Col Morton reports that he heard firing in the direction of Iuka early this morning   a few shot apparently 6 or 12 pdrs"   Telegram received, *ibid.*

5. On Sept. 11, USG telegraphed to Brig. Gen. John A. Logan. "Order all the Troops formerly belonging to Genl. McArthurs Division immediately back. They should march by the way of Pocahontas"   Copy, *ibid.*, 17th Army Corps, 3rd Division, Telegrams Received. On the same day, Logan, Jackson, telegraphed to USG. "I have ordered the troops of Genl McArthur command as you directed Hurlbut has not as yet been heard from   he must have traveled slow—"   Telegram received, *ibid.*, Dept. of the Mo., Telegrams Received. On the same day, Brig. Gen. Leonard F. Ross, Bolivar, telegraphed to USG. "your order for the troops belonging to Genl mcarthurs division to return to Corinth is rec'd—Do you intend that I shall send the third ohio and one section of Howells second 2d Ills battery with them   if so one of our posts will be without guns to defend it— had I not better send a small cavalry force along   if you think best I will send some of my cavalry as far as pocahontas with them—"   Telegram received, *ibid.* On Sept. 12, Logan telegraphed to USG. "Col Crocker left Bolivar this morning with his command for corinth by way of Pocahontas   Hurlburt has not been heard from   I sent from Bolivar to Somerville yesterday"   Telegram received, *ibid.* On Sept. 14, USG telegraphed to Logan. "Nothing has been heard here from Col. Crocker's Command. Enquire from Bolivar when he left & when last heard from, and answer"   Copy, *ibid.*, 17th Army Corps, 3rd Division, Telegrams Received. On the same day, Logan telegraphed to USG. "Genl Ross telegraphs that Col Crockers force left Bolivar on Friday morning   heard he-ard from yesterday morning two miles west of middleton   delayed by broken wagons cavalry not returned." Telegram received, *ibid.*, Dept. of the Mo., Telegrams Received. On Sept. 16, Maj. John A. Rawlins telegraphed to Brig. Gen. Stephen A. Hurlbut. "Send them by Land Via Chenpella"   Telegram received, *ibid.*, District of West Tenn., 4th Division, Telegrams Received.

On Sept. 15, Rawlins issued Special Orders No. 195. "Col. M. M. Crocker, 13th Regt. Iowa Vol. Infy, is hereby assigned temporarily to command an expedition Eastward to be composed of one regiment to be detailed by Gen. Ord, the 8th Wisconsin, and 11th Missouri and such other troops of Brig. Gen. Rosecran's command as may be found east of Glendale. Col. Crocker will report to Major Gen. Ord for instructions before leaving and afterwards report to and receive instructions from Gen. Rosecrans, reporting by telegraph from Burnsville." DS, *ibid.*, RG 94, Special Orders, District of West Tenn.; copies, *ibid.*, RG 393, USG

Special Orders; DLC-USG, V, 15, 16, 82, 87; Crocker Papers, IaHA. *O.R.*, I, xvii, part 2, 218. On Sept. 15, Rosecrans telegraphed to USG. "Col Crocker has not yet reported—I am told the train going to Iuka leaves in fifteen 15 minutes but whether with troops or not do not know   Have sent a dispatch to Col Mower from whom I have not yet heard to conduct his movement as a reconnoisance should Col Crocker go out he will consider these his orders if he ranks Mower" Telegram received, DNA, RG 393, Dept. of the Mo., Telegrams Received; copy, *ibid.*, Army of the Miss., Telegrams Sent. *O.R.*, I, xvii, part 2, 219. On the same day, Rosecrans telegraphed to USG. "Col mower 11th Mo who commands those troops is a brave & gallant & sensible commder   he is the senior officer of the second (2d) Brigade of stanlys division   I do not think it right that Crocker should be sent to Command & my three (3) regts Turned over to Genl Ord   that it should be the reverse & the command go with the bulk of the troops is to me clear beyond a question—" Telegram received, DNA, RG 393, Dept. of the Mo., Telegrams Received; copy, *ibid.*, Army of the Miss., Telegrams Sent. On the same day, Rosecrans telegraphed to USG. "all right   he will find col mower a pretty good man—" Telegram received, *ibid.*, Dept. of the Mo., Telegrams Received; copy, *ibid.*, Army of the Miss., Telegrams Sent.

6. See telegram to Brig. Gen. John A. Logan, Sept. 9, 1862, note 2.

7. On Sept. 13, Rosecrans telegraphed to Rawlins. "The following statement of J M Leonard is forwarded for the information of the Genl Comdg   I left Iuka on sunday   staid one night near Danville—Wendsday went to Rienzi where I was detained by the provost Marshall for three hours   after being released I went to within 2 miles of Ripley & staid all night at strongs house   learned positively there were not troops at Ripley   thursday morning I left for Guntown having learned that Price's forces were at Baldwin & guntown & some troops were at Boonville   Continued within four miles of Guntown where I staid all night in an old vacant house   saw no person to talk with   left friday morning & came back towards Boonville traveling nighboring roads until I struck the Rienzi & Guntown road   here I was halted by four cavalry pickets who ~~stripped~~ questioned me very closely & stripped my clothes off & searched them after which I satisfied them I was a Loyal citizen to the Confederate states   they disharged me to go home & directed the route to avoid the federal pickets   I learned from these pickets that Price's forces were at Guntown Baldwin & Boonville Eighty thousand (80,000) strong   I left & came up to Mr Covingtons & stopped to feed. he informed me that Prices forces were up between Boonville & Rienzi that he had very large army   I came up leaving Boonville four miles to my right by farm roads & came into the Renzi & Boonville Road four & half miles south of Rienzi when I was arrested by the federal pickets & brought to Rienzi   every one I talked with of the citizens were of the opinion price was going to attack Corinth very soon. they have scouts running in Every direction forcing Every man who can carry arms to go to the army   most Every man is away from his hom   I am certain there is no army moving to Ripley or In that direction or I should have learned of it   There had been good strong force up there a few days ago of cavalry & Infantry   Everybody said that Prices forces were on the rail road—" Telegram received, DNA, RG 393, Dept. of the Mo., Telegrams Received.

8. On Sept. 14, Hamilton telegraphed to USG and Rosecrans. "Capt Wilcox returned here with Eleven (11) Co's cavalry   Encountered ~~pickets~~ Rebel pickets at Barnetts on the right this moring   He captured four (4) Con-

federate soldiers who say Prices forces were at Peytons Mills this morning Thirty Thousand (30,000) strong. This shows a movement east of the Rebel Army. The rumbling of wagons as of Artillery heard during the night. The Inhabitants near Peytons Confirm the report of movement if this is true he is either marching on Iuka or getting in my rear—" Telegram received, *ibid*.

9. Barnett Knob, about eight miles east of Jacinto, Miss.

10. This may have been Paden, seven miles south of Barnett Knob.

To Julia Dent Grant

Corinth, Sept. 14th/62

MY DEAR JULIA,

I have not written to you for more than a week because I had written twice[1] for you to go either to La Fayette[2] or Detroit and did not know but you would be off before the next Tuesday, mail day, would come round when you could receive a letter. But not has yet come from you in response. I hope you have gone, or if not, will go soon. I would rather advise Detroit as the most preferable place. You have more acquaintances there, a good healthy place, and good schools for the children.

We have been very much threatened here for a week or more back and if the rebels had come in when they first threatened they would have found us very weak in consequence of the heavy drafts that had been made on me at other points for troops, and the extended line I was then protecting. Now however it is different. I am concentrated and strong. Will give the rebels a tremendious thrashing if they come. If they do not come will not say what I intend doing.

I shall move my Head Quarters to Jackson soon in all probability.[3] It is a much more central position to my command. Maj. Rawlins has returned in general good health but not able to ride on horseback Rowley is absent, in bad health.[4] Hillyer has not yet returned.[5] The remainder of my staff are well.—Have you heard anything from Covington? I do not hear a word from home. They must be badly frightened. I do not think really there is the least danger either there or at Louisville.—You will see the greatest fall in a few weeks of rebel hopes that was ever known. They have made a bold effort, and with wonderful success, but it is a spasmodic effort without anything behind to fall back on. When they do begin to fall all resources are at an end and rebellion will soon show a rapid decline. If I should see any signs of a short quiet I will try to get off for a few days and will go wherever you may be.

My general heath is good but still like it was when you left: a short appetite and a loss of flesh. From being some fifteen or twenty pounds above my usual weight I am now probably below it. I am begining to have those cold night sweats again which I had a few years ago.—Kisses for yourself and children.—I got those articles you sent me.

ULYS.

ALS, DLC-USG.

    1. These letters have not been found.
    2. USG visited Col. Joseph J. Reynolds and his family in La Fayette, Ind., in June, 1861. See letter to Julia Dent Grant, June 17, 1861.
    3. See telegram to Maj. Gen. Edward O. C. Ord, [*Sept. 23?*], 1862.
    4. On Aug. 28, 1862, 1st Lt. Theodore S. Bowers issued Special Orders No. 177. "Corporal, John Clark, Co. "D," 16th Regt Wis Vol. Infy. and Private, Peter Fries, 3rd Ohio Battery, having been properly reported to these Head Quarters as being Insane, it is hereby, Ordered, That Capt. Wm R. Rowley, Aid-de-Camp, proceed with said Insane Soldiers to Washington, D. C. and deliver them over to the proper authorities of the Government Insane Hospital in that City. Capt. Rowley will detail such Assistants as he may require." DS, DNA, RG 94, District of West Tenn., Special Orders; copies, *ibid.*, RG 393, USG Special Orders; DLC-USG, V, 15, 16, 82, 87.
    5. On Aug. 29, Col. William S. Hillyer, St. Louis, telegraphed to USG. "Sent my family to Newark   Just learned wifes mother dead   must go to Newark   get me leave of absence twenty 20 days   ans' immediatly" Telegram received, DNA, RG 94, Staff Papers, William S. Hillyer. On Sept. 19, Hillyer wrote to his wife that he had returned to USG's hd. qrs. the day before. Copy, Mrs. Theodore McCurdy Marsh, Springfield, N. J.

To Richard Yates

Head Quarters, Dist. of West Ten.
Corinth, Sept. 14th 1862

Hon. R. Yates
Gov.r of Illinois,
Springfield Ill.
Sir:

Enclosed herewith I send you a true copy of a letter from Asst. Surgeon Wesley Humphrey 52d Ill. Vols. with the endorsements thereon.

Dr. Wesley Humphrey seems to have reported for duty, in good faith, on the strength of telegraphic notice of his appointment from the Adjt. Gen. of the state, and has done good service ever since. Receiving no Commission and another Dr. being subsequently Commissioned for the same position has deprived Dr. H. from receiving compensation for his services notwithstanding he was regularly mustered in by order of Maj. Gen. Halleck.

I respectfully refer this to you because one of these Asst. Surgeons are illegally in service, and from the endorsement made by order of Maj Gen. Halleck it would seem to be that officer holding your commission, it being subsequent to the appointment of the former.

very respectfully
your obt. svt.
U. S. Grant
Maj. Gen.

ALS, Records of 52nd Ill., I-ar. On July 22, 1862, Wesley Humphrey wrote to Maj. Nathaniel H. McLean discussing the problems involved in his muster into the service. On April 5, Humphrey had been offered an appointment as asst. surgeon, 52nd Ill. On April 10, Humphrey accepted the appointment, and, learning about the battle of Shiloh, joined his regt. Although his commission did not arrive, he was mustered in by a U.S. officer. Later, a member of the medical board of Ill. asked him some questions. The board later informed him that he had not passed, but Humphrey wrote that he did not know the interview was an examination. Governor Richard Yates soon commissioned another man to fill the same office. Copy, *ibid*. On July 22, USG forwarded Humphrey's letter to "Gen Head Quarters." Copy, *ibid*. On July 23, Capt. William McMichael for Maj. Gen. Henry W. Halleck ruled Humphrey's muster valid and wrote that "he cannot be removed from office unless by the regular methods prescribed by law" Copy, *ibid*. On Sept. 14, Maj. John A. Rawlins issued Special Orders No. 194. "The Commanding Officer of the 52nd Regt. Ill. Vols. will muster Asst. Surgeon, Humphrey as the Asst. Surgeon of said Regiment until otherwise directed by competent authority, Dr. Humphrey having been duly appointed by the Governor of Illinois and mustered into service by orders from the Commdg. Officer of the Department. Any subsequent Commission given to another to fill the place is null and void, there being no vacancy." DS, DNA, RG 94, Special Orders, District of West Tenn.; copies, *ibid*., RG 393, USG Special Orders; DLC-USG, V, 15, 16, 82, 87. Humphrey served as asst. surgeon, 52nd Ill., until May 21, 1863, when he was appointed surgeon, 1st Ala. (later 55th U.S. Colored Inf.).

To Maj. Gen. Henry W. Halleck

———

Grants Hd Qrs
near Corinth Miss
Sept. 16th [*15 1862*] 8. a m

MAJ GEN H. W. HALLECK
GEN IN CHIEF

For ten (10) days or more the enemy have been hovering on our front in reported large force—I have watched their moves closely until I could concentrate my forces—All are now in good shape—Hurlbuts division has come from Memphis to Bolivar & about 6.000 troops from Bolivar brought here[1]—Gen Price is south east from us near Bay Springs moving north east.[2] It is reported that Van Dorn & Breckinridge are to join and attack.[3] From the best information they cannot reach here under four (4) days. My view is they are covering a move to get Gen Price into East Tennessee.[4] If I can I will attack Price before he crosses Bear Creek.[5] If he can be beaten there it will prevent either the design to go north or to unite forces and an attack here

U. S. GRANT
Maj Gen Comdg

Telegram received, DNA, RG 94, Generals' Papers and Books, Telegrams Received by Gen. Halleck; copies (dated Sept. 16, 1862), *ibid.*, RG 107, Telegrams Collected (Bound); *ibid.*, Telegrams Received in Cipher; *ibid.* (dated Sept. 15), RG 393, USG Hd. Qrs. Correspondence; DLC-USG, V, 4, 5, 7, 8, 88. Dated Sept. 16 in *O.R.*, I, xvii, part 2, 220. On Sept. 17, Maj. Gen. Henry W. Halleck telegraphed to USG. "Do everything in your power to prevent Price from crossing the Tennessee river. A junction of Price & Bragg in Tenn or Ky would be most disastrous. They should be fought while separate." ALS (telegram sent), DNA, RG 107, Telegrams Collected (Bound); copies, *ibid.*, RG 393, USG Hd. Qrs. Correspondence; DLC-USG, V, 4, 5, 7, 8, 88. *O.R.*, I, xvii, part 2, 222.

1. See telegram to Brig. Gen. John A. Logan, Sept. 9, 1862, and letter to Brig. Gen. William S. Rosecrans, Sept. 14, 1862.

2. Bay Springs, Miss., about thirty miles southeast of Corinth. On Sept. 15, Brig. Gen. Charles S. Hamilton, Jacinto, telegraphed to USG. "Prisoners captured last night confirm the movement of Prices army to Tennessee   cavalry left Baldwin on Wednesday Evening followed by Infantry & Artillery   the rears camped between Bay Springs & Maretta last night—Army Estimated by all the soldier at thirty (30) to forty (40) thousand   we have quiet a number of prisoners—All quiet here"   Telegram received, DNA, RG 393, Dept. of the Mo., Telegrams Received. On the same day, Col. John V. D. Du Bois, Rienzi, telegraphed to USG. "I have seen Gen Hamilton dispatch of 8 a m today but do not know if Bridge at Baldwin is destroyed   will send to Baldwin immediately   I heard this morning from some orders passing to Col Mizners that the (3d) Third Mich cavlry had reoccupied Iuka   Telegraph reparers are working on the wires—"   Telegram received, *ibid.* Also on Sept. 15, Du Bois telegraphed to USG. "Serg't & 6 men from Col Lee's command just returned   Col Lee reports the man perfectly reliable & that he went from Boonville on ~~Saturday~~ the south road to Marietta—The Cavalry command which was at Boonville on Saturday moved down this road on the Road six (6) miles south of Boonville—A command of Infantry & Artillery under McCullough came on the same road   these companies with others were encamped last night three (3) miles north east of Marietta. The Serg't captured two (2) rebel soldiers on the edge of their camp from them & scouting we learned that the camp extended toward Bay Springs. Force estimated by prisoners at Twelve Thousand (12000). On Friday troops left Guntown with Price & encamped in the vicinity of Bay Springs by road six (6) miles south of Marietta. Soldiers & citizens all state that the command of Price is moving to some point on the Tenn' River"   Telegram received, *ibid.* On the same day, USG telegraphed to Maj. Gen. Edward O. C. Ord. "The Cavalry sent from here have returned—they Went Within Three (3) miles of Burnsville and met fifth 5th ohio Cavalry returning   no Enemy at Burnsville" Telegram received, Ord Papers, CU-B.

3. As the army of Maj. Gen. Sterling Price pushed northward toward Iuka, Maj. Gen. Earl Van Dorn with a force of between 9,000 and 10,000 men moved toward Holly Springs, Miss., and Grand Junction, Tenn. His aim was to dislodge U.S. forces from western Tenn. and Ky. *O.R.*, I, xvii, part 2, 697, 701, 703–4. On Sept. 4, Maj. Gen. William T. Sherman, Memphis, wrote to Maj. John A. Rawlins that he believed C. S. A. troops were moving north to attack Bolivar or "threaten your communications." He sent out cav. to intercept them. Copy, DLC-William T. Sherman. *O.R.*, I, xvii, part 2, 201–2. On Sept. 12, Sherman

wrote to Rawlins that C. S. A. troops had reached Holly Springs with a force estimated at 9,000. *Ibid.*, pp. 215–16. On Sept. 13, Sherman wrote to Rawlins that he had sent out cav. to intercept and harass the enemy. *Ibid.*, pp. 217–18; *ibid.*, I, xvii, part 1, 57–60. On Sept. 16, USG telegraphed to Brig. Gen. John A. Logan. "If the Rebel Cavalry are in north of the Hatchie, I want you and Hurlbut to pocket them if possible. Telegraph Hurlbut of their presence." Copy, DNA, RG 393, 17th Army Corps, 3rd Division, Telegrams Received.

4. Price had originally intended to dislodge Rosecrans from USG's left, then follow him toward Nashville to effect a junction with Gen. Braxton Bragg. Van Dorn wanted Price to assist him in an attack on USG's hd. qrs. at Corinth, however; and when Rosecrans moved westward from Iuka, Price agreed to cooperate with Van Dorn. *O.R.*, I, xvii, part 2, 698, 702, 705–6.

5. On Sept. 15, Rosecrans telegraphed to USG. "Your dispatch received immediate orders will be given as to Subsistence but this Army or what is left of it has already been under orders to keep three (3) days rations in Haversacks & two (2) more in wagons. We have now one hundred (100) rounds per man Fifty (50) more will take thirty (30) wagon loads of Ammunition" Telegram received, DNA, RG 393, Dept. of the Mo., Telegrams Received; copy, *ibid.*, Army of the Miss., Telegrams Sent. On the same day, Rosecrans telegraphed again to USG. "You have had hamiltons dispatch this morning—we ought to send out a train with a regt to as near Iuka as the car will take us—Push a telegraph office at Burnsville & rush the Three (3) regts already out in that direction on Iuka & down to the south of it   one reg't which went out during the night was murphy's   the other the 11th Missouri Col Mower Comdg   they are on their way   the 39th Ohio half way between here & Burnsville south of the R R at Mrs Stricklains   have three days rations" Telegram received, *ibid.*, Dept. of the Mo., Telegrams Received; copy, *ibid.*, Army of the Miss., Telegrams Sent. On Sept. 16, Ord telegraphed to USG. "Shall I order the artillery from Batteries b & c and the purdy road to this division & assigned Larys & Madisons battery—" Telegram received, *ibid.*, Dept. of the Mo., Telegrams Received.

To Brig. Gen. William S. Rosecrans

Corinth, Sept. 15th 1862

GEN. ROSECRANS,

I send herewith a letter which I wish you to have sent through by "flag of truce" to Gen. Price, or Commanding officer South of us.

Just at this time I do not much like to be sending, flags of truce, but these prisoners that I am now ~~having~~ asking to exchange for have not been sent home and I am desirous of effecting the exchange before they are sent.

Yours &c—

U. S. GRANT

Maj. Gen.

P.S. Put up the letter to the Confed. Gen. and send such note as you may deem fit as to the officer & escort you think necessary to be bearers.

U. S. G.

ALS, IC. On Sept. 15, 1862, Brig. Gen. William S. Rosecrans telegraphed to USG. "Yours inclosing list of Prisoners paroled & to be exchanged is received. I dispatch the letter to Col Du Bois with orders to send it down by a handsome escort. the officers to slected for shrewdness and gentlemanly deportment. They are instructed to obtain if possible and bring back a reply." ALS, DNA, RG 393, Dept. of the Mo., Telegrams Received. *O.R.*, I, xvii, part 2, 219. On Sept. 16, Col. John V. D. Du Bois, Rienzi, telegraphed to USG and Rosecrans. "Col Hatch flag of truce returned this moment   I have sent reply to you   Col Hatch Reports he went to Baldwin via R R from six miles south of Boonville   all the trestle work at the sawmill of 20 mile creek is up except five hundred (500) feet—The timbers for this 500 feet are there ready to put up—The Bearings of Mud sills are all ~~of mud sills~~ ready laid or embedded—to accept the shoe the R R can be put in perfect order from Boonville to Baldwin in 6 hours   Everything is there bolts spikes & all   the forces in Baldwin are 2 regts of Infantry 1 light battery— & a battallion of Infantry   I said they looked as if they had just got off the train   They were a green looking set officers & men & acknowledged they had never been in a fight—They refused to let him pass further & the comdg officer sent the letter which I have forwarded to you by special messenger—if there is a reply it will be sent by them—"   Telegram received, DNA, RG 393, Dept. of the Mo., Telegrams Received. On Sept. 15, Col. John W. Portis, 42nd Ala., Baldwin, Miss., wrote to USG. "so soon as I communicate with Maj Gen Price I will send an answer under a Flag of Truce to Rienzi." ALS, *ibid.* On Sept. 18, Maj. Gen. Sterling Price wrote to USG. "I have the honor to acknowledge the receipt of your proposition to exchange prisoners which have been paroled by us respectively, and to say that having already forwarded to Vicksburg the names of all those connected with this Army whom you have paroled so that they might be embraced in the exchange which is being effected there it is impossible for me to accede to your proposition"   Copy, *ibid.*, RG 109, Price's Division, Army of the Miss., Letters Sent. *O.R.*, II, iv, 529.

To Julia Dent Grant

―――――

Corinth, Sept. 15th 1862.

DEAR JULIA,[1]

. . . and so stated and asked Mary to pay you a visit in that case.

As to you not geting letters how can you blame them? Mary has written[2] . . . a single one there, at this time, that I care for you or the children being with.

I got a letter from White this evening cooly telling me that he could pay nothing and advising that his debt on the city property should be paid and thereby save both the farm and that. This would make the house cost $1200 now due on it, $120 interest due and the $150 which you loaned. At this time I do not feel like making any such investment. White also wanted me to give him a letter of introduction to Gen. Steele enabling him to get to Helena to transact business and make money. It would be a grand idea for me to introduce persons of doubtful loyalty into our frontier posts! If he asks you anything about it you can say that his letter was received but I do not intend to answer it.

If I could get away for a week or two I would have a settlement with Mr. White that would end our business.

I am very well but hard worked. There has been two nights within a week that I did not get a single hours sleep and no night that I get over about five.

There is a large force hovering around us for the last ten days and the grand denouiment must take place soon, probably before you get this. My troops have been so scattered that it has taken all my efforts to get them up and save all the public property. All is now in good position. What I say of these matters I do not want you to read to anyone.

Kiss the children for me. I hope your answer will say that you are going to Detroit, and dont let us have any more letters that will cause [—]

Good night, I have written pages of very important instructions, all of which things I write myself notwithstanding what is said by Hillyer's friends, and without any of my staff knowing what I am going to write until after it is done. Hillyer never has given grounds for such a report because often when I have asked him to write something for me which might as well be done by any member of my staff as myself he has declined saying that no one could put anything pertaining to military matters in so concise a for and explain so fully all that was wanted, without possibility [of mi]ssinterpritation, as myself. No Gen. officer in the Army, I will ~~bar~~ venture to say, comes so near doing their own writing as myself with the exception of Halleck.

ULYS.

ALS, DLC-USG.

1. The bulk of the leaf containing the first and second pages of this letter has been torn away.

2. Due to the tearing away of the bulk of this page, on the next line the words "for an answer," appear at the end of the line. For the remainder of the page, only the last word, or part of the last word, of each line remains. These are: "cting . . . hown . . . than . . . who . . . faults . . . duct, . . . then. . . . ame . . . our . . . you . . . rebels . . . re . . . or . . . situated . . . ould . . . ences, . . . hools . . . xceedingly . . . en"

To Maj. Gen. Edward O. C. Ord

Head Quarters Dist. of West Tenn.
Corinth, Sept. 16th 1862.

MAJ. GENL. ORD
COMDG. POST.
GEN.

On the strength of Colonel Mower's[1] telegram I deem it advisable to send our forces to within supporting distance of him.

If Genl. Ross can move, his forces had better go to Glendale,[2] or either side of there where water can be found, and be on the alert to give assistance if required.

Capt. Reynolds can furnish any teams they may require.

Respectfully &c

U. S. GRANT

Maj. Genl.

Copy, DNA, RG 94, War Records Office, Union Battle Reports. *O.R.*, I, xvii, part 1, 118.

1. Joseph A. Mower of Conn. served as private in the Mexican War. Commissioned 2nd lt., 1st Inf., on June 18, 1855, he served in the U.S. Army until appointed col., 11th Mo., on May 3, 1862. On Sept. 16, Lt. Col. Edward Prince, 7th Ill. Cav., Burnsville, Miss., telegraphed to Brig. Gen. William S. Rosecrans. "an orderly sent to Col Mower says that our forces are falling back from Iuka towards Burnsville that they have fought the enemy all day & that Price is at Iuka with about 15000 fifteen thousand   dont rely on this second—" Telegram received, DNA, RG 393, Dept. of the Mo., Telegrams Received. On the same day, Rosecrans telegraphed to USG. "The following just been rec'd from Col Mower & is the latest information we have   dated Burnsville   I have already reported to that the people in the vicinity say, Price is at Iuka with a strong force   I dont know whether it is reliable or not   I am going to see   signed J A MOWER Col 11th Mo Vols   Hamilton reports nothing new   all quiet in his vicinity   cavalry officers think Price is on the fulton & Iuka road—Scouts are out to ascertain the fatcs   are expected in soon—DoBois reports all quiet in his vicinity" Telegram received, *ibid. O.R.*, I, xvii, part 2, 220. On the same day, Maj. Gen. Edward O. C. Ord sent USG a copy of a telegram from Col. Alexander Chambers, 16th Iowa, Burnsville. "We arrived here at two A M & ~~camped~~ camped in the train. I sent a company 2 miles towards Iuka on the Rail Road who report Picquet of the Enemy there—up to this time the wire has been down between here & Glendale & although in operation the party to repair it has not returned—as soon as it does the command will move toward Iuka but Picquets had to be reinforced this morning. Col Mower who commands thinks they are making for our rear from reports of scouts—the 3d Mich Cavalry is not at Iuka   citizens here report Price at Iuka with a force ranging from ten (10) to fifteen (15) Thousand—" Telegram received, DNA, RG 393, Dept. of the Mo., Telegrams Received.

Also on Sept. 16, Prince telegraphed to USG. "A picket party just come in & who was stationed about one (1) mile down the Jacinto road reports that Quite a large column of cavalry has crossed said road going west perhaps (200)—. . . P. S.—my 24 men are determined & will kill 2 to one—" Telegram received, *ibid.* On the same day, Rosecrans telegraphed to USG. "You have the telegram from DuBois   I have directed Col Gilbert to move up the 39th Ohio from Johnson's 4 miles north of Jacinto to Harvys mill about 2 miles south of Burnsville where there is a blind road leading to Iuka to post himself advantageously then send forward three co's to reconnoitre & cut off the cavalry that burned the train & send up a company to burnsville—Prince is to notify Genl Ross & col mowry of what has happened that those is coming—I think things will work out—I now find our stores were wagoned down towards Bay Springs—our cavalry heard the train moving down & saw those who had seen the packages with our marks on them   Only one regt of Infantry & one (1) of cavalry has gone from Dubois— Shall more be moved tonight or await further instructions"   Telegram received, *ibid. O.R.*, I, xvii, part 2, 221. Also on Sept. 16, Rosecrans telegraphed to USG. "The orders are all out   Col Mizner will direct one Regt of cavalry to move this afternoon from Reinzi   Do you not think it would be best to leave one battallion of Cavalry to cover that front & conceal movement   I will direct the Infantry to begin to move this P M"   Telegram received, DNA, RG 393, Dept. of the Mo., Telegrams Received. *O.R.*, I, xvii, part 2, 221. On the same day, Rosecrans telegraphed to USG. "Do I understand ~~that~~ you that I am to go up by rail to support Mowry or that you send up 1400 men for that purpose   I will consult Dubois about that move tonight   Hamiltons position is a good support to any thing of that sort"   Telegram received, DNA, RG 393, Dept. of the Mo., Telegrams Received. *O.R.*, I, xvii, part 2, 221.

2. Glendale, Miss., on the Memphis and Charleston Railroad, about six miles southeast of Corinth.

To Brig. Gen. Thomas J. McKean

Head Quarters Dist of West Tenn
Corinth, Miss. Sept. 16th 1862

BRIG. GEN THOMAS. J. McKEAN
COMMANDING POST
CORINTH, MISS:
GENERAL:

By Special Orders, I have assigned you to the command of this Post, contingent upon moving out with the main force to meet the enemy.

This command will include all troops not actually moved from their present camps, to-wit: Two Regiments at Danville; one Regiment and two companies of Cavalry at Kossuth;[1] one Regiment and one company of Cavalry at Chewalla; and about fifteen hundred men from Gen. Ross' command, and the first United States Infantry, with heavy guns. Besides these, there will be two or three other Regiments from Gen. Ord's command, the locality and position of which he is instructed to inform you.

The object is to defend this place against any raids that may be attempted, and particularly to guard against the near approach of a large force before information can reach me, and the return of the main body affected.

Miner details cannot be given as to how this is to be done, but I feel great satisfaction in being able to leave these in so competent hands.

At least one locomotive, and a full train of cars, should be kept here ready to move at all times. The Chief Quartermaster should also have ready at least one hundred teams to be called into service any moment they may be required.

Instructions have been given that the troops should have three days rations in their Haversacks, but it would be well to see that these are complied with.

You are authorized to use as Staff Officers Capt. Reynolds, Chief Quartermaster; Capt. Prime, chief Engineer; the Assistant Quartermaster of the Post; Lieut. Lyford, Chief of Ordnance,[2] and Lieut Callender,[3] now not on any special duty.

Capt. Prime is well acquainted with the officers of the Railroad, and also, with the localities occupied by the troops composing the forces for the defences of Corinth.

You will direct all Negroes coming into Corinth to Capt. Prime, to be put at work on the fortifications.[4] The women and children can be sent to the negro camp established East of the city

Respectfully, &c

U. S. GRANT

Maj. Gen. Com'd'g

LS, NjP. On Sept. 16, 1862, in order to consolidate troops at Corinth, USG telegraphed to Lt. Col. William W. Belknap. "You will immediately return to your regiment at this place, bringing with you all recruits." [W. W. Belknap ?], *History of the Fifteenth Regiment, Iowa Veteran Volunteer Infantry,* . . . (Keokuk, Iowa, 1887), p. 203. On Sept. 17, USG telegraphed to Brig. Gen. John A. Logan. "If you can send five or six hundred men down here tomorrow to stay a day or two do so—Send them if the transportation can be got." Copy, DNA, RG 393, 17th Army Corps, 3rd Division, Telegrams Received. On the same day, Logan, Jackson, telegraphed to USG. "I will send the men at once—" Telegram received, *ibid.*, Dept. of the Mo., Telegrams Received. On the same day, USG wrote to Brig. Gen. James M. Tuttle. "As soon as the 81st Ill. Vols. are replaced by another regiment, or can be dispensed with at Cairo order them to Jackson to report to the Commanding officer for assignment." ALS, Tuttle Papers, IaHA. Logan added an undated endorsement. "We are threatened on every side for

Gods sakes send these men as soon as possible" AES, *ibid*. Commanded by Col. James J. Dollins, the 81st Ill. was sent to join USG's army on Oct. 8.

1. Kossuth, Miss., about ten miles southwest of Corinth. On Sept. 5, Brig. Gen. William S. Rosecrans telegraphed to USG. "I think a matter of great importance for you to occupy Kossuth by a good regt of infantry they will have nothing to meet but the moral effect on the present movements will be fine the 7th Kansas will be there by day after tomorrow morning—a squadron of cavalry might go with infantry" Telegram received, DNA, RG 393, Dept. of the Mo., Telegrams Received. *O.R.*, I, xvii, part 2, 204.

2. Stephen C. Lyford of N. H., USMA 1861, was commissioned 2nd lt., June 24, 1861. After serving near Washington, D.C., he was transferred to the Dept. of the Mo. in Nov., and served as an ordnance officer under Maj. Gen. Henry W. Halleck and USG. He was appointed chief of ordnance, Dept. of the Tenn., on July 11, 1862.

3. 1st Lt. Byron M. Callender, 1st Mo. Light Art.

4. On Sept. 16, Capt. Frederick E. Prime, Corinth, wrote to USG. "I understand cotton is being shipped by R. Road. I have to request in conformity with your letter of instructions to me that no cotton be shipped from here until further orders. The whole of the cotton will be needed for defensive purposes as soon as I can get men to put it in position I regret to state that it will take some time to put Corinth in a Defensive condition I have met General Ord on the subject twice & have ridden round the ground so as to obtain his ideas. I shall endeavour to conform thereto to the best of my ability, though professionally I do not agree with him. But considering the paucity of the garrison, I shall do all I can to give them the necessary cover." ALS, James S. Schoff, New York, N. Y. On the same day, Brig. Gen. James B. McPherson, Corinth, telegraphed to USG. "I have got to send cars to Columbus from here to bring down supplies can I load the cars with cotton so as not to send them through ŧ empty—" Telegram received, DNA, RG 393, Dept. of the Mo., Telegrams Received.

To Brig. Gen. James M. Tuttle

———

Head Quarters, Dist. of West Ten
Corinth, Sept. 16th 1862

BRIG. GEN. TUTTLE
COMD.G DIST. OF CAIRO
GEN.

I send by bearer,—Col. J. Riggin Jr. two Confederate Lieuts F. Wilkinson & R. N. Harding, prisoners of war.

You will detain them until properly exchanged.

The conditions upon which prisoners are kept are to issue to them soldiers fare, where confined, or if paroled they live at their own expens.

Respectfully &c.
U. S. GRANT
Maj. Gen.

P.S. They are not to be paroled to go out of the free states and only to the corporate limits of any one town within them
U S G

ALS, Tuttle Papers, IaHA.

To Maj. Gen. Edward O. C. Ord

Head Quarters, Dist. of West Ten.
Corinth, Sept. 17th 1862

MAJ. GEN. ORD,
CORINTH MISS,
GEN.

We will get off all our forces now as rapidly as practicable. I have dispatched Rosecrans that all our movements now would be as rapid as ~~possible~~ compatible with prudence informing him at the same time of where your troops now are and that those not yet of would be at and near Glendale to-night, you probably with them.[1]

I directed Rosecrans to give me his routes and will inform you of them. Take an Opperator with you who has a packet instrument which can be attached to the wires any place ~~if~~ desired if there is such an one.

I will leave to-morrow for Burnesville[2] if to-day does not develop something to make a different plan necessary.

Respectfully &c.
U. S. GRANT
Maj. Gen.

ALS, ICarbS. *O.R.*, I, xvii, part 1, 118.

On Sept. 17, 1862, Brig. Gen. William S. Rosecrans telegraphed frequently to USG. "Stanleys Division marches tonight for Davenport mills near Jacinto where all the regts meet Hamilton moves forward tonight—I will not leave here until 8 A M tomorrow in order to get all the news—I will then move to Jacinto & connect my head Quarters with Burnsville & Rienzi By lines of vidette posts for Prompt & rapid communication with your Head Quarters—DuBois could & ought to send a couple of companies to occupy & keep Jacinto in order The 7th Kansas will watch the front it seems our flag of truce bearers did not see the troops they report at Baldwin—" Telegram received, DNA, RG 393, Dept. of the Mo., Telegrams Received; copy (dated Sept. 18), *ibid.*, Army of the Miss., Telegrams Sent. Dated Sept. 17 in *O.R.*, I, xvii, part 2, 222. "Hamilton has sent out Mizner with a regt of Infantry all our cavalry—under Mizner towards Barnetts on the Jacinto & Iuka Road—The only thing we can do to prevent Price passing through the defiles of Bear creek east is to push that Division on him & follow it with all Stanlys force while Ross makes a strong demonstration on his front—This is safe for a day or two if we can keep spies from Running to Breckenridge & Van [*Dorn*] if Price & you can hold your hand against [*them.*] I can pursue with my entire force which includes Dubois & Danville will be about 13.000 of all army—" Telegram received, DNA, RG 393, Dept. of the Mo., Telegrams Received; copy (dated Sept. 18), *ibid.*, Army of the Miss., Telegrams Sent. Dated Sept. 17 in *O.R.*, I, xvii, part 2, 222.

"Misners dispatch just in reports that the cannonading of our reconnoitiry party ceased at 4.40 last evening & that about eight oclock last evening a very large fire was seen in the direction of Iuka the distance is 20 miles Mizner has gone to feel of them since four 4 A M My suspicions are that some houses & stores have been burned in Iuka the place abandoned & that Price has crossed the Defiles of Bear Creek & will pass the Tennessee before it rises at the shoals if possible if not will proceed at once to above Decatur near Whitesburg" Telegram received, DNA, RG 393, Dept. of the Mo., Telegrams Received; copy (dated Sept. 18), *ibid.*, Army of the Miss., Telegrams Sent. Dated Sept. 17 in *O.R.*, I, xvii, part 2, 222–23. "Am dispatching orders for Hamilton to follow Mizners advance & hang on the skirts of Price if you approve I will dispose to follow with my entire force & including DuBois command or Col Chambers Reg't in Lieu thereof" Telegram received, DNA, RG 393, Dept. of the Mo., Telegrams Received; copy, *ibid.*, Army of the Miss., Telegrams Sent. *O.R.*, I, xvii, part 2, 223. "Which shall I take col Chambers Regt or DuBois command including Danville—" Telegram received, DNA, RG 393, Dept. of the Mo., Telegrams Received; copy, *ibid.*, Army of the Miss., Telegrams Sent. "The following just rec'd from Burnsville—I am going to send in a prisoner who gave himself up to our skirmishers yesterday he gives some very valuable information according to his statement Price is trying to draw our troops out from corinth when VanDorn & Breckenridge will attack that place—" Telegram received, *ibid.*, Dept. of the Mo., Telegrams Received. *O.R.*, I, xvii, part 2, 223. "Col Mizner has returned from his reconnoisance road directly east from Jacinto & all south clear as far as Peytons mills & probably all together so one company cavalry proceeded within 2 & half miles of Iuka & found no pickets captured 2 prisoners captains one (1) an Englishman & one a School Teacher in bentonville Arkansas he says Price has two divisions each brigade of 4 regts & six (6) batteries & 10 Regts of cavalry & is aiming to go north through Western Ky—a deserter from Iuka says he was there this morning—Great pains ought to be taken to ascertain tonight whether they are gone or not—He says Breckenridge has certainly gone to Holly Springs & will move on to bolivar—If our troops move by Jacinto they will not be ready to fight before Day after tomorrow morning if by burnsville about The same time with less fatigue but probably worse roads   I propose to move by Barnetts" Telegram received, DNA, RG 393, Dept. of the Mo., Telegrams Received; copy, *ibid.*, Army of the Miss., Telegrams Sent. *O.R.*, I, xvii, part 2, 224.

"Have just arrived at Jacinto.   ~~shall~~ there will be a courier line from there to my Hd.Qrs. at Davenport's   as soon as Stanley comes up we shall move on to near Barnetts, probably tonight—Courier lines will be open   stations all the way down from Burnsville—Nothing new from the front   Hamilton has no doubt of Price's being ~~there~~ at Iuka" Telegram received, DNA, RG 393, Dept. of the Mo., Telegrams Received. *O.R.*, I, xvii, part 2, 223. "Have ordered Reg't trains spare baggage of this army to some suitable point within the lines at Corinth to be parked defensively guarding by convalescents unfit for duty   March placed under the command of a responsible officer—The sick are to go to the Genl Hospital where our med' Director will see them provided for—I think it would be best to have few tent flies to be kept for each company in view of the storm—The deserter from the Rebels at Iuka is an Irishman from Co F Second Texas   left last night   he reports Price there with all his force—Regts number from 250 to 350 —Armstrongs cavalry about 15.000 five (5) four (4) gun batteries & two 2 heavy rifled pieces captured from us at Shiloh—The two (2) still larger went west   Price was to have left Iuka on yesterday morning—had we not pursue him with our reconnoitring force destined for up the Tennessee valley—Rations were ordered for five 5 days—Breckenridge & Van Dorn are to leap in on Corinth from the west as soon as we get out after Price   as to his statement of Prices command & position I have no doubt   Col Mowers reconnoisance was ably conducted & came to within 300 yards of their main line of Infantry Murrays division in order of battle   the loss of the Train was wholly owing to the risk of the conductor who ran out after Mower had been gone—some hours & was done by armstrongs entire cavalry force which come west a few miles south of the rail road to threaten Mower's flank—" Telegram received, DNA, RG 393, Dept. of the Mo., Telegrams Received; copy (dated Sept. 18), *ibid.*, Army of the Miss., Telegrams Sent. Dated Sept. 17 in *O.R.*, I, xvii, part 2, 223–24. "Have just rec'd the following from Genl Hamilton   Jacinto 9½ P M—Price & His whole force is in Iuka we have captured a lot of Prisoners wagons mules & ordnance stores—some of the prisoners just from Iuka—" Telegram received, DNA, RG 393, Dept. of the Mo., Telegrams Received; copy, *ibid.*, Army of the Miss., Telegrams Sent. *O.R.*, I, xvii, part 2, 224. "As price is an old wood pecker it would be well to have a watch set to see if he might not take a course down the Tennessee towards Eastport in hope to find the means of crossing—Have you any look out towards Hamburg landing" Telegram received, DNA, RG 393, Dept. of the Mo., Telegrams Received; copy, *ibid.*, Army of the Miss., Telegrams Sent. *O.R.*, I, xvii, part 2, 224.

1. This telegram has not been found.
2. Burnsville, Miss., on the Memphis and Charleston Railroad, about twelve miles southeast of Corinth, and about seven miles northwest of Iuka.

To Maj. Gen. Edward O. C. Ord

Head Quarters Corinth—Sept 17th 1862

Major Genl. Ord.

Some Citizens have just come to see me on a pass given them by the s[t]upid provost Marshal at Bolivar (for which I have ordered the arrest of the provost) and tell me they had no occasion to use their passes on the entire road not having seen a United States soldier until they arrived near Corinth—

Please send word to Genl. McKean to have this attended to and stop all ingress & egress with or without passes—

Respectfully &c
U S. Grant.
Majr Genl.

Copy, McKean Papers, Miss. Dept. of Archives and History, Jackson, Miss. On Sept. 17, 1862, Maj. John A. Rawlins telegraphed to Brig. Gen. Stephen A. Hurlbut, Bolivar. "To arrest W. H. Thurston provost marshall for granting passes to citizens to go to Corinth." DNA, RG 393, 16th Army Corps, District of West Tenn., 2nd Division, Register of Letters Received. On the same day, Hurlbut telegraphed to Rawlins. "Capt Thurston is arrested   no orders are here to prevent citizens from going to Corinth & he states that he has issued no passes except to sutlers or others connected with Rosses command—" Telegram received, *ibid.*, Dept. of the Mo., Telegrams Received.

To Brig. Gen. Stephen A. Hurlbut

Corinth Miss
Sept 17th 1862

Genl S. A. Hurlbut

Make a Demonstration towards Grand-Junction and Grenada —show a Large wagon train and let it Leak out that a Large force may be Expected to move from ~~Torrent~~ Memphis and Helena towards the same Point with the View of Getting on to the Yazoo[1]—to Destroy Looks that are underway of Construction as Gun Boats   let it be understood also that large Reinforcements are Expected from Columbus to take your Place. I do not want you to go far away

U. S. GRANT

Maj Genl

Telegram received, DNA, RG 393, District of West Tenn., 4th Division, Telegrams Received. On Sept. 18, 1862, Brig. Gen. Stephen A. Hurlbut, Bolivar, telegraphed to USG. "The roads below me are impractible for artillery from heavy rains which is still impending. Gen Ross artillery & wagon trains are here in my charge & without forage   in all we have forty five hundred (4,500) animals & forage must be sent by rail as heretofore ordered.   the country around cannot supply them except for a day or two   I presume do not wish my entire command to demonstrate & I shall therefore send five Reg'ts of Infantry one (1) battallion of Cavalry & twelve (12) pieces as soon as the roads will admit. I wish instructions how far to proceed & would prefer them by messenger as there will be ample time before these clay hills are passable—" Telegram received, *ibid.*, Dept. of the Mo., Telegrams Received; copy *ibid.*, District of West Tenn., Letters Sent. *O.R.*, I, xvii, part 2, 226–27. On Sept. 18, USG telegraphed to Hurlbut. "You need not leave Bolivar but make a show of going. Keep a look out towards Holly Springs. Information just received shows that Breckenridge has certainly moved up there & may move on you. Will retain Ross forces." Telegram received, DNA, RG 393, District of West Tenn., 4th Division, Telegrams Received. On Sept. 19, Hurlbut telegraphed to USG. "I move Lamans Brigade five (5) Regts Infantry twelve (12) peices Artillery & two (2) battalions of 2d Ills Cavalry towards Grand Junction tomorrow morning with instructions not to engage unless the advantage on our side but if an opening occurs to break in & destroy bridge at Davis ~~Creek~~ Mill   I hold the other Brigade to support them if over matched" Telegram received (misdated Sept. 9), *ibid.*, Dept. of the Mo., Telegrams Received; copy, *ibid.*, District of West Tenn., Letters Sent. *O.R.*, I, xvii, part 2, 228.

1. The Yazoo River in Miss. joins the Mississippi River a few miles above Vicksburg.

To Col. John V. D. Du Bois

Hd Qrs   Sept 17th 1862

COL DUBOIS

all the troops now at Jacinto will be off in the morning—it would be well for you to occupy it with 2 or 3 companies   if Genl

Rosecrans has not already directed I want you to keep a look out as far to your front & to the west as possible—inform us at Burnsville by telegraph if any move towards us is made & in case you have to fall back on Corinth inform Genl McKean or what commandr here of what information you have and obstruct the roads in every way you can as you fall back—in this respect you will know what to do in the absence of instructions

U S GRANT
Maj Genl

Telegram, copy, Justin G. Turner, Los Angeles, Calif. John V. D. Du Bois of N. Y., USMA 1855, reached the rank of 1st lt. before the Civil War. He then served successively in Kan. and Mo., becoming chief of art., Dept. of the Mo., Feb. 21, 1862, and col. and additional aide-de-camp, July 17. After Maj. Gen. Henry W. Halleck left Corinth, Du Bois had no fixed duties until Sept. 8, when he assumed command of a brigade in the Army of the Miss. Jared C. Lobdell, "The Civil War Journal and Letters of Col. John Van Deusen Du Bois, April 12, 1861 to October 16, 1862," *Missouri Historical Review*, LX, 4 (July, 1966), 436–59; LXI, 1 (Oct., 1966), 22–50.

To Jesse Root Grant

Corinth Mississippi
September 17th 1862

DEAR FATHER,

A letter from you and one from Mary was received some time ago which I commenced answer in a letter addressed to Mary, but being frequently interrupted by matters of business it was laid aside for some days, and finally torn up.—I now have all my time taxed. Although occupying a position attracting but little attention at this time there is probably no garrison more threatened to-day than this.

I expect to hold it and have never had any other feeling either here or elswhere but that of success. I would write you many particulars but you are so imprudent that I dare not trust you with them; and while on this subject let me say a word. I have not an enemy in the world who has done me so much injury as you in your efforts in my defence.[1] I require no defenders and for my sake let me alone. I have heard this from various sources and persons who have returned to this Army and did not know that I had parents living near Cincinnati have said that they found the best feeling existing towards every place except there. You are constantly denouncing other General officers and the inference with people naturally is that you get your impressions for me.

Do nothing to correct what you have already done but for the future keep quiet on this subject.

Mary wrote to me about an appointment for Mr. Nixon![2] I have nothing in the world to do with any appointments, no power to make and nothing to do with recommending except for my own Staff. That is now already full.

If I can do anthing in the shape of lending any influence I may possess in Mr. Nixons behalf I will be most happy to do so on the strength of what Mary says in commendation, and should be most happy if it could so be that our lot would cast us near each other.

I do not know what Julia is going to do. I want her to go to Detroit and board. She has many pleasant acquaintances there and she would find good schools for the children.

I have no time for writing and scarsely to look over the telegraphic columns of the newspapers.

My love to all at home.

Ulys.

ALS, James S. Schoff, New York, N. Y.

1. See letter to Jesse Root Grant, April 26, 1862.
2. The 1860 census listed John S. Nixon of Covington, Ky., as a thirty-seven-year-old lawyer born in Ohio. See letter to Jesse Root Grant, April 26, 1862.

To Mary Grant

———

Corinth, Sept. 17th 1862

DEAR SISTER,

Although but little time for writing I have penned a hasty letter to father this evening which you can read and turn over to him.

I have not been very well for several weeks but so much to do that I cannot get sick. We have been very active here for some time. Daily skirmishing takes place at our outposts. Before you receive this probably stiring news will reach you from this command.

You will see by my letter to father much that I would have written in this but is now not necessary as you will read it.

Your brother
ULYS.

ALS, IaHA.

To Brig. Gen. Leonard F. Ross

———

Corinth, Sept. 18th 1862

GEN. ROSS, ~~IUKA~~, BURNSVILLE

Gen. Ord is on his way to Burnsville. Left here last night. I start in a few minuets by rail to join you.

Throw out reconnoitering party towards Iuka and follow them slowly. Gen. Rosecrans is following the enemy closely on his flank. Captured yesterday a number of prisoners and an ordnance train of the enemies.

U. S. GRANT
Maj. Gen.

ALS, ICarbS. On the reverse of this letter USG wrote a note to Brig. Gen. Thomas J. McKean. "If the telegraph, to Bethel is not working by 12½ O'clock a train of cars should be sent North ~~to guar~~ with three comp.ys of Infantry to guard the portion of the road threatened by Price's Cav.y" ALS, *ibid.*

To Brig. Gen. William S. Rosecrans

Headquarters. Dist. West. Tennessee
Burnsville. Miss. Sept. 18th 1862

GENERAL ROSECRANS:

General Ross' command is at this place. McArthurs Division is north of the road 2 miles to the rear, and Davies' Division South of the road nearby. I sent forward two Regiments of Infantry with Cavalry by the road, north of rail-road towards Iuka, with instructions for them to Bivouac for the night at a point which was designated, about four miles from here, if not interrupted, and have the Cavalry feel where the enemy are. Before they reached the point of the road (you will see it on the map, the road north of the Rail-road) they met what is supposed to be Armstrongs Cavalry.

The Rebel Cavalry was forced back and I sent instructions then to have them stop for the night where they thought they could safely hold—

In the morning troops will advance from here at 4½ A.M. An anonymous dispatch just received states that Price, Magruder,[1] and Breckenridge have a force of 60.000 between Iuka and Tupelo.—This I have no doubt is the understanding of Citizens, but I very much doubt their information being correct.

Your reconnoissances prove that there is but little force south of Corinth for a long distance and no great force between Bay-Springs and the rail-road

Make as rapid an advance as you can, and let us do tomorrow all we can—It may be necessary to fall back the day following.

I look upon the shewing of a Cavalry force so near us as an indication of a retreat, and they a force to cover it.

15 minutes to 7 P. M.

U. S. Grant.
Major. General.

Telegram, copies, DNA, RG 94, War Records Office, Union Battle Reports; *ibid.*, RG 393, USG Hd. Qrs. Correspondence; DLC-USG, V, 4, 5, 7, 8, 88. *O.R.*, I, xvii, part 1, 66. According to these sources, USG's telegram was sent in reply to a telegram to him of Sept. 18, 1862, from Brig. Gen. William S. Rosecrans. "One of my spies in from Beardons, on the Bay Spring road tells of a continuous movement since last friday of forces Eastward. They say Van Dorn is to defend Vicksburg, Breckenridge to make his way to Kentucky, Price to attack Iuka or go to Tennessee.—If Prices forces are at Iuka the plan I propose is to move up as close as we can tonight, conceal our movements, Ord to advance from Burnsville, commence the attack, and draw their attention that way, while I move in on the Jacinto & Fulton roads, massing heavily on the Fulton Road, and crushing in their left, cutting off their retreat Eastward. I propose to leave in ten minutes for Jacinto from whence I will dispatch you by line of Videttes to Burnsville. Will await a few minutes to hear from you before I start. What news from Burnsville?" Copies, DNA, RG 94, War Records Office, Union Battle Reports; *ibid.*, RG 393, USG Hd. Qrs. Correspondence; DLC-USG, V, 4, 5, 7, 8, 88. *O.R.*, I, xvii, part 1, 66.

On the same day, Rosecrans telegraphed to USG. "Your dispatch recd   Genl Stanley & Div arrived after dark having been detained by falling in the rear of Ross through fault of guide. Our Cavalry Six Miles this side of Barnetts—Hamiltons 1st Brigade, Eight—2d Brigade nine miles this side Stanley near Davenports Mill. We shall move as early as practicable say 4½ o'clock A. M. This will give twenty miles march for Stanleys Div. to Iuka—shall not therefore be in before one or two O'clock, but when we come in will endeavor to do it strongly   Troops are in good order. Should there be any reason to believe the enemy not in Iuka you will adress us by Vidette line which will follow Head Qrs at short intervals. Col Mizner will establish scouts south east of us. Everything so far goes to show that their movement has taken place on the road from Marietta that passes above Bay Springs, which he will cause to be examined early to-morrow morning & the reconnoisance will extend if practicable over onto Fulton & Iuka road." Telegram received, DNA, RG 393, Dept. of the Mo., Telegrams Received; copies (incomplete), *ibid.*, USG Hd. Qrs. Correspondence; *ibid.*, RG 94, War Records Office, Union Battle Reports; DLC-USG, V, 4, 5, 7, 8, 88. *O.R.*, I, xvii, part 1, 66; *ibid.*, I, xvii, part 2, 227. According to his report, USG "dispatched to General Ord giving him the substance of the above, and directions not to move on the enemy until Rosecrans arrived, or he should hear firing to the South of Iuka." See letter to Col. John C. Kelton, Oct. 22, 1862. USG later recalled that: "I immediately sent Ord a copy of Rosecrans' dispatch and ordered him to be in readiness to attack the moment he heard the sound of guns to the south or south-east." *Memoirs*, I, 411. No communication from USG to Maj. Gen. Edward O. C. Ord of Sept. 18 has been found. On the other hand, Ord included in his report a message from Col. Clark B. Lagow of Sept. 19 which was received about 10:00 A.M. "I send you dispatch received from Rosencrans late in the night. You will see that he is behind where we expected him. Do not be too rapid with your advance this morning unless it should be found the enemy are evacuating." Copy, DNA, RG 94, War Records Office, Union Battle Reports. *O.R.*, I, xvii, part 1, 118.

On Sept. 18, Rosecrans again telegraphed to USG. "I telegraphed to Capt Simmons last night to send rations to Col Mower ross having taken ten thousand which I had ordered thus preventing mowers movement until his rations arrived the telegraph dispatch was not delivered until today—Have ordered Mower to move down & join stanly making arrangements for his rations to follow him— The road & darkness prevented Stanly from making progress until this morning We shall all be concentrated at Jacinto by abt 2 oclock & move forward to the vicinity of the bay springs road tonight—" Telegram received, DNA, RG 393, Dept. of the Mo., Telegrams Received. *O.R.*, I, xvii, part 2, 227.

On Sept. 18, John C. Van Duzer, telegraph superintendent, Cairo, telegraphed to USG. "The reports from Washington this evening contain intelligence of general engagement on 16th near Sharpsburg, between rebel army under General Lee and Union forces. Hotly contested all day and renewed on morning of 17th, rebels having been re-enforced during the night by Jackson's army and Union army by 30,000 men from Washington, and entire force on both sides engaged until 4 p. m., at which time Hooker gained position, flanked rebels, and threw them into disorder. Longstreet and his entire division prisoners. General Hill killed. Entire rebel army of Virginia destroyed, Burnside having reoccupied Harper's Ferry and cut off retreat. General Hooker slightly wounded. Action very sanguinary. Requisitions for surgeons and hospital supplies larger than ever before. Latest advices say entire rebel army must be captured or killed, as Potomac is rising and our forces pressing the enemy continually." *Ibid.*, p. 230. On the same day, Col. William S. Hillyer sent this dispatch to Ord to read to his troops. *Ibid.* Ord, "by permission of General Grant," at midnight, sent the dispatch to Col. Mortimer D. Leggett for transmission to C. S. A. forces, who were urged to avoid "useless bloodshed." *Ibid.*, pp. 229–30. The C. S. A. reply is *ibid.*, p. 230. Probably about this time, USG sent an undated message to Rosecrans. "The following message just rcvd. McClellan has driven the rebels out of Maryland with Tremendous slaughter Genl Lee taken prisoner" Copy, Justin G. Turner, Los Angeles, Calif.

1. In May, C. S. A. Maj. Gen. John B. Magruder of Va., USMA 1830, had been assigned to command forces west of the Mississippi River, but these orders were countermanded and Magruder remained in Va. until, on Oct. 10, 1862, he was assigned to command the District of Tex.

To Maj. Gen. Henry W. Halleck

Burnsville Miss 9 30 a m [*Sept.*] 19th [*1862*]

GENL H W HALLECK

GENL IN CHIEF U S A

Your dispatch directing that Price should not be permitted to get into Tennessee[1] is just rec'd. My forces are now here   Enemy's pickets & ours within a few hundred yards   Genl Rosecrans is South of the Enemy's movement on him whilst Ord attacks from the west. Corinth is well watched at a long distance out & unless the approach of a large force on that place should call us back I think it will be impossible for Price to get into Tennessee

I will do all in my power to prevent such a catastrophe

U. S. GRANT.

Maj Genl Comd'g

Telegram received, DNA, RG 94, Generals' Papers and Books, Telegrams Received by Gen. Halleck; *ibid.*, RG 107, Telegrams Collected (Bound); copies, *ibid.*, Telegrams Received in Cipher; *ibid.*, RG 393, USG Hd. Qrs. Correspondence; DLC-USG, V, 4, 5, 7, 8, 88. *O.R.*, I, xvii, part 2, 227–28.

1. See telegram to Maj. Gen. Henry W. Halleck, Sept. 15, 1862.

To Maj. Gen. Henry W. Halleck

Burnsville Miss Sept. 19th [*1862*] 7 35 P. M

MAJ GEN H. W. HALLECK

GEN IN CHIEF

Before leaving Corinth I instructed Genl Hurlbut at Bolivar to make a great fuss at preparing for a move & to let word leak out that he expected large reinforcements there and at Memphis when a combined movement would be made on Grenada & the Yazoo to destroy boats on that river.[1] The object of this is obvi-

ous but was before your dispatch² for this very move to be made
real

U S GRANT
Maj Gen'l

Telegram received, DNA, RG 94, Generals' Papers and Books, Telegrams
Received by Gen. Halleck; copies, *ibid.*, RG 107, Telegrams Received in Cipher;
ibid., RG 393, USG Hd. Qrs. Correspondence; DLC-USG, V, 4, 5, 7, 8, 88.
O.R., I, xvii, part 2, 228. On Sept. 22, 1862, 10:40 A.M., USG telegraphed to
Maj. Gen. Henry W. Halleck. "Will try to set an Expedition on foot for the
destruction of rebel boats in the Yazoo. Do I understand that I am have the
co-operation of some of Steele's forces? Cavalry particularly." Telegram received,
DNA, RG 94, Generals' Papers and Books, Telegrams Received by Gen. Halleck;
ibid., RG 107, Telegrams Collected (Bound); copies, *ibid.*, Telegrams Received
in Cipher; *ibid.*, RG 393, USG Hd. Qrs. Correspondence; DLC-USG, V, 4, 5, 7,
8, 88. *O.R.*, I, xvii, part 2, 232. On Sept. 23, Halleck telegraphed to USG.
"Arrange with Genl Curtis at St Louis in regard to Steele's cooperation. New
troops will be sent you as soon as they can be spared." ALS (telegram sent),
DNA, RG 107, Telegrams Collected (Bound); copy, *ibid.*, RG 108, Telegrams
Sent. *O.R.*, I, xvii, part 2, 234. See letter to Maj. Gen. Henry W. Halleck,
Sept. 24, 1862.

    1. See telegram to Brig. Gen. Stephen A. Hurlbut, Sept. 17, 1862.
    2. On Sept. 18, Halleck had telegraphed to USG. "Genl Butler reports from
New Orleans that the enemy are constructing two iron clad boats high up the
Yazoo river, & thinks they can be reached by a small land force from Memphis or
Helena. Consult with Genl Steele & commander of flotilla & if possible destroy
these vessels before their completion." ALS (telegram sent), DNA, RG 107,
Telegrams Collected (Bound); copies, *ibid.*, RG 393, USG Hd. Qrs. Correspond-
ence; DLC-USG, V, 4, 5, 7, 8, 88. *O.R.*, I, xvii, part 2, 225; *O.R.* (Navy), I,
xxiii, 362.

To Maj. Gen. Edward O. C. Ord

———

Burnsville 3.30. a m
sept. 20th 1862

GEN. ORD

Dispatch just received from Rosecrans. He is two miles south
of Iuka where he met the enemy in force last evening and was
engaged two hours with a loss on our side of some men and two
or three pieces of Artillery.

You must engage the ene[my] as early as possible in the morning bringing your forces as well together as possible being careful however to ~~have~~ leave sufficient guard in the hills up North to prevent the rebel Cavalry geting on our flank.

U. S. Grant
Maj. Gen

ALS, Ord Papers, CU-B. On Sept. 19, 1862, Brig. Gen. William S. Rosecrans sent three telegrams to USG. At 6 A.M., he sent one telegram received at 9 A.M. "Troops are all on the way, in fine spirits by reason of news—Eighteen miles to Iuka—but think I shall make it by time mentioned 2 o.clock P M. If Price is there he will have become well engaged by time we come up & if so twenty Regiments, and thirty pcs. cannon will finish him. Hamilton will go up Fulton & Iuka road, Stanley up Jacinto road from Barnetts & when we get near will be governed by circumstances. Cav. will press in on the right to cut off their retreat, if you can spare any of the 7th Ill. Cav. send them up to report on front as soon as possible— Country on our side is open; closed on yours." Telegram received, DNA, RG 393, Dept. of the Mo., Telegrams Received. *O.R.*, I, xvii, part 1, 69. At 12:40 P.M., Rosecrans telegraphed from "Barnett's." "Reached here at 12—Cavalry advance drove pickets from near here. Met another stand at about one mile from here— Hamilton's Division is advancing—Head of column a mile to the front now—Head of Stanley's column is here—Hatch at Peyton's Mills—Was skirmishing with cavalry. Killed orderly sgt & brough up his book—belongs to Faulkner—num- bered 45 men for duty—Cavalry gone east towards Fulton road—one hour—one of Hamilton's brigades went over to Cartersville. it will turn up into Jacinto & Iuka road above widow Moore's—Cols. Dickey & Lagow arrived here half an hour ago—says you have had no skirmishing since ~~Brig. Genl. U.S.A.~~ three o'clock—" Telegram received, DNA, RG 393, Dept. of the Mo., Telegrams Received; copy, *ibid.*, RG 94, War Records Office, Union Battle Reports. *O.R.*, I, xvii, part 1, 69. At 10:30 P.M., Rosecrans sent a third telegram from "2 miles South of Iuka." "We met the enemy in force just above this point. The engage- ment lasted several hours. We have lost two or three pieces of artillery. firing was very heavy—You must attack in the morning and *in force*. The ground is horrid, unknown to us and no room for developement. couldn't use our artillery at all, fired but few shots—Push in onto them until we can have time to do some- thing We will try to get a position on our right which will take Iuka" Tele- gram received, DNA, RG 393, Dept. of the Mo., Telegrams Received. *O.R.*, I, xvii, part 1, 67.

Although the letter to Maj. Gen. Edward O. C. Ord written at 3:30 A.M., Sept. 20, appears to have been written in response to the third telegram from Rosecrans, USG's official report states that Rosecrans's telegram did not arrive until 8:35 A.M., Sept. 20, and incorporates a different letter to Ord sent at 8:35 in response. See letter to Col. John C. Kelton, Oct. 22, 1862. No copy of the 8:35 letter to Ord has been located outside the official report, and the documentary evidence indicates that Rosecrans's third telegram did reach USG shortly before 3:30 A.M., that USG sent Ord instructions at 3:30 based upon Rosecrans's tele- gram, and that the 8:35 A.M. letter included in the official report is a reconstruction based on memory of the letter actually sent earlier. USG's statement in his

Memoirs (I, 412) that he learned of the battle of Iuka at "a late hour of the night" and ordered Ord to attack "early in the morning" is more consistent with the 3:30 A.M. message than that of 8:35 A.M.

An undated telegram from Ord to USG may have been sent on the morning of Sept. 20. "there appears to be an irregular ~~and or~~ canonading going on south of Iuka   in case you can spare the Regiments in Town send them to me via the direct road to Iuka—I shall try and get in upon the enemy by 10 oclock not having one road of approach may be later   Genl McArthur has not reported and I do not exactly know where his command is but apprehend that he came this way via the ridge Road"   Telegram received, DNA, RG 393, Dept. of the Mo., Telegrams Received.

General Field Orders No. 1

Head Quarters District of West Tennessee
Corinth, Miss Sept 20th 1862

GENERAL FIELD ORDER No 1

The General commanding takes pleasure in congratulating the two wings of the Army, commanded respectively by Maj Genl Ord and Maj Genl Rosecrans upon the eneray alacrity and bravery displayed by them on the 19th and 20th inst. in their movements against the enemy at Iuka. Although the enemy was in numbers reputed far greater than their own; nothing was evinced by the troops but a burning desire to meet him whatever his numbers and however strong his position

With such a disposition as was manifested by the troops on this occasion, their commanders need never fear defeat against anything but overwhelming numbers.

While it was the fortune of the command of Gen Rosecrans on the evening of the 19th inst to engage the enemy in a most spirited fight for more than two hours, driving him with great loss, from his position, and winning for themselves fresh laurels, the command of Gen Ord is entitled to equal credit for their efforts in trying to reach the enemy and in diverting his attention

And while congratulating the noble living, it is meet to offer our condolence to the friends of the heroic dead, who offered their lives a sacrifice in defence of constitutional liberty, and in their fall rendered memorable the field of Iuka

> By Command of Maj Genl U. S. Grant
> JNO A. RAWLINS
> A A Genl

Copy, DNA, RG 393, Dept. of the Tenn., General Orders; *New York Times*, Oct. 4, 1862. The reference to Maj. Gen. William S. Rosecrans in these orders, and their late appearance in the *New York Times*, suggest that they were prepared later than the purported date. In testimony before the Committee on the Conduct of the War, April 22, 1865, and in a report to the AGO, June 15, 1865, Rosecrans stated that he had been notified of his promotion on Sept. 20, 1862. *HRC*, 38-2-142, "Rosecrans's Campaigns," III, 20; DNA, RG 94, ACP, William S. Rosecrans. The first documents signed by Rosecrans as maj. gen. are dated Sept. 21, and the date on which USG's hd. qrs. learned of the promotion is unknown. The absence of these orders from several of USG's book records invites speculation that they were reconsidered and withdrawn because of the undue credit given to the troops of Maj. Gen. Edward O. C. Ord.

To Maj. Gen. Henry W. Halleck

Iuka Miss.
Sept 20th 1862

MAJ GEN H W HALLECK
GEN IN CHIEF

Gen Rosecrans with Stanleys & Hamiltons[1] Divisions & Misners[2] Cavalry attacked Price South of this village about two hours before dark yesterday & had a sharp fight until ~~no~~ night closed in. Genl Ord was [to] the north with an armed force of about 5.000 men had some skirmishing with Rebel Pickets. This morning the fight was renewed by Genl Rosecrans who was nearest to the town but it was found that the Enemy had been evacuating during the night going south[3]—Hamilton & Stanley with the Cavalry are in full pursuit—This will no doubt break up the Enemy & possibly force them to abandon much of their artillery Loss on either side in killed & wounded is from four 4 to five hundred[4]—The Enemy's loss in arms tents &c will be large—

We have about 250 prisoners. I have reliable information that it was Price's intention to move over East of me. In that he has been thwarted   Among the Enemy's loss are Gen'l Little[5] killed & Genl Whitfield[6] wounded   I cannot speak too highly of the energy & skill displayed by Genl Rosecrans in the attack & of the endurance of the troops under him   Genl Ords command showed untiring zeal but the direction taken by the Enemy prevented them taking the active part they desired   Price's force was about 18.000[7]

U. S. GRANT

Maj. Gen'l

Telegram received, DNA, RG 107, Telegrams Collected (Bound); copies, *ibid.*, RG 94, War Records Office, Union Battle Reports; *ibid.*, RG 393, USG Hd. Qrs. Correspondence; DLC-USG, V, 4, 5, 7, 8, 88. *O.R.*, I, xvii, part 1, 64. For USG's formal report of his role in the battle of Iuka, see letter to Col. John C. Kelton, Oct. 22, 1862.

1. Charles S. Hamilton of N.Y., USMA 1843, resigned from the U.S. Army on April 30, 1853, with the rank of 1st lt. and bvt. capt., then settled in Fond du Lac, Wis., as a farmer and flour manufacturer. Appointed col., 3rd Wis., on May 11, 1861, and confirmed as brig. gen. to rank from May 17, Hamilton served in the Army of the Potomac until removed by Maj. Gen. George B. McClellan, who called him "not fit to command a Division." Lincoln, *Works*, V, 208–9, 227. On March 19, 1863, Hamilton was confirmed as maj. gen. to rank from Sept. 19, 1862, the date of Iuka. For Hamilton's role at Iuka, see *O.R.*, I, xvii, part 1, 89–93; Hamilton, "The Battle of Iuka," *Battles and Leaders of the Civil War*, eds., Robert Underwood Johnson and Clarence Clough Buel (New York, 1887), II, 734–36; Hamilton to James R. Doolittle, Sept. 25, 1862, Doolittle Papers, WHi.
2. John K. Mizner of Mich., USMA 1856, served in the 2nd Dragoons before the Civil War and was appointed col., 3rd Mich. Cav., on March 7, 1862. During the battle of Iuka he was chief of cav., Army of the Miss., commanding cav. division. *O.R.*, I, xvii, part 1, 113–15.
3. On Sept. 20, Brig. Gen. William S. Rosecrans wrote to USG. "The enemy occupying a tongue of land between two roads skirted by woods, made great demonstrations of flanking us right & left, appeared to be establishing batteries in front, halting & dressing up. Meanwhile their train was moving to the rear but could not tell in what direction.   about 4 a. m. it began to be obvious that a movement of greater magnitude to resist your or my attack was going on. I watched their movements all night, but the fastnesses of their position prevented my learning anything definite until daylight, when skirmishers were ordered forward, and soon ascertained they were retreating. Stanly with 37th Ohio section of artillery & Mizners Cav are pushing them rapidly, Mizner ~~Cav~~ has ~~been~~ ordered up cav on the Russellville road, while his main force is pushing in on an oblique road leading from battlefield to Fulton road. The sound of their trains had not died

away when we began to move   what sort of a rear guard they have cannot say
Men are pushing forward as fast as excessive fatigue will admit." ALS, DNA,
RG 393, Dept. of the Mo., Telegrams Received. *O.R.*, I, xvii, part 1, 70–71. On
the same day, at 8 :45 A.M., Rosecrans wrote to USG. "Dispatched you this morng
at 7 o'c to go by Iuka, but orderly said rebels were there—Have sent it by courier
line—Night closed on us before we had more than eight six regiments engaged,
some of them but slightly—The rebels were in position on a high ridge running
to a point at the forks of the roads where we had to attack them—and commanding
the only cross road connecting Fulton & Jacinto roads—The fight was sharp at
this point where they captured the battery—reported now not to have been carried
off—but left in the woods—Our loss will probably amount to 400 killed &
wounded—Rebels were obliged to leave many of their dead on the field. They
made great noise of establishing batteries in the woods during the night & massing
troops   It excited my suspicions—I watched the movements all night, but could
do nothing until daylight when skirmishers going out reported enemy retreating
—Cav'ly & Infantry were promptly put in motion to pursue—Cavalry just report
seeing rebel train & Infantry on Jacinto Fulton road moving south   Genl Stanley
has reached Iuka I believe but having [recd] no report from him I can give no
orders—should it prove [so I shall order] Hamiltons Division to face about march
to Barnett's, Stanley's to follow, and endeavor to cut off his retreat south & drive
him into the defiles of Bear Creek—Iuka is deserted. Column retreating on Fulton
towards Russelville road. Have ordered Hamilton to go to Barnett's   [will order]
Stanley to follow. Cavalry will go in advance supported by a fresh regiment"
ALS, DNA, RG 393, Dept. of the Mo., Telegrams Received. *O.R.*, I, xvii,
part 1, 71. Brig. Gen. James B. McPherson added an undated endorsement to this
message. "1½ Miles from Iuka   Genl. Ord is moving on Iuka as rapidly as possible and will wait orders there—"   AES, DNA, RG 393, Dept. of the Mo.,
Telegrams Received. *O.R.*, I, xvii, part 1, 71.

Also on Sept. 20, at 9 :45 A.M., Rosecrans wrote to USG. "Rebels left all
their sick and wounded at this place, part of their little camp equipage—They are
retreating with all possible speed—Stanley follows them directly, and Hamilton
endeavors to cut them off from the Bay Springs road—The men double quick with
great alacrity—Genl Little killed—Genl Whitfield wounded—The rebel loss
estimated by themselves 400 to 500 killed & wounded—They have left many in
the hospitals, many on the ground, which is covered with their dead, some fully
¾ of a mile from where engagement took place—We shall bring our wounded into
the town at once—please order Hospital stores & attendants for 500 sick &
wounded—Why did you not attack this morning ?" ALS, DNA, RG 393, Dept. of
the Mo., Telegrams Received. *O.R.*, I, xvii, part 1, 70. This telegram was endorsed by McPherson. "I have opened this & read   communicated the contents to
Genl. Ord"   AES, DNA, RG 393, Dept. of the Mo., Telegrams Received. *O.R.*,
I, xvii, part 1, 70. Maj. Gen. Edward O. C. Ord also endorsed this telegram. "We
are out of Rations [to-ni]ght   We didnt hear any sounds of the battle last P M—
Started with sound of 1st guns for town   Gen. McArthur got tangled up among
the hill roads & caused me some delay—but I was within 3½ miles at 7. A. M—
took position there as per orders till I could hear frm Gen Rosecrans." AES, DNA,
RG 393, Dept. of the Mo., Telegrams Received. *O.R.*, I, xvii, part 1, 70.

4. On Sept. 22, USG telegraphed to Maj. Gen. Henry W. Halleck. "In my
dispatch of the twentieth (20) our loss was over estimated & the rebel loss were
under estimated   we found two hundred & sixty one of their dead upon the field

while our loss in killed will be less than one hundred (100)—" Telegram received, DNA, RG 94, Generals' Papers and Books, Telegrams Received by Gen. Halleck; *ibid.*, RG 107, Telegrams Collected (Bound); copies, *ibid.*, RG 393, USG Hd. Qrs. Correspondence; DLC-USG, V, 4, 5, 7, 8, 88. *O.R.*, I, xvii, part 1, 64. U.S. losses are tabulated as 141 killed, 613 wounded, and 36 captured or missing. *Ibid.*, p. 78. Almost all C. S. A. losses occurred in the 1st Division, for which Brig. Gen. Louis Hébert reported 86 killed, 408 wounded, and 199 sick left at or near Iuka. *Ibid.*, p. 126. But Capt. William M. Wiles, provost marshal, Army of the Miss., reported C. S. A. losses as 385 killed, approximately 350 wounded, and 703 captured. *Ibid.*, p. 80.

5. Lewis H. Little of Md. served in the U.S. Army 1839–61, resigning at the rank of capt. He served on the staff of Maj. Gen. Sterling Price, was confirmed as brig. gen. on April 16, 1862, and was killed at Iuka while commanding the 1st Division. In Civil War period documents his name is usually given as Henry Little.

6. John W. Whitfield of Tenn., lt. col., 2nd Tenn., in the Mexican War, moved to Independence, Mo., in 1853; served as Kans. territorial delegate 1854–57, and as land office register at Doniphan, Kans., 1857–61. He was wounded at Iuka while col., 27th Tex. Cav., also known as the 1st Tex. Legion.

7. The effective strength of Price's command was approximately 14,000. *Battles and Leaders*, II, 736.

To Col. John V. D. Du Bois

Burnsville Sept 20 [*1862*]

Col Dubois

Rosecrans met the Enemy last night & had a 2 hours fight without any particular result—some fighting on the left with ords command also—Dont fail to keep a look out to inform me if there should be a movement either to reinforce Price or to attack Corinth

U S Grant
Maj Gen'l

Telegram, copy, Justin G. Turner, Los Angeles, Calif. On Sept. 19, 1862, Col. John V. D. Du Bois, Rienzi, Miss., telegraphed to USG. "Prices order for forward movement allows 3 tent flies to 100 men & 3 wagons to 1000 men—Couldent find out anything about rations   Lost 8 men day before yesterday   none escaped —all quiet" Telegram received, DNA, RG 393, Dept. of the Mo., Telegrams Received. At 9:40 P.M., Sept. 20, Du Bois telegraphed to USG. "Picked men sent to Baldwin drove pickets to within 2 two or 3 three miles where force proved too strong against them. Captured five Soldiers & brought in 7 seven Citizens for various causes.   principally to prevent Lieut Home of 7th Kansas captured by guerrillas from being killed   Have papers up to the 18th from Mobile & Secesh mail   soon as examined will report—The 7th Kansas have had every man in the saddle for two days—Col Lee deserves much credit"   Telegram received, *ibid*.

To Brig. Gen. Stephen A. Hurlbut

Corinth Sept 21st [*1862*]

Genl Hurlbut.

Do not leave Bolivar without a sufficient force to hold, if you think Lauman in danger. Send what force you can to his relief. Let me know any further information you get.

U. S. Grant
Maj Genl.

Telegram, copy, DNA, RG 393, District of West Tenn., 4th Division, Telegrams Received. On Sept. 21, 1862, USG telegraphed again to Brig. Gen. Stephen A. Hurlbut, Bolivar. "Give all the Assistance you can   protect the Post but remember that force mounted to the front are to a Great Extent Protection   dont delay to send a Portion of your forces to [t]he assistance of Lauman"   Copy, *ibid*. At 11:00 A.M., Sept. 21, Hurlbut telegraphed to Maj. John A. Rawlins. "Genl Lauman & Command five miles from Grand Junction   Cavalry advanced as far as Grand Junction finding no enemy but best information that portion of force lately in vicinity had left in direction of Corinth leaving about twenty five hundred (2 500) at Davis Mills. Lauman has orders to attack if secure of the results & destroy Davis Mills & will probably do so this night or tomorrow morning. I learn from scouts that Villipigue & Jacksons Cavalry left Day before yesterday for East probably Corinth. Force at Davis Mills under Command of Gen Bowen"   Telegram received, *ibid*., Dept. of the Mo., Telegrams Received. *O.R.*, I, xvii, part 2, 231.

Also on Sept. 21, Hurlbut telegraphed three times to USG. "Genl Lauman is attacked 10 miles below here as I learn by orderly sent in by Col Noble with verbal message   I have 5 Regts here   shall I move them from this post   answer at once"   "Genl Lauman sends me a verbal message by an orderly that the Enemy are flanking him on [his] left & is rapidly falling back   he [is] 6 miles below shall I move the rest of [the] division out or wait for him to come   the stores here are of great value & I dislike leaving them without guard   answer at once"   "Gen Lauman command has returned all safely   the Cavalry & some Infantry followed close up as far as VanBuren where a few well directed shots Scattered them   further particulars will be sent by mail tomorrow."   Telegrams received, DNA, RG 393, Dept. of the Mo., Telegrams Received. *O.R.*, I, xvii, part 2, 231. See telegram to Brig. Gen. Stephen A. Hurlbut, Sept. 22, 1862. See also *O.R.*, I, xvii, part 1, 140–43.

To Col. John V. D. Du Bois

Burnsville [*Sept.*] 21 [*1862*]

Col DuBois

Hamilton & stanley with the cavy Pursued price yesterday morning south—They will probaly be in Jacinto & merge to-day   some of ords forces are ~~spread~~ already back to Corinth & all will be there today

U S Grant
Maj Gen

Telegram, copy, Justin G. Turner, Los Angeles, Calif. On Sept. 21, 1862, Col. John V. D. Du Bois, Rienzi, twice telegraphed to USG. "I can find no sign of the enemes retreating South West on The road   They went North—" "Not a word   have Sent 2. Messengers   Neither returned—" Telegrams received, DNA, RG 393, Dept. of the Mo., Telegrams Received.

On Sept. 21, at 1 A.M., Maj. Gen. William S. Rosecrans, Jacinto, wrote to USG. "If you can let me know that there is a good opportunity to cross the Rail Road & march on Holly Springs to cut off the forces of Buck Van Dorn I will be in readiness to take everything   if we could get them across the Hatchie they would be clean up the spout" ALS, *ibid. O.R.*, I, xvii, part 1, 71. On the same day, Rosecrans again wrote to USG. "Your dispatch recd   I have already, order Mizener to mass his cavalry at Peyton Springs & South of Jacinto   Hamiltons Division to take post on the Jacinto & Burnsville Road, Stanley camps one mile East of Davenports mill—My head Quarters will be in Jacinto tonight. Price short of Provisions retreats towards Fulton   Breckenridge & Van Dorn were certainly distined to some kind of cooperation in this move, & what they are about I cannot tell but we will try to whip them in detail if we can catch them— Have ordered four days supplies for our army to be at Jacinto tonight if possible —~~Capt Taylor~~   The rebel killed was far more than we thought.   yestrday they had collected the dead for burial 200 yds in rear of their little hospital where they were found yestrday covered with Tarpaulins   There 16 where Col Stanton 3d Ark. was lying were collected by the rebels to be carried down to the same point   My count was 99   these with the 162 makes 261 rebels killed. This at the usual allowance would make them ~~944~~ wounded.   our men found bloody rags &c along the line of their march." ALS, DNA, RG 393, Dept. of the Mo., Telegrams Received. *O.R.*, I, xvii, part 1, 72.

On Sept. 22, Rosecrans telegraphed to USG. "We arrived here tonight Chickasaw encamped from the rebels at Bay Springs & rejoined us tonight   He heard one Lt say to another than they were going to the place they came from either Baldwin Gun town or Tupelo   The prisoners were taken to the rear on the morning to be out of the way in the fight which they were told was to come off next day   The train was started out at 3 a. m. as Price went back with a part of the advance guard. When they found out that they were retreating some of the officers said Now we have all these forces up here   if Breckenridge & Van Dorn dont attack Memphis well throw up our commissions." ALS (telegram sent), DNA, RG 393, Dept. of the Mo., Telegrams Received. *O.R.*, I, xvii, part 2, 233. "Chickasaw" mentioned above is identified as L. H. Naron, a scout, *ibid.* On Sept. 23, Rosecrans telegraphed to USG. "Information shows that only two (2) Regts of Prices troops had reached the R R last evening   Rear guard at least staid at Bay Springs yesterday   country all clear & quiet to four (4) miles below Blickland & west to the Hatchie   shall put a brigade of stanly's division at Rienzi—tomorrow   am getting full information of the routes by which we should march down   anxiously await news from you—oh' that corinth could be left to take care of itself"   Telegrams received (2), DNA, RG 393, Dept. of the Mo., Telegrams Received. *O.R.*, I, xvii, part 2, 234.

On Sept. 22, Du Bois, Rienzi, twice telegraphed to USG. "Baldwin reinforced by Falkners Cavalry & one regt of infantry   citizens came up from Baldwin tonight   attack of night before last was by about three Hundred (300) cavalry   Price said to be at Day Springs"   "Not unless the force of guerrillas towards Riply is ~~is~~ stronger than I think—My opinion about line of rebels retreat was only for your information"   Telegrams received, DNA, RG 393, Dept. of the Mo., Telegrams Received. On Sept. 24, Du Bois telegraphed to USG. "Col Lee's scouts returned reports the scout was three (3) miles this side of Baldwin at Daylight   found camp on 20 mile c[reek] east side of R R   from sound of drums at Reville judged 3 Regts of Infantry   they have no pickets. They then went to a point four 4 miles N E of Marietta   found heavy camps there—then skirted towards Bay Springs   camps along the whole route—Prices army there the morning of the 23d En'route from Boonville south. They heard at Day light & for 2 hours afterwards very heavy firing both Artillery & Infantry   The Rebels have no scouts a strange fact.   a force of Falkners men were at Blackland—"   Telegram received, *ibid.* On Sept. 24, 1st Lt. Theodore S. Bowers, Corinth, sent a copy of this telegram to Maj. John A. Rawlins, Jackson. Telegram received, *ibid.*

To Col. Jesse Hildebrand

Head Qrs Dist of West Tenn
Corinth Sept 21st 1862

COL J HILDEBRAND
COMD.G FORCES
ALTON ILL
SIR

Your letter regarding the release of two Prisoners Col Neely and Fintress is just received,

The letter you received was genuine but feeling a doubt you did just right to enquire before acting.

I would now add to the number a Mr Hancock[1] (Capt) aso from Boliver

Respetfuly &c
U. S GRANT
Maj Genl

Copy, DNA, RG 249, Letters Received. Col. Jesse Hildebrand noted on the letter that the three prisoners were released on Sept. 25, 1862. Copy, *ibid*. See letter to Col. Jesse Hildebrand, Sept. 11, 1862. On Sept. 22, USG wrote to Hildebrand. "You are authorized to release Rufus Adams, Sent from this place to the Alton Prison by my order, in him takeing the prescribed Oath." Copy, DNA, RG 249, Letters Received. Hildebrand noted on the letter that the prisoner refused to take the oath on Sept. 27. Copy, *ibid*. On Sept. 24, USG wrote to Hildebrand. "You are authorized to release Jerome B Hill a Political Prisoner from Boliver Tennessee on the usual oath prescribed in such case's" Copy, *ibid*. Hildebrand noted on the letter that the prisoner refused to take the oath on Sept. 27. Copy, *ibid*. See letter to Col. Jesse Hildebrand, Oct. 3, 1862.

1. Thomas H. Hancock, Bolivar, Tenn., arrested on Aug. 11.

To Maj. Gen. Henry W. Halleck

Grant's Hd Qrs near Corinth 10 30 a m [*Sept.*] 22 [*1862*].

GENL H W HALLECK
GENL IN CHF U S A

I would respectfully request that some of the new Regts now organizing be sent to this Command   They could be of great service guarding rail road & posts that must be occupied & where they would be behind Breastworks. At Memphis one Regt could be well Employed without arms in manning the siege guns

U S GRANT M G C

Telegram received, DNA, RG 94, Generals' Papers and Books, Telegrams Received by Gen. Halleck; *ibid.*, RG 107, Telegrams Collected (Bound); copies, *ibid.*, Telegrams Received in Cipher; *ibid.*, RG 393, USG Hd. Qrs. Correspondence; DLC-USG, V, 4, 5, 7, 8, 88. *O.R.*, I, xvii, part 2, 232.

To Maj. Gen. Henry W. Halleck

Near Corinth Miss Sept 22th 1862

MAJ GEN H W HALLECK
GENL IN CHIEF

Boliver is now threatened with an attack from Villipigue, a portion of Breckenridges forces and possibly some other troops They marched in three columns from Davis Mills[1] about seven miles South of Grand Junction and will reach today Eight miles south of Bolivar   They have twenty Regts Infantry One thousand Cavalry Five Batteries Artillery   Hurlbut will be so reinforced tonight as to hold the place if attacked and to take the iniative if threatened and not attacked   I shall go to Jackson to morrow and Bolivar if necessary.

U S GRANT
Maj Genl

Telegram received, DNA, RG 107, Telegrams Collected (Bound); copies, *ibid.*, Telegrams Received in Cipher; *ibid.*, RG 393, USG Hd. Qrs. Correspondence; DLC-USG, V, 4, 5, 7, 8, 88. *O.R.*, I, xvii, part 2, 233. See following telegram.

  1. Davis' Mill, Miss., on the Mississippi Central Railroad at the Tenn. state line.

To Brig. Gen. Stephen A. Hurlbut

                Corinth [*Sept.*] *22* [*1862*]

GENL. HURLBUT.

  The last of Gen Ross Command is now just leaving[1] I am going to Jackson ~~and~~ also if the enemy are leaving prepare to pursue them with nearly all your force Bolivar will be sufficiently guarded with the troops arriving there tonight

               U S GRANT
               Maj Genl

Telegram, copy, DNA, RG 393, District of West Tenn., 4th Division, Telegrams Received. On Sept. 22, 1862, Brig. Gen. Stephen A. Hurlbut sent three telegrams to USG. "My cavalry pickets have been to the creek near VanBuren eight miles south & report the camp of Rebels broken up they are supposed to have returned they were 10.000 strong as reported their precise course not known went off in 3 bodies it would be well to look closely to the R R tonight I have every precaution taken against flank attack & think I am too strong in front in the morning early I shall report further & ask orders if report is favorable to move down" Telegram received, *ibid.*, Dept. of the Mo., Telegrams Received. *O.R.*, I, xvii, part 2, 232. "On yesterday morning at 2 A.M. the Conferate forces in three columns moved out from Davis' Mills about twenty regiments of Infantry, five batteries of Artillery, about one thousand Cavalry. They followed Lauman up to Middleburg nine miles from here and ran trains up there. I think last night Van Dorn, Villipigue, Bowen, Ruske and Col. Helmes are along. They may drive back to Wolf River for water but I expect an attack They started with one day's rations. This information from an intelligent deserter. There is fine water near Van Buren about eight miles and I expect them to Camp there to-day. If they do not fall back to Davis Mills they will of course attack. I desire orders. I shall of course hold this place, unless ordered to the contrary, to the last extremity The force as reported is very heavy. Breckinridge with one of his Brigades has gone to Chattanooga." Telegram received, DNA, RG 393, 16th Army Corps, Miscellaneous Papers; *ibid.*, Dept. of the Mo., Telegrams Received. *O.R.*, I, xvii, part 2, 232–33. "My patrols advises me that the enemy is concentrating in large force eight (8) miles on the Grand Junction Road I think they will attack early in the morning" Telegram received, DNA, RG 393, Dept. of the Mo., Telegrams Received. *O.R.*, I, xvii, part 2, 233. Reports of the expedition from Bolivar to Grand Junction, Tenn., are *ibid.*, I, xvii, part 1, 140–43. On Sept. 23, C. S. A. Maj. Gen. Earl Van Dorn wrote to Maj. Gen. Sterling Price. "I came within one hour day before yesterday of cutting off Hurlbut's division from Bolivar." *Ibid.*, I, xvii, part 2, 710.

1. Earlier on Sept. 22, USG telegraphed to Hurlbut. "hold Bolivar if Possible. I will commence at once Sending Ross force back to you, in the mean time will Instruct Logan to spare you all the force Possible" Copy, DNA, RG 393, District of West Tenn., 4th Division, Telegrams Received. On Sept. 22, Brig. Gen. James B. McPherson, Corinth, telegraphed to USG. "About 8. Oclock or as soon after ~~as~~ the Columbus train arrives & I can get them unloaded & ready to start back." Telegram received, *ibid.*, Dept. of the Mo., Telegrams Received. On the same day, Maj. Gen. Edward O. C. Ord, Corinth, telegraphed to USG. "Genl Ross has gone & the two co's sharp shooters here it will be very annoying to a good Col to break up his Reg't & create a necessity for me to order a new Reg't as Provost guards—" Telegram received, *ibid.*

To Maj. Gen. Stephen A. Hurlbut

Jackson [*Sept. 23, 1862*]

GENL HURLBUT.

You need not move now but keep a watch on those fellows at Davis Mills & if they remain there few days we may be able to move out & attack them if necessary I can bring a few thousand troops from corinth sufficient to whip them if they stand or to destroy the Road if they Run

U. S. GRANT
Maj Genl

Telegram received, DNA, RG 393, District of West Tenn., 4th Division, Telegrams Received. On Sept. 23, 1862, Maj. Gen. Stephen A. Hurlbut, Bolivar, telegraphed to USG. "Two (2) loads of Ross troops have come the others will not be in before night the Enemy have unquestionably from all reports fallen back to Davis Mills about ten thousand (10 000) strong Cavalry are out in pursuit. I could move this morning because Ross troops did not arrive and the Enemy have a days start do you wish me to move on La grange & Davis Mills with my own Division my stock is out of Forage & I must send this afternoon for a supply into the country" Telegram received, *ibid.*, Dept. of the Mo., Telegrams Received. *O.R.*, I, xvii, part 2, 234. On the same day, Hurlbut again telegraphed to USG. "The enemy are crossing at Davis Mills   our Cavalry followed to a mile from Grand Junct & found them gone   I have received notice of promotion to Maj Genl with orders to report to Genl Wright Cincinnatti   I do not wish to leave this ~~district~~ division nor this district. Will they take me away" Telegram received, DNA, RG 393, Dept. of the Mo., Telegrams Received.

On Sept. 23, Brig. Gen. Grenville M. Dodge, Trenton, Tenn., telegraphed to Maj. John A. Rawlins. "A Deserter from the 7th Kentucky under Breckinridge came in here this morning is a man I know. He left Davis Mill on Cold Water Friday Morning   Breckinridge was then there with Eight Thousand (8000). Two of the Kentucky Regiments had been ordered South their time being out and the officers were afraid that they would desert if they came North. He says they were going to Tennessee & Kentucky to join Bragg   there was a large force of Conscripts & released Prisoners at Jackson when they left that place and that they had been furloughed sixty Days   About one hundred (100) left with this man   several have come in   He reports Jacksons Cavalry between Sumerville & Memphis and that they caught several of his Party"   Telegram received, *ibid.* *O.R.*, I, xvii, part 2, 235.

To Maj. Gen. Edward O. C. Ord

By Telegraph from Jackson [*Sept. 23?*] *1862*

To Maj Gen Ord
    I will go to St Louis tomorrow   before starting will make the order for you to command the 2d ~~of~~ Division of the District Head Quarters here or at Bolivar at your discretion   my Head Quarters will be here[1]

U S Grant
Maj Gen Comdg

Telegram received, Ord Papers, CU-B. On Sept. 24, 1862, Maj. John A. Rawlins issued General Orders No. 83. "The District of West. Tenn. will, until otherwise directed, be divided into four Divisions, as follows: The First Division, Commanded by Major Genl. W. T. Sherman, will embrace all the territory south of the Hatchee, and west of Bolivar occupied by our troops. Head Quarters at Memphis. The Second Division will embrace all the territory south of the Kentucky line and to the Hatchee on the West, and Bethel Station on the East, including Bolivar south of the Hatchee Major Gen. E. O. C. Ord, Commanding. It will be the duty of the Commanding Officer of the second Division to guard all the Railroads within his District. Head Quarters will be at Jackson or Bolivar, at the option of the Commander. The Third Division, Major Gen. W. S. Rosecrans, Commanding, will embrace all the territory now occupied by the Army of the

Miss. and by the forces at present Commanded by Major Gen. Ord, Head Quarters at Corinth, Miss. It will be the duty of this Division to guard the Railroad, South from Bethel and east from Chewalla, so far as the country is occupied by our troops. The Fourth Division, Brig. Gen. J. F. Quinby, Commdg. will be composed of what are now known as the District of Cairo and of Miss., including Forts. Henry and Donelson, and exclusive of that portion lying in the State of Tenn. and along the line of the Railroads." Copies, DLC-USG, V, 12, 13, 14, 95; DNA, RG 393, USG General Orders; *ibid.*, Dept. of the Tenn., General and Special Orders. *O.R.*, I, xvii, part 2, 237.

While sending his telegram to Maj. Gen. Edward O. C. Ord, USG probably sent a similar telegram to Maj. Gen. William S. Rosecrans. On Sept. 23, Rosecrans telegraphed to USG. "Your dispatch received will you please designate in your orders what forces will be subject to my command. Sorry you are going even for one day how soon ~~do~~ will you return—when shall I go up to Corinth" Telegram received, DNA, RG 393, Dept. of the Mo., Telegrams Received. On Sept. 28, Rosecrans telegraphed to USG. "My dear General, there ought to be a large store house at Columbus for repair our small arms. We captured about fifteen hundred (1.500) of the Rebels. Mostly Harpers Ferry, 69. I wish you would authorize me to organize the troops left under my command as the army of the Miss. I want to give a proper position to McArthur by reorganizing them. Do you think you will be able to give me seven new regiments to make these divisions full." Copy, *ibid.*, Army of the Miss., Telegrams Sent. On Sept. 29, Rosecrans telegraphed to USG. "All our books our stationary &c is headed army of the Mississippi I am very anxious to retain the name cannot McKeans & Davis Division's be attached & we still retain the old name—" Telegram received, *ibid.*, Dept. of the Mo., Telegrams Received; copy, *ibid.*, Army of the Miss., Telegrams Sent.

1. On Sept. 26, Rawlins, Corinth, issued General Orders No. 84. "From and after this date the Head Quarters of the District of West. Tenn. will be at Jackson, Tenn. where all reports and returns required by Army Regulations and existing orders, will be made." Copies, DLC-USG, V, 12, 13, 14, 95; DNA, RG 393, USG General Orders; *ibid.*, Dept. of the Tenn., General and Special Orders. *O.R.*, I, xvii, part 2, 240. On Sept. 27, Rawlins issued Special Orders No. 204. "Capt. E. D. Osband, Commanding Genl. Grant's Escort, will proceed with his command at once to Jackson, Tenn. via, Bethel taking with him his Camp and Garrison Equipage and escorting Head Quarters train. Upon his arrival at Jackson, he will report to District Head Quarters for orders" DS, DNA, RG 94, District of West Tenn., Special Orders; copies, *ibid.*, RG 393, USG Special Orders; DLC-USG, V, 15, 16, 82, 87.

To Maj. Gen. Henry W. Halleck

———

Head Quarters, Dist. of West Ten.
Jackson, Sept. 24th 1862

Maj. Gen. H. W. Halleck,
Gen. in Chief
Washington D.C.
Gen.

Your dispatch of the 23d is received.[1] The enemy being driven from his position in front of Bolivar by the rapid return of troops drawn from there to reinforce Corinth, and everything now promising quiet in our front for a short time I shall go to St. Louis in person to confer with Gen. Curtis.[2]

To communicate readily with the gunboat fleet, and Gen. Sherman at Memphis, I would have to visit Columbus, and to go to St. Louis will keep me away but little if any longer from my post than if I should not go. It will also save the possibility of any plan leaking out through the telegraph offices on the route.

Another reason for my going is the fact that for several weeks my health has not been good and although improving for the last few days I feel that the trip will be of benefit to me.

Hoping that my course will meet with your approval

I Am Gen. very respectfully
your obt. svt.
U. S. Grant
Maj. Gen.

ALS, IHi. *O.R.*, I, xvii, part 2, 235.

1. See telegram to Maj. Gen. Henry W. Halleck, Sept. 19, 1862.
2. See telegram to Maj. Gen. Henry W. Halleck, Aug. 16, 1862.

To Maj. Gen. Henry W. Halleck

———

Columbus Ky [*Sept.*] 24 [*1862*].

MAJ GEN HALLECK
GENL

I wish to order Genl Quinby into the field but before going
he says a short leave of absence is necessary to arrange for his
family   May I give it

U. S. GRANT
Maj Genl

Telegram received, DNA, RG 94, Generals' Papers and Books, Telegrams
Received by Gen. Halleck; *ibid.*, RG 107, Telegrams Collected (Bound). *O.R.*,
I, xvii, part 2, 238. On Sept. 25, 1862, Maj. Gen. Henry W. Halleck telegraphed
to USG. "Do as you deem best with Genl Quinby. What of Price's army? Do
you hear anything from Nashville or Buell's army?" ALS (telegram sent), DNA,
RG 107, Telegrams Collected (Bound); telegrams received (3), *ibid.*, RG 393,
Dept. of the Tenn., Telegrams Received. *O.R.*, I, xvii, part 2, 238. See following
telegram.

On Sept. 29, Halleck wrote to USG. "From information received here of
Brig Genl Quinby's conduct at Columbus, especially in regard to trade & the
surveyor of Cairo, I am induced to believe that he is not a suitable person to command that post. If upon investigation you concur with me, give him a command
in the field, and put some competent officer in his place." LS, DNA, RG 108,
Letters Sent by Gen. Halleck (Press).

On Sept. 28, Brig. Gen. Isaac F. Quinby, Columbus, Ky., telegraphed to
Brig. Gen. Grenville M. Dodge, Trenton, Tenn. "Major Genl Grant is here &
wishes you to come up by the Todays Train—" Telegram received, Dodge
Papers, IaHA; typescript, *ibid.* On Sept. 29, USG, Columbus, telegraphed to Maj.
John A. Rawlins. "Issue an order assigning Brig Genl Dodge to the command of
fourth Division Dist of West Tenn during the tempory absence of Genl Quinby
Hd Qrs at Columbus—" Copies, DLC-USG, V, 1, 2; DNA, RG 393, USG
Letters Sent; typescript, Dodge Papers, IaHA. These instructions were embodied
in Special Orders No. 206, District of West Tenn., Sept. 29. DS, *ibid.*; copies,
DLC-USG, V, 15, 16, 82, 87; DNA, RG 94, District of West Tenn., Special
Orders; *ibid.*, RG 393, USG Special Orders. *O.R.*, I, xvii, part 2, 242.

On Sept. 2, Quinby had telegraphed to USG. "I have not heard from my
application of the twenty eighth 28th for twenty 20 days leave   may I expect it—"
Telegram received, DNA, RG 393, Dept. of the Tenn., Miscellaneous Letters
Received. On Sept. 10, 1st Lt. Theodore S. Bowers issued Special Orders No. 190.
"The District of Mississippi, Commanded by Brig. Gen. Quinby, and the District
of Cairo, Brig. Gen. J. M. Tuttle, Commdg, are hereby merged into one District
to be Known and designated as the District of Mississippi to be commanded by
Brig. Gen. J. F. Quinby, through whom all reports required by regulations and
existing orders, will be made." DS, *ibid.*, RG 94, District of West Tenn., Special

Orders; copies, *ibid.*, RG 393, USG Special Orders; DLC-USG, V, 15, 16, 82, 87. *O.R.*, I, xvii, part 2, 211.

On Sept. 26, Private William Thirds, 76th Ill., hospital steward at Columbus, wrote to President Abraham Lincoln complaining of the return of a slave to his master by authority of Quinby. ALS, DNA, RG 94, Letters Received. On Oct. 20, Col. Edward D. Townsend forwarded the letter to USG for report, and, on Oct. 26, Rawlins forwarded it to Quinby. ES, *ibid.* On Oct. 27, Quinby wrote to Rawlins. "A few days before the date of the transaction complained of Mr. R R. Taylor a confirmed and almost helpless invalid, a resident of Ballard County Ky: whose loyalty to the federal government is and has been throughout, above suspicion applied to me for permission to look for a negro man who had recently left him. I gave him the desired permit, assuring him that if he found his negro, and could persuade him to go home no obstacles should be thrown in his way—that unless he employed force no force would be opposed to him. After the lapse of about an hour Mr. Taylor returned to my office and reported that he had found his man but that the soldiers, inated I have reason to believe by a commissioned officer, would not permit the negro though willing to leave, to accompany his master, and threatened Mr. Taylor with violence if he attempted to take him. I advised him to go home for a few days to allow the excitement to subside which he did. On his return several days afterwards he was referred to Lt. Col. Duff 2d Ill. Arty, who did issue the order of which a copy was sent the President though it was neither dictated by nor submitted to my Staff   as he acted in accordance with my understood wishes I assume all criminality if any which attaches thereto. . . . " ALS, *ibid.* On Oct. 28, USG endorsed Quinby's letter. "Respectfully returned to the Adj. Gen. of the Army Washington D. C." AES, *ibid.* On June 9, 1863, Col. Joseph Holt, judge advocate gen., endorsed these documents. "In view of the explanation offered by Brig Gen Quinby, it is suggested that this complaint against him should not be further considered. The object of his action was doubt-less in good faith, not to restrain the freedom of the negro named but to prevent it from being restrained by others. If his course was misconceived, it was certainly free from all taint of insubordination, & it is not believed that it calls for the formal rebuke of the government—"   AES, *ibid.*

On Nov. 20, Quinby wrote to Asst. Secretary of War Peter H. Watson indignantly defending his conduct in arresting two correspondents, including one for the *Chicago Tribune*, at Cairo, and ordering them to print retractions of objectionable stories. LS, *ibid.* On the same day, USG endorsed this letter. "Respectfully forwarded to Headquarters of the Army Washington, D. C." ES, *ibid.* Also forwarded was a letter of Nov. 9 from Watson to Quinby requesting an explanation of this incident. ALS, *ibid.*

To Maj. Gen. Henry W. Halleck

St. Louis, Sept. 25th 1862

Maj. Gen. H. W. Halleck, Gen. in Chief
Washington D. C.

I do not hear a word from Buell's Army. Price was defeated from going east of the Tennessee river but I understand that Breckenridge has gone by way of Mobile and Chatanooga.

The rebels come up to within eight miles of Bolivar but finding the place so strongly reinforced fell back to Davis' Mills first and finding our Cavalry in such hot pursuit left there for further south in great haste. I wrote from Jackson the object of my coming to St. Louis. Will leave in the morning.

U. S. Grant
Maj. Gen.

ALS (telegram sent), DNA, RG 393, Dept. of the Mo., Telegrams Received; telegram received, *ibid.*, RG 107, Telegrams Collected (Bound). *O.R.*, I, xvii, part 2, 238.

On Oct. 29, 1862, Col. John C. Kelton wrote to USG. "I am directed by the General-in-chief to forward to you the enclosed copy of a letter from F. A. Dick Esqr. to the Att'y General. Your report of the battle of Iuka was received this morning" ALS, DNA, RG 108, Letters Sent by Gen. Halleck (Press). On Sept. 28, Franklin A. Dick, St. Louis, wrote to Attorney General Edward Bates. "Seeing it stated that the late attack by Rosecrans upon Price at Iuka failed, for want of co-operation by Genl Grant, I consider it my duty to state, that General Grant was drunk in St. Louis on Friday the 26th instant. I did not see him myself, ~~by~~ but Henry T. Blow met & talked with him, and stated to me, that the Genl was 'as ~~drunk~~ tight as a brick' Believing, as I do, that much of our ill success results from drunken officers, I intend to do my ~~part~~ duty in reporting such crime upon their part, so that the facts may reach those who have power to apply the remedy. . . . I make this fact as to Grant known, because I have heard it denied that he now drinks—If drunk in St. Louis on the 26th, he may be drunk in command of his army a few days later." ALS, NIC. On Oct. 2, Bates endorsed the letter. "Respectfully referred to the Sec.y. of War. Mr Dick is a lawyer of fair standing, at St Louis, & brother in law to Frank Blair." AES, *ibid.* On Oct. 4, Asst. Secretary of War Peter H. Watson referred the letter to Maj. Gen. Henry W. Halleck. AES, *ibid.* On Nov. 10, USG wrote to hd. qrs., U.S. Army. "Relative to his being drunk in St Louis Sept. 26-62" DNA, RG 108, Register of Letters Received. Sparse newspaper comment on USG's visit to St. Louis mentioned that he was accompanied by Col. T. Lyle Dickey and Col. Clark B. Lagow, and that USG looked "remarkably well, although bearing some marks of the fatigues of his summer campaign." *New York Times*, Oct. 5, 1862.

To Maj. Gen. Edward O. C. Ord

By Telegraph from St Louis 10.30 P m Sept 25 *1862*

To Gen Ord

Gen Hurlbut telegraphs me that Rebels are strongly reinforced and threaten him[1]   watch in that direction & if necessary reinforce him all you can. Communicate with Genl Rosecrans also—

U. S Grant
Maj Genl

Telegram received, Ord Papers, CU-B; copies, DLC-USG, V, 1, 2; DNA, RG 393, USG Letters Sent. *O.R.*, I, xvii, part 2, 239. On the bottom of the telegram received, Maj. John A. Rawlins added a note. "The dispatch from Gen. Hurlbut was forwarded ̶f̶r̶ to Gen Grant yesterday. The above is his reply thereto." ES, Ord Papers, CU-B.

1. On Sept. 25, 1862, Maj. Gen. Stephen A. Hurlbut, Bolivar, telegraphed to USG. "Negro in from near Grand Junction reports hearing his master say that enemy have received heavy reinforcements from Holly Springs & other points in Mississippi & that they will move northward & cut the railroad between Corinth & this place then attack here ̶t̶h̶e̶r̶e̶   he has evidently heard this   the information is of value as to the proposed point of attack on road but the probability is toward some point east of Jackson   there were three hundred (300) irregular cavalry in Somerville yesterday"   Telegrams received (2), DNA, RG 393, Dept. of the Mo., Telegrams Received. *O.R.*, I, xvii, part 2, 238. On the same day, Hurlbut again telegraphed to USG. "A large body of cavalry—estimated by citizens at 2,000 probably 1000 passed today by Andersons Mill east enquiring for Simpsons Ferry on Hatchie half way between Van Buren & here   The force was followed up by my cavalry patrol who agree that it is a large body of men. I am of opinion an attack is designed on R Road & if they have taken direction designated somewhere in the vicinity of Bethel or perhaps Purdy   They had four days rations"   Telegrams received (3), DNA, RG 393, Dept. of the Mo., Telegrams Received; copy, *ibid.*, 16th Army Corps, Miscellaneous Papers. *O.R.*, I, xvii, part 2, 238. On the same day, USG telegraphed to Hurlbut. "I have communicated to Ord & Rosecrans. the substance of your telegram and instructed that you be reinforced to any extent that may be necessary   communicate with Ord until my return"   Copies, DLC-USG, V, 1, 2; DNA, RG 393, USG Letters Sent. *O.R.*, I, xvii, part 2, 239.

Also on Sept. 25, USG telegraphed to Col. Isham N. Haynie, Bethel, Tenn. "Gen Hurlbut telegraphs that One Thousand Rebel cavelry passed East—yesterday toward Simpson ferry. Look out for attack on Rail Road near Bethel. Communicate with Genl Ord"   Telegram received, DNA, RG 393, Dept. of the Mo., Telegrams Received. Perhaps Haynie was absent, for in an undated message received at Cairo on Sept. 26, Col. William R. Morrison, Bethel, telegraphed to USG. "We are on the look out and ready"   Telegram received, *ibid*.

To Brig. Gen. Lorenzo Thomas

Headquarters Dist. of West. Tenn.
Corinth. Miss. Sept. 26. 1862.
Brig. General L. Thomas.
Adjutant General of the Army
Washington. D. C.
General:

I have the honor to transmit herewith, Proceedings of a General Court Martial in the cases of Colonel F. L. Rhoads, 8th Regiment Illinois Volunteers and 1st Lieutenant C. E. Harvey, 12th Regiment Michigan Vols.

Also General Orders. No. 82. from these Headquarters, publishing same.

I am, General,
Very Respectfully
Your Obt. Servant
U. S Grant
Major General Commanding

LS, DNA, RG 153, KK 233. On Sept. 26, 1862, USG endorsed the court-martial proceedings of Col. Frank L. Rhoads, 8th Ill. "Respectfully forwarded to Headquarters of the Army, Washington D. C." ES, *ibid*. On the same day, USG signed an identical endorsement on the court-martial proceedings of 1st Lt. C. E. Harvey, 12th Mich. ES, *ibid*. On Sept. 22, Maj. John A. Rawlins issued General Orders No. 82 reporting the charges, pleas, verdict, and decision of the commanding officer in both cases. Copies, DLC-USG, V, 12, 13, 14, 95; DNA, RG 393, District of West Tenn., General Orders.

The documents discussed above typify considerable paperwork involving USG in late 1862. On Sept. 14, USG wrote to Brig. Gen. Lorenzo Thomas enclosing court-martial proceedings for Maj. Stephen Walsh, 15th Mich., Lt. John Considine, 15th Mich., Capt. Patrick O'Connor, 17th Wis., Capt. William Grant, 11th Iowa, and also General Orders No. 78, Aug. 25, reporting the trials. LS, *ibid.*, RG 153, KK 223. On Sept. 4, USG endorsed the record of Walsh. "Respectfully forwarded to Hd. Qurs of the Army, Washington. D. C" ES, *ibid.* On Sept. 14, he similarly endorsed the records of O'Connor and Considine. ES, *ibid.*

Also on Sept. 14, USG wrote to Thomas enclosing court-martial proceedings for privates James McGrath, 18th Ill., John Page, 11th Ill., Edward Kelly, 8th Ill., 1st Lt. Benjamin F. Berry, 29th Ill., 2nd Lt. A. T. Lake, 25th Ill., and General Orders No. 70, Aug. 4, reporting the trials. ES, *ibid.*, KK 220. On Sept. 14, USG endorsed the record of Lake. "Respectfully forwarded to Head Quarters of the Army at Washington, for decision of the President" ES, *ibid.*, KK 252. Col. Joseph Holt, judge-advocate-gen., noted that approval of the president was not necessary in time of war, and on Sept. 26, Col. Edward D. Townsend, AGO, endorsed the proceedings back to USG. AES, *ibid.* The other endorsements in this group by USG were identical to that for Lake, but in each case the final words were crossed out and USG added his decision. For McGrath he noted: "Approved Alton"; for Page: "Approved to be confined in Alton Penitentiary. No evidence of stealing the pistol"; for Kelly: "Sentence approved To be confined with his regiment."; for Berry: "Approved and reinstated on recommendation of the Court with repremand." AE, *ibid.*, KK 220.

Also on Sept. 14, USG wrote to Thomas enclosing court-martial proceedings for Capt. Joseph M. Anderson, 80th Ohio, 1st Lt. William W. McAmon, 24th Mo., Capt. Lafayette M. Rice, 24th Mo., and General Orders No. 5, 3rd Division, Army of the Miss., reporting the trials. LS, *ibid.*, KK 219. Each transcript bore the standard endorsement, all dated Sept. 14. ES, *ibid.*

Also on Sept. 14, USG endorsed the transcript of the proceedings of the court-martial of Private James Weldon, 7th Ill. Cav. ES, *ibid.*, KK 288. In this case, Holt added an endorsement stating that the record failed to show that the judge advocate was sworn; below this, President Abraham Lincoln noted: "Not approved" AES, *ibid.* Also on Sept. 14, USG endorsed the transcript of the proceedings of the court-martial of Private James Keefe. ES, *ibid.*, LL 42. On Aug. 14, Brig. Gen. William S. Rosecrans had endorsed this transcript. "Respectfully forwarded recommending the confirmation of the sentence—and the prisoner be ordered to be confined in some prison north of the Ohio until his case or his friends can have time to show if he be insane" AES, *ibid.* On Oct. 24, Lincoln added his endorsement. "Suspended according to the suggestion of Gen. Rosecrans" AES, *ibid.*

On Sept. 22, USG endorsed individually a group of transcripts of the proceedings of military commission trials of citizens which had been forwarded by Brig. Gen. Isaac F. Quinby: George M. Anderson, Thomas P. Connor, Jacob A. Fowler, Thomas Knight, William L. McElmurry, Montgomery Robinson, James A. Snow, Joseph C. Taylor, James Thomason, and Thomas York. ES, *ibid.*, LL 875. All were eventually returned to USG, in part because the endorsements were written in the wrong place; the verdicts were overruled on procedural grounds, and, on Sept. 23, 1863, USG again endorsed each case. ES, *ibid.* Also on Sept. 22, 1862, USG endorsed the proceedings of a military commission in the case of Elijah Cheek. ES, *ibid.*, KK 237. See *Calendar*, Aug. 25, 1862. Also on Sept. 22, USG endorsed the court-martial proceedings involving Capt. Herman Stack, 44th Ill., 2nd Lt. Joseph Clancy, 14th Wis., and 1st Lt. Eliphas Kisner,

22nd Ohio. ES, DNA, RG 153, KK 236. On the same day, USG endorsed the records of a military commission convened by Maj. Gen. William T. Sherman in Memphis which tried twenty-six cases of soldiers and civilians on charges ranging from murder to calling Sherman "ornary." ES, *ibid.*, KK 285. The case of Sely Lewis, convicted as a smuggler and spy, was endorsed by Lincoln. "So far as the sentence in this case relates to the accused as a spy, it is disapproved, the Commission not having jurisdiction. of the offence. The sentence of death is mitigated to imprisonment for the term of six months commencing on this day." AES, *ibid.* See *O.R.*, II, iv, 661–62.

On Sept. 25, USG individually endorsed the transcripts of the proceedings of the courts-martial of five privates. ES, DNA, RG 153, KK 239.

Before Sept., 1862, USG had been involved in the convening of courts and commissions, but approval and announcement of sentences and referral of papers to Washington was the prerogative of Maj. Gen. Henry W. Halleck. On April 22, USG endorsed the transcript of the proceedings of the court-martial of Maj. John McDonald, 8th Mo., later active in the Whiskey Ring. "Respectfully refered to Hd Qrs. Dept. of the Miss." AES, *ibid.*, II 929. By late Sept., USG's handling of such paperwork was so much a matter of routine that further endorsements and letters of transmittal will not be noted in these pages except when the cases or persons involved were significant, or when the involvement of USG varied from normal routine. Since the letter to Thomas, Sept. 26, used as text, was prepared at Corinth on a day when USG was elsewhere, his involvement with it was probably limited to providing a signature.

To Maj. Gen. Edward O. C. Ord

———

By Telegraph from Columbus [*Sept. 27*] 1862

To Maj Gen Ord Corinth

I will be in Columbus for two or three days   Comunicate with me here if any thing of importance occurs

U S Grant
Maj Gen Comdg

Telegram received, Ord Papers, CU-B. On Sept. 27, 1862, Maj. Gen. Edward O. C. Ord, Jackson, Tenn., telegraphed to USG. "I have turned over the command at Corinth to Genl Rosecrans with my old division still there until you can designate where they shall go   A scout of McArthurs Cavalry 270 strong under Lt Col McDermont was supprised by about 200 Guerrillias on the Hatchie 8 miles west of Chewalla at davis bridge just at dark on the 25th   the horses were unsaddled & men scattered cutting corn   no guards out.   about a hundred escaped that night, including Capt. Fords company which had just arrived & was not unsaddled   after McDermot Ford & the Major of the 11th Ills had retreated in great haste & confusion a captain rallied some fifty men on a ford & sent for help which was sent them yesterday. I shall Quarter here inspect Bolivar & the Rail Road tomorrow" Telegram received, DNA, RG 107, Telegrams Collected (Unbound); copy, *ibid.*, RG 94, War Records Office, Union Battle Reports. *O.R.*, I, xvii, part 1, 143–44. The report of Sept. 25 from Lt. Col. John McDermott to Brig. Gen. John McArthur is *ibid.*, p. 144.

On Sept. 27, Maj. Gen. Stephen A. Hurlbut telegraphed to USG. "From the best information I can get the forces of the enemy encamped at Davis' Mill South of Grand Junction have gone Eastward" Telegram received, DNA, RG 393, Dept. of the Mo., Telegrams Received. *O.R.*, I, xvii, part 2, 240.

Also on Sept. 27, Maj. Gen. William S. Rosecrans telegraphed to USG. "Col Lee 7th Kansas has just telegraphed M the capture of a liut & private & of cavalry near Baldwin on picket duty   examined seperatly they report that most of the infantry & cavalry have moved west supposed to holly springs   if they concentrate there we & memphis will both be threatened unless steele does something   memphis will be in danger if not well fortified.   my dear General more cavalry is indispensible to use & our regiments should be filled up" Telegram received, DNA, RG 393, Dept. of the Mo., Telegrams Received; copy, *ibid.*, Army of the Miss., Telegrams Sent. On the same day, Rosecrans again telegraphed to USG. "From Negroes & deserters report to date of rebels. His advance guard is at Baldwin. Price at Tupello fortifying. Maurys division of three brigades have gone to Holly Springs. Genl. McKean sends report of a scout. Van Dorn & Villippigue reported at Grand Junction with forty Regts. poorly supplied with artillery & Q-M stores   Intends making a feint on Bolivar but a real attack on Corinth soon as they want stores. Price is expected to cooperate   He says one hundred & fifty rebels & recruits are in Montezuma. If they have forty Regts. will be eighteen ~~hund~~ thousand & five hundred 18500 men. Price has 13000 including Maurys" Telegram received, *ibid.*, Dept. of the Mo., Telegrams Received; copy, *ibid.*, Army of the Miss., Telegrams Sent.

On Sept. 28, Rosecrans telegraphed to USG. "Scouts from Genl Kean confirms my Telegraph of Price movement to Ripley   the Seminary Building was engaged for his Head Quarters   I shall move all Stanlies Division to Rienzi & from thence I think to Kossuth unless you have views differing from mine" Telegram received, *ibid.*, Dept. of the Mo., Telegrams Received; copy, *ibid.*, Army of the Miss., Telegrams Sent. *O.R.*, I, xvii, part 2, 241. On the same day, USG, Columbus, telegraphed to Rosecrans. "Send Stanley's division to Kossuth if you deem it necessary." Copy, DNA, RG 393, Army of the Miss., Telegrams Received.

To Maj. Gen. Henry W. Halleck

Columbus Ky
Sept 28th 11. a. m. [<i>1862</i>]

MAJ GEN H. W. HALLECK
GEN IN CHIEF.

To make a move on the Yazoo River promise successful it will be necessary to have some of the New Regts at Memphis to take the place of Sherman's Division. I will want Shermans Division & some of my command at Bolivar to move on Grenada to attract attention in that direction whilst Steel moves across from a point below not yet determined upon to do the work designed— can you send the new Troops

U S GRANT
Maj Genl

Telegram received, DNA, RG 94, Generals' Papers and Books, Telegrams Received by Gen. Halleck; *ibid.*, RG 107, Telegrams Collected (Bound); copy, *ibid.*, Telegrams Received in Cipher. *O.R.*, I, xvii, part 2, 240–41.

In order to communicate with Maj. Gen. William T. Sherman, USG issued special orders on Sept. 26, 1862. "Col W. S. Hillyer A. D. C. will proceed forthwith to Memphis Tenn and report to Maj. Gen. Sherman on special business and return to this place without unnecessary delay—" DS, Robert C. W. Hillyer, San José, Costa Rica. Although datelined "Jackson," these orders were written by USG in St. Louis, and this accounts for their unnumbered status, absence from book records, and issuance by USG.

Further indications of consultation on plans appear in a letter of Sept. 30 from Sherman to USG. "Yours of the 27th. is this moment received. I am not in possession of authentic data as to the exact location of the Enemy's fleet of Boats in the Yazoo or the road leading thereto. I am certain however that General Steele & Capts Phelps & Gwinn of the navy knows all about it. My study has been mostly confined to the country between this and Grenada. I feel certain that the two Railroads that branch from Grenada northward can and should be broken preliminary to operations against any point of the Yazoo near its mouth. Almost the entire force of the Enemy about Vicksburg has been moved North, except the released prisoners, who are being rearmed and reorganized back of Vicksburg. If Steele was to move on Panola, I could meet him there and we could jointly cross over to the Central Road at a point below Oxford, where there are several very high pieces of ~~tressel~~ trestle work requiring for repairs timbers of a length that could not be replaced in a long time. I have this from undoubted authority and indicate their several positions on a Map herewith. With these Roads broken a comparatively light force could operate between the Mississippi & Yazoo, and could destroy the Boats laying in the latter. The Yazoo is now very low and those

Boats are surely blockaded for five months, yet, giving ample time. My force here is now 8122 of which say 7000 are good effective men   I have been drilling these very hard, and the Infantry & Artillery are in fine order. The Cavalry too is in better train & drill than at any former period. Our fort is drawing to completion and five thousand new troops could hold the works, leaving me my Division for field operations   You will have heard of the operations of Guerrillas on the River. They have done little actual execution, but a good deal of mischief. I am determined to spare no efforts to check all such efforts or attempts on the Boats. I send up a Regiment today to bring from Randolph some Guns which I thought Col. Bissell had already moved, but which are reported there. The Guns are spiked but still might be repaired and put in position much to our detriment   Breckinridge has surely gone to Kentucky, via Jackson, Meridian, Chattanoga &c.   he took with him only about 3000 Kentuckians. Van Dorn is near Grand Junction. They are building a bridge there showing their desire to operate by Rail Road. This makes it important this Central Road should be broken below the Tallahatchie and Helenae is the best point to start from, and the same force can accomplish the other object, viz the destruction of the Boats in the Yazoo. I will write to Gen Steele for all the information he possesses on this point   I had a flag of truce yesterday from Genl. Hindman at Little Rock from which I infer Holmes has gone north from there altho the bearer of the flag said he was at Little Rock sick   I would be obliged if you if you would claim the 13th Infty for me. Wright took it after it had been relieved by my 77 Ohio, whereby I lost both, not a fair trade; I doubt not they have a enough troops at Cincinati now, and can well spare the Battalion   You know well that this is a magnificent place for assembling and organizing troops and strategically far better than Helena for operations on the River. We are all very healthy whereas I hear there is much sickness at Helena. I would like to have you send a Division of new Regiments here, they could soon be made efficient   My own opinion is that after discovering the exact point at which the boats in the Yazoo lie, whilst a force moves from here and Helena against Oxford., the Gunboats & transports should threaten Vicksburg as though an attack was intended, while a comparatively small force can land at some point below Gaines Landing and strike across to the Yazoo. Of course the movements of all should be prescribed as to time and kept absolutely secret, so that the Enemy could not guess at your purposes.   the first Vicksburg and the real attack on the Rail Road and Yazoo." Copies, DNA, RG 94, Generals' Papers and Books, William T. Sherman, Letters Sent; DLC-William T. Sherman. *O.R.*, I, xvii, part 2, 244-45.

To Maj. Gen. Henry W. Halleck

Corinth Miss
Sept 30th 5 30 P M [*1862*]

MAJ GEN HALLECK
GENL IN CHIEF

Price is now at Ripley Van Dorn at Somerville[1] and Villipigue at Salem[2]   It looks as if Van Dorn was trying to effect a lodgement on the Mississippi above Memphis   Threatened at all other points I cannot send out forces to drive him away   If Helena troops could now be sent across the River I think they would meet with no difficulty in getting to Grenada and perhaps down on to the Yazoo

U S GRANT
Maj Gen

Telegram received, DNA, RG 94, Generals' Papers and Books, Telegrams Received by Gen. Halleck; *ibid.*, RG 107, Telegrams Collected (Bound); copies, *ibid.*, Telegrams Received in Cipher; *ibid.*, RG 393, USG Hd. Qrs. Correspondence; DLC-USG, V, 4, 5, 7, 8, 88. *O.R.*, I, xvii, part 2, 243.

On Sept. 29, 1862, Maj. Gen. William S. Rosecrans, Corinth, telegraphed to Maj. John A. Rawlins. "I have not reported to the Maj Genl Comd'g the details of the pocahontas capture because full reports are not in yet—All but about forty 40) of our men have come in some seventy five (75) or eighty 80 horses & about as many carbines   the rebels are reported to have burned the pocahontas bridge completely & left some horses on this side   eight (8) Co's of 3rd Mich Cavalry are out there now & we shall have reports in soon.   stanly will be in Rienzi today   our scouts suprised & routed a party of shot gun cavelary 5 miles from Ruckersville yesterday—Nothing but Genl Report of Price moving West or south—" Telegram received, DNA, RG 393, Dept. of the Mo., Telegrams Received; copy, *ibid.*, Army of the Miss., Telegrams Sent. *O.R.*, I, xvii, part 2, 242. On the same day, Rosecrans telegraphed to USG. "Scout third 3d mich Cav' went to Jonesboro on the Pocahontas & Riply road found no enemy—stems from —Rumor that Van Dorn was already in Riply Price coming there—They were short of Rations & were going to Kentucky—our latest from Ripley was to saturday night   Van Dorn was not there then   Scouts from Rienzi have gone to Ripley   not yet in—what news have you   anything to render it advisable to move Stanly to Kossuth & Hamilton to Rienzi tomorrow—" Telegram received, DNA, RG 393, Dept. of the Mo., Telegrams Received; copy, *ibid.*, Army of the Miss., Telegrams Sent.

On Sept. 30, Maj. Gen. Stephen A. Hurlbut telegraphed to USG. "My best information is that with the exception of a strong advance guard at Davis Mills' a large portion of the Enemy have gone East below Salsbury. I think Van Dorn is in camp below Lagrange say at Ammons Bridge & so down Wolf River to Moscow with a cavalry advance guard near Somerville. It would be well, to look to the bridge partly constructed by me over the Hatchie 7 miles south of Brownsville. My Cavalry patrols go daily within 10 miles of Somerville but report no force but Guerrillas'—" Telegram received, *ibid.*, Dept. of the Mo., Telegrams Received. *O.R.*, I, xvii, part 2, 243. On the same day, Rosecrans sent four telegrams to USG. "Nothing further heard   have you heard anything"   "We have no maps of the country N. W. of us, will you please direct some one to collect all that is known or can be found out from our men of the south tier of counties between us & Grand Junction—Direct Genl Ross to call for information from all officers who can tell anything of it. We ~~who~~ want to know if the Rebels can harbor & subsist between Pocahontas & Grand Junction—" "News in this A M no signs of the Enemy at Hatchie Crossing yesterday. Rumors continue to come as the following from Hamilton—A citizen scout just in says he saw a secesh soldier who he knew, who says Price VanDorn & Breckenridge had effected a junction & would go to Tennessee through Purdy—Stanly says citizen Scouts report Price from Ripley— would rest in Ripley   Dont know where he would go from thence. My reason for proposing to put Stanly at or near Kossuth is that he would cover all the Hatchie crossings except heavy forces as far as Pocahontas—Hamilton would then move at least one Brigade from Rienzi—look out from S E from Bolivar—" "Citizen in great haste from near Jonesboro reports from a young man arrested near there. Rebels twenty thousand (20,000) strong near there advancing on Pocahontas— Will order Hamilton up. Stanly to Kossuth.   reconoissance to Hatchie crossing —cavalry towards Ruckerville   some one on Telegraph lines between here & Bethel   patrol out—" Telegrams received, DNA, RG 393, Dept. of the Mo., Telegrams Received; copies, *ibid.*, Army of the Miss., Telegrams Sent. The third of these telegrams is in *O.R.*, I, xvii, part 2, 243.

    1. Somerville, Tenn., about forty miles east of Memphis.
    2. Salem, Miss., about forty miles west of Corinth.

To Maj. Gen. Henry W. Halleck

H'd Qrs near Corinth Miss
Oct 1st 1862

MAJ GEN H. W. HALLECK
GEN IN CHIEF

    For several days there has been a movement of the Rebels south of my front which left it in doubt whether Corinth or Bolivar was to be the point of attack. It is now clear that Corinth is the point & that from the west or south west—Price. Van Dorn. Villipigue & Rust[1] are together. Rust commands Breckinridge's

forces the latter having gone to Kentucky by Mobile & Chattanooga taking three Regiments with him.[2] My position is precarious but hope to get out of it all right

U S GRANT

Maj Genl

Telegram received, DNA, RG 94, Generals' Papers and Books, Telegrams
Received by Gen. Halleck; *ibid.*, RG 107, Telegrams Collected (Bound); copies,
ibid., RG 393, USG Hd. Qrs. Correspondence; DLC-USG, V, 4, 5, 7, 8, 88.
O.R., I, xvii, part 2, 250.

1. Albert Rust, born in Va. in 1818, settled in El Dorado, Ark., and was
elected a state legislator (1842–48, 1852–54) and U.S. Representative (1855–57,
1859–61). Entering the Civil War as col., 3rd Ark., he was promoted to brig.
gen. as of March 4, 1862. On Sept. 8, he was assigned to command the 4th Brigade
of Maj. Gen. John C. Breckinridge, but commanded the 1st Brigade of Maj. Gen.
Mansfield Lovell at the battle of Corinth. *Ibid.*, pp. 697, 898–99; *ibid.*, I, xvii,
part 1, 375, 407–10, 416–21.

2. On Oct. 1, Maj. Gen. William S. Rosecrans telegraphed to USG transmitting a telegram from Brig. Gen. David S. Stanley, Rienzi, Sept. 30. "Spaulding
just returned, he went to Hatchie.   no rebels & is satisfied from good information
that there are none 3 miles beyond—Three prisoners of 4th Alabama Breckenridges command caught—Breckinridge has gone to Ky with 3 Ky Reg'ts, his
division is commanded by Genl Rust. Price Villipigue & Rust are all together &
camped on the Pocahontas road. Villipigue & Rust bro't up 15.000 men. Reported
Rebel force 40.000. Prisoners dont know where they are going—" Telegram
received, DNA, RG 393, Dept. of the Mo., Telegrams Received; copy, *ibid.*,
Army of the Miss., Telegrams Sent. *O.R.*, I, xvii, part 2, 251.

Also on Oct. 1, Rosecrans telegraphed frequently to USG. "Rebel Cavalry
have made their appearance at Youngs bridge & upper & lower from 2 to 5 miles
from Chewalla—The bridges were burned by our troops last night—Your body
guard Ford's Cavalry are reported to have run in the most disgraceful manner—
Have ordered McKean to send a brigade to sustain the Chewalla command & feel
the Enemy if he comes in sight—" "Dubois with Drawn from Rienzi to Danville   Cavalry reg't camped at Rucker mill between Clear Creek & Jacinto—No
news from Lee's reconnoisance supported by two (2) Regts of Infantry—Stanly
not yet reported himself in position to   Hamilton divisions concentrated & Davis
& McKean on chewalla road except Crocker who is near here—How far are the
Rebels advancing—Demonstration on chewalla amounted to nothing—" "Report from Chewalla four (4) P M   infantry—& Cavalry force of rebels appeared
south of Tuscumbia at youngs bridge—if they advance on Bethel stanly from position near Kossuth can cut off their retreat or if he should be wanted with me
Hurlbut can do the same—" Telegrams received, DNA, RG 393, Dept. of the
Mo., Telegrams Received; copies, *ibid.*, Army of the Miss., Telegrams Sent.
O.R., I, xvii, part 2, 251–52. "Your Dispatches rec'd   will send up all cars we
can spare—Will Telegraph you about Stanly—by the help of God we will use
them up if they get inside—" "Please send an order for the mustering officer at
once. The Alabamians & Mississippians are becoming discouraged at the delay &

unless immediately mustered in will go away—" Telegrams received, DNA, RG 393, Dept. of the Mo., Telegrams Received; copies, *ibid.*, Army of the Miss., Telegrams Sent. "I desire permission to send Dr Carpenter 5th Iowa In charge of Body wounded officers going home on leave   he is to return at once"   "Will you please let Lieut Lyford stay here until we see how this affair will turn   I have lost my aid Capt Greenwood who died on Monday evening & will need a little help   dont know the roads at all above here" Telegrams received, *ibid.*, Dept. of the Tenn., Miscellaneous Letters Received; copies, *ibid.*, Army of the Miss., Telegrams Sent.

To Maj. Gen. Stephen A. Hurlbut

Head Quarters U. S. Grant
Oct 1st—[*1862*]

MAJ GENL HURLBUT.

If Van Dorn is in West of you it will not do to be detach too much of your force to look after the Rebels about Pocahontas— I have instructed Rosecrans to follow them ~~up~~ if they move towards Bolivar.

U. S. GRANT
Maj Genl

Telegram received, DNA, RG 393, District of West Tenn., 4th Division, Telegrams Received. On Oct. 1, 1862, Maj. Gen. Stephen A. Hurlbut, Bolivar, telegraphed to USG. "There is Evidently a movement eastward going on in front of me the particulars of which I have not yet been able to obtain—" Telegram received, *ibid.*, Dept. of the Mo., Telegrams Received. *O.R.*, I, xvii, part 2, 250. On the same day, USG again telegraphed to Hurlbut. "Genl Rosecrans has not yet moved—you need not move until further orders—Rebels are now said to have their advance near Chewalla" Telegram received, DNA, RG 393, District of West Tenn., 4th Division, Telegrams Received. On the same day, Hurlbut telegraphed to USG. "Both Dispatches rec'd of your orders given—" Telegram received, *ibid.*, Dept. of the Mo., Telegrams Received. See following telegram.

To Maj. Gen. Stephen A. Hurlbut

U. S. Grants Office
Jackson 7.30 P M. [*Oct. 1, 1862*]

MAJ GEN HURBUT.

It is now evident that an attempt will be made to cut the communication between here & Both Corinth & Bolivar   should this prove successful & your position become untenantable retreat with all you can & destroy the balance   Your line of march in such event might be here or Bethel to be determined by Events

U. S. GRANT
Maj Genl.

Telegram received, DNA, RG 393, District of West Tenn., 4th Division, Telegrams Received.

To Maj. Gen. William S. Rosecrans

Head quarters department of West. Tenn.
Jackson Tenn. Oct. 2nd 1862

MAJ. GENL. ROSECRANS,

Inform yourself as well as possible of the strength and position of the enemy and if practicable—move on them as you propose.

Inform me if you determine to start and I will give you all the aid possible from Boliver. Bethel is now strong and can also give some assistance in case of such a move.

U. S. GRANT.
Maj. Genl.

Telegram received, Rosecrans Papers, CLU. On Oct. 2, 1862, Maj. Gen. William S. Rosecrans telegraphed to USG. "My troops are all concentrated in nearly the position given last night, have ordered Col Lee to examine best points for crossing the Hatchie   what do you think of the plan of my moving with my entire command save with perhaps 6 Regts & crossing Hatchie say near Ruckerville or higher up as report may show & push those fellows to the wall" Telegram received, DNA, RG 393, Dept. of the Mo., Telegrams Received; copy, *ibid.*, Army of the Miss., Telegrams Sent. *O.R.*, I, xvii, part 2, 254.

To Maj. Gen. William S. Rosecrans

By Telegraph from Grants Head Qrs [*Oct. 2*], *186*[*2*]

To Gen Rosencrans

If your Information is such as to lead you to think it probable for the Road north of you to be cut before the proper hour for the cars to pass, they had better Return to night This judge of for yourself the Rebels undoubtedly Build a Bridge across the Hatchie in probably with the Intention crossing a force to cut the Road. Watch them well and if a chance occasions to attack do it & Hulbert will help you.[1] let me know in time to give the signal. the Rebels Are said to have come with 3 days Rations! at 11 Oclock nothing but Pickets this side the Hatchie Bethel forces captured several of them, three (3) of them to day[2]

U. S. Grant

Maj Gen

Telegrams received (2), Rosecrans Papers, CLU. On Oct. 2, 1862, Maj. Gen. William S. Rosecrans telegraphed to USG. "The cavalry took 50 privates one (1) cap't & chaplain prisoners at Ruckersville yesterday after killing one & wounding several—Captured an ambulance & mules with sick Officer a rebel picket was killed at Duncan's Mill. A column of Infantry is reported beyond Youngs bridge. The prisoners were paroled. I fear this attack will disconcert them & check their advance—" Telegram received, DNA, RG 393, Dept. of the Mo., Telegrams Received; copy, *ibid.*, Army of the Miss., Telegrams Sent; *ibid.*, RG 94, War Records Office, Union Battle Reports. *O.R.*, I, xvii, part 1, 148–49.

1. On Oct. 2, Maj. Gen. Stephen A. Hurlbut, Bolivar, telegraphed to USG. "One company of my cavalry went out today 18 miles on the north purdy road within 6 miles of Clinton, no one in that quarter—I have ordered another reg't from Ross command to reinforce Pickets on rail road north" Telegram received, DNA, RG 393, Dept. of the Mo., Telegrams Received. On the same day, 1:00 P.M., Hurlbut telegraphed to Maj. John A. Rawlins. "I have just received reliable information as I think from an intelligent Union man near Grand Junction confirm-

ing the previously reported fact that Price Van Dorn & Villepigue have united near Ripley and are now at Pocahontas probably 18,000. strong—He also reports that Genl. Pillow is at Holly Springs with from 6, to 8000 men principally exchanged prisoners and is fortifying that place The talk among the men with whom he conversed is that they propose an attack on this point coming in by the way of Spring Creek which is in fact the weakest part of the line. I send a rough Diagram of the relative positions—If they move on this place they must show their flank to Rosecrantz force and as they cannot well surprise us—are liable to be taken in the act. As I am liable to be removed at any time would it not be well for Maj. Genl Ord to come down and fully examine the ground" Telegram received, *ibid*. *O.R.*, I, xvii, part 2, 253. On the same day, Hurlbut wrote to Brig. Gen. Leonard F. Ross. "By dispatch just received from General Grant I am informed the railroad has been cut 6 miles south of Bethel. You will re-enforce Engelmann's pickets with another regiment tonight, and use every caution as to the security of our communication north. The cavalry which went on the north Purdy road went out 18 miles; found no traces of an enemy." *Ibid*.

Also on Oct. 2, J. A. Van Buskirk, conductor, Bethel, sent a telegram, presumably to USG. " . . . ~~We were~~ 6 miles south of here by two 2 of our track repairers that came from near Ramer station stating that frt train was fired into at Ramer they judge by report about one hundred shots and a report like train off the track Telegraph poles cut mail train backed up to Bethel" Telegram received (incomplete), DNA, RG 393, Dept. of the Mo., Telegrams Received. On the same day, Col. Michael K. Lawler, Bethel, telegraphed twice to USG. "I sent three (3) co's last night to the bridges south of this place & they are all safe—I have sent a battalion to ascertain when the road was broken & what has become of the train & to return & remain at the bridges as soon as I hear I will telegraph you—" "I will order back the train to Jackson as soon as it arrives here from Ramer—It carried a battallion of soldiers to that place to see what has become of the previous train attacked at that place—" Telegrams received, *ibid*.

2. On Oct. 2, Col. Isham N. Haynie, Bethel, sent three telegrams to USG. "Lt Hays scouts just arrived from one mile of Pocahontas captured 3 of Prices men soldiers & 2 suspicious citizens Lt Hays reports that Rebels are building a bridge & it is almost ~~done~~ completed across the Hatchie. There is no force except Pickets on this side of Hatchie. Prisoners report that Price's army are thirty or thirty five thousand under Price Villipigue & Van Dorn.—Breckenridge at Tupello. Forces of Rebels said to be under marching orders. The bridge just being ready this morning about 11 oclock Dont know where their orders were to march to. Prisoners dont know where the Rebel cavalry is. Rebels came from Bolivar by Ripley to Pocahontas with 3 days rations. Col Lawler requests 2 guns one a 24 pound Howitzer & another gun & five hundred (500) more men ammunition for same—" "Your message to Genl Rosecrans sent copy by 2 trusty couriers —I also sent copy of my message to you relative to report of drums & moving of wagons up state line road—" "Our forces near ~~where at~~ the bridges you instructed me to guard the place where the road has been attacked is four (4) miles further toward Corinth at Ramer" Telegrams received, *ibid*., Dept. of the Tenn., Telegrams Received. On the same day, Capt. Robert R. Townes, Jackson, asst. adjt. gen. for Brig. Gen. John A. Logan, transmitted to USG two telegrams sent by Haynie to Logan. "Druner one of the men captured to day says that he heard the Rebel wagons Drums & Guns this morning from sun up till 11 Oclock going up the State line Road toward Chiwalla toward youngs Bridge on Tuscumbia that

on yestarday Davis Bridge was repaired over Hatchie & Wagons passed in that direction over it   this would bring them up near to Ramer" "Col Lawler has taken the passenger train and sends half of a Regiment down near to Ramer to see after the Freight train & look after the Rebels who are in there" Telegrams received, *ibid.*, Dept. of the Mo., Telegrams Received. See also *O.R.*, I, xvii, part 2, 253.

To Brig. Gen. Grenville M. Dodge

By Telegraph from Corinth [*Oct. 2*] *1862*

To Genl Dodd

Mr Mellen[1] is here.   he says that he orders were not to detain articles mentioned in your Telegraph but to have them labelled Supervised & permitted to the Parties claiming &c that none others received them   in case they are not received by the Parties to whom consigned they were to be returned

U. S. Grant
Major Genl

Telegram received, DNA, RG 393, Dept. of the Mo., Telegrams Received. On Oct. 2, 1862, Brig. Gen. Grenville M. Dodge, Columbus, Ky., telegraphed to Maj. John A. Rawlins. "An order was issued here this morning by Mr Mellen from Treasury Dep't prohibiting the shipping of all Mdze by R R or Express including the goods & packages of all kinds sent to Officers by Express without they carried with them the permit of the Custom House at St. Louis or Cairo instructing both not to recognize the permit of Comd'g Officers.   should not the stores for Officers in the field go forward   they are not contraband" Telegram received, *ibid.*

1. William P. Mellen, special agent of the U.S. Treasury Dept.

To Maj. Gen. Stephen A. Hurlbut

Jaxon [*Oct.*] 3rd [*1862*]

GENL HURLBUT

the following Dispatch just Recd   the two (2) couriers sent last night are here   got to Corinth safely   Delivered dispatches was attacked today coming back   Lost one [horse]   they are fighting at Corinth   Rebels Investing it close at Hand—couriers lost Dispatches sent me by Genl Rosecrans   the Genl told the Couriers that if he lost it it was not much

U. S. GRANT

Maj Genl

Telegram received, DNA, RG 393, District of West Tenn., 4th Division, Telegrams Received. The information transmitted was embodied in a telegram of Oct. 3, 1862, from Col. Isham N. Haynie, Bethel, to USG. *O.R.*, I, xvii, part 2, 258. Earlier on the same day, Haynie had telegraphed to USG. "They have not returned nor have I heard of them—"   Telegram received, DNA, RG 393, Dept. of the Tenn., Telegrams Received.

Also on Oct. 3, Haynie telegraphed frequently to USG. "Dr. Grimes and Captain House, in charge of scouts sent toward Pocahontas and Chewalla, confirm reports before made—enemy are moving toward Corinth; are crossing Tuscumbia at Evans' old bridge. Sharp cannonading not far off from Chewalla to-day for two hours, from 8 to 10. Scouts captured a contraband from rebel army. He says the rebels say they go to Corinth and then to join Bragg's army. The two regiments are *en route* as ordered."   "Burchfield, arrived across from toward Corinth, has just come in on hand-car; reports the track of railroad torn up 5 miles beyond Ramer and 6 miles from Corinth; says there are 800 there of Falkner's cavalry. Three bridges near Chambers said to be burned. Burchfield says he heard cannon at or below Corinth, or between Corinth and Chewalla; says they are fighting. Would it not be well to send a train here, so in case send down men to Chambers to drive out rebels? If you send train, send tools to repair road also; tools are burned."   "Passenger train back here; freight train supposed safe through. Three hundred rebels came in to the railroad; freight got by them; rebels then took up rail and cut telegraph; our force, Seventeenth Wisconsin, ran them off. No killed reported as yet."   "General McPherson and myself think troops can be sent by rail to Ramer, 11 miles this side of Corinth, and infantry can go by road from there to Corinth. Lawler is *en route* to a point 3 miles below Ramer; will probably be at Ramer by the time your train gets there." *O.R.*, I, xvii, part 2, 257–58. On the same day, Col. Michael K. Lawler, Bethel, telegraphed to USG. "Shall we expect a train to carry the regt's to Chambers station or shall they march   the distance is 16 miles by R R & the roads are reported bad—please answer—The troops will be ready immediately—"   Telegram received, DNA, RG 393, Dept. of the Mo., Telegrams Received.

Two telegrams of Oct. 3 from Haynie to Brig. Gen. John A. Logan, Jackson, were apparently copied for USG. "Report by a Citizen from in the Hatchie this morning says the Enemy in large force over there extending from Pocahontas up to Davis Bridge   they are said to have been crossing at Davis Bridge yesterday with ten thousand (10.000) on this side   Citizens say the Rebels are ~~marching~~ making for Corinth the Road they are on from that supposition   No news yet from our Scouts in towards Pocahontas"   "Our Scouts from towards Savana bring in 7 Paroled Prisoners from Braggs army taken at Mumfordsville   they want to go to their Home between Ripley & Oxford Miss   ought they to be allowed to go now   had we not better send them around by Bolivar"   Copies, *ibid.*, Dept. of the Tenn., Telegrams Received.

To Maj. Gen. Stephen A. Hurlbut

U. S. Grant Office
By Telegraph from Jackson [*Oct.*] 3rd *1862.*

To Maj Genl Hurlbut

Have you heard further from the Rebels towards Corinth. the wire & Road being cut I cannot hear except by Courier. If you have no enemy near you to the south or east move out four (4) Brigades towards Pocahontas with three (3) days rations & threaten the ~~enemys~~ enemies rear.

U. S. Grant
Maj Genl

Telegram received, DNA, RG 393, District of West Tenn., 4th Division, Telegrams Received. On Oct. 3, 1862, Maj. Gen. Stephen A. Hurlbut, Bolivar, Tenn., telegraphed to USG. "My cavalry has not yet come in from Expedition these Morning—the infantry & artillery will leave at three (3) A M in morning & go to Pocahontas. if not further—" Telegram received, *ibid.*, Dept. of the Mo., Telegrams Received. On the same day, Hurlbut sent three additional telegrams to USG. "I have sent a heavy ~~force~~ cavalry reconnoisance toward Pocahontas. My own Division has only 2 Brigades each of 5 Reg'ts. Ross has 4 Brigades   I will hold 8 Regts ready to march as soon as I hear from the Roads south & west   No further news from Pocahontas. It is reported that the Exchanged prisoners from Vicksburg are arriving at Davis' Mills." "I understand it to be my duty to relieve Rosecrans at all hazards if he is in at Corinth   I cant return before Sunday P M the distance being 46 miles   on reaching Davis Bridge I shall of course know whether the Enemy are repulsed or not   if not repulsed I propose to cut through   If repulsed to destroy their line of retreat in this direction"   "Cavalry have just come in   have been within 4 miles of Pocahontas—Cavalry rear guard of Enemy left there at 10 A M today.   the main force crossed the Hatchie at Davis Bridge yesterday P M & last night for Corinth—number not ascertained but large—Heard no firing From somerville—it is reported that about 800 cavalry are there—I shall move with my whole Division to Pocahontas or in that direction early in the morning but have no expectation that I can do more than demonstrate unless Rosecrans has beaten Price in which case I shall be in good position—Genl Ross remains here with his command." Telegrams received, *ibid.* *O.R.*, I, xvii, part 2, *255–56.*

To Maj. Gen. Stephen A. Hurlbut

Jaxon [*Oct.*] 3rd 1862

MAJ GENL HURLBUT

firing was heard this A-M for two (2) hours near Chewalla I think however you will be in time starting at three (3) in the morning.   don't be later and keep up a line of couriers with Bolivar & by Telegraph with me—if when you get to Davis Bridge¹ you should find the Enemy Retreating Destroy it & Harrass their crossing in every way   take four (4) more Regiments with you   I will send two (2) from here that can go

U. S. GRANT
Maj Genl

Telegram received, DNA, RG 393, District of West Tenn., 4th Division, Telegrams Received. On Oct. 3, 1862, Maj. Gen. Stephen A. Hurlbut telegraphed to USG. "My column will move at 3 oclock A M in marching order with 3 days provisions   I have ordered Genl Ross to select 2 Regts from his command with the 2 that will arrive will be brigaded together & move at the same hour—a line of couriers will be kept up to Genl Ross who will telegraph to you—" Telegram received, *ibid.*, Dept. of the Mo., Telegrams Received. *O.R.*, I, xvii, part 2, *255–56.*

1. Davis's Bridge crossed the Hatchie River in Tenn. about two miles north of the Miss. state line.

To Maj. Gen. Stephen A. Hurlbut

Jackson [*Oct.*] 3rd 1862

GENL HURLBUT

two *2* Regts will Reach you by twelve thirty *12.30* Oclock. be ready to start on their arrival—the following Dispatch just Recd from Bethel̶l̶   scouts came in Late this ~~morning~~ P-M from towards chewalla say they are fighting in the Direction of Corinth south of and near to Chewalla.   all of the Scouts up to Sun down confirm the Previous Reported movements of Rebel forces.   one Regt of cavalry Remain at Pocahontas.   no news from Corinth except as above

U. S. GRANT
Maj Genl

Telegram received, DNA, RG 393, District of West Tenn., 4th Division, Telegrams Received. On Oct. 3, 1862, Maj. Gen. Stephen A. Hurlbut telegraphed to USG. "I am ready to move at 3 oclock   shall move & do any regt's report to me—" Telegram received, *ibid.*, Dept. of the Mo., Telegrams Received; copy, *ibid.*, District of West Tenn., 4th Division, Letters Sent.

To Maj. Gen. Stephen A. Hurlbut

U S Grants Office
Jackson [*Oct.*] 3rd [*1862*]

MAJ GENL HURLBUT.

No troops will be sent you. Go with what you have got   Four (4) Regiments have gone from here to Corinth by the Mobile & Ohio R. R. & will be in Corinth by sunrise. Rush as rapidly as possible. Take the two (2) Regiments from Ross command.

U. S. GRANT
Maj Genl

Telegram received, DNA, RG 393, District of West Tenn., 4th Division, Telegrams Received. On Oct. 3, 1862, USG again telegraphed to Maj. Gen. Stephen

A. Hurlbut. "go on with the troops you can take from Bolivar   I will send four (4) Regiments from here to Corinth Direct"   Telegram received, *ibid*. On the same day, Hurlbut telegraphed to USG. "What troops have you sent & where have you sent them. I expected 2 Regts by your recent dispatch   Are they coming or not   ans ?" Telegram received, *ibid*., Dept. of the Mo., Telegrams Received.

To Maj. Gen. William S. Rosecrans

Head quarters. Dept. of West Tenn.
Jackson Tenn. Oct.r 3d 1862

MAJ. GENL. ROSECRANS,

Genl. Hurlbut will move today towards the enemy. We should attack if they do not. Do it soon. More forces will arrive in front of Bolivar, and their assistance cannot be had from that quarter   Fight!

U. S. GRANT.
Maj. Genl.

Telegram, copies, Rosecrans Papers, CLU; DNA, RG 393, Army of the Miss., Telegrams Received. On Oct. 3, 1862, USG again telegraphed to Maj. Gen. William S. Rosecrans. "Genl. Hurlbut will be in the enemy's rear with a large force by tomorrow at ten oclock." Telegram received, Rosecrans Papers, CLU. An almost identical message is misdated Sept. 3. Copies, *ibid*.; DNA, RG 393, Army of the Miss., Telegrams Received.

On Oct. 3, Rosecrans telegraphed to USG. "dispatch recd   the left of our line rests in the new works near the seminary our right on the old Rebel works where the Pittsburg Road passes through there   the Rebels appear to be massed between the two rail roads north west   our scouts have been out some distance to the front & Report Rebels have withdrawn either to feed or to attack you" Telegram received (misdated Oct. 4), *ibid*., Dept. of the Mo., Telegrams Received; copies, *ibid*., RG 94, War Records Office, Union Battle Reports; (dated Oct. 3) *ibid*., RG 393, Army of the Miss., Telegrams Sent. Misdated Oct. 4 in *O.R.*, I, xvii, part 1, 161. On Oct. 3, Rosecrans telegraphed to USG. "the Enemy came in on the Chewalla road this morning and made a demonstration on our left on McKean division   the leading Brigade commanded by Col Oliver acted feebly & fell back   McArthur has now taken command & is pushing forward to make strong reconnoisance   We are now holding our position & pushing cavalry rconnoisance up the Bolivar & Purdy road   also main Purdy Road east of the rail road   no developments have yet appeared on that front   scouts report the Enemy on both sides the rail road last night near Chewalla   one unusually reliable gives their entire force not exceeding thirty thousand and is satisfied that they intend to make their main move on Bolivar will endeavor to communicate again as soon as there is anything new & if we find the force not meant for Corinth or we are in position to do it shall move on them steadily & firmly with everything we can spare . . .P S the Enemy have since come in on the Chewalla road and have driven in Davis left our men did not act or fight well I think we shall handle them we are at the outer line of works." Telegram received (misdated Oct. 4), DNA, RG 393, Dept. of the Mo., Telegrams Received; copies (dated Oct. 3), *ibid.*, Army of the Miss., Telegrams Sent; *ibid.*, RG 94, War Records Office, Union Battle Reports. *O.R.*, I, xvii, part 1, 160. At 11 :30 P.M. on Oct. 3, Rosecrans telegraphed to USG. "from advanced position at exterior batteries reported to you this morning our troops slowly drew in and concentrated. the Rebel attack between rail roads north west Davies Division the right of McKeans were the only troops really engaged it was bush wacking our troops knowing nothing of the ground although many of them have been here Hamilton attempted to swing in from the purdy road west-ward but it was late in the Evening and he was too far advanced to the north our left McKean & Stanly occupies Primes new line right Hamilton & Davies rests north of the town on the rebel works stretches across to join Stanly in the bottom near Hallecks old head quarters they appear to be still in the angle of the roads if they fight us tomorrow I think we shall whip them if they go to attack you we shall advance upon them— . . . Genl Hackelman killed" Telegram received (misdated Oct. 4), DNA, RG 393, Dept. of the Mo., Telegrams Received; copy, *ibid.*, RG 94, War Records Office, Union Battle Reports. *O.R.*, I, xvii, part 1, 160–61.

On the same day, Rosecrans wrote to Brig. Gen. Thomas A. Davies. "Dispatches from Genl. Grant have been recd. which indicate the enemy have moved in on State line Road, eight (8) miles north of us." Copy, DNA, RG 393, Army of the Miss., Letters Sent.

To Col. Jesse Hildebrand

Head Quarters, Dist. of West Ten
Jackson October 3d 1862

Col. J. Hildebrand
Comd.g Alton Ill.
Sir:

Yours of the 28th ult. is received. You did right in not releasing Hill & Adams who refused to take the oath.[1]

I now want Jas. C. Fleming, R. G. Crawford, Jas. Collins, Thos. Harris and Calvin Bolls, all political prisoners from Bolivar Ten. released on their taking the proper oath.[2]

I would also like to have released W. A. Smith from Burnsville Miss. on the same terms.

> Respectfully &c.
> U. S. Grant
> Maj. Gen.

ALS, DNA, RG 249, Records of Prisoners Confined at Alton. See letter to Col.
Jesse Hildebrand, Sept. 21, 1862.

1. On Oct. 1, 1862, Brig. Gen. Leonard F. Ross, Bolivar, wrote to USG.
"I respectfully recommend the release of Jerome Hill a clerk by occupation now
confined in the Military Prison at Alton Ills, having been sent there from this
place—" ALS, DNA, RG 109, Union Provost Marshals' File of Papers Relating
to Individual Citizens. On Oct. 3, Maj. John A. Rawlins endorsed this letter.
"The Major General Commanding sent a communication to Colonel Hildebrand,
Commanding Military Prison at Alton, instructing him to release the within
named prisoners, Jerome Hill and one other named Adams, on condition that they
should take the oath of allegiance, which they refused to do, and consequently
remain prisoners." ES, *ibid*. See letter to Col. Jesse Hildebrand, Oct. 16, 1862.
2. On Oct. 7, Capt. William R. Rowley wrote to the commanding officer,
Alton Military Prison. "I am desired by Maj. General U. S. Grant, Comdg.
Distr. of West Tenn. to request you to release all the Political prisoners heretofore sent to Alton from the town of Bolivar Tenn, together with one by the name
of Strahon sent from Jackson Tenn, upon their Taking the Oath of Allegiance.
Capt. A. D. Ray of Co. "H" 26th Ala. Vols. who was sent from this District is to
be considered as a Prisoner of War, and as such entitled to be exchanged. He may
if he desires it, be paroled for 30 Days and proceed down the River to effect his
exchange for that of Capt. James Rouse of Co. "C" 45th Ills. Vols. who is now on
parole at St. Louis.—" Copy, DNA, RG 109, Unfiled Abstracts. Statements concerning the arrest of Calvin Boles, James Collins, and R. G. Crawford at Bolivar
on Aug. 11 are *ibid*. In letters to Brig. Gen. Jeremiah C. Sullivan, Dec. 27, and
to Capt. Thomas H. Harris, Jan. 13, 1863, Brig. Gen. Mason Brayman, Bolivar,
discussed the continuing disloyal conduct of James C. Fleming, Reverend W. C.
Gray, Jerome B. Hill, and R. P. Neely. ALS, *ibid*., Union Provost Marshals' File
of Papers Relating to Two or More Civilians. See letter to Col. Jesse Hildebrand,
Sept. 11, 1862.

To Julia Dent Grant

Jackson Tennessee
October 3d 1862

DEAR JULIA

I returned here from St. Louis just in time to find my presence very much required. Price, Van Dorn and Villapigue were marching North in seperate columns to attack some portion of my command. It was impossible to say whether it was Bolivar or Corinth. I have been kept busy watching their progress. They have now all concentrated and are preparing to attack Corinth with their combined forces. Making preparations to receive them, and giving the necessary orders, has kept me so busy, with other duties that are necessarily forced on me, so that I did not find time to write to you two days ago as I should have done. I hope however that this will reach you on Teusday next. Before that I expect another great battle to be fought by the troops under my command.—I hope they will be victorious, and expect it, but they have to meet a superior force.

I hope this will find you well.

I regret very much that the children are loosing all this time from school!   you can however stay where you are or go to Galena since this seems to be your determination.

Give my love to all at Wishten-Wish. Kisses for yourself and the children.

ULYS.

ALS, DLC-USG.

To Maj. Gen. Henry W. Halleck

Grants Hd Qrs Jackson Tenn
Oct 4th [*1862*] 11 30 A M

Maj Gen Halleck
Gen in Chief

The Rebels are now massing on Corinth in the north west angle of the R. R There was some fighting yesterday Rosecrans informs me that his troops occupy from College Hill to Pittsburg road on the Enemies old works—Genl McPherson has gone with a fine Brigade raised from troops here and Trenton to his relief[1] Probably reached Corinth by seven this morning Hurlbut is moving on the Enemies flank from Bolivar I have given every aid possible

U S Grant M G.

Telegram received, DNA, RG 94, Generals' Papers and Books, Telegrams Received by Gen. Halleck; *ibid.*, RG 107, Telegrams Collected (Bound); DLC-Robert T. Lincoln; copies, DNA, RG 107, Telegrams Received in Cipher; *ibid.*, RG 393, USG Hd. Qrs. Correspondence; DLC-USG, V, 4, 5, 7, 8, 88. *O.R.*, I, xvii, part 1, 154.

1. On Oct. 3, 1862, Brig. Gen. James B. McPherson, Bethel, Tenn., twice telegraphed to USG. "Arrived here all right will go on towards Corinth early tomorrow morning & if possible reach that place—scouts report fighting at or near Corinth today—" "Your Dispatches rec'd I will be in readiness on arrival of troops one company of Tennessee Cavalry went with Col Lawler and Col Haynie has just ordered out another company which I will send on immediatly to meet one at or near Ramer station" Telegrams received, DNA, RG 393, Dept. of the Mo., Telegrams Received. On the same day, Maj. John A. Rawlins issued Special Orders No. 210. "Brig. Genl. J. B. McPherson is hereby assigned to the command of the two Brigades, commanded respectively by Col. M. K. Lawler and Col. John D. Stevenson, and will proceed without delay and with all possible dispatch to Corinth, Miss. and report to Major Gen. Rosecrans, Commanding." DS, *ibid.*, RG 94, District of West Tenn., Special Orders; copies, *ibid.*, RG 393, USG Special Orders; DLC-USG, V, 15, 16, 82, 87. *O.R.*, I, xvii, part 2, 257.

On Oct. 4, Col. Isham N. Haynie wrote and telegraphed frequently to USG. "The Courier came the farmington road Thence 11 miles in purdy road thence into Bethel passing south of Purdy at Farrs Mills. Courier left Corinth at 5. oclock p. m—Knows no more of Gen McPherson than I have reported." "~~Ceapt~~ Capt Houstons scouts just in from near Chewalla reports heavy cannonading since day break this a m. it began at first between Corinth & Chewalla is it seemed &

appears to have receded from then until Capt Houston left it ceased south-westerly from Chewalla some distance   cannonading ceased at 10 to 11 oclock— . . . message had no time to it" Telegrams received, DNA, RG 393, Dept. of the Tenn., Telegrams Received. "Courier says General McPherson had not got in, but would be in tonight; thinks he sent in messengers. This is all he knows. He further says General Oglesby is getting along finely; also that Price this a. m. was clear into the city, but was driven back up toward the southwest with terrible loss; ours small." "Courier just in from Corinth reports heavy fighting yesterday; killed and wounded quite heavy. Rebels inside of western breastworks. He brings the following message in cipher." "A message in cipher arrived here from Corinth about 1 o'clock this morning. It was impossible to communicate with the operator at your headquarters; we have not yet been able to get him, now 7 o'clock; the line being in good order it must be the fault of the operator. The cipher message was for this reason sent to Henderson, and from there by courier to you; I feel it to be my duty to call this remissness to your attention." *O.R.*, I, xvii, part 2, 258–59. "I inclose you a dispatch rcd just this minute recd from your Jackson operator   I know that no insolence from any one will be tolerated, when indulged against those who simply desire to do what necessity requires from them   I reported the operator to you because I was sure somebody was remiss— I cannot send the original cipher without your man—I hope no message will be allowed from operators to me as I have nothing to do with them   my business is & has been official with my superiors" ALS, DNA, RG 393, Dept. of the Tenn., Telegrams Received. "This courier left Lawler at 8 o'clock and went into Corinth. When he left Colonel Lawler he (Colonel Lawler) was making for the Blue Cut, 1 mile this side, northwest of the blacksmith's shop. McPherson had not at that time joined Lawler. Courier heard a conversation between a colonel and General Rosecrans; from that he says he learned Van Dorn's forces were up northwest of Corinth, along near to the railroad, on the west side, not far from the blacksmith's shop, in the northwest angle of the railroad. General Rosecrans had ordered at 2 p. m. three regiments and some batteries out in that direction. Van Dorn's men had not fallen back like Price's. Courier understood from conversation of General Rosecrans with the colonel (don't know his name) that Van Dorn had sixty or seventy guns. General Rosecrans said if Van Dorn held that position he should open on him with his siege guns soon. As courier came on here he heard cannon, about 9 o'clock." *O.R.*, I, xvii, part 2, 258–59.

To Maj. Gen. Stephen A. Hurlbut

By Telegraph from U. S. Grants office Jackson
[*Oct.*] 4th *1862* 9-45 a m

To Genl Hurlbut

Rosecrans is now back in the works   I have instructed him to follow up the Enemy should they turn to attack you. The com-

bined force of the Enemy does not Exceed thirty Thousand
30.000   he must be whippe[d]

U. S. GRANT
Maj Genl

Telegram received, DNA, RG 393, District of West Tenn., 4th Division, Telegrams Received. On Oct. 4, 1862, Maj. Gen. Stephen A. Hurlbut twice telegraphed to USG, first from "Porters Creek" at 11 A.M., then from "Camp on Muddy." "The command has reached this place 12 miles—rather tired   I shall rest & push on to Davis Bridge tonight, no news from the Enemy"   "I arrived here this Evening at five (5) P M after an exhausting march of twenty two (22) miles. We have driven in the Pickets of Enemy up to Davis Bridge where my Cavalry encountered two (2) Reg'ts of Rebel Cavalry at Sunset & fell back   Took 2 prisoners who report a large force between Davis' & Chewalla—The bridges are deceitful & if the Hatchie bridge is destroyed or the Tuscumbia I cannot advance—I shall move as rapidly as possible but see no ground to believe that I can rea[ch] Corinth tomorrow—A citizen reports Davis bridge destroyed   if the game is up & I shall return to save my own command—"   Telegrams received, *ibid.*, Dept. of the Mo., Telegrams Received. *O.R.*, I, xvii, part 2, 259.

Also on Oct. 4, Brig. Gen. Leonard F. Ross, Bolivar, telegraphed frequently to USG. "Your dispatch rec'd & will be forwarded to Genl Hurlbut at once. The troops desired will be ready to move at such time in the morning as you may direct   Our scouts have returned from north of the Hatchie. They went 14 miles towards Bethel & same distance north west across Clover Creek   both parties report all quiet. Our scouts towards Grand Junction & Somerville not yet returned   so far as I can judge no reinforcements are needed at this point at present. Please se advise me when General Ord will start"   "Citizens considered reliable state the Rebels destroyed bridge over the Hatchie near Pocahontas night before last—There were 2 companies of Rebel cavalry in Somerville last night & still hover near there, but no heavy force is reported in that Region—"   "I have seven 7 companie[s] of cavalry about four hundred 400 men   most of them are out as pickets—I am withdrawing them to be used as patrols & scouts & supplying their place with infantry—The rail Road to Toons is well guarded   they cant get through in that direction"   "Eight loads of Forage will answer for the next five days." Telegrams received, DNA, RG 393, Dept. of the Mo., Telegrams Received. On the same day, Maj. Gen. Edward O. C. Ord, Bolivar, telegraphed to USG. "The operator at Jackson will give you important telegram just recd by me from Trenton. I am off now." Telegram received, *ibid.*

To Maj. Gen. Stephen A. Hurlbut

U. S. Grants Office
By Telegraph from Jackson [*Oct.*] 4th *1862.*

To Maj Gen Hurlbut.

Make all dispatch. Rosecrans condition is precarious. The enemy are massed in the North West angle of the Rail Roads You are late but may yet be of service. I regret that you did not leave one day earlier

U. S. Grant
Maj Genl.

Telegram received, DNA, RG 393, District of West Tenn., 4th Division, Telegrams Received.

To Maj. Gen. William S. Rosecrans

Headquarters Dept. of West Tenn.
Jackson Tenn. Oct. 4th 1862

Maj Genl. Rosecrans

If the enemy fall back push them with all force possible and save Hurlbut who is now on the way to your relief. The Corinth and Bolivar forces must act in concert.

Hurlbut is not strong enough alone to handle the rebels without very good luck. Dont neglect this warning. I can reinforce no more from this on—hence you will see the vital importance of yours and Hurlbuts forces acting in conjunction and send forces messag in.

U. S. Grant.
Maj. Genl.

Telegram, copy, DNA, RG 393, Army of the Miss., Telegrams Received. On Oct. 4, 1862, Maj. Gen. William S. Rosecrans telegraphed to USG. "Your dispatch rec'd   Enemy opened fire with artillery this morning close in probably to cover their retreat—heavy reconnoisance ordered on the road for advance cavalry scouts to the front   We wish to find his movements & position whether he moves back on chewalla road or crossing the Tuscumbia—Had a hard battle this morning on north East front   Enemy penetrated the town but were repulsed with heavy loss,   have not renewed the combat. Tr[oops are] in old position. The Batteries ar[e] rather better posted & will I trust be better supported—Hope & trust—" Telegram received, *ibid.*, Dept. of the Mo., Telegrams Received; copies, *ibid.*, Army of the Miss., Telegrams Sent; *ibid.*, RG 94, War Records Office, Union Battle Reports. *O.R.*, I, xvii, part 1, 161. On the same day, Rosecrans again telegraphed to USG. "Dispatch received telling me to follow Rebels   shortly after this morning Price made a ferce & determined attack on our right—Van Dorn & Lovell on our left   the contest lasted until eleven (11) & one half oclock & was very deadly to the enemy—They drove in our centre some of them penetrated to the Corinth House—Davis division was seized with a perfet panic which the commander shared—Hamilton whose left ~~on~~ was on the main line of their attack, [*held*] His ground in all but one spot & made an advance secured the centre with two first rate regts—Col sullivan gave us time to bring batteries into action & saved the day on that side—Van Dorn & Lovell made a most determined attack on the extreme right on the Chewalla road from [stonney]—they were led to the attack through the abaattis   two of them reached the contrascarp of the Ditch   the other two (2) stopped not fifty (50) paces from it—all that Grape & cannister could do was tried but when it reached this point a charge was ordered when it became a race between the twenty seventh (27) Ohio & the Eleventh (11) Missouri—this was too much for the staggered columns   many fell down & held up their hands for mercy—they are badly beaten on both fronts—left their dead & wounded on the field & are in full retreat—Our loss though serious especially in officers is nothing like that of the Rebels—Brig General Hackleman fell bravely fighting at the head of his Brigade yesterday shot through the jugular vein—Cols Kirby smith Gilbert, Mower wounded not mortally—Genl Oglesby dangerously wounded   the number killed I cannot now tell.   their killed & wounded are strewn along the road for five (5) miles out where they had a hospital   We have between seven hundred (700) & one thousand (1000) prisoners—Not counting wounded—McPherson has reached here with his force—we move at daylight in the morning—" Telegram received, DNA, RG 393, Dept. of the Mo., Telegrams Received; copy, *ibid.*, Army of the Miss., Telegrams Sent.

On Oct. 4, USG telegraphed to Maj. Gen. Edward O. C. Ord. "Rosencrans Telegraphs that Price attacked this morning but was Repulsed with Heavy Loss" Telegram received, Ord Papers, CU-B. On Oct. 3, Ord, Columbus, Ky., had telegraphed to USG. "Gen Steele's command is ordered to Pilot Knob—He is anxious not to go there—So Genl Tuttle who I find here tells me—I think you could get them by telegraphing to Washington—I will be down in the morning—" Telegram received, DNA, RG 393, Dept. of the Mo., Telegrams Received. See telegram to Maj. Gen. Henry W. Halleck, Oct. 5, 1862.

To Richard Yates

————

Head Quarters, Dist. of West Ten
Jackson, Oct. 4th 1862

HON. YATES,

I take great pleasure in confirming the opinion expressed by Gen. Logan of the qualifications of Capt. Wheaton and his fitness for the promotion asked.

It would afford me great pleasure, and add very much to the efficiency of the 63d regiment, if Capt. Wheaton should be appointed to the command of it.

Your Truly
U. S. GRANT
Maj. Gen.

ALS, Records of 63rd Ill., I-ar. USG's letter was accompanied by a petition of Oct. 3, 1862, of officers of the 63rd Ill. and an undated endorsement of Brig. Gen. John A. Logan. *Ibid.* Capt. Lloyd Wheaton, 8th Ill., was later promoted to maj. in his own regt.; Joseph B. McCown was appointed col., 63rd Ill.

To Maj. Gen. Henry W. Halleck

————

Grant's Head Quarters Jackson Tenn
8 a m [*Oct.*] 5th [*1862*]

MAJ GEN HALLECK.

Yesterday the Rebels under Van Dorn Price & Lovell[1] were repulsed from their attack on Corinth with great slaughter   The enemy are in full retreat leaving their dead and wounded on the field.

Rosecrans telegraphs that the loss is serious on our side particularly in Officers but bears no comparison with that of the Enemy   Gen Hackleman[2] fell while gallantly leading his Brigade   Genl Oglesby dangerously wounded.[3] McPherson reached

Corinth with his command yesterday   Rosecrans pursued the
retreating Enemy this morning & should he attempt to move
towards Bolivar will follow him to that place   Hurlbut is at the
~~Hatchie~~ Natchie with five or six thousand men & is no doubt
with the pursuing column

From seven hundred to a thousand Prisoners besides wounded
are left in our hands.

U. S. GRANT

M G Comd'g

Telegram received, DLC-Robert T. Lincoln; DNA, RG 94, Generals' Papers
and Books, Telegrams Received by Gen. Halleck; *ibid.*, RG 107, Telegrams Collected (Bound); copies, *ibid.*, RG 393, USG Hd. Qrs. Correspondence; DLC-USG,
V, 4, 5, 7, 8, 88. *O.R.*, I, xvii, part 1, 155. On Oct. 7, 1862, Maj. John A. Rawlins
issued General Orders No. 88 congratulating U.S. troops on their victory. Copies,
DLC-USG, V, 12, 13, 14, 95; DNA, RG 94, War Records Office, Union Battle
Reports; *ibid.*, RG 393, USG General Orders. *O.R.*, I, xvii, part 1, 159. On
Oct. 11, Maj. Gen. William S. Rosecrans telegraphed to USG. "Our movement
will be completed by tomorrow night unless some extraordinary accidents   Your
Genl Order 88 rec'd, the part expressing the hope that good feeling will exist
between Ord's command & my own amazes me   so far as I know there was
nothing even to suggest the thought that it might be otherwise, under such circumstances the part is to be regretted because our troops knowing there was no
foundation for it in them will be led to think there is some elsewhere." Telegram
received, DNA, RG 393, Dept. of the Mo., Telegrams Received; copies, *ibid.*,
Army of the Miss., Telegrams Sent; *ibid.*, RG 94, War Records Office, Union
Battle Reports. *O.R.*, I, xvii, part 1, 165.

1. Mansfield Lovell of D. C., USMA 1842, resigned from the U.S. Army
on Sept. 18, 1854, with the rank of bvt. capt. and later moved to New York City,
where he was deputy street commissioner when the Civil War began. Appointed
C. S. A. maj. gen. as of Oct. 7, 1861, he commanded at the surrender of New
Orleans, and, on Sept. 8, 1862, was assigned command of a division by Maj. Gen.
Earl Van Dorn. Lovell's report of the battle of Corinth is *ibid.*, pp. 404-6.

2. Pleasant A. Hackleman, born in Franklin County, Ind., in 1814, was a
lawyer and newspaper editor of Rushville, Ind., twice an unsuccessful candidate
for U.S. Representative, the second time as a Republican. Appointed col., 16th
Ind., on May 16, 1861, he was promoted to brig. gen. on April 28, 1862. See
Calendar, Aug. 17, 1862. On Oct. 13, Rosecrans telegraphed to USG. "I wish
permission to send Cap't Randall A A G. to Convey the remains of his Genl
P H Hackleman to his home"   Telegram received, DNA, RG 94, Staff Papers;
copy, *ibid.*, RG 393, Army of the Miss., Telegrams Sent. On the same day,
Rawlins telegraphed to Rosecrans. "You will grant permission to Captain Randall
A. A. G. to convey the remains of Genl. Hackleman to his home. General Order
No. 208. from these Head quarters is recinded as per request." Copy, *ibid.*,
Telegrams Received.

3. See telegram to Abraham Lincoln, Oct. 10, 1862, note 4.

To Maj. Gen. Henry W. Halleck

Hd. Qrs. Jackson Tenn
Oct 5th 62 1862

MAJ GEN HALLECK
GEN IN CHIEF

Genl Ord who followed Hurlbut and took command met the Enemy today on South side of Hatchie as I understand from dispatch and drove him across the stream and got possession of the heights with our troops.[1]

Ord took two Batteries & about two hundred prisoners   A large portion of Rosecrans forces were at Chewalla. At this distance everything looks most favorable and I cannot see how the Enemy are to escape without losing everything but their ~~side arms~~ small arms   I have strained everything to take into the fight an adequate force & to get them to the right place

U S GRANT M G

Telegram received, DLC-Robert T. Lincoln; DNA, RG 94, Generals' Papers and Books, Telegrams Received by Gen. Halleck; *ibid.*, RG 107, Telegrams Collected (Bound); copies, *ibid.*, RG 393, USG Hd. Qrs. Correspondence; DLC-USG, V, 4, 5, 7, 8, 88. *O.R.*, I, xvii, part 1, 155.

1. On Oct. 5, 1862, 6 P.M., "Hospital near Pocahontas," Maj. Gen. Edward O. C. Ord telegraphed to USG. "I joined the column and took command at 7½ oclock this A. M., and found that Genl Hurlbut had driven ~~the~~ in the enemy's videttes & had skirmished considerably in the afternoon of the 4th. I also found that he made excellent arrangements for the advance of today. About half a mile from our camp of last night the enemy began to dispute our advance, first with cavalry ~~& artillery~~ to which their Infantry & artillery in force were soon added—the road narrow & winding through swamp & jungle & over precipitous ridges across which at times the artillery was with difficulty dragged by hand, was one of the most dangerous to attempt in the face of an enemy I have ever seen. They took advantage of every swamp & jungle for their infantry, & every ridge for their artillery, from which we successfully drove them, generally at the double quick, for five (5) miles to & across the Hatchie, at Davis Bridge over which & up the steep beyond we pushed them so rapidly that they had not time to burn the bridge. In driving the enemy we took two Batteries & have them, & at the River captured between 200 and 300 prisoners, among whom are Field Officers and an Aid De Camp of Genl Van Dorn, who commanded the enemy. ~~Therefore~~ On account of the fact that we had frequently to attack across open fields & up hills whilst the enemy were under dense cover, we have lost Quite a number of officers

& men & have several hundred wounded, probably a greater number than have the Enemy. Genl Veach was very badly contused by a spent ball striking him in the side. I will send you Regimental list of Killed and wounded as soon as they can be brought in. Genl Hurlbut has Cavalry in pursuit of the enemy who moved off to the south about four O'Clock this afternoon. Our Infantry which started from Bolivar at 3 oClock A. M. yesterday marched 26 miles and to day fighting 5 miles over this country, under a fire at short range for 7 hours, being too much fatigued to pursue today, besides it will take until dark to bring in the wounded. The troops in their charge over the miserable Bridge at Davis' & up the steep beyond, exposed to a murderous fire of shell, grape & cannister, with 3 of their Batteries playing upon them at cannister range, however, proved that wherever their officers dare to lead them, the men will go. Generals Hurlbut, Veach & Lauman, the former commanding the Division, the latter two Brigades, did not confine themselves alone to their duties as commanders, but did everything that men could do to make victory complete. Gallant officers! so ~~well~~ much praised of them is entirely unecessary. To their respective staff officers I must, also, add my sincere thanks for the zeal & energy with which they discharged their arduous duties throughout the day. To the officers of the Line & the men from what I have seen of them today, I can only say that should the fortunes of war continue them under my command, it will be my pride to win their confidence. Genl Veach pushed the enemy with great vigor & success in front until their forces were so much increased that it became necessary to bring up our reserve under command of Genl Lauman which I ordered at once, whereupon the enemy were driven from their last stronghold. Genl Lauman, showing by his coolness, energy and courage, that the front was his proper place. Genl Hurlbut has reported to me that he has gathered about 900 arms already, thrown away by the enemy in their retreat, and expects to collect a large number tomorrow. The names of 289 prisoners have already been registered, and they are still being brought in. From the nature of the country over which we fought it is impossible to arrive at an accurate estimate of the number of the enemy, but this may be infered from the number of arms thrown away, the quantity of their artillery, and the fact that a portion of their forces engaged against us were not at Corinth. Guns are heard to night in the direction of Corinth. Genl Hurlbut will push forward early tomorrow morning, as it is presumed Genl Rosecrans is harrassing the rear of the enemy. My personal staff—Division Surg S B. Davis Capt Sharpe & Lt Brown A. D. C. and Capt Hotaling 2nd Ill Cavalry & A. D. C. were, by turns, Colonels of Regiments or Captains of Batteries, cheering and leading the men through the thickest of the fight.   they always took the shortest line to danger on the field, & were always on hand when wanted—I commend to the consideration of the Government" Telegram received (incomplete), DNA, RG 393, Dept. of the Mo., Telegrams Received; copy, *ibid.*, RG 94, War Records Office, Union Battle Reports. *O.R.*, I, xvii, part 1, 302–3.

On the same day, 2:10 P.M., Capt. Alexander B. Sharpe, aide to Ord, telegraphed to Maj. Gen. William S. Rosecrans through USG. "We have been fighting all A. M. and have driven the enemy across Davis Bridge on the Hatchie; they are contesting the ground at every point and Van Dorn's forces are increasing rapidly   If you can possibly produce a diversion do so. . . . P. S.—Gen Ord is [severely] wounded and General Hurlbut is in command." Copy, DNA, RG 94, War Records Office, Union Battle Reports. *O.R.*, I, xvii, part 1, 301–2. A similar message from Sharpe to USG is *ibid.*, p. 303.

On Oct. 6, Col. William L. Sanderson, Bolivar, telegraphed to USG. "Gen Ord will be here about 3 o clock P. M. He wishes to go directly through to Jackson if the regular train cannot start on his arrival can he have an extra train from Jackson." Telegram received, DNA, RG 94, War Records Office, Dept. of the Tenn.

Also on Oct. 6, Ord wrote to Secretary of War Edwin M. Stanton recommending Surgeon Samuel B. Davis, 15th Iowa, for a U.S. commission; USG endorsed this letter. *Ibid.*, RG 107, Register of Letters Received. On Oct. 8, Maj. John A. Rawlins issued Special Orders No. 210 sending Ord and Davis to Carlisle, Pa., so that Ord might recover, and assigning Maj. Gen. Stephen A. Hurlbut to succeed to Ord's command. DS, *ibid.*, RG 94, District of West Tenn., Special Orders; copies, *ibid.*, RG 393, USG Special Orders; DLC-USG, V, 15, 16, 82, 87. *O.R.*, I, xvii, part 2, 268.

On Nov. 14, Brig. Gen. John McArthur wrote to Stanton that since Davis was currently act. medical director of a division, his appointment as asst. surgeon must have been an error. ALS, DNA, RG 94, Letters Received. On Nov. 15, USG endorsed this letter. "As Dr. Davis is already a Regimental Surgeon it is presumable that there has been some mistake in tendering him the position of Asst. Surgeon." AES, *ibid.* On Nov. 25, Brig. Gen. William A. Hammond, surgeon gen., endorsed this letter, stating that Davis had been properly recommended for asst. surgeon by a board of examiners. Formally nominated as asst. surgeon on Jan. 19, 1863, and as surgeon on Feb. 12, Davis was confirmed at the higher rank on Feb. 19.

To Maj. Gen. Henry W. Halleck

Head Quarters, Dist. of West Ten
Jackson, October 5th 1862

Maj. Gen. H. W. Halleck,
Gen. in Chief
Washington D. C.
Gen.

I deem it a matter of great importance in this District to have organized a Corps of experienced rail-road Engineers and builders. Repairs are constantly being required and if we should penetrate further into the Southern country other roads would have to be fixed up.

To take charge of such a Corps a man of experience in Superintending such work would be required, and one in whos hands I can place the management of the rail-roads under my jurisdiction.

I would state in this connection that Gen. McPherson is exceedingly anxious to take an active command and I think it a great misfortune to have such a man without an important military command. I would feel more strengthened to-day if I could place McPherson in command of a Division than I would to receive a whole Brigade of the new levies.

I would respectfully ask authority to place Col. Geo. G. Pride in this position.[1]

I know that he has the requisite experience, and the energy and ability to fill the place admirably. Col. Pride served on my Staff as a volunteer Aid at the battle of Shiloh, and some time since. I can vouch for his ability.

To make Col. Pride eligible for the position, and to entitle him to the position; also to give him the proper command over men as well as that he may come under proper Military restrictions, I would respectfully ask that he be commissioned by the President, with the rank of Col.

I Am Gen. very respectfully
your obt. svt.
U. S. Grant
Maj. Gen.

ALS, Abraham Lincoln Book Shop, Chicago, Ill. *O.R.*, I, xvii, part 2, 262. On Oct. 13, 1862, Maj. Gen. Henry W. Halleck wrote to USG. "Your letter of the 5th inst in relation to the management of Rail Roads in your command has been received & laid before the Secty of War. Genl McPherson should be relieved & assigned to his proper command, and if you have no other officer suitable for the superintending of the Roads you are authorized to employ a civil engineer paying him suitable compensation from the proceeds of the roads   It is impossible to give him a military commission as the law allowing additional Aides is repealed Perhaps it may be revised when Congress meets again. No difficulty is encountered on other roads from the Supt not having military rank." ADf, DNA, RG 94, Generals' Papers and Books, Drafts of Letters Sent by Gen. Halleck; LS, *ibid.*, RG 108, Letters Sent by Gen. Halleck (Press); copies, *ibid.*, RG 393, USG Hd. Qrs. Correspondence; DLC-USG, V, 4, 5, 7, 8, 88. *O.R.*, I, xvii, part 2, 276.

1. See letter to Capt. Nathaniel H. McLean, April 9, 1862, note 17. On Oct. 13, George G. Pride, Washington, telegraphed to Maj. John A. Rawlins. "Gen Halleck leaves the Rail Road entirely to Gen Grant   He has written Him —He says Gen Grant can appoint me if He choose   Telegraph me 5th Avenue Hotel New York if I am appointed"   Telegram received, DNA, RG 94, Staff

Papers, George G. Pride. On Oct. 14, Pride, New York, sent a similar telegram to Rawlins. Telegram received, *ibid*. On Oct. 16, Pride wrote to Rawlins. "I reached Washington all right and found Gen Halleck and all hands feeling gay about the fight, and having the kindest and most ardent regard for General Grant —Gen Halleck remarked that he wished his other Generals 'would do as well—' —He went to see the Secretary of War about making me col—, but said there was no law or he would—Said he would write Gen Grant that he could hire a civil engineer and place in charge, remarking that would 'make you all right'— I telegraphed you from Washington, and also from here asking you to ~~write~~ telegraph me here if I was to have charge—. Gen Grant told me, that even if the commission was not given, if Gen Halleck was willing he would give me the charge of the R. Rds &c—Please write me and telegraph me to St. Louis so I may know next week what to depend on, as I want to engage some good men—Gen Grant is *all right* in this section you may depend—Kelton said we were to have at once 7 new regiments—and more afterwards—They seem to think we cannot do much in *advance* until Buel comes up within some reasonable distance—Please telegraph me to the Planters House, St. Louis so soon as this reaches you— . . . I recd no despatch here." ALS, *ibid*. On Oct. 21, Pride, St. Louis, telegraphed to Rawlins. "Arrived this morning   have rec'd no dispatch or letter from you at all" Telegram received, *ibid*., RG 393, Dept. of the Mo., Telegrams Received.

On Nov. 1, Rawlins issued Special Orders No. 5. "Brig Genl J. D. Webster is hereby appointed General Superintendent of the Military Railroads of this Department and in all matters appertaining thereto he will have, possess and exercise the same authority as that confered upon Genl McPherson by orders from Headquarters Department of the Mississippi. The Engineer Regiment of the West will be under his command with such Officers, soldiers and Citizens as it may be necessary to employ from time to time   Col George B. Pride is appointed Chief Engineer of Military Railroads and will have charge of the repair and re-construction of the road-beds, bridges and tracts of all Railroads in this Department. The Mechanics, and laborers required will be furnished from the Engineer Regiment and will be under his command while so engaged. He will have authority to engage Citizen employees when necessary. Requisitions for materials and funds necessary for repairing and building Railroads will be made by him on the Quarter Masters Department. All contracts with citizen employees and all requisitions for materials and funds will be subject to the approval of the Commanding General" Copies, DLC-USG, V, 26; DNA, RG 393, Dept. of the Tenn., General and Special Orders; *ibid*., Special Orders; (printed) Oglesby Papers, IHi. *O.R.*, I, xvii, part 2, 315. Pride, however, never received an appointment in the U.S. Army.

On Oct. 27, Col. Joseph D. Webster, Cairo, telegraphed to USG. "Will be in Jackson tomorrow   if you wish an immediate decision I will take the Road—" Telegram received, DNA, RG 393, Dept. of the Tenn., Telegrams Received.

To Maj. Gen. William S. Rosecrans

———

Head quarters dept. of West Tenn.
Jackson Tenn. Octr. 5th 1862

M AJ. G ENL. R OSECRANS,

Firing has been going on all day towards the Hatchie Crossing. It is plainly heard at Bolivar and was also reported by scouts from Bethel who had been out towards Pocahontas.[1]   ·

I have ordered additional forces to support Hurlbut[2]—but he will require your aid. Push the enemy to the wall. Were any officers of rank on Rebel side killed.[3]

U. S. G RANT.
Maj. Genl.

Telegram, copy, Rosecrans Papers, CLU.

On Oct. 5, 1862, Maj. Gen. William S. Rosecrans telegraphed twice to USG. "Dispatch from Hamilton 11 a. m   flag of truce from Van Dorn requesting permission to bury the dead dated Chewalla answered   ample provision has been made—Where is Hurlbut   Now is his time to pitch in. If they stand this side of Chewalla we shall fight where there is no water." "Dispatch recd—I sent my compliments to Maj. Genl Van Dorn Comdg Conferate forces & told him that ample provision had bee[n] made for the Burial of the dead." Telegrams received, DNA, RG 393, Dept. of the Mo., Telegrams Received; copies, *ibid.*, Army of the Miss., Telegrams Sent; *ibid.*, RG 94, War Records Office, Union Battle Reports. *O.R.*, I, xvii, part 1, 161–62. On the same day, Capt. Charles E. Farrand, asst. adjt. gen. for Rosecrans, telegraphed to USG. "News from the front   Enemy reported 3 hours ahead breaking for to the Tuscumbia for water—Rebel cavalry reported in your old camp to the south"   Telegram received, DNA, RG 393, Dept. of the Mo., Telegrams Received; copy, *ibid.*, RG 94, War Records Office, Union Battle Reports. *O.R.*, I, xvii, part 1, 162.

On Oct. 5, USG sent two additional telegrams to Rosecrans. "How stands now the two armies—are you pursuing? I told you that heavy firing was heard towards the Hatchie Crossing a good part of the day." "You are in receipt of Ords dispatches. The Rebels are now north of the Hatchie and if you do not bag the most of them it will be your fault. Troops must push on tonight." Copies, Rosecrans Papers, CLU. On Oct. 5, Rosecrans again telegraphed to USG. "Your dispatches about Ords engagement received. We will push on with all speed. I thought we had done so already but am displeased to report slow progress." Copy, DNA, RG 393, Army of the Miss., Telegrams Sent. "McArthur pursued the enemy 5 & half miles with small force   was reinforced in the night with 5 Regiments—He was encamped within short distance of two Regmts of enemy rear guard   McKean followed at day light with Balance of Division support[ed] by Hamiltons division. McPherson Stanly & Davies were to start at daylight but through error were delayed. They take route north of Rail Road towards ~~to~~ Pocahontas balance south. Now is the time for Steele to pitch in while they are all looking this way. Rebel prisoners talk of reinforcements & fighting again" "Leading divisions arrived at Chewalla   no news from McPherson since 12 M. enemies rear guard overtaken beyond Chewalla road repairing a bridge to go over—Progress very slow   McKean on the way   order us forage at once or our animals will starve" Telegrams received, *ibid.*, Dept. of the Mo., Telegrams Received; copies, *ibid.*, Army of the Miss., Telegrams Sent; *ibid.*, RG 94, War Records Office, Union Battle Reports. *O.R.*, I, xvii, part 1, 162.

On Oct. 4, USG had telegraphed to Brig. Gen. Grenville M. Dodge, Columbus, Ky. "Send no more forage or stores here until directed   direct quarter master & commissary to this effect" Telegram received, DNA, RG 393, Dept. of the Mo., Telegrams Received. On Oct. 5, USG telegraphed to Dodge. "Load every car that you can spare with forage and send it in the morning   large supplies of forage are required immediately" Telegram received, *ibid.* On the same day, Dodge telegraphed to USG. "Gen Rosecrans telegraphs for subsistence stores for sick & wounded at Corinth   shall I send these as far first break in road or to what ~~point~~ place" Telegram received, *ibid.* An undated telegram from USG to Dodge was probably sent on Oct. 5. "Send subsistence stores to Bethel & we can then designate where to put them off" Telegram received, *ibid.* On the same day, Maj. John A. Rawlins telegraphed to Dodge. "Permit forage in any quantity to come over the road but no other freights" Telegram received, *ibid.* On Oct. 5, USG again telegraphed to Dodge. "Forbid all citizens from coming down the road for a few days. They cannot get to Corinth at present on account of Breaks in the road & they would be placed at useless expense & trouble by coming now. You can let this be published" Telegram received, *ibid.* On Oct. 7, Dodge telegraphed to Rawlins that wives and families of wounded officers wanted to go to Corinth, and on Oct. 8, Rawlins telegraphed to Dodge cancelling the restriction on citizen travel. Telegrams received, *ibid.*

On Oct. 5, USG telegraphed to Brig. Gen. Leonard F. Ross the text of the last two telegrams from Rosecrans printed above. "the following Dispatches Received from Genl Rosecrans   . . . Genl Ords Dispatches have been forwarded to Genl Rosecrans with orders to push forward without Delay or Referral to fatigue of troops to Divert Enemies attention & capture him if Possible" Telegram received, *ibid.*, District of West Tenn., 4th Division, Telegrams Received. On the same day, Ross, Bolivar, twice telegraphed to USG, first at 4:00 P.M. "I shall be on my way to join Genl Ord within an hour leaving Col Sanderson in command   no cannonading heard for the last hour." "Cannonading has been heard for the last hour in a South Easterly direction and is now Quite lively—" Telegrams received, *ibid.*, Dept. of the Mo., Telegrams Received. On the same day, Capt. Francis A. Dallam, Bolivar, telegraphed to USG. "Genl Ross left this p. m at 5 oclock with 12th Wisconsin & 47th Ills 5 companies of 22nd Ind one Company of Cavalry & two pieces of artillery to support Genl Ord   the 76th Illinois has just arrived" Telegram received, *ibid.*

On Oct. 6, 11:00 A.M., "Battle Ground of the Hatchie," Ross telegraphed to Dallam. "I arrived here at three oclock this A. M the fighting all over—the victory dicisive the enemy greatly demoralized & retreating in a southerly direction. Rosecrans supposed to be in pursuit—A dense smoke is rising in the south & the impression is that the enemy is destroying train. Over three hundred prisoners taken & more arriving—shall probably return in the morning—The wounded &

prisoners will soon be sent in—Our troops all did well . . . P. S. If the enclosed information has not been sent to Genl Grant send it." Telegram received, *ibid.*

On Oct. 4, Rawlins telegraphed to Dodge. "Reinforcements have been sent from this place, to Corinth leaving it much exposed   send forward at once all the troops you can possibly spare & if you need cars from Columbus they can be sent from here. Answer the number of troops you can send & cars needed"   Telegram received, *ibid.* On Oct. 4, Dodge telegraphed twice to USG. "I have one whole reg't & part of two (2) regts here   will send the full reg't 76th Ills. at one (1) today—" "The 76th has just left—" Telegrams received, *ibid.* On the same day, Dodge telegraphed to Rawlins. "There is at Humboldt in my old division one (1) full Reg't 12th Wis a part of 54 Ills & about 300, armed ~~Ten~~ Tenn' troops with a battery   the 12 Wisconsin is a fine Regt—" Telegram received, *ibid.* On Oct. 7, Dodge telegraphed to Rawlins. "The 81st & 124th Ills regt will be in here tonight   do they go forward" Telegram received, *ibid.* On Oct. 8, USG telegraphed to Dodge. "Send the 2 new Regiments just arrived to Jackson   there are five (5) more yet to arrive   the next two 2 you may send to Trenton & Humboldt" Telegram received, *ibid.* On Oct. 9, USG telegraphed to Dodge. "The regiments that arrived at Columbus this afternoon you will send forward to Trenton tonight if possible—" Telegram received, *ibid.* On the same day, Dodge telegraphed to USG. "Train will start for Trenton in one hour—" Telegram received, *ibid.*

Also on Oct. 4, Brig. Gen. James M. Tuttle, Cairo, telegraphed to Rawlins. "I have but one regiment for all duty here   have a large lot Rebel prisoners to guard   Have telegraphed Gov Yates to send reinforcements   How is the fight going" Telegram received, *ibid.* On Oct. 5, Tuttle telegraphed to USG, then to Rawlins. "I have suceeded in getting Genl Wright to request Gov. Yates to send you seven (7) new Reg'ts as reinforcements in my call—shall I order them. How goes the fight   of course you whipped them good!—" "Does Genl Grant want the seven (7) Regt's. of Gov Yates—Governor says he will send them if wanted immediately—" Telegrams received, *ibid.* On Oct. 8, Tuttle twice telegraphed to USG. "Gov Yates is sending seven (7) Regiments   two (2) of them have gone on from here balance to leave soon   I have Telegraphed Him and Gen Wright & Maj Gen Halleck contents of your dispatch for twenty (20) Regiments also Gov Hayward of Iowa & Gen Curtis to know if they have any that can be spared if Gen Halleck orders." "Curtis has ordered all Steeles forces to Ironton Mo. Except Carr's Division. They are now on the way—Genl Steele passed through here this morning—I inform you for the reason that I think you ought to know it—" Telegrams received, *ibid.*

1. On Oct. 5, Col. Isham N. Haynie, Bethel, twice telegraphed to USG, the second time at 3:00 P.M. "Courier came just now. Artillery heard in the direction of Pocahontas, and, I think, just east of that place. Possibly, if Hurlbut is out, it may be him; he has forces moving threatening the rebels. None of my scouts are in yet from that direction." Misdated Dec. 5 in *O.R.*, I, xvii, part 2, 387. "Gen Rosecrans directs me to send a ~~messenger~~ message by carrier to Gen Hurlbut—Can you advise me of the probable whereabouts of Gen Hurlbut" Telegram received, DNA, RG 393, Dept. of the Tenn., Telegrams Received.

2. On Oct. 5, 5:00 A.M., Maj. Gen. Stephen A. Hurlbut, Big Muddy, Tenn., telegraphed to USG. "The Column is moving toward to the Hatchie Bridges & levees across the Muddy very bad & have to be repaired. Three Regm of Cavalry

are near Hatchie ~~we~~ shall disperse them as soon as infantry & artillery can reach them—Despatch from Gen Ross that provision train will be here today with Maj Gen Ord'' Telegram received, *ibid.*, Dept. of the Mo., Telegrams Received. *O.R.*, I, xvii, part 2, 263.

3. On Oct. *5*, Rosecrans telegraphed to USG. "The following are among the Rebel officers killed and wounded Col Pritchard 3rd Mo severely wounded— Col Johnson 20th Arkansas killed—Col Daily 18th Ark severely wounded—Col Rodgers 20th Texas killed—Col Martin Comdg 4th Brigade 1st Division killed Maj Jones 20th Ark killed—Col McClain 37th Mississippi mortally wounded'' Telegram received, DNA, RG 393, Dept. of the Mo., Telegrams Received; copies, *ibid.*, Army of the Miss., Telegrams Sent; *ibid.*, RG 94, War Records Office, Union Battle Reports. *O.R.*, I, xvii, part 1, 161.

To Maj. Gen. Henry W. Halleck

Hd. Qrs Gen Grant
Jackson Tenn [*Oct. 6*] 12.20 P M [*1862*]

MAJ GENL HALLECK
GEN IN CHF.

Genls Ord & Hurlbut came on the Enemys yesterday & Hurlbut, having driven in small bodies the day before, after seven (7) hours hard fighting drove the enemy five (5) miles back across the Hatchie towards Corinth capturing two (2) Batteries about three hundred prisoners & many small arms. I immediately apprised Rosecrans of these facts & directed him to urge on the good work. Following dispatch just rec'd from ~~Chewalla~~ Chewalla ~~Oct 6 1862~~ Oct. 6th. To Maj Gen Grant.

"The Enemy are totally routed throwing everything away. We are following sharply

Signed W. S. ROSECRANS''[1]

Under previous instructions, Hurlbut is also following McPherson in the lead of Rosecran's column. Rebel Genl Martin said to be killed.[2]

U S GRANT
M G Comdg

Telegram received, DNA, RG 94, Generals' Papers and Books, Telegrams
Received by Gen. Halleck; *ibid.*, RG 107, Telegrams Collected (Bound); copies,
ibid., RG 393, USG Hd. Qrs. Correspondence; DLC-USG, V, 4, 5, 7, 8, 88.
O.R., I, xvii, part 1, 155. On Oct. 10, 1862, Maj. Gen. Stephen A. Hurlbut sent
to Maj. John A. Rawlins a lengthy report of the battle of the Hatchie. LS, DNA,
RG 94, War Records Office, Union Battle Reports. *O.R.*, I, xvii, part 1, 305–7.

    1. Telegram received, DNA, RG 393, Dept. of the Mo., Telegrams
Received.
    2. Col. John D. Martin, commanding the 4th Brigade, 1st Division, Army
of the West, was killed Oct. 3 in the battle of Corinth.

To Maj. Gen. Stephen A. Hurlbut

BY TELEGRAPH FROM Jackson [*Oct. 6*] *1862*

To GENL HURLBUT
    Return with your command as soon as you can Bringing your
Wounded with you   a Portion of it should return at once

U S. GRANT

Maj Genl

Telegram received, DNA, RG 393, District of West Tenn., 4th Division, Telegrams Received. On Oct. 6, 1862, USG again telegraphed to Maj. Gen. Stephen
A. Hurlbut. "Retain all Prisoners. Parole none" Telegram received, *ibid.* On
the same day, Hurlbut telegraphed to USG. "I am compelled to send back for
transportation for my wounded I am out of rations the enemy have twenty
four hours start & are fleeing light & cannot be ~~sent~~ overhauled by my command—
Rosecrans is in Pursuit as I am told but my command is too much crippled in
wounded men & Dead artilley Horses to follow." Telegram received, *ibid.*, Dept.
of the Mo., Telegrams Received. *O.R.*, I, xvii, part 2, 267. On Oct. 7, 9:30 P.M.,
Hurlbut, Bolivar, telegraphed to USG. "I have the honor to report that I have
returned to this point. My First Brigade is now at Porter's Creek, 13 miles. The
Second Brigade, with balance of wounded I captured, artillery, and guns, is at
Muddy. Both brigades will be here to-morrow. I received dispatch from General
Rosecrans at Ruckersville dated 10 A. M. urgently requesting to me proceed
south but the state of command ~~by~~ & your orders had determined that question.
We had no ink or paper in the division on this trip so that official reports cannot
be made until camp is reestablished— . . . P. S. My surgeons demand Ice for the
wounded say for 200 men Will you order it from Columbus at once." Telegram
received (incomplete), DNA, RG 393, Dept. of the Mo., Telegrams Received.
O.R., I, xvii, part 2, 268. On the same day, Maj. John A. Rawlins telegraphed to

Brig. Gen. Grenville M. Dodge, Columbus, Ky., asking him to send ice. Telegram received, DNA, RG 393, Dept. of the Mo., Telegrams Received.

Earlier on Oct. 7, Brig. Gen. Leonard F. Ross, Bolivar, twice telegraphed to USG. "I returned last night Genl Hurlbut will be in tonight the wounded are arriving—The Prisoners 350 in number will be in about 10 oclock. Have you any orders in relation to them" "In regard to the two (2) Regiments sent here 12th Wisconsin & 76th Ills are they to remain here and if so who will they report to" Telegrams received, *ibid.*

Also on Oct. 6, USG twice telegraphed to Maj. Gen. William S. Rosecrans. "Oweing to the great number of wounded men with Genl Hurlbuts command I have been compelled to order his return. Be governed by this circumstance in your pursuit." "Retain all prisoners: Parole none." Copies, Rosecrans Papers, CLU.

To Maj. Gen. William S. Rosecrans

Head quarters Dept. of West Tenn.

Jackson Tenn. Oct. 6th 1862

GENL. W. S. ROSECRANS.

Following received from Bethel. Prisoners from Prices army brought in this A. M. by my scouts from near Chewalla—say the Rebels admit a loss of four thousand (4.000) and that Genl. Martin was killed.

They saw his body. They report Price' army in a state of starvation. Really the looks of the men confirm it.

No news of the Rebels movements this morning.[1]

U. S. GRANT.

Maj. Genl.

Telegram, copies, Rosecrans Papers, CLU; DNA, RG 393, Army of the Miss., Telegrams Received. An undated telegram of Maj. Gen. William S. Rosecrans to USG datelined "on Road" was probably sent early on Oct. 6, 1862. "From end of wire 2 miles east of Chewalla. Our advance at Tonnys low bridge of Tuscumbia. Had sharp skirmish last evening. At dark Rebels driven from a very strong & high hill. Was with the advance under McPherson. At daylight this morning, after left, heard a solitary gun. I think it the rebel signal for their rear guard to quiet come stand our ~~crossing~~ advance, on crossing Tuscumbia 3 miles from Pocahontas Bridge to be repaired at all the crossings above—" Telegram received, *ibid.*, Dept. of the Mo., Telegrams Received. On Oct. 6, Rosecrans sent two additional telegrams to USG, the first datelined "Cheneys Mill Bridge," the second "on Road." "From best information. Rebel rear guard passed Hatchie this morning before 10 oclock   burned the bridge   they are aiming for Holly Springs. Hurlbut reports himself too much cut up to pursue—McPhersons Brigade & McKeans & Stanlys Divisions here. Hamiltons four (4) miles off—Bridge built   part of the troops across. We shall pursue them—"   "Have you anything further from Men, or any orders for me   am at end of Telegraph wire going forward to Woodwards thence to Hatchie crossing   please answer before I leave —Have ordered Rail Road track to cleared & in working order to Hocks crossing also telegraph wire to be repaired"   Telegrams received, *ibid.*; copies, *ibid.*, RG 94, War Records Office, Union Battle Reports. *O.R.*, I, xvii, part 1, 162–63.

1. See *ibid.*, I, xvii, part 2, 267. On Oct. 6, Col. Isham N. Haynie, Bethel, again telegraphed to USG. "Seven prisoners from Price's army, General Moore's brigade, are just brought in by scouts, and they report that the whole brigade, five regiments, Forty-second Alabama, Thirty-fifth Mississippi, Second Arkansas Regiments, and one Texas regiment threw away their arms at Davis' Bridge and every man scattered. This occurred when Hurlbut first attacked their rear. They are a miserable, squalid, starved set. What shall I do with them? Lieutenant Grimes, who is in charge of scouts, reports the woods filled with them." *Ibid.*

To Maj. Gen. William S. Rosecrans

Head quarters Dept. of West Tenn.
Jackson Tenn. Octr. 6th 1862

MAJ. GENL. ROSECRANS,

Your dispatch received. No further orders to give. You will avail yourself of every advantage and capture and destroy the Rebel army to the utmost of your power. Ord will be back here tonight wounded.

Hurlbut left in command. All news recd. cheering and all parts of the army have behaved nobly.

U. S. GRANT.
Maj Genl.

Telegram, copies, Rosecrans Papers, CLU; DNA, RG 393, Army of the Miss., Telegrams Received.

To Maj. Gen. Henry W. Halleck

Jackson Tenn 12 10 P M
Oct. 7, 1862.

MAJ GENL HALLECK.

What shall be done with prisoners taken in the late engagement?

Our advance in pursuit followed enemy's main column into Jonesboro[1] last night. I have ordered their return.

U S GRANT
M G Comdg

Telegram received, DNA, RG 94, Generals' Papers and Books, Telegrams Received by Gen. Halleck; *ibid.*, RG 107, Telegrams Collected (Bound); copies, *ibid.*, RG 393, USG Hd. Qrs. Correspondence; DLC-USG, V, 4, 5, 7, 8, 88. On Oct. 8, 1862, Maj. Gen. Henry W. Halleck telegraphed to USG. "Why order a return of your troops? Why not reinforce Rosecrans & pursue the enemy into Miss, supporting your army on the country?" ALS (telegram sent), DNA, RG 107, Telegrams Collected (Bound); copies, *ibid.*, RG 108, Telegrams Sent; *ibid.*, RG 393, USG Hd. Qrs. Correspondence; DLC-USG, V, 4, 5, 7, 8, 88. *O.R.*, I, xvii, part 1, 156. See telegrams to Maj. Gen. Henry W. Halleck, Oct. 8, 1862. On Oct. 7, USG again telegraphed to Halleck. "If possible have McPherson made Major Genl   He should be made at once to take rank above others who may be promoted for the late battles." Telegram received, DNA, RG 94, Letters Received; *ibid.*, RG 107, Telegrams Collected (Bound); copies, *ibid.*, RG 108, Telegrams Received in Cipher; *ibid.*, RG 393, USG Hd. Qrs. Correspondence; DLC-USG, V, 4, 5, 7, 8, 88. *O.R.*, I, xvii, part 2, 267. On Oct. 8, Halleck again telegraphed to USG. "Prisoners of war will be paroled and delivered to the enemy at some point within his lines. A receipted list must be taken in duplicate and one copy sent to Adjt Genl in order to effect an exchange. Genl Wright says he has placed seven (7) Ill regiments at your command   A large body of new levies will be collected as soon as possible at Memphis. Genl McPherson is promoted. Report others who deserve it." ALS (telegram sent), DNA, RG 107, Telegrams Collected (Bound); telegram received, *ibid.*, RG 393, Dept. of the Tenn., Telegrams Received. *O.R.*, I, xvii, part 2, 268–69; *ibid.*, II, iv, 606. See following telegram.

1. Jonesborough, Miss., about eighteen miles east of Corinth.

To Maj. Gen. William S. Rosecrans

Head quarters Dept. of West Tenn.
Jackson Tenn. Octr. 7th 1862

Maj. Genl. Rosecrans,

Genl. Hurlbut took with him three (3) days rations and I forwarded to him (3) three days more by wagons. If they are out now they must have wasted them.

Sherman cannot leave Memphis   He has not got the force to do it. I would have had him on the way before this time if it had been practicable. You should have communicated with Sherman through me and not direct.

Hurlbut loss had been severe and he is in a country where nothing can be had except by sending to Bolivar, twenty six (26) miles over bad roads. You need not send him supplies as he will be back in Bolivar tonight.

Every regiment that could possibly be spared from Columbus to this place, has already been sent you and Hurlbut. Our condition was fully reported to Genl Halleck as soon as the advance of the enemy was known—and several day before the attack Genl. Wright was also requested to order new Regts. from Illinois. I understand that seven (7) new regts. are to come. Genl. Halleck has been written and telegraphed to several days since on the subject. of McPherson.[1] I want you to give him a Div.

We can do nothing with our weak forces but fall back to our old places. Order the pursuit to cease.

U. S. Grant.
Maj. Genl.

Telegram, copies, Rosecrans Papers, CLU; DNA, RG 393, Army of the Miss., Telegrams Received. On Oct. 7, 1862, Maj. Gen. William S. Rosecrans sent three telegrams to USG. "Since my last McPherson occupied Jonesboro at nine oclock last night—out of rations having followed the main column of the precipitate retreat of the enemy   Hurlbut reports himself out of provisions & too much crippled to follow the enemy   I have ordered rations sent to Cypres for him & have begged him not to return to Bolivar until I can communicate with Sherman. I want him appear to threaten the enemy   I think Sherman should to go to Holly Springs by all means & that the road should be opened to take supplies to him   think it could be done without much trouble—Telegraph line should ~~the~~ be put up   the superintendent should immedy supply himself with a ~~key~~ large stock of wire & supplies of all kinds that may be needed in the work. I repeat it is of the utmost importance to give the enemy no rest ~~by~~ day or night but push him to Mobile & Jackson—~~Do~~ Beg the authorities north to send us more troops   ship everything you can   now is our time   we must give the enemy no time to reinforce or recruit Every nerve must be strained   everything will be sent to see that our troops lack nothing of the necessaries to keep them going   among other things rolling stock and material for repairs are needed   a civilian must take the place of McPherson he is needed in the field   he adds twenty per cent to my troops he commands Telegraph Quinby to come or send him down with all you can" Telegram received, *ibid.*, Dept. of the Mo., Telegrams Received; copy, *ibid.*, RG 94, War Records Office, Union Battle Reports. *O.R.*, I, xvii, part 1, 164. "Do not I entreat you call Hurlbut back   let Him send away His wounded   it surely is easier to move the sick and wounded than to remove both. I propose to push the Enemy so that we need but the most trifling guards behind us. Our advance is beyond Ruckersville. Hamilton will seize the Hatchie ~~Road~~ crossing on the Riply Road tonight. A very intelligent Honest young Irishman Ambulanced Driver deserted from the Rebels says that they wished to go together to Rail Road near Tupelo where they will meet the nine thousand (9000) exchanged Prisoners but He says they are much scattered and demoralized. They have much Artillery" Telegram received, DNA, RG 393, Dept. of the Mo., Telegrams Received; copies, *ibid.*, Army of the Miss., Telegrams Sent; *ibid.*, RG 94, War Records Office, Union Battle Reports. *O.R.*, I, xvii, part 1, 163. "Midnight your 8.30. P. M. received. Our troops occupy Ripley. I must deeply dissent from your views as to the policy of pursuit. We have defeated routed and demoralized the army which holds the lower Miss Valley. We have the two R. Roads leading down into the Gulf through the most populous part of the state into which we can now pursue them by the Miss. or the Mo. & Ohio. The effect returning to our old position will be to give them up the only corn country which they have west of Alabama—including the Tuscumbia Valley and to permit them to recruit their forces advance and occupy the old ground reducing us to the occupation of a defensive position barren and worthless on a long front of which they can harrass us until bad weather precludes any effectual advance except on the Rail. Roads— when time fortifycations and rolling stock will render them superior to us. Our force including what can be spared with Hurlbut, will garrison Corinth and Jackson and enable us to push them. Our advance will cover even Holly springs which will be ours when we want it—and what is needful is to continue to push and whip them. We have whipped them and should now push them to the wall—all the force in Miss. and capture all the rolling stock of the R. R. then west of alabama & of Mobile. Braggs Army alone could repair the damage. We have it in our power to do them   But I beseech you to send everything   Push them while they are broken hungry weary and illsupplied. Draw everything from Memphis to help move on Holly Springs. Let us concentrate and appeal to the Governors of the States to rush down twenty (20) or thirty (30) new Regiments to hold our rear and we can make a triumph of our start." Copies, DNA, RG 393, Army of the Miss., Telegrams Sent; *ibid.*, RG 94, War Records Office, Union Battle Reports. *O.R.*, I, xvii, part 1, 163–64.

1. See letter to Maj. Gen. Henry W. Halleck, Oct. 5, 1862, and preceding telegram.

To Maj. Gen. Henry W. Halleck

———

Jackson Tenn 9 a m [*Oct. 8, 1862*]

MAJ GEN HALLECK.

Rosecrans has followed Rebels to Ripley   troops from Bolivar will occupy Grand Junction tomorrow   with reinforcements rapidly sent in from the new levies I can take every thing on the Mississippi Central Road   I ordered Rosecrans back last night but he is so averse to returning, that I have directed him to remain still until you can be heard from

U S GRANT
M G C

Telegram received, DNA, RG 94, Generals' Papers and Books, Telegrams Received by Gen. Halleck; *ibid.*, RG 107, Telegrams Collected (Bound); copies, *ibid.*, RG 393, USG Hd. Qrs. Correspondence; DLC-USG, V, 4, 5, 7, 8, 88. *O.R.*, I, xvii, part 1, 156.

To Maj. Gen. Henry W. Halleck

———

Jackson Tenn
Oct 8th 62

MAJ GEN HALLECK
COMDR IN CHIEF

Before telegraphing you this morning for reinforcements to follow up our victories I ordered Genl Rosecrans to return   He showed such reluctance that I consented to allow him to remain until you could be heard from, if further reinforcements could be got—

On reflection I deem it idle to pursue farther without more preparation and have for the third time ordered his return

U S GRANT
Maj Gen

Telegram received, DNA, RG 94, Generals' Papers and Books, Telegrams Received by Gen. Halleck; *ibid.*, RG 107, Telegrams Collected (Bound); copy, *ibid.*, Telegrams Received in Cipher. *O.R.*, I, xvii, part 1, 156.

To Maj. Gen. Henry W. Halleck

Jackson Tenn
Oct 8—7 30 P M [*1862*]

MAJ GEN HALLECK
GEN IN CHIEF

An Army cannot subsist itself on the country except in forage   They did not start out to follow but a few days and are much worn out, and I have information not only that the Enemy have reserves that are on their way to join the retreating column, but that they have fortifications to return to in case of need. The Mobile Road is also open to the Enemy to near Rienzi and Corinth would be exposed by the advance   Although partial success might result from further pursuit disaster would follow in the end. If you say so however it is not too late yet to go on and I will join the moving column and go to the farthest extent possible Rosecrans has been reinforced with everything at hand, even at the risk of this Road against raids—

U S GRANT
Maj Gen

Telegram received, DNA, RG 94, Generals' Papers and Books, Telegrams Received by Gen. Halleck; *ibid.*, RG 107, Telegrams Collected (Bound); copies, *ibid.*, Telegrams Received in Cipher; *ibid.*, RG 393, USG Hd. Qrs. Correspondence; DLC-USG, V, 4, 5, 7, 8, 88. *O.R.*, I, xvii, part 1, 156.

To Maj. Gen. Henry W. Halleck

Head Quarters, Dist. of W. Ten.
Jackson, Oct. 8th 1862,
Respectfully forwarded to Head Quarters of the Army with the remark that there is undoubtedly a large illegal and contraband trade going on on the Mississippi river.

I have ordered a river police until some decision is made in this matter.

U. S. GRANT
Maj. Gen

AES, DNA, RG 36, Special Agents, Reports and Correspondence. Written on a letter of Oct. 7, 1862, from Maj. Robert B. Jones, 34th Ind., New Madrid, to Brig. Gen. Grenville M. Dodge. "The Shipping of salt to the rebels is a common occurrence by certain boats in the St. Louis and Memphis trade. It is shipped by quantities and landed at points where there is no military post and conveyed to the interior and Arkansas. The Belle Memphis and Platt Valley are suspected of being engaged in this trade. It is well known that quantities of salt have been landed at Point Pleasant, Gayosa and Ashport which have been delivered to the rebel and guerrilla authorities, and it is impossible to ~~know~~ learn of it until after it is beyond our reach. This trade ought to be subjected to more stringent rules. Perhaps an order forbidding boats to land at these points might remedy the abuse in part—but they will ship these contraband articles of salt & whiskey to wood landings and unusual points on the river. But the most effective way to prevent these illegal shippments would be the establishment of Provost Guards upon the boats engaged in this illegal traffic. There is no mistake but what the rebels are getting all the salt they need, by some means or other." ALS, *ibid*. On Oct. 8, Dodge endorsed this letter. "Respectfully Reffered to Maj Gen U. S. Grant. there is no doubt of the truth of the within statement and there is no way to prevent this illegal traffick except by seizing all such articles upon any boat destined—for any point between Cairo & Memphis. I respectfully request that such order be issued" AES, *ibid*. On Oct. 22, Maj. Gen. Henry W. Halleck added an endorsement. AES, *ibid*. On Oct. 23, the letter was transmitted from the War Dept. to the Treasury Dept. AES, *ibid*. On Oct. 22, Halleck wrote to USG. "Major R. B. Jones' letter of the 7th inst in relation to illicit trade in salt & c on the Miss. river is received. The attention of the Treasury Dept will be called to this matter with the suggestion that 'Aids to the revenue,' be placed on such steamers. You will take measures to assist in suppressing this illegal trade & punishing the guilty parties." ADfS, *ibid*., RG 94, Generals' Papers and Books, Drafts of Letters Sent by Gen. Halleck; ALS, *ibid*., RG 108, Letters Sent (Press).

On Oct. 9, Maj. John A. Rawlins wrote to Dodge. "The communication of Major Jones commanding Post at New Madrid, referred by you to these Headquarters, in relation to the shipments of salt to the Rebels, and landing it at points where there is no Military Post, below Columbus on the Mississippi River, is received. To guard against this you will place a sufficient number of men on each steamer suspected of being so engaged, under command of a commissioned officer, with instructions to seize any salt or any other goods that may be attempted to be landed, in violation of the orders of the Treasury Department, and return with the Boats or Boats that may be so engaged to Columbus, where they will be held until further orders. The Steamers will be required to furnish the transportation and such facilities as the men may require for cooking their rations : Also, to report on each trip the quantities and kinds of goods landed, under Treasury Permits and the points at which they are landed." LS, *ibid.*, RG 393, District of Western Ky., Unentered Letters Received. On Oct. 6, Rawlins had telegraphed to Dodge. "It is reported here that salt is being sold at various points on the Mississippi River near Randolph & is daily being hauled through ~~tro~~ Brownsville in 4 horse teams to the Confederate Army   please instruct the forces at Fort Pillow to investigate the matter & seize & turn over to the quarter master Dept any salt & other articles contraband of war that are laibel to get into the possession of Rebels"   Telegram received, *ibid.*, Dept. of the Mo., Telegrams Received. On Oct. 8, Rawlins telegraphed to Dodge. "the name of One of the parties engaged in sending Salt from a point on the Mississippi River to the Rebels Telegraphed you on October 6th   Bawdin a merchant at Ashport   he is said to be the principal Operator   you will inform the commandant at Fort Pillow"   Telegram received, *ibid.* On Oct. 19, Dodge telegraphed to Rawlins. "There appears to be continually trouble in relation to the boats running in the Cairo & Columbus trade in connection with the R. R ~~to the serv~~ Co   The service would be greatly benefited if the R R Co or the Chf Q M should put in a chertered boat to do [a]ll the business   can this b[e] done"   Telegram received, *ibid.*

On Sept. 24, Capt. Charles A. Reynolds, Corinth, telegraphed to Rawlins. "Two or three hundred Barrels of Salt was Brought here from Hamburg   it is more than the Gov't want   shal it be turned over to the owners   some citizens claiming to be Union men want to make small purchases." Telegram received, *ibid.*

To Maj. Gen. Stephen A. Hurlbut

By Telegraph from Jackson [*Oct. 8*] *1862*

To Genl Hurlbut

Let Ross go out & send light force forward to Davis Mills & Destroy Road as suggested by you   this will cover Rosencrans which I am now sending orders for the third time to return—I will not send to fixed-up wire & Repair Road as Indicated in my Dispatch of this morning[1]

U. S. Grant
Maj Genl

Telegram received, DNA, RG 393, District of West Tenn., 4th Division, Telegrams Received. On Oct. 8, 1862, Maj. Gen. Stephen A. Hurlbut, Bolivar, Tenn., telegraphed to USG. "The train with all the wounded came through from the Hatchie last night I have taken Houses for their accommodations" Telegram received, *ibid.*, Dept. of the Mo., Telegrams Received.

On Oct. 9, 2:30 P.M., Hurlbut telegraphed to USG. "Have just heard from Ross. his advanced guard went into Grand Junction about sunrise too late for a surprise on Davis' mills—The main body at 9 a m were at Van Buren nine (9) miles from Junction. Scouts report two Thousand (2000) infantry & three (3) hundred cavalry at Davis Mills infantry exchanged prisoners not well armed Ross has thirty three hundred (3 300) infantry ~~exchanged prisoners not well ar~~ four hundred (400) Cavalry & sixteen (16) pieces of artillery—I have ordered him to crown the heights on Wolf River near Lagrage & push forward & destroy the bridge or force them to destroy it & return.—I still think they will burn it in pesence of Ross force I will send his report by Train—" Telegram received, *ibid. O.R.*, I, xvii, part 2, 271. On Oct. 10, Hurlbut telegraphed to USG. "Gen Ross is on his return having thouroughly destroyed Bridge at Davis—only twenty five cavalry found who fled—I regret that the bridge was not saved—" Telegram received, DNA, RG 393, Dept. of the Mo., Telegrams Received. *O.R.*, I, xvii, part 2, 274.

1. On Oct. 8, Maj. John A. Rawlins telegraphed to Hurlbut. "Rosecrans is still in pursuit. He is now at Ripley. Send General Ross with the entire force at Bolivar, excepting your Division, out to Grand Junction to repairing Railroad in his rear to carry supplies. They must get off this evening without fail. I will send men and tools from here to-night to aid in repairing the Road" Telegram received, DNA, RG 393, District of West Tenn., 4th Division, Telegrams Received. On Oct. 8, Hurlbut telegraphed to USG. "Order for Ross movement received Second Ills Cavalry one (1) Regt & one (1) section will move flying light to seize Davis Mills Bridge The rest of the column will follow rapidly. I think Mack's Reg't 76th Ills had better remain here & perhaps the 12th Wisconsin Mack has no Haversacks for provisions—" Telegrams received (2), *ibid.*, Dept. of the Mo., Telegrams Received. *O.R.*, I, xvii, part 2, 269. On Oct. 9, Rawlins telegraphed to Hurlbut. "The 12th Wisconsin & 76th Ills will remain at Bolivar, let the 12th Wisconsin send for their camp & garrison equippage You may assign the 76th to your Division. Instructions have been sent you in regard to Prisoners." Telegram received, DNA, RG 393, District of West Tenn., 4th Division, Telegrams Received. See telegram to Maj. Gen. Stephen A. Hurlbut, Oct. 9, 1862. On Oct. 12, Col. George E. Bryant, 12th Wis., Humboldt, Tenn., telegraphed to USG. "I have already turned over to Q M here the horses & accoutrements as was ordered by Maj Gen Hurlbut I shall start at sunrise with detachment for Bolivar." Telegram received, DNA, RG 393, Dept. of the Mo., Telegrams Received. On the same day, Col. James J. Dollins, 81st Ill., Humboldt, telegraphed to Rawlins. "Col Bryant with the remainder of his reg't leaves for Bolivar tomorrow cant I keep Capt Maxeys Co mounted Infantry here it is important as they know the country well near Brownsville that is infested by Guerillas they are just in from a scout & report some valuable information have no other effectives mentioned" Telegram received, *ibid.*

On Oct. 8, USG telegraphed to Hurlbut. "all I want of the present movement from Bolivar is to cover the Return of Rosecrans who has Remained out too long

& against orders & to Destroy the Bridge at Davis Mills which will be a Good Job. let them return as soon as it is done" Telegram received, *ibid.*, District of West Tenn., 4th Division, Telegrams Received. On Oct. 8, Hurlbut telegraphed to USG. "I have just heard from Holly Springs. There are no forces there.—All left on Sunday There is about one company of Cavalry at Davis Mills to destroy the Rail Road Bridge if we move. Everything in shape of force above Wolf River has moved south—I am of opinion that the route of Van Dorns army is complete and that Pillows force late at Holly has caught the panic. Ross moves tonight & will await further orders at La Grange & Grand Junction which he is ordered to occupy by morning—" Telegram received, *ibid.*, Dept. of the Mo., Telegrams Received. *O.R.*, I, xvii, part 2, 269.

To Maj. Gen. William S. Rosecrans

Head quarters Dept. of West Tenn.
Jackson Tenn. Octr. 8th 1862

MAJ. GENL. ROSECRANS.

I have ordered Hurlbut to Grand Junction with orders to repair his R. Road to his rear. Part of Engineer Regt. goes from here tonight to do the work.

I have strained every string to get new troops but as yet have got two Regiments.

Hold where you are until further orders from me. With out further reinforcements to hold our rear it would be folly to push on. I will make other efforts to get them.

U. S. GRANT
Maj. Genl.

Telegram, copies, Rosecrans Papers, CLU; DNA, RG 393, Army of the Miss., Telegrams Received. On Oct. 8, 1862, USG again telegraphed to Maj. Gen. William S. Rosecrans. "Return to Corinth as first ordered." Copies, *ibid.*

On the same day, Rosecrans, Ripley, 9:45 P.M., telegraphed to USG. "Your two (2) dispatches rec'd. the last highly gratifying—Dispositions will be made in conformity & I will remain here—have ordered Telegraph line to be extended to Pocahontas & repaired to Grand Junction—Please order R. R to be repaired to Pocahontas & Grand Junction—You are misinformed as to me having communicated with Sherman as I have never presumed to do so except so far after having been informed by you as to his whereabouts—I sent word to Hurlbut wishing him to tell Sherman where we were & asking co'operation   I should not think of communicatig with him in any official way except through you. Please order a large number of cavalry & artillery horses to be ready   many are now needed. Cavalry has suffered very severely by last week's labor & for forage—" Telegram received, *ibid.*, Dept. of the Mo., Telegrams Received; copy, *ibid.*, RG 94, War Records Office, Union Battle Reports. *O.R.*, I, xvii, part 1, 164–65. The "highly gratifying" telegram has not been located. It was probably in response to the second USG telegram that Rosecrans telegraphed to Maj. John A. Rawlins from Jacinto on Oct. 9. "The dispatch of the Maj Genl Comd'g dated the 8th inst' directing our return to Corinth is just rec'd   I shall take the most prompt & officious measures to carry the orders into Execution with as little predjudice as practicable to the interest of the service"   Telegram received, DNA, RG 393, Dept. of the Mo., Telegrams Received; copy, *ibid.*, RG 94, War Records Office, Union Battle Reports. *O.R.*, I, xvii, part 1, 165. Also on Oct. 8, 9:45 P.M., Rosecrans telegraphed to USG. "I have to report that our advance occupied Ripley last night before (11) oclock—Enemy formed there line of battle yesterday afternoon expecting us to attack them but recd before night   Genl Hamilton occupied Renzi & having rec'd provisions marched from there to Hatchie crossing on Ripley road today whence he has been ordered to take post at Nowlins crosseroads coming our communication with Rienzi & Kossuth   the troops will then be McArthur on the right, Stanly next McPherson covering the town   Cavalry division has been ordered to recruit furnishing minimum number of scouts—" Telegram received, DNA, RG 393, Dept. of the Mo., Telegrams Received; copy, *ibid.*, RG 94, War Records Office, Union Battle Reports. *O.R.*, I, xvii, part 1, 164.

Another telegram from Rosecrans to USG, also datelined at Ripley, 9:45 P.M., is entered in records as of Oct. 9, but context suggests that Oct. 8 is more likely. "I consider it nearly certain that Tilghman with the Prisoners has gone to Holly Springs & that Price has gone to join him. I shall soon hear further information. I will be in Corinth soon under a big show of remaining with all my force   I will take immediate measures to put in the best state of defence, to be left while I reorganize my forces." Telegram received (undated), DNA, RG 393, Dept. of the Mo., Telegrams Received; copy, *ibid.*, Army of the Miss., Telegrams Sent; *ibid.*, RG 94, War Records Office, Union Battle Reports. *O.R.*, I, xvii, part 1, 165.

To Maj. Gen. William T. Sherman

By TELEGRAPH FROM Jackson [*Oct.*] 8 *1862*

To MAJ GEN SHERMAN
CARE GEN DODGE—

Rosecrans is following the enemy—Hurlbut will follow from Bolivar tonight   if you can spare any portion of your force to push on towards Oxford send them   the R Road in rear of

Hurlbut will be repaired to carry supplies as fast as troops move.
I will do all I can to have reinforcements sent you

U S Grant
Maj Genl

Telegram received, DNA, RG 393, Dept. of the Mo., Telegrams Received. This
telegram was sent in care of Brig. Gen. Grenville M. Dodge, Columbus, Ky. On
Oct. 8, 1862, USG telegraphed to Dodge. "Has Dispatch to Gen Sherman gone
yet   if not hold it until further directions are sent from here"   Telegram
received, *ibid*. On the same day, Maj. John A. Rawlins telegraphed to Dodge.
"Do not send Shermans message at all   retain it"   Telegram received, *ibid*.
    Also on Oct. 8, Dodge wrote to his wife inserting "the despatch I got from
Grant." "Hurlbut cometh up with the enemy yesterday at noontide, and whipped
them exceedingly and driveth them across the Chawalla, then established his army
upon the heights thereat; upon hearing which Gen. Grant rejoiceth and is of
exceeding great joy, and asketh: 'how can the enemy flee? and how can they
supply themselves with food and raiment where they now lyeth?' He also compliments in the battle of Corinth. Gen. Ord commandeth the pursuing forces and
countless numbers of federal troops from Dodge's division probably reached him
this morning." Typescript, Dodge Papers, IaHA.

To Maj. Gen. Stephen A. Hurlbut

By Telegraph from Jackson [*Oct.*] 9 1862.

To Maj Genl Hurlbut
    Prisoners of War will be paroled and delivered to the enemy
inside of their lines under flag of truce. A receipted list must be
taken in duplicate & one copy sent to Adjutant General in order
to effect an exchange

U. S. Grant
Maj Genl

Telegram received, DNA, RG 393, District of West Tenn., 4th Division, Telegrams Received. On Oct. 9, 1862, USG again telegraphed to Maj. Gen. Stephen
A. Hurlbut. "Take all side arms from Prisoners before sending them south."
Telegram received, *ibid*. On Oct. 8, Hurlbut had telegraphed to USG. "Have
many prisoners   please instruct me as to my course in relation to them—"   Telegram received, *ibid*., Dept. of the Mo., Telegrams Received. On Oct. 9, Hurlbut
wrote to USG. "I have no camp kettles or other utensils for prisoners and sug-

gest that they be removed at once to Alton or some other point or if kept here that necessary utensils be furnished—there are none here. As soon as Ross returns I shall send the 12th Wisconsin back to Humboldt. I expect a report from Ross every moment which will be forwarded. What disposition shall I make of the 76th Illinois? I am short one regiment in my division and would like to have them in my second brigade. The 52d Indiana has not joined me yet. I suppose it is at Fort Pillow" Copy, *ibid.*, District of West Tenn., 4th Division, Letters Sent. *O.R.*, I, xvii, part 2, 270–71.

On Oct. 9, Maj. John A. Rawlins telegraphed to Brig. Gen. Grenville M. Dodge, Columbus, Ky. "Prisoners of war will be paroled and delivered to the enemy inside of their lines under flag of Truce & receipted list must be taken in duplicate and one (1) copy sent to adjt Genl in order to effect an Exchange the prisoners sent to Columbus you will send by steamer to Memphis with a copy of these instructions to Maj Genl Sherman" Telegram received, DNA, RG 393, Dept. of the Mo., Telegrams Received. On Oct. 9, USG telegraphed to Dodge. "Take all side arms from Prisoners before sending them South" Telegram received, *ibid.* On the same day, Dodge telegraphed to Rawlins. "are there any prisoners of war coming up today and how many—" Telegram received, *ibid.* Rawlins drafted his reply below Dodge's telegram. "Five Hundred left here for Columbus at ten Oclock today—" ADfS, *ibid.*; telegram received, *ibid.* On Oct. 12, Maj. Gen. William T. Sherman wrote to Rawlins. "I received last night at the hands of Col. Baldwin of the 57. Illinois Infty a letter of Genl. Dodge at Columbus, with a copy of your dispatch to him of Oct. 9. touching the Prisoners of War ordered to be sent me for exchange. The order involved in the dispatch is to deliver the prisoners to the Enemy within their lines taking Duplicate Receipts &c. The Enemys Lines are very indefinite at this time. Holly Springs is the nearest place where I could expect to find an Officer, although a few days since a Maj Ballintine was at Bohalia 35 miles S. E. of Memphis. To have marched these prisoners out would have required a guard of a Regiment for they are disposed to escape. On their way fr. Columbus to Memphis five did actually escape. Some eight or ten claimed to have deserted to us and near two hundred want to take the oath and remain I have learned from Captain Lazelle 8 U. S. Infty who took the prisoners of War from Cairo to Vicksburg that the agent there for exchange of Prisoners was very technical and would receipt for none unless delivered in person, although I understand they claim credit for all of ours picked up & parolled in every manner of way. Beliving also that the cartel for exchange stipulates for their delivery at or near Vicksburg I have concluded to send them down under a flag of Truce and a Guard. I accordingly had the boat 'Dacotah' coaled & provisioned & have dispatched her for Vicksburg giving the Officer in Command Capt. Swan of the 57. Ills full instructions as to his flag, the means of delivery, receipts &c & have instructed him to claim credit for the five who escaped on the way here. I also addressed a note to Commander Phelps at present Flag Officer at Helena, asking him if in his judgement he deemed it prudent that he send an escort along. I would suggest the propriety of assembling at Columbus all your prisoners of War, & when ready to send them all to Vicksburg. That is the point named in the cartel & it is to our interest to keep these prisoners away from Holly Springs for a while as also to have our Boats make occasional trips down the River. The landing & marching prisoners of War through Memphis & the country back would be attended with scens that should be avoided. I believe the Generals & higher officers of the Confederate Army would respect an escort to prisoners under a Flag but these Guerrillas would not, and the exhirbitions of popular feelings in Memphis are such an occasion might lead to serious results Hoping this may action will meet the General's approval" Copy, *ibid.*, RG 94, Generals' Papers and Books, William T. Sherman, Letters Sent.

To Maj. Gen. William S. Rosecrans

Head quarters Dept. of West. Tenn.
Jackson Tenn. Octr. 9th 1862

MAJ. GENL. ROSECRANS.

You will have to get back to Corinth with great caution. I am credibly informed that Price has been joined by a large force estimated at twenty-thousand, (20.000).

Probably however not more than half that.

U. S. GRANT
Maj. Genl.

Telegram, copies, Rosecrans Papers, CLU; DNA, RG 393, Army of the Miss., Telegrams Received.

On Oct. 9, 1862, 8:00 A.M., Maj. Gen. William S. Rosecrans, Corinth, telegraphed to USG. "If forage is not sent us immediately our animals will die. This trip has worked them down and we have had sent us three hundred (300) sacks. We require three thousand (3,000) sacks per day. The case is critical and something must be done. Please let the steam on the Quarter masters Department." Copy, *ibid.*, Telegrams Sent. On Oct. 11, USG telegraphed to Rosecrans. "I have ordered quarter master at Columbus to load up train of forage and send it forward by extra train. Quartermaster here also directed to push forage on to Corinth." Copy, *ibid.*, Telegrams Received. Also on Oct. 11, Capt. Charles W. Lyman, Columbus, telegraphed to USG. "I have used all the cars for the last few days for soldiers & commissary stores—shall work them all night loading forage & will send a large amount tomorrow to Corinth also som to Jackson." Telegrams received (2), *ibid.*, Dept. of the Mo., Telegrams Received.

On Oct. 9, USG telegraphed to the commanding officer, Columbus. "Forward supplies to this place without delay, we are now nearly out" Telegram received, *ibid.* On the same day, Brig. Gen. Grenville M. Dodge, Columbus telegraphed to USG. "We will send one hundred & twenty five thousand (125000) complete Rations by mornings train and have as many more ready to go forward the next day." Telegram received, *ibid.* On Oct. 11, USG telegraphed to Dodge. "let all Sanitary goods come over the rail road free and to the exclusion of every thing else" Telegram received, *ibid.*

To Abraham Lincoln

Jackson Tenn 10 45 P M [*Oct. 10, 1862*]

THE PREST U. S.

Your dispatch recd.[1] I cannot answer it as fully as I would wish[2] Paloled now eight thirteen 813 Enlisted Men & forty three (43) Commissioned Officers in good health   seven hundred Confederate wounded already to Iuka. Paroled three fifty (350) wounded   paroled still at Corinth   Cannot tell the number of dead yet. About Eight hundred Rebels already buried— Their loss in Killed about Nine to one of ours. The ground is not yet cleared of their unburied dead. Prisoners yet arriving by Every wagon Road & train[3]   This does not include Casualties where Ord attacked in the rear. He has three fifty (350) well prisoners besides two batteries & small arms in large numbers. Our loss there was between four & five hundred (500)   Rebel loss about the same   Genl Oglesby is shot through the breast & ball lodged in the spine.[4] Hopes for his recovery. Our Killed & wounded at Corinth will not Exeed Nine hundred (900) Many of them slightly

U. S GRANT
Maj Genl

Telegram received, DLC-Robert T. Lincoln; DNA, RG 94, Generals' Papers and Books, Telegrams Received by Gen. Halleck; (2) *ibid.*, RG 107, Telegrams Collected (Bound); copies (dated Oct. 9, 1862), *ibid.*, RG 393, USG Hd. Qrs. Correspondence; DLC-USG, V, 4, 5, 7, 8, 88. *O.R.*, I, xvii, part 1, 156–57. Although USG had previously joined in signing petitions and writing recommendations to President Abraham Lincoln, the telegrams of Oct. 8–10 are the beginning of direct military communication between the two.

1. On Oct. 8, Lincoln telegraphed to USG. "I congratulate you and all concerned on your recent battles and victories—How does it all sum up? I especially regret the death of Gen. Hackelman; and am very anxious to know the condition of Gen. Oglesby, who is an intimate personal friend." ALS (telegram sent), RPB; telegram received, DNA, RG 393, Dept. of the Tenn., Telegrams Received. Lincoln, *Works*, V, 453. On Oct. 9, Maj. John A. Rawlins issued General Orders No. 89 embodying the telegram from Lincoln. Copies, DNA, RG 94, War Records Office, Union Battle Reports; DLC-USG, V, 95. *O.R.*, I, xvii, part 1, 159–60.

Copies (misdated Oct. 7), DLC-USG, V, 12, 13, 14; DNA, RG 393, USG General Orders; (printed) Oglesby Papers, IHi.

2. On Oct. 9, Rawlins issued General Orders No. 90. "All Commanders of Posts within this Dist., who have not already done so, will cause duplicate certified lists of all prisoners heretofore paroled by them, to be made out, and one copy forwarded to the Adjutant General of the Army. The other copy they will retain. It is desirable that this should be done with as little delay as practicable." Copies, DLC-USG, V, 12, 13, 14, 95; DNA, RG 393, USG General Orders; (printed) Oglesby Papers, IHi.

3. On Oct. 9, Col. Patrick E. Burke, 14th Mo., Corinth, telegraphed to USG. "Paroled now 813 enlisted men, 43 commissioned officers, in good health; about 700 Confederate wounded, already sent to Iowa, paroled; 350 wounded paroled here; cannot tell the number of dead yet. About 800 Confederates already buried; their loss about eight or ten to one of ours. Prisoners arriving by every wagon road and train; will send full reports as soon as possible. No return yet from the hospitals. The woods stink yet with unburied dead. Oglesby shot through the breast and ball lodged in the spine; hope for his recovery. No news from Rosecrans. I understand Hamilton's division, my regiment, and others left Rienzi yesterday at 4 p. m. for the west; nothing authentic from them. Hillyer is here. Shall I send any wounded Confederates to Saint Louis? Our hospitals are full of them. McKean telegraphs me he will be here this night." *O.R.*, I, xvii, part 2, 270; *ibid.*, II, iv, 608.

4. On Oct. 6, Surgeon John G. F. Holston telegraphed to Rawlins. "Genl Oglesby wounded by musketry ball not found   perhaps it is near spine   no bleeding   breathing difficult   slightly easier than yesterday   Will perhaps get well, am wounded doing well—confed wounded dressed rapidly, their wounded much worse than ours—Men not so good as ours—all operations performed   all the sick cared for   rapidly organizing—no confusion or suffering—one hundred & fifty (150) men examined to be discharged   can they have immediate furloughs & pay sent after them   the order No 209 rec'd today   surgi Wirtz not here so I still act—" Telegram received, DNA, RG 393, Dept. of the Mo., Telegrams Received. On Oct. 9, Holston telegraphed to USG. "Gen Oglesby is easier   his medical attendants feel sanguine of his recovery—I have scarcely any hope—The Ball is not found, and interferes seriously with the most important functions of life resperation and circulation   his ease is deceptive only the waning of his powers but I hope to have erred." Telegram received, *ibid*. On Oct. 10, Holston telegraphed to Rawlins. "Genl Oglesby case I had re-examined by surgeon Norman Gay this morning   Pulse 120 ~~twenty~~ one hundred & twenty lying down breathing forty in the minute   Great distress—the doctor agrees with my opinion telegraphed yesterday   no reasonable hope of recovery, my personal Estimate founded upon examination of the battl field on the morning of the fifth 5th Gives our dead two hundred fifty to three hundred—Enemies dead I Estimated up-ward of fifteen hundred though many others scattered about did not come under my observation   there are more likely two thousand, wounded soldiers, one thousand wounded traitors fifteen hundred. ours are doing well   the majority of theirs will die   half are dead already   numbers of prisoners last night exclusive of wounded above fifteen hundred   hourly more coming—I am pleased to find that my independent—Estimate agrees closly with that of the military authorities —Gen Rosecrans pushing ahead—~~I~~ can I not soon be relieved of my present irksome condition, acting with all responsibility & no credit—" Telegram received,

ibid. On Oct. 11, Rawlins issued Special Orders No. 218. "Brig General R. J. Oglesby, having been dangerously wounded at the late battle of Corinth, has leave of absence, for the purpose of proceeding to Decatur Illinois, where he will report by letter to these Headquarters, and to the Adjutant General of the Army, Washington, D. C." DS, Oglesby Papers, IHi; DNA, RG 94, District of West Tenn., Special Orders; copies, *ibid.*, RG 393, USG Special Orders; DLC-USG, V, 15, 16, 82, 87. See Silas T. Trowbridge, "Saving a General," *Civil War Times Illustrated*, XI, 4 (July, 1972), 20–25.

On Oct. 2, Rawlins had issued General Orders No. 87 assigning Surgeon Horace R. Wirtz as chief medical director, District of West Tenn. Copies, DLC-USG, V, 12, 13, 14, 95; DNA, RG 393, USG General Orders; (printed) Oglesby Papers, IHi. *O.R.*, I, xvii, part 2, 255. On Oct. 11, Holston telegraphed to Rawlins. "Oct. 5th Rec'd Gen Grants order by Med Director Wirtz to remain here as as acting Medical Director   Just now rec'd ordr from Gen Rosecrans forthwith to proceed to Jackson & report to Gen Grant for orders   What shall I do   I am quite unwell"   Telegram received, DNA, RG 393, Dept. of the Mo., Telegrams Received.

On Nov. 1, 4:30 P.M., USG telegraphed to Maj. Gen. Henry W. Halleck. "I respectfully recommend the promotion of Brig Genl Oglesby." Telegram received, *ibid.*, RG 94, ACP, 0112 CB 1863; *ibid.*, RG 107, Telegrams Collected (Bound); copies, *ibid.*, RG 393, Dept. of the Tenn., Hd. Qrs. Correspondence; DLC-USG, V, 5, 8, 24, 88. *O.R.*, I, lii, part 1, 297. Nominated on Feb. 9, 1863, and confirmed on March 9, Richard J. Oglesby ranked as maj. gen. from Nov. 29, 1862.

To Maj. Gen. Henry W. Halleck

Jackson Tenn
Oct 10th 9 30 P M 1862

MAJ GEN H. W. HALLECK
GEN IN CHIEF.

Light draft Boats can go to Fort Henry, from there there will be no difficulty reaching Clarksville. Will go by Donelson should the Cumberland River be too high to ford.

U. S. GRANT
Maj Genl

Telegram received, DNA, RG 94, Generals' Papers and Books, Telegrams Received by Gen. Halleck; *ibid.*, RG 107, Telegrams Collected (Bound); copies, *ibid.*, RG 393, USG Hd. Qrs. Correspondence; DLC-USG, V, 4, 5, 7, 8, 88. *O.R.*, I, xvii, part 2, 274. On Oct. 9, 1862, Maj. Gen. Henry W. Halleck telegraphed to USG. "Governor Johnson is very desirous that troops be sent to

Clarksville. How far is the Cumberland navigable, and how could troops be sent to Clarksville." ALS (telegram sent), DNA, RG 107, Telegrams Collected (Bound); telegram received, *ibid.*, RG 393, Dept. of the Tenn., Telegrams Received. *O.R.*, I, xvii, part 2, 270. On Oct. 12, Col. William W. Lowe, Fort Henry, telegraphed to USG. "The Cumberland River is not navigable for any kind of Steamboats   Troops had better be sent to this point & marched from here to Clarksville. The distance is about forty five (45) miles"   Telegram received, DNA, RG 393, Dept. of the Mo., Telegrams Received.

To Maj. Gen. William S. Rosecrans

Head quarters dept. of West Tenn.
Jackson Tenn. Octr. 11th 1862
MAJ. GENL. ROSECRANS,
Prisoners will be paroled and sent south of our lines as directed in my previous dispatch to you. Those sent to Benton Barracks were—under orders from Maj. Genl. Halleck—stopped at Columbus and sent to Memphis with same instructions to Maj Genl Sherman as. sentenced in my dispatch to you.
U. S. GRANT
Maj. Genl.

Telegram, copies, Rosecrans Papers, CLU; DNA, RG 393, Army of the Miss., Telegrams Received. Earlier on Oct. 11, 1862, USG telegraphed to Maj. Gen. William S. Rosecrans. "Paroled prisoners should all be sent south of our lines and delivered to some officer of the southern army and a receipt taken. The receipt should be taken on duplicate rolls of prisoners and one rolls sent to Adjt. of the army and the other retained." Copies, *ibid.* On Oct. 11, Rosecrans telegraphed to USG. "We have been paroling the Prisoners & sending them north to a depot for exchange—the wounded are sent to Iuka hospital   this Hospital is regarded within our Lines   We have one of our Surgeons there   I have notified the Confedrate troops that either they must not come there or they must take care of their Sick & wounded [th]emselves—If you wish I will send the Remaining Prisoners as you desire south but would it not be well to let the remainder go with those already sent to Benton Barracks—We hav[e] already burried 1146 Rebels & have 2116 Prisoners besides which I know of 300 more on their way in." Telegram received, *ibid.*, Dept. of the Mo., Telegrams Received; copies, *ibid.*, Army of the Miss., Telegrams Sent; *ibid.*, RG 94, War Records Office, Union Battle Reports. *O.R.*, I, xvii, part 1, 166.

On Oct. 13, Rosecrans telegraphed to USG. "I am informed on what I consider good authority that Paroled Prisoners sent Home are detailed for Provost guard & garrison duty—would it not be well for you to send a flag of truce down to Oxford on the subject   I will correct in the Paroles here after   Please also ask for the exchanges of Maj Cromwell 47th Ill for Maj Thomas Holmes 35th Miss —Maj C is much wanted in the Reg't since the death of Col Thrush"   Telegram received, DNA, RG 393, Dept. of the Mo., Telegrams Received; copy, *ibid.*, Army of the Miss., Telegrams Sent. On Oct. 14, Rosecrans telegraphed to USG. "Another cause for remonstrance with the Confederate authorities is that our Prisoner report that they do not give them food for a Day or two after they are first taken and then a very inadequate and inferior allowance   their attenuated features bear testimony to the fact that they are treated more as criminals than as Prisoners of War"   Telegram received, *ibid.*, Dept. of the Mo., Telegrams Received; copy, *ibid.*, Army of the Miss., Telegrams Sent. *O.R.*, II, iv, 620. On the same day, Rosecrans telegraphed to Maj. John A. Rawlins. "Please ask the Gen whether I shall make those recruiting detail which were ordered by special order one eighty seven (187) Dist Tenn & which have been deferred because we could not stop nor spare the men   The lists are ready   if the Gen wishes will forward them at once"   Telegram received, DNA, RG 393, Dept. of the Mo., Telegrams Received; copy, *ibid.*, Army of the Miss., Telegrams Sent. Also on Oct. 14, Rosecrans telegraphed to USG. "Please order the Pay Masters down here at once while we have a breathing spell   all of us Officers & Men are in want"   Telegram received, *ibid.*, Dept. of the Mo., Telegrams Received; copy, *ibid.*, Army of the Miss., Telegrams Sent. On Oct. 11, Rosecrans had telegraphed to USG. "Please order some paymaster here.   all the reg'ts are to concentrate here to refit & there never will be a better opportunity to pay them—"   Telegrams received (2), *ibid.*, Dept. of the Mo., Telegrams Received; copy (undated), *ibid.*, Army of the Miss., Telegrams Sent. On Oct. 14, Rawlins telegraphed to Rosecrans. "The detailing prisoners as Provost Guard and for Garrison duty— is clearly a violation of the cartel entered into between their Government and the United States   You will send a Flag of Truce—make this violation of the cartel reference and their treatment of our prisoners—Maj. Cromwell of the 47th Ills. Vols. for Maj Thomas Holmes of the 35th Miss. the subject of your communication. If the commanding Officers of Regiments or Detatchments have any assurance that the details for recruiting service can accomplish anything you will order them to proceed   Where they cannot you will return the order revocation. There are no Pay Masters here. Have asked that a sufficient number be ordered here at once." Copy, *ibid.*, Telegrams Received.

On Oct. 14, Maj. Charles T. Larned, chief paymaster, District of Ky., wrote to USG. "I regret very sincerely that in response to your plea for payment of your army, I can only explain why it is impossible to gratify you.—Ex nihilo nihil— The Treasury Department with all its multiplication of Labor and ingenuity, is unable to create money ripidly enough to keep the machinery of this District running. I have labored at Washington in person and by proxy, & have accumulated letter upon letter & telegram upon telegram arguing the urgent need of funds & imploring their instant transmission:—yet the results of many weeks of such efforts were instantly absorbed in the recent partial payment of Genl. Buell's army, & I am now bankrupt, the latest telegram from Washington, informing me that 'it is impossible to say when more money can be forwarded—'   As the troops of Gen. Buell, unpaid since April 30th, claim a proper preference over your own, who have been a shorter time without pay, than any others in the District, you will appreciate the reasons why I can give you no assurances whatever as to an early settlement with your command." Copy, *ibid.*, Letters Received. On Oct. 21, Rawlins endorsed this letter. "Respectfully referred to Maj Gen W. S. Rosecrans, for his information." ES, *ibid.*

To Maj. Gen. William S. Rosecrans

Head quarters dept. of West Tenn.
Jackson Tenn. Octr. 11th 186[2]

Maj. Genl. Rosecrans.

Order McPherson to report to me on his arrival at Corinth. I want to give him an important command at Bolivar.

Send me the names of such officers as you think could be promoted in the order of preference. I want all directed to send on such a list.

U. S. Grant.
Maj. Genl.

Telegram, copies, Rosecrans Papers, CLU; DNA, RG 393, Army of the Miss., Telegrams Received. On Oct. 12, 1862, Maj. Gen. William S. Rosecrans telegraphed to Maj. John A. Rawlins. "Your orders in reference to M McPherson & his troops duly rec'd and will carried into effect on the arrival of Gen McPherson & his command" Telegram received (undated), *ibid.*, Dept. of the Mo., Telegrams Received; copy, *ibid.*, Army of the Miss., Telegrams Sent. *O.R.*, I, xvii, part 2, 275.

On Oct. 11, Rawlins issued Special Orders No. 218. "Major Gen. McPherson, immediately upon reaching Corinth, will turn over his command to Col. Lawler and report himself in person to these Head Quarters." Copies, DLC-USG, V, 15, 16, 82, 87; DNA, RG 393, USG Special Orders. *O.R.*, I, xvii, part 2, 275. On Oct. 14, Rawlins issued Special Orders No. 221. "Maj Genl J B. McPherson is hereby assigned to the Command of the U. S. Forces at Bolivar Tenn and will report to Maj Genl Hurlbut Comdg 2nd Div Disct West Tenn." DS, DNA, RG 94, District of West Tenn., Special Orders; copies, *ibid.*, RG 393, USG Special Orders; DLC-USG, V, 15, 16, 82, 87. *O.R.*, I, xvii, part 2, 277.

On Oct. 11, Brig. Gen. Leonard F. Ross, Bolivar, telegraphed to USG. "On my return last evening I rec'd from the secc'y of war a leave of absence for twenty (20) days when will it suit you to have me leave—" Telegram received, DNA, RG 393, Dept. of the Mo., Telegrams Received. On Oct. 14, Ross telegraphed to USG. "Gen McPherson has not yet arrived—do you wish me to wait for Him I am anxious to leave as early as you think advisable—having some business in Jackson would like to go that far this P. M. if you have no objections" Telegram received, *ibid.* Rawlins drafted a reply at the foot of this telegram. "Will let you know this afternoon" ADfS, *ibid.*

To Maj. Gen. William S. Rosecrans

Head quarters ~~Army of the Miss.~~
Jackson Tenn. Oct. 11th 1862

MAJ. GENL. ROSECRANS.

On the return of troops to Corinth send Lawler and his two Regts. and Stevens[1] and his two regiments back here to join their old brigades.

The 1st Kansas may be retained—attaching it to the weakest Brigade in McKean's Division. I am now promised a large force of new troops   They will mostly go to Memphis.

U. S. GRANT
Maj. Genl.

Telegram, copy, DNA, RG 393, Army of the Miss., Telegrams Received. Also on Oct. 11, 1862, USG sent two additional telegrams to Maj. Gen. William S. Rosecrans. "Get in reports of the Battle of Iuka as soon as possible— I want to make out my report. Also those of Corinth Battle." Copies, *ibid.*; Rosecrans Papers, CLU. "Permit the body of Captain Ward to be transported over the road to Columbus." Copy, DNA, RG 393, Army of the Miss., Telegrams Received. On Oct. 8, W. W. Huntington, Columbus, Ky., had telegraphed to Maj. John A. Rawlins. "Packard with chettands Boy and myself ~~are~~ are here and cant get any further   Can you help us" Telegram received, *ibid.*, Dept. of the Mo., Telegrams Received. On the same day, Rawlins telegraphed to Brig. Gen. Grenville M. Dodge. "How will Permit messr Packard Huntington & Chetlains son & also mr alva Ward with coffin for Capt Ward Deceased but inform him that Capt Wards remains will have to be interred at Corinth for the present as the remains of Officers and soldiers are prohibited by orders from passing over the rail road from Corinth" Telegram received, *ibid.*

1. John D. Stevenson, born in Staunton, Va., in 1821, attended the College of South Carolina, practiced law in Mo., then served as capt., Mo. Mounted Vols., in the Mexican War. After a career as a lawyer-politician in St. Louis, Stevenson was commissioned col., 7th Mo., on June 1, 1861. His report as brigade commander of the pursuit after the battle of Corinth is in *O.R.*, I, xvii, part 1, 370–72.

To Maj. Gen. William S. Rosecrans

Head quarters Dist of West Tenn.
Jackson Tenn. October 13th 1862

Maj. Genl. Rosecrans

We must ascertain if Johnson is in our front and if so it will become necessary to abandon Corinth and concentrate the whole force at Bolivar. We will see from his move what to do ourselves and will give him a tremendous thrashing some place.

Substance of your dispatches has been sent Genl. Sherman.

U. S. Grant.
Maj. Genl.

Telegram, copy, DNA, RG 393, Army of the Miss., Telegrams Received. On Oct. 13, 1862, Maj. Gen. William S. Rosecrans telegraphed to USG. "Gen McPherson arrived last night   no signs of an Enemy   pushed Cavalry 17 miles on the Oxford Road   nothing but stragglers.—Enemy have gone to Oxford except a few Regiments to Tupelo   A Rumor is going currency among the Secesh that Johnson with forty thousand (40 000) men from Virginia has arrived at Oxford—it must receive prompt attention   Pocahontas is a Key which ought to be occupied in case the Rebels dispose a portion of their Virginia forces to push in here   it would be a strong move   tell Sherman to put Spies in ~~in~~ motion   I will do the same to find out all I can"   Telegram received, *ibid.*, Dept. of the Mo., Telegrams Received; copy, *ibid.*, Army of the Miss., Telegrams Sent. *O.R.*, I, xvii, part 2, 276.

Also on Oct. 13, USG telegraphed to Maj. Gen. Henry W. Halleck. "Genl Rosecrans reports a rumor that Johnson with forty thousand (40 000) men have arrived at Oxford   Should reports prove true I will concentrate my forces at Bolivar & be prepared to meet him—"   Telegram received, DNA, RG 94, Generals' Papers and Books, Telegrams Received by Gen. Halleck; *ibid.*, RG 107, Telegrams Collected (Unbound); copies, *ibid.*, Telegrams Received in Cipher; *ibid.* (dated Oct. 12), RG 393, USG Hd. Qrs. Correspondence; DLC-USG, V, 4, 5, 7, 8, 88. Dated Oct. 13 in *O.R.*, I, xvii, part 2, 276. C. S. A. Gen. Joseph E. Johnston was not assigned to command in the West until Nov. 24. *Ibid.*, pp. 757–58.

On Oct. 14, Rosecrans telegraphed to USG. "The following is from a most reliable source.—Much conversation with men from central Albama & Mississippi Satisfiy me that forage & Provisions are not to be had via Tuscoolosa   letters from there say flour is forty (40) Dollars per Bbl bacon forty (40) cts per pound coffee & sugar not to be had   Corn crop short and in parts none—Breckenridge with Seven thousand (7000) men at Chattanooga—Price was to have joined Bragg   Much discontent with Van Dorn—a General depression in regard to the safety of Bragg.—"   Telegram received, DNA, RG 393, Dept. of the Mo., Telegrams Received; copy, *ibid.*, Army of the Miss., Telegrams Sent.

To Brig. Gen. Grenville M. Dodge

BY TELEGRAPH FROM Jackson [*Oct. 15*] *1862*

To GEN DODGE

If practicable send troops from Columbus & paducah to occupy Caseyville for a few days and drive out the rebels. Inform yourself well however ~~to~~ of their probable strength before going Caseyville not being in this military Dist it is not desirable that troops sent there should remain more than a few days

U S GRANT
Maj Genl

Telegram received, DNA, RG 393, Dept. of the Mo., Telegrams Received. On Oct. 15, 1862, Brig. Gen. Grenville M. Dodge telegraphed to USG. "Genl Tuttle telegraphs the following—Steam Boat Hazel Dell just arrived from Evansville was stopped seven (7) hours at Caseyville by Large force of Guerrillas— Mails niggers goods taken off of her and several officers & soldiers taken prisoners" Telegram received, *ibid*. On Oct. 16, Dodge telegraphed to Maj. John A. Rawlins. "A force from Evansville In'd left Caseyville yesterday morning in pursuit of the Guerrillas that captured the Boat.   another gang took a boat 5 miles above Smithland yesterday. Released it after taking what they wanted   I have sent Gun Boat & a force after them—" Telegram received, *ibid*. On the same day, Dodge again telegraphed to Rawlins. "The Tug boat Watts reports that he left Caseyville yesterday morning. The mail taken from the Hazel Dell has been recovered. Johnson & his forces left Tuesday at Ten (10) A. M. our forces in pursuit.   before leaving he stopped the Steamer Campbell with 200 Infantry to relieve In'd Troops at Smithland   was stopped by Johnson & ordered to surrender   the Capt refused & landed his troops on Ill Shore at Battery rock. The Steamer Exchange with 600 Infantry and 2 Guns soon arrived from Evansville & landed above the town. They are the troops now in pursuit" Telegram received, *ibid*.

To Brig. Gen. Lorenzo Thomas

Head Qrs Disct of West Tenn
Jackson Tenn, Oct 16, 1862

ADJT GENL OF THE ARMY
WASHINGTON D. C.
GENL

Enclosed herewith I send you a few replies in answer to a circular calling for report of success of recruiting parties sent from this command in compliance to Genl Orders No 36 from Head Qrs of the Department of the Miss.[1] It is not in my power to compell the return of these parties but as they seem to be rendering no service to the Government I would recommend that that they be ordered to join their Regiments or companies without delay.

Very Respcty
Your Obt Sevt
U. S. GRANT
Maj Genl

Copies, DLC-USG, V, 4, 5, 7, 8, 88; DNA, RG 393, USG Hd. Qrs. Correspondence. On Oct. 10, 1862, USG endorsed a letter. "Order these recruiting officers back to their regiments." AES, *ibid.*, District of West Tenn., 4th Division, Letters Received. Written on a letter of Sept. 26 from Lt. Col. Charles M. Ferrell, 29th Ill., Jackson, Tenn., requesting the return of two officers and ten men from recruiting duty since only thirty-six recruits had been reported and none had yet arrived. LS, *ibid.* On the same day, USG endorsed another letter. "Order the return of these officers & men" AES, *ibid.*, 16th Army Corps, Miscellaneous Papers. Written on a letter of Sept. 26 from Col. Addison S. Norton, 17th Ill., Bolivar, Tenn., requesting the return of men from his regt. sent on recruiting service. ALS, *ibid.*

On Oct. 30, Col. Albert L. Lee, 7th Kan. Cav., Corinth, telegraphed to Maj. John A. Rawlins. "Will you inform me if Gen Grant has given the permission requested for granting officers and men to proceed on recruiting service for 7th Kansas Vols Inf'y   the Papers were sent some days ago—if not will you request him to act upon it & greatly oblige" Telegram received, *ibid.*, Dept. of the Tenn., Telegrams Received. On the same day, USG telegraphed to Lee. "Recruiting details made out and sent to Gen'l Hamilton yesterday" Copies, DLC-USG, V, 18, 30; DNA, RG 393, Dept. of the Tenn., Letters Sent.

1. General Orders No. 36, Dept. of the Miss., June 23, established procedures for recruiting service, which included a stipulation that not more than two

commissioned officers and four enlisted men from each regt. be detailed. Copy (printed), *ibid.*, RG 94, Dept. of the Miss., General Orders.

To Maj. Gen. William T. Sherman

Head Quarters, Dist. of W. Ten
Jackson Oct. 16th 1862

MAJ. GEN. W. T. SHERMAN
COMD.G MEMPHIS TEN.
GEN.

Permit me to introduce to you Mr. E. Parkman, one of the few Union citizens of this place. Mr. Parkman goes to Memphis on private business of his own and is entitled to all the curticies extended to citizens of the revolted states.

Very Truly yours
U. S. GRANT
Maj. Gen.

ALS, DLC-William T. Sherman.

To Col. Jesse Hildebrand

Head Quarters Dist of West Tenn
Jackson Oct 16th 1862

COL HILDEBRAND
COMD.G ALTON ILL
COL,

There is confined at Alton I understand one Nimrod P Graham whos residences is near Pocahontas Tennessee. Mr Graham has been confined for no serious offence and therefore I would recommend his discharge on takeing the usual oath. The Young man Gerome Hill who I once before wrote to have discharged, can now be discharged on the same condition's or declining that he may be paroled to go South of our lines by the way of Memphis. He is said to be in delicate health without much prospect of Liveing many months and his people are most excellent Union Citizens which is an other reason for this leniency

Respectfully &c
U. S GRANT
Maj. Gen.

Copy, DNA, RG 249, Letters Received. See letter to Col. Jesse Hildebrand, Oct. 3, 1862.

To Mary Grant

Jackson Ten.
October 16th 1862

DEAR SISTER,

I received your letter by due course of mail and expected before this to have answered one of your questions in the shape of an official report. That is the part where you ask me the part I played at the battle of Iuka. When the reports of subalterns come in I will make my report which no doubt will be published and will be a full answer to your question.[1] I had no more to do with troops under Gen. Ord than I had with those under Rosecrans but gave the orders to both. The plan was admirably laid for catching Price and his whole Army but owing to the nature of the ground, direction of the wind and Gen. Rosecrans having been so far behind where he was expected to be on the morning before the attack it failed. In the late battles we have gained such a moral advantage over them however with Van Dorn and Lovell added that I do not know but it may have all been for the better.

I have written to Julia to come down here and spend a short time. It will probably be but a short time that she can stay but so long as I remain here this will be a pleasant place for her.—If the children have not already been sent to Covington I told her to bring them with her. The last letter I received she said that she was about sending them to Covington.

I believe you have now got it all quiet on the Ohio!² I hope it will soon be so every place els. It does look to me that we now have such an advantage over the rebels that there should be but little more hard fighting.

Give my love to all at home. Write often and without expecting eith[er] very prompt or very long replies.

Ulys.

ALS, PPRF.

1. See letter to Col. John C. Kelton, Oct. 22, 1862.
2. On Sept. 15, 1862, C. S. A. Lt. Gen. Edmund Kirby Smith led his troops to the outskirts of Covington, Ky., but soon withdrew, having accomplished his diversionary purpose.

To Maj. Gen. Henry W. Halleck

Jackson Tenn
Oct 17th 8 15 P. M. [*1862*]

Maj Gen H. W. Halleck
Gen in Chief.

My effective force is 48.500 exclusive of extra duty men located as follows 4.800 in Kentucky & Illinois—7.000 in Memphis—19.200 from Union city south besides Corinth forces —Latter 17.500.

Another attack soon is inevitable. Reinforcements necessary to keep up the confidence of our men as well as to give sufficient strength to meet the Enemy. The Enemy are largely reinforced

U. S. Grant

Telegram received, DNA, RG 94, Generals' Papers and Books, Telegrams Received by Gen. Halleck; *ibid.*, RG 107, Telegrams Collected (Bound); copies, *ibid.*, Telegrams Received in Cipher; *ibid.*, RG 393, USG Hd. Qrs. Correspondence; DLC-USG, V, 4, 5, 7, 8, 88. *O.R.*, I, xvii, part 2, 279. On Oct. 17, 1862, Maj. Gen. Henry W. Halleck telegraphed to USG. "What is the condition of affairs in your Dept? Am anxious to know, as Gov. Johnson & Genl Curtis are asking for more troops." ALS (telegram sent), DNA, RG 107, Telegrams Collected (Bound); telegram received, *ibid.*, RG 393, Dept. of the Tenn., Telegrams Received. *O.R.*, I, xvii, part 2, 279.

To Maj. Gen. William S. Rosecrans

Head quarters Dept. West Tenn
Jackson Tenn. Oct. 18th 1862

MAJ. GENL. ROSECRANS

If you deem the man reliable to send south send him by all means. We want to get all the information possible of the present strength and future plans of the enemy.

Send all the convalescents of the 1st and 4th Divisions to Louisville but try to have them go in a body as near as possible. Do not have them go day by day.

U. S. GRANT
Maj. Genl.

Telegram, copy, DNA, RG 393, Army of the Miss., Telegrams Received. On Oct. 18, 1862, Maj. Gen. William S. Rosecrans telegraphed to USG. "I can send a man to Prices head Quarters who will give him any information we may desire and will bring us back all He can learn—What would you like to have done with him—I sent the Flag of truce yesterday by Col Ducat Capt Lyford & a Doctor & forty (40) men Will send you copy of my letter—Was sick yesterday but better today" Telegram received, *ibid.*, Dept. of the Mo., Telegrams Received; copy, *ibid.*, Army of the Miss., Telegrams Sent. On the same day, Rosecrans telegraphed to USG. "There are large numbers of convalesents & others stragglers from the 1st & 4th Div of this Army now here at Jackson: & Columbus shall I send them on to Louisville or not" Telegram received, *ibid.*, Dept. of the Mo., Telegrams Received; copy, *ibid.*, Army of the Miss., Telegrams Sent.

On Oct. 17, Absalom H. Markland, Post Office Dept. agent, Cairo, telegraphed to USG. "Pleas cause to be detailed some reliable man for post master at Corinth in place of one Truesdale who I understand is neither an officer nor private of the Army—" Telegram received, *ibid.*, Dept. of the Mo., Telegrams Received. On Oct. 20, Markland telegraphed to USG. "Can you recommend a thoroughly reliable & competent citizen of Jackson for Post Master at that Point it is desirable to open the office regularly" Telegram received, *ibid.*

On Oct. 18, USG telegraphed to Rosecrans. "Send Truesdale up here   I want to see him." Copy, *ibid.*, Army of the Miss., Telegrams Received. On the same day, Rosecrans telegraphed to USG. "He will come up in the morning.— I have ordered the works for the defense of Corinth to be completed at once and will put six thousand (6.000) Men at work on Monday   I have a great mind to come up and see you in the Moring   I want to tell you about some promations which ought to be made and other things   I will not send up official reccomendations until I get in full reports   They are coming in—Any news from McPhersons Front"   Telegram received, *ibid.*, Dept. of the Mo., Telegrams Received; copy, *ibid.*, Army of the Miss., Telegrams Sent. Also on Oct. 18, USG telegraphed to Rosecrans. "Come up if you can leave." Copy, *ibid.*, Telegrams Received. On the same day, Rosecrans telegraphed to USG. "The Dr thinks I had better keep my today as I have had an attack of Diarrhea   I will therefore not be up today   Col Moore Col Dubois & Col Crocker ought to be made Brigadiers   some changes are demanded imperitively by the interests of the service   of these I will speak or write soon   a man leaves this morning for the South"   Telegram received (dated Oct. 19), *ibid.*, Dept. of the Mo., Telegrams Received; copy (dated Oct. 18), *ibid.*, Army of the Miss., Telegrams Sent.

To Brig. Gen. Grenville M. Dodge

By TELEGRAPH FROM Jackson [*Oct.*] 18 *1862*

To GEN DODGE

If as I have reason to hope four 4 more Regiments should be sent from the north to this District retain the first to relieve the 76[1] whose time is now expirring the 2d to relieve the 62 Head quarters at Kenton[2] & forward the balance here.   the 62d will in that case report here for further Directions as to destination

U S GRANT
Maj Genl

Telegram received, DNA, RG 393, Dept. of the Mo., Telegrams Received. On Oct. 19, 1862, USG telegraphed to Brig. Gen. Grenville M. Dodge. "Relieve the 3 months Regiments with the new one just arrived   Telegraph the Adjt Genl of Ill. to know where he will have this Regt sent be mustered & if they will take their arms accoutrements & camp equipage with them." Telegram received, *ibid.* On Oct. 25, USG telegraphed to Dodge. "Should reinforcements arrive, the first Regiment will be sent to relieve Col. True at Kenton. The second will be retained at Columbus, and the regiment now here sent to Corinth. After that all that arrive will come here." Copies, DLC-USG, V, 18, 30; DNA, RG 393, Dept. of the Tenn., Letters Sent.

1. The 71st Ill. was meant. On Oct. 20, Maj. John A. Rawlins telegraphed to Dodge. "the arms camp & garrison equipage of the 71st Ills Regt to be mustered out of service and who are to be releived by the 109th will be turned over to the 109th   No attention will be paid to any answer you may receive from The adjt Genl of the state of Illinois in reply to that part of the communication you was directed to send him in reference to the arms & accoutrements of said 71st Ills" Telegram received, *ibid.*, Dept. of the Mo., Telegrams Received.

2. Kenton, Tenn., on the Mobile and Ohio Railroad, approximately midway between Trenton and Union City.

To Maj. Gen. Henry W. Halleck

Jackson Tenn [*Oct.*] 19 [*1862*]

Maj Gen Halleck.

We have Faulkner three of his officers & twelve men   how shall they be treated   they claim to be regulars in the Army & entitled to Exchange   I think the officers at least should be held

U S Grant

M. G.

Telegram received, DNA, RG 94, Generals' Papers and Books, Telegrams Received by Gen. Halleck; *ibid.*, RG 107, Telegrams Collected (Bound); copies, *ibid.*, RG 393, USG Hd. Qrs. Correspondence; DLC-USG, V, 4, 5, 7, 8, 88. *O.R.*, I, xvii, part 2, 281. On Oct. 21, 1862, Maj. Gen. Henry W. Halleck telegraphed to USG. "I know nothing of Faulkner and his officers & therefore can give no special directions. To what point do you wish new troops to be sent, Columbus or Memphis?" ALS (telegram sent), DNA, RG 107, Telegrams Collected (Bound); copies, *ibid.*, RG 108, Telegrams Sent; *ibid.*, RG 393, USG Hd. Qrs. Correspondence; DLC-USG, V, 4, 5, 7, 8, 88. *O.R.*, I, xvii, part 2, 283. On Oct. 21, USG telegraphed to Halleck. "I want first five Regts sent to Columbus not to Memphis" Telegram received, DNA, RG 94, Generals' Papers and Books, Telegrams Received by Gen. Halleck; *ibid.*, RG 107, Telegrams Collected (Bound); copies, *ibid.*, RG 393, USG Hd. Qrs. Correspondence; DLC-USG, V, 4, 5, 7, 8, 88.

On Oct. 18, Brig. Gen. Grenville M. Dodge, Columbus, Ky., telegraphed to Maj. John A. Rawlins. "Cox Faulkner and three hundred (300) Rebel Cavalry attacked Island 10 yesterday at Daylight   our forces whipped the Enemy taking Col Faulkner Capt R M Merriweather Capt H B Blooeman Adj't L H Johnson & twelve (12) enlisted men prisoners   the Enemies loss in killed & wounded is severe   our loss three (3) killed   Maj McNeal with Reinforcements from New Madrid has crossed Reel Foot Lake below the Obion and thinks He will cut off their retreat" Telegram received, DNA, RG 393, Dept. of the Mo., Telegrams Received; copy, *ibid.*, RG 94, War Records Office, Union Battle Reports. *O.R.*,

I, xvii, part 1, 460. The report of Maj. Quincy McNeil, 2nd Ill. Cav., on this skirmish is *ibid.*, pp. 460–61.

On Oct. 19, Maj. Gen. Stephen A. Hurlbut, Jackson, telegraphed to USG. "Part of the 4th Ill's Cavalry and Fosters company are on an expedition after the fragment of Faulkners band   as soon as they return they will be sent forward—" Telegram received, DNA, RG 393, Dept. of the Tenn., Telegrams Received. On Oct. 19, Dodge telegraphed to Rawlins. "Shall I send Col Faulkner & the officers & men taken with Him to Memphis   they claim to be regular confederate officers & soldiers—" Telegram received, *ibid.*, Dept. of the Mo., Telegrams Received. On Oct. 21, USG telegraphed to Dodge. "I have heard nothing from Gen Halleck in reply to my enquiry as to the disposition to be made of Faulkner & his men. You may send them under escort to Alton" Telegram received, *ibid.*

On Nov. 4, Col. W. W. Faulkner, Alton, wrote to USG. "I cant understand why it is myself & men are kept in close confinement here, for so long a time when others are being paroled or exchanged; We are sent here as prisoners of War subject to the first exchange of prisoners, but there is no telling when that exchange will take place unless hasened by your orders. I should like to get the matter arranged as soon as possible either sent to Vicksburg, or if there is no exchange to be effected very soon if you will order me to Jackson to report to you then I can arrainge it satisfactorily either by going under a flag of Truce from Bolivar or any other way you direct.   if you will give this your earliest attention, you will very greatly oblige" ALS, *ibid.*, Dept. of the Tenn., Telegrams Received. On Nov. 13, Faulkner again wrote to USG complaining that he was held as a political prisoner though properly in the C. S. army and eligible for parole and exchange. *Ibid.*, Register of Letters Received; DLC-USG, V, 21. See letter to Lt. Gen. John C. Pemberton, Dec. 15, 1862. Faulkner should not be confused with Col. William C. Falkner, grandfather of novelist William Faulkner. See Andrew Brown, "The First Mississippi Partisan Rangers, C. S. A.," *Civil War History*, I, 4 (Dec., 1955), 388.

To Maj. Gen. William S. Rosecrans

Head quarters Dept. of the West Tenn.
Jackson Tenn. October 19th 1862

Maj Genl Rosecrans.

Order all captured and surplus arms or accoutrements to this place. Also send Lyford here. I want his services for a few days.

U. S. Grant
Maj Genl.

Telegram, copy, DNA, RG 393, Army of the Miss., Telegrams Received. On Oct. 19, 1862, Maj. Gen. William S. Rosecrans telegraphed to USG. "Lyford has gone with the Flag of truce—I will send up the Arms as fast as possible—am better" Telegram received, *ibid.*, Dept. of the Mo., Telegrams Received; copy, *ibid.*, Army of the Miss., Telegrams Sent. On the same day, Maj. Gen. James B. McPherson, Bolivar, Tenn., telegraphed twice to USG. "Orders were given yesterday morning to the ordnance officer here to have all the captured and surplus arms picked up and sent to Jackson" "News from the front indicate all quiet no force reported farther north than Davis Mills six (6) miles below Grand Junction where a cavalry force Armstrong it is supposed to be A brigade of Infantry at Salem & a large force concentrating at Holly Springs I can send four hundred cavalry in the direction of Brownsville they had better cross" Telegrams received, *ibid.*, Dept. of the Mo., Telegrams Received.

On Oct. 21, Rosecrans telegraphed to USG. "I send you the following from Col Dubois at Rienzi for what it shows—The report is current through the Jumpertown & Ripley coutry that Genl Johnston has arrived at Holly Springs & taken command large reinforcements from albama conscripts & exchanged prisoners expected to have arrived some people reported that an a advance had been made from Holly Springs the commecment of another move on Corinth—Holly Springs is being intrenched—We are pushing our works—Flag out four days & have not returned—Cant you send capt Prime some three hundred (300) contrabands by next train or soon they are much wanted—" Telegram received, *ibid.*; copy, *ibid.*, Army of the Miss., Telegrams Sent. On the same day, Rosecrans telegraphed to Maj. John A. Rawlins. "I have the pleasure to report for the information of Maj Gen Comdg the Dept the safe return of our Flag of truce from the Head Quarters of Maj Gen Van Dorn at Holly Springs—No answer could be obtained because Gen Van Dorn has been relieved by Gen Pemberton to whose Head Quarters at Jackson Miss the Dispatch was sent—Van wants his Aid de Camp from exchanged for a Capt sent in on Parole I have sent the letter of Van Dorn to you by mail Will forward a written report of bearer of Flag so soon as it can be procured" Telegram received, *ibid.*, Dept. of the Mo., Telegrams Received; copy, *ibid.*, Army of the Miss., Telegrams Sent.

General Orders No. 91

———

Head Quarters Dist. of West Tenn.
Jackson, Tenn. Oct. 21st 1862.

GENERAL ORDERS No. 91.

The Commanders of the several Divisions of this Military District will regulate and enforce trade within their respective Divisions in strict conformity to the Regulations of the Treasury Department concerning commercial intercourse with insurrectionary States or sections, dated August 28. 1862., and General Orders No. 119, A. G. O. War Department, respecting the same.

All permits given by them, conforming to said Trade Regulations and Orders will be valid, without approval at these Head Quarters.

Permits for articles in packages for the use of officers and persons connected with the Army, and not for sale, may be given by Post commanders. In such cases, however, a suitable officer will be designated to receive such packages and see that they are delivered to no one but the party obtaining the permit, and that they contain nothing but what is authorized. Post commanders will be held strictly responsible for a faithful compliance with the regulations and orders referred to in the issuing of these permits:

By Command of Maj. Genl. U. S. Grant
JNO. A. RAWLINS
Asst Adj't Genl.

Copies, DLC-USG, V, 12, 13, 14, 95; DNA, RG 393, USG General Orders; *ibid.*, RG 366, 2nd Special Agency, Book Records; (printed) Oglesby Papers, IHi. A collection of documents concerning trade in military districts furnished by Secretary of War Edwin M. Stanton to the Committee on the Conduct of the War on Jan. 29, 1863, includes those mentioned in USG's orders. HRC 37-3-108, III, *557–620*. See *ibid.*, p. 613.

To Maj. Gen. Henry W. Halleck

Jackson Tenn [*Oct.*] 21. [*1862*]

MAJ GEN HENRY W. HALLECK
GENL IN CHF U S A
GENERAL

I respectfully recommended promotion for the following officers for meritorious services & Qualifications for their advancement

Brig Gen C. S. Hamilton, Col C C Marsh 20th Ills, Col M M Crocker 13th Iowa Col J A Mowrie 11th Mo. Col M D Leggett 78th Ohio Col John D. Stevenson 7th Mo & Col Jno E. Smith 45th Illinois.

U S GRANT M G

Telegram received, DNA, RG 107, Telegrams Collected (Bound); *ibid.*, RG 94, ACP, G402 CB 1863; copies, *ibid.*, RG 393, USG Hd. Qrs. Correspondence; DLC-USG, V, 4, 5, 7, 8, 88. *O.R.*, I, lii, part 1, 293. Charles S. Hamilton was confirmed on March 9, 1863, to rank as maj. gen. from Sept. 19, 1862. Marcellus M. Crocker, Mortimer D. Leggett, C. Carroll Marsh, Joseph A. Mower, John E. Smith, and John D. Stevenson were all nominated as brig. gen. to rank from Nov. 29; all were eventually confirmed except Marsh. On Sept. 25, the officers of the 78th Ohio prepared a petition to President Abraham Lincoln for the promotion of Leggett, later favorably endorsed by Brig. Gen. Leonard F. Ross, Brig. Gen. John A. Logan, and Maj. Gen. Edward O. C. Ord. On Oct. 1, USG endorsed the petition. "I can fully endor[se] Col. Leggett as eminantly qualified for the promotion asked. He has served under my command since the battle of Fort Donelson and I can answer knowingly for him being one of my ablest commanders." AES, DNA, RG 94, 364 ACP 1882.

To Col. John C. Kelton

Head Quarters, Dist. of W. Ten.
Jackson, Oct. 21st 1862.

Col. J. C. Kelton
Washington D. C.
Col.

I am just in receipt of your letter of the 16th inst. calling my attention to a violation of Gen. Order No 114 in ordering Col. Dickey and Capt. Reynolds to Washington, D. C.

Capt. Reynolds was a case when it was of high pecuniary interest to the Government that he should go to Washington and New York Cities and the other I looked upon also as of special interest to the service.

I acknowledge however that I did wrong in sending them without proper authority, or authority properly obtained, and can only say in extenuation that I was ~~only~~ looking alone to the good of the service.

Very respectfully
your obt. svt.
U. S. Grant
Maj. Gen.

ALS, IHi. On Oct. 16, 1862, Col. John C. Kelton wrote to USG. "The General-in-chief has directed me to call your attention to a violation of a General order of the War Dept No 114, which has occurred at your Head Quarters, in ordering Col. Dickey, Chief of Cavalry, on your staff, and Capt Reynolds A. Q. Mr. to this city." ALS, DNA, RG 108, Letters Sent by Gen. Halleck (Press).

On Sept. 27, USG, Columbus, Ky., had telegraphed to Maj. John A. Rawlins. "Order Col Dickey to Washington to procure arms for our cavalry   the Col. will be in Jackson today and can give you the ditails of instructions he should have—I will not probably be down for two days"   Copies, DLC-USG, V, 1, 2; DNA, RG 393, USG Letters Sent. On Sept. 28, Rawlins issued Special Orders No. 205 embodying these instructions. DS, *ibid.*, RG 94, District of West Tenn., Special Orders; copies, *ibid.*, RG 393, USG Special Orders; DLC-USG, V, 15, 16, 82, 87.

On Oct. 18, Brig. Gen. James W. Ripley, chief of ordnance, wrote to USG. "I have to acknowledge your Requisition for 2750 Cavalry Carbines and accoutrements, for various Regiments of your command, and to inform you of the measures which have been taken to supply the articles called for: to which have been added 200 cartridges per gun. Orders have been given to the under named officers to issue to 'Col T. Lyle Dickey, Chief of Cavalry Dist of West Tennessee, Via Columbus, Ky.' ... As all the Sharp's Carbines ordered to be issued are not on hand, the officer who is to issue those from Washington Arsenal, has been instructed to make each issue in the order, in which they are stated above and all the officers have been directed to make the issues as soon as possible and to send the stores by fast transportation. I regret that it was not possible to furnish all Sharp's Carbines, but the Burnside & the Smith Carbines which have been in part substituted are reliable cavalry arms. Be pleased to cause proper directions to be given to the transportation agents at Columbus so that the arms may reach the troops for which they are intended, without delay." LS, DNA, RG 393, District of West Tenn., Letters Received. See following telegram.

On Oct. 8, Rawlins issued Special Orders No. 215. "Capt. C. A. Reynolds, chief Quartermaster, Dist of West. Tenn. will proceed to Washington City without delay for the purpose of procuring funds for this District: He will then proceed to New York City and collect certain drafts, and deposit the funds with the Assistant Treasurer in New York. Immediately on completion of the said business, Capt C. A. Reynolds will report himself in person to these Headquarters" DS, DNA, RG 94, District of West Tenn., Special Orders; copies, *ibid.*, RG 393, USG Special Orders; DLC-USG, V, 15, 16, 82, 87.

To Maj. Gen. William S. Rosecrans

Headquarters Dept. of West Tenn
Jackson Tenn. Oct. 21st [*1862*]

Maj Genl. [*Rosecrans*]

Your remarkably telegram is just recd. If the troops commanded by you are not a part of my command what troops are?

The Eastern Dist. is the same to me and I have no partiality for any portion of it, over any other portion. That Col. Dickey is the Senior Cav. officer in the whole district or department as I understand by telegraph he now is and as such I sent him to Washington to see if he could do by his personal presence what I had failed to do by corrispondence. All the arms obtained by Col. Dickey will be distributed over my command where most needed. Genl, I am afraid from many of your dispatches that you regard your command giving privileges held by others commanding geographical divisions this is a mistake.

U. S. Grant
Maj Genl

Telegram, copy, DNA, RG 393, Army of the Miss., Telegrams Received.
Earlier on Oct. 21, 1862, USG had telegraphed to Maj. Gen. William S. Rosecrans. "Genl, are you in receipt of or have you any rifles for cavalry on the way for use of troops at Corinth. If so how many? I remember hearing you say something on the subject and want to know so as to know how to distribute when arrive." Copy, *ibid.* On the same day, Rosecrans telegraphed to USG. "The ass't secc'y of War in reply to an urgent Telegraph for cavalry arms which I sent to Mr Stanton sends a list (27 00) to be sent to Col Dickey Chief of Cavalry for various detachments of Cavalry of your command but not one for the four (4) Reg'ts which have been fighting on your front—I appeal to you for justice towards these men they if any should have arms—Two thousand (2 000) pistols & fifteen hundred (1500) carbines are required to arm them properly—" Telegram received, *ibid.*, Dept. of the Mo., Telegrams Received; copy, *ibid.*, Army of the Miss., Telegrams Sent.
On Oct. 21, Rosecrans again telegraphed to USG. "Your reply to my dispatch about cavalry arms just rec'd. I cannot say what the wires conveyed but my dispatch was written to say that Mr Watson supt secy of war telegraphed that arms for cavalry have been shipped Col Dickey for certain Regts and companies naming them to the number of 2700 two thousand seven hundred.—Not one (1) being for the four 4 Regts serving under my command—and as they are as much yours as the others and have been on the front & fighting the enemy in force nearly all summer I think they ought to be the first served not the last & I asked you to do them Justice could I have done less & without direlection of duty—I am amazed at the tenor of your dispatch—You have had no truer friend no more loyal subordinate under your command then myself—Your dispatch does me the grossest injustice I now say to you if you have any suspicions at at varience with this declaration or if my position towards you is to receive a share of coloring different from this—either from the influences—the suspicions or jealousies of mischief makers winesellers & mouse catching ~~politictions~~ politicians or from any other cause I ask you to tell me so frankly & at once as a favor to myself & the service—" Telegram received, *ibid.*, Dept. of the Mo., Telegrams Received; copy, *ibid.*, Army of the Miss., Telegrams Sent. On the same day, Rosecrans

again telegraphed to USG. "I was promised *nine* hundred (900) Revolving Arms by Mr Stanton after being referred by Gen Halleck to Callender. Of these four hundred & thirty nine (439) were sent some six (6) weeks ago. Nothing since nor any news from them—the following is the dispatch to which my Telegram of this morning referred. Washington   Oct 20th 1862—Dispatch of the 19th relating to arms received   the four hundred & thirty nine (439) Colts Revolving Rifles were all on hand the 18th on Requisition of Maj Gen Grants chief of Cavalry   the following Breech loading Carbines complete were sent to Columbus for the use of the following Reg'ts . . . This requires no comment. Please give an early answer to my last dispatch for my own good & that of the service"   Telegram received, *ibid.*, Dept. of the Mo., Telegrams Received; copy, *ibid.*, Army of the Miss., Telegrams Sent. For communications between Rosecrans and the War Dept., Oct. 19–23, see *O.R.*, I, xvii, part 2, 181–91.

To Maj. Gen. William S. Rosecrans

Head quarters Dept. of West Tenn.
Jackson Tenn. Oct. 21st 1862

Maj Genl. Rosecrans.

My dispatch was but a proper reply to yours of this date and others from you equally objectionable. The leaky lecture of some in your staff or in confidential relation to you as evidenced by newspaper correspondents and their attempt to keep up an invideous distinction between the armies of the Miss and the Tenn. are detrimental to the good feeling that should exist between officers & men as well as improper and should not be allowed Your ordering Rebel prisoners to Benton Barracks and paroling prisoners to go within our lines to St Louis was unauthorized by me & looked like ignoring higher authority[1]

Maj Genl. U. S. Grant

Telegram, copy, DNA, RG 393, Army of the Miss., Telegrams Received. On Oct. 21, 1862, Maj. Gen. William S. Rosecrans telegraphed to USG. "My sending away Paroled Prisoners to Benton Barracks was in conformity with previous custom and in supposed accordance with your views of the propriety of clearing them out of Corinth as rapidly as possible. As soon as made aware of different orders or views they were promptly carried out—The only person I authorized to leave for St Louis was Dr Scott not a Prisoner who called on you and took a message from you—Your dispatch complaining of the action is the first intimation I have had of your disapproval—A Capt Tobin was paroled & permitted to go north while I was absent at Ripley but neither with my consent or approval No other instance have come to my knowledge. That part of your dispatch which refers to News Paper Reporters & leaky members of my staff showing the existance of any desire or even any sentiment at these Head Quarters of keeping up a distinction of feeling and spirit ~~of my command~~ between the Troops of my command or the rest of your Troops as if they were not an integral part thereof I answer that no such feeling has ever existed at these Head Quarters No countenance either directly or indirectly has been given to such an idea nor was I aware that such an idea was abroad until I saw indications of it from members of your Staff and in your own orders—I regard it as the offspring of sentiments than those of a desire for justice or the good of the service and sincerely hope that you do not participate therein. There are no Head Quarters in these United States less responsible for what News Paper correspondents and Paragraphists say of operations than mine this I wish to be understood to be distinctly applicable to the affairs of Iuka and Corinth after this declaration I am free to say that if you do not meet me frankly with a declaration that you are satisfied I shall consider my power to be useful in this Department ended." Telegram received, *ibid.*, Dept. of the Mo., Telegrams Received; copy, *ibid.*, Army of the Miss., Telegrams Sent. *O.R.*, I, xvii, part 2, 283; *ibid.*, II, iv, 639.

On Oct. 22, Maj. John A. Rawlins telegraphed to Rosecrans. "On the 25th of August General Orders No. 77. was issued and sent you requiring a full and minute report of the number-kind-quality and Caliber of the Arms ammunition accoutrements and ordnance property of each arm of the service in this district and estimate of the kind and number of each required. The 25th of Septem. a letter was written you calling your attention to the fact that no such report from your command had yet been received and directing that they be sent on at once. Up to this time no reports have been received from you. Your attention is again called to the subject." Copy, DNA, RG 393, Army of the Miss., Telegrams Received. On the same day, Rosecrans telegraphed to Rawlins. "I think 2 Reports have been sent since the order one (1) of the whole five (5) Divisions of the Army of the Miss' and one later. One report of your letter a copy of the latter & one for the artillery & cavalry will be forwarded tomorrow morning. I regret the apparent neglect as I ordered prompt compliance with the orders—" Telegram received, *ibid.*, Dept. of the Mo., Telegrams Received; copy, *ibid.*, Army of the Miss., Telegrams Sent.

On Oct. 19, Col. Mortimer D. Leggett, Bolivar, had written to Rawlins. "I have been exceedingly vexed and pained of late, to witness the apparently determined effort, in a *single* direction, to revive and strengthen an unjust popular prejudice, against Major Genl. U.S. Grant. The infamous falsehoods and hellish malignity originated against the General just after the battle of Shiloh,—originated partly to excuse the disgraceful cowardice of poltroon officers, and partly to satisfy the popular demand for a victim, have left the public mind, both in the army, and among our friends at home, in fit condition to be readily excited against Major Genl. Grant. Gen Grant's army were winning laurels, even *before* the late battles, merely because they *had not been driven back*,—and when our arms at Bolivar, Meadon, Iuka, Corinth and the Hatchie, had uniformly proved so successful, it was a gross outrage for the minions of a newly fledged Major Genl., not only to attempt an exclusive appropriation (or rather, absorbtion) of all the honors, but, by irresponsible assertions, and mysterious insinuations, to attempt to awaken & deepen, former prejudices against the General to whom naturally and rightfully the first honors belonged. Major Genl. Rosecrans, is undoubedly an excellent officer—and I hope, for his honor, and the honor of his state, that he is not a party in this hellish attempt to ruin Genl Grant,—but the evidence is such, that I cannot rid my mind of the conviction that he must be, at least, *privy* to the whole devilish scheme. It *may* be, that the sin is *only* at the door of the Cincinnati Commercial Correspondent 'W. D. B.' (*Wm D. Bickham*, late clerk of the Ohio Senate and one of the Satelites of old Ben. Stanton, Lt Gov. of Ohio, and Gen Grant's *bitterest* enemy.) if so, Major Genl. Rosecrans will yet do partial justice by dismissing said Bickham from his confidence & army. But I *fear* that the inordinate ambition of Rosecrans, leads him to seek the downfall of Grant, hoping that thereby he may ~~seek~~ succeed to the command of the department—a position for which he is not, and never can be, fitted:—for while he is a brave, dashing officer, a good fighter, & well calculated to inspire his men with enthusiasm, yet he lacks the business talant, and comprehensiveness of judgment, needed in the command of a department. Major—cannot that thing be crushed? Is it not time for officers to begin to understand that there is a point beyond which even the patience & endurance of Gen. Grant must not be pushed? His meekness under abuse might do for St. Paul, or old Stephen, but it is hardly demanded of a Millitary officer especially as the *service* must suffer when he suffers. He is without doubt *the best* department commander in the field, and while such ungenerous—heartless efforts, cannot hurt *him* at the Head Quarters of the Army at Washington—yet they may shake the confiden[ce] of his troops, & thereby, weaken them, and ultimately ruin him & them together. Were I at Corinth a few days, my acquaintance with the parties there would enable me to get at the root of the matter, but I am not there. It would seem that a friendly note to Gen Rosecrans from you would bring the subject sufficiently before him, to induce his sense of justice to repair a *wrong* which at least he has *permitted* For Heaven's sake do *something* in the matter." ALS, *ibid.*, Dept. of the Mo., Telegrams Received.

1. On Oct. 19, Maj. Gen. Samuel R. Curtis, St. Louis, telegraphed to USG. "I call your attention to the fact that rebel paroled prisioners have come through your lines to these Hd Quarters Dr Scott was sent back yesterday & private Bacon here today will be put in imprisonment if he does not take an oath of allegiance & ~~leave~~ give bond to my satisfaction for his good Behavior I do not understand that paroled enemies are to remain in our lines but on their own side Dr. Scott came with a provost Marshall pass or parole from Gen Rosecrans Hd Quarters—" Telegram received, *ibid.*; copy, *ibid.* O.R., II, iv, 635. On Oct. 20, USG telegraphed to Curtis. "I have given no authority for paroled prisoners to go north. None have been permitted to go who declined being paroled. But wanted to ~~th~~ take the oath of allegiance & get where they could not be made to Serve again" Copy, DNA, RG 393, Dept. of the Mo., Telegrams Received. *O.R.*, II, iv, 637.

To Col. John C. Kelton

Headquarters, Dist. of West. Tenn.
Jackson, Tenn. Oct. 22nd 1862

COLONEL J. C. KELTON
ASST. ADJT. GENERAL
WASHINGTON, D. C.
COLONEL:

I have the honor to make the following report of the Battle of Iuka, and to submit herewith such reports of subordinates as have been received.[1]

For some ten days or more, before the final move of the Rebel Army, under General Price, Eastward, from the Mobile & Ohio Rail-road, it was evident that an attack upon Corinth was contemplated, or some change to be made in the location of that Army. This caused great vigilance to be necessary on the part of our Cavalry, especially that to the southern front under Colonel Mizner. The labor of watching, with occational skirmishing, was most satisfactorily performed, and almost every move of the enemy was known as soon as commenced

About the 11th of September, Price left the rail-road, the Infantry and Artillery probably moving from Baldwin,[2] their Cavalry from roads north of Baldwin, towards Bay Springs. At the latter place a halt of a few days seemed to have been made, likely for the purpose of collecting stores and reconnoitering our Eastern flank. On the 13th of September the enemies Cavalry made their appearance near Iuka, and were repulsed by the small Garrison, under Colonel Murphy of the 8th Wisconsin Infantry, still left there to cover the removal of stores, not yet brought in to Corinth. The enemy appearing again in increased force on the same day, and having cut the Rail-road and Telegraph between there and Burnsville, Colonel Murphy thought it prudent to retire to save his forces.[3] This caused a considerable amount of Commissary stores to fall into the hands of the enemy, which, properly, should have been destroyed. Prices whole force then soon congregated at Iuka.—Information brought in by scouts as to the intention of the enemy was conflicting. One report was that Price wanted to cross Bear Creek and the Tennessee river for the purpose of crossing Tennessee and getting into Kentucky. Another, that Van-Dorn was to march by the way of Ripley and attack us on the Southwest, whilst Price would move on us from the East or Northeast. A third, that Price would endeavor to cross the Tennessee and if pursuit was attempted, Van Dorn was in readiness to attack Corinth.

Having satisfied myself that Van Dorn could not reach Corinth under four days with an Army embracing all Arms, I determined to leave Corinth with a force sufficient to resist Cavalry and to attack Price at Iuka. This I regarded as eminently my duty, let either of the theories of the enemy's plans be the correct solution.

Accordingly on the 16th, I gave some general directions as to the plan of operation. General Rosecrans was to move on the south side of the rail-road to opposite Iuka, and attack from that side with all his available force, after leaving sufficient force at Rienzi and Jacinto to prevent a surprise on Corinth from that direction. Major General Ord was to move to Burnsville and from there take roads North of the Rail-road and attack from that side.

General Ord having to leave from his two Divisions, already very much reduced in numbers from their long continued service, and the number of Battles they had been in, the garrison at Corinth (he also had one Regiment of Infantry and squadron of Cavalry at Kossouth, one regiment of Infantry and one Company of Cavalry at Chewalla, and one regiment of Infantry that moved under Colonel Mower and joined General Rosecrans' command), reduced the number of men of his command, available for the expedition to about (3000) Three Thousand.

I had previously ordered the Infantry of General Ross' command at Bolivar, to hold themselves in readiness to move at a moments warning.—had also directed a concentration of cars at Jackson to move these troops.[4] Within twenty four hours from the time a dispatch left Corinth for these troops to "come on" they had all arrived, 3400 in number: this, notwithstanding a locomotive was thrown off the track on the Mississippi Central Road, preventing the passage of other trains for several hours. This force was added to General Ord's command making his entire strength over 6000 to take into the Field. From this force two Regiments of Infantry and one section of Artillery was taken, about 900 men, for the Garrison, or rear guard, to be held at Burnsville. Not having General Ord's report these figures may not be accurate.

General Rosecrans was moving from Jacinto Eastward with about 9000 men, making my total force with which to attack the enemy about 15.000. This was equal to or greater than their numbers as I estimated them.

General Rosecrans, at his suggestion, acquiesced to by me, was to move, Northward from his eastern march in two columns. One under Hamilton was to move up the Fulton[5] & Eastport road, the other under Stanley, on the Jacinto road from Barnetts.

On the 18th, General Ord's command was pushed forward, driving in the enemies pickets and capturing a few prisoners, taking a position within six miles of Iuka. I expected from the following dispatch that General Rosecrans would be near enough by the night of the 18th to make it safe for Ord to press forward on the morning of the 19th and bring on an engagement.

"Sept. 18th 1862

To GENERAL GRANT.

One of my spies in from Reardons, on the Bay Spring road tells of a continuous movement since last friday of forces Eastward. They say Van Dorn is to defend Vicksburg, Breckenridge to make his way to Kentucky, Price to attack Iuka or go to Tennessee.—If Prices forces are at Iuka the plan I propose is to move up as close as we can tonight, conceal our movements, Ord to advance from Burnsville, commence the attack and draw their attention that way, while I move in on the Jacinto & Fulton roads, massing heavily on the Fulton Road, and crushing in their left, cutting off their retreat Eastward. I propose to leave in ten minutes for Jacinto from whence I will dispatch you by line of Videttes to Burnsville. Will await a few minutes to hear from you before I start. What news from Burnsville?

(Signed) W. S. ROSECRANS
Brig. General"

To which was sent the following in reply:

"Headquarters, Dist. West. Tennessee
Burnsville, Miss. Sept. 18th 1862

GENERAL ROSECRANS:

General Ross' command is at this place. McArthurs Division is north of the road 2 miles to the rear, and Davies' Division South of the road nearby. I sent forward two Regiments of Infantry with Cavalry by the road, north of rail-road towards Iuka, with instructions for them to Bivouac for the night at a point which was designated, about four miles from here, if not interrupted, and have the Cavalry feel where the enemy are. Before they reached the point of the road (you will see it on the map, the road north of the Rail-road) they met what is supposed to be Armstrongs Cavalry.

The Rebel Cavalry was forced back and I sent instructions then to have them stop for the night where they thought they could safely hold—

In the morning troops will advance from here at 4½ A. M. An anonymous dispatch just received states that Price, Magruder, and Breckenridge have a force of 60.000 between Iuka and Tupelo.—This I have no doubt is the understanding of Citizens, but I very much doubt their information being correct.

Your reconnoissances prove that there is but little force south of Corinth for a long distance and no great force between Bay-Springs and the rail-road

Make as rapid an advance as you can, and let us do tomor-

row all we can—It may be necessary to fall back the day
following.

I look upon the shewing of a Cavalry force so near us as
an indication of a retreat, and they a force to cover it.
15 minutes to 7. P. M.

> (Signed)   U. S. GRANT.
> Major General."

After midnight the following dispatch was received:

> "Headquarters Encampment.
> Sept. 18th 1862.
>
> GENERAL:
> Your dispatch received: General Stanley's Division ar-
> rived after dark having been detained by falling in the rear
> of Ross through fault of guide   Our Cavalry six miles this
> side of Barnetts, Hamiltons 1st Brigade eight, 2nd Brigade,
> nine miles this side, Stanleys near Davenports Mills. We
> shall move as early as practicable, say 4½ A. M. This will
> give 20 miles march for Stanley to Iuka. Shall not therefore
> be in before one or two O'Clock. But when we come in will
> endeavor to do it strongly.
>
> (Signed)   W. S. ROSECRANS.
> Brig. General. U. S. A."

Receiving this dispatch as I did late at night and when I
expected these troops were far on their way towards Iuka, and
had made plans accordingly, caused some disappointment, and
made change of plan necessary. I immediately dispatched to
General Ord giving him the substance of the above, and directions not to move on the enemy until Rosecrans arrived, or he
should hear firing to the South of Iuka. Of this change General
Rosecrans was promptly informed by dispatch sent with his return Messenger. During the day General Ord returned to my
Headquarters at Iuka, and in consultation we both agreed that it
would be impossible for General Rosecrans to get his troops up
in time to make an attack that day. The General was instructed,
however, to move forward driving in the enemy's advanced

guards, but not to bring on an engagement unless he should hear firing. At night another dispatch was received from Genl. Rosecrans,[6] dated from Barnetts; about eight miles from Iuka, written at 12:40. P. M. stating that head of column arrived there at 12.M. Owing to the density of the forests and difficulty of passing the small streams and bottoms, all communications between General Rosecrans and myself had to pass far around.—near to Jacinto—even after he had got. on the road heading north. For this reason his communication was not received until after the engagement. I did not hear of the engagement, however, until next day, although the following dispatch had been promptly forwarded.

> "Headquarters, Army of the Mississippi
> 2 Miles South of Iuka, Sept. 19th/62.
> 10½ P. M.
>
> GENERAL:
>
> We met the enemy in force just above this point. The engagement lasted several hours. We have lost two or three pieces of Artillery—Firing was very heavy. You must attack in the morning and in force. The ground is horrid—unknown to us, and no room for development. Couldn't use our Artillery at all: fired but few shots   Push in onto them until we can have time to do something. We will try to get a position on our right which will take Iuka.
>
> (Signed)   W. S. ROSECRANS
> Brig. Genl. U. S. A."

This dispatch was received at 8:35 A. M. on the 20th and the following immediately sent:

> "Burnsville, Sept. 20th 1862
> 8:35. A. M.
>
> GENERAL ORD:
>
> Get your troops up and attack as soon as possible. Rosecrans had two hours fighting last night, and now this morning again, and unless you can create a diversion in his favor he may find his hands full.

Hurry your troops all possible.
(Signed)   U. S. GRANT.
Maj. General"[7]

The statement that the engagement had commenced again in the morning was on the strength of hearing Artillery. General Ord hearing the same, however, pushed on with all possible dispatch without awaiting orders.

Two of my Staff, Colonels Dickey and Lagow had gone around to where Genl. Rosecrans was and were with him during the early part of the engagement. Returning in the dark and endeavoring to cut off some of the distance, they became lost and entangled in the woods, and remained out over night, arriving at Head Quarters next morning about the same hour that General Rosecrans' Messenger arrived.[8] For the particular troops engaged and the part taken by each Regiment I will have to refer you entirely to the accompanying reports of those officers who were present.

Not occupying Iuka afterwards for any length of time, and then not with a force sufficient to give protection for any great distance around (the Battle was fought about two miles out) I cannot accompany this with a Topographical Map. I sent however a map showing all the roads and places named in this report. The country between the road traveled by General Ord's command to some distance south of the rail-road, is impassable for Cavalry, and almost so for Infantry. It is impassable for Artillery, southward to the road traveled by General Rosecrans' command. Soon after dispatching General Ord, word was brought by one of my Staff, Colonel Hillyer that the enemy were in full retreat. I immediately proceeded to Iuka and found that the enemy had left during the night taking every thing with them except their wounded and the Artillery captured by them the evening before, going south by the Fulton road. Generals Stanley and Hamilton were in pursuit.

This was the first I knew of the Fulton road being left open to the enemy for their escape. With it occupied no route would have been left them except East, with the difficult bottom of Bear-Creek to cross or Northeast with the Tennessee River in their front, or to conquer their way out. A partial examination of the Country afterwards convinced me, however, that troops moving in seperate columns by the routes suggested could not support each other until they arrived near Iuka. On the other hand an attempt to retreat would, according to programme have brought General Ord with his force on the rear of the retreating Column.

For casualties and captures see accompanying reports.

The Battle of Iuka foots up as follows:

On the 16th of September we commenced to collect our strength to move upon Price at Iuka in two columns. The one to the right of the Rail-road commanded by Brigadier General, now Major General, W. S. Rosecrans: the one to the left commanded by Major General E. O. C. Ord. On the night of the 18th the latter was in position to bring on an engagement in one hours march: The former from having a greater distance to march and through the fault of a guide was twenty miles back. On the 19th by making a rapid march, with hardy, well disciplined and tried troops arrived within two miles of the place to be attacked. Unexpectedly the enemy took the iniative and became the attacking party. The ground chosen was such that a large force on our side could not be brought into action. But the bravery and endurance of those brought in was such, that, with the skill and presence of mind of the officers commanding, they were able to hold their ground until night closed the conflict. During the night the enemy fled leaving our troops in possession of the field with their dead to bury and wounded to care for. If it was the object of the enemy to make their way into Kentucky they were defeated in that. If to hold their position until Van Dorn could come up on the South West of Corinth and make a simultaneous attack they were defeated in that. Our only defeat was in not capturing the entire Army, or in destroying it as I had hoped to do.

It was a part of General Hamilton's command that did the fighting directed entirely by that cool and deserving officer. I commend him to the President for acknowledgement of his services.

During the absence of these forces from Corinth that post was left in charge of Brig. General T. J. McKean.[9] The southern front beyond Jacinto to Rienzi was under the charge of Colonel Du Bois with a small Infantry and Cavalry force. The service was most satisfactorily performed, Colonel Du Bois showing great vigilance and efficiency. I was kept constantly advised of the movements of flying bodies of Cavalry that were hovering in that front.

The wounded, both friend and enemy are much indebted to Surgeon J. G. F. Holsten,[10] Medical Director for his untiring labors in organizing Hospitals, and providing for their every want.

I cannot close this report without paying a tribute to all the officers and soldiers composing this command. Their conduct on the march was exemplary and all were eager to meet the enemy. The possibility of defeat I do not think entered the mind of a single individual, and I believe this same feeling now pervades the entire Army which I have the honor to command.

I neglected to mention in the proper connection, that to cover our movement from Corinth and to attract the attention of the enemy in another direction, I ordered a movement from Bolivar towards Holly Springs.[11] This was conducted by Brig. General Lawman, whose report is herewith submitted.[12]

Before completing this report the report of Maj. Gen. Ord was received and accompanies this.[13]

> I am, Colonel.
> Very Respectfully
> Your Obt. Servt
> U. S. GRANT
> Maj. Genl.

LS, DNA, RG 94, War Records Office, Union Battle Reports. *O.R.*, I, xvii, part 1, 64–69. On Oct. 25, 1862, USG wrote to Col. John C. Kelton. "In my report of the battle of Iuka I speak of Col. Murphy abandoning Iuka on the 16th of Sept. I should have said 13th   Will you do me the kindness to make the correction before the report becomes public." ALS, IHi. No copy of USG's report has been found in which this error occurs.

1. U.S. Army reports of Iuka are in *O.R.*, I, xvii, part 1, 68–119; C. S. A. reports are *ibid.*, pp. 119–37.

2. Baldwyn, Miss., on the Mobile and Ohio Railroad, about thirty miles south of Corinth.

3. See letter to Brig. Gen. William S. Rosecrans, Sept. 14, 1862. On Sept. 14, Brig. Gen. David S. Stanley arrested Col. Robert C. Murphy, and, on the next day, filed charges against him of "Misbehaving himself in the presence of the Enemy," and "Shamefully abandoning a post which he had been commanded to defend." Copy, DNA, RG 153, Court-Martial Case KK 303, Robert C. Murphy. On Sept. 23, Murphy sent to Maj. John A. Rawlins a lengthy defense of his conduct at Iuka. LS, *ibid.* On Sept. 28, Maj. Gen. William S. Rosecrans endorsed this letter. "Respectfully forwarded. The movements of the army prevented the calling of a court martial until to-day for Col. Murphy's trial. It will doubtless gratify him to have this forwarded. I think extreme fright and want of judgement of Col. M so manifest as to need no comment. For example says that he formed line facing west ward expecting a fight at Burnsville and when he learned that two cos of Sharp shooters were there he still remained in order of battle one hour until Capt Webster requested him to 'get out of his way'—He never went to t[he] telegraph office nor did anything to know if his retreat was not sufficient—Nor did wait for further orders   he got out of the way of Capt Webster and got prosperously into Farmington—"   AES, *ibid.* On Oct. 2, Rawlins endorsed this letter. "The Major General Command'g from a careful examination of the within statement of Colonel Murphy, in the absence of other evidence, is of the opinion that he was justified in his action in the evacuation of Iuka: but the opinions of the officers under whose immediate command he was at the time, being adverse, deems it for the good of the service as well as justice to Colonel Murphy, that the trial before Court Martial on the charges preferred should proceed." ES, *ibid.* On Oct. 16, Murphy was acquitted, but in announcing the verdict and returning Murphy to duty, Rosecrans in General Orders No. 144, Oct. 23, also announced his disapproval of the verdict. Copy (printed), *ibid.*

4. On Sept. 17, Brig. Gen. James B. McPherson telegraphed to USG. "Train will be ready tomorrow at 12 oclock   we can take our horses   will have a platform made so that we can get them out at almost any point—"   Telegram received, *ibid.*, RG 393, Dept. of the Mo., Telegrams Received.

5. Fulton, Miss., about thirty-seven miles south of Iuka.

6. See telegram to Brig. Gen. William S. Rosecrans, Sept. 18, 1862.

7. See letter to Maj. Gen. Edward O. C. Ord, Sept. 20, 1862.

8. On Sept. 19, at 2 P.M., from "Barnetts," Col. Clark B. Lagow sent a message to "Genl.," presumably USG. "Your dispatch to Genl. Rosecrans recd. He will move up at once. Col Dickey & I will go with him, the Orderly' we send to accompany our guide back will show you the shortest way to this place or to where Genl Rosecrans will be—all quiet in front"   Telegram received, DNA, RG 393, Dept. of the Mo., Telegrams Received. On Sept. 21, Col. T. Lyle Dickey wrote to his wife. " . . . Col Lagow & I were sent by Gen Grant to visit Gen Rosecrans & explain to him the plan of operations—We went south ten or twelve miles & then turned north East & over-took Gen Rosecrans at a farm house 7½ miles from Iuka—His army was stretched along the road—some five miles—the head of the column being within 5 miles of Iuka & skirmishing with rebel Cavalry —We dined with Gen Rosecrans & then rode with him to the head of his column —which (the column) was in mean time ~~had been~~ advancing—& at about 1½

miles south west of Iuka—the head of the column encountred the enemy in force about an hour before sundown   Our troops came forward in double quick and the roar of canon & rattle of Muskety became loud rapid & general—on both sides   The shells burst around us—the bullets whisted through the air & it began to sound like some of the sharp passages at the battle of shiloh—Col Lagow & myself after witnessing the battle for half an hour—(our folks holding their ground firmly) set out for Gen Grants Head Quarters at Burnsville to report the state of affairs & have Ords army push on in the Morning—As we rode back for three miles we met our troops pressing eagerly forward & heard the roar of battle till it was quite dark—From this point our route lay through a deep forest—over steep hills & low bottoms—with a blind winding path—It soon became pitch dark —& although clear star-light night—in the woods it was very dark   In our progress we lost the road & traveled a mile by the north star our only guide through grape vines—briers & fallen trees brush piles &c—atlength my horse which was ahead halted & putting his nose down refused to go forward—I told Col Lagow that my horse refused to go—that we had doubtless come to some obstruction— He said 'Let me try it' & spurred his horse past me & to his surprise plunged horse & man down a perpendicular bank five feet high into the bed of a creek— The horse fell flat on his side & caught Lagow's leg under him—They both grunted & got up again & found they were not seriously hurt—We could find no crossing & had to build a fire—tie our horses & lie down in the woods till day-light—At day-light we mounted & galloped seven miles to Burnsville   Couriers had been sent by a more circuitous, had reached Gen Grant about 3. O'clock A. M. Saturday giving him word of the engagement—and Gen Grant had ordered Gen Ord to advance at day-light & attack the enemy from the north . . ." ALS, Wallace-Dickey Papers, IHi.

9. See letter to Brig. Gen. Thomas J. McKean, Sept. 16, 1862.

10. John G. F. Holston, born in Germany, appointed surgeon on Aug. 3, 1861, served as medical director, District of West Tenn. See *Calendar*, June 25, 1862; telegram to Abraham Lincoln, Oct. 10, 1862, note 4.

11. See telegram to Brig. Gen. Stephen A. Hurlbut, Sept. 17, 1862.

12. Printed in *O.R.*, I, xvii, part 1, 140–41.

13. Copy, DNA, RG 94, War Records Office, Union Battle Reports. *O.R.*, I, xvii, part 1, 117–19.

To Maj. Gen. Henry W. Halleck

Jackson Tenn Oct 23 10 a m [*1862*]

Henry W. Halleck
General in chf

It is now certain that the Rebels have been largely reinforced at Holly Springs and are strongly fortifying   Pemberton[1] in

Command, Tillghman[2] in Command of exchanged prisoners. They are reinforced by conscripts Alabama & Texas troops. Is it not probable that Bragg will come this way?

U. S. GRANT

Maj. Genl

Telegram received, DNA, RG 94, Generals' Papers and Books, Telegrams Received by Gen. Halleck; *ibid.*, RG 107, Telegrams Collected (Bound); copies, *ibid.*, RG 393, USG Hd. Qrs. Correspondence; DLC-USG, V, 4, 5, 7, 8, 88. *O.R.*, I, xvii, part 2, 290.

On Oct. 22, 1862, Maj. Gen. William S. Rosecrans telegraphed to USG. "Some of our Scouts from the far front say report & surmises Prevail that forces from Alabam conscripts etc & from Vicksburg are concentrating at Holly Springs intending to make another push at our lines—they say Corinth but do not think so—eight hundred (800) Troops reported remaining at Vicksburg   rest gone to reinforce Price   They are fortifying Holly Springs" Telegram received, DNA, RG 393, Dept. of the Mo., Telegrams Received; copy, *ibid.*, Army of the Miss., Telegrams Sent. On Oct. 23, Rosecrans again telegraphed to USG. "I dont value Price's conscripts but I greatly value them Alabama troops.   beware of Bragg   it is nearly time for a few car loads of his troops to arrive, depend upon it   unless Buell is sharper than heretofore we shall have the Devil to pay here—Please answer my personal dispatch—" Telegram received, *ibid.*, Dept. of the Mo., Telegrams Received; copy, *ibid.*, Army of the Miss., Telegrams Sent. *O.R.*, I, xvii, part 2, 291.

On Oct. 22, Maj. Gen. William T. Sherman wrote to USG. "A merchant of undoubted character is just in from Holly Springs which he left yesterday at 10 A.M. He brought many letters from the various officers to St Louis & California some of which were examined. Price is there with all the Missouranies many of whom are known to us personally. Van Dorn & Lovell are ordered to Richmond. No other Divisions or Brigades have joined them since the battle of Corinth but they claim that they have received 10000 men from various quarters Blyth has about 700 Cavalry on the Hernando Road & Line of Cold Water. Jackson has 4500 & Cavalry at my old Camp on Cold Water near Holly Springs. The Infantry is Camped all about the town & all seem to be in high spirits. Pemberton is now in Command. On balancing all the accounts received I dont think they can attack but will await attack. They may occupy Davis Mills but if you advance LaGrange is the Point   The aggragete force at Holly Springs I should judge to be about 23.000 all told. Cavalry now in good order, Infantry only so so. Clothing poorly & scarce of blankets & shoes, plenty of Corn meal & beef, all esle scarce. The letters claim that Bragg whipped Buell taking 17000 prisoners   No firing on our boats since since the Gladiator, and I think we should not hesitate to make the Country feel the full effects of all such attempts   I am just going to review two of my Brigades, which are in fine order" Copy, DNA, RG 94, Generals' Papers and Books, William T. Sherman, Letters Sent. *O.R.*, I, xvii, part 2, 288–89. On Oct. 21, Sherman had written at length to Maj. John A. Rawlins incorporating similar information concerning C. S. A. movements. Copy, DNA, RG 94, Generals' Papers and Books, William T. Sherman, Letters Sent. *O.R.*, I, xvii, part 2, 285–86.

On Oct. 29, Col. William S. Hillyer wrote to Sherman. "I am directed by Gen'l. Grant to acknowledge the receipt of your report of the 21st, and letter of the 22d, and to say to you His information is that Bowen is moving north of the Hatchie with the evident intention of getting on to the Mississippi river to cut off navigation. An expedition will be sent to cut him off, from here. A flag of truce from Corinth went into Holly Springs last week, they allowed our officers to stay in town from Sunday at 3, oclock P. M., till 10, A. M Monday. They were taken to the Hotel and allowed every liberty. Van Dorn threw no restraint around them, and seemed perfectly indifferent how much they learned. Our officers estimated the force there at not over 25000. The enemy are beginning to move now, Price is at Ripley.—Information is in that troops are going south, possibly going to Mobile. The General heartily approves your course in expelling secession families as a punishment and preventive example for Guerillas firing into boats. He would also recommend that if it becomes necessary to distribute food to the poor and destitute families, or to unemployed contrabands, to make an assessment on the better provided secession citizen to pay the expenses. Rosecrans has been ordered to Cincinnati to receive further orders; this is greatly to the relief of the General, who was very much disappointed in him. This matter the General will explain to you when he sees you. He much regrets that Hurlbut is ordered away, and has telegraphed to have the order countermanded. Adjt. General Fuller of Illinois telegraphed to-day that in addition to eight (8) Regiments heretofore sent, the Regiment—(the 103d) is under orders to move Wednesday, the 111th & 95th, within four days afterward. He further telegraphs that ten more Regiments can be forwarded in next ten days if paid and armed. The General will try and send troops to you, possibly not more than one Brigade armed and one Regiment without arms to take charge of Siege Guns. The General has abandoned all idea of the troops expedition. He find Curtis indisposed to cooperate with him. From the Newspapers and other reports it is probable that McClernand will go to Helena and lead whatever expedition may move from there, and report to Curtis. As soon as the promised reinforcements arrive the General will make arrangments for a forward move and will then send a staff officer to inform you fully of plans, and how he desires your cooperations." Copies, DLC-USG, V, 18, 30; DNA, RG 393, Dept. of the Tenn., Letters Sent. *O.R.*, I, xvii, part 2, 307–8. On Nov. 1, Sherman wrote to Rawlins at length in response to this letter, and concluded: "I note the Generals allusion to Rosecrans & was somewhat surprised, though convinced. I hope Hurlbut & McPherson will be retained in the Dept." Copy, DNA, RG 94, Generals' Papers and Books, William T. Sherman, Letters Sent. *O.R.*, I, xvii, part 2, 857–58.

1. John C. Pemberton of Pa., USMA 1837, resigned from the U.S. Army with the rank of capt. and bvt. maj. on April 29, 1861. The decision of Pemberton, a Pa. Quaker, to fight for the South is discussed in John C. Pemberton, *Pemberton: Defender of Vicksburg* (Chapel Hill, 1942), chap. IV. Appointed brig. gen. as of June 17, 1861; confirmed as maj. gen. on Jan. 14, 1862; then confirmed as lt. gen. on Oct. 13, he assumed command on Oct. 14 of C. S. A. forces in Miss., east La., and southern Tenn. *O.R.*, I, xvii, part 2, 728.

2. C. S. A. Brig. Gen. Lloyd Tilghman, captured at Fort Henry and later exchanged, had been assigned to prepare other exchanged prisoners for C. S. A. service. *Ibid.*, II, iv, 852–53.

To Maj. Gen. Henry W. Halleck

Jackson Tenn [*Oct.*] 23d 6 37 P M [*1862*]

MAJ GEN HALLECK

A dispatch just in says our Cavalry under Maj Madd[1] run into Haywoods[2] partizan Rangers Seven (7) Miles west of Brownsville   Killed one Captain, Captured about forty prisoners Sixty horses & mules & a wagon load of Arms Completely breaking up the parties   I will send these Men to Alton

U. S GRANT

Maj Gen

Telegram received, DNA, RG 94, Generals' Papers and Books, Telegrams Received by Gen. Halleck; *ibid.*, RG 107, Telegrams Collected (Bound); copies, *ibid.*, RG 94, War Records Office, Union Battle Reports; *ibid.*, RG 393, USG Hd. Qrs. Correspondence; DLC-USG, V, 4, 5, 7, 8, 88. *O.R.*, I, xvii, part 1, 461.

At 8 A.M., Oct. 21, 1862, Maj. John J. Mudd, "On road 12 miles north west of Brownsville," wrote to USG. "I am out on order of Genl McPherson. I do not think it safe to send couriers to him, will you advise him by wires that we found a detachment or several squads of rebels in Brownsville yesterday. They fled on our approach   a few shots as they ran.   we took several prisoners and twenty or thirty horses and mules of Jacksons and Pinsons Cavalry.   one of Jacksons Lieuts.   we are now on trail of Haywards command. They are not many hours ahead   no casualties"   ALS, DNA, RG 393, District of West Tenn., 4th Division, Letters Received.

On Oct. 23, Capt. William T. Clark, Bolivar, telegraphed to Maj. Gen. James B. McPherson. "Cavalry expedition ran over Haywood seven Miles west of Brownsville. Killed one Captain   scattered them in every direction   Captured 40 prisoners 60 horses and wagon load of arms. Will be in tomorrow noon"   Telegram received, *ibid.*, Dept. of the Tenn., Telegrams Received.

1. John J. Mudd, born in Mo. in 1820, was commissioned maj., 2nd Ill. Cav., as of Sept. 23, 1861. Wounded at Fort Donelson, he was unfit for regular cav. duties until Sept., 1862. See Newton Bateman and Paul Selby, *Historical Encyclopedia of Illinois and Biographical Memoirs* (Chicago, 1917), I, 392; endorsement to Brig. Gen. Lorenzo Thomas, Dec. 31, 1862.

2. Capt. Robert W. Haywood commanded a co. of Tenn. cav. See *O.R.*, I, lii, part 2, 305; letter to Maj. Gen. Earl Van Dorn, Nov. 19, 1862.

To Maj. Gen. William S. Rosecrans

———

Head quarters dept. of West Tenn.
Jackson Tenn. Oct. 23d 1862

MAJ. GENL. ROSECRANS,
The following dispatch is just this moment received.

Washington Oct. 23d 1862

MAJ. GENL. GRANT.
You will direct Maj Genl Rosecrans to immediately repair to Cincinnati where he will receive orders.
(Signed.   H. W. HALLECK.
Comd.r in Chief.[1]

Turn over your command to Hamilton. I will send Quimby to take his division.[2] Can you get in your report of the "Battle of Corinth" before Starting. I would like to have it if possible.

I predict an important command where in the course of events we may cooperate.

U. S. GRANT
Maj. Genl.

Telegram, copy, DNA, RG 393, Army of the Miss., Telegrams Received. On Oct. 23, 1862, Maj. Gen. William S. Rosecrans telegraphed to USG. "Your Dispatch rec'd   your directions will be complied with—I think the Report may be finished by tomorrow night—I propose to leave next Day A. M." Telegram received, *ibid.*, Dept. of the Mo., Telegrams Received.

On the same day, Rosecrans telegraphed to USG. "Awaiting action from the President I have appointed 1st Lt. C. R. Thompson Brussels Engineer Regiment Actg. Aide de Camp. I wish your permission for him to accompany me. Also six (6) Orderlies belonging to companies D. & C. 4th U.S. Cavalry now serving with Genl Buell—left here by Genl Pope   I wish them to accompany me to Cincinnati where they can rejoin their Regiment. They have had no pay since they have been separated from their companies." Copy, *ibid.*, Army of the Miss., Telegrams Sent. On Oct. 24, USG telegraphed to Rosecrans. "Lt R. C. Thompson Brissells Engnr. Regiment has permission to accompany you as Aide de Camp. The six Orderlies belonging to companies D. &. C. 4 U.S. Cavalry will also accompany you." Copy, *ibid.*, Telegrams Received.

On Oct. 22, Rosecrans had written at length to Maj. Gen. Henry W. Halleck discussing his differences with USG and requesting a change of assignment. *O.R.*, I, xvii, part 2, 286–87. On Oct. 28, Rosecrans telegraphed to USG. "My orders are to relieve Gen Buell and assume command of the Dept of the Cumberland and

We are to co-operate so far as possible to support each others operations   please keep me advised & I will do the same for you   I will go to Louisville tomorrow" Telegram received, DNA, RG 94, War Records Office, Dept. of the Tenn. *O.R.*, I, xvi, part 2, 650.

    1. ALS (telegram sent), DNA, RG 107, Telegrams Collected (Bound); telegram received, *ibid.*, RG 393, Dept. of the Tenn., Telegrams Received. *O.R.*, I, xvii, part 2, 290.
    2. On Oct. 24, Brig. Gen. Charles S. Hamilton telegraphed to USG. "Rose-crans suggests that immediate steps be taken that Brig Genl Buford do not return to this command   if he comes back he will take the command of the Division from Quinby   please telegraph what steps are taken in this matter"   Telegram received, DNA, RG 393, Dept. of the Mo., Telegrams Received; copy, *ibid.*, Army of the Miss., Telegrams Sent. Actually, Brig. Gen. Isaac F. Quinby, appointed as of March 17, ranked Brig. Gen. Napoleon B. Buford, appointed as of April 15. Hamilton had recently criticized Buford for occupying the wrong position during the battle of Corinth. *O.R.*, I, xvii, part 1, 205, 209, 254.

To Maj. Gen. William S. Rosecrans

Head quarters Dept. of West Tenn.
Corinth Miss. Octr. 23d 1862

MAJ. GENL ROSECRANS.

    The Signal Corps when here proved rather a nuisance with-out being of service. I have also sent off all signal operators and would not like now to send for them again.

U. S. GRANT.
Maj Genl.

Telegram, copy, DNA, RG 393, Army of the Miss., Telegrams Received. On Oct. 23, 1862, Maj. Gen. William S. Rosecrans had telegraphed to USG. "Would it not be well to apply for a detail from the U.S. Signal Corps   there are frequently instances when it would be of great service"   Telegram received, *ibid.*, Dept. of the Mo., Telegrams Received; copy, *ibid.*, Army of the Miss., Telegrams Sent.
    On Dec. 26, Capt. John W. De Ford, act. signal officer, Cairo, wrote to USG. "By direction of Capt. O. H. Howard—Chief-Acting Signal Officer, in your dep't. I have the honor to request that any officers which you may detail upon Signal duty, pursuant to extract from 'Special Orders No 364,' (a copy of which is here-with enclosed) be taken from the 'Right Wing, 13th Army Corps,' or that portion of your forces engaged in the combined land & naval operations now pending against Vicksburg, & that they be ordered to report to the Chief-Acting Signal Officer at Maj. Gen. W. T. Sherman's—Headquarters, instead of Cairo, Ill. Capt.

Howard's Hd. Qurs. are with Genl. Sherman & the expedition—" ALS, *ibid.*, Dept. of the Tenn., Letters Received. AGO Special Orders No. 364, Nov. 28, required USG to send ten officers and twenty-five enlisted men suited for signal corps duty to Cairo. Copy, *ibid.*

To Maj. Gen. Edward O. C. Ord

[*Oct. 24, 1862*]

Gen. Rosecrans is ordered to Cincinnati to receive orders. I suspect he is going to take Buells place. Have had no intimation of the fact but Buells failure to come up with Bragg, whether his fault or not, will raise such a storm that he will probably have to give way. . . . It is a great annoyance to gain rank and command enough to attract public attention. I have found it so and would now really prefer some little command where public attention would not be attracted towards me.

The Collector, LXXVII, 7–9 (1964), 15. According to the description of contents, USG acknowledged receipt of the report of Maj. Gen. Edward O. C. Ord of the battle of Iuka and expressed hope that he would soon recover and rejoin his command. No reply to this letter has been found, but on Nov. 24, 1862, Ord, Carlisle, Pa., telegraphed to USG. "Yours of sixteenth 16 just recd. I am offered a military commission at Cincinnate or would accept your offer with pleasure & go to Jackson, wound is drying & I can walk a little" Telegram received, DNA, RG 393, Dept. of the Tenn., Telegrams Received. Ord served Nov. 24, 1862–May 10, 1863, on a military commission investigating the campaigns of Maj. Gen. Don Carlos Buell, then rejoined USG's command on June 18.

To Maj. Gen. William S. Rosecrans

Head quarters dept. of West Tenn.
Jackson Tenn. Oct. 24th 1862

MAJ. GENL. ROSECRANS

Returns of the forces of this department are demanded at Washington immediately

Have returns of ~~all~~ your command of all arms made out and sent in at once up to the present time.

As you are doubtless busily engaged in making preparations to leave you will give the matter in charge of Genl. Hamilton. Returns must be in within three (3) days from this date.

U. S. GRANT
Maj. Genl.

Telegram, copy, DNA, RG 393, Army of the Miss., Telegrams Received. On Oct. 24, 1862, Maj. Gen. William S. Rosecrans telegraphed to USG. "Your dispatch received. Your directions will be complied with. I think the report may be finished by tomorrow night. I propose to leave next day noon." Copy, *ibid.*, Telegrams Sent. On the same day, Rosecrans again telegraphed to USG. "I will not leave here until day after tomorrow morning because I should I gain no time by it would have to lay over in Cairo" Telegram received, *ibid.*, Dept. of the Mo., Telegrams Received; copy, *ibid.*, Army of the Miss., Telegrams Sent.

On Oct. 24, Brig. Gen. Lorenzo Thomas had telegraphed to USG. "Send us returns of your command for Congress in triplicate immediately acknowledge telegram" Telegram received, *ibid.*, Dept. of the Tenn., Telegrams Received; copies, *ibid.*, RG 94, Letters Sent; *ibid.*, RG 107, Telegrams Collected (Unbound); *ibid.*, RG 393, USG Hd. Qrs. Correspondence; DLC-USG, V, 4, 5, 7, 8, 88. On the same day, USG telegraphed to Thomas. "Despatch received will send the returns Soon as possible." Telegram received, DNA, RG 107, Telegrams Collected (Bound); copies, *ibid.*, RG 393, USG Hd. Qrs. Correspondence; DLC-USG, V, 4, 5, 7, 8, 88.

On Oct. 25, Rosecrans addressed three separate letters to Maj. John A. Rawlins recommending the promotion of Col. Thomas W. Sweeny, 52nd Ill., to brig. gen., the promotion of Col. John V. D. Du Bois to brig. gen., and the promotion of Brig. Gen. David S. Stanley to maj. gen. Copies, DNA, RG 393, Army of the Miss., Letters Sent. In response to the first letter, on Oct. 26 USG telegraphed to Maj. Gen. Henry W. Halleck. "I would respectfully recommend Col. T. W. Sweeney 52nd Ill for promotion" Telegram received, *ibid.*, RG 107, Telegrams Collected (Bound); copies, *ibid.*, RG 393, Dept. of the Tenn., Letters Sent; DLC-USG, V, 5, 8, 24, 88. On Oct. 29, USG endorsed the second letter. "Respectfully forwarded to the Headquarters of the Army Washington, D. C." ES, DNA, RG 94, Letters Received. On Oct. 30, USG added an identical endorsement to the third letter. ES, *ibid.* All were nominated as requested to rank from Nov. 29, but Du Bois was not confirmed by the Senate.

To Brig. Gen. Grenville M. Dodge

———

Jackson, October 24th 1862

GEN. DODGE
COLUMBUS KY.

Permit me to introduce to your acquaintance Mr. S. A. Hudson of Burlington Iowa.

Mr. Hudson is a cousin of mine on a visit to see and learn all he can of the scenes made memorable and sad within the last year. He will probably spend a day in Columbus. Attention paid Mr. Hudson I will regard as a personal favor to myself.

Respectfully &c
U. S. GRANT
Maj. Gen.

ALS, CoHi. Silas Alonzo Hudson of Burlington, Iowa, was the son of Susan A. Grant, older sister of Jesse Root Grant (the father of USG), and of Bailey Washington Hudson. See letter to Silas A. Hudson, Nov. 15, 1862.

General Orders No. 1

———

Head Quarters, Department of the Tennessee,
Jackson, Tenn., Oct. 25th, 1862

GENERAL ORDERS, NO. 1.

In compliance with General Orders No. 159, A. G. O., War Department, of date October 16th, 1862, the undersigned hereby assumes command of the Department of the Tennessee, which includes Cairo, Fort Henry and Fort Donelson, Northern Mississippi and the portions of Kentucky and Tennessee west of the Tennessee River.

Head Quarters of the Department of the Tennessee will remain, until further orders, at Jackson, Tennessee.

All orders of the District of West Tennessee, will continue in force in the Department.

U. S. GRANT.

Major General Commanding.

Copies, DLC-USG, V, 13, 14, 95; DNA, RG 393, Dept. of the Tenn., General and Special Orders; (printed) *ibid.*, RG 94, Dept. of the Tenn., General Orders; (printed) Oglesby Papers, IHi. *O.R.*, I, xvii, part 2, 294. On Oct. 26, 1862, Maj. John A. Rawlins issued General Orders No. 2. "The Geographical Divisions designated in General Orders No. 83 from Head Quarters District of West Tennessee, of date September 24th 1862, will hereafter be known as Districts. The first Division will constitute the 'District of Memphis,' Major General W. T. Sherman commanding. The second Division, the 'District of Jackson,' commanded by Major General S. A. Hurlbut. The third Division, the 'District of Corinth,' Brig. General C. S. Hamilton commanding. The fourth Division, the 'District of Columbus,' commanded by Brig. General T. A. Davies. The army heretofore known as the 'Army of the Mississippi,' being now divided and in different Departments, will be discontinued as a separate Army. Until Army Corps are formed, there will be no distinctions known, except those of Department, Districts, Divisions, Posts, Brigades, Regiments and Companies." Copies, DLC-USG, V, 13, 14, 95; DNA, RG 393, Dept. of the Tenn., General and Special Orders; (printed) *ibid.*, RG 94, Dept. of the Tenn., General Orders; (printed) Oglesby Papers, IHi. *O.R.*, I, xvii, part 2, 297.

On Oct. 29, USG wrote to Brig. Gen. Lorenzo Thomas. "I have the honor to transmit herewith copies of my General Orders Nos 1 & 2. Department of the Tennessee." Copy, DLC-USG, V, 88.

To Brig. Gen. Lorenzo Thomas

———

Head Quarters, Dept. of W. Ten.

Jackson, Oct. 25th 1862

BRIG. GEN. L. THOMAS
ADJ. GEN. OF THE ARMY
WASHINGTON D. C.
GEN.

I would respectfully request, if compatible with the interests of public service, that 1st Lieut. Joshua W. Sharp of the 130th regiment, Pa Vols, be ordered to report to me as one of my regular Aid-de-Camps.

There are now two vacancies on my Staff

> I am Gen. very respectfully
> your obt. svt.
> U. S. GRANT
> Maj. Gen

ALS, DNA, RG 94, Vol. Service Division, Letters Received. On Nov. 10, 1862, Col. Edward D. Townsend wrote to USG. "The General-in-chief U S A, directs me to acknowledge the receipt of your communication of the 25th Ult. and respectfully to inform you that he considers it incompatible with the interests of the service to detach Lieutenant Sharp 130th Penna Voluntiers, from the command to which he belongs." Copy, *ibid.*, Letters Sent. See letter to Julia Dent Grant, Aug. 26, 1861.

To Col. John C. Kelton

> Headquarters, Department of the Tennessee
> Jackson, Tennessee, Oct. 25th 1862

COLONEL J. C. KELTON
ASST. ADJT. GENERAL
WASHINGTON. D. C.
COLONEL:

I have the honor to transmit herewith my official Report of the "Battle of Iuka" fought on the 19th day of September 1862, and the following official papers relating to the same, viz:

1st   General Rosecran's Report of the Battle and the following enclosures, viz.

> 1st   General Hamilton's Report of the part taken by the 3rd Division and (12) twelve enclosures.
>
> 2nd. General Stanley's Report of the part taken by the 2nd Division & (15) fifteen enclosures.
>
> 3rd. Colonel Mizner's Report of the part taken by the Cavalry Division, & (4) four enclosures.
>
> 4th. Colonel Lathrops Report of the part taken by the Artillery.

5th. Captain Simmon's Report of the Commissary Stores captured at Iuka

6th. Captain Taylors' Report of the Quartermasters Stores captured

7th. Medical Directors Report of the Killed, Wounded, & missing

8th. Provost Marshals Report of the Enemys killed, wounded and parolled Prisoners.

9th. Chief of Ordnance Report of the quantity and kind of Ordnance and Ordnance Stores captured.

2nd. Major General Ord's Report of the part taken by the Forces under his command.

3rd. The Report of Surgeon John G. F. Holston, Medical Director of the number of Wounded.

4th. Reports of Brig. General Lawman and four enclosures.

> I am, Colonel
> Very Respectfully
> Your Obt. Servt.
> U. S. GRANT
> Maj. Genl.

LS, DNA, RG 108, Letters Received. See letter to Col. John C. Kelton, Oct. 22, 1862. For the reports enclosed, see *O.R.*, I, xvii, part 1, 64–119, though not all are printed.

To Maj. Gen. Samuel R. Curtis

> Jackson Tenn.
> [*Oct. 25th 1862*]

MAJ GENL CURTIS

New Madrid being out of my dept I would like to withdraw the detachment of troops I have there as soon as ~~pos~~ they can be relieved. will, you send troops to relieve them.

> U. S. GRANT
> Maj Genl

Telegram, copy, DNA, RG 393, Dept. of the Mo., Telegrams Received. On Oct. 25, 1862, Maj. Gen. Samuel R. Curtis telegraphed to USG. "Despatch received   Cant spare troops. from New Madrid at present"   Telegram received, *ibid.*, Dept. of the Tenn., Telegrams Received; copy, *ibid.*, Dept. of the Mo., Telegrams Sent. On the same day, USG telegraphed to Curtis. "The troops at New Madrid are detachments from other troops of my command. If they cannot remain subject to my order, I must remove them"   Copies, DLC-USG, V, 18, 30; DNA, RG 393, Dept. of the Tenn., Letters Sent; *ibid.*, Dept. of the Mo., Telegrams Received.

On Nov. 21, Brig. Gen. Thomas A. Davies telegraphed to Curtis that by USG's order troops at New Madrid were to be moved to Island No. 10. Although Curtis protested that these troops were under his command, they were moved anyway. Curtis then protested to Washington in a long telegram embodying the previous telegrams on the subject. Telegram received, *ibid.*, RG 107, Telegrams Collected (Bound). *O.R.*, I, xvii, part 2, 356. A copy of this telegram sent to Davies was forwarded by him to Lt. Col. John A. Rawlins. Telegram received, DNA, RG 393, Dept. of the Tenn., Telegrams Received.

On Oct. 23, Brig. Gen. Grenville M. Dodge, Columbus, Ky., telegraphed to Rawlins. "The Platte Valley reports a Stern Wheeler Captured at mouth of Big Obion River   I send reinforcements last night   more gone today   the Platte Valley moved all gov't Stores at Island No 10 on to the Island   I have requested a GunBoat to go down"   Telegrams received (2), *ibid.*, Dept. of the Mo., Telegrams Received. On Oct. 24, Dodge telegraphed to Rawlins. "Two thousand (2000) of Jacksons cavalry are reported within 12 miles of Island 10 also a large force back of New Madrid   the Expedition has returned from Osceola   captured large amount of goods & salt hid back of the town in the woods—"   Telegram received, *ibid.* On Oct. 23, USG telegraphed to Dodge. "Send infantry & a section of artillery to reinforce new Madrid   I will send an expedition from here for the relief of Island 10"   Telegram received, Dodge Papers, IaHA.

In a similar case, USG encountered difficulties in removing troops from Smithland, Ky. On Nov. 12, Davies telegraphed to Rawlins. "In obediance to your orders I have ordered the troops at Smithland to join their respective commands & ordered transportation accordingly. I have this moment received advice from commanding officer at Smithland sent there by Gen Boyle that these troops will not be permitted to leave without an order from Genl Wright £   I rec'd a similar telegram from Gen Boyle—what shall be done—"   Telegram received, DNA, RG 393, Dept. of the Tenn., Telegrams Received; copy, *ibid.*, Hd. Qrs. District of Columbus, Telegrams Sent. A protest of the same date of Capt. Alexander C. Semple was endorsed to USG by Maj. Nathaniel H. McLean. "Respectfully referred to Maj. Gen. Grant: Com'dg Dept. of the Tenn. with the request that Gen'l Davies be instructed to correct his order of which a copy is enclosed herewith." Copies, DLC-USG, V, 25; DNA, RG 393, Dept. of the Tenn., Endorsements. On Nov. 18, Rawlins endorsed this letter to Davies. "Respectfully referred to Gen'l Davies who will make the correction necessary to conform to the facts. Smithland is not in this Department." Copies, *ibid.*

To Maj. Gen. James B. McPherson

Jackson Tenn Oct 25th 1862

MAJ GENL MCPHERSON
BOLIVAR TENN
GEN:

Your Dispatch received.[1] I have dispatched Hamilton to hold his troops in readiness with three (3) day's provisions in Haversacks to be ready either for a move or for defence of Corinth.

Hold yours in the same way. The move of Price may be to cover the balance of the army in a move on Corinth, should either place be attacked ten regiments can be spared from the line of the Rail-road to re-inforce you with.

U. S. GRANT
Maj Genl

Telegram, copies, DNA, RG 393, District of West Tenn., 4th Division, Letters Received; *ibid.*, Dept. of the Tenn., Letters Sent; DLC-USG, V, 18, 30. *O.R.*, I, xvii, part 2, 294. On Oct. 25, 1862, Maj. John A. Rawlins wrote to Maj. Gen. Stephen A. Hurlbut. "You will have two (2) Brigades of the troops at this place in readiness to move at a moments notice, with three (3) days rations in their haversacks, and one hundred (100) rounds of ammunition to each man." LS, DNA, RG 393, District of West Tenn., 4th Division, Letters Received; copies, *ibid.*, Dept. of the Tenn., Letters Sent; DLC-USG, V, 18, 30. *O.R.*, I, xvii, part 2, 293.

1. Two telegrams of Oct. 25 from Maj. Gen. James B. McPherson to Hurlbut are found in USG's records, the first received at 7:50 P.M. "The patrol sent out on the Grand Junction road to day reports that Jacksons' cavalry was at Grand Junction yesterday & Prices' forces a few miles below Saulsbury. It looks very much as though Price was making a movement this way. I sent out a Battalion of the 5th Ohio Cav'y: this afternoon with instructions to go beyond: Middleburg & ascertain all they could about the disposition & movements of the enemy. Will telegraph you every thing of importance." "Maj. Hayes has just returned from his scout to Middleburg & reports the cavalry in that vicinity. A couple of companies of cotton burners. He also reports the significant fact that the R. R. bridge at Davies Mills has been repaired & that a very large force of Prices' army was four miles below Grand Junction last night. No further news of them could be obtained to day." Telegrams received, DNA, RG 393, Dept. of the Tenn., Telegrams Received. The second of these telegrams is printed as addressed to USG in *O.R.*, I, xvii, part 2, 293.

To Maj. Gen. James B. McPherson

———

Jackson Tenn. Oct 25, 1862

MAJ GEN'L J. B. MCPHERSON
BOLIVAR TENN

Three of the men under Maj Mudd straggled from their command whilst out, and went to several houses and pillaged everything they could carry away. One place they went to, was the house of a Mr. Rodgers, who has been a most loyal man from the beginning. They frightened his family nearly to death, carried off his daughters jewelry and some small articles, tore up his private papers &c. In talking to each other one of them was called Anthony and one Frank. If these men can be identified have them put in irons and brought to trial

U. S. GRANT
Maj Gen'l

Telegram, copies, DLC-USG, V, 18, 30; DNA, RG 393, Dept. of the Tenn., Letters Sent. On Oct. 25, 1862, Maj. Gen. James B. McPherson telegraphed to USG. "Dispatch received in relation to outrages of three men of Major Mudds command and the matter will be thoroughly investigated" Telegram received, *ibid.*, Telegrams Received.

To Brig. Gen. Charles S. Hamilton

———

Jackson Tenn. Oct 25, 1862

GEN'L C. S. HAMILTON
CORINTH MISS

General Quimby will probably be in Corinth tomorrow,[1] and General Dodge as soon as relieved by General Davies.[2] Can't you get up an expedition to go down the Rail Road, and destroy it far to the South? If done the Cavalry should go in force to Tupelo, or further South, supported by a Division of Infantry as far down as Guntown or that vicinity

U. S. GRANT

Telegram, copies, DLC-USG, V, 18, 30; DNA, RG 393, Dept. of the Tenn., Letters Sent; *ibid.*, Army of the Miss., Telegrams Received. *O.R.*, I, xvii, part 2, 293. On Oct. 25, 1862, Brig. Gen. Charles S. Hamilton telegraphed to Maj. John A. Rawlins. "Can you inform me when to expect Generals Quimby and Dodge—" Telegram received, DNA, RG 393, Dept. of the Tenn., Telegrams Received; copy, *ibid.*, Army of the Miss., Telegrams Sent.

1. On Oct. 25, Brig. Gen. Isaac F. Quinby, Columbus, Ky., telegraphed to USG. "I have made my arrangemts for going to Corinth tomorrow   have been almost Sick with a Cold or should have gone down before" Telegram received, *ibid.*, Dept. of the Tenn., Telegrams Received.

2. On Oct. 24, USG telegraphed to Brig. Gen. Grenville M. Dodge, Columbus, Ky. "I have ordered Gen ~~Davits~~ Davies to relieve you in the command of the 4th Division   remain 1 day or as long as may be necessary to post Gen Davies in the localtion of different posts of his command orders &c   you will then report here for orders" Telegram received, Dodge Papers, IaHA. In a telegram dated Oct. 25 in a book record copy, but undoubtedly sent Oct. 24, USG telegraphed to Maj. Gen. William S. Rosecrans. "Would, Genl. Davies like the command of the 4th Geographical Dist. Hd. qrs. at Columbus Ky. I could then send Quimby and Dodge to Corinth   I will send Quimby at any rate and would like him to command a Div." Copy, DNA, RG 393, Army of the Miss., Telegrams Received. On Oct. 24, Rosecrans telegraphed to USG. "Genl Davis replies as follows—If it be the wish of the commanding Genl of department that I should take command of the fourth (4th) Georphical district it will be agreeable to me—" Telegrams received (2), *ibid.*, Dept. of the Mo., Telegrams Received; copy, *ibid.*, Army of the Miss., Telegrams Sent. On Oct. 27, Dodge telegraphed to USG. "Gen Davies releived me this P. M   I shall remain here tomorrow when I will report as ordered—" Telegram received, *ibid.*, Dept. of the Tenn., Telegrams Received; (undated) *ibid.*, Dept. of the Mo., Telegrams Received.

To Brig. Gen. Charles S. Hamilton

Jackson Tenn. Oct 25th 1862

GENL C. S. HAMILTON

I was aware of the destruction of the Rail Road for a considerable distance south of Rienzi. If practicable it should be destroyed south of Tupelo. By moveing on the small force at that they will be likely to destroy the road south themselves, as well as the stores they have there.

My information is that the enemy have but a small force at Tupelo

U. S. GRANT

Telegram, copies, DLC-USG, V, 18, 30; DNA, RG 393, Dept. of the Tenn., Letters Sent; *ibid.*, Army of the Miss., Telegrams Received. *O.R.*, I, xvii, part 2, 292. On Oct. 25, 1862, USG again telegraphed to Brig. Gen. Charles S. Hamilton. "Make your preparations, and execute the suggestions made in my former dispatch as rapidly as possibly" Copies, DLC-USG, V, 18, 30; DNA, RG 393, Dept. of the Tenn., Letters Sent; *ibid.*, Army of the Miss., Telegrams Received. *O.R.*, I, xvii, part 2, 292. On Oct. 25, Hamilton had telegraphed to USG. "I find on investigation the road is entirely destroyed from Rienzi to Baldwin from Baldwin to Tupello there is no Trestle work the Timbers for bridge over Twenty (20) mile Creek are out but not put together and are green There are five bridges destroyed below Rienzi" Telegram received, DNA, RG 393, Dept. of the Tenn., Telegrams Received; copy, *ibid.*, Army of the Miss., Telegrams Sent. On the same day, Hamilton telegraphed to USG. "W. S. R goes up Tomorrow What you suggest can be done" Telegram received, *ibid.*, Dept. of the Tenn., Telegrams Received; copy, *ibid.*, Army of the Miss., Telegrams Sent.

To Brig. Gen. Charles S. Hamilton

———

Jackson Tennessee Oct. 25th 1862

GEN'L C. S. HAMILTON
CORINTH MISS.

Price is moving with considerable force towards Bolivar he is now about four miles South of Grand Junction. Hold your troops in readiness for defence where they are or to move with three day's rations in Haversacks as may be required. All other moves will be suspended until this blows over.

It may be possible that this is to cover a move on Corinth (be prepared) I can reinforce you with ten regiments from here if it becomes necessary

U. S. GRANT

Telegram, copies, DLC-USG, V, 18, 30; DNA, RG 393, Dept. of the Tenn., Letters Sent; (dated Oct. 24, 1862) *ibid.*, Army of the Miss., Telegrams Received. *O.R.*, I, xvii, part 2, 293. On Oct. 25, Brig. Gen. Charles S. Hamilton sent three telegrams to USG. "It is believed here that Price has been largely reinforced from Texas and Arkansas There are all indications that he is moving this way Deserters say he is going to attack Corinth. I have ordered large Cavalry forces to scout to the west. Am pushing the fortifications as fast as possible." Copy, DNA, RG 393, Army of the Miss., Telegrams Sent. "Reports in from Cavalry Scouts at Pocahontas and beyond no apparant movement by Price—Two (2) trains each day from Mobile to Tupelo & back leave Mobile at 7 & 7 35 A M leave Tupelo at 8 45 & 9 30 A M" Telegram received, *ibid.*, Dept. of the Tenn., Telegrams Received; copy, *ibid.*, Army of the Miss., Telegrams Sent. "Dispatch received. Will be ready. A Catholic priest just arrived from Huntsville says the rebels there had news that Mobile was attacked. Price may be causing a movement in that direction." *O.R.*, I, xvii, part 2, 293.

Also on Oct. 25, USG telegraphed to the commanding officers, Humboldt, Trenton, and Columbus. "Hold one (1) Regiment at Columbus & the Infantry not detached on Rail Road guard from Trenton & Humbolt with 3 days rations in Haversacks ready to move if ordered." Telegram received, DNA, RG 393, Dept. of the Mo., Telegrams Received; copies, *ibid.*, Dept. of the Tenn., Letters Sent; DLC-USG, V, 18, 30. *O.R.*, I, xvii, part 2, 293. On the same day, Col. James J. Dollins, Humboldt, Tenn., telegraphed to Maj. John A. Rawlins. "The 81st Ills Vols here have no Haversacks & could never get them but will go if ordered any time" Telegram received, DNA, RG 393, Dept. of the Tenn., Telegrams Received. On Oct. 26, Dollins telegraphed to USG. "Would like to stay here now till I finish the fortifications am getting along very well with them have a hundred contrabands at work on them Please answer" Telegram received, *ibid.* On the same day, Col. John I. Rinaker, Trenton, Tenn., telegraphed to USG. "The only Infantry at Trenton is 122d Ills has no tents not a particle of transportation not an ambulance. without half supply of Blankets." Telegram received, *ibid.* On the same day, Brig. Gen. Grenville M. Dodge, Columbus, Ky., telegraphed to Rawlins. "I have here only parts of but two (2) Regts will have them ready—" Telegram received, *ibid.*

To Commanding Officer, Bethel, Tenn.

Jackson Tenn Oct 25, 1862

COMD'G OFFICER BETHEL TENN.

Complaints are constantly coming to me of depredations committed by Hurst's men on Citizens through the country. They go about the country taking horses whereever they find them. They must desist from this practice or I will disband the whole concern. When horses are claimed by citizens, and there is no satisfactory reason why they should be taken, have them returned.

U. S. GRANT.

Copies, DLC-USG, V, 18, 30; DNA, RG 393, Dept. of the Tenn., Letters Sent. On Oct. 25, 1862, Col. William R. Morrison, Bethel, Tenn., telegraphed to Maj. John A. Rawlins. "What you say of Hursts men is true   they are made up of deserters from Rebels & other bad men. Here where many of them have private grievances it is impossible to control them because impossible to prove anything. Most of the horses were taken before they came into camp & have been returned but I believe in many cases people dont complain restrained by fear—I have more than once presented this matter to Gen Logan & will venture to send you communications direct by Mail stating facts more fully tomorrow—These men ought to be removed from here—"   Telegram received, *ibid.*, Telegrams Received.

On Oct. 25, Maj. Gen. Stephen A. Hurlbut wrote to Rawlins. "The papers returned to me in case of Fielding Hurst justify a Court Martial. I would respectfully inquire if the said Hurst is a Commissioned officer of the U. States & if so what his rank is—I have no evidence that he is & it may make a question if he be not" ALS, *ibid.*, District of West Tenn., 4th Division, Letters Received. On Oct. 28, Rawlins endorsed this letter. "Col. Hurst assumes to act under the authority of the Governor of the State of Tennessee, who is authorized by the President of the U. S. to accept troops, and will be regarded and treated as in the service, and subject to the same regulations." ES, *ibid.*

On Oct. 20, USG telegraphed to Maj. Gen. William S. Rosecrans. "By what Authority did Col. Mizner rder Col. Hurst to organize his Regt. of West Tenn. Cav. This Regt. is on duty in Hurlbut Division and subject to his orders." Copy, *ibid.*, Army of the Miss., Telegrams Received. On the same day, Rosecrans telegraphed to USG. "Col Mizner informs me that Col Hurst reported to him at Ripley as from Bethel then supposed to be in my command and received orders from Col Mizner for his return via Corinth via his old Post   since then Col Hurst addressed a letter to Col Mizner asking Permission to move to Clayton Station giving reasons that He could better organize his Reg't there. Col Mizner says He replied expressing his approbation of the reasons given but has not presumed to give Col Hurst any orders nor has he supposed Himself authorized to order Col H since Bethel was decided to be out of this Division"   Telegram received, *ibid.*, Dept. of the Mo., Telegrams Received; copy (misdated Oct. 17), *ibid.*, Army of the Miss., Telegrams Sent.

On Nov. 11, Hurlbut telegraphed to USG. "Their is one Battalion of (1st) First Tenn Cavalry at Bolivar awaiting organization.   will you send Colonel Dickey to Bolivar for that purpose." Copy, *ibid.*, District of West Tenn., 4th Division, Letters Sent. See telegram to Andrew Johnson, July 25, 1862.

To Maj. Gen. Henry W. Halleck

Jackson Tenn
Oct 26th 8 40 a m [18]62

MAJ GEN H. W. HALLECK
GEN IN CHIEF

The Rebel Army is again moving, probably on Corinth. They have been reinforced with the exchanged prisoners. Troops from Texas & Arkansas and conscripts—We will be attacked in a few days—Is it not possible to send the Helena force or some other reinforcements here?

U. S. GRANT
Maj Gen'l

Telegram received, DNA, RG 94, Generals' Papers and Books, Telegrams Received by Gen. Halleck; *ibid.*, RG 107, Telegrams Collected (Bound); copies, *ibid.*, Telegrams Received in Cipher; (dated Oct. 25, 1862) *ibid.*, RG 393, USG Hd. Qrs. Correspondence; DLC-USG, V, 4, 5, 7, 8, 88. Dated Oct. 26 in *O.R.*, I, xvii, part 2, 296. On Oct. 27, Maj. Gen. Henry W. Halleck telegraphed to USG. "The Governor of Ill. has been directed to send you as many troops as possible. Genl Curtis is begging for reinforcements to be sent to Helena. Be prepared to concentrate your troops in case of an attack. For a cartel ship to receive deserters is a violation of the laws of war." ALS (telegram sent), DNA, RG 107, Telegrams Collected (Bound); telegrams received (2), *ibid.*, RG 393, Dept. of the Tenn., Telegrams Received. *O.R.*, I, xvii, part 2, 298. See following telegram.

On Oct. 27, Maj. Gen. Horatio G. Wright telegraphed to USG. "Under instructions from the Gen in Chief I have requested Gov Yates to send all available troops in Illinois to report to you at Columbus   if not required they are to proceed to Helena" Telegram received (dated "26"), DNA, RG 393, Dept. of the Tenn., Telegrams Received; copy, *ibid.*, Dept. of the Ohio (Cincinnati), Telegrams Sent. For correspondence between Halleck and Wright, Secretary of War Edwin M. Stanton, Governor Richard Yates of Ill., and Maj. Gen. John A. McClernand concerning reinforcements for USG, see *O.R.*, I, xvii, part 2, 298–300, 302–3, 308–10; *ibid.*, I, xvi, part 2, 656–58. McClernand believed that these troops would be under his command.

On Oct. 28, USG telegraphed to Ill. AG Allen C. Fuller. "I am informed that reinforcements have been ordered here from Illinois. When may I look for them? Public interest requires that they should be sent promptly." Copies, DLC-USG, V, 18, 30; DNA, RG 393, Dept. of the Tenn., Letters Sent. *O.R.*, III, ii, 692. On the same day, Fuller telegraphed to USG. "In addition to eight (8) Regiments heretofore sent you the hundred & third (103) is under orders & will move Wednesday   the hundred & eleventh (111) which will move Friday & the ninety fifth (95) which will move Monday next—ten (10) more Regiments can be forwarded in next ten (10) Days if paid & armed   Can you supply any Good Arms to a few of our Regiments"   Telegram received, DNA, RG 393, Dept. of the Tenn., Telegrams Received.

On Oct. 31, Brig. Gen. James M. Tuttle, Cairo, telegraphed to USG. "The 103d Ills just reported here   their orders is a telegram to report to Cairo   I knew nothing of them until their arrival—What shall I do with them—They have no tents   will have to issue them here—"   Telegram received, *ibid.* On the same day, Maj. John A. Rawlins telegraphed to Tuttle. "You will issue tents to the 103rd Ills Regt and send it Jackson"   Copies, *ibid.*, Letters Sent; DLC-USG, V, 18, 30. Also on Oct. 31, Col. Robert Allen, St. Louis, telegraphed to USG. "Do any of the Wis' Regts ordered to Cairo go to Columbus   the 29th & 32d are now on their way [to] Corinth by rail—"   Telegram received, DNA, RG 393, Dept. of the Tenn., Telegrams Received. On the same day, USG telegraphed to Allen. "All regiments ordered to Cairo will come to Columbus, where orders will await them"   Copies, DLC-USG, V, 18, 30; DNA, RG 393, Dept. of the Tenn., Letters Sent.

To Maj. Gen. Henry W. Halleck

Jackson [*Oct.*] 26th [*1862*]

GEN HALLECK

Capt Swan[1] of the 57th Ill in charge of transport Carrying exchanged prisoners & under a flag of truce brought back with him Six Confederate deserters & two Negroes from Vicksburg & delivered them to Gen Tuttle, to whom I have telegraphed to hold them till further order   Is not this a Violation of a flag of truce

U S. GRANT
M. Genl

Telegram received, DNA, RG 94, Generals' Papers and Books, Telegrams Received by Gen. Halleck; *ibid.*, RG 107, Telegrams Collected (Bound); copies, *ibid.*, RG 393, Dept. of the Tenn., Letters Sent; DLC-USG, V, 5, 8, 24, 88. *O.R.*, II, iv, 654.

Brig. Gen. James M. Tuttle, Cairo, had sent an undated telegram to USG. "Capt Swan fifty seventh Ill in charge of transport with Prisoners to Vicksburg with Flag of truce brought off six (6) confederate deserters from Vicksburg also two 2 Negroes will be subject of complaint for violation of flag of truce   what shall I do   parts and transport are all here"   Telegram received, DNA, RG 393, Dept. of the Mo., Telegrams Received. On Oct. 26, 1862, USG telegraphed to Tuttle. "Hold the Negroes and prisoners at Cairo till further orders"   Copies, *ibid.*, Dept. of the Tenn., Letters Sent; DLC-USG, V, 18, 30. On Nov. 3, Tuttle telegraphed to USG. "Transport with prisoners for Vicksburg will leave tomorrow   shall I send the six (6) prisoners that deserted at Vicksburg & the two (2) negroes that were stolen under flag of truce—Have you any prisoners to send down—" Telegram received, DNA, RG 393, Dept. of the Tenn., Telegrams Received.

1. William S. Swan of Chicago was appointed capt., 57th Ill., on Dec. 30, 1861. On Nov. 7, 1862, Lt. Col. John A. Rawlins issued Special Orders No. 11. "Capt Wm. S. Swan 59th Regt Illinois Inf Vols will at once rejoin his Regt at Corinth, Miss, and remain with it in arrest untill further orders. Any explanation he may have to make will be addressed to the Adjutant General of the Army, Washington, D. C. and forwarded through these Headquarters." DS, *ibid.*, RG 94, Dept. of the Tenn., Special Orders; DLC-USG, V, 16, 26, 27, 87. Swan's explanation, dated Nov. 14, reached USG's hd. qrs. on Nov. 25, and was forwarded to the AGO. *Ibid.*, V, 21; DNA, RG 393, Dept. of the Tenn., Register of Letters Received; *ibid.*, RG 94, Register of Letters Received. On Nov. 25, Rawlins issued Special Orders No. 29 releasing Swan from arrest. DS, *ibid.*, Dept. of the Tenn., Special Orders; copies, *ibid.*, RG 393, Dept. of the Tenn., Special Orders; DLC-USG, V, 16, 26, 27. On Dec. 14, Capt. Theodore S. Bowers endorsed charges against Swan preferred by Capt. Edgar M. Lowe, 9th Ill. "Charges not sustained. The statement of Capt Swan was sent to the Gen'l in Chief of the Army who approved the action of the General Com'd'g in releasing Capt. Swan, and restoring him to duty." Copies, *ibid.*, V, 25; DNA, RG 393, Dept. of the Tenn., Endorsements.

To Maj. Gen. Henry W. Halleck

Head Quarters, Dept. of Ten.
Jackson Oct. 26th 1862

MAJ. GEN. H. W. HALLECK
GEN. IN CHIEF
WASHINGTON D. C.
GEN.

You have never suggested to me any plan of opperations in this Department and as I do not know anything of those of commanders to my right or left. I have none therefore that is not independent of all others forces than those under my immediate command.

As situated now, with no more troops, I can do nothing but

defend my positions and I do not feel at liberty to abandon any of them without first consulting you.

I would suggest however the destruction of the rail-roads to all points of the compas from Corinth by the removal of the rails to this place or Columbus and the opening of the road from Humboldt to Memphis. The Corinth forces I would move to Grand Junction and add to them the Bolivar forces except a smal garrison there. With small reinforcements at Memphis I think I would be able to move down the Mississippi Central road and cause the evacuation of Vicksburg and be able to capture or destroy all the boats in the Yazoo river.

I am ready however to do with all my might whatever you may direct, without criticism.

I see in the papers ~~that reached here yesterday~~ of Saturday that Gen. Curtis has refused permits to $30.000 worth of liquors ~~that~~ which had been authorized to be shipped to Memphis, among it 750 bbls. of whiskey to one of my Staff. As no member of my staff has ever engaged, since entering the army, in any speculation by which to make a dollar I care nothing for the publication, but as the information could have been derived only from Gen. Curtis' Hd Qrs. I think it a matter requiring explaination. I telegraphed Gen. C. for the explaination but he has not replied.[1]

The facts are these: I gave a Mr. Farrington,[2] an undoubted Union citizen of Memphis, permission to ship $7.000 worth of liquor to Memphis, ~~with subject to Gen~~ subject to all Treasury restrictions   Finding that these stores could not be got out of St. Louis without Gen. Curtis approval Farrington asked Col. Pride, who has never been more than a Vol. Aid on my staff, to introduce him. From this has sprung the report. I would respectfully suggest that my permits be good for all articles coming into this Dept. subject only to Treasury regulations and orders of those above me.

I am now holding New Madrid with detachments from troops of this command which Gen. Curtis has assumed controll over, and coolly informs me that he cannot spare them.[3] I would respectfully suggest that both banks of the river be under one command.

> I am Gen. very respectfully
> your obt. svt.
> U. S. Grant
> Maj. Gen. Com

ALS, IHi. *O.R.*, I, xvii, part 2, 296–97.

1. On Oct. 25, 1862, USG telegraphed to Maj. Gen. Samuel R. Curtis. "I see by telegraph from St Louis that a member of my staff had a permit to ship seven hundred and fifty (750) barrels of liquor to Memphis which you refused to let go, no such permit has been granted here & you will oblige me by giving the name of the party having the permit." Copies, DNA, RG 393, Dept. of the Mo., Telegrams Received; (misdated Dec. 25) Curtis Papers, IaHA. No record of a reply has been found.

Although USG issued orders prohibiting shipment of liquor into his command for commercial purposes (see *Calendar*, Aug. 23, 1862), Memphis was an exception. On Aug. 17, Col. William S. Hillyer issued permits, on USG's authority, for R. A. Peebles and for Daniel Able and Co. to ship liquor from Cairo to Memphis since Maj. Gen. William T. Sherman authorized the opening of the saloons of Memphis. ADS, DNA, RG 366, Special Agents, Reports and Correspondence. On Dec. 17, these permits were sent to Secretary of the Treasury Salmon P. Chase by special agents William P. Mellen and W. D. Gallagher, who complained that they violated Treasury regulations. LS, *ibid.*

On Sept. 25, Mellen wrote to USG. "I visited Corinth on the 18th inst. hoping to see you but you were down the road, *engaged*, and I cannot get nigh you in result. I wish to call your attention to the 8th section of the 'regulations' inclosed herewith. Your written request or that of some person on your staff by you will be required as a condition precedent to permitting any shipment of 'intoxicating drink,' to any place throughout or in the Department and this as it now stands includes all wines, malt liquors, bitters &c. I desire to consult with you as to your wishes in this and some other matters. Through the officers in command of military posts in your Department I find that upon *their* recommendation of any shipment of liquor to points *therein* for their *individual use* Customs officers always grant the permits.—If this is your wish and you will so report yourself to me, I will direct all officers to grant *such* permits upon *such* certificates. I presume also that you may wish to delegate the power which you are authorized to do at certain places in your department, for recommending shipments of wines and liquor to persons therein for *general* purposes. If so, and you will inform me what places and to whom therein you have confided the authority I will instruct the surveyors to grant permits as may be recommended by the persons named by you. This will prevent unauthorized persons from deceiving the officers of the customs and will also prevent question by the officers of the customs when a certificate is presented from an authorized officer as to his authority to give it. I would suggest also that as in many cases 'license fees' have been demanded by officers for recommending shipments, of from $10 to $50, which of course they pocket themselves, your authority to them to grant certificates of recommendation expressly forbids their receiving any fee or compensation therefor. Otherwise a fee in each case is a temptation to make them numerous. I hope to hear from you at your earliest convenience, and to see you before long" ALS, *ibid.*, Letters Sent (Press). On Oct. 14, Sherman received a letter of J. P. Maguire requesting permission to ship liquor to Memphis, which USG had endorsed. "All trade is subject to the regulations of the treasury Dept." Copies, *ibid.*, RG 393, 15th Army Corps, Register of Letters Received; *ibid.*, RG 94, Generals' Papers and Books, William T. Sherman, Register of Letters Received. On Nov. 14, Sherman received a letter from Col. John Riggin, Jr., authorizing R. D. Nabers to ship liquor to Memphis "if consistent with Treasury Rules." Copy, *ibid.* See letter to Maj. Gen. Henry W. Halleck, Sept. 7, 1862.

2. On Nov. 4, U.S. Treasury Agent David G. Barnitz, Cincinnati, wrote to Mellen. "Our friend Matt. Farrington obtained an order from Genl. Sherman at Memphis for his bill of liquors which was also approved by Genl. Tuttle at Cairo. They were shipped from St. Louis to Cairo, and about one half of them were sent down to Memphis. Before the other half could be shipped, a telegraphic order came from *Genl Curtis* at St. Louis, ordering the Provost Marshall at Cairo to stop them, which was accordingly done, and when I left Cairo, Farrington was about going to Jackson to see Genl. Grant about it. How *Grant* will relish the interference of *Curtis* in his District, I cannot say, but I think he will not approve of it." ALS, DNA, RG 366, Correspondence of the General Agent.

3. See telegram to Maj. Gen. Samuel R. Curtis, Oct. 25, 1862.

To Brig. Gen. Charles S. Hamilton

Jackson Tenn. Oct 26, 1862.

GEN'L. C. S HAMILTON
CORINTH MISS

Unless you are promoted, you cannot retain your present command. I recommended you by telegraph some days ago for the promotion.[1]

Should Ord return as he expects to do, it would give me four Maj Gen'l senior to yourself and I would be compelled to place one at Corinth. In that case I would divide the army at Corinth into two wings, reinforced if possible, and of course you would have one wing.

No further news from the front

U. S. GRANT
Maj Gen'l

Copies, DLC-USG, V, 18, 30; DNA, RG 393, Dept. of the Tenn., Letters Sent. On Oct. 26, 1862, Brig. Gen. Charles S. Hamilton telegraphed to USG. "Am I likely to remain in command here I want to know & if so I will organize a staff &c. I have nothing new. Have you?" Telegram received, *ibid.*, Telegrams Received; copy, *ibid.*, Army of the Miss., Telegrams Sent.

1. See telegram to Maj. Gen. Henry W. Halleck, Oct. 21, 1862. Hamilton wrote frequently to Senator James R. Doolittle of Wis. about his promotion; letters of Sept. 25, Oct. 22, Nov. 20, 1862, Jan. 7, 30, Feb. 11, 1863, WHi. On Jan. 16, 1863, President Abraham Lincoln nominated Hamilton as maj. gen. to rank from Sept. 19, 1862.

To Brig. Gen. Lorenzo Thomas

Head Quarters, Dept. of Ten.
Jackson Oct. 27th 1862

BRIG. GEN. L THOMAS
ADJ. GEN. OF THE ARMY
WASHINGTON D. C.
GEN.

I would respectfully request that Maj. J. A. Rawlins A. A. Gen. on my Staff, and Capt. R. W. Rowley, the latter at this time an additional Aid-de-Camp on the Staff of[1] and assigned to me, be promoted, the former to the rank of Lt. Col. and the latter to the rank of Maj. in conformity with the 10 Section of an Act of Congress embraced in Gen. Orders No 91 from the War Dept. of the 29th of July 1862.

I would also ask that Capt. Chas. A. Reynolds A. Q. M. Chief Qr. Mr. of this Dept. and Capt. J. P. Hawkins C. S. Chief Com.y be each promoted to the rank of Lt. Col. and 1st Lt. T. S. Bowers A. D. C. be promoted to the rank of Capt. in accordance with the same provisions.

I am Gen. Very respectfully
your obt. svt.
U. S GRANT
Maj. Gen

ALS, Mrs. Walter Love, Flint, Mich. Each promotion requested by USG was announced by AGO General Orders No. 181, Nov. 1, 1862, effective the same day.

1. The name of Maj. Gen. George B. McClellan was omitted at this point.

To Brig. Gen. Lorenzo Thomas

Jackson Tenn [*Oct.*] 28 [*1862*]

GEN L THOMAS

The order will be sent by Mail   The sentence in the case of Sergt Charles Braffit has not been carried into effect   Was ordered to be confined in the Military Prison at Alton, Ill. & now awaits the decision of the Prest

U. S. GRANT

Telegram received, DNA, RG 107, Telegrams Collected (Bound); copies, *ibid.*, RG 393, Dept. of the Tenn., Hd. Qrs. Correspondence; DLC-USG, V, 5, 8, 24, 88. On Oct. 28, 1862, Brig. Gen. Lorenzo Thomas telegraphed to USG. "The copy of General Orders number seventy six District of West Tennessee relating to sentence of Court Martial in case of Sergeant Charles Braffitt fifth Ohio Cavalry is not with the proceedings, or on file in this office. Has the sentence been carried into effect, or how does the case stand?" Copies, *ibid.*; *ibid.*, RG 94, Letters Sent. On Oct. 28, Maj. John A. Rawlins telegraphed to Brig. Gen. Charles S. Hamilton. "In June a Court Martial at Corinth sentenced Sergeant Charles Braffitt, of the 5th Ohio Cavalry, then in 2d Div. commanded by Gen'l. Davies, to be shot. The order publishing the Court Martial postponed the execution of the sentence, and directed that the prisoner be confined in the Alton Prison until further orders. Please ascertain at once what has been done to him" Copies, DLC-USG, V, 18, 30; DNA, RG 393, Dept. of the Tenn., Letters Sent; *ibid.*, District of Corinth, Telegrams Received. On the same day, Hamilton telegraphed to Rawlins. "No such Regt. as the 5th Iowa Cavalry in this command. Is it not the 5th Ohio. Cavly? No records of such sentence at these Hd. quarters. Please answer." Copy, *ibid.*, Telegrams Sent. On Oct. 29, Hamilton telegraphed to Rawlins. "Charles Braffit—a sergeant of the 5th Ohio Cav.ly Vols. under sentence of death was sent to Alton Illinois with other prisoners Septem. 17th 1862." Copy, *ibid.*

To Maj. Gen. Henry W. Halleck

Jackson Tenn
Oct 28th 8 10 P. M. [*1862*]

Maj Gen H. W. Halleck
Gen in chief.

The following dispatch is just received from Brig Gen Davis at Columbus Ky.

The Expedition to Clarkson Mo 34 miles from New Madrid under command of Capt Rogers[1] Co K 2nd Illinois Artillery has been eminently successful dispersing the Guerrillas killing 10 mortally wounding 2 capturing Col Clarke[2] [in] command Captain & 3 Lieutenants 3 Surgeons 37 men 70 stand of arms 42 horses 13 mules 2 wagons [a] large quantity of ammunition burning their barracks & magazine totally breaking up the whole concern—No loss on our side"

U S Grant
Maj Genl

Telegram received, DNA, RG 94, Generals' Papers and Books, Telegrams Received by Gen. Halleck; *ibid.*, RG 107, Telegrams Collected (Bound); copies, *ibid.*, RG 393, Dept. of the Tenn., Hd. Qrs. Correspondence; DLC-USG, V, 5, 8, 24, 88. A copy of the telegram of Oct. 28, 1862, from Brig. Gen. Thomas A. Davies to Maj. John A. Rawlins is in DNA, RG 393, Hd. Qrs. District of Columbus, Letters Sent. On Oct. 29, Davies wrote to Rawlins reporting the expedition in greater detail. Copy, *ibid. O.R.*, I, xiii, 338.

1. Benjamin F. Rodgers of Jacksonville, Ill., was mustered in as capt., Battery K, 2nd Ill. Light Art., on Dec. 31, 1861.
2. C. S. A. Col. Henry E. Clark later stated that as a recruiting officer he had collected twenty-one organized cos. and portions of several others before his capture, along with twenty-three men, on Oct. 26, 1862, at Clarkston, Mo. *Ibid.*, I, xxii, part 1, 1079.

To Maj. Gen. James B. McPherson

Headquarters Dep't of the Tenn.,
Jackson, Oct. 28. 1862

GEN'L MCPHERSON,
BOLIVAR, TENN

Hamilton's scouts, also one of Price's escort, report troops moving south. This would look as if Mobile was threatened. If you can find out anything from the front do it.

U. S. GRANT.
Maj. Gen'l.

Copies, DLC-USG, V, 18, 30; DNA, RG 393, Dept. of the Tenn., Letters Sent. *O.R.*, I, xvii, part 2, 301. On Oct. 28, 1862, Maj. Gen. James B. McPherson, Bolivar, telegraphed to USG. "A man by the name of Robinson, who lives near Grand Junction and left there last night, reports to me that infantry were moving south from Holly Springs, though there was a large force of cavalry about Davis' Mill. I have scouts out, and will, I hope, know shortly whether this is the case. I sent Colonel Johnson, with two companies of cavalry, one regiment of infantry, and a section of artillery, yesterday afternoon in the direction of Somerville to make a thorough reconnaissance. He has not returned; will probably be in to-night or to-morrow. My patrols on the Grand Junction road have returned, after going 3 miles south of Van Buren, and report everything quiet and no enemy to be seen or heard from." *Ibid.* See *ibid.*, I, lii, part 1, 295–96.

Earlier on Oct. 28, Brig. Gen. Charles S. Hamilton had telegraphed to USG. "Cavalry scouts in from Chewalla tonight report troops have left, Holly Springs going south. Also confirmed by one of Prices Escort who left Holly Springs on Sunday." Copy, DNA, RG 393, District of Corinth, Telegrams Sent. *O.R.*, I, xvii, part 2, 301.

On Oct. 27, Maj. John A. Rawlins transmitted to USG a telegram from McPherson to Maj. Gen. Stephen A. Hurlbut. "The reconnoitering party under Col. Leggett has returned safely. The infantry went 2½ miles south of Van Buren; at this point the Cavalry was divided into three detachments. One went to Saulsbury, one to Grand Junction capturing a picket of four men a short distance this side of the Junction, and driving the balance out of the town, and the 3d went through New Castle to within 4 miles of La Grange, the reconnoisance developed the fact that there is no force of the enemy except Cavalry this side of Davis Mills. About four hundred (400) Cavalry are reported to have gone on to Estinola whether for the purpose of crossing the Hatchie and interfering with the Rail Road or not, I have not yet ascertained" Copy, DNA, RG 393, Dept. of the Tenn., Telegrams Received. *O.R.*, I, xvii, part 2, 299.

To Brig. Gen. Charles S. Hamilton

———

Headquarters Dept., of the Tenn
Jackson, Tenn., Oct. 28, 1862

GEN'L. HAMILTON,
CORINTH, MISS.

Stop all Recruiting from Volunteer regiments for the regular service, and order back to their companies any that have already so enlisted. If there is to be any enlisting from Volunteer regiments, I will publish the orders regulating it in this Department. I see by the papers however that the order will be countermanded, and all soldiers so enlisted will be ordered back as I am now directing.

U. S. GRANT.
Maj. Gen'l

Telegram, copies, DLC-USG, V, 18, 30; DNA, RG 393, Dept. of the Tenn., Letters Sent; *ibid.*, District of Corinth, Telegrams Received.

On Nov. 17, 1862, Maj. Gen. Stephen A. Hurlbut telegraphed to USG. "Officers of Regular service are enlisting men from 7th Wisconsin battery at Humboldt   I suppose it cannot be helped but It will cripple the battery & reduce it below standard of six gun battery   I await your orders—" Telegram received, *ibid.*, Dept. of the Tenn., Telegrams Received. On the same day, USG telegraphed to Hurlbut. "Require all men already enlisted into the Regular Army to return to their Companies, and inform Officers engaged in that kind of recruiting service, that they will be arrested, and if necessary be put in close confinement if found engaged in taking men from this Department without my authority" Copies, DLC-USG, V, 18, 30; DNA, RG 393, Dept. of the Tenn., Letters Sent.

On Dec. 26, Col. Edward D. Townsend wrote to USG. "I am instructed to acknowledge the receipt of a letter dated November 29. 1862. from Capt. J. R. Edie, 15th U. S. Infantry. to you with your indorsement, and to request that you will not offer any obstacles to the enlistment of Volunteers into the regular army unless in a case of Emergency   I enclose for your information General Orders 154 and 162 from the War Department which are still in force. If the men referred to have been properly enlisted in accordance with General Orders, 154 and 162, you will please send them at once to the 15th U. S. Infantry, with their Discriptive Lists and account of pay and clothing" Copies, DLC-USG, V, 5, 8, 24, 88, 93; DNA, RG 393, Dept. of the Tenn., Hd. Qrs. Correspondence; *ibid.*, Military Division of the Miss., War Dept. Correspondence. See *O.R.*, III, ii, 654, 676.

To Brig. Gen. Charles S. Hamilton

Jackson, Tenn, Oct. 28. 1862

BRIG. GEN. HAMILTON
CORINTH, MISS.

The party cannot come in—say to them you will receive their communication and refer it to me.

U. S. GRANT.
Maj. Gen'l.

Telegram, copies, DLC-USG, V, 18, 30; DNA, RG 393, Dept. of the Tenn., Letters Sent; *ibid.*, District of Corinth, Telegrams Received. On Oct. 28, 1862, Brig. Gen. Charles S. Hamilton telegraphed to USG. "Flag of truce has arrived at Chewalla outposts with communication from Van Dorn to Rosecrans. Bearer is instructed to deliver dispatches here in person. I send out Col. Mizner to receive Dispatch—which I say will be referred to you. I wish to avoid their coming to this place." Copy, *ibid.*, Telegrams Sent. *O.R.*, I, xvii, part 2, 300–1. On the same day, Hamilton telegraphed to Col. John K. Mizner. "Maj. Genl. Grant telegraphs that the communication must be referred to him at Jackson and that the party cannot enter Corinth. Answer this dispatch." Copy, DNA, RG 393, District of Corinth, Telegrams Sent. On the same day, Mizner telegraphed to Hamilton. "Col. Major is at house two miles from here refreshing himself. I go to him immediately. Genl. Grants instructions received." Copy, *ibid.*, Telegrams Received. On the same day, Hamilton telegraphed to USG. "Have sent out Col. Mizner to meet flag of truce with Authority to receive communication and to say it will be referred to you. Oweing to temporary absence of Genl. Rosecrans the party will not come in. Two scouts just in went within twelve miles of Grand Junction where they found pickets. Saw a man living between Grand Junction and Saulsbury who reports nothing but Cavalry north of Holly Springs. Could hear of no Inf. except at Holly Springs   Armstrong at Salem. Great numbers of men on short furloughs through the country. The talk was of a movement on Bolivar if any was made." Copy, *ibid.*, Telegrams Sent.

To David Tod

Headquarters, Dep't. of the Tenn.
Jackson, Tenn., Oct. 28th 1862

Hon. David Todd
Gov. of the State of Ohio
Your Dispatch of 23d inst., received and the following sent:

"Jackson 23d Oct. 1862

Maj. Gen'l. Wright,
Cincinnati Ohio,"

"Please order Lieut. Col. Haskin,[1] 63d Ohio Vols., now at Marietta, to rejoin his Regiment or send me his resignation."

U. S. Grant.
Maj. Gen'l."

Telegram, copies, DLC-USG, V, 18, 30; DNA, RG 393, Dept. of the Tenn., Letters Sent. On Oct. 28, 1862, Governor David Tod of Ohio telegraphed to USG. "Did you receive my Telegram of the Twenty third (23) inst asking you to order Lieut Col Haskins of the 63rd Regt O. V I to join his Reg't   Please answer" Telegram received, *ibid.*, Telegrams Received.

1. Alexander L. Haskins, commissioned maj., 63rd Ohio on March 3, 1862, was commissioned lt. col. on Aug. 5, but the latter was later revoked, and Haskins was discharged on March 20, 1863. On Dec. 13, 1862, Col. John W. Sprague, 63rd Ohio, wrote to USG's hd. qrs. concerning the resignation of Haskins for medical reasons. *Ibid.*, Endorsements; DLC-USG, V, 25. On Dec. 15, USG endorsed this letter. "Respectfully forwarded to Head Quarters of the Army Washington D. C. and recommend that he be honorably discharged"   Copies, *ibid.*

To Maj. Gen. Henry W. Halleck

Jackson Tenn Oct 29 [*1862*] 4 P M

HENRY W HALLECK
GENL IN CHF

Everything now indicates an early attack on Bolivar or Corinth. The Rebels have been largely reinforced & are moving precisely as they did before the last attack   Price is at Ripley Whilst a force is in front of Bolivar with Cavalry thrown out in large force toward Somerville. I will be ready to do all that is possible with the means at hand   Reinforcement not arrived—

U S. GRANT

Telegram received, DNA, RG 94, Generals' Papers and Books, Telegrams Received by Gen. Halleck; *ibid.*, RG 107, Telegrams Collected (Bound); copies, *ibid.*, RG 393, Dept. of the Tenn., Hd. Qrs. Correspondence; DLC-USG, V, 5, 8, 24, 88. *O.R.*, I, xvii, part 2, 302–3.

To Maj. Gen. Henry W. Halleck

Jackson Tinn Oct 29 [*1862*] 4 30 P M

HENRY. W HALLECK
GEN IN CHF

112 furloughs granted by Genl Curtis to men of my command is just recd. Has authority been granted since General orders Number 78 to give furloughs?

U S GRANT
Maj Genl

Telegram received, DNA, RG 94, Generals' Papers and Books, Telegrams Received by Gen. Halleck; *ibid.*, RG 107, Telegrams Collected (Bound); copies, *ibid.*, RG 393, Dept. of the Tenn., Hd. Qrs. Correspondence; DLC-USG, V, 5, 8, 24, 88. *O.R.*, I, xvii, part 2, 303. On Oct. 30, 1862, Maj. Gen. Henry W. Halleck telegraphed to USG. "Reinforcements for your army are moving from Wisconsin, Minnesota & Illinois. Furloughs to men in your command given by

Genl Curtis are null & void. They should not be recognised. Order No 78 is still in force." ALS (telegram sent), DNA, RG 107, Telegrams Collected (Bound); telegram received, *ibid.*, RG 393, Dept. of the Tenn., Telegrams Received. *O.R.*, I, xvii, part 2, 308.

On Oct. 25, USG had telegraphed to Halleck. "Can I have authority to furlough wounded men who cannot be fit for duty under 30 or 60 days?" Telegram received, DNA, RG 94, Generals' Papers and Books, Telegrams Received by Gen. Halleck; *ibid.*, RG 107, Telegrams Collected (Bound); copies, *ibid.*, RG 393, Dept. of the Tenn., Hd. Qrs. Correspondence; DLC-USG, V, 4, 5, 7, 8, 88.

To Maj. Gen. Stephen A. Hurlbut

Headquarters, Department of the Tenn.,
Jackson, Oct. 29, 1862.

MAJ. GEN'L. HURLBUT,
COMDG. DIST. OF JACKSON.

I am just informed of a movement across the Hatchie of a large force of cavalry, with some artillery and Infantry under Bowen, evidently with the intention of getting on the River some place to intercept navigation. They are said to be now in the neighborhood of Brownsville. If this is so we will want one Brigade of Infantry, with a section of artillery and all the cavalry that can be spared from here and Humboldt to get in their rear and cut them off.

The forces should move towards Brownsville until they found the direction of the enemy, and then pursue them by the most practicable route. They should go with very little baggage, taking three days rations in Haversacks and seven days in wagons. Forage will have to be obtained on the route, giving receipts as provided for in General Orders. The expedition should be conducted by an efficient officer.

U. S. GRANT
Major Gen'l.

Copies, DLC-USG, V, 18, 30; DNA, RG 393, Dept. of the Tenn., Letters Sent. *O.R.*, I, xvii, part 2, 305. In accordance with USG's instructions, Maj. Gen.

Stephen A. Hurlbut wrote to Col. C. Carroll Marsh to prepare an expedition. *Ibid.*, p. 306. On Oct. 29, 1862, George G. Pride wrote to Hurlbut. "The Troops ordered to move under Col Marsh need not move until further orders from here— The news we get is that the enemy have not crossed the Hatchie—" ALS, DNA, RG 393, District of West Tenn., 4th Division, Letters Received. *O.R.*, I, xvii, part 2, 306.

To Maj. Gen. James B. McPherson

Head Qrs. Dept of the Tenn
Jackson Tenn Octr 29. 1862

MAJ GENL McPHERSON
BOLIVAR TENN

Hamilton has just learned the following from one of Roddy's[1] men now a prisoner

Roddy is ordered to Kentucky, will cross the river at Muscle Shoals,[2] en route to Bragg, Roddy moved from Big Springs on Friday   Joe Johnson is reported at Columbus with large force, and is intending to co operate with Price moving to the west of Corinth. No supplies and very little force at Tupolo. Price's movements already commenced.

Signd   ELI WHITEHURST[3]

If it demonstrated that Bolivar is the part of attack, Hamilton is instructed to move by way of Bethel with three Divisions to your support.   should Corinth be attacked, be in readiness to move by same route, with all the force that can be spared   I will send ten regiments from the line of Rail road to the point of attack

U. S. GRANT
Maj Genl

Copies, DLC-USG, V, 18, 30; DNA, RG 393, Dept. of the Tenn., Letters Sent. *O.R.*, I, xvii, part 2, 306–7. On Oct. 29, 1862, USG twice telegraphed to Maj. Gen. James B. McPherson. "I have ordered one Regiment of Cavalry from Corinth to report to you" "Citizens from Brownsville report Jackson, with 9000 Cavalry in neighborhood of Somerville. Your forces in that direction if not strong enough to meet them had better be withdrawn" Copies, DLC-USG, V, 18, 30; DNA,

RG 393, Dept. of the Tenn., Letters Sent. The second telegram is in *O.R.*, I, xvii, part 2, 307.

1. In 1861, Philip D. Roddey of Ala., whose background is rather obscure, organized and led a cav. co., the Tishomingo Rangers. In late 1862, he was commissioned col., 4th Ala. Cav. See *DAB*, XVI, 70–71.
2. Muscle Shoals on the Tennessee River in Ala. east of Florence.
3. A copy of the telegram of Oct. 29, 1862, from Brig. Gen. Charles S. Hamilton to USG embodying this information is in DNA, RG 393, District of Corinth, Telegrams Sent.

To Brig. Gen. Charles S. Hamilton

Head Qrs Dept of the Tenn
Jackson Tenn Oct 29 1862

Gen Hamilton
Corinth Miss

Immediately on my return from Corinth I telegraphed Quarter Master at Columbus to send you forage by any train.[1] He replied that he had no more forage but telegraphed to St Louis for it, received the reply that they were out there[2]

I telegraphed then Gen Allen[3] the necessity for pushing it on rapidly. No reply from him yet. If he cannot send it, I will send to Illinois and purchase independently

Reliable Union men from Brownsville think Bolivar will be the point of attack. We must watch closely   If Bolivar is the point, then Divisions of your command must march upon them by way of Bethel. If Corinth is attacked you will be assisted from there and ten Regiments from along the road   Captain Prime may remain for the present[4]

U S Grant
Maj General

Telegram, copies, DLC-USG, V, 18, 30; DNA, RG 393, Dept. of the Tenn., Letters Sent; *ibid.*, District of Corinth, Telegrams Received. *O.R.*, I, xvii, part 2, 304. On Oct. 29, 1862, Brig. Gen. Charles S. Hamilton telegraphed to Maj. John A. Rawlins. "We have not a particle of forage here. If our communication is cut, we shall loose our transportation from starvation. I hope every means may be used to get us twenty days supply ahead. It is of vital importance. Let all the places along the R. Road where forage can be had—collect forage in the country —and all other forage be sent here. None here in a circuit of fifteen miles." Copy, DNA, RG 393, District of Corinth, Telegrams Sent. On the same day, Hamilton sent two telegrams to USG. "Flag of truce dispatches were delivered over six (6) miles beyond Chewalla. They are from Pemberton and Van Dorn. Are of no importance. Will send contents by tomorrows mail. Everything confirms the movement of part of Price and Van Dorns army south by rail. I shall try to get up a magazine of forage from the country. I think much can be had along the Rail Road about Bethel and beyond, if we can have a train of cars to bring it in." Copy, *ibid. O.R.*, I, xvii, part 2, 304. "If Captain Prime can be relieved from going to Boliver and Jackson I should be very glad. The works here are getting on slowly and I regard his presence indispensable until they are well towards completion." Copy, DNA, RG 393, District of Corinth, Telegrams Sent.

On the same day, Hamilton wrote to USG. "I desire to call your attention to the letters of Van Dorn sent by the 'Flag of truce'   You can perhaps answer the question propounded as to the exchange of Captain Silence for Van Dorn's Aide   I cannot but think the making of Iuka a hospital for Confederate prisoners was very ill advised—Under the terms of the Cartel, we are obliged to deliver prisoners within the lines of the opposing Army   This involves the necessity of sending them from Iuka by ambulance to Baldwin, for those who cannot march, or bringing them back through Corinth to be sent to Columbus or to Holly Springs   I do not want to bring them back this way. Van Dorn's language that 'Ink is liable to the vicissitudes of war' can be construed only that it is liable to capture and that the stores sent there for the use of the Rebel sick and wounded are liable to seizure as also would be the running Stock of the rail road used in communicating and furnishing that hospital with supplies   I wish you would suggest some plan by which the whole thing can be shifted off our hands   Many of the prisoners leave daily and go where they choose   This has been the case with those who have sufficiently recovered to move   Of this I do not care but I do not like the idea of being burdened with the care of that place as a hospital unless it may fairly be considered as not liable to capture while so occupied   My idea would be to move all the wounded by rail through Corinth at night to be sent to Vicksburgh via Columbus   Please write me your views with such instructions as may suggest themselves to you   An answer on this subject, and also that of the exchange of Capt. Silence may be the means of sending another Flag of truce' to the rebel lines" Copy, *ibid.*, Letters Sent. *O.R.*, II, iv, 663. See letter to Maj. Gen. Earl Van Dorn, Nov. 19, 1862.

1. On Oct. 28, Hamilton telegraphed to USG. "I regard it of the first importance to have at least twenty (20) days forage on hand at this point. Can it be supplied? I want to get the sick and wounded away soon   Please push the hospitals." Copy, DNA, RG 393, District of Corinth, Telegrams Sent. *O.R.*, I, xvii, part 2, 301. On the same day, USG telegraphed to Hamilton. "I have telegraphed to have forage forwarded as rapidly as possible. I will refer the other matter to the Medical Director immediately" Copies, DLC-USG, V, 18, 30; DNA, RG 393, Dept. of the Tenn., Letters Sent; *ibid.*, District of Corinth, Telegrams Received. On the same day, USG telegraphed to Capt. Charles W. Lyman, Columbus, Ky. "Ship Forage to Corinth by every train that goes. We want a supply laid up there. At present they are out, and have been on short allowance

for some time." Copies, DLC-USG, V, 18, 30; DNA, RG 393, Dept. of the Tenn., Letters Sent.

2. Also on Oct. 28, Lyman telegraphed to USG. "A few hundred sacks of grain arrived this morning all that I have had for three (3) Days which is now on the Cars for Corinth and will go forward tomorrow   have Telegraphed to St Louis for Forage and am answered none there" Telegram received, *ibid.*, Telegrams Received.

3. On Oct. 29, USG telegraphed to Col. Robert Allen. "Corinth is without forage and none at Columbus to send   Teams now go twelve miles to obtain it   can you send a supply ?" Copies, DLC-USG, V, 18, 30; DNA, RG 393, Dept. of the Tenn., Letters Sent. On Oct. 30, Rawlins issued Special Orders No. 3. "The Maj Genl Commanding the District of Jackson, will send out foraging parties from the several stations of his command, for the purpose of obtaining forage for Government animals a ten days supply of which will be kept constantly on hand. The parties will be placed in charge of intelligent and responsible commissioned Officers who will receipt to the owners or claimants for amount & kind of forage taken, and keep an accurate account of the same, making return thereof to the Disct of Post Quarter Master, who will duly return and account for said forage, stating the authority for the seizure in his receipts and returns. Forage so seized will be issued by Quarter Masters on proper Forage Returns in same manner as forage purchased by the Government. Pillaging strictly forbidden under penalties prescribed in existing orders." Copies, DLC-USG, V, 16, 26, 27, 87; DNA, RG 393, Dept. of the Tenn., Special Orders.

4. On Oct. 27, USG had telegraphed to Col. C. Carroll Marsh. "Send all the Picks Spades and Shovels which can be spared to Capt Prime Corinth by earliest Train" Copy, *ibid.*, 17th Army Corps, 3rd Division, Telegrams Received. On Nov. 2, USG telegraphed to Capt. Frederick E. Prime. "Get the works in condition to be pushed forward without your presence and join me as soon as possible" Copies, DLC-USG, V, 18, 30; DNA, RG 393, Dept. of the Tenn., Letters Sent.

To Brig. Gen. Charles S. Hamilton

Jackson Octr 29. 1862

GEN HAMILTON
CORINTH MISS

I am inclined to think that a part of the force from Holly Springs has gone South either to Mobile or to come round by way of Tupelo, to get in on the east of us, and their presence in Ripley is a cover. They might also move a column from there in conjunction with the order.

I have information of a large force of Cavalry with some

Artillery and infantry are now attempting to cross the Hatchee near Brownsville, evidently with the intention of getting on to the river for the purpose of stopping navigation   I will attend to them

U S GRANT
Maj General

Telegram, copies, DLC-USG, V, 18, 30; DNA, RG 393, Dept. of the Tenn., Letters Sent; *ibid*., District of Corinth, Telegrams Received. *O.R.*, I, xvii, part 2, 305. On Oct. 29, 1862, Brig. Gen. Charles S. Hamilton telegraphed to USG. "News in which seems reliable that part of Price's forces were at Ripley yesterday preparing for another move on this place." Copy, DNA, RG 393, District of Corinth, Telegrams Sent. *O.R.*, I, xvii, part 2, 304.

To Brig. Gen. Charles S. Hamilton

Head Qrs Dept of the Tenn.
Jackson Tenn Octr 29. 1862

GEN HAMILTON
CORINTH MIS

The 16th Wisconsin can be consolidated in the way Col Allen[1] proposed, that is by the resignation of the surplus Officers.

The surplus Officers should be sent over the road and non commissioned Officers should be transferred to the remaining companies, until they are filled to the maximum number, one from each broken company, and three (3) as representatives of the remaining companies, can be ordered on recruiting service with Col Allen

No order has yet been made for the consolidation because the application has not yet come in, I will make it however and send it down to day[2]   Dodge will be down to day

U. S. GRANT.
Maj General

Telegram, copies, DLC-USG, V, 18, 30; DNA, RG 393, Dept. of the Tenn., Letters Sent; *ibid*., District of Corinth, Telegrams Received. On Oct. 29, 1862, Brig. Gen. Charles S. Hamilton telegraphed to USG. "Have any orders been issued relating to consolodating the 16th Wisconsin. The consolodation has been made by the Colonel & shall the surplus Officers & N. C. officers leave here without orders from you, Should they be passed over the Road—Will Genl Dodge be here today" Telegram received, *ibid.*, Dept. of the Tenn., Telegrams Received; copy, *ibid.*, District of Corinth, Telegrams Sent.

On Oct. 23, Capt. Temple Clark, Corinth, sent to Maj. Gen. William S. Rosecrans a long report of alleged cowardice by Capt. George Fox, 16th Wis., during the battle of Corinth. Fox withdrew his co. from a skirmish Clark had ordered. "I enquired of Captain Fox the reason for his retreat, and if he had received any orders to fall back; he replied; that he had received no orders, but had returned because the fire of the enemy was too heavy, that two or three squads had fired upon his company, that his company knew nothing about skirmishing, having and that the skirt of his coat had been hit by one of the enemy's balls, that none of his men had been killed or wounded, that the men who retreated with him came back by his order, that the rest of his company was still advanced as skirmishes having received no orders from him to fall back" LS, CSmH. On Oct. 29, Maj. John A. Rawlins endorsed this letter. "Respectfully returned to Brig Gen. Hamilton Commanding District of Corinth, who will refer this case to a Board of Examiners or a Court Martial" ES, *ibid.*

1. On Oct. 22, USG endorsed a petition to President Abraham Lincoln, prepared Oct. 16, recommending Col. Benjamin Allen, 16th Wis., for promotion. "Col. Allen is well known to me as an able cool and valuable officer upon whom promotion would be well bestowed." AES, DNA, RG 94, ACP, A264 CB 1863.

2. The reorganization of the 16th Wis. was announced in Special Orders No. 7, Dept. of the Tenn., Nov. 3. Copies, DLC-USG, V, 16, 26, 27, 87; DNA, RG 393, Dept. of the Tenn., Special Orders.

To Brig. Gen. Charles S. Hamilton

Jackson Tenn Octr 29, 1862

GEN HAMILTON
CORINTH MISS

Order one Regiment of Cavalry from your command to Bolivar.[1] They will march by way of Bethel   It would also be well to occupy Pocohontas with one Division and one Regiment of Cavalry. This would make a good lookout for an attack on either Bolivar or Corinth and would protect the Bridge at Davis, if we should want to use it or enable us to destroy it for use of the enemy

U. S. GRANT
Maj General

Telegram, copies, DLC-USG, V, 18, 30; DNA, RG 393, Dept. of the Tenn., Letters Sent; *ibid.*, District of Corinth, Telegrams Received. *O.R.*, I, xvii, part 2, 305. On Oct. 29, 1862, Brig. Gen. Charles S. Hamilton telegraphed to USG. "I have ordered the 7th Ills Cavalry to move early ~~in the~~ tomorrow with 3 days rations   it is the strongest Regt I have   They go by way of Bethel. I can send a Division to Pocahontas on Saturday   cannot well spare them before without seriously interefering with fortifications. I doubt there being any Rebel force in Ripley   Shall know certain in the morning—" Telegram received, DNA, RG 393, Dept. of the Tenn., Telegrams Received; copy, *ibid.*, District of Corinth, Telegrams Sent. On Oct. 27, Maj. Gen. James B. McPherson wrote to Maj. Gen. Stephen A. Hurlbut urging the transfer of inf. and cav. from Corinth to Pocahontas, Tenn. *O.R.*, I, xvii, part 2, 299–300. On Oct. 29, Hurlbut sent this letter to USG's hd. qrs. with a favorable endorsement. Copy, DNA, RG 393, District of West Tenn., 4th Division, Endorsements.

1. On Oct. 29, Hamilton telegraphed to USG. "Cant you get a Cavalry Brigadier   Col Misner is not worth a damn" Telegram received, *ibid.*, Dept. of the Tenn., Telegrams Received; copy, *ibid.*, District of Corinth, Telegrams Sent. On the same day, USG telegraphed to Hamilton. "If you dont like Mizner as chief of Cavalry select his Regiment to go to Bolivar and take one of your other Colonels as Chief. I have no Cavalry Genl, and in fact but one General commanding a Brigade this side of Memphis" Copies, DLC-USG, V, 18, 30; DNA, RG 393, Dept. of the Tenn., Letters Sent; *ibid.*, District of Corinth, Telegrams Received. On Oct. 30, Hamilton telegraphed to Maj. John A. Rawlins. "Will the cavalry Regt ordered to Bolivar make reports through McPherson or him—is it permanently detached—" Telegram received, *ibid.*, Dept. of the Tenn., Telegrams Received; copy, *ibid.*, District of Corinth, Telegrams Sent. On the same day, USG telegraphed to Hamilton. "The Cavalry Regiment is permanently detached." Copy, *ibid.*, Telegrams Received.

To Brig. Gen. James M. Tuttle

Jackson Octr 29, 1863[2]

GENL TUTTLE
CAIRO ILL.

I have just received a letter from my cousin Silas Hudson, saying that you expected to be called into the field, and that you are not able for it. I have no idea of moving you from your present position except on your application, knowing well that as soon as able you will want to take the field.

U. S. GRANT
Maj Genl.

Copies, DLC-USG, V, 18, 30; DNA, RG 393, Dept. of the Tenn., Letters Sent. See telegram to Maj. Gen. Stephen A. Hurlbut, Nov. 12, 1862.

To Commanding Officer, Union City, Tenn.

———

Jackson Tenn Oct 29 1862

COMMANDING OFFICER
UNION CITY TENN

Keep all paroled prisoners out of our lines   If they come in arrest them and send them to Cairo for safe keeping

U. S. GRANT
Maj Genl.

Copies, DLC-USG, V, 18, 30; DNA, RG 393, Dept. of the Tenn., Letters Sent. On Oct. 29, 1862, Capt. John W. True, 54th Ill., Union City, Tenn., telegraphed to Maj. John A. Rawlins. "There are three Paroled Prisoners here asking for transportation to Memphis   their Paroles are sworn to before a justice of the peace in Kentucky   there is a Goodly number of them in this country here. We do not know that their Paroles are good simply a piece of writing—had we better hold them   the Col desires to have some instructions in the matter"   Telegram received, *ibid.*, Telegrams Received.

To Allen C. Fuller

———

Jackson, Tenn, Oct. 29th 1862

COL. AND ADJ'T. GENERAL FULLER,
OF ILLINOIS, SPRINGFIELD ILL'S.

COL.

We have a large amount of captured arms. The Ordnance Officer will report to you to-morrow the number of Regiments that can be properly armed here. I would like to have one Regiment sent to Memphis, without arms, to take charge of siege guns in fortifications.

U. S. GRANT, Maj. General.

Copies, DLC-USG, V, 18, 30; DNA, RG 393, Dept. of the Tenn., Letters Sent. On Oct. 29, 1862, Ill. AG Allen C. Fuller telegraphed to USG. "The one hundred sixteenth (116) Regt Col Kinney and Capt Vaughn's Battery of light Artillery have just been ordered to Columbus Ky to report to you." Telegram received, *ibid.*, Telegrams Received. On Oct. 30, Fuller telegraphed to USG. "The Ninety fifth (95th) Regt Col Church at Rockford has just been ordered to Columbus Ky—" Telegram received, *ibid.*

On Oct. 30, 2nd Lt. Stephen C. Lyford, Cairo, telegraphed to USG. "There are only about one thousand Arms of all descriptions here and those not fit for issue—Arms and accoutrements at this Post have been ordered by Asst Secy of War to be held subject to Gen Ketchums orders and now Maj Gen McClernand orders them to be held for Him   those orders should have passed through Head Quarters or at least I should have been notified of their issue at Washington   before Telegraphing fully I wait further instructions   Please answer immediately what to do" Telegram received, *ibid.* On the same day, USG telegraphed to Lyford. "No Order was ever received here effecting the arms at Cairo   Telegraph the Adjutant Genl the number of Regiment we can arm here without reference to that Order"   Copies, DLC-USG, V, 18, 30; DNA, RG 393, Dept. of the Tenn., Letters Sent.

To Edwin M. Stanton

Head Qrs. Dept. of the Ten.
Jackson, Oct. 30th 1862

HON. E. STANTON
SEC. OF WAR
WASHINGTON D. C.
SIR:

Jno. A Rawlins who addresses you in behalf of D. Sheehan, Esq. at present a Political prisoner, is Asst. Adj. Gen. on my staff.

Maj. Rawlins is a man of as much influance in the Northern portion of Ill. as any one of his age hailing from that section. From the firing of the first gun at Fort Sumpter to the present hour his heart and soul has been in favor of a vigorous prossecution of this war. Before entering the service no man made more strenuous efforts to encourage enlistments.

I refer you to the Hon. E. B. Washburn for any information that you may want as to the standing of Maj. Rawlins.

Mr. Sheehan is a Law partner of Maj. Rawlins hence the interest he feels in procuring an early trial.

I can assure you the Maj. does not ask any sympaty for his partner in business if he should be proven guilty of treason to his Government.

> I am sir, very respectfully
> your obt. svt.
> U. S. GRANT
> Maj. Gen.

ALS, IHi. On Oct. 30, 1862, Maj. John A. Rawlins wrote to Secretary of War Edwin M. Stanton protesting the arrest of David Sheean, Rawlins's law partner in Galena. Rawlins enclosed the letter of USG printed above and letters of Maj. Gen. Stephen A. Hurlbut, Brig. Gen. John A. Logan, and Capt. William R. Rowley, which also praised Rawlins. LS, DNA, RG 94, Baker-Turner Records, 205T. See James Harrison Wilson, *The Life of John A. Rawlins* (New York, 1916), pp. 102–3; John A. Marshall, *American Bastille* (Philadelphia, 1882), pp. 451–62.

To Col. John C. Kelton

Headquarters, Department of the Tenn.
Jackson, Tenn, Oct. 30th 1862

COLONEL J. C. KELTON,
ASST. ADJT. GENERAL,
WASHINGTON, D. C.,
COLONEL:

I have the honor to submit the accompanying reports of the Battles of Corinth and of the Hatchie, fought on the 3rd, 4th and 5th inst., together with a short statement of the preperations made to receive the enemy, and of orders given previous to and during the engagement.

From information brought in by scouts, w[ho] were constantly kept out by General Rosecrans, from Corinth, and General Hurlbut, from Bolivar, it was evident for a number of days before the final attack upon Corinth that that place, or Bolivar, was to be assailed. From the dispositions made by the enemy of his forces, it was impossible to tell which place would be the one selected for the attack.

My main bodies of troops were at these two places; but to reinforce one from the other would have invited an attack upon the weaker place. I was compelled, therefore, to leave my forces where they were until the enemy fully exhibited his plans.

At this time Price was at Ripley with his force. Van Dorn was at La-Grange, with Cavalry thrown out to the neighborhood of Somerville, and Villipigue (and Lovell probably) at Salem. With the disposition made of his Cavalry, Van Dorn was enabled to move from La-Grange to Ripley without being discovered. This I learned on the 30th inst. by dispatches from both Gen. Rosecrans and Gen. Hurlbut. This demonstrated clearly a design on the part of the enemy to attack Corinth. I accordingly notified General Rosecrans, commanding Corinth, of the probable intention of the Rebels to try to get in north of Corinth and cut the road between that and Bethel, and directed him to concentrate all his forces at or near Corinth, instructions having been previously given him to break up Iuka, and bring his forces in the neighborhood of Corinth, and at the same time directed Genl. Hurlbut commanding Bolivar, to watch the movements of the Enemy to the East and Northeast of Bolivar, and if a chance occurred to attack him with all the force he could spare, holding his entire force in readiness for action.

To save the Bridge, six miles south of Bolivar, I ordered two Regiments from here under Colonel Lawler. It had the desired effect and compelled the enemy to cut the road nearer Corinth, and where the damage could not be made serious.

General Rosecrans was immediately informed of this disposition of troops. He was also directed to send back to Jackson all cars and locomotives   This I regarded as a necessary precaution and subsequent events proved it to be so. I also ordered ~~back~~ troops from Bolivar to increase the force on the important bridges North of that place. On the 2nd I permitted the train to run to Corinth, but informed Gen. Rosecrans that the enemy had crossed the Hatchie with the intention of cutting the Railroad and directed him to send the train back that night; that the enemy's pickets only were then across the stream; and also told him, if opportunity occurred, to attack, but to inform me so that I might order Bolivar forces to his assistance.

There was no attack made on the 2nd however, but General Rosecrans pushed out towards Chewalla, where he was attacked on the following day.

On the 3rd, I ordered Genl. Hurlbut who had been previously ordered to be in readiness to move at any moment, to march upon the enemy's rear by way of Pocahontas; also, sent two Regiments from here, under Colonel Stevenson, of the 7th Mo., to join Colonel Lawler at the Bridge, six miles south of Bethel, and put the whole under General McPherson, with directions to reach Corinth at the earliest possible moment. Owing to the cutting of the railroad and telegraph on the 2nd, the train of cars sent on that day could not return and all communication between Genl. Rosecrans and myself had to be sent by Couriers from Bethel. The enemy occupying the direct road to Corinth, compelled the Couriers to take a circuitous route by way of Farmington, thus seperating General Rosecrans and myself some seven or eight hours.

For the Battles fought on the 3rd, 4th, and 5th, see accompanying reports. Not having been present, I can only judge of the conduct of the troops by these reports and the results.

I had informed Genl. Rosecrans where Generals Ord and Hurlbut would be, and directed him to follow up the enemy the moment he began to retreat; to follow him to Bolivar if he should fall upon Ord's command and drive it that far. As shown by the reports, the enemy was repulsed at Corinth at 11 A. M. on the 4th and not followed until next morning.

Two days hard fighting without rest, probably, had so fatigued the troops as to make earlier pursuit impracticable. I regreted this as the enemy would have been compelled to abandon most of his artillery and transportation in the difficult roads of the Hatchie crossing, had the pursuit commenced then.

The victory was most triumphant as it was, however, and all praise is due officers and men for their undaunted courage and obstinate resistance against an enemy outnumbering them as three to two.

When it became evident that an attack would be made, I drew off from the guard along the line of the rail-road, all the troops that could possibly be spared, (Six Regiments) to reinforce Corinth and Bolivar. As before stated, four of these were sent under General McPherson to the former place and formed the advance in the pursuit. Two were sent to Bolivar and gave that much additional force to be spared to operate on the enemy's rear.

When I ascertained that the enemy had succeeded in crossing the Hatchie, I ordered a discontinuance of the pursuit. Before this order reached them, the advance Infantry force had reached Ripley and the Cavalry had gone beyond, possibly twenty miles. This I regarded, and yet regard, as absolutely necessary to the safety of our Army. They could not have possibly caught the Enemy before reaching his fortifications at Holly Springs and where a Garrison of several thousand troops were left that were not engaged in the Battle of Corinth. Our own troops would have suffered for food, and suffered greatly from fatigue. Finding that the pursuit had followed so far and that our forces were very much scattered I immediately ordered an advance from Bolivar, to be made to cover the return of the Corinth forces. They went as far south as Davis' Mills, about seven miles south of Grand Junction, drove a small rebel garrison from there and entirely destroyed the railroad bridge at that place

The accompanying reports show fully all the casualties and other results of these Battles

> I am, Colonel.
> Very Respectfully
> Your Obt. Serv't.
> U. S. GRANT.
> Maj. Genl. Commanding.

LS, DNA, RG 94, War Records Office, Union Battle Reports. *O.R.*, I, xvii, part 1, 157–59.

To Brig. Gen. Thomas A. Davies

Jackson Tenn Oct 30 1862

GEN DAVIES
COLUMBUS KY.

Where you can suppress Guerillas with the force at your command do it.

This one back of Hales Landing[1] should be broken up as soon as you can send the troops. Where Citizens give aid and comfort to these fellows who amuse themselves by firing into them, arrest them.

U. S. GRANT
Maj Genl.

Telegram, copies, DLC-USG, V, 18, 30; DNA, RG 393, Dept. of the Tenn., Letters Sent. *O.R.*, I, xvii, part 2, 309. On Oct. 30, 1862, Brig. Gen. Thomas A. Davies telegraphed to Maj. John A. Rawlins. "From information rec'd there is a band of guerrillas about 9 miles back from Hales landing Tenn' They have been committing depredations of various kinds—They have a boat 4 miles up the Obion River at a place known as Burghers ferry The same band fired into the Forrest Queen—A Mr Kusgrave living at Hale's is implicated as furnishig supplies to the Rebels although heretofore claiming to be loyal—" Telegram received, DNA, RG 393, Dept. of the Tenn., Telegrams Received; copy, *ibid.*, Hd. Qrs. District of Columbus, Telegrams Sent. On Oct. 31, Davies telegraphed to Rawlins. "The expedition down the has started with 250 Infantry—50 Cavalry, to take on at New Madrid 1 Co Cavalry & one section of Artillery under command of Capt Rogers in Steamer 'Tecumseh' " Copy, *ibid.*

1. Hale's Landing or Hale's Point, Tenn., at the mouth of the Obion River. On Oct. 15, Brig. Gen. Grenville M. Dodge, Columbus, Ky., telegraphed to Rawlins. "Col Baldwin from Memphis reports that five hundred men left Hales Point last night to cut the R R—the Guerrillas along the river are thick & troublesome Burn't considerable cotton above Randolph" Telegram received, *ibid.*, Dept. of the Mo., Telegrams Received.

To Brig. Gen. Thomas A. Davies

———

By Telegraph from Jackson Oct 30, 1862.

To Genl Davies

I doubt much finding morgan[1] at Hopkinsville or any other force in near the number represented   your forces should move cautiously however as if the whole number represented were there and ascertain from the people as much as they can of the enemy   if morgan is there he will likely run   it [*is not*] his policy to fight but to plunder & interrupt our lines of communications as much as possible

U. S. Grant

Telegram received, DNA, RG 107, Telegrams Collected (Unbound); copies, *ibid.*, RG 393, Dept. of the Tenn., Letters Sent; DLC-USG, V, 18, 30. *O.R.*, I, xvii, part 2, 310.

On Oct. 29, 1862, Maj. John A. Rawlins telegraphed to Brig. Gen. Thomas A. Davies. "Send Troops from Paducah & from Cairo if nessary under command of Genl Rawson to Eddyville to attack Morgan at Hopkinsville   order at same time all the avaible force at Ft Henry & Ft Donelson to cooperate with him   they will act in concert   you can communicate by telegraph with Paducah & Ft Henry   have ordered the Telegraph operatores at these places to remain at their Post" Telegram received, DNA, RG 107, Telegrams Collected (Unbound); copies, *ibid.*, RG 393, Dept. of the Tenn., Letters Sent; DLC-USG, V, 18, 30. *O.R.*, I, xvii, part 2, 303. On Oct. 29, Davies wrote to Brig. Gen. Thomas E. G. Ransom and to Col. William W. Lowe instructing them to participate in this operation. *Ibid.*, pp. 303–4. A copy of the instructions to Lowe was telegraphed to Rawlins. Copy, DNA, RG 393, Hd. Qrs. District of Columbus, Letters Sent.

On Oct. 30, Davies telegraphed to Rawlins. "Gen Ransom reports that he can furnish 2500 men (infantry) 60 cavalry & a section of Artillery from Paducah, Genl Tuttle reports that he cannot furnish any troops has scarce enough for Guard duty   Col Lowe at Fort. Donelson. can furnish 13th and 5 companies of cavalry, but Gen Ransom reports that they cannot form a junction except at Hopkinsville   He wishes to know if Lowe shall move out cautiouly while he holds the enemy in front, in advance of him   He thinks with the reinforcements from Fort Henry, he will be able to hold till Lowe can come up. ~~What do you of it.~~ Will this do" Copy, *ibid. O.R.*, I, xvii, part 2, 309. On the same day, Rawlins telegraphed to Davies. "The Plan proposed is satisfactory" Telegram received, DNA, RG 107, Telegrams Collected (Unbound). On Oct. 30, Davies telegraphed to Rawlins. "The total force to attack Morgan 250 Infantry one (1) section of artillery & 60 cavalry from Paducah   From Ft Henry (350) Infty & 150. cavalry   from Donelson about 400 Infty—Total 1000 Infty 200 cavalry & one (1) section artillery, is this force sufficient. The Expedition is in motion   all I know of Morgans forces is what I sent you—" Telegram received, *ibid.*, RG 94, War Records Office, Military Division of the Miss. *O.R.*, I, xvii, part 2, 309.

1. John H. Morgan, born in Huntsville, Ala., but long associated with Lexington, Ky., attended Transylvania College briefly, and served as a private, 1st Ky. Cav., in the Mexican War. He led a co. he had organized in 1857, the Lexington Rifles, into C. S. A. service; on April 4, 1862, he was appointed col., 2nd Ky. Cav. After a dramatic raid on Lexington on Oct. 18, Morgan rested three days at Hopkinsville, Ky., at the end of the month, leaving before U.S. forces had assembled to attack him. Basil W. Duke, *History of Morgan's Cavalry* (Cincinnati, 1867), p. 292.

To Brig. Gen. Charles S. Hamilton

Head Qrs Dept of Tennessee
Jackson Tenn Oct 30 1863[2]

GEN HAMILTON
CORINTH MISS

Ammunition can be obtained from Ordnance officer here. All Discharge papers from the Department have to come here

When the Carbines now ordered for this command arrive about one thousand (1000) of them can go to your command

U. S. GRANT
Maj Genl

P. S   Order Capt. Williams 1st Infantry to take command of the 7th Ill Vols[1]

Telegram, copies, DLC-USG, V, 18, 30; DNA, RG 393, Dept. of the Tenn., Letters Sent; *ibid.*, District of Corinth, Telegrams Received. On Oct. 30, 1862, Brig. Gen. Charles S. Hamilton telegraphed to USG. "Enemy had strong Cav. pickets yesterday five miles East of Ripley on the Rienzi road—too strong to be driven in by our scout. 38th Alabama was sent to Mobile by Pemberton on the 21st   Another train has been put on the road between Mobile and Tupelo. I looks as though the force at Ripley was covering a movement over the Mobile and Ohio Road." Copy, *ibid.*, Telegrams Sent. *O.R.*, I, xvii, part 2, 310. On the same day, Hamilton again telegraphed to USG. "The Pickets 5 miles East of Ripley prove to have been our own party   DuBois had a party of Cavalry in Ripley one hour   no Rebels there but Baxters Cavalry in camp 5 miles west of Ripley   People about Ripley agree in reporting that Ten to Fifteen Thousand men passed through Ripley for Mobile   Shall I send Capt Jarnswath to St. Louis for Ammunition. Shall I send discharge papers to your Hd Qrs." Telegram received, DNA, RG 393, Dept. of the Tenn., Telegrams Received; copy, *ibid.*, District of Corinth, Telegrams Sent.

1. On Oct. 30, Brig. Gen. David S. Stanley telegraphed to USG. "Will you order Capt. Geo. A. Williams to take command of the 47th Ills. Vols. The Captain is elected colonel of the Regt. unanimously and the matter is referred to the Governor of Ills. The Regt. needs the Captains immediate attention." Copy, *ibid.* George A. Williams of N. Y., USMA 1852, served in Tex. and as an instructor at USMA before the Civil War. Nominated as capt. in Dec., 1861, he was soon assigned to the Army of the Miss. under Maj. Gen. John Pope, where he remained through the Corinth campaign. On Nov. 22, 1862, Lt. Col. Samuel R. Baker, 47th Ill., recommended the appointment of Williams as col.; on Nov. 24, USG endorsed this letter. "I would most respectfully but urgently recommend the promotion of Capt. G. A. Williams to the Colonelcy of the 47th Ill. Vol. Infantry. Capt. Williams, at the request of the officers of this regiment, is now in command of it. With such a commander this regiment could not fail to be one of the best in service" AES, Records of 47th Ill., I-ar. Although Williams temporarily commanded the 47th Ill., he was never officially recognized as col. See letter to Maj. Gen. Henry W. Halleck, Nov. 2, 1862.

To Col. Jesse Hildebrand

Hd Qrs. Dept. of the Ten.
Jackson Oct. 30th 1862

Comd.g Officer, Alton Ill. &
Provost Marshal Gen. Dept. of the Mo.
Sirs:

I send Col. J. Riggin Jr. A. D. C. to Alton and St. Louis for the purpose of investigating the charges against Political prisoners sent from my command either by my order or the order of officers under me.

Such persons as he may ask to have released I will be obliged to you if you will release them on their taking the prescribed oath.

Very respectfully
your obt. svt.
U. S. Grant
Maj. Gen. Com

ALS, DNA, RG 94, Staff Papers, John Riggin, Jr. On Nov. 5, 1862, Col. John Riggin, Jr., wrote to Col. Jesse Hildebrand. "In accordance with my written instructions from Maj Genl Grant Comd.g Department of the Tennissee as contained in the letter from Him in your Posession I have designated on the roll of Political Prisoners from said Department, furnished me by you such as I deem Proper to have released. You will release those so designated upon their takeing the Proscribed oath 'Such of said Prisoners to be released as you may believe unable to reach their homes or friends without, you will furnish with transportation" Copy, *ibid.*, RG 249, Letters Received. Names of prisoners released by Riggin are included on a "Roll of Prisoners of War Discharged from Alton Military Prison during the month of November 1862," *ibid.*, RG 109, Prison Records, Alton, Ill.

On Nov. 15, Col. William S. Hillyer wrote to Hildebrand. "I am directed by Maj Gen Grant Comg this Dept to request that you would release W. H. Hawkins of Co G 22 Regt Tenn Vols sent to the military Prison at Alton from this Dept during this month. Mr Hawkins was arrested as a member of a guerilla band, but it appears that he belongs to the Confederate cavalry & was arrested while approaching our lines under a flag of truce. Let his release be immediate and unconditional and let him be furnished with transportation to Trenton Tenn or such other point as he may desire." ALS, *ibid.*, RG 249, Letters Received. Along with a protest of W. H. Hawkins, "Adjt Tenn River Battn," Nov. 12, Hillyer's letter was forwarded on Nov. 20 by Capt. Henry W. Freedley, Alton, to Col. William Hoffman, commissary gen. of prisoners, with an explanation that Hawkins had been sent to Sandusky. LS, *ibid.* On Nov. 19, Freedley wrote to Hoffman of conditions at Alton, complaining that both USG and Maj. Gen. Samuel R. Curtis had exceeded their authority by ordering the release of prisoners. ALS, *ibid.* *O.R.*, II, iv, 734–35. On Nov. 27, Hoffman wrote to Secretary of War Edwin M. Stanton enclosing both these letters from Freedley and also copies of USG's earlier letters to Hildebrand. LS, DNA, RG 249, Letters Received. *O.R.*, II, iv, 761.

To Col. John C. Kelton

Headquarters, Department of the Tennessee

Jackson, Tennessee Oct. 31st 1862

COLONEL J. C. KELTON.

ASST. ADJT. GENERAL.

WASHINGTON, D. C.

COLONEL.

I have the honor to transmit herewith my official Report of the Battles of Corinth and of the Hatchie, fought on the 3rd 4th & 5th inst. and the following official papers relating to same, viz:

Reports of the Battle of Corinth

Major General W. S. Rosecrans' Report and Maps

Brig. Gen. C. S. Hamilton's Report and Sixteen enclosures.
Brig. Gen. D. S. Stanley's Report and sixteen enclosures.
Brig. Gen. T. A. Davies' Report and eighteen enclosures.
Brig. Gen. John McArthur's Report and eight enclosures.
Colonel J. K. Meizner's (3rd Mich. Cav.) Report and one enclosure.
Captain Williams' Report of part taken by Seige Artillery.
Major Powell's Report of Light Artillery and five enclosures.
Major General J. B. McPherson's Report and one enclosure.
List of Honorable Mentions, and eleven enclosures
Casualties—Sixteen Enclosures.
Surgeon Campbell's Report as Acting Medical Director.
Report of Yates' Sharp Shooters.
Report of Provost Marshal
Report of Surgeon J. G. F. Holston acting Med. Director of the District.
    The Battle of the Hatchie.
Maj. Genl. E. O. C. Ord's dispatch from Field of Battle.
Maj. Genl. S. A. Hurlbut's Report
Brig. Genl. J. C. Veach's Report
Brig. Genl. J. G. Lauman's Report.
Major Hayes' Report (15th Ohio Cavalry)
Major. C. C. Campbell's Report of Artillery in action.
List of Prisoners captured and paroled.

> I am, Colonel
> Very Respectfully
> Your Obt Serv't
> U S. GRANT.
> Major General Com'd'g

LS, DNA, RG 94, War Records Office, Union Battle Reports.
    On Nov. 13, 1862, USG wrote to Col. John C. Kelton. "I have the honor to transmit herewith Brig Genl T. J. McKeans Report of the part taken by the 6th Division in the Battle of Corinth   It was not in at the time of fowarding the other reports"   Copies, DLC-USG, V, 5, 8, 24, 88; DNA, RG 393, Dept. of the Tenn., Hd. Qrs. Correspondence.

To Brig. Gen. Charles S. Hamilton

Head quarters Bolivar[1] [*Oct. 31,*] 1862
BRIG GENL. HAMILTON

If it will retard the work of fortifications by sending a Division to Pocahontas you need not send them at present. Pocahontas however is a strong position and troops there besides keeping Guerrillas from getting in north of the Hatchie would be in position to reinforce either this place or Corinth. When they go out I want the telegraph immediately entended from Chewalla to Pocahontas.

U. S. GRANT
Maj. Genl.

Telegram, copy, DNA, RG 393, District of Corinth, Telegrams Received. On Oct. 31, 1862, Brig. Gen. Charles S. Hamilton telegraphed to USG. "News just in that one Regt of Rebel Cavalry was at or near Pocahontas yesterday evening probability Falkners Negroes in from Ripley no troops there" Telegram received, *ibid.*, Dept. of the Tenn., Telegrams Received; copy, *ibid.*, District of Corinth, Telegrams Sent. On the same day, Hamilton again telegraphed to USG. "If everything remains quiet will it be necessary to send a Division to Pocahontas the Earthwork of the Fortification will be nearly complete by tomorrow night but the Stockading will require a week yet, it is a large job if you do not deem it important, I will keep the division here until the work is all done.—" Telegram received, *ibid.*, Dept. of the Tenn., Telegrams Received; copy, *ibid.*, District of Corinth, Telegrams Sent.

1. For an account of USG's review of troops at Bolivar on Oct. 31, see letter from Bolivar, Nov. 1, in *New York Herald*, Nov. 7, 1862.

To Maj. Gen. Henry W. Halleck

Jackson Tenn Nov 1st [*1862*]

MAJ GEN H W HALLECK
GEN IN CHF

I would respectfully ask to have Capt Dubarry assigned here as Chf Commissary with rank of Lt Col   Capt Hawkins has not joined   I wish to withdraw his Name

U S GRANT
M Gen'l

Telegram received, DNA, RG 108, Letters Received; *ibid.*, RG 107, Telegrams Collected (Bound); copies, *ibid.*, RG 393, Dept. of the Tenn., Hd. Qrs. Correspondence; DLC-USG, V, 5, 8, 24, 88. On Nov. 4, 1862, Maj. Gen. Henry W. Halleck telegraphed to USG. "The Commissary objects to the exchange of capt DuBarry for Capt. Hawkins, as the former cannot be spared from Cincinnati." ALS (telegram sent), DNA, RG 107, Telegrams Collected (Bound); copy, *ibid.*, RG 108, Telegrams Sent. On Nov. 5, USG telegraphed to Halleck. "As I cannot have Capt Dubarry I renew my application for promotion of Capt Hawkins" Telegram received, *ibid.*, RG 107, Telegrams Collected (Bound). On Nov. 6, Col. Edward D. Townsend, AGO, telegraphed to USG. "Lieut. Colonel Hawkins appointed November 1. 62, and appointment forwarded to Jackson, Tenn." LS (telegram sent), *ibid.*, Telegrams Collected (Unbound); copies, *ibid.*, RG 393, Dept. of the Tenn., Hd. Qrs. Correspondence; DLC-USG, V, 5, 8, 24, 88.

On Oct. 15, Col. Thomas J. Haines, St. Louis, had telegraphed to USG. "Will Ship today Fifteen Hundred (1500) Bushels Potatoes and Six Hundred (600) onions to Columbus—I understand that Capt DuBarry has been ordered to Cincinnati. If so would it be agreeable to you to have Capt Hawkins ordered to report to you—" Telegram received, DNA, RG 393, Dept. of the Mo., Telegrams Received. On Oct. 24, Haines telegraphed to USG. "Hawkins will report to you   he has delayed in order to see Mrs Canby   shall I still continue to furnish your dept." Telegram received, *ibid.* On Oct. 29, Haines telegraphed to USG. "Do you wish more than seven hundred thousand (70.0 000) rations to be kept on hand at Corinth   if not please so inform Capt Cox   Hawkins will leave tomorrow if Gen Canby arrives as expected   can I continue to have reports of stores on hand at Columbus sent to me   it will be of service and I will be able to keep a good supply for your army" Telegram received, *ibid.* On the same day, USG telegraphed to Haines. "Six-hundred thousand (600,000) rations is enough to have at Corinth. Report of stores on hand at Columbus will be sent you as usual." Copies, DLC-USG, V, 18, 30; DNA, RG 393, Dept. of the Tenn., Letters Sent. On the same day, USG telegraphed to Capt. John C. Cox, Columbus, Ky. "Six-hundred thousand (600,000) rations will be sufficient to keep on hand at Corinth. Keep Col. Haines informed of amount of stores on hand, so as to draw all your supplies from him." Copies, *ibid.* On the same day, Cox telegraphed to USG. "Your dispatch is received   my System is to send Col Haines weekly an inventory of stores on hand and information as to what date the diffrent Posts are supplied" Telegram received, *ibid.*, Telegrams Received.

On Oct. 31, Cox wrote to USG requesting a leave of absence, and, on the same day, USG endorsed the letter. "Approved and respectfully forwarded to Head Quarters of the Army. Capt. Cox has been a most faithful and efficient officer in the discharge of his duties as C. S. and I would be pleased to see this favor granted him." *Charles Hamilton Auction Number 41*, April 23, 1970, p. 26.

On Nov. 1, USG telegraphed to Cox. "I wish you would get a supply of Potatoes, Onions, Whiskey and Beer for delivery to different Commissaries It is absolutely necessary that these articles should be had, at least in sufficient quantities for the Hospitals. I am expecting Hawkins today, and will then have published the orders you ask for" Copies, DLC-USG, V, 18, 30; DNA, RG 393, Dept. of the Tenn., Letters Sent. On the same day, Cox telegraphed to USG. "I am moving heaven & earth to get supplies of potatoes & onions from arrangiment made yesterday I am confident a more liberal supply may be expected very soon but at excessive prices potatoes 80 & 85¢ Onions 1.25—the whisky shall be forthcoming, but Beer it is impractible to procure within the dept—" Telegram received, *ibid.*, Telegrams Received.

On Nov. 6, USG telegraphed to Lt. Col. John P. Hawkins. "Ration out tomorrow night—Wagon train has gone to-day to Middleburg Station to bring up 100000 Rations. If Capt Strickler has passed Middleburg Station direct him to go back to that point" Copies, DLC-USG, V, 18, 30; DNA, RG 393, Dept. of the Tenn., Letters Sent. On the same day, Hawkins, Jackson, telegraphed to Lt. Col. John A. Rawlins. "Two hundred head of beef cattle will leave Corinth with train today also a number from Bolivar for Grand Junction how are the supplies with you Capt Stickler will go through with a train saturday morning he is now below Bolivar at the station" Telegram received, *ibid.*, Telegrams Received. On the same day, R. H. Thomas, Bolivar, telegraphed to USG. "Eight (8) car loads of commissary stores were forwarded from here to Middleburg last night & unloaded at that point—by order of capt J. P Hawkins C. S. Capt strickle is there—I will send fourteen (14) car loads to Middleburg station on the arrival of train from Jackson the stores will be sent as fast as possible" Telegram received, *ibid.* On Nov. 7 or 8, USG telegraphed to Hawkins. "As soon as cars run here get forward 800.000 rations with all dispatch, come down on an early train" Copy (dated Nov. 7), DLC-USG, V, 18; copies (dated Nov. 8), *ibid.*, V, 30; DNA, RG 393, Dept. of the Tenn., Letters Sent.

On Nov. 11, Townsend telegraphed to USG. "If Captain A. E. Strickler commissary subsistence in your command can be spared the secretary of war directs that he be ordered to report to General Rosecrans—" ALS (telegram sent), *ibid.*, RG 107, Telegrams Collected (Bound); copies, *ibid.*, RG 94, Letters Sent; (dated Nov. 12) *ibid.*, RG 393, Dept. of the Tenn., Hd. Qrs. Correspondence; DLC-USG, V, 5, 8, 24, 88. On Nov. 8, Maj. Gen. William S. Rosecrans telegraphed to Secretary of War Edwin M. Stanton requesting that Capt. Abraham E. Strickle, commissary, be ordered to duty under Rosecrans to supervise the baking of bread. *O.R.*, I, xxi, part 2, 27. On Nov. 5, Strickle, Bolivar, telegraphed to USG. "I am here with 19 cars loaded with Subsistence stores they will go forward as soon as the trestle will permit other trains are behind & will go forward immediatly after this—" Telegram received, DNA, RG 393, Dept. of the Tenn., Telegrams Received. On Nov. 8, Strickle, Grand Junction, telegraphed to USG. "I am unloading a train of provisions here the train will come forward soon as unloaded" Telegram received, *ibid*. No reply to Townsend's telegram has been found; later orders and correspondence indicate that Strickle remained in USG's command.

To Maj. Gen. Stephen A. Hurlbut

Head Quarters, Dept. of the Ten.
Jackson Nov. 1st 1862

Maj. Gen. Hurlbut
Comd.g Dist. of Jackson,
Gen.

As it is probable that I may move forward from Bolivar it will be necessary to send forward the regimental trains. You may forward them in the morning sending four men with each team. Regimental Quartermasters should accompany them and Fosters[1] Cavalry or some good company in addition.

Instruct the officer in charge to fill each wagon with corn on the route giving receipts as required in Gen. Orders.

Respectfully &c.
U. S. Grant
Maj. Gen.

ALS, DNA, RG 393, District of West Tenn., 4th Division, Letters Received. On Nov. 1, 1862, Maj. William R. Rowley wrote to Maj. Gen. Stephen A. Hurlbut. "You will have four Regiments of Infantry ready to move by rail to Bolivar on to morrow morning under the command of Brig. Gen'l J A Logan who on his arrival at that place will assume command of the Division lately commanded by Brig Gen Ross including the four regiments sent from this place" ALS, *ibid*. *O.R.*, I, xvii, part 2, 313.

1. Capt. John S. Foster, 4th Ohio Independent Cav.

To Maj. Gen. James B. McPherson

———

Head Quarters Dept of the Tennessee
Jackson Nov 1. 1862

Maj. Gen McPherson
Bolivar Tenn

Prepare to move forward on Monday,[1] leaving four Regiments and one Battery at Bolivar, Hamilton starts tomorrow for Grand Junction

Take three (3) days rations in Haversacks and three days in Wagons   Five (5) Regiments will go down to night and to morrow to reinforce you. Gen Logan will take command of Ross' Division

Preparations should be made for repairing the Rail Road and Telegraph. You give orders for the former and I will attend to the latter

U. S. Grant
Maj Genl.

Telegram, copies, DLC-USG, V, 18, 30; DNA, RG 393, Dept. of the Tenn., Letters Sent. *O.R.*, I, xvii, part 2, 314. On Nov. 1, 1862, Maj. Gen. James B. McPherson telegraphed to USG. "Dispatches rec'd   have telegraphed Maj Tweedal Engineer Regt to send down four companies with arms & tools to repair Rail Road if that many men can be spared & finish the bridge already commenced over the Obion River—if that many men cannot be spared he is to send as many as he can"   Telegram received, DNA, RG 94, War Records Office, Dept. of the Tenn. *O.R.*, I, xvii, part 2, 314.

1. Nov. 3.

To Maj. Gen. James B. McPherson

Head Quarters Dept of the Tennessee
Jackson Nov 1. 1862

MAJ GEN MCPHERSON
BOLIVAR TENN

I have ordered Hamilton to hold three Divisions in readiness to move towards Bolivar tomorrow morning. If you ascertain, that an attack is threatening inform me of the fact and I will start them at once. I will send four Regiments from here at once

U S GRANT
Maj Genl

Telegram, copies, DLC-USG, V, 18, 30; DNA, RG 393, Dept. of the Tenn., Letters Sent. *O.R.*, I, xvii, part 2, 314. On Nov. 1, 1862, Maj. Gen. James B. McPherson telegraphed to USG. "Col Leggett has just rec'd following dispatch —Grand Junction to Col Leggett—Large force of infantry & cavalry here—They will attack you   cavalry now moving   I saw you last Tuesday   cant get to Bolivar—the Dispatch was brought in by a negro about a half an hour ago & col Leggett thinks it is from a man who is perfectly reliable—I shall immediately send four (4) companies of cavalry down on the Road to Reconnoitre   my patrols that went out this morning have not reported yet"   Telegram received, DNA, RG 94, War Records Office, Dept. of the Tenn. *O.R.*, I, xvii, part 2, 313.

On the same day, USG again telegraphed to McPherson. "The moment you hear from the front inform me. If the enemy are moving on you I want to put the troops in motion"   Copies, DLC-USG, V, 18, 30; DNA, RG 393, Dept. of the Tenn., Letters Sent. *O.R.*, I, xvii, part 2, 314. On the same day, McPherson telegraphed to USG. "Major Mudd started at half past three this P. M. with four companies of cavalry on reconnoisance towards Grand Junction—I have heard nothing from him yet—he was cautioned to be on the alert & to send back couriers if anything important transpird   my patrols which went out this morning went below Van Buren & returned just before dark without seeing or learning anything of the Enemy   I will advise you immediately if I learn anything important"   Telegram received, DNA, RG 94, War Records Office, Dept. of the Tenn. *O.R.*, I, xvii, part 2, 314.

To Brig. Gen. Charles S. Hamilton

Head Quarters Dept of the Tennessee
Jackson Nov 1 1862

GENL HAMILTON
CORINTH MISS

Start in the morning, move on Grand Junction keeping a good lookout to the South of you. If you find the enemy have moved North of that place, you can change your direction towards Bolivar

McPherson will also move to the point, starting next day.

Establish a line of couriers from Chewalla to enable me to communicate with you

U. S. GRANT
Maj Genl.

Telegram, copies, DLC-USG, V, 18, 30; DNA, RG 393, Dept. of the Tenn., Letters Sent; *ibid.*, District of Corinth, Telegrams Received. *O.R.*, I, xvii, part 2, 311–12. On Nov. 1, 1862, Brig. Gen. Charles S. Hamilton telegraphed to USG. "You say in your dispatch if I find the Enemy have moved south of Holly Springs I will change my direction towards Bolivar ought it not to read north instead of south Will try & reach Pocahontas with the head of my column tomorrow" Telegram received, DNA, RG 393, Dept. of the Tenn., Telegrams Received; copy, *ibid.*, District of Corinth, Telegrams Sent. On the same day, USG telegraphed to Hamilton. "My dispatch Should be read North of Grand Junction instead of South of Holly Springs. My dispatch reads north on examination" Copies, DLC-USG, V, 18, 30; DNA, RG 393, Dept. of the Tenn., Letters Sent; *ibid.*, District of Corinth, Telegrams Received. *O.R.*, I, xvii, part 2, 312.

Also on Nov. 1, Hamilton telegraphed to USG. "Your dispatch is received. Everything will be in readiness. Please give some instructions about the route to be followed. Rosecrans carried of the maps that are most needed" Copy, DNA, RG 393, District of Corinth, Telegrams Sent. *O.R.*, I, xvii, part 2, 312. On the same day, USG telegraphed to Hamilton. "The route will be by ~~Rochester~~ Pocohontas It will be of the utmost importance in case of a move to seize on Davis' Brigade and the Bridge at Pocohontas at once with a cavalry force. Instruct the telegraph operators to keep the offices open until six oclock tonight" Copies, DLC-USG, V, 18, 30; DNA, RG 393, Dept. of the Tenn., Letters Sent; *ibid.*, District of Corinth, Telegrams Received. *O.R.*, I, xvii, part 2, 312.

Also on Nov. 1, Hamilton telegraphed to USG. "If I do not find it necessary to move towards Bolivar from Pocahontas I will follow the State line road to Grand Junction. What arrangments shall I make for supplies Six days are not enough. Shall I have trains follow or will it be shorter to get supplies from Bolivar." Copy, DNA, RG 393, District of Corinth, Telegrams Sent. On the same day, USG telegraphed to Hamilton. "Supplies will be got forward from Bolivar. The Cars run now to within ten miles of Grand Junction, and the ~~amount~~ moment troops pass the break in the road repairers will go to work to complete it" Copies, DLC-USG, V, 18, 30; DNA, RG 393, Dept. of the Tenn., Letters Sent; *ibid.*, District of Corinth, Telegrams Received.

To Brig. Gen. Charles S. Hamilton

Jackson Nov 1. 1862

GENERAL HAMILTON
CORINTH MISS

I have before me a Jackson Miss paper which makes no mention of the fall, not even of attack upon Mobile It may be so however, we will make the move indicated in my former dispatch, and if practicable drive the enemy from Holly Springs. Corinth will then be covered

U S GRANT
Maj Genl

Telegram, copies, DLC-USG, V, 18, 30; DNA, RG 393, Dept. of the Tenn., Letters Sent; *ibid.*, District of Corinth, Telegrams Received. *O.R.*, I, xvii, part 2, 312. On Nov. 1, 1862, Brig. Gen. Charles S. Hamilton twice telegraphed to USG. "Negroes in from the south at Rienzi report Mobile taken—" "A Mobile paper of 26th says all troops were ordered from Columbus to Mobile—Negroes from Ripley & Boonville report Mobile captured—our Gunboat had run past the forts & shelled the city which had surrendered the other boats were engaged with the forts. is it not likely the Rebels are evacuating Holly Springs and covering it by a feint on Bolivar The bridges will be seized tonight I think the Rebels will concentrate their forces on the Rail Road from Vicksburg to Montgomery no feint towards Pocahontas—" Telegrams received, DNA, RG 393, Dept. of the Tenn., Telegrams Received; copies, *ibid.*, District of Corinth, Telegrams Sent.

To Brig. Gen. Charles S. Hamilton

Jackson Nov 1 1862

GEN HAMILTON
CORINTH MISS

There is indications that Bolivar will be attacked within 48 hours

Have three Divisions of your command ready to move tomorrow morning with three days rations in haversacks and three days in wagons   Take as little baggage as can be possibly got along with   Do not move without further directions but be ready at the time stated

U S GRANT
Maj Gen

Telegram, copies, DLC-USG, V, 18, 30; DNA, RG 393, Dept. of the Tenn., Letters Sent; *ibid.*, District of Corinth, Telegrams Received. *O.R.*, I, xvii, part 2, 312.

To Brig. Gen. Charles S. Hamilton

Jackson Nov 1 1862

GEN HAMILTON
CORINTH MISS

Capt. Silver[1] is now here on Parole and anxious to be released; on notice of his release by proper authority, the aide to General Van Dorn will also be released. You may send by first Flag of truce, the unconditional release of the aide referred to to be delivered on receiving a like release for Capt. Shivers

The wounded prisoners from Iuka may be brought in under a Flag of Truce and sent here to be disposed of.

U S GRANT
Maj Genl.

P. S. Name of Aide, Lieut C. Sullivan[2]

Telegram, copies, DLC-USG, V, 18, 30; DNA, RG 393, Dept. of the Tenn., Letters Sent; *ibid.*, District of Corinth, Telegrams Received. See telegram to Brig. Gen. Charles S. Hamilton, Oct. 29, 1862.

    1. Capt. S. O. Silence, 1st Tenn. Cav. See letter to Maj. Gen. Earl Van Dorn, Nov. 19, 1862. On Oct. 17, 1862, Col. James J. Dollins, 81st Ill., Humboldt, Tenn., telegraphed to Maj. John A. Rawlins. "Robert & Edward Taylor Citizens are [h]ere   they are both prominent men   Guerrillas have been encamped in the vicinity of where they live for the last three (3) months & capt Hawood is now raisng a reg't in that siction   Edward Taylor swears he never will take the oath of allegiance   what shall I do with them—Capt silence of the Tennesse Cavalry was captured near their houses   am I authorized to levy upon their slaves to build fortifications   I will bind the Taylors or hold them   [I do] with them as you order   please ans:—" Telegram received, DNA, RG 393, Dept. of the Mo., Telegrams Received. On Oct. 17, Dollins again telegraphed to Rawlins. "There is ten (10) Guerrillas here who have been in the Guard house for some time   can they be exchanged for Capt Silence of the tennessee Cavalery   he is needed badly in his co.   he is reported to be at Holly Springs   Please ans:" Telegram received, *ibid.*

    2. E. Clement Sulivane of Miss., appointed 1st lt. and aide-de-camp as of Oct. 29, 1861, served on the staff of his uncle, Maj. Gen. Earl Van Dorn, until his capture at the battle of the Hatchie.

To Col. Jesse Hildebrand

Head Quarters of the Tenn
Jackson Nov 1st 1862

COMDG OFFICER
ALTON ILL
SIR

    The sentence against S. E. Grider & D. Collins was confined on the 12th of August 1862. Their term of imprisonment was for three months, and of cource commenced the day of confirmation. Although they were not sent to Alton for near a month after that time. You will please release them on the 12th inst by reason of expiration of sentence

Respectfully &c
U S GRANT

Copy, DNA, RG 109, Alton Military Prison, Letters Received.

To Col. George P. Ihrie

Head Quarters Dept of the Tenn
Jackson Nov 1 1862

Col Ihrie
Corinth Miss

I have already pushed the Quartermaster on the subject of clothing

I made no detailed report of the battle of Corinth but left that for those who were engaged. I said nothing about the interior line of entrenchments nor of those who constructed them. I would be glad to forward a report from Capt Prime on the subject together with my remarks expressing my appreciation of his services. I intend to recommend Capt Prime and Col Williams for Brigadiers in a special communication[1]

U S Grant
Maj Gen

Telegram, copies, DLC-USG, V, 18, 30; DNA, RG 393, Dept. of the Tenn., Letters Sent. On Nov. 1, 1862, Col. George P. Ihrie telegraphed to USG. "I would like to accompany Hamiltons command Have you any objections We are all on the rampage down here & such eagerness for the fray I never saw before" Telegram received, *ibid.*, RG 94, Generals' Papers and Books, George P. Ihrie. On the same day, USG telegraphed to Ihrie. "I would like to have you accompany Hamilton, you have my permission to go." Copies, DLC-USG, V, 18, 30; DNA, RG 393, Dept. of the Tenn., Letters Sent. On Oct. 22, Ihrie, Cairo, telegraphed to USG. "I inspect this post including all the Departments to day, as I do not feel well I will join you tomorrow unless you particularly wish me to go to Henry & Donelson Please answer." Telegram received, *ibid.*, Dept. of the Mo., Telegrams Received. At the foot of the telegram, Maj. John A. Rawlins drafted a reply in USG's name. "You need not go to Ft Henry & Donelson," ADf, *ibid.* On Oct. 31, Ihrie, Corinth, telegraphed to USG. "Reviewed McArthurs Division today creditable performance save one (1) Batt'y of light artillery.—Inspected 1st brigade of said Div today. Arms in fine condition accoutrements servicable. plenty Ammunition. said deficient of clothing. Knapsacks Haversacks & Canteens. plenty tents. By all means have Ale issued to Regts & Genl Hospital—" Telegram received, *ibid.*

1. See letter to Maj. Gen. Henry W. Halleck, Nov. 2, 1862.

To Lt. Col. William L. Duff

Head Quarters Dept of the Tennessee
Jackson Nov 1. 1862

Col. Duff
Chief of Artillery
Corinth Miss

I have been telegraphing ever since the battle of Corinth urging supplies of forage forward, and at last had Gen Allen telegraphed to know if he would supply me, if not we would set up for ourselves, and buy at Cairo, independent of the St. Louis authorities. I think forage can be got on the line of the road to be travelled. I will see if any can be got here and if so will send it to Chewalla tomorrow

U. S. Grant
Maj Genl

Copies, DLC-USG, V, 18, 30; DNA, RG 393, Dept. of the Tenn., Letters Sent. William L. Duff, born in Scotland, was mustered in as lt. col., 2nd Ill. Light Art., on Jan. 30, 1862, and was announced as chief of art. in General Orders No. 6, Dept. of the Tenn., Nov. 11. For an accusation that Duff supplied liquor to USG, see Benjamin P. Thomas, ed., *Three Years with Grant as Recalled by War Correspondent Sylvanus Cadwallader* (New York, 1955), pp. 70–72. On Nov. 1, Duff telegraphed to Lt. Col. John A. Rawlins. "I have inspected the artillery of Genl McArthurs & Genl Quinbys Division   with the exception of one battery they are in condition to take the field in every respect except are in miserable condition for want of forage & about to march through a country entirely bare   Can anything be done to remedy this, all animals that have seen appear to be suffering from the same cause & will eventually give out if moved—"   Telegram received, DNA, RG 393, Dept. of the Tenn., Telegrams Received. Also on Nov. 1, Rawlins telegraphed to Capt. Lyne S. Metcalf, Corinth. "The General commanding directs that all the forage that can be spared be sent to Chewalla tomorrow morning. Capt Lyman telegraphs me he sent a full train of forage to Corinth today   answer me what you can do"   Copies, DLC-USG, V, 18, 30; DNA, RG 393, Dept. of the Tenn., Letters Sent.

To Maj. Gen. Henry W. Halleck

Jackson Tenn
Nov. 2nd 11. A M 1862

Maj Gen H. W. Halleck
Gen in Chief

I have commenced a movement on Grand Junction with three 3 divisions from Corinth and two from Bolivar. Will leave here tomorrow evening and take command in person. If found practicable I will go on to Holly Springs and may be Grenada completing Railroad & Telegraph as I go. Bolivar has been threatened for some days but it may be a feint to cover a retreat

U. S. Grant
Maj Genl Comdg

Telegram received, DNA, RG 94, Generals' Papers and Books, Telegrams Received by Gen. Halleck; *ibid.*, RG 107, Telegrams Collected (Bound); copies, *ibid.*, Telegrams Received in Cipher; *ibid.*, RG 393, Dept. of the Tenn., Hd. Qrs. Correspondence; DLC-USG, V, 5, 8, 24, 88. *O.R.*, I, xvii, part 1, 466–67. On Nov. 3, 1862, Maj. Gen. Henry W. Halleck telegraphed to USG. "I approve of your plan of advancing upon the enemy as soon as you are strong enough for that purpose. The Minn & Wisconsin regts should join you very soon & the Governor of Ill. has promised ten regts this week. I have directed Genl Curtis to reinforce Helena & if they cannot operate on Little Rock they can cross the river and threaten Grenada. I hope for an active campaign on the Miss. this fall. A large force will ascend the river from New Orleans. Genl Stanley will be sent to Genl Rosecrans as chf of cavalry." ALS (telegram sent), DNA, RG 107, Telegrams Collected (Bound); copies, *ibid.*, RG 108, Telegrams Sent; *ibid.*, RG 393, Dept. of the Tenn., Hd. Qrs. Correspondence; DLC-USG, V, 5, 8, 24, 88. *O.R.*, I, xvii, part 1, 467.

On Nov. 2, Lt. Col. John A. Rawlins wrote to Maj. Gen. Stephen A. Hurlbut. "Major General U. S. Grant directs me to say to you that he will start to the front to-morrow in person, and that he desires you to remain at Jackson until further orders." LS, DNA, RG 393, District of West Tenn., 4th Division, Letters Received.

To Maj. Gen. Henry W. Halleck

————

Head Quarters, Dept. of the Ten.
Jackson Nov. 2d 1862

MAJ. GEN. H. W. HALLECK
GEN. IN CHIEF,
WASHINGTON D. C.
GEN.

I would respectfully recommend to the President, and ask your approval, the Promotion of Col. T. Lyle Dickey, 4th Ill. Cavalry, Capt. F. E Prime, Corps of Engineers and Geo A. Williams 1st U. S. Infantry to the rank of Brig. Gen.

In making these recommendations I do it entirely upon the merits of the officers named and their fitness for the positions ask for them.

Neither of these officers are aware of this recommendation nor have they asked either directly or through friends. It is made solely with the view of advancing the interests of service and of rewarding meritorious officers.

I am Gen very respectfully
your obt. svt.
U. S. GRANT
Maj. Gen.

ALS, Mrs. Walter Love, Flint, Mich. None of the officers named was nominated as requested. For the status of Capt. George A. Williams, see telegram to Brig. Gen. Charles S. Hamilton, Oct. 30, 1862, note 1.

To Maj. Gen. James B. McPherson

————

Jackson Nov 2nd 1862

MAJ GEN MCPHERSON
BOLIVAR TENN

Hamilton started this morning, is moving on Grand Junction. He will put himself in communication with you tomorrow. Start in the morning and try to arrange as to have both columns reach Grand Junction about the same time. I will join you tomorrow night or this next day. Supplies will be sent from Bolivar as far as possible for further want. Two additional Regiments will reach Bolivar tonight or tomorrow   This will give a garrison for Van Buren[1] or other available points on the road.

Every arrangement will be made to forward other reenforcement if we should go far south   Reenforcements are also going to Sherman and we may look for him. Cavalry should be well thrown out to the West.

Have you any further news from the front

U S GRANT
Maj Gen

Copies, DLC-USG, V, 18, 30; DNA, RG 393, Dept. of the Tenn., Letters Sent. *O.R.*, I, xvii, part 2, 317. On Nov. 2, 1862, Maj. Gen. James B. McPherson twice telegraphed to USG. "Will be ready to start at daylight tomorrow monday morning—shall I start?—Genl Brayman remains in command of the post with four (4) Regts of Infantry Battery of Artillery & the 5th Ohio Cavalry also all but three (3) Co's of Hursts first Tennessee cavalry—I have made three brigades of the 4th Div' & have 2 Brigades of the third Division for Genl Logan—Have put a new Regt into each of the brigades—" "Patrols report all quiet on the front—Everything is arranged to start tomorrow morning   will move so as to reach Grand Junction at the same time with Hamilton." Telegrams received, DNA, RG 94, War Records Office, Dept. of the Tenn. *O.R.*, I, xvii, part 2, 317.

1. Van Buren, Tenn., about ten miles south of Bolivar.

To Maj. Gen. James B. McPherson

Jackson Nov 2nd 1862

MAJ GEN McPHERSON
BOLIVAR TENN

Two hundred (200) rounds of ammunition is required to be carried at all times with troops moving. Lyford will be down to-day[1] and will be instructed about keeping up any further supply of ammunition that may be required. About six (6) wagons per Regiment had better be taken and all the ambulances. There will be two more Regiments reach you today from Columbus, making seven in all.

U S GRANT
Maj Gen

Telegram, copies, DLC-USG, V, 18, 30; DNA, RG 393, Dept. of the Tenn., Letters Sent. On Nov. 2, 1862, Maj. Gen. James B. McPherson telegraphed to USG. "Major Mudd reached Grand Junction at 11 P M last night found no rebels there about one thousand (1000) cavalry passed through Grand Junction a day or two ago & it is reported that fifteen hundred (1500) are in camp one (1) mile from lagrange—it is undeniably true that Rebal cavalry are in camp there but the number is probably exaggerated I shall be ready to move tomorrow morning at sunrise as I understand it we are to move light say two (2) wagons to a Regt one (1) to carry ammunition & the other provisions &c I propose to take along two hundred (200) Rounds of ammunition per man—" Telegram received, *ibid.*, RG 94, War Records Office, Dept. of the Tenn. *O.R.*, I, xvii, part 2, 317–18.

1. On Nov. 1, USG telegraphed to Brig. Gen. James M. Tuttle. "Send Lieut. Lyford chief of Ordnance down by train tomorrow" Copies, DLC-USG, V, 18, 30; DNA, RG 393, Dept. of the Tenn., Letters Sent. In a telegram dated "11," 2nd Lt. Stephen C. Lyford, Grand Junction, reported to USG. "Think I will have to put ammunition at Lagrage no suitable buildings here may find one at Davis mills go down this moring—" Telegram received, *ibid.*, Telegrams Received.

To Maj. Gen. Horatio G. Wright

BY TELEGRAPH FROM Jackson Tenn
[*Nov. 2, 1862*]

To MAJ GENL WRIGHT

Col Taylor 5th Ohio Cavalry with over three hundred recruits for his regiment, will you do me the favor to order him to his regiment. If he can get horse equipments in Cincinnati it would be an accommodation.

U S GRANT
Maj Genl

Telegram received, DNA, RG 393, Army of the Ohio, Letters Received; *ibid.* Dept. of the Ohio (Cincinnati), Telegrams Received; copies, *ibid.*, Dept. of the Tenn., Letters Sent; DLC-USG, V, 18, 30. On Nov. 7, 1862, Maj. Nathaniel H.

McLean endorsed this telegram. "Respectfully referred to Lt H. Porter Chief of Ordnance Dept of the Ohio, who will furnish the horse equipments if they can be spared." AES, DNA, RG 393, Army of the Ohio, Letters Received. 1st Lt. Horace Porter added an undated endorsement. "I have but 95 Sets of horse equipments on hand. I put in a requisition for 1200 two weeks ago but have heard nothing in regard to it, and cannot tell how soon they will be here." AES, *ibid.*

To Brig. Gen. Thomas A. Davies

Jackson Tenn Nov 2nd 1862

Gen Davies
Columbus Ky

Are any new Regiments on their way here   I want two Regiments to go to Bolivar including any that may be on the road at this time. If there are not two on the road now send Starrings'[1] Regiment and detain one to arrive in its place. As previous directed send four Regiments in all arriving on suitable transports to Memphis.[2] After sending two (2) Regiments to Bolivar send one (1) to Kenton and one to Union City to relieve those two (2) Regiments and order them to report here to Gen Hurlbut   all others arriving will be sent to Jackson for further orders.

U S Grant
Maj Gen

Telegram, copies, DLC-USG, V, 18, 30; DNA, RG 393, Dept. of the Tenn., Letters Sent. *O.R.*, I, xvii, part 2, 319. On Nov. 2, 1862, Brig. Gen. Thomas A. Davies telegraphed to Lt. Col. John A. Rawlins. "The (32) Wis Vol leave immediaty for Memphis—" Telegram received, DNA, RG 393, Dept. of the Tenn., Telegrams Received; copy, *ibid.*, Hd. Qrs. District of Columbus, Telegrams Sent.

Also on Nov. 2, Davies telegraphed to Rawlins. "Last night an attempt was made to fire the public buildings in this place   The new commissary building was fired under the floor but fortunately was extinguished   This is the 3rd time that the public property here has been set on fire & a dertimination seems to possess some one to accomplish its destruction   I have taken such steps as will I think thoroughly prevent the recurrence   I fear now more now from some wooden buildings in the vicinity being sit on fire to spread to them—than any other cause—would it not be well to destroy them or remove them than run this risk—I would like instructions" Telegram received, *ibid.*, Dept. of the Tenn., Telegrams Received; copy, *ibid.*, Hd. Qrs. District of Columbus, Telegrams Sent.

On the same day, USG telegraphed to Davies. "If the removal of any houses is necessary for the security of public stores have them removed" Copies, DLC-USG, V, 18, 30; DNA, RG 393, Dept. of the Tenn., Letters Sent. See letter to Maj. Gen. Stephen A. Hurlbut, Nov. 3, 1862.

On Nov. 3, Davies sent three telegrams to Rawlins. "I have telegraphed to Gen Tuttle to enquire if there are any more troops on the way down—The following list of Regts here—72d Ill present for duty 425 enlisted men—109th Ills present for duty 151 enlisted—72d Ills sick extra duty & arrest 199 enlisted men —109 sick extra duty & arrest 104 enlisted men 72d absent detached &c 209 enlisted men 109th Ills absent detached service 651 enlisted men 72d Ills aggregate present & absent 833 men enlisted men—72d Ills aggregate present & absent 906 enlisted men The 111th 940 all here—Gen Tuttle says there are no more on the way" Telegram received, DNA, RG 393, Dept. of the Tenn., Telegrams Received. Authorship of this telegram is attributed to Capt. Julius Lovell, asst. adjt. gen. to Davies, *ibid.*, Hd. Qrs. District of Columbus, Telegrams Sent. "I am compelled to go to Island 10 today to see to some defenses they have progressing from what I learn I think some changes are necessary—capt Lovell will attend to all business—" Telegram received, *ibid.*, Dept. of the Tenn., Telegrams Received; copy, *ibid.*, Hd. Qrs. District of Columbus, Telegrams Sent. "The 109 Ills leave here for Jackson in about an hour. Thare are 2 companies on expedition which will be sent on arrival" Copy, *ibid.*

1. Frederick A. Starring of Chicago was mustered in as maj., 46th Ill., on Dec. 31, 1861, but resigned one month later to accept the same rank in the 2nd Ill. Light Art. On Aug. 21, 1862, he was mustered in as col., 72nd Ill., also known as the 1st Chicago Board of Trade Regt.

2. On Nov. 1, USG telegraphed to Davies. "Send four Regiments of Infantry arriving by steamers suitable for carring them to Gen Sherman at Memphis Should any Cavalry be sent send that to Memphis" Copies, DLC-USG, V, 18, 30; DNA, RG 393, Dept. of the Tenn., Letters Sent. *O.R.*, I, xvii, part 2, 311. On Nov. 1, Davies telegraphed to Rawlins. "Telegraph rec'd from Gen Tuttle that two Regt's will be down tonight for Gen. Grant one (1) left this morning—" Telegram received, DNA, RG 393, Dept. of the Tenn., Telegrams Received; copy, *ibid.*, Hd. Qrs. District of Columbus, Telegrams Sent. On the same day, Rawlins telegraphed to Davies. "You will relieve the 109th Illinois Vols now at Columbus by one of the newly arrived Regiments, and send them forward to Bolivar Tenn" Copies, DLC-USG, V, 18, 30; DNA, RG 393, Dept. of the Tenn., Letters Sent. On the same day, Davies telegraphed twice more to Rawlins. "The 111th Ills has arrived here, transportation can not be furnished them, untill 4 Oclock A M the 2 Nov." Copy, *ibid.*, Hd. Qrs. District of Columbus, Telegrams Sent. "agreeable to orders I shall retain the 111th Ills & send forward the 109th as soon as they can be got together I expect more troops tonight & hope to send a reg't tomorrow in place of the 111th Ills—" Telegram received, *ibid.*, Dept. of the Tenn., Telegrams Received; copy, *ibid.*, Hd. Qrs. District of Columbus, Telegrams Sent.

To Brig. Gen. Charles S. Hamilton

Jackson Tenn Nov 2nd 1862

GEN HAMILTON
CORINTH MISS

Have just heard from Grand Junction there is a camp of say 2000 Cavalry at La Grange Tenn three miles from the Junction and probably a small force at Davis's Mills seven miles south, I think the enemy are evacuating Holly Springs, We will asertain at all events. You should have 200 rounds of ammunition per man with you   Lyford will see that any further supply that may be required is got up. Further supply of provisions will be looked after by way of Bolivar[1]

U S GRANT
Maj Gen

Telegram, copies, DLC-USG, V, 18, 30; DNA, RG 393, Dept. of the Tenn., Letters Sent; *ibid.*, District of Corinth, Telegrams Received. *O.R.*, I, xvii, part 2, 315–16. On Nov. 2, 1862, Brig. Gen. Charles S. Hamilton telegraphed to USG. "Troops are moving   have you anything more from the front—" Telegram received, DNA, RG 393, Dept. of the Tenn., Telegrams Received.

1. On Nov. 2, USG telegraphed to Capt. John C. Cox, Columbus, Ky. "Send additional supplies to Bolivar. Three Divisions and seven additional Regiments have been sent there" Copies, DLC-USG, V, 18, 30; DNA, RG 393, Dept. of the Tenn., Letters Sent. On the same day, Cox telegraphed to USG. "Order received   will load tomorrow 125.000. Rations" Telegram received, *ibid.*, Telegrams Received. On Nov. 4, Col. William S. Hillyer, Jackson, telegraphed to Brig. Gen. Mason Brayman, Bolivar. "Mr Walker Train Master is sending three trains to Bolivar tonight loaded with Commissary stores & it is important that they should be unloaded at once as stores & troops are waiting at Columbus" Copy, Brayman Papers, ICHi.

To Brig. Gen. Charles S. Hamilton

Jackson Nov 2nd 1862

GEN C S HAMILTON
CORINTH MISS

I have sent directions to Lieut Lyford to forward the ammunition mentioned in your dispatch. One of my staff is now in Memphis with instructions for Gen Sherman to move out under certain contingencies depending on information he may receive.[1] We cannot calculate on his cooperation however on account of the length of time it takes to communicate. I am sending reenforcements to Sherman and also to Bolivar. New Regiments are now arriving rapidly

U S GRANT
Maj Gen

Telegram, copies, DLC-USG, V, 18, 30; DNA, RG 393, Dept. of the Tenn., Letters Sent; *ibid.*, District of Corinth, Telegrams Received. *O.R.*, I, xvii, part 2, 316. On Nov. 2, 1862, Brig. Gen. Charles S. Hamilton telegraphed to Lt. Col. John A. Rawlins. "Dont fail to have the ammunition for the heavy artillery sent down by the train today   does Genl Sherman cooperate in this movement." Telegram received, DNA, RG 393, Dept. of the Tenn., Telegrams Received.

Before leaving Corinth on Nov. 2, Hamilton sent two additional telegrams to USG. "The three divisions are already gone. I shall move at noon. I have ordered an additional supply of ammunition to follow us but will rely on Bolivar for provisions." "My advance will reach the Tuscumbia to-night near Pocahontas. I shall probably stay at Chewalla to-night, and will endeavor to open communication with McPherson to-morrow. I shall have information to-morrow direct from Jackson, Miss. If the enemy shall prove to be in force at Holly Springs the co-operation of Sherman is of the utmost importance." *O.R.*, I, xvii, part 2, 316.

Also on Nov. 2, USG telegraphed to Hamilton, Chewalla. "Did you leave anyone at Corinth to finish up report to be laid before Congress. This report is called for by the Adj Genl." Copies, DLC-USG, V, 18, 30; DNA, RG 393, Dept. of the Tenn., Letters Sent. On the same day, Hamilton telegraphed to USG. "Genl Dodge remains with his Division—" Telegram received, *ibid.*, Telegrams Received.

1. On Nov. 2, Lt. Commander James W. Shirk, Columbus, Ky., telegraphed to USG. "General Sherman asked me to telegraph you that he had confirmatory reports that the enemy were evacuating Holly Springs and going south to Meridian and toward New Orleans and Mobile, and that he would send some other news to you in a few days." *O.R.*, I, xvii, part 2, 318.

To Brig. Gen. Charles S. Hamilton

Jackson Tenn Nov 2nd 1862

Gen Hamilton
Chewalla Tenn

McPherson will start in the morning, will hold back so as to reach Grand Junction at the same time with you. I will be there.

U S Grant
Maj Gen

Communicate with McPherson by telegraph from Chewalla to Bolivar   carriers at both ends to carry dispatches. After you pass Pocahontas start couriers for Van Buren nine miles south of Bolivar.

U. S. G.

Telegram, copies, DLC-USG, V, 18, 30; DNA, RG 393, Dept. of the Tenn., Letters Sent; *ibid.*, District of Corinth, Telegrams Received. On Nov. 2, 1862, Brig. Gen. Charles S. Hamilton, Chewalla, telegraphed to USG. "Troops will come on the Tuscumbia to-night. I shall stop 4 miles beyond this point. Tell me how I can best communicate with McPherson to-morrow. Negroes bring in the rumor that Price has gone to Mobile." *O.R.*, I, xvii, part 2, 316. On the same day, 11:00 P.M., Hamilton, "4 Miles West of Chewalla," telegraphed to USG. "Yours rec'd   shall reach Porters creek tomorrow & Grand Junction the following Afternoon   have communication with McPherson by Telegraph & Courier, will meet him at Van Buren tomorrow   I am very glad you will be on hand—No signs of the Enemy in front—"   Telegram received, *ibid.*, Dept. of the Tenn., Telegrams Received; copy, *ibid.*, District of Corinth, Telegrams Sent. *O.R.*, I, xvii, part 2, 317. On Nov. 3, 10:30 A.M., from "Davis' Bridge Hatchie," Hamilton telegraphed to USG. "Cavalry scouts from Ruckersville just in, report having met a citizen of Holly Springs who says Price is still there in force but quiet—We shall reach Porters Creek in good season to-day." Copy, DNA, RG 393, District of Corinth, Telegrams Sent. *O.R.*, I, xvii, part 2, 318.

General Orders No. 4

Head Quarters, Department of the Tennessee,
Jackson, Tenn., November 3rd 1862.

GENERAL ORDERS, No. 4.

It has been reported to the General Commanding that many families within the limits of the Military Guards of this Department are in a suffering condition—lacking food and clothing—and without any possible means of earning or procuring support. People not actively engaged in rebellion should not be allowed to suffer from hunger, in reach of a country abounding with supplies. The Government, never the cause of this state of affairs, should not be subjected to the burden of furnishing the necessary relief, but the weight should fall on those, who, by act, encouragement or sympathy, have caused the want now experienced. It is therefore ordered:

1. The necessary expenses for the relief needed must be borne by sympathizers with the rebellion.

2. District Commanders throughout this Department will cause the extent of these wants to be ascertained and the necessary supplies to be procured and distributed.

3. To this end, District Commanders will cause all persons known to be disloyal within reach of their respective Commands, to be assessed in proportion to their relative ability to pay, and cause such assessments to be collected and discreetly applied. Assessments may be paid in money or supplies.

4. A suitable Chaplain or other commissioned officer, will be appointed at each Post where it may be necessary to distribute supplies under this order, who shall have charge of the distribution of supplies and who shall be held responsible for the faithful performance of his duties, and that no supplies are unworthily bestowed.

5. Commissaries of Subsistence will be allowed to sell provisions at the rates charged officers, to such persons as are desig-

nated to distribute them, on certificates that they are for such purpose, and are necessary to save suffering.

6. Officers collecting assessments will keep an accurate account of all monies and provisions so collected, and from whom, and send their accounts through their immediate Commanding Officers to the Chief Commissary of the Department, to be audited.

The Chief Commissary of the Department will designate in a circular, how the abstract of such sales is to be kept and returned.

By Command of Major General U. S. Grant.
JNO. A. RAWLINS,
Assistant Adjutant General.

Copies, DLC-USG, V, 13, 14, 95; DNA, RG 393, Dept. of the Tenn., General and Special Orders; (printed) *ibid.*, RG 94, Dept. of the Tenn., General Orders; (printed) Oglesby Papers, IHi. *O.R.*, I, xvii, part 2, 319–20.

To Maj. Gen. Stephen A. Hurlbut

Head Quarters Dept of the Tenn
Jackson Tenn Nov 3d 1862

MAJ GEN HURLBUT
COMM'DG DIST OF JACKSON
GENERAL:

Enclosed I send you copy of dispatch sent Gen Davies last evening. If Starring's Regiment is not among the first two arriving here, send it to Corinth when it does arrive. Send two Regiments to Bolivar as soon as praticable without taking them from here. When that is done detain all other new Regiments at this place. Assign the first one so detained to Col Lawler's Brigade and require Lawler to relieve the 8th Illinois from road duty. Assign the next one to Col Stevenson's Brigade and require him to hold his troops in readiness for a foward movement at any time. When this done all other troops can be assigned to Col Lawlers command without being Brigaded leaving the subject to further orders.

U S GRANT
Maj Gen

P. S. In my absence any change you may find necessary for the public safety even to the reenforcement of Corinth which is out of your District you can make

I will inform Gen Dodge that he is to communicate directly with you.[1] A line of couriers will be kept up between my Hd qrs and the telegraph, through this I desire to be kept informed of everything that it is important should be communicated to me

U. S. G.

Copies, DLC-USG, V, 18, 30; DNA, RG 393, Dept. of the Tenn., Letters Sent. *O.R.*, I, xvii, part 2, 318–19. For the enclosure, see telegram to Brig. Gen. Thomas A. Davies, Nov. 2, 1862.

1. On Nov. 3, 1862, USG wrote to Brig. Gen. Grenville M. Dodge. "I leave here for the front today. In my absence communicate directly with Gen Hurlbut who is directed to reenforce you if such a thing should become necessary." Copies, DLC-USG, V, 18, 30; DNA, RG 393, Dept. of the Tenn., Letters Sent; Dodge Papers, IaHA.

To Maj. Gen. William T. Sherman

Jackson Nov 1[3] 1862

MAJ GEN SHERMAN
MEMPHIS TENN

Troops from Corinth marched on Grand Junction yesterday from Bolivar today. I go forward with the advance   will push on to Grenada if possible opening Railroad and Telegraph as we advance. I have ordered four Regiments to Memphis   will order more if the reenforcements sent me justify it. If communication can be opened with you by courier I will do it.

If your hear of my forces passing Holly Springs and can put a force on the Railroad to repair it, start towards Grenada repairing the road as the troops advance.

A demonstration made to the South-east at once, would give the idea of a formidable movement to the front particularly as you will be receiving reenforcements and I also in considerable numbers.

The amount arrived and to arrive will not amount to less than 30.000 men.

The news of these reenforcements coming cannot be kept from the enemy of course

U S GRANT

Maj Gen

Copies (misdated Nov. 1, 1862), DLC-USG, V, 18, 30; DNA, RG 393, Dept. of the Tenn., Letters Sent. *O.R.*, I, xvii, part 2, 315. Copy (dated Nov. 3), DNA, RG 393, Hd. Qrs. District of Columbus, Telegrams Sent. On Nov. 3, Maj. Gen. William T. Sherman wrote to USG. "I extract from a letter received last evening from Mr H——, who lives on the Yazoo, whose information hitherto has been reliable—'I this morning met a gentlemen from Richmond, Va., from whom I received the following information: "officials and others greatly disappointed about Bragg's retreat from Kentucky. All quiet at Mobile, Genl. Villipigue gone to Port Hudson instead of Meridian. Federals have landed a force at mouth of Bayou Manchac: a fight is anticipated at an early day between them and forces at Port Hudson. More troops have been sent to Genl. Villipigue at Port Hudson. Troops at Port Hudson supposed to be about 16,000. General M. L. Smith at Vicksburg is soon to be reinforced. A plan of a fortification has been agreed on, and placed under the supervision of Capt. Brown, late of Gun Boat Arkansas, to be made at the mouth of the Yazoo. 10,000 men to be sent there; the largest guns of the Confederacy to be used; active preparations are being made at Holly Springs for a move of some kind: It is supposed that the attack on Mobile was merely a feint to draw Rebel troops there to give Federals a chance to march up ~~in~~ the Mississippi. All anxiety and fears are now for a south movement.' " I will send out two parties to Holly Springs today, as contraband traders & hope to get reliable information from them. The party representing having seen artillery on the cars from Holly springs south, continues to renew her assertions. I want to test her information. The 32nd Wisconsin has just arrived and I will post them outside the Fort, near where Gen. Veatch was encamped, and will leave room there for a whole Brigade, if you propose to give me a real Brigadier, otherwise I will take one of my present Colonels—Buckland or Stuart, both officers of merit & experience. I will organize a 4th Brigade and divide my command into two Divisions of two ~~two~~ Brigades each, one inside of Fort Pickering and one outside; the former under the immediate command of Brig. Gen. Denver and the other under the command of Brig. Genl. M. L. Smith, on the outside of Memphis. In case of a movement, I can go forward with, say three Brigades, leaving one to hold the Fort. By mixing the old and new Regiments, I secure the advantage of association

and experience already gained. Col. Hilyer went up yesterday, and can explain
fully how satisfactory every thing is here. I feel no uneasiness about Memphis,
for to take it, the enemy would have to sacrifice more men than they can afford."

Copies, *ibid.*, RG 94, Generals' Papers and Books, William T. Sherman, Letters
Sent; (2) DLC-William T. Sherman.

To Maj. Gen. Henry W. Halleck

Lagrange Miss[1]
Nov. 4th 8. P. M. 62

MAJ GEN H W. HALLECK
GEN˙IN CHIEF.

Troops from Corinth & Bolivar reached here today   occupy
the line of Scott Creek & Wolf River[2] from two & half miles
South of Grand Junction to a short distance west of Lagrange.
Gen McPherson Com'dg Right wing Hamilton Marcy[3]   will
remain here[4] for few days to get up stores by Railroad & to
reconnoitre the front perfectly   Enemys Pickets occupied this
place on our arrival & two 2 captured Bridges over Woolf river
at this place are safe   Gen Sherman moves out from Memphis to
attract attention in that direction. My moving force will be about
31.000

U S GRANT Mj Gen

Telegram received, DNA, RG 94, Generals' Papers and Books, Telegrams
Received by Gen. Halleck; *ibid.*, RG 107, Telegrams Collected (Bound); copies,
ibid., Telegrams Received in Cipher; *ibid.*, RG 393, Dept. of the Tenn., Hd. Qrs.
Correspondence; DLC-USG, V, 5, 8, 24, 88. *O.R.*, I, xvii, part 1, 467.

    1. An error: Tenn. was intended.
    2. The Wolf River rises in northern Miss. and crosses the Tenn. state line
at a point equidistant from Grand Junction and La Grange, Tenn.
    3. "Marcy" is a telegraphic error for "the left."
    4. On Nov. 3, 1862, USG, Bolivar, telegraphed to Julia Dent Grant. "Went
six Miles beyond Bolivar and returned   Will go to Lagrange tomorrow & probably send for you on thursday" Telegram received, DLC-USG. On Nov. 5,
Lt. Col. John A. Rawlins, La Grange, telegraphed to Capt. Theodore S. Bowers,
Jackson. "Move every thing belonging to Hd Qrs including Printing ~~Office~~ Press
to this place where Hd Qrs of the Dept will for the present be established. Come
forward on first through train   The Genl says for Mrs Grant to come with you

Your report of what you have done is all satisfactory" Telegram received, DNA, RG 393, Dept. of the Tenn., Telegrams Received. On Nov. 9, Col. T. Lyle Dickey wrote to his wife. "On last Monday I started with Gen Grant & Staff for La Grange The army was already moving—part from Corinth under Gen Hamilton & part from Bolivar under Gen McPherson We went that day to Bolivar & on tuesday (the day of the election) we marched 25 miles to La Grange going in at the Head of the Column—with only a small squad of cavalry as advance guard—The Rebel pickets were in town when we arrived—Our entry was wholly unexpected—The Rebels fled & our boys chased & captured a lieut. & sergeant —Gen McPherson took the right occupying Lagrange & Gen Hamilton the left— occupying the camps on Davis Creek (or Scott Creek) where Gen Hurlbut sojourned in June On tuesday wednesday—I rode with Gen Grant through the different camps & country—Our soldiers were doing a great deal of plundering—" ALS, Wallace-Dickey Papers, IHi.

To Brig. Gen. Charles S. Hamilton

Head Quarters Dept of the Tenn
LaGrange Nov 4th 1862

GEN C S HAMILTON
COMM'DG LEFT WING ARMY IN THE FIELD
GENERAL:

Please get your men in camp as comfortbly as you can on the stream 2½ miles south of Grand Junction. McPherson will form a line almost connecting with you extending down Wolf river west of this place. Seize on the bridges between you and Holly Springs if they are still standing and if not upon the places where they were and organize working parties to rebuild them and repair the roads leading to them. Send out tomorrow a large Cavalry reconnoisance supported by Infantry towards Holly Springs with a lookout towards Ripley. McPherson will send from here a force to drive out some Cavalry that are now in towards Somerville. Halleck advises me that a large force is moving up from New Orleans also that Helena force may move towards Grenada[1] Sherman will also be out. They now sending me reenforcements as rapidly as the road can transport them. I have sent Sherman some. The telegraph and Railroad will be complete. I hope to visit your camp some time tomorrow. Let your teams collect all the forage they can but in an orderly manner. Send in charge of foraging parties Officers who can be relied upon to maintain order. I will probably go round to see you tomorrow

U S GRANT
Maj Gen

Copies, DLC-USG, V, 18, 30; DNA, RG 393, Dept. of the Tenn., Letters Sent. *O.R.*, I, xvii, part 2, 320.

1. See telegram to Maj. Gen. Henry W. Halleck, Nov. 2, 1862.

To Maj. Gen. Stephen A. Hurlbut

BY TELEGRAPH FROM Lagrange [*Nov.*] 5 *1862*

To MAJ GEN HURLBUT

Direct Col Lawler to relieve the 20th Ills and send it here as soon as possible. As soon as one new Regt reaches Jackson cause the 8th Ills to be relieved and send Stevensen forward with his brigade of three (3) regiments. I can attach another regiment to it here   Let them bring their camp & garrison equipage Trains march through with escort of three men to each wagon. Dissolve the court Martial now in session at Jackson & order the Officers to their regiments. Order Lieut Carter[1] to report to Gen Logan. Order Capt Fort[2] to supply regimental Trains to new regiments arriving from the supply Train of first division. When Trains are so supplied teamsters must be taken from the troops having the teams or Negroes, and the present ~~drivers~~ teamsters sent back to their regiments

U. S. GRANT
Maj Genl

Telegram received, DNA, RG 393, District of West Tenn., 4th Division, Telegrams Received; copies, *ibid.*, Dept. of the Tenn., Letters Sent; DLC-USG, V, 18, 30. On Nov. 6, 1862, Maj. Gen. Stephen A. Hurlbut, Jackson, telegraphed to

USG. "Lawler has but two regiments in his brigade the 31st having gone with Gen'l Logan. only one regt. the 109th has reached Bolivar. the 119th will come down to day destined by your former order. to Bolivar. If they go to Bolivar I must relieve the 20th with one of Lawlers Regiments. shall I stop that regiment here and relieve the 8th with it so as to send Stevenson forward. No troops are reported yet as coming down and if I send the 20th and Stevensons Brigade it will leave two light regiments of Infantry here. not enough for guard duty." Copy, DNA, RG 393, District of West Tenn., 4th Division, Letters Sent. *O.R.*, I, xvii, part 2, 323. On the same day, USG telegraphed to Hurlbut. "Stop the 119th at Jackson and bring down there. Also one of the four regiments between Humboldt and Union City. Three regiments I think enough to guard that line" Telegram received, DNA, RG 393, District of West Tenn., 4th Division, Telegrams Received; copies, *ibid.*, Dept. of the Tenn., Letters Sent; DLC-USG, V, 18, 30. On the same day, USG again telegraphed to Hurlbut. "Order Capt Holcomb of the 45th Ills now on duty at Jackson & Lieut J Johns of the 31st Ill now at Bethel to join their Regts" Telegram received, DNA, RG 393, Dept. of the Tenn., Miscellaneous Letters Received; copies, *ibid.*, Letters Sent; DLC-USG, V, 18, 30.

On Nov. 7, Hurlbut telegraphed to USG. "The Twentieth are ready to move as soon as the road is open. I will send Stevenson's brigade directly after, or, if you order it, will march them by land. Does General McPherson need Foster's cavalry? If so, will send it through. My cavalry force here is very small. What shall be done with the Engineer Regiment?" *O.R.*, I, xvii, part 2, 326. On the same day, USG telegraphed to Hurlbut. "Send Engr Regt. on Rail as far as possible & then march them to this place Keep capt Fosters company of cavalry Send Stevensons brigade Monday next" Telegram received, DNA, RG 393, District of West Tenn., 4th Division, Telegrams Received; copies, *ibid.*, Dept. of the Tenn., Letters Sent; DLC-USG, V, 18, 30.

On Nov. 8, USG telegraphed to Hurlbut. "When the 106th Ills Vols arrive detain them at Jackson and have their arms repaired" Telegram received, DNA, RG 393, District of West Tenn., 4th Division, Telegrams Received; copies, *ibid.*, Dept. of the Tenn., Letters Sent; DLC-USG, V, 18, 30. On Nov. 11, Hurlbut telegraphed to USG. "The 106th has come down with austen rifles calibre 54 defective & worthless there are arms enough here as I am informed to supply them shall I do so—" Telegram received, DNA, RG 393, Dept. of the Tenn., Telegrams Received. On the reverse of this telegram, USG drafted an order. "Direct Ordnance officer at Jackson to exchange these arms." ANS, *ibid.* On the same day, in USG's name, a telegram was sent to Capt. James P. Harper, ordnance officer, Jackson. "You will exchange the arms of the 106th Ill in accordance with Genl Hurlbuts directions" Copies, DLC-USG, V, 18, 30; DNA, RG 393, Dept. of the Tenn., Letters Sent.

1. Possibly 2nd Lt. Julian Carter, Battery E, 2nd Ill. Light Art.

2. Greenbury L. Fort, born in Ohio in 1825, a lawyer and politician of Lacon, Ill., rose from 2nd lt. to capt., 11th Ill., during 1861, and was confirmed as asst. q. m. and capt. on March 24, 1862. See *Calendar*, April 21, 1862.

To Col. Robert Allen

Head Quarters Dept of the Tenn
La Grange Tenn Nov 5th 1862

GEN R ALLEN
CHIEF QUARTERMASTER
JACKSON TENN

I have directed Capt Reynolds not to make any purchases of lumber until further orders, the stores are required for immediate use   please fill his requisition for them at the earliest possible moment. Send Capt Eddy to Memphis   he is much needed there.[1] Capt Tighe[2] I would like to have here

U S GRANT
Maj Gen

Telegram, copies, DLC-USG, V, 18, 30; DNA, RG 393, Dept. of the Tenn., Letters Sent. On Nov. 4, 1862, Col. Robert Allen, St. Louis, twice telegraphed to USG. "Very heavy requisitions for Lumber to build Barracks at Jackson have been recd not approved by you. Do you order the same.   a large ~~lumber~~ number of stores are also required." "Capt Eddy is ordered by the Adjutant General of the Army to Memphis. Do you want Capt Tighe to go also." Telegrams received., (1st) *ibid.*, Telegrams Received; (2nd) *ibid.*, Miscellaneous Letters Received.

1. On Oct. 29, USG had telegraphed to Capt. Asher R. Eddy, St. Louis. "Captain Reynolds Chief Qr. M., is absent and reported dead, if true I want you here as Chief, if not true, report at Corinth." Copies, DLC-USG, V, 18, 30; DNA, RG 393, Dept. of the Tenn., Letters Sent. The information about Capt. Charles A. Reynolds was incorrect.

On Oct. 30, Maj. Gen. William S. Rosecrans telegraphed to USG. "Capt Taylor Vols says you want him. Gen Halleck authorised me to bring him along   if you wish him as chief Q M it will give the promotion I could give—Let me know" Telegram received, *ibid.*, RG 94, Staff Papers. On the same day, USG telegraphed to Rosecrans. "I do not want capt Taylor as chief   I am scarce of Q. M. but will send him to you as soon as his place can be filled   cant you send me on[e] in his place" Telegram received, *ibid.*, RG 393, Dept. of the Cumberland, Telegrams Received; copies, *ibid.*, Dept. of the Tenn., Letters Sent; DLC-USG, V, 18, 30. On Oct. 31, Rosecrans telegraphed to USG. "I find no availabe q m to send you   maj Gen Halleck directed me by telegraph to take Capt Taylor Vols with me   please send him at once as I am obliged to have a Chief Q M for this dept—" Telegram received, DNA, RG 94, Staff Papers; copy, *ibid.*, RG 393, Dept. of the Cumberland, Telegrams Sent. On Nov. 1, USG telegraphed to Rosecrans. "I have ordered Capt Taylor to report to you at once." ADf (in the hand of Lt. Col. John A. Rawlins), *ibid.*, RG 94, Staff Papers; telegram received, *ibid*. On Oct. 31, Brig. Gen. Charles S. Hamilton had telegraphed to USG. "Have you an energetic Quarter Master to take capt Taylors place as chief Q M here—Taylor is appointed Lieut Col on Roscrans Staff—if you have one I shall be glad of him—" Telegram received, *ibid*., RG 393, Dept. of the Tenn., Telegrams Received; copy, *ibid*., District of Corinth, Telegrams Sent. On Nov. 1, Rawlins telegraphed to Hamilton. "You will relieve Capt Taylor A. Q. M. at Corinth and order him to report to Maj Gen Rosecrans at Louisville without delay" Copies, DLC-USG, V, 18, 30; DNA, RG 393, Dept. of the Tenn., Letters Sent; *ibid*., District of Corinth, Telegrams Received.

2. John H. Tighe, born in Ireland, was appointed asst. q. m. and capt. on May 12, 1862.

To Maj. Gen. Henry W. Halleck

Gen Grants H'd Qrs
Grand Junction Tenn
Nov. 6th 7. A M 1862

MAJ GEN H. W. HALLECK
GEN IN CHIEF.

Send sixteen (16) Regiments of Infantry and all Cavalry & Artillery to Memphis   this will give two full Divisions to move from there & leave a sufficient garrison—I want seven (7) Regiments here to fill private organizations—Stanley is the only General to his division & I have no one to take his place that can be spared   Will relieve him as soon as possible[1]

U. S. GRANT
Maj Genl

Telegram received, DNA, RG 94, Generals' Papers and Books, Telegrams Received by Gen. Halleck; *ibid*., RG 107, Telegrams Collected (Bound); copies, *ibid*., Telegrams Received in Cipher; *ibid*., RG 393, Dept. of the Tenn., Hd. Qrs. Correspondence; DLC-USG, V, 5, 8, 24, 88. *O.R.*, I, xvii, part 1, 467–68. On Nov. 5, 1862, Maj. Gen. Henry W. Halleck telegraphed to USG. "Had not troops sent to reinforce you better go to Memphis hereafter? I hope to give you twenty thousand additional men in a few days." ALS (telegram sent), DNA, RG 107, Telegrams Collected (Bound); copies, *ibid*., RG 108, Telegrams Sent; *ibid*., RG 393, Dept. of the Tenn., Hd. Qrs. Correspondence; DLC-USG, V, 5, 8, 24, 88. *O.R.*, I, xvii, part 1, 467.

1. See telegram to Maj. Gen. Henry W. Halleck, Nov. 2, 1862. On Nov. 7, Maj. Gen. William S. Rosecrans, Bowling Green, Ky., telegraphed to USG.

"The War Department has ordered Genl. Stanley here. He is to command our Cavalry. He is much needed. Please send him as soon as you can. You will do a most necessary thing for the service—" Copy, DNA, RG 393, Dept. of the Cumberland, Telegrams Sent. Dated Nov. 8 in *O.R.*, I, xx, part 2, 27. On Nov. 11, Lt. Col. John A. Rawlins issued Special Orders No. 15 sending Maj. Gen. David S. Stanley to Rosecrans and assigning Brig. Gen. Leonard F. Ross to Stanley's division. DS, DNA, RG 94, Dept. of the Tenn., Special Orders; copies, *ibid.*, RG 393, Dept. of the Tenn., Special Orders; DLC-USG, V, 16, 26, 27, 87. *O.R.*, I, xvii, part 2, 343.

To Maj. Gen. William T. Sherman

———

Hd Qrs Dept of the Tenn
LaGrange Tenn Nov 6th 1862

Maj Gen W T Sherman
Comm'dg Dist of Memphis
Memphis Tenn

A dispatch just received from Gen Halleck promises me reenforcements to the number of 20,000, men to be sent immediately and suggests sending them to you[1] I have asked to have sixteen Regiments of Infantry and all the Artillery and Cavalry that may come to be sent that way. The remainder I want sent here to fill the present organization at present reduced by taking out Railroad guards. I am also instructed to detail one commissioned Officer from each Ohio Regiment to report to the Adj Gen of the State to take charge of drafted men to fill up their respective Regiments[2]—You may regard this as an order for making the detail from your command. The expectation of these reenforcements will cause a delay in my movements and will render a demonstration from Memphis unnecessary for the present unless our reconnoisance should demonstrate that the enemy are evacuating Holly Springs. I will not move from here under a week or ten days and will try and communicate with you in the meantime. I have already been reenforced to such an extent that I feel no doubt of the result if I should advance now, but as so many are coming it is more prudent perhaps to avail myself of our whole strength. I am also informed by Gen Halleck that a large force of our troops are moving north from New Orleans. Also that the Helena force is being augmented and if not praticable to go to Little Rock, they will be instructed to cross the Mississipi and march on Granada[3]

Of course I can make nothing but independent moves with this command being governed in that by information received from day to day until I am fully informed of when and how all these other forces are moving so as to make the whole cooperate. If you have not yet moved out under the instructions sent by way of Columbus it will not be necessary to do so now. If you have moved you can go back to Memphis and await re-enforcements and instructions.

Send me any information you may have received from Holly Springs within the last week.

There is no doubt but that Villipugue has left there with his command either for Mobile Meridan or Vicksburgh. A small force has also been sent to occupy points on the river where the enemy hold both banks and we hold neither to prevent desertions. The enemy at Holly Springs is now estimated at 30000 men in rather a disorganized condition. I can now move from here with a force sufficient to handle that number without gloves

> I am Very Respectfully
> Your Obedt Sevnt
> U S GRANT
> Maj Gen

Copies, DLC-USG, V, 18, 30; DNA, RG 393, Dept. of the Tenn., Letters Sent. *O.R.*, I, xvii, part 2, 322–23. On Nov. 8, 1862, Maj. Gen. William T. Sherman wrote to USG. "Yours of november 6th from LaGrange, was brought to me by Captain Newell, 3rd. Michigan Cavalry, last night, he having ridden by circuitous routes and reached me without serious opposition. Yet I fear his return ~~might~~ may be hazardous and I have ordered Col. Grierson, 6th. Ills. Cavalry, to escort him back with about 300 select Cavalry and in going and returning to do certain things that will be of advantage to the service. He will show you his instructions. I have not yet received the instructions via Columbus referred to in yours of november 6th, but am prepared on short notice to do anything you may require. As yet but one Regiment has reported to me—the 32nd Wisconsin, Col. Howe— a strong regiment of good material, well armed and equipped. By the reduction of transportation under recent orders, I will have enough wagons for double my force and since the incursions of morgan & Kirby, Smith into Kentucky, & Stuart's Raid into Penn. in which they took horses of private owners, we should no longer hesitate to replenish our stock in the country we operate in, giving owners simple receipts to be settled for at the conclusion of hostilities, according to the circumstances of each case. I deem it good policy now to encourage the non–combatant population to trade with Memphis their cotton and corn for such articles of groceries and clothing as they need for their families and servants. Many of them are justly indignant at their own armies and partizans for burning their cotton by the sales of which alone they can realize the means of purchase of the articles they absolutely need to maintain their suffering families, and I would like some expression of opinion from you on this policy. Of course a part of these supplies will fall into improper hands, but the time must come when the inhabitants must choose their rulers, and even I now donot fear their choice, if protected from their Confederate armies & Bandits. Some of them of course make loud complaints against our troops for burning rails and stealing potatoes &c., but I tell them plainly these are the inevitable accompaniments of armies, for which those who provoked war & appealed to it, are responsible & not ~~us~~. we. I am satisfied a change of opinion is rapidly growing here which I endeavor to foster & encourage. On Monday next a Union Club will come out in public, will decorate their houses with our flag and have a public procession, speeches &c., I will attend of course and aid them with every means to produce effect. The advance of your army to LaGrange will have an admirable effect. All my information goes to the belief that the Rebel force at Holly Springs is reduced by detachments to the South, so that it no longer threatens W. Tenn. Some farmers just in, report Holly Springs evacuated, but I am not satisfied on that point. I have out two good men who ought to be back in a day or two, whose report I will get through to you by some safe means. I will keep my force well in hand but will make a demonstration towards Cold Water tomorrow &c., to gain information and withdraw attention from you. I do not believe that there is in Arkansas, a force to justify the armies of Schofield, Steele & Hovey (at Helena) remaining quiet and would advise the latter, to threaten Grenada & the Yazoo, by all means. I will rapidly organize Brigades & equip all Regiments coming to me, and be prepared to act with promptness the moment I learn the part you design me to play. Cols. McDowell 6th Iowa, Stuart 55th Ills. & Buckland 72nd Ohio, are fully competent to take Brigades and I will so dispose of them, unless you send me Brigadiers duly commissioned. Cols. Hilyer & Lagow of your staff recently here, will tell you fully of all figures, numbers and facts that I deem imprudent to trust by this route. I have already ordered one officer of every Ohio Regiment to proceed with dispatch to Columbus, Ohio, to bring back the drafted men for the Ohio Regiments —7 in number. Health of troops good and every thing as well as I could wish. I will write to Genl. Hovey at Helena, telling him of your movements & asking him to gather all information he can of the Country towards Grenada. Deserters come in constantly, one is just now in from Cold Water, where he was a picket. He did not know you were at LaGrange, and said he deserted because he did not wish to go further south. Heard that Price was to go to Jackson, Miss. but he had not been to Holly Springs for 5 Days. . . . I send you our morning papers,— one of Mobile, Nov. 3, & Grenada Nov. 5." Copies, DNA, RG 94, Generals' Papers and Books, William T. Sherman, Letters Sent; (2) DLC–William T. Sherman. *O.R.*, I, xvii, part 2, 860–62.

1. See preceding telegram.

2. On Nov. 5, Maj. Thomas M. Vincent, AGO, telegraphed to USG. "Old Ohio regts of your command are to be filled with drafted men   please detail an officer from each of said Regts to report to Supt volunteers Recruiting service Columbus to take charge of drafted for his regt and conducts it to its command" Telegram received, DNA, RG 393, Dept. of the Tenn., Telegrams Received; copies, *ibid.*, RG 94, Vol. Service Division, Letters Sent; *ibid.*, RG 393, Dept. of the Tenn., Hd. Qrs. Correspondence; DLC-USG, V, 5, 8, 24, 88. An LS (telegram sent), DNA, RG 107, Telegrams Collected (Bound), indicates that an identical telegram was sent to Maj. Gen. George B. McClellan and to Maj. Gen. William S. Rosecrans.

3. See telegram to Maj. Gen. Henry W. Halleck, Nov. 2, 1862.

To Brig. Gen. James M. Tuttle

Head Quarters Dept of the Tenn
LaGrange Tenn Nov 6th 1862

GEN TUTTLE
CAIRO ILL'S

There is man by the name of Eaton connected with the Post Surveyor's Office in some way at Cairo who interferes with packages coming to Officer's here. I am told that he took a box from the express office some weeks ago marked for Mrs Gen Hamilton Fon-du-lac Wisc which cannot be brought to light. I wish you would make inquiries about him and inform Mr Eaton that I want no more interference from him outside his duties. If I violate any Treasury regulation let him report it but not interfere over my permit

U S GRANT
Maj Gen

Telegram, copies, DLC-USG, V, 18, 30; DNA, RG 393, Dept. of the Tenn., Letters Sent. On Nov. 6, 1862, Brig. Gen. James M. Tuttle telegraphed to USG. "The man Eaton is at Columbus   I have sent your dispatch to Gen Davies—The election returns are megre but indicate large Democratic gains—New York New Jersey are democrate Ills doubtful   Arnold Washburne & Lovejoy elected Frank Blair reported beat, both the Woods elected in N. Y. I will send you more news in morning—" Telegram received, *ibid.*, Telegrams Received.

On Oct. 25, Brig. Gen. Charles S. Hamilton had telegraphed to Maj. John A. Rawlins. "A small box sent by me to my wife Mrs C S Hamilton Fond Du Lac Wisconsin by express has been stopped at Cairo by Custom House officer   Will you do me the favor to have it forwarded   nothing Contraband in it"   Telegram received, *ibid.*; copy, *ibid.*, District of Corinth, Telegrams Sent. On Nov. 16, Brig. Gen. Thomas A. Davies telegraphed twice to Hamilton stating that the box had been found with some maps removed, and that an investigation was underway. Copies, *ibid.*, Telegrams Received; *ibid.*, Hd. Qrs. District of Columbus, Telegrams Sent.

Special Field Orders No. 1

———

Headquarters, 13th Army Corps
Dept of the Tennessee
In Field, LaGrange, Tenn, Nov 7th 1862

SPECIAL FIELD ORDERS No 1

It is with extreme regret that the General Commanding has had his attention called to the gross acts of vandalism committed by some of the men composing the two wings of the Army on the march from Corinth and Bolivar to this place.

Houses have been plunder'd and burned down, fencing destroyed and citizens frightened without an enquiry as to their status in this Rebellion, cattle and hogs shot and Stock driven off without any observance of the rules prescribed in General Orders for taking such property for public use.

Such acts are punishable with death by the Articles of War and existing orders. They are carculated to destroy the efficiency of an army and to make open enemeis of those who before if not friends were at least non combatants.

Officers are more to blame for these acts of violence than the men who commit them and in furture will be held to a strict accountability. If they will perform their duty obedience can be enforced in the ranks.

In furture marches all men will be kept in the ranks and Regimental Commanders held accountable for thier good conduct. It is the duty of Regimental Commanders and within their power, if they are worthy of the position they hold, to enforce attention to duty on the part of Company Commanders.

All deriliction of duty within any Regiment in furture will be reported by Brigade Commanders, through the proper channels, to Headquarters of the Wing to which they belong to the end that the offenders may be brought to trial or immediate dismissal from the service and public disgrace.

All men who straggle from their Companies and are captured by the enemy will be reported to General Headqua[rters] so that they may dishonorably discharged, whereby they will forfeit all back and furture pay and allowances, and Government will be protected from exchanging a captured in actual conflict for one who by his worthlessness and disregard for the good of the service has become a captive

This order will be read on parade before each Regiment and Detachment for three (3) sucessive evenings.

By order of Maj. Genl. U S. Grant.

JNO A RAWLINS

Asst. Adjt. General

DS, DNA, RG 94, Dept. of the Tenn., 13th Army Corps, General Orders; copies, *ibid.*, RG 393, Dept. of the Tenn., General and Special Orders; *ibid.*, Special Orders; DLC-USG, V, 26, 27. *O.R.*, I, xvii, part 2, 326–27.

On Nov. 9, 1862, Lt. Col. John A. Rawlins issued Special Field Orders No. 2 authorizing stoppage of pay for soldiers in units guilty of such "depredations." DS, DNA, RG 94, Dept. of the Tenn., 13th Army Corps, General Orders; copies, *ibid.*, RG 393, Dept. of the Tenn., General and Special Orders; *ibid.*, Special Orders; DLC-USG, V, 26, 27. *O.R.*, I, xvii, part 2, 331–32. On Nov. 6, USG wrote to Brig. Gen. Charles S. Hamilton. "Col. Oliver of a Michigan Regiment ordered the immediate release of prisoners sent to him by me for confinement and punishment for the offense of pillaging, and this without taking the names of the offenders or reporting the fact. I wish you would enquire if this is the fact and if so arrest him, by my order, reporting to me the result of the enquiry . . . " *Charles Hamilton Auction No. 74*, Jan. 17, 1974, p. 37. For an account of these "depredations" emphasizing Hamilton's responsibility, see letter of "Spur," Grand Junction, Nov. 7, in *Missouri Republican*, Nov. 12, 1862.

To Maj. Gen. Henry W. Halleck

La Grange Tenn.
Nov. 7. 1862.

MAJ GEN H W HALLECK,
GENL-IN-CHIEF—

I will make a reconnoissance in force tomorrow towards Holly Springs. Will not attack or advance however unless it is ascertained that the Enemy are evacuating, until re-inforcements are up—

Will have the railroad complete to Davis Mills on Monday

I have not the slightest apprehension of a reverse from present appearances.

U. S. GRANT,
Maj. Gen. Comd'g

Telegram received, DNA, RG 94, Generals' Papers and Books, Telegrams Received by Gen. Halleck; *ibid.*, RG 107, Telegrams Collected (Bound); copies, *ibid.*, Telegrams Received in Cipher; *ibid.*, RG 393, Dept. of the Tenn., Hd. Qrs. Correspondence; DLC-USG, V, 5, 8, 24, 88. *O.R.*, I, xvii, part 1, 468.

On Nov. 7, 1862, Col. George P. Ihrie, La Grange, wrote to Maj. Gen. James B. McPherson. "I am directed, by Maj. Genrl. Grant, to communicate to you the following: 'To-morrow (the 8th inst.) you will make a reconnoisance in force, with one Division, in the direction of Holly Springs, with two days rations in haversacks, taking the Westerly roads. Genrl. Hamilton, with similar force, will coöperate with you, taking the Easterly roads, and join you, on the main road to Holly-Springs, about ten miles from this place. You will particularly note the topography of the country, and send copy of map to these Hd. Qrs. The cavalry of your Division will report to Col. Lee, 7th Kansas Cavly., at Davis' Mill to-morrow, at 10 A. M.; and, the Cavalry portion will be pushed as near Holly Springs as possible, to ascertain the force, position and movements of the enemy, as also the location of roads and water. It is not necessary you should accompany the reconnoisance in person: exercise your own discretion, in the matter. Should you be satisfied Holly Springs is being evacuated, and it can be occupied, without an engagement, take it, and send back couriers for supplies. You will caution Commanders of Regiments against acts of vandalism & against straggling; and hold officers to a strict accountability for violation of instructions or neglect of duty.' " ALS, Ritzman Collection, Aurora College, Aurora, Ill. *O.R.*, I, xvii, part 2, 324.

To Brig. Gen. Grenville M. Dodge

———

La Grange Nov. 7th 1862.

Brig Genl Dodge
Corinth

Baxters[1] Cavalry amounts to but little and can be driven off any time with two or three companies   Our cavalry sometimes act timidly and run at the sight of a horseman, without stopping to see what there is. Cant you send two additional Companies from Corinth

U. S. Grant,
Maj Genl

Copies, DLC-USG, V, 18, 30; DNA, RG 393, Dept. of the Tenn., Letters Sent. On Nov. 7, 1862, Brig. Gen. Grenville M. Dodge telegraphed to Lt. Col. John A. Rawlins. "Capt Gainbles Rogers Holcombes & Porters Cos of faulkners cavalry mentioned at Holly Springs sunday were order to dismount & act as Infty they left Holly Springs on their way home   Jackson cavalry in pursuit   a portion of them were at Ripley yesterday   two (2) Regts of cavalry are this side of Guntown   shall I attack them—"   Telegram received, *ibid.*, Telegrams Received.

1. See telegram to Brig. Gen. William S. Rosecrans, Aug. 14, 1862.

To Brig. Gen. Charles S. Hamilton

———

La Grange, Ten.
Nov. 7th 1862
9″ 10′ P. M.

Brig. Gen C. S. Hamilton,

Your note just rec'd. If the news it contains prove reliable the troops leaving to-morrow will not return and wagons should be held in readiness to take one or two days rations to Holly Springs on Sunday.

I have received no papers to-day. An ambulance will go after the Mail to-morrow.

yours Truly

U. S. GRANT

Maj. Gen.

P. S. I have now got up my Chief Eng. and constructionest on the rail-road and Supt. of telegraph with abundance of operators.[1] Work in both these departments will go on lively hereafter. Provisions will reach you to-night.

U. S. G.

ALS, deCoppet Collection, NjP. On Nov. 7, 1862, Brig. Gen. Charles S. Hamilton wrote to USG. "Quinby's division is selected for the reconnaissance tomorrow. If McPherson does not go in person Quinby will be in command. Will the cavalry be under his orders? What time should the division start, and can it be furnished with a guide? I have none. The movement will have to be postponed unless the provision train gets up to-night. I hear nothing of it as yet. I shall post Stanley's division at Davis' Mill to-morrow, so as to more completely cover the ground between McPherson and me. It will also cover the bridges there and relieve the cavalry now required to hold them. Please let me know if McPherson goes out in command of the reconnaissance. The only thing I get confirmatory of an evacuation is the story of a negro who heard Price say if many more men deserted he would not be able to get his trains off. I somewhat doubt the story. Send me, if you please, papers of the 5th, if you have them, and also results of elections in the States of New York, Illinois, and Wisconsin. What do you learn of the provision train?" *O.R.*, I, xvii, part 2, 325. On the same day, Col. George P. Ihrie wrote to Hamilton. "General Grant directs me to say to you McPherson goes in person   Cavalry under the immediate command of Col Lee but subject to the orders of the commanding Officer   Start as early as possible—have no guide, take Mr Scott residing at Scott Creek near where the troops crossed with you   Fifty-five wagon loads of Subsistence Stores will reach you tonight. No papers of the 5th yet received   no further election news received . . . If you can['*t*] get Scott impress a guide" Copies, DLC-USG, V, 18, 30; DNA, RG 393, Dept. of the Tenn., Letters Sent. Also on Nov. 7, 7:15 P.M., Hamilton wrote to USG. "Two deserters arrived here from Fifth Kentucky Infantry; left Holly Springs on Wednesday—the day before yesterday—and say the wagons of the army had already gone and that the wagons were removing the sick and that evacuation was the order of the day. They got news of our movement on Tuesday night; that we were 50,000 strong, moving from Bolivar, Corinth, and Memphis, and orders were given to evacuate the next morning. These two men were examined separately, each telling the same story. They were twelve-months' men, whose time was out in September, and this is the first chance they have had to get away. Quinby will get away by 8 a. m. if we get rations in the night. . . . They report much sickness in Price's army. Please send me papers of the 5th, if any have arrived." *O.R.*, I, xvii, part 2, 326.

On Nov. 7, Maj. Gen. James B. McPherson, La Grange, telegraphed to USG.

"Provision Train just in—Wagons were loaded in Such a manner that the Train could not be divided—Am having Fifty wagons loaded to be sent to Genl. Hamilton to night—No Commissary came down with the Train, and I have detailed Lt. Gillespie of the 41st Ills, to act as Commissary and issue the rations—" Telegram received, DNA, RG 393, Dept. of the Tenn., Telegrams Received. On the same day, Lt. Col. John A. Rawlins telegraphed to McPherson. "I am instructed by Maj Gen Grant to say that half of the wagons loaded with rations now on the road from Middleburg will be sent to Gen Hamilton's command that you please send some Cavalry to the Junction of the LaGrange and Grand Junction road with instructions to Officer in charge of the train to that effect so that the wagons for Gen Hamilton may be sent to Grand Junction" Copies, DLC-USG, V, 18, 30; DNA, RG 393, Dept. of the Tenn., Letters Sent. See letter to Maj. Gen. James B. McPherson, Nov. 8, 1862.

On Nov. 6, USG had telegraphed to the commanding officer, Corinth. "You will send a Company of Cavalry with Gen Hamilton's wagon train as escort as far as Bethel where they will be relieved" Copies, DLC-USG, V, 18, 30; DNA, RG 393, Dept. of the Tenn., Letters Sent. On Nov. 7, USG telegraphed to Brig. Gen. Mason Brayman, Bolivar. "You will immedy send to ~~thise~~ this point all Teams belonging to Troops now here." Telegram received, Brayman Papers, ICHi; copies, DLC-USG, V, 18, 30; DNA, RG 393, Dept. of the Tenn., Letters Sent. On Nov. 8, Brayman telegraphed to USG. "The Teams will be sent at once   the 17th Regt. left this morning. I wish capt Klinck to leave some articles of immediate necessity here" Telegram received, *ibid.*, Telegrams Received. Also on Nov. 8, Brig. Gen. Grenville M. Dodge, Corinth, telegraphed to USG. "Genl Hamilton's wagon train has gone—under escort of 3 three companies of 7th Kansas cavalry & at least five hundred (500) Infty belonging to his divisions   the cavalry were ordered to report to the command at Grand Junction   do you intend to have them return from Bethel—" Telegram received, *ibid.* On Nov. 9, Rawlins telegraphed to Dodge. "The troops sent from Corinth as escort to Genl Hamiltons will not return" Copies, DLC-USG, V, 18, 30; DNA, RG 393, Dept. of the Tenn., Letters Sent. On Nov. 8, USG telegraphed to the commanding officer, Bethel. "Upon the arrival of Genl Hamiltons wagon train you will send with then a Cavalry company as escort to Bolivar releiving the company that accompanies them from Corinths" Copies, *ibid.* On Nov. 9, Col. Isham N. Haynie, Bethel, telegraphed to USG. "There are six hundred (600) wagons on the train here convoyed by three squadrons of cavalry of one hundred & eighty 180 men in all   my company here numbers less than forty (40) men for duty but I have sent them out   will that do to relieve the three (3) squadrons and guard so many wagons—" Telegram received, *ibid.*, Dept. of the Mo., Telegrams Received. On the same day, USG telegraphed to Haynie. "When I directed you to send a Company of Cavaly with wagon train, I did not know that there were troops to come with them from Corinth   Your company is not wanted   the other troops come all the way." Copies, DLC-USG, V, 18, 30; DNA, RG 393, Dept. of the Tenn., Letters Sent.

1. On Nov. 7, USG, La Grange, telegraphed to Brayman. "You will furnish the Telegraph Superintendent with the Teams necessary to transport his material from Bolivar to this place" Telegram received, Brayman Papers, ICHi. See following telegram.

To Col. Joseph D. Webster

Hd Quarters Dept of the Tennessee
La Grange Nov 7th 1862

GENERAL[1] J. D WEBSTER
JACKSON TENN

Remain at Jackson and set the Rail Road going on proper
time and in general working order before coming down

I will telegraph you when an advances is to made   it will
necessary to give a few hours personal attention to the working
of affairs there daily for a while

U. S GRANT
Maj Genl.

Telegram, copies, DLC-USG, V, 18, 30; DNA, RG 393, Dept. of the Tenn.,
Letters Sent. On Nov. 7, 1862, Maj. Gen. Stephen A. Hurlbut, Jackson, had telegraphed to USG. "Some person must be appointed to take charge of the Rail Road
as it stands there is no systim or order. It must be done at once"   Copy, *ibid.*,
District of West Tenn., 4th Division, Letters Sent. *O.R.*, I, xvii, part 2, 326.

On Nov. 8, USG telegraphed to Col. Joseph D. Webster. "There will be a
detail of Officers from Hamiltons command reach Jackson to day on their way to
Corinth after their Regimental baggage   send and extra train with them and
keep sufficient cars to bring their baggage. When ready let the same cars come
immediately here without unloading"   Copies, DLC-USG, V, 18, 30; DNA,
RG 393, Dept. of the Tenn., Letters Sent. On Nov. 9, USG telegraphed to Webster. "Let an engine return from Bolivar to LaGrange to night and bring a train
of loaded cars that have been laying at Bolivar for two three days with camp and
garrison equipage that it is absolutely necessary to have here at once. Men are
suffering"   Copies, *ibid.* On Nov. 10, USG telegraphed to Webster. "Some
twelve cars of baggage destined for this place was left at Bolivar   Can it not be
forwarded through to day"   Copies, *ibid.*

1. Although USG had already recommended Webster for promotion to brig.
gen., he was not nominated until Feb. 12, 1863. See letter to Abraham Lincoln,
Dec. 28, 1862. Perhaps through misunderstanding, USG began to address him
as brig. gen. on Nov. 1, 1862. For Webster's assignment as superintendent of
military railroads, see letter to Maj. Gen. Henry W. Halleck, Oct. 5, 1862, note 1.

To Elihu B. Washburne

La Grange Tennessee
November 7th 1862

Hon. E. B. Washburn
Galena Ill.
Dear Sir;

Not having much of special note to write you since your visit to Jackson, and knowing that you were fully engaged, I have not troubled you with a letter. I write now a little on selfish grounds.

I see from the papers that L. Swett is to be called near the President in some capacity.[1] I believe him to be one of my bitterest enemies. The grounds of his enmity I suppose to be the course I pursued whilst at Cairo towards certain contractors and speculators who wished to to make fortunes off of the soldiers and Government and in which he took much interest whether a partner or not.

He called on me in regard to the rights of a Post Sutler for Cairo, (an appointment not known to the law) whom he had got appointed.

Finding that I would regard him in the light of any other Merchant who might set up there; that I would neither secure him a monopoly of the trade nor his pay at the Pay table for such as he might trust out, the Sutler never made his appearance. If he did never made himself known to me.

In the case of some contracts that were given out for the supply of forage, they were given, if not to the very highest bidder, to far from the lowest, and full 30 pr. cent higher than the articles could have been bought for at that time.

Learning these facts I immediately annulled the contracts.[2]

Quite a number of car loads of grain and hay were brought to Cairo on these contract, and a change of Quartermasters having taken place in the mean time the new Quartermaster would not receive it without my order, except at rates he could then get the same articles for from other parties. This I refused to give.

The contractors then called on me and tried to convince me that the obligation was binding but finding me immovable in the matter asked if Gen. Allen's approval to the contract would not be sufficient. My reply was in substance that Gen. Allen was Chief Quartermaster of the Department and I could not controll him. They immediately left me and thinking over the matter it occured to me that they would go immediately to St. Louis and present their contract for approval without mentioning the objection I made to it. I then telegraphed to Gen. Allen the facts and put him on his guard against these men. For some reason however my dispatch did not reach St. Louis for two days. Gen. Allen then replied to it stating that these parties had been to him the day before and knowing no objection to the contract he had approved it.

The parties then returned to Cairo evidently thinking they had gained a great triumph. But being no money to pay at that time and the bad repute the Quartermasters Department was in they were afraid to take vouchers without my approval. They again called on me to secure this. My reply to them was that they had got their contract without my consent, had got it approved against my sence of duty to the Government, and they might go on and deliver the forage and get their pay in the same way. I would not approve a voucher for them under that contract if they never got a cent. Hoped they would not. This forced them to abandon the contract and to sell the forage already delivered for what it was worth.

Mr. Swett took much interest in this matter and wrote me one or more letters on the subject, rather offensive in their manner. These letters I have preserved but they are locked up in Mr. Safford's safe in Cairo.

I afterwards learned from undoubted authority that there was a combination of wealthy and influential citizens formed, at the begining of this war, for the purpose of monopolizing the Army contracts. One of their boasts was that they had sufficient influance to remove any General who did not please them.

The modus operandi for geting contracts at a high rate I sup-

pose was for a member of this association to put in bids commencing at as low rates as the articles could be furnished for, and after
they were opened all would retire up to the highest one who was
below any outside person and let him take it. In many instances
probably they could buy off this one for a low figure by assuring
him that he could not possibly get the contract, for if he did not
retire it would be held by the party below.

You will see by the papers that I am on the move. If troops are
furnished me to keep open my lines of communication there will
be no delays in this Department. Once at Grenada I can draw
supplies from Memphis and save our present long line.

I do not see my report of the battle of Iuka in print![3] As the
papers in Gen. Rosecrans interest have so much misrepresented
that affair I would like to see it in print. I have no objection to
that [or] any other Gen. being made a hero of by the press, but
I do not want to see it at the expense of a meritorious portion of
the Army. I endeavored in that report to give a plain statement
of facts, some of which I would never have mentioned had it not
become necessary in defense of troops who have been with me
in all, or nearly all, the battles where I have had the honor to
command. I have never had a single regiment disgrace itself in
battle yet except some new ones at Shiloh that never loaded a
musket before that battle.

I recommended Maj. Rawlins for promotion to a Lieut.
Colonelcy, a promotion which he is entitled to by law. His merit
would entitle him to a Brigadier Generals commission. Nothing
has been heard from it yet. Will you do me the favor to look to
this matter when you visit Washington. I also recommended
Rowley for the position of Maj. and to be transfered from Gen.
Halleck's staff, as additional aid, to mine as regular aid.[4]

All my military family are well and desire to be remembered
to you.

yours truly
U. S. GRANT

ALS, IHi.

1. Leonard Swett, born in Turner, Maine, in 1825, attended Waterville College for three years, studied law, and served in the Mexican War with the 5th Ind. After establishing a law practice at Bloomington, Ill., he became closely associated with Abraham Lincoln in both law and politics. During an unsuccessful campaign for U.S. Representative in 1862, Swett was the victim of a rumor circulated by his opponents that he had gone to Washington "to assume a responsible position near the President." *Illinois State Journal*, Oct. 17, 18, 1862.

2. See letters to Capt. John C. Kelton and to Capt. Reuben B. Hatch, Jan. 2, and to Maj. Robert Allen, Jan. 3, 1862.

3. See letter to Col. John C. Kelton, Oct. 22, 1862.

4. See letter to Brig. Gen. Lorenzo Thomas, Oct. 27, 1862.

To Maj. Gen. James B. McPherson

———

Head Quarters Dept of the Tenn
LaGrange Nov 8th 1862

MAJ GEN McPHERSON
COMM'DG RECONNOISANCE
GENERAL.

Your dispatch is received   well done so far. I hope it will turn out as well throughout   My hope rather favors remaining at Holly Springs. The opportunity of attacking there is better than it would be with the Tallahatchie between. The only particular advantage I can see for having the rebels abandon Holly Springs is that we would then cover Corinth somewhat better   I will hold two Divisions in readiness tomorrow should you require reenforcements. Take no risk for a general engagement   we are not ready for that. Send in your prisoners in the morning under a proper escort.

U S GRANT
Maj Gen

Copies, DLC-USG, V, 18, 30; DNA, RG 393, Dept. of the Tenn., Letters Sent. *O.R.*, I, xvii, part 2, 328. On Nov. 8, 1862, Maj. Gen. James B. McPherson sent two telegrams to USG, datelined respectively: "In the Field, 5½ miles from La Grange, 11:45 a. m.," "Lamar, 3 p. m." "My column is all united at this point, where the road from Grand Junction comes in. The cavalry under Colonel Lee have just arrived, and have gone on in advance. I have established a courier post 4½ miles from La Grange, at the forks of the road. General Quinby's division will not be up for two or three hours. I shall, however, push on cautiously to Lamar or vicinity. Would it not be well to keep a strong lookout on the Moscow road? Some few of the rebel pickets have been seen." "Have just reached this point. The advance under Colonel Lee had some pretty sharp skirmishing with rebel cavalry a short distance beyond here. I shall halt my column here until General Quinby comes up, unless I hear something definite from the front." *Ibid.* On the same day, USG telegraphed to McPherson. "The provision train did not go to Genl Hamiltons last evening consequentely Quinby may be more behind than you expect. I sent out towards Moscow some hours ago" Copies, DLC-USG, V, 18, 30; DNA, RG 393, Dept. of the Tenn., Letters Sent.

On Nov. 8, Brig. Gen. Charles S. Hamilton telegraphed to USG at 9:45 A.M. "No rations yet, and I cannot learn anything of the train. Commissaries were out all night watching for it. Of course Quinby cannot move until he gets food for his men. Our supplies were out last night." Telegram received, *ibid.*, Telegrams Received. On the same day, Lt. Col. John A. Rawlins wrote to Hamilton. "I am directed by Genl U.S. Grant, to send you the copy of dispatch from Genl. McPherson and to say you will hold one of the remaining Divisions in your command in readiness to move at a moments notice" Copies, DLC-USG, V, 18, 30; DNA, RG 393, Dept. of the Tenn., Letters Sent. On the same day, Rawlins wrote to Brig. Gen. John A. Logan. "You will hold your Division with the exception of the Regiment detailed of Provost Guards in readiness to move at a moments notice" Copies, *ibid.*

Also on Nov. 8, McPherson, Lamar, Miss., sent two additional telegrams to USG at 8:15 P.M. and 10:30 P.M. "We have had quite a skirmish a mile and a half in advance of this point, and captured ~~seventy two~~ 72 prisoners, among whom are ~~eight~~ 8 commissioned officers, principally due to the cavalry under Colonel Lee. We have two ~~hundred~~ wounded, and the enemy fifteen. The inclosed sketch will give you an idea of our position, and the manner in which the rebel cavalry were captured. Col. Lee kept on the straight road past "A" some distance and made a detour around to "B," coming in on the flank of the rebel column as it was being driven back from "A" by the infantry of Col. Johnsons brigade. Genl Quimby has not yet come up, though I am expecting him every moment. The reports as to whether the rebels have left Holly Springs and Cold Water are very conflicting. Some say the infantry has all gone; others, that they are there in strong force. The prisoners generally say that we will be *whipped* tomorrow, and that if we expect to get to 'Cold Water' without a heavy fight, we are very much mistaken. A man told Col. Johnson this evening that the order was given to evacuate Holly Springs, but that some *General* came up and put a stop to it, saying they would fight there, they could not better their position by falling back. Col. Lee is in advance and may report something more definite; if so, I will let you know immediately." "We have captured ~~forty~~ 40 more of the enemy, and killed ~~sixteen~~ 16 that we know of. Col. Lee's pickets are in Hudsonville. The enemy know we are out with a force which they estimate at ~~fifteen hundred~~ 15,000 ~~thousand~~. It is still uncertain whether the enemy are in strong force at 'Cold Water.' Colonel Lee is instructed to push forward cautiously in the morning, and if possible ascertain what is there." Copies, *ibid.*, RG 94, War Records Office, Union Battle Reports. *O.R.*, I, xvii, part 1, 486–87.

To George G. Pride

LaGrange Nov 8th 1862

COL G G PRIDE
BOLIVAR TENN

Use the Engineer Regt to the best advantage. You will be the Judge of that   Keep the saw Mill going   I do not know about the water station here, but beleive it is all right

U. S. GRANT,
Maj Genl.

Telegram, copies, DLC-USG, V, 18, 30; DNA, RG 393, Dept. of the Tenn., Letters Sent. On Nov. 8, 1862, George G. Pride, Bolivar, telegraphed to USG. "I think we will run through in the morning—Shall work tonight   the obine bridge is nearly finished but the men of the engineer reg't who were raising it have been ordered forward—it should be finished now   may I order them to remain—it takes about thirty 30   Engr Regt have been running a saw mill in Jackson & I think if we can keep it going with the same force it will help very much—That will leave us in the front with (250). I wait here for answer & shall return to the bridge.   is the water station at Lagrange in working order—" Telegram received, *ibid.*, Telegrams Received.

To Maj. Gen. Henry W. Halleck

Lagrange Tenn
Nov 9 2 P M 62

MAJ GEN H W HALLECK
GEN IN CHIEF

Ten (?) [*Two*] Divisions and twelve hundred cavalry are now out on reconnoissance towards Holly Springs   The whole under Col Lee[1] Seventh Kansas—Had two skirmishes yesterday in which they took one hundred and two prisoners & killed 17 that they saw   Our reported loss two wounded—Rebels commenced evacuating Holly Springs last Thursday,[2] but Pemberton come up & turned them back[3]   This army should be supplied with fifteen thousand (15,000) muskets & accoutrements complete of uniform pattern, delivered at Jackson to supply recruits & replace arms requiring repairs   this number would enable us by making some changes to have more uniformity of calibre in the different Regts   May I expect forces from New Orleans and Helena to cooperate?

U S Grant M G

Telegram received, DNA, RG 94, Generals' Papers and Books, Telegrams Received by Gen. Halleck; *ibid.*, RG 107, Telegrams Collected (Bound); copies, *ibid.*, Telegrams Received in Cipher; *ibid.*, RG 393, Dept. of the Tenn., Hd. Qrs. Correspondence; DLC-USG, V, 5, 8, 24, 88. *O.R.*, I, xvii, part 1, 468. On Nov. 8, 1862, 7:50 p.m., USG again telegraphed to Maj. Gen. Henry W. Halleck. "Reinforcements are arriving very slowly   If they do not come on more rapidly I will attack as I am   But one Regt has yet reached Memphis"   Telegram received, DNA, RG 94, Generals' Papers and Books, Telegrams Received by Gen. Halleck; *ibid.*, RG 107, Telegrams Collected (Bound); copies, *ibid.*, Telegrams Received in Cipher; *ibid.*, RG 393, Dept. of the Tenn., Hd. Qrs. Correspondence; DLC-USG, V, 5, 8, 24, 88. *O.R.*, I, xvii, part 1, 468. On Nov. 10, Halleck telegraphed to USG. "Five regiments and one battery left Ill for Memphis last week; six or seven more will leave this week. Others will be sent from Ohio & Kentucky. Memphis will be made the depot of a joint military & naval expedition on Vicksburg. Your requisitions for arms must be made through the Ordnance Dept. If not attended to, report that fact. There is a scarcity of first class, and each army must take its proportion of lower classes." ALS (telegram sent), DNA, RG 107, Telegrams Collected (Bound); telegram received, *ibid.*, RG 393, Dept. of the Tenn., Telegrams Received. *O.R.*, I, xvii, part 1, 468–69.

On Nov. 9, USG telegraphed to Brig. Gen. James M. Tuttle, Cairo. "Report to me what troops have passed down in the last three days and where ordered   also report as fast as troop go forward"   Copies, DLC-USG, V, 18, 30; DNA, RG 393, Dept. of the Tenn., Letters Sent. On the same day, Tuttle telegraphed to USG. "Regts that have left here in last three days—95th—113th—106th—116th—and 83d Indiana   I have sent them all to Columbus by order of Gen Davies   I dont know what he has done with them—I find some Regts with a kind of loose order to report to Gen McClernand   the 83d Indiana & 2 Wisconsin Regts that went down are the ones   I have sent them all to Davies   Gen McClernand is not here & I have heard nothing from him on the subject   I understand today from Gen Washburne that he will be here in about (19) days—The ninety third (93) one hundred fourteen (114) & one hundred twenty seventh (127) and mercantile battery are to be here tonight with orders for Memphis.—" Telegram received, *ibid.*, Telegrams Received.

Also on Nov. 9, USG telegraphed to Brig. Gen. Thomas A. Davies, Columbus, Ky. "What was done with the 83rd Indiana and two Wisconsin Regiments" Copies, DLC-USG, V, 18, 30; DNA, RG 393, Dept. of the Tenn., Letters Sent. On the same day, Davies telegraphed to USG. "The 83d Ind Vols was sent to Memphis to report to Sherman   the 2d Wisconsin has not reported here   I do not know when it is   I send to Jackson at 5 in the morning the 106th Ills—" Telegram received, *ibid.*, Telegrams Received; copy, *ibid.*, Hd. Qrs. District of

Columbus, Telegrams Sent. On the same day, Ill. AG Allen C. Fuller telegraphed
to USG. "The one hundred third (103) one hundred eleventh (111) one hundred
nineteenth (119) ninety fifth (95) and one hundred & thirteenth (113) and
Vaughns Battery have been sent to Columbus   The one hundred sixth (106)
one hundred fourteenth (114) ninety third (93) one hundred sixteenth (116)
one hundred twentieth (120) & Tooleys Battery to Memphis   I will send you
four (4) or five (5) Regts this week to Memphis—"   Telegram received, *ibid.*,
Dept. of the Tenn., Telegrams Received.

 1. Albert L. Lee of Elwood, Kans., was appointed maj., 7th Kans. Cav., on
Oct. 29, 1861, and promoted to col. on May 17, 1862. On Nov. 11, 10:30 P.M.,
USG telegraphed to Halleck. "One hundred and thirty four prisoners were taken
by Col Lee 7th Kansas Cavalry & 16 Rebels killed. Our loss two wounded. Col
Lee is one of our best cavalry officers   I earnestly recommend him for promotion"
Telegram received, *ibid.*, RG 94, Generals' Papers and Books, Telegrams
Received by Gen. Halleck; *ibid.*, RG 107, Telegrams Collected (Bound); copies,
ibid., RG 94, ACP, L298 CB 1863; (dated Nov. 12, 1862) *ibid.*, RG 393, Dept.
of the Tenn., Hd. Qrs. Correspondence; DLC-USG, V, 5, 8, 24, 88. Dated
Nov. 11 in *O.R.*, I, xvii, part 1, 469. Also on Nov. 11, USG telegraphed to Brig.
Gen. Charles S. Hamilton. "I have recommend Col. Lee by telegraph for promo-
tion"   Copies, DLC-USG, V, 18, 30; DNA, RG 393, Dept. of the Tenn., Letters
Sent; (dated Nov. 12) *ibid.*, District of Corinth, Telegrams Received. Lee was
nominated on Jan. 19, 1863 (confirmed March 9), to rank as brig. gen. from
Nov. 29, 1862.
 On Nov. 22, Lee sent to Hamilton's adjt. a report of his capture of Ripley,
Miss., on Nov. 20, and of operations in Tippah County later that day which led
to the capture of sixty men. LS, *ibid.*, RG 94, War Records Office, Union Battle
Reports. *O.R.*, I, xvii, part 1, 490–91. On the same day, Hamilton endorsed this
report. "I respectfully forward this report—with list of prisoners, as well as
prisoners themselves. I consider the expedition a brilliant one, and Col Lee
deserving of all praise & promotion"   AES, DNA, RG 94, War Records Office,
Union Battle Reports. On Dec. 14, USG added an endorsement. "Respectfully
referred to Head Quarters of the Army, Washington, D. C." ES, *ibid.*
 2. Nov. 6.
 3. After learning of USG's advance, C. S. A. Lt. Gen. John C. Pemberton
joined the army of Maj. Gen. Earl Van Dorn at Holly Springs, probably on Nov. 6.
Advised by Gen. Braxton Bragg to withdraw his army beyond the Tallahatchie
River, Pemberton evacuated Holly Springs on Nov. 9. *O.R.*, I, xvii, part 2, 743–45.

To Maj. Gen. Stephen A. Hurlbut

By Telegraph from Lagrange [*Nov.*] 9 *1862*

To Gen Hurlbut

Have you relievid one Regiment from Road duty between Humboldt and Union City. I think two Rgiments will be sufficient with the cavalry and artillery   They now have one battalion at Union City one at Kenton one at Trenton one at Humboldt   make this change & send the relieved Rgiments here

U. S. Grant
Maj Genl

Telegram received, DNA, RG 393, District of West Tenn., 4th Division, Telegrams Received; copies, *ibid.*, Dept. of the Tenn., Letters Sent; DLC-USG, V, 18, 30. On Nov. 9, 1862, Maj. Gen. Stephen A. Hurlbut telegraphed to USG. "The change of Regts on road duty between Humboldt & Union City will be made on Monday" Telegram received, DNA, RG 393, Dept. of the Tenn., Telegrams Received.

Much of USG's correspondence on Nov. 8–9 involved gathering troops and supplies. On Nov. 8, USG telegraphed to Brig. Gen. Thomas A. Davies, Columbus, Ky. "Send one of the Columbus, Batteries here as soon as possible" Copies, DLC-USG, V, 18, 30; DNA, RG 393, Dept. of the Tenn., Letters Sent. On the same day, Davies twice telegraphed to USG. "Dispatch recd   Vaughns 3d Ills battery was sent forward at (4.) oclock this morning to report to Genl Hurlbut at Jackson   will send degolyer Michigan battery to you today—" "Train just left with battery of artillery on board for Lagrange—" Telegrams received, *ibid.*, Telegrams Received; copies, *ibid.*, Hd. Qrs. District of Columbus, Telegrams Sent. On the same day, Brig. Gen. Grenville M. Dodge, Corinth, telegraphed to USG. "I rec'd the following dispatch   Springfield Nov 8 to Brig Genl. Dodge   The one hundred and thirteen (113) Col Hoge left Chicago last Evening and the one hundred & sixth (106) this Evening from here for Columbus   their arms are unsevicable   I trust you will have them repaired or exchanged   signed Allen C. Fuller—" Telegram received, *ibid.*, Dept. of the Tenn., Telegrams Received.

On Nov. 9, USG telegraphed to Brig. Gen. Mason Brayman. "Order the 20th Ills now at Middleburg immediately forward to this place" Telegram received, Brayman Papers, ICHi; copies, DLC-USG, V, 18, 30; DNA, RG 393, Dept. of the Tenn., Letters Sent. On the same day, Brayman wrote to Lt. Col. John A. Rawlins. "Yesterday Gen. Hulburt ordered that none go forward to Lagrange, except officers of Genl. Grant's Staff, and persons having his (Genl. Hulburt's) Special order. This morning he permits officers and soldiers to join their commands. I am carrying out his orders, but not permitting Regimental quartermasters Stores—nor sutlers to go until I am better advised as to the reasons of the restriction. The 17th went forward yesterday. Shall I send another Regt. to guard the Railroad? I have one guarding north, & but two others here—two batteries, and fragments of cavalry regiments. I am receiving and obeying orders, direct from Major Generals Grant, McPherson & Hurlburt. No clothing yet, but there may be." ADfS, Brayman Papers, ICHi.

Also on Nov. 9, USG telegraphed to commanding officer, Paducah. "Send eight Woodruffs guns with amunition and everything complete, men and all to memphis Tenn   Can the 11th Illinois be spared?   is so send it here"   Copies, DLC-USG, V, 18, 30; DNA, RG 393, Dept. of the Tenn., Letters Sent. On the same day, Lt. Col. Lloyd D. Waddell, 11th Ill., Paducah, telegraphed to USG. "There are but six (6) guns here—The 11th Ills are all away with Gen Ransom they number only (200) men   I have but the Kentucky Vols here Cavalry   What am I to do   ans?"   Telegram received, *ibid.*, Telegrams Received. On the same day, USG telegraphed to Surgeon Edward C. Franklin, Mound City, Ill. "Send Burton Parson of 33rd Indiana here   also send back convalescents as rapidly as they are fit for duty"   Copies, DLC-USG, V, 18, 30; DNA, RG 393, Dept. of the Tenn., Letters Sent. On Nov. 11, Franklin telegraphed to USG. "Burton Parsons was returned yesterday   I am sending to their Regts about eighteen (18) convalescents per day & shall continue sending as fast as they are fit for duty" Telegram received, *ibid.*, Telegrams Received.

Also on Nov. 9, USG telegraphed to Lt. Col. John P. Hawkins, Jackson. "Is there a provisin train now on the way here? Provisions are now required at the Junction"   Copies, DLC-USG, V, 18, 30; DNA, RG 393, Dept. of the Tenn., Letters Sent. On the same day, Hawkins telegraphed to USG. "A large lot of provisions will reach LaGrage as soon as trains pass through"   Telegram received, *ibid.*, Telegrams Received. On the same day, Capt. Charles W. Lyman, Columbus, Ky., telegraphed to USG. "Am informed that Complaints have been made by Commissary Cox   all cars are turned over to me every day by Rail Road Company   Capt Cox has had & shall continue to have all the cars he can load   on the 7th seventh he asked for forty three (43) & loaded twenty five with assistance of forty (40) of my men   on the 8th eighth he asked for all & loaded none, on inquiry I find he has not got the stores to ship   am holding all the cars today for him"   Telegram received, *ibid.* On the same day, USG telegraphed to Col. William Myers, St. Louis. "Send fifty feet two inch lead pipe in charge of special Messenger by Rail Road to come here on first train"   Copies, DLC-USG, V, 18, 30; DNA, RG 393, Dept. of the Tenn., Letters Sent.

On Nov. 10, Col. James J. Dollins, 81st Ill., Humboldt, telegraphed to USG. "Have just rec'd an order to move and report to you   I regret much to have to say to you that I was thrown from my horse this Evening & badly hurt   hope you will pardon me for telegraphing direct to you   Will send my Regt but greatly prefer to go with it myself which I regret to say is impossible at present   please answer—"   Telegram received, *ibid.*, Telegrams Received. On the same day, USG telegraphed to Dollins. "Send your Regiment on under the officer next to you present." Copies, DLC-USG, V, 18, 30; DNA, RG 393, Dept. of the Tenn., Letters Sent.

On Nov. 10, Hurlbut wrote to USG. "The 81st Illinois from Humboldt is under marching orders for La Grange. Gen'l Brayman wants another regiment and says he has to do Rail Road duty south. I can send him one in a day or two. The Mills at Davis Mill and the steam mill at G Junction ought to be seized for use, also McConns Mills near moscow. They can be made to grind cob & corn at least for horses instead of long forage which will be scarce. The country between La Grange and Somerville has plenty of forage." Copy, *ibid.*, District of West Tenn., 4th Division, Letters Sent. *O.R.*, I, xvii, part 2, 337. On Nov. 12, Hurlbut telegraphed to USG. "The Eighty first (81st) Ill Regt has just left Humboldt for La grange" Telegram received, DNA, RG 393, Dept. of the Tenn., Telegrams Received; copy, *ibid.*, District of West Tenn., 4th Division, Letters Sent.

To Maj. Gen. Stephen A. Hurlbut

By Telegraph from Lagrange [*Nov.*] 9 *1862*

To Maj Gen Hurlbut

Refuse all permits to come south of Jackson for the present The Isrealites especially should be kept out   what troops have you now exclusive of stevensons brigade

U S Grant
Maj Genl

Telegram received, DNA, RG 393, District of West Tenn., 4th Division, Telegrams Received; copies, *ibid.*, Dept. of the Tenn., Letters Sent; DLC-USG, V, 18, 30. *O.R.*, I, xvii, part 2, 330. On Nov. 9, 1862, Maj. Gen. Stephen A. Hurlbut twice telegraphed to USG. "I have stopped all civilians below Bolivar without special permit from here until I receive orders from you that the road is to be open to the public. All the Transportation & more will be required for some days to move troops & supplies" Telegram received, DNA, RG 393, Dept. of the Tenn., Telegrams Received; copy, *ibid.*, District of West Tenn., 4th Division, Letters Sent. "My force at Jackson now consists of the following. (18th) Eighteenth Illinois Infantry. (29th) Twenty Ninth Illinois Infantry. (95th) Ninety Fifth Illinois Infantry. (119th) One Hundred & Nineteenth Illinois Infantry. (14th) Fourteenth Ohio Battery. Co "G" 1st Illinois Artillery. (14th) Fourteenth Indiana Battery. (3d) Third Batallion Eleventh Illinois Cavalry. Co "A" Second Illinois Cavalry. (12th) Co "H" Twelfth Illinois Cavalry. Fosters Independent Cavalry. Col. Stevensons 4th Brigade   Will move on Monday Morning." Copy, *ibid.* *O.R.*, I, xvii, part 2, 331. On Nov. 10, Hurlbut telegraphed to Brig. Gen. Mason Brayman. "Genl Grant has ordered that no civilians go below this point except on orders from these Head Quarters. You will place a guard at the Depot & enforce the order rigidly." Telegram received, Brayman Papers, ICHi.

On Nov. 10, USG wrote to Col. Joseph D. Webster. "Give orders to all the conductors to all the conductors on the road that no Jews are to be permitted to travel on the Rail Road southward from any point   They may go north and be encouraged in it but they are such an intolerable nuisance. That the Department must be purged for them" Copies, DLC-USG, V, 18, 30; DNA, RG 393, Dept. of the Tenn., Letters Sent. *O.R.*, I, xvii, part 2, 337.

To Brig. Gen. Charles S. Hamilton

LaGrange, Nov 9th 1862

GENL HAMILTON

The following dispatch Just received from Genl. McPherson; written 8½ a m[1]

You will send out carriers at once to find Quinby and direct him to Lamar[2] He should have reported ere this to McPherson leave the stores mentioned to find him and hurry him up. It will be that he has taken the Ripley road which is all wrong.

U. S. GRANT.

Maj Genl

Copies, DLC-USG, V, 18, 30; DNA, RG 393, Dept. of the Tenn., Letters Sent. *O.R.*, I, xvii, part 2, 330. On Nov. 9, 1862, 10:30 A.M., Brig. Gen. Charles S. Hamilton, "Scott's House," wrote to USG. "Stanley's division has been ready to move since dawn. If he moves to support Quinby, McArthur will relieve his pickets at the river-crossings. My aide, Lieutenant Pearce, has just got back from Corinth, and has brought the printing-press and material from Corinth. You had better take the whole for use at your headquarters; it is on the cars at the Junction. If Stanley moves I will probably go with him, though on my return last night I was attacked with dysentery and am very weak this morning. Ought not a depot of provisions to be established at the Junction to-day? Only 45 wagons came to my command, and Quinby took all the bread, there being only enough for his division. We shall get along if we can draw from the Junction this evening or in the morning." *Ibid.*, p. 329. On the same day, Lt. Col. John A. Rawlins wrote to Hamilton. "Stanleys Division will not be required to move only in case the enemy should come out. and attack   put forces in front in force. You can send your trains to Grand Junction, as that is probably the most convenient place to draw your supplies, taking in consideration the facilities for unloading the cars   They will be there to day without fail   There is a printing press connected with these Head Quarters. You can retain the one you speak of if you need it." Copies, DLC-USG, V, 18, 30; DNA, RG 393, Dept. of the Tenn., Letters Sent. *O.R.*, I, xvii, part 2, 329–30.

1. On Nov. 9, 8:30 A.M., Maj. Gen. James B. McPherson, Lamar, wrote to USG. "One of our men who was taken prisoner near Jackson about five weeks ago made his escape from the rebel lines and came in this morning. He says there are about 30,000 infantry, artillery, and cavalry at Coldwater; that they commenced evacuating Holly Springs, but Pemberton came up on Thursday and put a stop to it, ordering the troops all back. They had out five regiments of cavalry yesterday, which were all driven back. Colonel Lee is advancing his cavalry cautiously to find out the truth of the matter. I cannot hear anything of General Quinby, though I have sent several couriers to find him. The prisoners are just

starting in." Misdated Nov. 8, *ibid.*, pp. 327–28. On Nov. 9, USG wrote to McPherson. "I have sent word to Hamilton to send out, for Quimby and direct him to you. If the enemy is found in strong force at Cold Water return sending Col Lee with the Cavalry from Hamiltons Columns to hunt Quimby up and direct his return" Copies, DLC-USG, V, 18, 30; DNA, RG 393, Dept. of the Tenn., Letters Sent. *O.R.*, I, xvii, part 2, 331. On the same day, 1 P.M., McPherson wrote to USG. "We have discovered the enemy drawn up in line of battle, 10,000 strong, on a hill across Coldwater, under Pemberton; 10,000 are under Price, a short distance below Holly Springs, and 13,000 at Abbeville. If our whole army was here we could go to Holly Springs, probably, without much of a fight. As it is, they are disposed to dispute our farther advance. I have made arrangements to fall back and will be in La Grange to-night. General Quinby came up about 9.30 a. m., having camped at Davis' Mill last night. Colonel Lee, of the cavalry, is a trump and no mistake. He has some more prisoners; altogether I think the number will amount to 150. I am going forward to see Colonel Lee, and will give you more detailed information when I come in." *Ibid.*

2. Lamar, Miss., on the Mississippi Central Railroad, about twelve miles southwest of Grand Junction, Tenn., and about twelve miles northeast of Holly Springs, Miss.

To Brig. Gen. Charles S. Hamilton

———

Lagrange Nov. 9th 1862

GEN. C. S. HAMILTON,

If the enemy will remain at Holly Springs it will satisfy me. I have instructed McPherson that he is to bring on no engagement but simply ascertain whether Holly Springs is being evacuated, and if so occupy it.

I am not advised of the order you refer to for troops to report to McClernand having been issued. I imagine if any such order has been issued it is to report to him as general forwarding officer, he having taken Ketchum's place, and that he is instructed to send them here. Gen. Halleck informed me that the Minnesota, Ill. and Michigan troops had been ordered to me. I have also received copy of special order for the 3d regular cavalry to report to me without delay.

If the enemy will hold on where they are we will let them lay until fully ready. Sherman will be able to join us with 20.000

men. I am not yet entirely decided whether I will have him move on the enemies rear or come East to Moscow and act with the troops here. My decission will depend a little on the answer I may receive from Gen. Halleck to a dispatch I sent him this morning. I have been making inquiries as to when the force promised from New Orleans may be looked for, and if that at Helena will move on Grenada. If it does it will be better to have it here.

Respectfully &c.

U. S. GRANT

Maj. Gen.

P. S. I have received copy of order for Gen. Wallace to report to me.[1] Dodge consequently will be here.[2] U. S. G.

ALS, NHi. On Nov. 9, 1862, noon, Brig. Gen. Charles S. Hamilton wrote to USG. "I have sent out parties to find Quinby. He camped at Davis' Mill last night. He had a map such as I have; was instructed to join McPherson at Lamar and to pick up a guide on the way. I cannot think he is out of the way, but if it shall prove so, he will speedily be brought back and set right. McPherson probably thought him nearer than Davis' Mill last night. I have little doubt the story brought by our man who escaped is entirely the correct one; it agrees with what McPherson said last night, as coming from the prisoners he had captured. If the enemy have concluded to stay at Coldwater would it not be well to let them remain there until we can bag them. A big haul now will be of the greatest importance at this juncture of affairs. An officer who came in this morning from Jackson says France and England have formally recognized the Confederacy. If such be the case battles, to have any importance, must be of the most decisive character, and we ought to run no risk, but make sure of great things. Have you heard from Sherman? A letter from Wisconsin to-day advises me that the Wisconsin regiments in the State, as also those of Pope's command, are ordered to McClernand. Is that so? If I am able to ride I will come over this p. m." *O.R.*, I, xvii, part 2, 330.

1. On Oct. 30, Brig. Gen. Lorenzo Thomas issued Special Orders No. 320. "Maj Genl Lewis Wallace U. S. Volunteers is hereby assigned to duty in the Dept of the Tennessee and will report in person to Maj Genl U. S. Grant at Corinth, Miss" Copy, DLC-USG, V, 93. *O.R.*, I, xvii, part 2, 308. On Nov. 10, Maj. Gen. Henry W. Halleck telegraphed to USG. "Major Genl Lewis Wallace will be ordered to Cincinnati as President of a Military Commission to meet at that place on the 17th inst. He will find the orders for the Commission at that place." ALS (telegram sent), DNA, RG 107, Telegrams Collected (Bound); telegram received, *ibid.*, RG 393, Dept. of the Tenn., Telegrams Received. On the same day, USG telegraphed to Brig. Gen. James M. Tuttle, Cairo. "When Genl Wallace arrives at Cairo inform him that Despatch just received from Washington says he is orderd to Cincinnatti, he will find orders there." Telegram

received, Wallace Papers, InHi; copies, DLC-USG, V, 18, 30; DNA, RG 393, Dept. of the Tenn., Letters Sent. On Nov. 14, Maj. Gen. Stephen A. Hurlbut, Jackson, telegraphed to USG. "Gen Wallace has not arrived consequently I have not delivered the orders" Telegram received, *ibid.*, Telegrams Received. On Nov. 13, Wallace wrote to his wife. "As the papers have doubtless apprised you, I am turned up in Cincinnati again. We reached Cairo at 2 O'clock day before yesterday. I hadn't stepped off the car before a telegram was put into my hand from Gen. Grant, directing, as per order from Washington, that I should return to Cincinnati, where orders were waiting me. You may guess my surprise! What could be the object of this movement? I racked my brain, but could find no solution of the mystery. Without waiting a moment I changed to the train going back, rode all the night, and got here a little after day break next morning. I called for my orders, but have as yet neither recd nor heard of them. My turning up here was a great astonishment to my friends. Some say I am to relieve Gen. Wright; others that I am to sit on the court ordered for the trial of Gen. Buel. This latter I suspect is true. Meantime I possess myself with as much patience as possible, and assume to be ready for any fate. To say truth, however, it is very vexatious to be thus kicked about from pillar to post. Still more mortifying is it to have Gen. Morris appointed a Maj. Gen. with a commission dated away back with a purpose to outrank me. So much for Gov. Morton's friendship. Will Lane doubt any longer? I say Morton is a hypocrite and double dealer." ALS, Wallace Papers, InHi. In later years, Wallace explained that "being again taken with the old longing to get back into the field, I determined to go down and see General Grant; possibly he might be prevailed upon to give me something to do." *Lew Wallace: An Autobiography* (New York and London, 1906), II, 641. Wallace had, of course, forgotten his orders to report to USG. Between 1862 and the time he wrote his *Autobiography*, Wallace had decided to shift blame for his failure to receive field command from Governor Oliver P. Morton of Ind. to Halleck. But on Nov. 3, William R. Holloway, private secretary to Morton, telegraphed to Morton, Washington. "If Lew. Wallace is ordered to Grant, have it changed to McClerland. He and Grant do not get along, and he desires to go with McClerland." Copy, Morton Papers, In. See letter to Maj. Gen. Henry W. Halleck, Dec. 14, 1862.

2. On Nov. 8, USG wrote to Brig. Gen. Grenville M. Dodge, Corinth. "When you are satisfied the enemy can be attacked and repulsed without endangering the post from other parties, do it. You can Judge of the propriety of attacking at Guntown better than I can Genl Wallace will probably relieve you in a day or two a Division then awaits you here" Copies, DLC-USG, V, 18, 30; DNA, RG 393, Dept. of the Tenn., Letters Sent. *O.R.*, I, xvii, part 2, 327. On Nov. 14, Dodge telegraphed to USG. "When Gen Hamilton left he left me in command of my Division only—my position now is rather embarassing there are troops on the R R ~~with~~outside of the Division that never have reported to me but when necessary I have issued orders to them & they promptly obeyed but they are no part of the Division I have taken no action in the matter I expected Genl Wallace along before this Will you instruct ~~me~~ in the matter—" Telegram received, DNA, RG 393, Dept. of the Tenn., Telegrams Received. On Nov. 15, Dodge again telegraphed to USG. "~~If h~~ a few days ago I rec'd a dispatch stating that I would be relieved here and was to join you is it the intention now that I shall leave here I make the enquiry to determine me in making a little different disposition of my forces which if any one is to releive soon I will not make"

Telegram received, *ibid*. On Nov. 14, USG had telegraphed to Dodge. "Your command embraces the District of Corinth. Special orders to that effect will reach you by mail." Copies, DLC-USG, V, 18, 30; DNA, RG 393, Dept. of the Tenn., Letters Sent; Dodge Papers, IaHA.

To Maj. Gen. Henry W. Halleck

Hd Qrs Lagrange Miss
Nov. 10th 7 45 P M 62

MAJ GEN H. W. HALLECK
GEN IN CHIEF.

Am I to understand that I lay still here while an Expedition is fitted out from Memphis or do you want me to push as far South as possible? Am I to have Sherman move subject to my order or is he & his forces reserved for some special service? Will not more ~~troops~~ forces be sent here?

U. S. GRANT
Maj Genl

Telegram received, DNA, RG 94, Generals' Papers and Books, Telegrams Received by Gen. Halleck; *ibid*., RG 107, Telegrams Collected (Bound); copies, *ibid*., Telegrams Received in Cipher; *ibid*., RG 393, Dept. of the Tenn., Hd. Qrs. Correspondence; DLC-USG, V, 5, 8, 24, 88. *O.R.*, I, xvii, part 1, 469. On Nov. 11, 1862, Maj. Gen. Henry W. Halleck telegraphed to USG. "You have command of all troops sent to your Dept, and have permission to fight the enemy when you please." ALS (telegram sent), DNA, RG 107, Telegrams Collected (Bound); telegram received (dated Nov. 12, 11:10 A.M.), *ibid*., RG 393, Dept. of the Tenn., Telegrams Received. The unmentioned subject of this telegraphic exchange was the projected expedition of Maj. Gen. John A. McClernand. See preceding letter.

On Nov. 24, U.S. Senator Lyman Trumbull of Ill. wrote to USG. "Since coming to Washington a few days ago, I have had a conversation with the President from which I gather that he expects great successes from the armies commanded by you & Gen Rosecrans—To a remark of mine that if let alone from Washington, you two commanders would soon clean out the South West & open the Mississippi river, he replied that you would be let alone except to be urged forward. This I was glad to hear, for my belief has been that we have had men enough for more than a year to have driven the rebel armies from the field, had they only been vigorously led against them. To my surprise I find even here in Washington that much more is expected of the Western armies than from those on the Potomac. The Eastern army surely is not inferior to that in the West either in numbers or equipments, so far from it, the choice arms and abundant supplies have been lavished on the army of the Potomac, while our troops in the West have often suffered for even the necessaries—As a Western man I take pride in our Western troops & the uniform and glorious successes which those under your command have everywhere achieved. Before coming to Washington, I had expected that the change of Commanders over the army of the Potomac, would be followed by a vigorous prosecution of the war & an advance which should speedily expel the enemy from Va—I hope so still, but do not find our friends as sanguine of success as I had expected—It is to the West & not the East that they look for brilliant successes—Your past career is a guaranty that you will do your whole duty without special inducements, but I could not refrain from letting you know that the Government and the country look especially to you & Gen. Rosecrans & the armies under your commands to crush the rebellion & save the Union; & besides I desired to express my admiration for the ability & skill with which you have led the army under your command—It would afford me pleasure to hear from you at any time, & to contribute any way in my power to your success." ALS, USG 3. On Nov. 26, McClernand, Springfield, wrote to Trumbull requesting information about "what is said and being done with regard to me and the enterprize with which my name has been lately connected." ALS, DLC-Lyman Trumbull. On Dec. 1, Trumbull wrote to McClernand that Secretary of War Edwin M. Stanton had spoken favorably of McClernand's expedition. ALS, McClernand Papers, IHi. On Nov. 26, McClernand had also written to U.S. Senator Orville H. Browning of Ill., as Browning mentioned in his letter of Dec. 2 to McClernand. "I have availed myself of the earliest opportunity to see the President, and have just returned from an interview with him. He says so far from any purpose of superceding you existing, both he and the Secretary of war are very anxious for you to have the command of the expedition, and intend to stand by you, and sustain and strengthen you. Go ahead—you are in no danger." ALS, *ibid.*

To Maj. Gen. Stephen A. Hurlbut

By Telegraph from Lagrange [*Nov.*] 10 *1862*

To Genl Hurlbut

You will have all prisoners now at Bolivar ready to go north in charge of an officer who will go in charge of prisoners from this place. Have a proper list made out   Hereafter you will send all prisoners to Cairo to await a cartelship going south.

U. S. Grant
Maj Genl

Telegram received, DNA, RG 393, District of West Tenn., 4th Division, Telegrams Received. On Nov. 10, 1862, an identical telegram signed by USG was received by Brig. Gen. Mason Brayman. Telegram received, Brayman Papers,

ICHi. Letterbooks, however, indicate that these telegrams were sent by Maj. William R. Rowley. Copies, DLC-USG, V, 18, 30; DNA, RG 393, Dept. of the Tenn., Letters Sent.

On Nov. 11, USG telegraphed to Brayman. "the Prisoners here will not leave till this Evening   I will let you know when ~~they~~ the train has started" Telegram received, Brayman Papers, ICHi. On Nov. 12, Col. George P. Ihrie telegraphed to Maj. Gen. Stephen A. Hurlbut. "Prisoners leave here today at noon"   Telegram received, DNA, RG 393, District of West Tenn., 4th Division, Telegrams Received. On Nov. 13, Brayman telegraphed to USG. "The prisoners to go to Columbus are waiting at the depot in a suffering condition   will your officer be here prepared to take them on board the train tonight—"   Telegram received, *ibid.*, Dept. of the Tenn., Telegrams Received. On the same day, Lt. Col. John A. Rawlins telegraphed to Brayman. "Officer in charge of Prisoners of War left Grand Junction at half past four oclock this afternoon   if he has not taken the Prisoners to be sent from Bolivar to Cairo you will Detail an officer and Guard to go in charge of them to Cairo & then turn them over to Genl Tuttle who has Instructions in the matter   train will leave here at 10-30 on which send them   send names of three"   Telegram received (incomplete), Brayman Papers, ICHi; copies, DLC-USG, V, 18, 30; DNA, RG 393, Dept. of the Tenn., Letters Sent.

To Maj. Gen. William T. Sherman

Head Quarters, Dept. of the Ten.
Lagrange Nov. 10th 1862

MAJ. GEN. W. T. SHERMAN
MEMPHIS TEN.
GEN.

Col. Grierson and company arived here yesterday about 4 P. M. without accident by the way.

Your policy of encouraging trade with the citizens I am satisfied with so long as the Treasury Department throws no more restrictions in the way than they do at present. But I think such articles as are of prime necessity for the supply of an army there should be some restrictions in. As we expect to advance Southward so soon however I do not deem any change from your present policy either necessary or advisable.[1]

McPherson returned last evening from a reconnaisance in force towards Holly Springs. The Cavalry had some sharp skirmishing resulting in the capture of about 130 of the Confederates with sixteen killed on their side, that our troops saw, and no doubt many wounded. Our loss was but two slightly wounded. Our cavalry was armed with revolving rifles and dismounted, whilst the enemy were mostly armed with shot guns and on horseback.

The reconnoisance was pushed to Coldwater and across it.

The facts ascertained from observation, from citizens, deserters·and prisoners is that on our arrival here Price commenced the evacuation of Holly Springs. Pemberton come up on Wednesday[2] evening and countermanded the order. The enemy now occupy Coldwater, a line in rear and Aberville[3]   The following is their organization.

Pemberton 4 Divisions
    Price 2 Divisions
        Maury[4]
        Bowen
    Russ Comd.g Lovells Division latter at Holly Springs sick
        Tilghman Div. relased prisoners
Russ 6000 men 3 Brigades 5 batteries 4 guns each
Tilghman 4000 men 2 Brigades 2 ''   2 ''   ''
Price 10000 men 2 Divisions No of guns not known
At Abberville there is 12 000 Militia.

There are no intrenchments at Cold Water. At Holly Springs ordinary Rifle pitts. They have no heavy guns.

Villepique[5] has gone to Port Hudson.[6] Directly after the Corinth fight about 10000 men went to Mobile.

Gen. Halleck informed me that there would be a movement North from New Orleans and that Curtis was directed to reinforce Helena and would be directed to move on Grenada if it was impracticable to go to Little Rock. I telegraphe[d] yesterday before receiving your letter to be more definitely informed of these different movements and desired particularly that the Helena force be required to cooperate with me.

I am now informed that six regiments have already left for Memphis and that five or six more will start immediately. This is Infantry alone. The 3d regular Cavalry and likely other regiments of Cavalry will also join you besides several batteries.

I think it will not be advisable for you to move until you can do it with two complete Divisions of twelve Infantry regiments each with a full proportion of Cavalry & Artillery. My plan was for you to move on Oxford, if the enemy remain where they now are, or some point south of the Tallehatchee. But on reflection I am more inclined to favor ~~the route~~ your occupying Moscow and all start together, especially if there should be a movement from Helena as desired.

When you can leave a force of four regiments of Infantry with ~~the~~ Artillery and about four companies of Cavalry at Memphis[7] I think you will be ready to move. Reinforcements may constantly be expected at Memphis after your departure hence this opinion.

I will not be able to send you any General officers unless possibly one to take command of the forces that will be left at Memphis. Steward[8] & Buckland[9] will both command Brigades, or even Divisions, as well as if they held the commissions which they should, and I hope will, hold.

We will of course supply ourselves from the country with every thing it affords necessary for the Army, giving receipts for the same to be settled at the close of hostilities. These receipts should set forth as far as practicable the status of the parties who are deprived of their property.

I will enclose with this some information just this minuet received. If ascertained to be true I may occupy Holly Springs for the purpose of finishing the rail-road as far South as possible and geting our supplies also as far in that direction as possible. We are now geting up rations rapidly and will keep on hand 1,000,000 ahead. The rail-road is completed to Davis' Mills and work progressing rapidly.

There were a number of matters I intended to write you when I commenced but being interupted so often I have forgotten them. I will communicate with you again before the final start is made.

> Yours truly
> U. S. GRANT
> Maj. Gen

ALS, Stephenson County Historical Society, Freeport, Ill. *O.R.*, I, xvii, part 2, 335–36. On Nov. 12, 1862, Maj. Gen. William T. Sherman wrote to USG. "Col Grierson got back last evening 24 hours from La Grange, having encountered nothing by the way. He brought me yours of the 10th with Enclosures which I read with great interest. Four new Regiments have reached me, Wisconsin 32nd Col. Howe (900)—Illinois 113 Col Hoge (850) Indiana 83 Col Spooner 800— Illinois 116 Col Tupper (900)—I have commenced 2 new Brigades 4th Col Stewart. 5th Col Buckland and shall make each Brigade of 5 Regiments, and arrange them into 2 Divisions Gens. Denver and Morgan L Smith. No Cavalry or artillery have yet reached me, but I am prepared to remain and arrange all the troops you have Indicated. I sent out under Buckland 4 Regts of Infantry. Thielman's Cavalry, 60 men, and 1 Co of Artillery Bowtons, toward Hernando to turn square to the left & appear in the Pidgeon Roost Road, Thence to Germantown to be out only, 5 days. I hear that as I Expected Hernando was Promptly abandonned, and I have no doubt at Holly Springs they were looking for my whole command on Tuesday   of Course I cannot expect to conceal my movements from this Quarter as I am watched by thousands of watchful eyes. I can move to Moscow in 2½ days, to Holly Springs in 3, or I could move via mount Pleasant so as to be in communication with you this Side of Coldwater, but I will await your Orders and act to the very letter according to your Orders. I have full confidence in the Spirit of my men, and the Officers are full of confidence & Zeal. If you have Some clever Brig. Genl. to command in Memphis it would be well for him to come as soon as possible that I may initiate him in the mysteries of the Place. I believe all the People here now feel impressed with the truth that Memphis is lost to the South *forever*. Gen. Hovey was here to day and says he will be ready to make his dash on Grenada the moment you give him the Signal. He proposes to march from Friar's Point to a point on Tallahatchie & then dispatch his Cavalry to break the Road. I do think Such a movement an indespensable part of your General plan, & Gen Hovey is very anxious to do his part. The quicker the better, as I fear Rains may make the Roads terrible. It is now raining. I hear good accounts from all west Tennessee, and many deserters come in from the Coldwater. If you are in Telegraphic communication with Illinois, you can expedite the removal of the new Regiments to Memphis. I promptly Sent the Ohio officers to their State to bring the drafted men. Admiral Porter Should also appear at Vicksburg coincident with our crossing the Tallahatchie"   Copies, DNA, RG 94, Generals' Papers and Books, William T. Sherman, Letters Sent; DLC-William T. Sherman.

1. See letter to Maj. Gen. William T. Sherman, Nov. 6, 1862.
2. Nov. 5.
3. Abbeville, Miss., on the Mississippi Central Railroad, about eighteen miles south of Holly Springs.
4. Dabney H. Maury of Va., USMA 1846, was dismissed from the U.S. Army, in which he held rank as capt., on June 25, 1861. He joined the C. S. Army as capt., but was quickly promoted. Nominated on March 6, 1863, as maj. gen. to rank from Nov. 4, 1862, he appears as maj. gen. on an official list dated Nov. 27. *O.R.*, I, xvii, part 2, 765. See *PUSG*, 1, 133*n*–34*n*.
5. C. S. A. Brig. Gen. John B. Villepigue died on Nov. 9 at Port Hudson.
6. Port Hudson, La., on the Mississippi River, about twenty miles north of Baton Rouge.
7. On Nov. 10, Lt. Col. John A. Rawlins wrote to Brig. Gen. Thomas A.

Davies, Columbus, Ky. "Company "M" 6th Ills Cavalry, Capt Sperry Comdg, at Birds Point, Misso, and Company "B," 6th Ills Cavalry at Paducah Ky Capt Morray Comdg, will be ordered to report to their Regiment without delay at Memphis Tenn also detach from Company K 2nd Ills Artillery Capt Smith Comdg, with orders to report to Colonel Grierson, Comdg 6th Ills Cavalry at Memphis Tenn at once Eight (8) Woodruff Guns (2 Pr's Cannon) with a full supply of Ammunition and one Lieutenant with Non-Commissioned officers and Privates, sufficient to man them. The Quartermasters Dep't will furnish River Transportation." LS, DNA, RG 393, District of Western Ky., Letters Received. This letter was recorded as written by USG. Copies, *ibid.*, Dept. of the Tenn., Letters Sent; DLC-USG, V, 18, 30.

8. For Col. David Stuart, 55th Ill., see letter to Capt. John C. Kelton, Jan. 22, 1862. Although nominated on Jan. 19, 1863, for promotion to brig. gen. as of Nov. 29, 1862, Stuart was not confirmed.

9. Ralph P. Buckland, born in Ravenna, Ohio, in 1812, practiced law at Lower Sandusky (now Fremont), Ohio, was for a time a partner of Rutherford B. Hayes, and served two terms in the Ohio Senate as a Republican. Appointed col., 72nd Ohio, on Jan. 10, 1862, he was confirmed on March 10, 1863, as brig. gen. to rank from Nov. 29, 1862.

General Orders No. 6

———

Head Quarters 13th Army Corps,
Dep't of the Tennessee,
LaGrange, Tenn. Nov. 11. 1862.

GENERAL ORDERS No. 6.

I. The following officers are announced as the Staff and Staff Corps of this Department, and will be recognized and obeyed accordingly:

Brig. Gen. J. D. Webster, Superintendent Military Railroads.

Lieut. Col. Jno. A. Rawlins, Ass't Adjutant Genl and Chief of Staff.

Col. T. Lyle Dickey, Chief of Cavalry.

Col. Wm. S. Hillyer, Aide-de-Camp and Provost Marshal General.

Col. Clark B. Lagow,[1] Aid-de-Camp and Acting Inspector General.

Col. George P. Ihrie, Aid-de-Camp and Acting Inspector General.

Col. John Riggin, Jr., Aid-de-Camp and Superintendent of
   Military Telegraphs.
Col. Geo. G. Pride, Chief Engineer of Military Railroads.
Lieut. Col. W. L. Duff, Chief of Artillery.
Lieut. Col. J. P. Hawkins, Chief of Subsistence Department.
Lieut. Col. C. A. Reynolds, Chief of Quartermasters Depart-
   ment.
Surgeon Horace R. Wirtz, Chief of Medical Department.[2]
Major William R. Rowley, Aid-de-Camp and Mustering
   Officer.
Captain T. S. Bowers, Aid-de-Camp.
Captain F. E. Prime, Chief of Engineers.
Lieut. James H. Wilson, Chief of Topographical Engineers.[3]
Lieut. S. C. Lyford, Chief of Ordnance Department.[4]

> By Command of Major General U. S. Grant
> JNO. A. RAWLINS
> Ass't Adj't Genl.

Copies, DLC-USG, V, 13, 14, 95; DNA, RG 393, Dept. of the Tenn., General
and Special Orders.

1. On Nov. 25, 1862, USG telegraphed to David Lagow, Evansville, Ill.
"Your brother Clark B Lagow is very ill   come on here immediately"   Copies,
DLC-USG, V, 18, 30; DNA, RG 393, Dept. of the Tenn., Letters Sent. On
Nov. 29, Lt. Col. John A. Rawlins issued Special Orders No. 33. "Col. Clark B.
Lagow, A. D. C on the staff of the General Commanding, will immediately proceed to his home at Palestine, Illinois, and upon recovery from his illness will
rejoin Headquarters, wherever the same may be"   DS, *ibid.*, RG 94, Dept. of
the Tenn., Special Orders; copies, *ibid.*, RG 393, Dept. of the Tenn., Special
Orders; DLC-USG, V, 16, 26, 27.
2. See telegram to Abraham Lincoln, Oct. 10, 1862, note 4. On Dec. 18,
USG telegraphed to Col. Robert C. Wood, asst. surgeon gen. "Since my dispatch
of this morning I have made inquiries about Surgeon Wirtz. I am satisfied the
high estimate in which I have hitherto held him is sustained. I would not wish a
change." Copies, *ibid.*, V, 18, 30, 91; DNA, RG 393, Dept. of the Tenn., Letters
Sent.
3. James H. Wilson of Ill., USMA 1860, after returning from service in
Ore., accompanied the Port Royal expedition as chief topographical engineer.
Although Wilson held rank only as 1st lt., Maj. Gen. John A. McClernand
expected him to play a key role in his Vicksburg expedition, and it was through
McClernand's influence that Wilson was sent west. James Harrison Wilson,
Under the Old Flag (New York and London, 1912), I, chap. iv; Wilson to
McClernand, Nov. 24, 1862, McClernand Papers, IHi. On Oct. 26, 1862, Maj.

Gen. James B. McPherson telegraphed to Rawlins requesting the assignment to his staff of Capt. John G. Klinck, asst. q. m., and Capt. Andrew Hickenlooper, 5th Ohio Battery. Telegram received, DNA, RG 393, Dept. of the Tenn., Telegrams Received. On Oct. 26, Rawlins wrote to McPherson. "Capt. Klinck and Hickenlooper have been ordered to report to you. Capt. Hickenlooper temporarily however. He will be relieved by Lieut J. H. Wilson, who has been ordered to report here when he arrives" Copies, *ibid.*, Letters Sent; DLC-USG, V, 18, 30. On Oct. 27, McPherson wrote to Rawlins. "You are a trump. I would rather have Wilson for my engineer than any officer I know. We are old friends; came home from California together last year." *O.R.*, I, xvii, part 2, 300. On Nov. 10, when Wilson arrived at La Grange, Tenn., Rawlins issued Special Orders No. 14 assigning him to duty with McPherson. DS, DNA, RG 94, Dept. of the Tenn., Special Orders; copies, *ibid.*, RG 393, Dept. of the Tenn., Special Orders; DLC-USG, V, 16, 26, 27. On Nov. 23, USG wrote to Maj. Gen. Henry W. Halleck requesting that Wilson remain in his command. DNA, RG 108, Register of Letters Received.

4. On Nov. 9, USG had telegraphed to Governor Richard Yates of Ill. "Has a colonel been appointed for the 7th Illinois Cavalry It is highly necessary that a good officer be appointed for the regiment and I would earnestly recommend Lieut S. C. Lyford of the Ordnance Dept." Copies, DLC-USG, V, 18, 30; DNA, RG 393, Dept. of the Tenn., Letters Sent. On Nov. 10, Ill. AG Allen C. Fuller telegraphed to USG. "Gov Yates is in Washington & no appointment can be made of Col. of 7th Cavalry until his return—" Telegram received, *ibid.*, Telegrams Received. Lt. Col. Edward Prince, 7th Ill. Cav., was promoted to col. as of June 1, 1862, although not mustered in at that rank until Feb. 1, 1863.

To Maj. Gen. Henry W. Halleck

Lagrange Tenn 9 20 P M [*Nov.*] 11th [*1862*]

Gen H. W. Halleck

The following dispatch just recd from Genl Davies at Columbus. The expedition Commanded by Brig Gen Ransom has proved a great success. It came up with Col Woodwards[1] Rebel force eight hundred strong near Garretsburg[2] had a short Engagement killed sixteen of his men Among them one Capt & Lieut wounding forty including one Captain & two Lieuts took twenty five prisoners all their horses & fifty mules. A large number of Arms & equipments half the Camps of Woodwards men including his own routing the whole concern & driving them out of the State of Kentucky. Our loss three killed & seven wounded[3]

U. S Grant
Maj Genl

Telegram received, DNA, RG 94, Generals' Papers and Books, Telegrams Received by Gen. Halleck; *ibid.*, RG 107, Telegrams Collected (Bound); copies, *ibid.*, RG 393, Dept. of the Tenn., Hd. Qrs. Correspondence; DLC-USG, V, 5, 8, 24, 88. *O.R.*, I, xx, part 1, 9.

    1. Lt. Col. Thomas G. Woodward, 1st Ky. Cav., commanding his regt. since the promotion of Col. Ben Hardin Helm on March 18, 1862.
    2. Garrettsburg, Ky., about fifteen miles southwest of Hopkinsville, practically at the Tenn. state line.
    3. A copy of this telegram of Nov. 11, addressed to Lt. Col. John A. Rawlins, is in DNA, RG 393, Hd. Qrs. District of Columbus, Telegrams Sent. In this copy, the C. S. A. officers killed and wounded are named, the number of captured horses is put at 100, and the last two words read "several wounded."

To Brig. Gen. Thomas A. Davies

LaGrange Tenn Nov 11 1862

Genl Davies
Columbus Ky

No more regiments are required at union city or Kenton. I neglected to telegrap you the change I had made in this respect. Troops generaly are to go to Memphis   if any come to Columbus without Special Order and not on boats suitable for carrying them to Memphis send them to Jackson   If the regiments are not started send then to Memphis   if they started direct them to keep on to Jackson

U. S. Grant,
Maj. Gel.

Copies, DLC-USG, V, 18, 30; DNA, RG 393, Dept. of the Tenn., Letters Sent. On Nov. 11, 1862, Brig. Gen. Thomas A. Davies telegraphed three times to Lt. Col. John A. Rawlins. "The 127th Ills left cairo at 12 m the 93d Ind at 8 P M   in accordance with Genl Grants instructions I shall send one (1) to memphis & one (1) to union city to relieve the Regt there—This will make the 4th Regt sent to Memphis as ordered one to union city & (1) to Kenton will complete Gen Grants instructions   please send instructions for regts arriving after these orders have been carried out—" "The following telegraph has been received from Adjt Genl Fuller   by direction of Maj Genl Halleck just rec'd the direction of your battery is changed to Memphis   you will therefore report to the Com'dg Officer at Memphis—This battery has arrived at Columbus   Shall I send it along?" "Six 6 Gun battery four (4) Rifle (2) brass guns (14) caissons (8) limbers with a direction to cap't Burrows Jackson nailed on a gun.   no order or men or any thing else came with them   what will be done with them   the reason they are not forwarded was that I thought men & horses might arrive belonging to them—" Telegrams received, *ibid.*, Telegrams Received; copies, *ibid.*, Hd. Qrs. District of Columbus, Telegrams Received. On the same day, Rawlins telegraphed to Davies. "Send the Battery to Memphis" Copies, DLC-USG, V, 18, 30; DNA, RG 393, Dept. of the Tenn., Letters Sent.

On Nov. 12, Davies telegraphed to Rawlins. "Troops sent from Columbus since nov 2d and battery Ill artillery 119 Ill (95) Ills (109) Ills and Degolyers Battery to Bolivar 32d Wisconsin (83d) Ind 93d Ills mercantile battery (127) Ills 120 Ills 114 Ills to Memphis 108 Ills to Jackson also 93d Ind just in for memphis—" Telegram received, *ibid.*, Telegrams Received; copy, *ibid.*, Hd. Qrs. District of Columbus, Telegrams Sent.

To Brig. Gen. Charles S. Hamilton

La Grange, Tenn., Nov. 11. 186[2]

GEN'L. HAMILTON,

Direct your troops to draw rations as soon as possible, to include the 20th and be prepared for an advance movement when ordered. To-morrow will be early enough to draw them.

U. S. GRANT,
Maj Genl.

Telegram, copies, DLC-USG, V, 18, 30; DNA, RG 393, Dept. of the Tenn., Letters Sent; *ibid.*, District of Corinth, Telegrams Received. *O.R.*, I, xvii, part 2, 342.

On Nov. 11, 1862, Brig. Gen. Charles S. Hamilton, "Cassetts House," wrote to USG. "States that the enemy retired to Tompkin's Mills 7 miles from Holly Springs: that Falkners Reg't is broken up; Send 6 prisoners in this morning." DLC-USG, V, 21. On the same day, USG telegraphed to Hamilton. "Your note about Faulkner confirms a dispatch received from Dodge. He said that Faulkner's men were going home, Jacksons cavalry in pursuit. Send all prisoners here. Is Lee out now?" Copies, *ibid.*, V, 18, 30; DNA, RG 393, Dept. of the Tenn., Letters Sent; *ibid.*, District of Corinth, Telegrams Received; Dodge Papers, IaHA. On the same day, Hamilton telegraphed to USG. "Colonel Lee is not out. He does not wish to start until the morning, and then to make his arrangements so as to enter Holly Springs just at daybreak. He is a little afraid his return may be embarrassed by a larger force of cavalry than he has. I have directed Quinby to send a brigade with one battery as far as Lamar to-morrow for Lee to fall back upon if pressed. Lee has had his scouts in the front to-day." *O.R.*, I, xvii, part 2, 342.

Also on Nov. 11, USG sent three additional telegrams to Hamilton. "I have just directed five companies of cavalry, to report to Col. Lee in the morning, and send a communication for you to furnish a Brigade and Battery, just as you dispatch states you have done" "I only wanted the advance made to Holly Springs in the event that Cold Water Rail Road bridge is standing. If that is down Quinby can return. My dispatch to you was in consequence of the Sup't. of Telegraph reporting that all the troops had left Davis' Mills." "Information just received from deserters proves that Tompkins Mills is evacuated, and that Cold Water bridge is still standing. If this is so the Brigade going out should remain there, and the balance of Quinbys, and one other Division move up as soon as possible." Copies, DLC-USG, V, 18, 30; DNA, RG 393, Dept. of the Tenn., Letters Sent; *ibid.*, District of Corinth, Telegrams Received. *O.R.*, I, xvii, part 2, 342–43. On the same day, Col. John V. D. Du Bois, chief of staff to Hamilton, telegraphed to USG. "Dispatch received and necessary orders given   Hamilton unwell   Quinby's & Ross' Division detailed—"   Telegram received, DNA, RG 393, Dept. of the Tenn., Telegrams Received.

To Maj. Gen. Henry W. Halleck

Head Quarters, Dept. of the Ten.
Lagrange Nov. 12th 1862

MAJ. GEN. H. W. HALLECK
GEN. IN CHIEF
WASHINGTON D. C.
GEN.

If it is the intention to permit this column push South by the Mississippi Central road, and supply it from Memphis by way of the Miss. & Ten. road after reaching Grenada it will be necessary to have six additional locomotives as early as practicable. Three of them should be sent to Memphis as all material for repairs would have to be taken from that end.

If there is no expectation of using this route three additional engines would still be required. I would respectfully request that they be ordered.

Our present force of engines is twenty-two of which eighteen are in working order, three of them being in the shops for repairs about one half the time.

At present we draw all our forage for this place from the country, and about one half of it for the balance of the Department, except the District of Memphis.

This supply will probably continue until the 1st of January when it may become necessary to bring a great part of it over the road.

> I am Gen. very respectfully
> your obt. svt.
> U. S. GRANT
> Maj. Gen.

ALS, IHi. *O.R.*, I, xvii, part 1, 469–70. See telegram to Maj. Gen. Henry W. Halleck, Nov. 13, 1862.

To Maj. Gen. Stephen A. Hurlbut

———

BY TELEGRAPH FROM Lagrange [*Nov.*] 12 *1862*

To GENL HURLBUT

All my reinforcements are going to Memphis and as Ohio & Kentucky have been added to the States directed to send forces here, I will have a much larger number there than in the Two wings here. It will be necessary therefore for me to help Sherman out in Generals a little   you may make your preparations to go in a few days as soon as I can appoint a successor to command the district

> U S GRANT
> Maj Genl

Telegram received, DNA, RG 393, District of West Tenn., 4th Division, Telegrams Received; copies, *ibid.*, Dept. of the Tenn., Letters Sent; DLC-USG, V,

18, 30. On Nov. 12, 1862, Lt. Col. John A. Rawlins telegraphed to Brig. Gen. James M. Tuttle, Cairo. "The General commanding desires to know if you feel sufficiently recovered in health to take the command of the District of Jackson. Your Headquarters at Bolivar or Jackson." Copies, *ibid.*, V, 18, 30; DNA, RG 393, Dept. of the Tenn., Letters Sent. On Nov. 13, Tuttle telegraphed to Rawlins. "I was well enough a few days ago to go to Jackson but I am confined to my bed now with very severe attack of flux   will probably be all right in a few days & will be pleased to get the Jackson division—or one in the field"   Telegram received, *ibid.*, Telegrams Received. On Nov. 14, USG telegraphed to Tuttle. "Will you be able to take command at Jackson within a day or two?" Copies, DLC-USG, V, 18, 30; DNA, RG 393, Dept. of the Tenn., Letters Sent. On Nov. 15, Tuttle telegraphed to USG. "My physician says I will not possibly be so as to leave my bed for four (4) days yet   I am very sick & getting no better yet   as soon as I take a turn for the better I will Teleg'h you, as I am very anxious to get away from here—" Telegram received, *ibid.*, Telegrams Received. On Nov. 17, Rawlins issued Special Orders No. 21 replacing Maj. Gen. Stephen A. Hurlbut at Jackson with Tuttle, and sending Hurlbut to Memphis. DS, *ibid.*, RG 94, Dept. of the Tenn., Special Orders; copies, DLC-USG, V, 16, 26, 27, 87. *O.R.*, I, xvii, part 2, 353.

On Nov. 17, Surgeon John P. Taggart sent to USG's hd. qrs. a statement that Tuttle was suffering from dysentery and would not be fit for duty for two weeks. DLC-USG, V, 21. On Nov. 17, USG telegraphed to Tuttle. "After receiving your dispatch saying that you would not be able to take the Command at Jackson, I ordered Genl J C Sullivan to that place   You will therefore retain command at Cairo" Copies, *ibid.*, V, 18, 30; DNA, RG 393, Dept. of the Tenn., Letters Sent. On Nov. 18, USG telegraphed to Tuttle. "I will order some one else to relieve Hurlbut. If your Physician thinks it unsafe for you to remain at Cairo, take a leave until you recover" Copies, *ibid.* On Nov. 18, Tuttle telegraphed to Rawlins. "Your Telegram ordering me to Jackson to relieve Gen Hurlbut came late last night   I am still sick so much so that I am not capable of doing any business   Capt Sample my A A G is now doing it all here—I am confined to my bed all the time   my surg tells me it is all brought about from my Donelson injuries & which they say will get worse as long as I stay in the service   I had finally concluded to tender my resignation as soon I get able to travel home as I am sure I will not be able for the field any more now & I have no ambition to be a *rear Genl*   now what shall I do   I am not able to get there & could do nothing if I was there   please answer" Telegram received, *ibid.*, Telegrams Received. On Nov. 19, Tuttle telegraphed twice to USG. "Am a little better this morning   have turned over command here to Col. Daugherty 22d Ills   think I will be able to go to Jackson Friday—Have had a bad time of it—" "Your dispatch of this morng recd   I sent you line this A M informg you that I would go down friday   I would have to go on a bed as I will not be able to set up by that time   if you send some one else you will greatly obj   am 2 sick to travel   if I had leave I w remain on duty here for the present as I have good A A G who can do all the work & not trouble me with it" Telegrams received, *ibid.* On Nov. 19, Rawlins issued Special Orders No. 23 assigning Brig. Gen. Jeremiah C. Sullivan to replace Hurlbut at Jackson. DS, *ibid.*, RG 94, Dept. of the Tenn., Special Orders; DLC-USG, V, 16, 26, 27, 87. *O.R.*, I, xvii, part 2, 355. Tuttle continued in service until June 14, 1864.

On Oct. 28, 1862, USG had telegraphed to Maj. Gen. Horatio G. Wright.

·"Is Genl Hurlbut necessary to your command   I would like to retain him if he is not—"   Telegram received, DNA, RG 393, Dept. of Ohio (Cincinnati), Telegrams Received; copies, *ibid.*, Dept. of the Tenn., Letters Sent; DLC-USG, V, 18, 30. On Oct. 29, Wright telegraphed to USG. "Gen Hurlbut is not necessary to this command and as far as I am concerned you can retain Him"   Telegram received, DNA, RG 393, Dept. of the Tenn., Telegrams Received; copy, *ibid.*, Dept. of Ohio (Cincinnati), Telegrams Sent. On the same day, George G. ·Pride sent Hurlbut a copy of Wright's telegram. ALS, *ibid.*, District of West Tenn., 4th Division, Letters Received.

On Nov. 2, USG had telegraphed to Capt. William T. Clark, Bolivar, Tenn. "Telegraph Gen McKean if you know where he is to join as soon as possible and take command of Hurlbuts old Division"   Copies, DLC-USG, V, 18, 30; DNA, RG 393, Dept. of the Tenn., Letters Sent. On the same day, Clark telegraphed to USG. "I have telegraphed Genl McKean"   Telegram received, *ibid.*, Telegrams Received. On Nov. 3, Brig. Gen. Thomas J. McKean, Cedar Rapids, Iowa, telegraphed to Rawlins. "I start tomorrow & will report without delay." Telegram received, *ibid.* On Nov. 11, Rawlins issued Special Orders No. 15, Dept. of the Tenn., assigning McKean to command the 4th Division, Right Wing. DS, *ibid.*, RG 94, Dept. of the Tenn., Special Orders; copies, *ibid.*, RG 393, Dept. of the Tenn., Special Orders; DLC-USG, V, 16, 26, 27, 87. *O.R.*, I, xvii, part 2, 343.

To Brig. Gen. Charles S. Hamilton

La Grange, Tenn., Nov. 12 1862.

GEN'L. HAMILTON,

Have you sent forward more than one Brigade? My instructions were that if Wolfe river Rail Road bridge is still standing and Holly Springs and Tompkins Mills[1] deserted, as I understand they are, these two Divisions were to be pushed forward. Answer if the two Divisions have already gone. If so I want telegraph office pushed forward, and a Brigade sent to Davis' Mills

U. S. GRANT,
Maj. Gen'l.

Telegram, copies, DLC-USG, V, 18, 30; DNA, RG 393, Dept. of the Tenn., Letters Sent; *ibid.*, District of Corinth, Telegrams Received. *O.R.*, I, xvii, part 2, 343. In a letter dated only Nov., 1862, noon, apparently written on Nov. 12, Brig. Gen. Charles S. Hamilton wrote to USG. "Only one brigade has moved, and that as a support for Lee. The other brigade of Quinby's is ordered to supply itself with rations for the whole division and be ready to move. Stanley's division is ordered to be ready to move forward with Quinby's Second Brigade, but not to move until we get reports from Colonel Lee that Holly Springs and Lumpkin's Mill were evacuated. I don't expect that report from Lee before to-morrow a. m. Colonel Lee will establish couriers every 3 miles and send back word. Wolf River Railroad Bridge is not standing. The country around Holly Springs is used up for forage, and if a command goes there before the bridge over Wolf River is completed it will be difficult to supply it with forage. The movement you ordered will take place, however, as soon as we hear from Colonel Lee that the enemy is across the Tallahatchie." *Ibid.*, pp. 343–44. On Nov. 12, Hamilton wrote to USG. "States that we will labor under difficulties in occupying Holly Springs before the RRd is opened.   wishes to speak with the Gen'l Comd'g on the Subject." DLC-USG, V, 21. On the same day, Hamilton telegraphed to USG. "No report from Lee as yet about the Coldwater bridge. Quinby is at Davis Mill with one brigade. I should like to have a telegraph Station there. Can an operator & instrument be sent down." Telegram received, DNA, RG 393, Dept. of the Tenn., Telegrams Received. *O.R.*, I, xvii, part 2, 344. On Nov. 11, USG had telegraphed to Brig. Gen. Isaac F. Quinby, Davis' Mill, Miss. "There are not here at present operators or instruments to send an Office to your Headquarters without breaking up one of the Offices already established. We now have five Offices, one at my Headquarters one at Gen'l. Hamilton's, one at Davis' Mills, one at La Grange Depot" Copies, DLC-USG, V, 18, 30; DNA, RG 393, Dept. of the Tenn., Letters Sent. On Nov. 13, 9:00 P.M., Hamilton telegraphed to USG. "The telegraph ~~officer~~ office at Davis Mill is one mile beyond Quinby's Hd Quarters. I directed Quinby to cut the wire beyond his Hd Qrs & establish the office near by—Quinby is on the Railroad—He replies to me that the operator refuses to move—Will you please order him to establish himself at Quinby's Hd Qrs—" Telegram received, *ibid.*, RG 107, Telegrams Collected (Unbound). See letter to Col. John C. Kelton, Dec. 3, 1862, note 3.

1. Apparently a reference to Lumpkin's Mill, Miss., mentioned frequently in correspondence of the time but omitted from maps. This correspondence indicates that Lumpkin's Mill was a few miles southeast of Holly Springs. William Lumpkin owned a large plantation three miles south of Holly Springs. Information from a W. P. A. interview of about 1938 supplied by Laura D. S. Harrell, Miss. Dept. of Archives and History, Jackson, Miss., Oct., 1973.

To Col. Joseph D. Webster

La Grange, Nov. 12. 1862

Gen'l. J. D. Webster,
Jackson, Tenn.,

I think it advisable to start no more trains from Jackson until the cars that are now clogging up the road and sidings are removed. Don't you think it advisable to have Walker, who understands making up trains, with you in the place of the man you have, who does not seem to understand it. If it is found that any employees are throwing obstacles in the way of the proper running of the road, discharge them and employ new men.

U. S. GRANT,
Maj. Gen'l.

Copies, DLC-USG, V, 18, 30; DNA, RG 393, Dept. of the Tenn., Letters Sent.
    On Nov. 12, 1862, George G. Pride, Grand Junction, telegraphed to USG. "Our train has been waiting here since 12 oclock to go north   Will probably get away in an hour   the trains are in a snarl & will be until learn not to send more than (1) Engine will pull"   Telegram received, *ibid.*, Telegrams Received.
    On Nov. 15, USG telegraphed twice to Col. Joseph D. Webster. "Refuse all permits to ship goods to this place for sale. Instruct railroad men that good cannot be brought here." "Direct some cars to be loaded with forage for Corinth." Copies, DLC-USG, V, 18, 30; DNA, RG 393, Dept. of the Tenn., Letters Sent. On the same day, Webster telegraphed to USG. "Is the quater master here to furnsh the forage for Corinth"   Telegram received, *ibid.*, Telegrams Received. On the same day, USG again telegraphed to Webster. "All the forage within fifteen miles of Corinth, is consumed, it must be furnished from Columbus." Copies, DLC-USG, V, 18, 30; DNA, RG 393, Dept. of the Tenn., Letters Sent.
    On Nov. 17, USG telegraphed to Webster. "Sutlers goods are not intended to be prohibited. Bolivar is not included in the order." Copies, *ibid.* On Nov. 18, USG telegraphed to Webster. "Hereafter the tariff of charges on all Military Rail Roads in this Department, will be six (6) cents per head per mile for passengers; ten (10) cents per bale per mile for Cotton, and twenty five (25) cents per ton per mile for all other freight"   Copies, *ibid.*

To Maj. Gen. Henry W. Halleck

Lagrange Tenn
Nov 13 1862 2 15 P M

MAJ GENL H W. HALLECK
GENL IN CHIEF

    Col Lee with cavalry entered Holly Springs this morning ~~with Cavalry~~ driving the enemys pickets from there and far beyond   He has taken about one hundred prisoners and killed and wounded many   Lee still in pursuit

The enemy are now south of the Tallahatchie   I do not deem it advisable to move from present position until prepared to follow up any success

Twelve additional Locomotives are required to supply the Army   Three at Memphis   Will you direct them ordered   Can I not have an Ordnance Officer from St Louis ordered to Memphis

U S GRANT
Maj Gen Comdg

Telegram received, DNA, RG 107, Telegrams Collected (Bound); copies, *ibid.*, Telegrams Received in Cipher; *ibid.*, RG 393, Dept. of the Tenn., Hd. Qrs. Correspondence; DLC-USG, V, 5, 8, 24, 88. *O.R.*, I, xvii, part 1, 470. On Nov. 15, 1862, Maj. Gen. Henry W. Halleck telegraphed to USG. "Twelve additional locomotives cannot be sent to you for they cannot be procured without seriously deranging other lines. It is not advisable to put rail roads in operation south of Memphis. Operations in northern Miss. must be limited to rapid marches upon any collected forces of the enemy, feeding as far as possible on the country. The enemy must be turned by a movement down the river from Memphis as soon as a sufficient force can be collected." ALS (telegram sent), DNA, RG 107, Telegrams Collected (Bound); copy, *ibid.*, RG 108, Telegrams Sent. *O.R.*, I, xvii, part 1, 470. Although no text of this telegram was copied in USG's book records, its arrival was noted in his register of letters received. DLC-USG, V, 21.

Also on Nov. 15, George G. Pride, Columbus, Ky., telegraphed to USG. "Will the locomotives be ordered at Washington   if so we ought to know how soon they will arrive that I can hurry the cars up to the same time. I shall send a man from here to see about the cars at once—Will it not be well to order a few Engines down from here & have a man to attend to urging them forward this week. We can hurry them up by that means this & materially for road from Memphis. Engines ordered from Washington I learn come on sooner by having a good man after four (4) or five (5) Engines.   he can hasten, it very much. Think I can get ~~four~~ three (3) or four (4) Rail Roads to alter some Engines to our gauge within ten (10) days—" Telegram received, DNA, RG 393, Dept. of the Tenn., Telegrams Received. On the same day, USG telegraphed twice to Pride. "I requested Gen'l. Halleck to order the locomotives, but have received no answer yet. We cannot send any cars from here to Memphis, all are required here." "Orders from Washington change plans. No work will be commenced from Memphis. Suspend orders for cars except such as have been commenced." Copies, DLC-USG, V, 18, 30; DNA, RG 393, Dept. of the Tenn., Letters Sent. Also on Nov. 15, Pride telegraphed to Lt. Col. John A. Rawlins. "We cannot obtain timber in time. report at Cincinnati St Louis or Chicago—The Ills Central R R have a million & half feet of bridge timber on hand which they keep for emergencies which will answer our purpose.   how can we get it   they of course do not want to sell it   Have you sent to Genl Wight and must I send a man from here about the cars or will Genl Wight attend to it—" Telegram received, *ibid.*, Telegrams Received. On the same day, USG again telegraphed to Pride. "The locomotives —twelve—will not be ordered nor road from Memphis repaired. Fifty additional cars will be sufficient, and much less bridge timber than we expected. Send word to agent sent to Ohio to this effect." Copies, DLC-USG, V, 18, 30; DNA, RG 393, Dept. of the Tenn., Letters Sent.

On Nov. 13, Col. Albert L. Lee, Holly Springs, wrote frequently to USG. "Day light." "I have just entered this city, & my pickets are polluting the 'sacred soil' some two miles below it. I found a considerable force of cavalry, but they 'skedaddled.' We charged their pickets 2 miles north of town capturing 4 & killing one man—No loss on our side. Rebel Infantry is below Tallahatchie cavalry at Lumpkins mills & vicinity. I shall send there this morning, Ls mills is 7 miles south—" ALS, *ibid.*, RG 94, War Records Office, Union Battle Reports. *O.R.*, I, xvii, part 1, 488–89. 8:00 A.M. "We have pursued the enemy four miles below this city, killing & capturing. I have taken prisoner a Captain, Commissary of Subsistence on Van Dorn's staff. He says VanDorn is not in arrest—I find a hospital 1½ miles from town with a number of convalescents. In all I have about one hundred prisoners & the 'work is going on' " ALS, DNA, RG 94, War Records Office, Union Battle Reports. *O.R.*, I, xvii, part 1, 489. 9:00 A.M. "All is still quiet here. My cavalry has gone to within 1½ miles of Lumpkins mills & reports cavalry in considerably force. They are driving the enemy with brisk skirmishing — I am gathering horses to mount my dismounted men & the rebels are on their knees" ALS, DNA, RG 393, Dept. of the Tenn., Telegrams Received. 11:00 A.M. "Have captured another Captain of rebel army & taken below a picket of 10 men, My forces are skirmishing briskly at Lumpkins mill—one man slightly wounded" ALS, *ibid.* 3:30 P.M. "I have been skirmishing with enemys cavalry all day—They have had up 5 Regiments. We have just ended an affair in some force, & they are now advancing on us opening with artillery. Gen Sullivan is here but thinks he may have exceeded orders & feels delicate about engaging in any fight now to hold his place. If you will allow me to express my opinion, we should be immediately reinforced or not expected to hold the place. I believe their infantry is mainly if not quite the other side of Tallahatchie   Some may be this side. I have been nearly to Lumpkins mill & their strong force of cavly followed me back. Have captured a Lieut & several men   Please send instructions to me immediately & to infantry behind me   Genl Sullivan decides to fall back to Coldwater fearing an engagement. I continue to occupy the place & shall do so till further orders" ALS, *ibid.*, RG 94, War Records Office, Union Battle Reports. *O.R.*, I, xvii, part 1, 489. On the same day, Rawlins wrote to Lee. "Your dispatch of 3.30 P. M., of to-day received. Gen'l. Hamilton was directed some hours ago to order your return, which orders have perhaps reached you. You will return at once, using necessary precautions to your old camp." Copies, DLC-USG, V, 18, 30; DNA, RG 393, Dept. of the Tenn., Letters Sent. Also on Nov. 13, 9:00 P.M., Lee wrote to USG. "An officer I sent this afternoon to examine the railroad bridges over Cold-Water has already reported to Genl Quinby that the two bridges were sound and the rails in order. He rode over the two bridges on a hand-car and went within two miles of Lamar   From what my men have seen and the statements of laborers on the road, I fully believe the road to be in perfect order from Holly Springs to Lamar. I learn the force of cavalry which attacked us this afternoon to consist of five (5) regiments, commanded by Jackson in person. In repulsing them we killed one officer and several of their men and horses. I think they have fallen back to Lumpkin's Mills. Our pickets are two miles south of the town. Their line of pickets is about ½ or ¾ mile in front of ours. In the attack to-day they used three (3) pieces of artillery. I have no good reason to believe, however, that their infantry (in force, at least) is this side of the Tallahatchee.

I learn Gen. Sullivan has fallen back near Lamar. I shall endeavor to hold this position until you desire it vacated. I think I can do it. I sent to Hd. Qrs by Gen. Sullivan seven commissioned officers captured to-day." ALS, *ibid.*, RG 94, War Records Office, Union Battle Reports. *O.R.*, I, xvii, part 1, 489–90.

On Nov. 14, Brig. Gen. Charles S. Hamilton telegraphed three times to USG. "I learn tonight that Faulkners cavalry is to be reorganized. The men are to be treated as deserters if they do not immediately repair to their old camp south west of Ripley. To-morrow is the first day of meeting. If Lees horses were not too tired, I would send him out   Thirty one prisoners will be sent over to you in the morning." ALS (telegram sent), DNA, RG 393, Dept. of the Tenn., Unregistered Letters Received; telegram received, *ibid.*, Telegrams Received. "Sullivan camped at Hudsonville last night and will reach Davis Mill by noon today   He has thirty six prisoners including seven officers." Copy, *ibid.*, Army of the Tenn., Left Wing, Telegrams Sent. "Sullivans Brig has just arrived   he is close behind   the prisoners will be sent up to you today   a large portion of them were convelescents & have been paroled   I will send in Lees report as soon as recd   Lee says the force opposed to him at Lumpkins mill was a Brig of Infantry with the cavaly of the whole army   the cannonade was from enemys guns   no loss sustained on our side"   Telegram received, *ibid.*, Dept. of the Tenn., Telegrams Received.

On Nov. 18, USG telegraphed to Hamilton. "Send Col Lee as your propose I will send Lieut. Wilson with him"   Copies, DLC-USG, V, 18, 30; DNA, RG 393, Dept. of the Tenn., Letters Sent; *ibid.*, District of Corinth, Telegrams Received. On Nov. 19, 1st Lt. James H. Wilson recorded in his diary that he had received a note from USG asking him to accompany Lee on a reconnaissance to Ripley. Historical Society of Delaware, Wilmington, Del. Lee's report of the expedition is in *O.R.*, I, xvii, part 1, 490–91. On Nov. 20, Hamilton wrote to USG's hd. qrs. "States that he has supported Lee. and directed a reconnoisance to the river. Will send out a reconnoisance under Quinby from near Waterford to the South East. Each reconnoisance will take 2 days but he will move ~~but~~ his camp to the S. E. if he can find water." DNA, RG 393, Dept. of the Tenn., Register of Letters Received; DLC-USG, V, 21.

To Brig. Gen. Charles S. Hamilton

La Grange, Nov. 13. 1862

BRIG. GEN'L. C. S. HAMILTON
COM'D'G. LEFT WING, & c.

Artillery firing was heard south from Moscow   I have no reconnoissance in that dirction. Have you heard anything further from Lee?

Direct him to return.

U. S. GRANT.
Maj. Gen'l.

Telegram, copies, DLC-USG, V, 18, 30; DNA, RG 393, Dept. of the Tenn., Letters Sent; *ibid.*, District of Corinth, Telegrams Received. *O.R.*, I, xvii, part 2, 346.
On Nov. 13, 1862, Brig. Gen. Charles S. Hamilton telegraphed to USG. "The following just recd from the front   I have my advance in camp south of the coldwater & my pickets two (2) miles further south   I have only come on flying pickets.   a gentleman just from Holly Springs informs me there is considerable cavalry there & a small amount of Infty   I shall move on the town at day light— I strongly recommend that at brigade & battery be advanced to Hundsonville at day light   the road is plain from our trail the town one & half 1½ miles north of coldwater   I may need a men to clear out Holly Springs & in such event it should be near   will you inform me if you conclud to move as I suggest   I am Genl Respy Your (signed) A L LEE Col Comdg Cav   sullivan has gone forward with his Brigade to Hudsonville   no word about the coldwater bridge yet—" Telegram received, DNA, RG 393, Dept. of the Tenn., Telegrams Received. On the same day, Hamilton again telegraphed to USG. "Sullivan sends word that the Coldwater Bridge is some distance off his route, but the citizens say the road has not been molested." *O.R.*, I, xvii, part 2, 346. On the same day, USG telegraphed to Hamilton. "Direct Sullivan & Lee to fall back to camp if not already done" Copy, DNA, RG 393, District of Corinth, Telegrams Received. On the same day, Hamilton wrote to USG. "I recalled Sullivan while you were here to-day. Have since learned that Sullivan went on to Holly Springs at Lee's request without orders. His orders were to go to Lamar, and in no event beyond Coldwater. Lee and Sullivan have both been recalled by courier from Holly Springs. Colonel Sanders, at Davis' Mill, reports five reports of cannon in the southwest at 3.30 p. m., apparently heavy caliber." *O.R.*, I, xvii, part 2, 346. Also on Nov. 13, 8:30 P.M., Hamilton again telegraphed to USG. "Sullivan reached Holly Springs at 12.30. I think he must have gone to Lees support at Lathams Mills and fired a few shots at the Cavalry engaged with Lee. But five shots were heard, and I do not doubt it was Sullivans artillery. The couriers recalling him and Lee ought to have reached them by 4 P M." Telegram received, DNA, RG 107,Telegrams Collected (Unbound), *O.R.*, I, xvii, part 2, 346.

To Brig. Gen. Charles S. Hamilton

La Grange; Nov. 13th 1862

GEN'L. HAMILTON,

I tried to get Paymasters here immediately after the battle of Corinth. Major Larned replied they had no funds   Hope they will have soon.[1] Gen'l. Allen says no blankets in St. Louis. I will make another effort.[2]

U. S. GRANT.
Maj. Gen'l.

Telegram, copies, DLC-USG, V, 18, 30; DNA, RG 393, Dept. of the Tenn., Letters Sent; *ibid.*, District of Corinth, Telegrams Received. On Nov. 13, 1862, Brig. Gen. Charles S. Hamilton telegraphed to USG. "Bitter & just complaints are rife in my command at the want of blankets & want of pay   hundreds of my men are without blankets these cold nights—cannot something be done to get up a supply immediately.   the effective as well as the discipline of the command will suffer greatly unless these wants are supplied soon—" Telegram received, *ibid.*, Dept. of the Tenn., Telegrams Received.

1. On Nov. 15, USG telegraphed to Maj. Charles T. Larned, Louisville, Ky. "Cannot the troops in this Department be paid soon?" Copies, DLC-USG, V, 18, 30; DNA, RG 393, Dept. of the Tenn., Letters Sent. On Nov. 20, Larned wrote to USG "Giving reasons why troops of this Dept. have not been paid." DLC-USG, V, 21. On Dec. 8, Larned telegraphed to USG. "I am prepared to send paymasters to your command   can they join you now & where   how many divisions Have you to be paid including Sherman Quinby & Hovey who I understand have moved to join you" Telegram received, DNA, RG 94, War Records Office, Dept. of the Tenn. On the same day, USG telegraphed to Larned. "Paymasters can come here by rail. I have Quinby's, Stanley's, now Ross', McArthur's, Logan's, McKean's Divisions and Sherman's command. Hovey will be found at Helena. Let Paymasters bring a portion of their funds in Eastern drafts." Copies, DLC-USG, V, 18, 30, 91; DNA, RG 393, Dept. of the Tenn., Letters Sent. On Dec. 6, Paymaster Isaac N. Cooke, Louisville, telegraphed to USG. "I expect to leave here on monday next for your Hd Qrs   I will have charge of the payment of your army & will remain permanently with you   I hope to have funds sufficient to pay to october 31st   will it be necessary to have an escort from Columbus to Hd Qrs   please write me at Columbus" Telegram received, *ibid.*, Telegrams Received. On Dec. 15, Cooke, Columbus, Ky., telegraphed to USG. "I am here with funds & pay masters for your Corps   would it not be better for me to go to Memphis & pay Sherman as I learn he is preparing to move" Telegram received, *ibid.*

2. On Nov. 13, USG telegraphed to Col. Robert Allen, St. Louis. "A portion of this command have no blankets, can they not be got immediately?" Copies, DLC-USG, V, 18, 30; DNA, RG 393, Dept. of the Tenn., Letters Sent. On

Nov. 14, Allen telegraphed to USG. "Sent a week since two thousand blankets to Capt Tighe Corinth will send you to Lagrange today five thousand will this suffice" Telegram received, *ibid.*, Telegrams Received. On the same day, USG telegraphed to Allen. "I think the blankets now coming will be sufficient." Copies, DLC-USG, V, 18, 30; DNA, RG 393, Dept. of the Tenn., Letters Sent. Also on the same day, USG telegraphed to Hamilton. "Two-thousand blankets will be here to-day or to-morrow, and five-thousand more in a few days." Copies, *ibid.*

To Maj. Gen. William T. Sherman

Head Quarters, Dept. of the Ten.
Lagrange Nov. 14th 1862

MAJ. GEN. W. T. SHERMAN,
MEMPHIS TEN.

After writing to you by Col. Grierson[1] I received a dispatch from Gen. Halleck stating that in addition to troops already ordered to this Department some from Ohio and Ky. were also ordered. All to be collected at Memphis from which place a combined Military & Naval expedition would move on Vicksburg.[2]

This taken in connection with the misterious rumors of McClernands command left me in doubt as to what I should do. I therefore telegraphed Halleck to know if that movement was to be made independent of mine here. If I was to lay still where I am, or to penetrate as far south as possible with the means at hand. He replied that all troops sent into the Department would be under my controll. Fight the enemy in my own way.[3]

From information brought in by spies sent from Corinth by Gen. Rosecrans before he left there the enemy are expecting reinforcements from Braggs Army and also from Virginia.[4] Have also been reinforced by Holmes[5] & Hindman.[6] This latter I do not credit.[7]

I think it advisable to move on the enemy so soon as you can leave Memphis with two full Divisions of twelve regiments of Infantry each and the proper proportion of other Arms. If troops should arive sufficiently rapidly to enable you to bring three Divisions it would be more advisable. The country through which you would pass would no doubt afford supplies of forage. I will have here provisions to furnish you on arrival. Also Ordnance stores. Not less than three hundred rounds per man should be brought from Memphis however.

Our reconnoisances have driven the enemy to beyond the Tallahatchee. Yesterday our Cavalry went six or seven miles beyond Holly Springs where they met five regiments of rebel Cavalry some Infantry and a battery. Col. Lee of the 7th Kansas Cavalry, one of the best Cavalry officers I ever saw, drove them back capturing killing & wounding a large number. He has now taken since we have been here some 250 prisoners, killed perhaps 50 and wounded a large number with a loss on his side of only three men wounded.

I am ready to move from here any day and will only await your movements. You can inform me by messenger what day you will start, with what force and by what route and I will make my calculation accordingly.

The route you should take will depend upon the force you can bring with you, the number of days supplies you can transport, and whether the enemy is materially reinforced.

If you can move with three Divisions and so as to reach Oxford with three days su[pplies,] I would say go there. But I am not advised whether the new regiments joining you are supplied with transportation. I presume they are not.

I will have here from five to six hundred wagons for a supply & Ordnance train and the road in runing order to beyond Holly Springs, probably to the Tallahatchee.

If you cannot move to Oxford, and I dont expect it, the next best place would be to move to Tallaloosa,[8] or water some place from six to ten miles West or Southwest from Holly Springs   I would then move to Holly Springs so as to reach there at the same time. All future plans could be aranged after our arrival at these positions. I have asked to have three Locomotives purchased and sent to Memphis with the view of having ~~that road~~

Grenada & Memphis road used. I have ordered Lauman, and will send Hurlbut to report to you in a few days.[9]

Let me hear from you, by special Messenger, as soon as possible. Any suggestions you have to make will be gladly received and duly concid[ere]d.

I am exceedingly anxious to do something before the roads get bad and before the enemy can entrenc[h] and reinforce.

Yours Truly

U. S. GRANT

Maj. Gen.

P. S. I enclose you Dodges summary of the information brought by Rosecrans' Spies.   U. S. G.

ALS, DLC-William T. Sherman. *O.R.*, I, xvii, part 2, 347–48. On Nov. 15, 1862, USG wrote to Maj. Gen. William T. Sherman. "Meet me at Columbus Ky. on Thursday next. If you have a good map of the country south of you take it up with you." ALS, DLC-William T. Sherman. At this meeting, USG confirmed the plans discussed in his letter of Nov. 14. *Memoirs*, I, 427; *Memoirs of Gen. W. T. Sherman* (4th ed., New York, 1891), I, 307–8. On Nov. 23, Sherman wrote to USG. "As soon as I arrived here I despatched an aid to Helena who brings me back an answer perfectly satisfactory from Gen. Steele who has reached Helena with Osterhaus' Division which added to the force there makes a heavy Command. I send you his letter which assures us that he will send Hovey with a large force on Grenada from Friar's Point, reaching the Tallahatchee about Charleston on next Monday   From that point they attack or threaten Grenada about Monday Tuesday & Wednesday. I will march tomorrow Wednesday according to Orders. Denver's Div. 2 Brigades 9 Regts of Inf. & 3 Batties of Artillery on Pigeon Roost Road to Bihalia & thence south to Tchullahoma reaching Bihalia Thursday & Tchullahoma Sunday. Smith's Division to Germantown Bihalia & Tchullahoma.   same forces as Denver's   Lauman's Division 8 Regts Infty. 3 Batteries & 4 Co's Cavalry will take the Hernando Road & turn East & join Denver at Bihalia   I will accompany the center column, keeping with me Grierson with 8 co's of cavalry   Hurlbut has joined, has been assigned command of the Post, garrisoned by 4 Reg'ts 1 Battery & Thielman's 2 Co's of Cavalry. I will instruct him to organize into Brigades & Divisions all troops arriving ready to move Inland if called for. I leave as a part of the garrison the sick & helpless of the moving column, maybe 1000 men in all better behind a parapet than in a Genl. Hospital   I have a very intelligent man in from Jackson who has been to Abbeville, Grenada, Mobile, Vicksburg, everywhere, no doubt of the fact, some little doubt of his sincerity but I believe he has large interests on the Yazoo which he is anxious to cover up. He wants to get *his* Cotton out *safe*. He brings me late papers which I send you   He says a Court of Inquiry acquitted Van Dorn & that he commands the Army of the Tallahatchee. Pemberton Comd'g Dept. at Jackson, Miss. Van Dorn over Price—Tighlman, Bowen, & Jackson, not a word of any of Bragg's or Holmes' forces.   he describes much feeling against Van Dorn for bad management or bad luck. They are fortifying all fords & ferries of the Tallahatchee especially about the Rail Road crossing, & today they are ordered to commence at Panola. But all this will cease when they hear of Hovey coming across from Helena. ~~Its~~ His strength and purpose will be magnified. Mr. H. thinks that the aggregate force of Van Dorn ~~to~~ does not reach 30.000, although he admits they are so scattered that it is hard to estimate. Van Dorn's Hd. Qrts are at Abbeville & the Tallahatchee is their line. I send this & enclosures by a special bearer of despatches. I hear of a rebel Cavalry Regiment at Somerville but suppose they will fall back as we advance. I have only Grierson's Cavalry with me." Copies, DNA, RG 94, Generals' Papers and Books, William T. Sherman, Letters Sent; (2) DLC-William T. Sherman. *O.R.*, I, xvii, part 2, 874.

1. See letter to Maj. Gen. William T. Sherman, Nov. 10, 1862.
2. See telegram to Maj. Gen. Henry W. Halleck, Nov. 9, 1862.
3. See telegram to Maj. Gen. Henry W. Halleck, Nov. 10, 1862.
4. On Nov. 12, Brig. Gen. Grenville M. Dodge, Corinth, telegraphed to USG. "Spies sent out by Gen Rosecrans have come in from Chattanooga Columbus Miss & Grenada Miss   I send their statements around by mornings train by messenger   the one from Grenada insist that Price is falling back—" Telegram received, DNA, RG 393, Dept. of the Tenn., Telegrams Received. On Nov. 13, Dodge wrote to USG's hd. qrs. "States that a number of secret service men who were employed by Gen'l Rosecrans have come in since he left and asks for funds to pay them with" DLC-USG, V, 21. See telegram to Maj. Gen. Henry W. Halleck, Dec. 3, 1862.
5. Theophilus H. Holmes of N. C., USMA 1829, resigned his commission as maj. in the U.S. Army on April 22, 1861. Nominated as C. S. A. brig. gen. on Aug. 1, maj. gen. on Nov. 21, and lt. gen. on Oct. 10, 1862, Holmes served without distinction in Va. before his assignment to command the Trans-Mississippi Dept. on July 16.
6. Thomas C. Hindman, born in Knoxville, Tenn., in 1825, served as 2nd lt., 2nd Miss., in the Mexican War, and later practiced law. First active in Miss. politics as a supporter of Jefferson Davis, in 1856 he moved to Ark., where he was elected to the U.S. House of Representatives in 1858. He served as col., 2nd Ark., and on Nov. 21, 1861, was nominated as brig. gen. After his confirmation as maj. gen. on April 19, 1862, he commanded the Trans-Mississippi District, Western Dept., until superseded by Holmes, who assigned him to command the District of Ark., then the 1st Army Corps, Army of the West.
7. Although requested on Nov. 11, and again on Nov. 19, to send 10,000 troops to Miss., Holmes did not do so. *O.R.*, I, xvii, 914, 921, 927–28.
8. Tallaloosa, Miss., on Pigeon Roost Creek, about six miles west of Holly Springs.
9. Brig. Gen. Jacob G. Lauman was sent to Memphis by Special Orders No. 21, Dept. of the Tenn., Nov. 13. DS, DNA, RG 94, Dept. of the Tenn., Special Orders; DLC-USG, V, 16, 26, 27, 87. See telegram to Maj. Gen. Stephen A. Hurlbut, Nov. 12, 1862.

To Maj. Gen. Horatio G. Wright

By Telegraph from Grants Head Qrs
Lagrange Miss [Nov.] 14 1862

To Maj Gen Wright

I understand there are at Dayton Ohio a great many R R cars we require two hundred additional cars here will you arrange to have them sent here I will arrange for the payment

U S. Grant
Maj Genl

Telegram received, DNA, RG 393, Dept. of the Ohio (Cincinnati), Telegrams Received; copies, *ibid.*, Dept. of the Tenn., Letters Sent; DLC-USG, V, 18, 30. This telegram was referred to Col. Thomas Swords, chief q. m., Dept. of the Ohio. DNA, RG 393, Dept. of the Ohio (Cincinnati), Register of Letters Received. On Nov. 26, 1862, USG telegraphed to Maj. Gen. Horatio G. Wright. "Please notify Col Swords that I will not want the cars—" Telegram received (misdated Nov. 28), *ibid.*, Telegrams Received; copies, *ibid.*, Dept. of the Tenn., Letters Sent; DLC-USG, V, 18, 30. See telegram to Maj. Gen. Henry W. Halleck, Nov. 13, 1862.

To George G. Pride

La Grange Tenn., Nov. 14. 1862

Col. G. G. Pride
St. Louis, Mo.

I have sent to Gen. Wright for the cars. A man had better go there however. Most if not all the money can be paid down from funds now on hand from earnings of the road. If lumber cannot be otherwise, we will get that from the Illinois Central by some means.

U. S. Grant.
Maj. Gen'l.

Telegram, copies, DLC-USG, V, 18, 30; DNA, RG 393, Dept. of the Tenn., Letters Sent. On Nov. 14, 1862, George G. Pride, Jackson, telegraphed to USG.

"It will be necessary to order one hunded cars more for these roads & fully the same No for Road south from Memphis at once   even more than these will be wanted directly—I learn that there are at dayton O a No. of cars in course of construction for an Ohio Road   will you Teleg. Gen Wright to take possession of them as necessity & our Quarter Master will arrange with the builders   shall I make my arrangements for material & organization for the Road south from Memphis   if postponed too long will delay very much   Telegraph me at Columbus   think we can pass Davis Mill & all Brgers souh to Holly Springs by tuesday   shall return tomorrow if possible"   Telegram received, *ibid.*, Telegrams Received. On the same day, USG sent two more telegrams to Pride. "Suspend all orders for cars or locomotives until you hear from me." "Will send for the cars. Make your arrangements for running both roads. I think however, that most of the bridges on the Memphis road will be safe. Bridge over Coldwater is standing." Copies, DLC-USG, V, 18, 30; DNA, RG 393, Dept. of the Tenn., Letters Sent.

To Maj. Gen. Henry W. Halleck

Lagrange Tenn
Nov. 15th 4 P. M 1862

Maj Gen H W Halleck
Gen in Chief.

Citizens south of us are leaving their homes & Negroes coming in by wagon loads. What will I do with them? I am now having all the cotton still standing out picked by them.

U. S. Grant
Maj Genl

Telegram received, DNA, RG 94, Generals' Papers and Books, Telegrams Received by Gen. Halleck; *ibid.*, RG 107, Telegrams Collected (Bound); copies, *ibid.*, RG 94, War Records Office, Union Battle Reports; *ibid.*, RG 393, Dept. of the Tenn., Hd. Qrs. Correspondence; DLC-USG, V, 5, 8, 24, 88. *O.R.*, I, xvii, part 1, 470. On Nov. 16, 1862, Maj. Gen. Henry W. Halleck telegraphed to USG. "The sectry of war directs that you employ the refugee negroes as teamsters, laborers, &"c, so far as you have use for them in the Quartermasters Dept, in forts rail roads, &"c; also in picking & removing cotton on account of the Government. So far as possibl[e] subsist them and your army on the rebel inhabitants of Mississippi." ALS (telegram sent), DNA, RG 107, Telegrams Collected (Bound); telegram received, *ibid.*, RG 393, Dept. of the Tenn., Telegrams Received. *O.R.*, I, xvii, part 1, 470–71.

USG had already inaugurated a new Negro policy. On Nov. 13, Lt. Col. John A. Rawlins issued Special Orders No. 17. "Chaplain Eaton of the 27th Regt

Ohio Infty Vols is hereby appointed to take charge of the Contrabands that come into Camp in the vicinity of this Post, organizing them into suitable companies for working, see that they are properly cared for, and set them to work picking, ginning and Baleing Cotton now out and ungathered in field. Suitable Guards will be detailed by Commanding Officers nearest where the parties are at work to protect them from molestation. For further instructions the Officer in charge of these laborers will call at these Head Qrs." Copies, DNA, RG 393, Dept. of the Tenn., Special Orders; DLC-USG, V, 16, 26, 27, 87. In John Eaton, *Grant, Lincoln and the Freedmen* (New York, 1907), p. 5, the orders are quoted correctly, but are designated Special Orders No. 15, Nov. 11. Since Eaton matched number and date correctly, and another version of Special Orders No. 17 (DS, DNA, RG 94, Dept. of the Tenn., Special Orders) lacks the section pertaining to Eaton, the orders may have been entered in USG's book records incorrectly. Eaton was born in N. H. in 1829, graduated from Dartmouth College, and became superintendent of schools in Toledo, Ohio, in 1856. In 1859, he left Toledo to attend Andover Theological Seminary, and after his ordination, served as chaplain, 27th Ohio. Eaton later stated (p. 6) that he never knew how his name came to USG's attention, but one small clue exists in a telegram of Nov. 12, 1862, from Col. John V. D. Du Bois, chief of staff to Brig. Gen. Charles S. Hamilton, to Rawlins. "Chaplain Eaton 27th Regt. Ohio Volunteers." Copy, DNA, RG 393, District of Corinth, Telegrams Sent. USG discussed the appointment of Eaton in *Memoirs*, I, 424–26.

On Nov. 14, Rawlins issued Special Field Orders No. 4. "Chaplain J Eaton Jr, of the 27th Regt Ohio Infantry Vols., is hereby appointed to take charge of all fugitive Slaves that are now or may from time to time come within the military lines of the Advancing Army in this vicinity, not employed and registered in accordance with General Orders, No 72, from Headquarters District of West Tennessee, and will open a camp for them at Grand Junction, Tenn, where they will be suitably cared for and organized into companies and set to work picking, ginning and baling all cotton now out standing in Fields. Commanding Officers of troops will send all fugitives that come within the lines, together with such teams, cooking utensils and other baggage as they may bring with them to Chaplain Eaton Jr at Grand Junction, Tenn.   one Regiment of Infantry from Brig. General McArthur's Division will be temporarily detailed as Guard in charge of such contrabands, and the Surgeons of said Regiment will be charged with the care of the sick. Commissaries of Subsistence will issue on the requisitions of Chaplain J Eaton Jr, omitting the coffee rations and substituting Rye." DS, DNA, RG 94, Dept. of the Tenn., Special Orders; copies, *ibid.*, RG 393, Dept. of the Tenn., Special Orders; *ibid.*, General and Special Orders; DLC-USG, V, 26, 27; (printed) Oglesby Papers, IHi. *O.R.*, I, lii, part 1, 301–2.

On Dec. 17, Rawlins issued General Orders No. 13. "Chaplain John Eaton, jr., of the 27th Regiment Ohio Volunteers, is hereby appointed General Superintendent of Contrabands for the Department. He will designate such Assistant Superintendents as may be necessary for the proper care of these people, who will be detailed for their duty by the Post or District Commander. All Assistant Superintendents will be subject to the orders of the Superintendent. It will be the duty of the Superintendent of Contrabands to organize them into working parties in saving cotton, as pioneers on railroads and steamboats, and in any way where their service can be made available. Where labor is performed for private individuals, they will be charged in accordance with the tariff fixed in previous orders.

When abandoned crops of cotton are saved for the benefit of Government, the officer selling the same will turn over to the Superintendent of Contrabands the same amount charged individuals. The negroes will be clothed, and in every way provided for, out of their earnings so far as practicable, the account being kept of all earnings and expenditures, and subject to the inspection of the Inspector General of the Department when called for. Such detail of men as may be necessary for the care and superintendence of the contrabands will be made by Post or Division Commander on application of the Superintendent; as far as practicable such men as are not fit for active field duty will be detailed. The Superintendent will take charge of all contributions of clothing, etc., for the benefit of negroes and distribute the same. All applications for the service of contrabands will be made on the General Superintendent, who will furnish such labor from negroes who voluntarily come within the lines of the army. In no case will negroes be forced into the service of the Government, or be enticed away from their homes except when it becomes a military necessity." Eaton, pp. 26–27. Although this document is not in USG's book records, its authenticity need not be challenged, since USG's copies may have been lost in the raid on Holly Springs, Dec. 20. See General Orders No. 11, Dec. 17, 1862.

On Sept. 18, 1:00 P.M., Brig. Gen. James M. Tuttle, Cairo, had telegraphed to Secretary of War Edwin M. Stanton. "Major-General Grant is sending here large lots of negro women and children, and directs me to ask you what to do with them. Parties in Chicago and other cities wish them for servants. Will I be allowed to turn them over to a responsible committee, to be so employed? If so, can I transport at Government expense?" *O.R.*, III, ii, 569. On the same day, 7:00 P.M., Stanton answered both questions favorably, but on Oct. 13 told Tuttle to send no more Negroes into Ill. *Ibid.*, pp. 569, 663. A clue to the reason for the change in policy is contained in a letter of Oct. 14 from David Davis to President Abraham Lincoln stating that the movement of Negroes from Cairo northward would "work great harm in the coming Election." ALS, DLC-Robert T. Lincoln. This blockade apparently led USG to appoint a superintendent of contrabands.

To Maj. Gen. Henry W. Halleck

Head Quarters 13th Army Corps
Dept. of the Tennessee
Lagrange Nov. 15th 1862

MAJ. GEN. H. W. HALLECK
COM.D.G CHIEF
WASHINGTON D. C.
GEN.

Permit me to renew some recommendations already made for promotions, and in doing so to say that those recommended have not only earned their promotion but are fully qualified for such commands as their increased rank would entitle them to. With some hitherto promoted this latter is not true of.

The following are the names I would suggest from this Dept. towit: Brig. Gen. C. S. Hamilton to be Maj. Gen. Col. M. M. Crocker, 13th Iowa Vols.[1] Col. J. D. Webster 1st Ill. Art.y[2] Col. T. Lyle Dickey, 4th Ill. Cavalry,[3] Col. M. D. Leggett 78th Ohio Vols. Col. C. C. Marsh 20th Ill.[4] Col. John E. Smith 45th Ill.[5] Col. H. T. Reid, 15th Iowa Vols.[6] Col. Ransom, 11th Ill.[7] Col. J. D. Stevenson 7th Mo.[8] Col. A. L. Lee 7th Kansas Cavalry,[9] Capt. F. E. Prime U. S. Engineer Corps & Capt. G. A. Williams 1st U. S. Inf.y[10] to be Brigadier Generals.

> I am Gen. very respectfully
> your obt. svt.
> U. S. GRANT
> Maj. Gen.

ALS, DNA, RG 94, ACP, G402 CB 1863. For other recent recommendations by USG for promotions to gen. officer, see telegram to Maj. Gen. William S. Rosecrans, Oct. 24, 1862, and telegram to Brig. Gen. Charles S. Hamilton, Oct. 29, 1862, note 1. On Oct. 25, 1862, USG endorsed a petition of Oct. 17 from Col. Gabriel Bouck, 18th Wis., and eleven other officers, to Maj. John A. Rawlins recommending Col. John M. Oliver, 15th Mich., for promotion to brig. gen. DS, DNA, RG 94, Letters Received. "Respectfully forwarded. The recommendations herei[n] are from parties who have had an opportunity of judging of Col. Olivers qualifications and claims for the promotion asked" AES, *ibid.*

1. See telegram to Maj. Gen. Henry W. Halleck, Oct. 21, 1862.
2. See letter to Edwin M. Stanton, March 14, 1862.
3. See letter to Maj. Gen. Henry W. Halleck, Nov. 2, 1862.
4. See telegram to Maj. Gen. Henry W. Halleck, Oct. 21, 1862.
5. See *ibid.* and letter to Abraham Lincoln, Aug. 11, 1862. In that letter, USG had also requested the promotion of Col. Isham N. Haynie, 48th Ill., but on Nov. 21, Haynie submitted his resignation. "Tendered 1st on account of important private business at home, 2nd thinks his claim to promotion has been overlooked" DNA, RG 393, Dept. of the Tenn., Endorsements; DLC-USG, V, 25. On Nov. 28, USG endorsed the resignation. "Respectfully forwarded to Headquarters of the Army. The reasons assigned for resigning I do not regard as well founded but an officer giving them would perhaps be better out of service than in it" Copies, *ibid.* On Dec. 14, Rawlins wrote to Haynie. "Your appointment as Brig. Genl. has been received. You will therefore turn over the command of the forces at Bethel to Col Wm R. Morrison, and report in person and without delay to these Hd Qrs. for orders." Copies, *ibid.*, V, 18, 30, 91; DNA, RG 393, Dept. of the Tenn., Letters Sent. On Dec. 23, President Abraham Lincoln nominated Haynie as brig. gen. as of Nov. 29. On Feb. 12, 1863, the nomination was

returned to Lincoln by the Senate. On the strength of his nomination, Haynie commanded the 1st Brigade, 3rd Division, 17th Army Corps, until March 6. *O.R.*, I, xxiv, part 3, 257.

On Nov. 22, 1862, Col. William R. Morrison, 49th Ill., resigned because he had been elected a U.S. Representative. DLC-USG, V, 21. On Nov. 28, USG endorsed the resignation. "Respectfully forwarded to Headquarters of the Army, not deeming the reasons assigned sufficient to justify a Department Commander in accepting a resignation, except in cases of Officers who are a detriment to the service which cannot be said of Col. Morrison. He is one of our best Officers" Copies, DNA, RG 393, Dept. of the Tenn., Endorsements; DLC-USG, V, 25. Morrison resigned as of Dec. 13. See Lincoln, *Works*, V, 486–87. On Dec. 23, Morrison, Bethel, telegraphed to USG. "The scare is over & bethel still is ours H̶o̶n̶ Hon W A Richarsdson telegraphed on 15th that my resignation was accepted on that day   will you give me permision to go home now as I am out of the service & yet my papers may not reach me for many days perhaps weeks   I dont think they are in a condition for doing business at Washn with dispatch just now" Telegram received, DNA, RG 393, Dept. of the Tenn., Telegrams Received; *ibid.*, RG 107, Telegrams Collected (Unbound).

6. Hugh T. Reid, born in Union County, Ind., in 1811, graduated from Bloomington College, studied law, then moved to Iowa, where he practiced law and served as president of the Des Moines Valley Railroad. Appointed col., 15th Iowa, as of Feb. 22, 1862, he fought with distinction at Shiloh. See *O.R.*, I, x, part 1, 288–90. Reid was nominated on March 13, 1863, as brig. gen. No previous recommendation by USG for Reid has been found; see following letter.

7. See letter to Elihu B. Washburne, June 19, 1862.

8. See telegram to Maj. Gen. Henry W. Halleck, Oct. 21, 1862.

9. See telegram to Maj. Gen. Henry W. Halleck, Nov. 9, 1862, note 1.

10. See letter to Maj. Gen. Henry W. Halleck, Nov. 2, 1862.

To Silas A. Hudson

Lagrange Ten.
Nov. 15th 1862

DEAR COUSIN,

Your letter was duly received and laid on my table, open, with the intention of answering it as soon as I could get time. By some means it got mislaid so that I cannot now find it. Expecting to read the letter again I did not burthen my memory with the name of your Nephew[1] of whom you spoke nor do I know where he is. If he is here tell him to call on me and I will see what can be done; if not here write to me again and I will ascertain if a place can be secured for him, and if so let him know.

Since you left me I have made a slight advance but as the enemy retreated from his position at Holly Springs without waiting an attack it is useless for me to pursue further until my reinforcements come up and are in hand. As the enemy falls back he increases in strength by gathering up his rail-road garrisons whilst I am weakened by leaving behind protection to my avenues of supply. Reinforcements are coming however to Memphis, within my Department, and I hope soon to have collected together such strength as to make my march onward. I regret that I cannot have some of the new regiments from your state.

I am glad that your Senators[2] are better disposed towards the confirmation of McPherson.[3] He belongs to a class of men that we have to few of. We cannot afford to loose them. Such men as McPherson, Sherman, Crocker, Hamilton and a few others I have got are worth more each than a Brigade of troops under such commanders as some that have been promoted.

I will write a letter to-day renewing my recommendations for Brigadier Generals.[4] Col. Reid's name will be embraced in the list.

It is but a few minuets now until the mail closes and I have another letter to write.

My regards to your family,   Write to me again and I will endeavor to find time to answer.

Yours truly

U. S. GRANT

Maj. Gen. Com

ALS, CoHi. See letter to Brig. Gen. Grenville M. Dodge, Oct. 24, 1862.

1. According to an unpublished inventory of the Hudson material in CoHi, prepared by Sidney G. Morse, 1970, family tradition identified this nephew as Private John B. Hudson, 12th Ohio, who rejected an offer of a staff appointment from USG because he believed that too many of USG's relatives had already advanced through family ties rather than merit. Peter T. Hudson, later appointed to USG's staff, although a brother of Silas A. Hudson, is more likely to be the person involved. See letter to Edwin M. Stanton, Nov. 27, 1862.
2. Presumably Iowa Senators James Harlan and James W. Grimes.
3. See letter to Maj. Gen. Henry W. Halleck, Dec. 14, 1862.
4. See preceding letter.

Special Field Orders No. 6

—————

Headquarters, 13th Army Corps.
Dept. of the Tennessee
LaGrange, Tenn, Nov 16th 1862.

SPECIAL FIELD ORDERS No 6.

The facts having been officially reported to the Major General Commanding, that a potion of the 20th Regt. Illinois Infantry Vols., did, on the night of the 7th day of November inst at Jackson, Tenn, break into the store of G M.[*W*] Graham & Co and take therefrom goods to the value $841.40 the property of said Graham & Co and did cut the tent of R B. Kent and N A. Bass, and take there from goods to the value of $345, the property of said Kent and Bass and burn and destroy the tent and poles, also the property of said Kent and Bass of the value of $56.25, all of which damages amount to the sum of $1,242.66, and it further appearing from said report that Capt C L. Page, Co. "D," Captain J M. North, Co. "E," Capt G W. Kennard, Co. "I," Lieutenants Harry King, Co. "B," Wm. Seas, Co. "C," John Edmonston, Co. "E," David Wadsworth Co. "F," J Bailey, Co. "F," Victor H. Stevens, Co. "H," R M. Evens, Co. "I," Charles Taylor, Co. "I," of said Regiment were absent from their commands at the time of the prepetration of these outrages, in violation of orders, and without cause, when they should have been present, and, also, that Capt Orton Frisbee, of Co. "H," acting in the capacity of Major and Capt John Tunnison of Co., "G," the senior captain, immediately after the commission of these depredations did not exercise their authority to ferret out the men guilty of the offences, but that, on the contrary Capt Tunnison interposed to prevent search and discovery of the parties really guilty, and that, Capt Frisbee after the commission of said depredations, being in command of the Regiment, remained behind twenty four hours after the Regiment marched, and the names of the individual parties guilty not having been disclosed it is therefore ordered.

1d That the said sum of twelve hundred and forty two dollars and Sixty Six cents be assessed against said Regiment and the Officers herein before named, excepting such enlisted men as were at the time sick in Hospital or absent with proper authority, that the same be charged against them on the proper Muster and Pay Rolls, and the amount each is to pay noted opposite his name thereon: the Officers to be assessed pro-rata with the men on the amount of their pay proper: and that the same so collected will be paid by the commanding Officer of the Regiment to the parties intitled to the same.

2d. That Capt Orton Frisbee[1] and Capt John Tunnison of the 20th Regt. Illinois Infy. Vols., for wilful neglect of duty and violation of orders are hereby mustered out the service of the United States to take effect this day.

By order of Maj. Genl U S. Grant,
JNO A R[AWLINS]
Asst. Adjt. Genl

DS, DNA, RG 94, Dept. of the Tenn., General Orders; copies, *ibid.*, RG 393, Dept. of the Tenn., Special Orders; *ibid.*, General and Special Orders; DLC-USG, V, 26, 27. *O.R.*, I, xvii, part 2, 349–50.

On Nov. 8, 1862, Maj. Gen. Stephen A. Hurlbut wrote to USG. "Last night the 20th Illinois broke into and robbed two stores near Depot while waiting transportation. I did not learn the facts until the regiment had left. I will forward proofs and reque[st] that the Regiment may turn out the guilty parties or damage be assessed against them. Officers as usual had abandoned their men." Copy, DNA, RG 393, District of West Tenn., 4th Division, Letters Sent. On Nov. 22, USG wrote to Brig. Gen. Lorenzo Thomas. "I have the honor to transmit herewith. copy of Special Feild Orders, No 6 of date November 16th, 1862, and report of Col. C. C. Marsh of depradations committed by the 20th Reg't. Illinois Vol's, on the 7th Inst at Jackson, Tenn. 8 inclosures" LS, *ibid.*, RG 94, Muster Rolls of Vol. Organizations, Civil War, 20th Ill. The enclosures are *ibid.*

1. On Dec. 8, Capt. Orton Frisbie wrote to USG asking a trial by military commission or court-martial. On Dec. 20, USG endorsed this letter. "This regiment is one of the best in the service. It was at the Battle of Fredericktown, Fort Donelson, Pittsburg Landing and Britton's Lane, and in all of them behaved most gallantly. At the latter place it was Commanded by Capt Frisbie who has had the immediate Command of it since (up to the date of depradations Committed at Jackson and permitted it to run down in its discipline. The Colonel being in Command of a Brigade and Lieut Col (unable for field duty) absent on recruiting service at that time. A. Court of inquiry was not Convened for the reason that the Army was on the move rendering it impracticable, which reasons still exist. The order alluded to was made after full investigation and report of Col. Marsh

Comd'g Brigade, and was deemed absolutely necessary to prevent further viola-
tion of Military discipline and violation of oft repeated orders. Attention is Called
to the order and proceedings in the Case which have been duly forwarded to
Headquarters of the Army at Washington D C." Copies, DLC-USG, V, 25;
DNA, RG 393, Dept. of the Tenn., Endorsements. On Dec. 28, USG endorsed
a similar letter from Frisbie. "Respectfully forwarded to Head quarters of the
Army Washington D. C. and attention invited to the endorsement on a similar
Case forwarded on the 20th Inst." Copies, *ibid.* See *Calendar*, Sept. 4, 1861.

To Brig. Gen. Lorenzo Thomas

Headquarters 13th Army Corps
Department of the Tennessee
La Grange, Tenn. Nov. 16. 1862

BRIG. GEN. L. THOMAS,
ADJUT. GEN'L OF THE ARMY
WASHINGTON D. C.
GENERAL:

I have the honor to acknowledge the receipt of a communication of Captain P. A. Taylor, of the 81st Regiment Ohio Inft.
Volunteers of date October 18. 1862, referred to me for report
by order of the Secretary of War of date 7th November inst.[1]
and in compliance therewith to submit the following:

At the suggestion of the Governor of the State of Ohio, the
following order was made, to-wit:

"Headquarters District of West Tennessee
Corinth, Miss. Aug 3, 1862

SPECIAL ORDERS, No. 152.

7. Companies "E." "H." "F." and "G." of the 81st
Regiment Ohio Volunteers, in the Army of the United States
having been reduced by casualties so materially as to render
their entire organization inefficient and inconvenient, will be
consolidated into two Companies. All the Company Officers
will be retained in command, except Captain C. M. Hughes
of Company "H;" Capt. R. B. Kinsell, of Company "G.;"
and 2nd Lieut. M. G. Bailey, who will be permitted honor-

ably to retire from the service.—The enlisted men of Companies "H." and "G" will be assigned and distributed to Companies "E." and "F" of said Regiment, in such proportion as to make them as nearly the same in numbers as practicable. The Non-Commissioned Company Officers will be appointed by the Colonel Commanding on the recommendation of the respective Commanders of said Companies "E." and "F" Captains C. M. Hughes and R. B. Kinsell, and Lieut M. G. Bailey will be permitted to resign, having signified their willingness so to do.

Col. Thomas Morten, of said Regiment will attend to the execution of this order.

By order of Maj. Gen. U. S. Grant
Jno. A. Rawlins
Assist. Adjut. Gen'l"

The Regiment was consolidated as directed by the order, the excess of officers tendering their resignations which were accepted, and forwarded to Headquarters of the Army, Washington. On the 20th day of October last, five hundred and sixty-two (562) recruits joined said Regiment, at Corinth, Miss., sent out by Governor Todd, of Ohio, making the present aggregate strength of the 81st Ohio 926 and Completing the Regimental organization.

I am, General
Very Respectfully
Your Ob't Sev't
U. S. Grant
Maj Genl

LS, DNA, RG 94, Vol. Service Division, Letters Received, T584 (VS) 1862.

1. In this letter, Capt. Peter A. Tyler, 81st Ohio, suggested that since the regt. was so reduced in number, the men should be mustered out in order to join other regts. or the existing regt. should be filled. ALS, *ibid.* On Nov. 7, 1862 Maj. Thomas M. Vincent endorsed this letter. "Respectfully referred to Major General U S Grant, Comdg 13th Army Corps for report   Please return this paper"   ES, *ibid.* On Oct. 20, Tyler wrote again to Secretary of War Edwin M. Stanton to report the arrival of 580 recruits. ALS, *ibid.*

To Brig. Gen. Charles S. Hamilton

La Grange, Tenn., November 16th 1862
Brig. Gen'l. C. S. Hamilton,
Com'd'g. Left Wing

Relieve Quinbys Division with one of the others, and direct him to move to Moscow, eight miles west of La Grange. I will send Cavalry from McPhersons command for him.

If I do not get over to see you to-morrow, I would like you to come here the next day.

U. S. Grant,
Maj. Gen'l.

Telegram, copies, DLC-USG, V, 18, 30; DNA, RG 393, Dept. of the Tenn., Letters Sent; *ibid.*, District of Corinth, Telegrams Received. *O.R.*, I, xvii, part 2, 349. On Nov. 16, 1862, Brig. Gen. Charles S. Hamilton telegraphed to USG. "Despatch recd. Ross will relieve Quinby early tomorrow morng   I will come & see you in the morng at 9 a. m. if you will be at home" Telegram received, DNA, RG 393, Dept. of the Tenn., Telegrams Received. On the same day, USG telegraphed to Hamilton. "I will be home" Copy, *ibid.*, District of Corinth, Telegrams Received.

On Nov. 15, Brig. Gen. Isaac F. Quinby telegraphed to USG. "All will be in readiness for you tomorrow   will have a dinner for you   best that can be served up here" Telegram received, *ibid.*, Dept. of the Tenn., Telegrams Received.

To George G. Pride

La Grange, Tenn., Nov. 16, 1862.

COL. G G. PRIDE
COLUMBUS, KY.,

Recent orders from Washington, will change former theories of repairs to railroads. I telegraphed you in St. Louis to suspend orders for locomotives and cars. We will not want any work done out from Memphis for the present. Telegraph to stop the purchase of cars except those already way.

U. S. GRANT,
Maj. Gen'l.

Telegram, copies, DLC-USG, V, 18, 30; DNA, RG 393, Dept. of the Tenn., Letters Sent. A telegram received, Parsons Papers, IHi, was received on Nov. 24, 1862, and this may indicate either that the telegram was delayed in reaching George G. Pride or that the copies in USG book records are misdated.

On Nov. 24, Pride, Chicago, telegraphed to USG. "Have arranged for six (6) locomotives & 200 cars without troubling other lines   have angaged such men as required   leave tonight Memphis via St Louis   Telegraphe me Columbus" Telegram received, DNA, RG 393, Dept. of the Tenn., Telegrams Received.

On Nov. 25, Pride, St. Louis, twice telegraphed to USG. "Returnd from Chicago & recd you despatch to suspend   I made arrangements in Chicago for enough rolling stock for road already in operation & from LaGrange to Memphis without detriment to existing lines   Shall I Countermand the above orders   have engagd such men as I require for shops at Memphis & some portion of materials are already on way   I wait orders here"   "Will cars run from Memphis to LaGrange   if so we will want the six locomotives & also the men I have engaged the changes in Locomotives are in progress for our use"   Telegrams received, *ibid.* On the same day, USG telegraphed to Pride. "The road from Memphis to LaGrange will not be built." Copies, DLC-USG, V, 18, 30; DNA, RG 393, Dept. of the Tenn., Letters Sent. See telegram to Maj. Gen. Henry W. Halleck, Nov. 13, 1862.

To Brig. Gen. Lorenzo Thomas

Headquarters, 13th Army Corps.
Department of the Tennesse[e]
L Grange, Tenn. Nov 17th 1862.

Brig Gen L Thomas
Adjutant General of the Army,
Washington D. C.
General

I have the honor to transmit herewith triplicate copies of the return of the forces under command for Oct 31st 1862. I hope to be able to forward a more full and satisfactory return by the meeting of Congress.

17 Regts of Infantry and 2 Batteries of Light Art'y have arrived since the 1st inst from which returns have not been recd.

I am General
Very Respectfully
Your obt servt
U S. Grant
Major General.

Copies, DLC-USG, V, 5, 8, 24, 88; DNA, RG 393, Dept. of the Tenn., Hd. Qrs. Correspondence. Figures for USG's command for this period are available from dept. returns for Oct. and Nov. 10, 1862. DS, *ibid.*, RG 94, Dept. of the Tenn., Returns. These are summarized in *O.R.*, I, xvii, part 2, 311, 337–42.

On Dec. 1, Brig. Gen. William F. Barry, inspector of art., wrote to USG requesting a detailed return of art. in his command. Copies, DLC-USG, V, 88; DNA, RG 393, 13th Army Corps, Letters Sent; *ibid.*, 16th Army Corps, 1st Division, Letters Received; McClernand Papers, IHi.

To Col. Lewis B. Parsons

By Telegraph from Lagrange Nov. 17 *186[2]*

To Col. L. B. Parsons
A Q M. St. Louis

Requisitions are forwarded to you today for six (6) locomotives & two hundred (200) cars—Gen'l Halleck telegraphs they cant get them in the East—Visit the roads in the northwst & west and get the roads to furnish each one (1) or two (2) and have them altered to five (5) feet guage and send to Memphis—Answer and keep us advised what we can depend upon—are in great haste

U. S. Grant
Maj Genl

Telegram received, Parsons Papers, IHi; copies (3), *ibid.*; (misdated Nov. 19, 1862), *ibid.* Lewis B. Parsons, born in Genesee County, N.Y., in 1818, graduated from Yale and Harvard Law School, practiced law in Alton, Ill. (1844–59), then was connected in several capacities (including president) with the Ohio and Mississippi Railroad. In the Civil War he first served on the staff of Maj. Gen. George B. McClellan, was appointed asst. q. m. and capt. as of Oct. 31, 1861, and on Dec. 9 was assigned to supervise all transportation of the Dept. of the Miss., retaining this duty after confirmation of his promotion to col. on July 17, 1862. Harry E. Pratt, "Lewis B. Parsons: Mover of Armies and Railroad Builder," *Journal of the Illinois State Historical Society*, XLIV, 4 (Winter, 1951), 349–54.

On Nov. 17, George G. Pride wrote to Parsons. "Gen Grant telegraphed you today that We needed Six Locomotives, and Two Hundred cars, and wished you to visit personally, roads in Indiana, Michigan and the Northwest and procure the Engines—Gen Halleck telegraphs they cannot be procured at the East—The supposition is, you can obtain one or two Engines from a road, and have them changed at their Shops to five feet guages   These Engines are needed at the shortest possible moment to open the road *South* from Memphis—of the cars We will want fifty platform cars, and the balance of the number box cars—Seventy five cars to be sent to Columbus and the rest to Memphis—The first you get to go to Memphis—also please order us five good hand cars for Memphis—The Northwest roads have not been called upon much for Engines, and they must help—We hope you will within two weeks start a portion of above on the way, as our army cannot move without them—They are a number of cars in course of construction at Dayton which might be taken—"   ALS, Parsons Papers, IHi. USG endorsed this letter "Approved." AES, *ibid.* On the same day, USG signed a special requisition for six locomotives and two hundred railroad cars. DS, *ibid.*

On Nov. 18, USG telegraphed to Col. Robert Allen, St. Louis. "Is Col

Parsons in St Louis? If not when will he return? I have ordered machinery from him." Copies, DLC-USG, V, 18, 30; DNA, RG 393, Dept. of the Tenn., Letters Sent. On Nov. 19, Capt. Charles Parsons, St. Louis, telegraphed to USG. "Col Parsons is in Ohio buying cars—He has engaged fifty Cars—H. M Woodward &C. here have forty (40) Twenty cars building which will be done in Thirty days —I have repeated your Message to Col Parsons" Telegram received, *ibid.*, RG 107, Telegrams Collected (Unbound).

On Nov. 20, Col. Lewis Parsons telegraphed to USG. "Your dispatch of the 19th inst, is received. I shall not wait your requisition but go to Chicago at once where I hope to get all you require. There are at least 10,000 Cars on the Rail-roads terminating there. Will you not be likely to want more & would it not be better to make requisitions on them for 500 Cars & 10 locomotives and take at once what you now require and others as wanted." Copies (3), Parsons Papers, IHi; telegram received, DNA, RG 107, Telegrams Collected (Unbound). An inspection of the contents of a telegram of Nov. 22 printed in *O.R.*, I, xvii, part 2, 355–56, as sent from Parsons to USG indicates that it must have been addressed to some other officer.

On Dec. 2, Parsons telegraphed to USG. "The Cars will begin to arrive at Cairo within a few days. Can I not deliver them at Columbus instead of Memphis? It can be done much sooner & cheaper, & Mr Stevens desires them so delivered, if satisfactory to you" ALS (telegram sent), Parsons Papers, IHi. On Dec. 3, USG telegraphed to Parsons. "Deliver Cars at Columbus Ky there is the place I want them" Telegram received, *ibid.*; copies, DLC-USG, V, 18, 30, 91; DNA, RG 393, Dept. of the Tenn., Letters Sent. On Jan. 28, 1863, Allen telegraphed to USG. "What is to be done with the six 6 locomotives & one hundred 100 cars purchased by your orders they are refused at Columbus" Telegram received, *ibid.*, RG 107, Telegrams Collected (Unbound).

To Brig. Gen. Charles S. Hamilton

La Grange Tenn Nov 18 1862

BRIG GENL C. S. HAMILTON
COMD'G LEFT. WING

McArthur has not yet sent a Regiment to Grand Junction to guard the Contrabands, and form the Provost Guard for that place The Regiment should take their camp equppage and go into Camp There was also a detail of three men from Genl Ross' Division ordered at the same time to report to Mr Eaton, in charge of Contrabands who have not yet reported.

U. S. GRANT
Maj Genl.

Copies, DLC-USG, V, 18, 30; DNA, RG 393, Dept. of the Tenn., Letters Sent. On Nov. 18, 1862, Chaplain John Eaton telegraphed to Lt. Col. John A. Rawlins. "Regiment ordered has arrived   the Col has recd no orders to releive the present provost & hospital guards" Telegram received, *ibid.*, Telegrams Received. See telegram to Maj. Gen. Henry W. Halleck, Nov. 15, 1862.

On Nov. 17, USG had telegraphed twice to the provost marshal, Grand Junction. "Send to their Regiments all Soldiers at the Junction, not in Hospital or otherwise properly detailed"   "The property of Mrs Smith at Grand Junction must be protected, and rails hauled by Government Teams and fence rebuilt by the troops. Mrs Smith is not only Union, but her husband on account of his sentiments, was forced to leave his home, and has been in our service for several months" Copies, DLC-USG, V, 18, 30; DNA, RG 393, Dept. of the Tenn., Letters Sent. On Nov. 19, Rawlins wrote twice to Lt. Col. John McDermott, 15th Mich., Grand Junction. "The guard on duty at Contraband Depot previous to your arrival, will be relieved and ordered to rejoin their Regiment at once" "Your Regiment will form the Garrison and Provost Guard for Grand Junction. One Company will be sufficient for the Provost Guard, and one of the Field officers if you have a full number should be appointed Provost Marshall, if not a Company officer will be selected. The remainder of the Regiment will form the Guard for the protection and control of the Contrabands in their Camp and when taken beyond our Guards to work   Chaplan J Eaton Jr's requisitions for troops to accompany working parties of these people when employed at labor will be respected. During the day Citizens will be permitted to pass to and fro without written passes unless you have reason to suspect them, and in that event they may be arrested and their cases reported to the Provost Marshall Genl at these Head Quarters. Permits may be given all loyal Citizens to travel on the Rail road   No officer or Soldiers will be permitted to travel on the Rail Road without a leave of absence, in case of a commissioned officer, or a discharge in case of a Soldier, in either case the evidence of permission, must be from these Head Quarters. Officers and Soldiers in the performance of duty may be required to travel on the Rail Road, but in all such cases they will have evidence of the duty upon which they are engaged with them   Such tools and Mechanics as your command affords in such work as Chaplan Eaton may desire to have done to enable him to carry out his instructions   Public teams with the Regiment may be employed in like manner" Copies, *ibid.* The second letter is misdated Dec. 19 in DLC-USG, V, 18; DNA, RG 393, Dept. of the Tenn., Letters Sent.

Perhaps intending to replace the regt. sent to Grand Junction, on Nov. 19, USG telegraphed to Maj. Gen. Stephen A. Hurlbut. "Send 95th regt Ills Vols to report to Gen Hamilton south of Grand Junction" Telegram received, *ibid.*, District of West Tenn., 4th Division, Telegrams Received; copies, *ibid.*, Dept. of the Tenn., Letters Sent; DLC-USG, V, 18, 30. On Nov. 20, Hurlbut wrote to Rawlins. "Fosters Cavalry will leave in the morning by land to report at La Grange. The 95th Illinois will leave by rail tomorrow at 8. A.M. to report at Grand Junction to General Hamilton   Notify him that he may have them conducted to camp" Copy, DNA, RG 393, District of West Tenn., 4th Division, Letters Sent. On Nov. 17, Hurlbut had written to USG. "Part of the 4th Illinois cavalry and Fosters company are on an expidition after the fr[a]gment of Falkmers band.   as soon as they return they will be sent forward." Copy, *ibid.* On the same day, Hurlbut wrote to Rawlins. "I beg to call the attention of Major General Grant to the condition of the 54th and 62d Illinois. at the upper end of the

Road, (from Union city to Trenton)   Both as a matter of health and discipline these regiments should be removed. I understand that their places were to be supplied by new troops, but none have been assigned. If the 7th Tennessee Infantry now, as I am Informed at Dresden, (by special order from Department Head quarters) is fit for purpose they might relieve the 54th and occupy the Obion bridges and swamps. It is possible that some other regiment may be designated to relieve the 62d. I do not consider it safe to reduce the garrison at Trenton or Humboldt any farther while the partisan rangers are reported in such force at Waverly. The 95th Illinois now here, is a good regiment, well armed, and in a fair state of drill, and if another regiment is required soon at the front, may be sent forward." Copy, *ibid*.

To Brig. Gen. Isaac F. Quinby

La Grange Tenn Nov 18 1862

BRIG GENL J F QUINBY
DAVIS MILLS MISS

You may permit all persons living at home to save their Cotton and bring it in for sale. Such persons as are known to be in the Southern Army or contributed directly and voluntarily to the support of the Rebellion, their cotton may be taken if they have any and sent here to be sold for the benefit of the Government[1] Persons who prefer taking their cotton to Memphis may be permitted to do so. Persons whose Negroes have run off, and have cotton yet to Pick will be allowed to hire the negroes in charge of Government here

U. S. GRANT
Maj Gen C.

Copies, DLC-USG, V, 18, 30; DNA, RG 393, Dept. of the Tenn., Letters Sent. *O.R.*, I, xvii, part 2, 354. On Nov. 18, 1862, 4 P.M., Brig. Gen. Isaac F. Quinby, Moscow, Tenn., telegraphed to USG. "The 2d Brigade of my Division reach here just at dark last night. The first Brig camped five miles back and came in at 7 oclk this Morning. I have occupied the day so far in examining my surroundings establishing Pickets &c. There is a large amount of Rail Road property here consisting of Wheels & ale axels together and Detached Locomotive ties &c   The people are taking cotton in large quantities to Memphis and bringing back all sorts of commodities, contraband and otherwise   I have stopped it until further orders. Have ordered all roads running south from Memphis & Charleston except that from here obstructed. All Teams coming from Charleston to report here, and teams taking cotton turned back.   there is some cotton about here unpicked, but a large amount picked & ginned and unginned. I have directed it to be kept until I receive your orders about it"   Copy, DNA, RG 393, 15th Army Corps, District of Corinth, Letters Sent. *O.R.*, I, xvii, part 2, 353–54. On the same day, Quinby also wrote to Lt. Col. John A. Rawlins concerning surplus teams. *Ibid.*, p. 354.

On Nov. 19, Quinby wrote to USG. "Major Nelson, Seventh Illinois Cavalry, reports the enemy's pickets on the two roads to the west of that running from this place to Holly Springs. The Seventh Illinois Cavalry is mostly armed with Smith's carbines, and for these there are but 6 rounds of ammunition each. I will obstruct all of these roads for 15 miles running south from the wagon road to Memphis, except the first, unless you should otherwise order. May I ask you to order ammunition for Smith's carbine—an excellent arm? There is much work for my small cavalry force; could use two companies more to advantage." *Ibid.*, p. 354. On Nov. 20, USG wrote to Quinby. "I will order the ammunition you ask for. Will also order two more companies of Cavalry to report to you. Obstruct the roads as you suggest, but leave the road to Holly Springs free, we will want to use that"   Copies, DLC-USG, V, 18, 30; DNA, RG 393, Dept. of the Tenn., Letters Sent.

1. On Nov. 1, USG wrote a pass. "Mrs M. Bradstreet of Cincinnati has permission to pass South to Vicksburg via the Mississippi river and return with a cargo of Cotton to Memphis Ten. The pass for Mrs B. being subject to the approval of the Secretary of State—Washington D C.—and the permit for the Cotton—subject to the approval of the Sec. of the Treasury." Copy, *ibid.*, RG 107, Letters Received. USG also endorsed this pass. "This conditional pass is given solely on the letter of Secretary Chase accompanying the application.—Without the endorsement of such authority, applications of this kind would not be entertained." Copy, *ibid.* On Oct. 8, Secretary of the Treasury Salmon P. Chase had written to E. P. Bradstreet, Cincinnati. "The Secretary of the Interior has referred to me for answer your letter to him of the 27th ulto asking whether your wife would be allowed. to go beyond the lines of our army in Mississippi to procure Cotton from her friends and relatives resident there, and bring the same north. The question of passing through the lines of the army is one exclusively within the control of the military authorities—Should they sanction the proposed transaction, their permit will be necessary to bring the cotton to a port open to commerce. Having arrived there under such authority, a permit or clearance from an officer of this Department will be required to ensure its further transit North or East: but no obstructions will be interposed on account of the source from which it was obtained. I enclose for your further information a copy of the 'Regulatio[ns] concerning Internal and coastwise Commercial Intercourse'" Copy, *ibid.*

On Nov. 13, Lt. Col. Charles A. Reynolds, chief q. m., Dept. of the Tenn., issued orders by authority of USG concerning the seizure and sale of cotton. Julian K. Larke, *General Grant and his Campaigns* (New York, 1864), pp. 139–40.

On Nov. 14, Quinby had telegraphed to Rawlins. "A negro wagon left here about noon today with 4 bales of cotton which Genl Hamilton had just ordered to be seized for Gov't benefit. he went to Lagrange with it—The speculators are reaping a harvest out of such transactions, would it not be well to regulate them or drive them out of the country—" Telegram received, DNA, RG 393, Dept. of the Tenn., Telegrams Received.

On Nov. 18, USG telegraphed to D. W. Fairchild, Jackson, Tenn. "You have permission to visit La Grange Tenn Your first despatch was answered" Copies, DLC-USG, V, 18, 30; DNA, RG 393, Dept. of the Tenn., Letters Sent. On Nov. 16, Fairchild had telegraphed to USG. "Will you send me permit to Come to LaGrange by this evenngs train" Telegram received, *ibid.*, Telegrams Received. On Nov. 21, Fairchild wrote to USG's hd. qrs. asking to purchase four government horses or mules to haul cotton. DLC-USG, V, 21. Sylvanus Cadwallader concluded a quarrel with cotton-buyer D. W. Fairchild by thrashing him; according to Cadwallader, this pleased USG. Benjamin P. Thomas, ed., *Three Years with Grant as Recalled by War Correspondent Sylvanus Cadwallader* (New York, 1955), pp. 22–23; Fairchild statement, Nov. 27, 1862, DLC-Cadwallader. For the burning of Fairchild's cotton at Holly Springs, see letter of "Junius," Holly Springs, Dec. 26, 1862, *New York Tribune*, Jan. 5, 1863.

On Nov. 18, Capt. Robert E. Bryant, La Grange, wrote to USG asking whether "a gentleman of wealth" from Indianapolis would be allowed to purchase cotton at La Grange. On Nov. 19, USG endorsed this letter. "All that is required is a Treasury Permit which can be obtained from the Surveyor of the Port at Cairo" Copy, DNA, RG 393, Dept. of the Tenn., Endorsements; DLC-USG, V, 25.

On Nov. 19, Rawlins issued General Orders No. 8. "In addition to permits from the Treasury Department, all persons are required to have a permit from the Local Provost Marshal at the Post, before purchasing Cotton or other Southern products in this Department, and shipping the same North. It will be regarded as evidence of disloyalty for persons to go beyond the lines of the Army to purchase Cotton or other products, and all contracts made for such articles, in advance of the Army, or for Cotton in the Field, are null and void, and all parties so offending will be expelled from the Department. Freight Agents on Military Railroads will report daily to the Post Provost Marshal all Cotton or other private property shipped by them, and when shipments are made by persons who have not the proper permits, notice will be given, by Telegraph, to the Provost Marshal at Columbus, Ky., who will seize the goods for the benefit of Government. The Federal Army being now in the occupancy of West Tennessee to the Mississippi line, and it being no part of the policy of the Government to oppress, or cause unnecessary suffering to those who are not in active rebellion, hereafter, until otherwise directed, licenses will be granted by District Commanders to loyal persons at all Military stations within the Department, to keep for sale, subject to the Treasury Regulations, such articles as are of prime necessity for families, and sell the same to all citizens, who have taken, or may voluntarily take, the oath of allegiance, and who have permits from the Provost Marshal, obtained under oath, that all goods to be purchased are for their own and for their family's use, and that no part thereof is for sale or for the use of any person other than those named in the permit. Permits so given will be good until countermanded, and all violations of trading permits will be punished by the forfeiture of the permit, fine and imprisonment, at the discretion of a Military Commission. Particular attention is called to existing orders prohibiting the employment or use of Government teams for hauling private property. All Cotton brought to stations or places for shipment in this Department, by Government teams, will be seized by the Quarter-Master's Department for the benefit of Government, and persons claiming such property expelled from the Department. It is made the duty of all officers and especially of Local Provost Marshals to see that this order is rigidly enforced." Copies, *ibid.*, V, 13, 14, 95; DNA, RG 393, Dept. of the Tenn., General and Special Orders; *ibid.*, RG 109, Union Provost Marshals' File of Papers Relating to Individual Civilians; (printed) Oglesby Papers, IHi. *O.R.*, I, lii, part 1, 302–3.

On Nov. 19, USG telegraphed to the commanding officers, Cairo and Columbus. "Pass all bagging and rope for baling Cotton through without regard to District or Department permits, so that Treasury Permits are obtained" Copies, DLC-USG, V, 18, 30; DNA, RG 393, Dept. of the Tenn., Letters Sent.

On Dec. 2, USG telegraphed to "All commanders." "Genl order No 8 restricting trade is suspende[d] retail trade in all articles not contraband of War will only be restricted as may be deemed for the good of the service in the judgement of the several district commanders" Telegram received, *ibid.*, 16th Army Corps, 4th Division, Telegrams Received; Brayman Papers, ICHi.

On Nov. 23, USG telegraphed to Brig. Gen. Jeremiah C. Sullivan. "There is said to be in Jackson a cotton buyer from Cincinnati by the name of Handy who at home is known as a secessionists He is reported to have made overtures by which he would smuggle ~~Quinine~~ through our lines Quinine Arrest him" Telegram received, DNA, RG 393, 16th Army Corps, 4th Division, Telegrams Received. *O.R.*, I, xvii, part 2, 357. See General Orders No. 11, Dec. 17, 1862.

To Maj. Gen. Earl Van Dorn

Head Quarters, Dept. of the Ten.
Lagrange Nov. 19th 1862

MAJ. GEN. E. A. VAN DORN
ABBERVILLE MISS.
GEN.

Your note of yesterday[1] in relation to Haywoods Cavalry[2] and the release of Lieut. Sullivan,[3] your Aid-de-Camp, is just received.

I will order the immediate release on parole of all of Capt. Haywoods men now in our hands.[4] You may regard the release of Lieut. Sullivan as final and complete and I will so regard that of Capt. Silence.[5]

Accompanying your letter was one from Chief of Cavalry W. H. Jackson relative to the seizure of two horses by Col. Lee from Hospital Steward and Medical Director to his command, and making enquiry whether this is to be regarded as a precedent.[6]

To this I only have to reply that it is following every prescedent that has come to my knowledge since the begining of this war. There has been no instance to my knowledge when one of our surgeons has been permitted, after capture, to retain his horse or even his private packet instruments. In the very last instance of the capture of one of our surgeons by southern troops, at Britton's Lane,[7] the Surgeon was deprived of his horse.

I am disposed however to deal as leniently as possible with all captives and am willing in future to adopt as a rule of action that none of the necessary camp & garrison equipments, or accompanyments, of that class of persons who, by agreement, are exempted from arrest as prisoners of war shall be taken. This of course to be mutual with both parties.[8]

> I am Gen. Very respectfully
> your obt. svt.
> U. S. GRANT
> Maj. Gen. Com

ALS, ICarbS. *O.R.*, II, iv, 729.

1. On Nov. 17, 1862, C. S. A. Maj. Gen. Earl Van Dorn, Abbeville, Miss., wrote to "The Commanding Officer, U. S. Forces—Near La Grange." "I have to reply in answer to your communication relative to Capt Haywoods Company of Partizan Rangers.—I have made necessary enquiries relative to this company, and find that he received full and proper authority to raise a Battalion of Cavalry, and that they belong regularly to the Confederate Service, and are entitled to all the rights of Confederate Troops. I wish to enquire if Capt S. O. Silence U. S. A., Recruiting Officer, 1st Tenn Cavalry, has been accepted in Exchange for Lt. C. Sullivan, my aid-de-camp, captured at Hatchie Bridge, and paroled? Capt S. O. Silence, U. S. A. was sent with Lt. Col. Ducal, U. S A. who bore a Flag of Truce to these Hd. Qrs. from General Rosecrans', about the 20th of October, 1862. I have also the honor to acknowledge the receipt of Captain T. W. Harris A. A. G and Capt Wm. Clark A. C. S captured at & near Holly Springs, who are recieved & acknowledged as prisoners of war and their names will be sent as others to the proper authorities for exchange" LS, DNA, RG 393, Dept. of the Tenn., Letters Received. *O.R.*, II, iv, 946–47. On Nov. 19, Brig. Gen. Leonard F. Ross, Davis' Mill, telegraphed to USG. "I have just forwarded to you a document addressed to the comdg officer of the U S forces at Lagrange   it was brought to

our outpost by an officer & escorted by 150 men. I am informed that he waits your reply" Telegram received, DNA, RG 393, Dept. of the Tenn., Telegrams Received. On Nov. 20, Ross telegraphed to Lt. Col. John A. Rawlins. "The answer to Flag of Truce has been forwarded by Capt Ryan" Telegram received, *ibid.*

2. See telegram to Maj. Gen. Henry W. Halleck, Oct. 23, 1862. On Oct. 24, Maj. Gen. Stephen A. Hurlbut referred to Rawlins an inquiry from Maj. Gen. James B. McPherson concerning prisoners of Haywood's Cav. AES, DNA, RG 393, District of West Tenn., 4th Division, Letters Received. On the same day, Rawlins endorsed this letter. "The within named prisoners will be sent to Alton, Ill. for confinement. They are not regarded as regular Cavalry" ES, *ibid.*

3. See telegram to Brig. Gen. Charles S. Hamilton, Nov. 1, 1862, note 2.

4. See following letter.

5. See telegram to Brig. Gen. Charles S. Hamilton, Nov. 1, 1862, note 1.

6. On Nov. 18, C. S. A. Col. William H. Jackson wrote a letter delivered to USG. "States that Col Lee in his raid on Holly Springs captured a Surgeon & Hos. Steward and asks if he is to take this as a precedent for his future operations, their horses and equipments being taken from them and they forced to walk back to their lines." DLC-USG, V, 21.

7. On Sept. 1, C. S. A. Act. Brig. Gen. Frank C. Armstrong skirmished with troops under Col. Elias S. Dennis, 30th Ill., at Britton's Lane, Tenn., near Denmark, about ten miles southwest of Jackson.

8. On Dec. 6, Rawlins wrote to Brig. Gen. Grenville M. Dodge. "The General Commdg. has communicated with the Genl Commdg. Confederate Forces, on the subject of Army Surgeons, who are captured, right to retain their horses and other private property indicating his willingness to let them take with them when released everything that is necessary to enable them to perform their vocation in the field; but has not yet received a reply and until he does their horses and Surgical instruments will be held, they having set the example in depriving our Surgeons when captured of such property." Copies, *ibid.*, V, 18, 30, 91; DNA, RG 393, Dept. of the Tenn., Letters Sent; Dodge Papers, IaHA. *O.R.*, I, xvii, part 2, 388–89; *ibid.*, II, v, 32–33. No reply has been found to USG's offer.

On Oct. 31, Brig. Gen. James M. Tuttle, Cairo, had telegraphed to USG. "Nine (9) rebel Surgeons are here from Louisville   are anxious to go South shall I send them to you to be put through lines   no boat going to Vicksburg for some time—" Telegram received, DNA, RG 393, Dept. of the Tenn., Telegrams Received. On the same day, USG telegraphed to Tuttle. "Send the Rebel Surgeons by the way of Memphis with a note with my directions to Genl. Sherman to let them out that way. He can send them in ambulances under a flag of truce to the nearest rebel Garrison if he chooses" Copies, DLC-USG, V, 18, 30; DNA, RG 393, Dept. of the Tenn., Letters Sent. On Nov. 1, Col. William W. Lowe, Fort Henry, telegraphed to Rawlins. "I hold as prisoners two (2) Surgeons belonging to Napiers command   shall I release them under the Genl Order with reference to surgeons—" Telegram received, *ibid.*, Telegrams Received. On Nov. 1, Rawlins telegraphed to Lowe. "Release the two (2) surgeons and send them south via Memphis" Copies, DLC-USG, V, 18, 30; DNA, RG 393, Dept. of the Tenn., Letters Sent.

To Col. Jesse Hildebrand

Head Quarters 13th Army Corps
Department of the Tennessee
La Grange Tenn Nov 20. 1862

Col J Hilderbrandt Comdg 77th Ohio Vols
In charge of Military Prison
Alton Ill

I have made the status of Capt. Haywoods Cavalry (known as Partisan Rangers) the subject of a communication under flag of truce, and learn that he and his men are recognized as regularly in the Confederate Service, and entitled to the same treatment as other prisoners of War

You will therefore please send such officers and men belonging to said Cavalry as were sent from this Department to the Military Prison at Alton, to Cairo Illinois, there to be detained until such time as a cartel ship is going to Vicksburg, when they will be sent to Vicksburg as paroled prisoners, until duly exchanged

U. S. Grant
Maj Genl.

Copies, DLC-USG, V, 18, 30; DNA, RG 393, Dept. of the Tenn., Letters Sent. See preceding letter.

To Maj. Gen. James B. McPherson

Columbus 21st Nov [*1862*]

GENL MCPHERSON

Is all quiet on the front   no boat has arrived here since Wednesday[1] and it is reported that quite a number of boats are aground between here and Memphis. Riggin[2] may be on one of those boats and Sherman consequently not have my order to meet me here[3]   unless there is immediate necessity of my return I will remain here until Saturday   answer

U S GRANT
Maj Genl

Telegram received, McPherson Papers, NjR. An undated telegram from USG to Maj. Gen. James B. McPherson was probably sent the next day. "I will leave here this evening   meet me at the cars at Grand Junction in the evening   Sherman will be with me"   ALS, *ibid*. USG wrote out this telegram three times in order to put it in cipher; its presence in the McPherson Papers, however, indicates hand delivery.

1. Nov. 19, 1862.
2. On Nov. 17, Col. John Riggin, Jr., Columbus, Ky., telegraphed to USG. "Have been waiting here 24 hours for boat   will be off in few minutes"   Telegram received, DNA, RG 393, Dept. of the Tenn., Telegrams Received.
3. See letter to Maj. Gen. William T. Sherman, Nov. 14, 1862.

To Brig. Gen. Lorenzo Thomas

Headquarters 13th Army Corps
Department of the Tennessee
LaGrange, Tenn. Nov 22nd 1862.

BRIG GENL. L THOMAS
ADJT GENL. OF THE ARMY
WASHINGTON, D. C.
GENERAL,

In the case of Lieut George H Morgan,[1] 18th Mo Vols.

refered to me by order of the Secretary of War of date Oct 15th 1862, I have the honor to report that being unacquanted with the facts, I refered the same to the Governor of the state of Mo, to whose endorsement I would respectfully invite your attention, also to Governor Gamble's endorsement in the similar case of Capt F M. Bell,[2] of same Regiment, as the only report I am able to make

      hoping that the case may be finally decided,

I remain General
Very Respectfully
Your obt Servt
U S GRANT
Major Genl.

Copies, DLC-USG, V, 5, 8, 24, 88; DNA, RG 393, Dept. of the Tenn., Letters Sent. On Sept. 28, 1862, 2nd Lt. George H. Morgan, 18th Mo., wrote a letter requesting official recognition of his status. On Oct. 15, this letter was endorsed to USG by the AGO. "Respectfully referred to Maj. Gen. U. S. Grant for report. On the muster roll for April 30th, 1862, he is reported dismissed." Copies, *ibid.*, Endorsements; DLC-USG, V, 25. On Nov. 4, USG endorsed this letter. "Respectfully referred to his Excellency H. R. Gamble Governor of the State of Missouri who will please furnish these Headquarters with any information he may possess on the subject of the within papers" Copies, *ibid.* On Nov. 12, Act. Mo. AG William D. Wood endorsed this letter. "Respectfully returned. Commissions were issued to Officers of 18th. Mo. Vols. in accordance with a Roster furnished by Col. Miller by order of Act. Gov. Hall. No orders were ever issued from the A. G. O. effecting this regiment. If orders were issued by Col. Miller in the name of the Act'g Governor they are void and of no effect. Information has been received at this office through Col Bonneville that he had instructions to muster the original officers of this regiment." Copies, *ibid.*

On Nov. 24, Maj. Thomas M. Vincent wrote to USG. "I am directed by the Secretary of War to enclose you, a copy of a letter to his Excellency the Governor of Missouri, in which reference is made to two sets of Officers for the 18th Missouri Volunteers. So soon as the Governor appoints the new officers, for which he has the authority of the War Department, You will please cause the others to be mustered out of service   A copy of this letter has been furnished his Excellency" LS, DNA, RG 393, Dept. of the Tenn., Letters Received.

On Dec. 11, USG endorsed a letter of Governor Hamilton R. Gamble of Mo., Oct. 29, "Requesting that the 18th, Mo. Vols be sent home to recruit and to reorganize" "The services of this regiment although it is much reduced in numbers cannot at present be dispensed with without great detriment to the service" Copies, *ibid.*, Endorsements; DLC-USG, V, 25.

On Dec. 6, Wood wrote to USG. "I have the honor to enclose herewith a Roster of the Officers appointed in 18th Infantry Mo. Vols. on the 4th inst. by his Excellency the Governor under authority from the Secretary of War, dated

24th ulto. In accordance with said authority and instructions furnished you on same date you will please cause the other remaining Officers to be mustered out of service and forward to this office a copy of the muster." Copy, DNA, RG 393, Dept. of the Tenn., Letters Received. On Jan. 9, 1863, Vincent wrote to USG. "I am directed to enclose herewith copies of papers in reference to the officers of the 18th Missouri Volunteers (Infantry) and to inform you that the said officers, alone, will be recognized. In accordance with instructions of December 26th. 1862, a copy of which were sent you, all other officers will be mustered out of service under your orders." LS, *ibid.*

1. Although George H. Morgan had served as 2nd lt., 18th Mo., since July 25, 1861, he was never commissioned due to the confusion between the officers appointed by the governor of Mo. and those appointed by the lt. governor. On Nov. 29, 1862, he tendered his resignation "on acc't of ill health." DLC-USG, V, 21.

2. Francis M. Bell, serving as capt., 18th Mo., since Aug. 1, 1861, like Morgan never commissioned, was eventually mustered out.

To Act. Rear Admiral David D. Porter

By Telegraph from Jackson [*Nov.*] *22 1862*
To Commodore Porter

Gen. Sherman will move from Memphis towards Holly Springs on Wednesday[1] next. I will move on Saturday following; Genl Steele will also move from Helena on Grenada early the coming week   Any cooperation on the part of your Fleet will be of great assistance   Please answer giving me your programme.

U. S. Grant
Maj Genl.

Telegram received, DNA, RG 45, Correspondence of David D. Porter, Telegrams Received. *O.R.* (Navy), I, xxiii, 496–97. David D. Porter, born in 1813, was the son of Capt. David Porter, distinguished in the War of 1812, the brother of Commander William D. Porter, who commanded the gunboat *Essex* on the Fort Henry expedition, and the brother of Capt. David G. Farragut, adopted by the Porter family. David D. Porter, who entered the U. S. Navy as midshipman in 1829, accompanied Farragut on his expedition to New Orleans and up the Mississippi River, and, on Oct. 1, 1862, was assigned to replace Act. Rear Admiral Charles H. Davis in command of the Mississippi Squadron with the rank of act. rear admiral. *Ibid.*, p. 388. Porter stated that soon after his arrival at Cairo he informed USG of plans of Maj. Gen. John A. McClernand to command an expedition against Vicksburg, and discussed plans for a Vicksburg campaign with USG at dinner at Cairo. *Incidents and Anecdotes of the Civil War* (New York, 1885), pp. 125–26; *The Naval History of the Civil War* (New York, 1886), p. 284. Reporters stated that USG had been in Cairo on Nov. 20–21. *Missouri Republican, Chicago Tribune,* Nov. 22, 1862. Porter's anecdotes, however, are frequently unreliable. *DAB,* XV, 88. On Nov. 12, Maj. Gen. William T. Sherman had written to Porter about USG's plans. *O.R.,* I, xvii, part 2, 862–63.

On Nov. 22, Porter telegraphed to USG. "I have sent a large force to the mouth of the Yazoo river with some light draft vessels to prevent the Enemy from erecting fortifications, with orders to hold the position until we are ready to land the army, there will be two (2) iron clads left at Helena The rivers are too shallow for our vessels. I have a few vessels here where will you have them—" Telegram received, DNA, RG 393, Dept. of the Tenn., Telegrams Received. *O.R.,* I, xvii, part 2, 356; *O.R.* (Navy), I, xxiii, 497. On Nov. 23, USG telegraphed to Porter. "I cannot say what is best to do with the vessels you have at Cairo—you will be a much better judge in this matter than me. Some Gunboats should and I suppose will accompany the Transports from Helena" Telegram received, DNA, RG 45, Correspondence of David D. Porter, Telegrams Received. *O.R.* (Navy), I, xxiii, 497.

1. Nov. 26.

To Lt. Gen. John C. Pemberton

Head Quarters Dept of the Tennessee
La Grange Tenn Nov 23, 1862

LIEUT. GENL J PEMBERTON
COMDG JACKSON MISS
SIR

Your letter of the 19th inst reached here yesterday, during my temporary absence from this place, hence the delay in answering

The goods you speak of sending for the use of your wounded now confined to Hospitals in Iuka, will be received at any point between here and Abbeyville, say Holly Springs, and sent by our conveyance in charge of some responsible Officer to their destination Should you prefer sending these articles by your own conveyance, then they can go from some point on the Mobile and Ohio Rail Road by way of Bay Springs

This route will be left free for your ambulances whilst engaged in removing the sick and wounded

> I am Very Respectfully
> Your obt Servant.
> U S GRANT
> Maj Genl.

Copies, DLC-USG, V, 18, 30; DNA, RG 393, Dept. of the Tenn., Letters Sent. *O.R.*, II, iv, 747. On Nov. 19, 1862, C. S. A. Lt. Gen. John C. Pemberton wrote to "General Officer Comdg United States Forces, S. W. Tennessee" "With your consent I desire to send for the use of the sick & wounded soldiers of the Confedr Army now in hospital at Iuka—some necessary clothing, and also one thousand dollars with which to purchase provisions suitable to their condition— Will you be good enough to inform me at what point they shall be delivered— The stores will be forwarded to Abbeville there to await your decision—I propose also to send, say once a week ambulances for such convalescents as it may be proper to remove—I desire General to express my thanks for the kind treatment which the Confederate Surgeon in charge informs me has been extended to our sick and wounded by the U. S. authorities—at Iuka—Requesting as early a reply as may be convenient—" ALS, DNA, RG 393, Dept. of the Tenn., Letters Received. *O.R.*, II, iv, 731. On the same day, Pemberton wrote another letter identically addressed concerning the status of Capt. W. W. Faulkner and nineteen other members of the Partisan Ranger Corps, C. S. Army, who had been imprisoned rather than exchanged. *Ibid.* This letter was not entered in USG's registers and received no reply. For a virtually identical letter of Dec. 13 addressed directly to USG and USG's reply, see letter to Lt. Gen. John C. Pemberton, Dec. 15, 1862.

To Brig. Gen. Charles S. Hamilton

———

Jackson Nov 23rd [*1862*]

GENL HAMILTON

Rebel cavalry to the number probably fifteen hundred 1500 is reported in the neighborhood of Sommerville. Send Lee to-day with such Cavalry as you can spa[re] & call on McPherson for any additional he may want.

> U S. GRANT
> Maj Genl.

Telegram, copy, DNA, RG 393, District of Corinth, Telegrams Received. On Nov. 23, 1862, Brig. Gen. Charles S. Hamilton telegraphed to USG.

"I have intelligence from private sources that turnpike bridge, over Tallahatchie, is destroyed. The rebels use floating bridge. Price is on this side of Tallahatchie and Pemberton at Abbeville." *O.R.*, I, xvii, part 2, 357.

On Nov. 22, Brig. Gen. Mason Brayman, Bolivar, telegraphed to USG and Maj. Gen. Stephen A. Hurlbut. "A. man just from Somervill—2000 Rebel Cavalry there   he was taken prisoner & made his escape about 6 oclock. They threw pickets & appeared to have encamped—a reinforcement is needed along the road from here to Jackson. I have only about 800 men here   have sent parties out on Somerville road"   Copy, DNA, RG 393, District of Columbus, Telegrams Received. On Nov. 23, Brayman telegraphed to Lt. Col. John A. Rawlins. "Soon after Genl Grant left here a gentlemen living on the Jackson road from Somerville called. He was captured yesterday near Somerville & paroled to report in 6 days at Mason Station   they are commanded by Richardson & are robbing & enforcing the conscription   He saw no Artillery or Infty." Telegram received, *ibid.*, Dept. of the Tenn., Telegrams Received. On the same day, Brayman telegraphed to USG and Maj. Gen. James B. McPherson. "A man from Somerville who knows Jackson says he is there with cavalry three (3) pieces of Artillery & several hundred Inf'ty waiting for reinforcements from further west of them & preparing to come in this direction   they probably intend to break both roads—" Telegram received, *ibid.*

On Nov. 23, Rawlins telegraphed to Brig. Gen. Isaac F. Quinby, Moscow. "Genl Brayman telegraphs that a man from Somerville, who knows Jackson, says that he is there with Cavalry 3 pieces of Artillery, and several hundred Infantry, waiting for reinforcements from further west of there, and preparing to come in this direction. They probably intend to break both roads. Have you or can you obtain any information of the truth of the same"   Copies, DLC-USG, V, 18, 30; DNA, RG 393, Dept. of the Tenn., Letters Sent. *O.R.*, I, xvii, part 2, 357. On the same day, Quinby telegraphed to USG. "I was informed just at dark that there was to-day a large rebel cavalry force at Hay's Bridge, about 6 miles west of this place. These, in connection with the report just received that Colonel Lee had already been sent toward Somerville, led me to believe that the rebel force has got south of the Wolf River. They could have been intercepted by sending out a force to guard Hay's Bridge. I will send out all of my disposable cavalry early to-morrow, hoping to catch them." *Ibid.* Also on Nov. 23, USG telegraphed to Quinby. "You can fit out an expedition to go to Somerville"   Copies, DLC-USG, V, 18, 30; DNA, RG 393, Dept. of the Tenn., Letters Sent. *O.R.*, I, xvii, part 2, 358. On the same day, USG telegraphed to Brig. Gen. Jeremiah S. Sullivan and Brayman. "A considerable force of Cavalry, from five hundred to one thousand, crossed the Tennessee river, and are now moving west. Look out for them on the Rail road"   Copies, DLC-USG, V, 18, 30; DNA, RG 393, Dept. of the Tenn., Letters Sent. *O.R.*, I, xvii, part 2, 358.

Also on Nov. 23, Rawlins telegraphed to Quinby. "You will please send forward to this place the team and Cotton taken from the gentlemen arrested this morning in advance of you pickets (on the way to Memphis) to report to the Provost Marshall here"   Copies, DLC-USG, V, 18, 30; DNA, RG 393, Dept. of the Tenn., Letters Sent. On the same day, Quinby telegraphed to Rawlins. "The team with cotton will be sent at once   I have had conflicting rumors of Jacksons—The man I sent you suspected of being a spy yesterday could give you information if he would. I sent out Cavalry to Mount Pleasant this morning   if Enemies cavalry is not found there I propose to send out tomorrow in the direction

of Somerville   will transmit all information worthy of credit without delay—"
Telegram received, *ibid.*, Telegrams Received.

On Nov. 24, Hamilton telegraphed to Rawlins. "Has Quinby recd three (3)
new Regts   if so he has 13 Regts   the next 3 Regs I desire to send to Gen
Ross   he has but (9)"   Telegram received, *ibid.* On the same day, Rawlins telegraphed to Hamilton. "The 72nd & one hundred & ninth 109th are the only Rgts
ordered to report to Quimby unless you sent the ninety fifth 95th to him. I can
see that it gives him more than was intended & it must be sent somewhere else
four additional Regts have been ordered from Columbus   when they arrive they
will be ordered to report to you"   Copy, *ibid.*, District of Corinth, Telegrams
Received.

Also on Nov. 24, Quinby telegraphed to USG. "There is a rebel encampment
seven (7) miles west of Somerville composed I supposed mostly if not entirely
of Guerrillas   shall I send out to break it up—"   Telegram received, *ibid.*,
Dept. of the Tenn., Telegrams Received. On the same day, USG telegraphed to
Quinby. "You may send out an expedition to break up Richardson's Camp near
Somerville"   Copies, DLC-USG, V, 18, 30; DNA, RG 393, Dept. of the Tenn.,
Letters Sent. *O.R.*, I, xvii, part 2, 359.

On Nov. 27, Quinby telegraphed to Rawlins. "A Report from Col Prince is
Just recd at   the Expedition is [a] Success   He has 2 Commissioned officers &
twenty one (21) privates prisoners and large amount of property   the destruction of Martins bridge and that at Lafayette must have prevented the Escape of
the rebels south   I will Send Col Princes report by a messenger"   Telegram
received, DNA, RG 393, Dept. of the Tenn., Telegrams Received. The report
of Lt. Col. Edward Prince, 7th Ill. Cav., Nov. 27, of a skirmish near Somerville,
Tenn., Nov. 26, is in *O.R.*, I, xvii, part 1, 526–27. On Dec. 15, USG forwarded
to the AGO, Washington, a report by Prince of an engagement, probably the
report cited above. DNA, RG 94, Register of Letters Received.

To Jesse Root Grant

Lagrange Ten.
Nov. 23d 186[2]

DEAR FATHER,

A batch of letters from Covington, and among them one from
you is just received.

I am only sorry your letter, and all that comes from you speaks
so condescendingly of every thing Julia says, writes or thinks.
You without probably being aware of it are so prejudiced against
her that she could not please you. This is not pleasing to me.

Your letter speaks of Fred.s illness. Fred is a big stout looking boy but he is not healthy. The difference that has always been made between him and the other children has had a very bad influence on him. He is sensitive and notices these things. I hope no distinction will be made and he will in time recover from his diffidence caused by being scolded so much.

I wish you would have a bottle of Cod liver oil bought and have Fred. take a table spoonful three times a day in part of a glass of ale each dose. Dr. Pope[1] of St. Louis says that he requires that treatmen[t] every little while and will continue to do so whilst he is growing. One of Mary's letters asks me for some explaination, about the Iuka battle. You can say that my report of that battle, and also of Corinth & the Hatchee went to Washington several weeks ago[2] and I suppose will be printed. These will answer her question fully.

Before you receive this I will again be in motion. I feel every confidance of success but I know that a heavy force is now to my front. If it is my good fortune to come out successfully I will try and find time to write Mary a long letter.

Julia joins me in sending love to all of you.

ULYSSES.

ALS, PPRF.

1. See *PUSG*, 1, 349n.
2. See letters to Col. John C. Kelton, Oct. 22, Oct. 30, 1862.

To Maj. Gen. Henry W. Halleck

La Grange Tenn
Nov. 24th 9. a m 1862

MAJ GEN H. W. HALLECK
GEN IN CHIEF.

Memphis has 18,252 men for duty—being well fortified 16.000 can be spared From other portions of Department troops cannot be spared except to move south on their present lines. I have contemplated attack upon Pemberton and given my orders accordingly. Sherman will move on Wednesday[1] and form junction with my forces south of Holly Springs on Sunday next Steele has been written to to threaten Grenada and Como Porter has sent some Gunboats to operate about the mouth of Yazoo. Must I countermand the orders for this movement? It is too late to reach Sherman or Steele before they will have moved.

Within the Dep't I have 72.000 men

U. S. Grant
Maj Genl Comdg

Telegram received, DNA, RG 94, Generals' Papers and Books, Telegrams Received by Gen. Halleck; *ibid.*, RG 107, Telegrams Collected (Bound); copies, *ibid.*, Telegrams Received in Cipher; *ibid.*, RG 393, Dept. of the Tenn., Hd. Qrs. Correspondence; DLC-USG, V, 5, 8, 24, 88. *O.R.*, I, xvii, part 1, 471. On Nov. 23, 1862, Maj. Gen. Henry W. Halleck had telegraphed to USG. "Report approximate number of men in your command, and number that can be sent down the river to Vicksburg, reserving merely enough to hold Corinth and West Tennessee." ALS (telegram sent), DNA, RG 107, Telegrams Collected (Bound); telegram received, *ibid.*, RG 393, Dept. of the Tenn., Telegrams Received. *O.R.*, I, xvii, part 1, 471. On Nov. 25, Halleck telegraphed to USG. "Proposed movements approved. Do not go too far." ALS (telegram sent), DNA, RG 107, Telegrams Collected (Bound); telegram received, *ibid.*, RG 393, Dept. of the Tenn., Telegrams Received. *O.R.*, I, xvii, part 1, 471.

1. Nov. 26.

To Brig. Gen. Charles S. Hamilton

La Grange Tenn. Nov 24. 1862

Brig Genl C S Hamilton
Comdg Left Wing

Your instructions for the move on Friday[1] will be sent over in a short time. Lee need not go, as he could not ascertain if the enemy are evacuating Tallahatchie in time for an earlier move. than we expect to make in any event.

U S Grant
Maj Genl.

Telegram, copies, DLC-USG, V, 18, 30; DNA, RG 393, Dept. of the Tenn., Letters Sent; (dated Nov. 26, 1862) *ibid.*, District of Corinth, Telegrams Received. *O.R.*, I, xvii, part 2, 359.

On Nov. 25, USG telegraphed to Brig. Gen. Charles S. Hamilton. "If the evacuation of Tallahatchie has taken place be prepared to follow with all your command" Copies, DLC-USG, V, 18, 30; DNA, RG 393, Dept. of the Tenn., Letters Sent; *ibid.*, District of Corinth, Telegrams Received. *O.R.*, I, xvii, part 2, 359. On the same day Hamilton sent five telegrams to USG. "Had lee better go out his men will be ready at 10 & half oclock but if we move on friday but little will be gained by his going today please answer—" "The following just recd from Moscow to Gen Quinby—It is Reported by negroes coming in that the Rebels are tearing up R R track at Colliersville & drawing off the Rails with teams M. ROCHESTER a.a.g.' " "Contraband from Tallahatchee reports enemy leaving there thinks they are moving on Vicksburg & that negroes are being collected to work at Vicksburg" "The report from the Talahatchie brot by contraband was telegraphed me by Gen Ross it was reported to him by officer on picket the contraband has gone to Grand Junction the picket officer is here & says the negro reported only hearsay & that he came from this side Holly springs but little credence can be given his report I propose to send" "I shall get more definate information in a few hours of the condition on Tallahatchie & if the report of the evacuation is probable I wish to follow it up with all the Cavalry & one or more Divisions of Infantry" Telegrams received, DNA, RG 393, Dept. of the Tenn., Telegrams Received.

1. Nov. 28.

To Brig. Gen. Jeremiah C. Sullivan

By TELEGRAPH FROM Lagrange Nov 25 *1862*
To GENL SULLIVAN.

Persue the Rebels that captured Henderson[1] until they are driven out of the state. Was any cars captured tell Genl Webster to place men on the road to repair it at once

U. S. GRANT
Maj Genl

Telegram received, DNA, RG 393, 16th Army Corps, 4th Division, Telegrams Received; copies, *ibid.*, Dept. of the Tenn., Letters Sent; DLC-USG, V, 18, 30. *O.R.*, I, xvii, part 2, 360. Jeremiah C. Sullivan, born in Madison, Ind., in 1830, the son of a prominent politician and judge, served in the U.S. Navy as midshipman (1848–54), then practiced law. His brother, Algernon S., a New York City attorney, in defending the capt. of a C. S. A. privateer in summer, 1861, corresponded with C. S. A. authorities and was himself imprisoned for six weeks.

Ibid., II, ii, 682–88. Jeremiah C. entered the Civil War on April 18 as capt., 6th Ind., advanced to col., 13th Ind., on June 19, and was confirmed as brig. gen. on April 28, 1862. Soon transferred to the West, he commanded a brigade in the Army of the Miss. until Nov. 17, then was assigned to command the District of Jackson. See letter to Maj. Gen. Stephen A. Hurlbut, Nov. 12, 1862. On Nov. 25, Sullivan sent three telegrams to USG. "I have just received the following dispatch: The rebel cavalry, about 400 strong, came into Henderson, captured the post, killed 1 man, took the balance of the company prisoners, burned the station-house and Mount Pinson Station and tank, and burned 74 bales cotton. I have ordered out one regiment and all the cavalry to proceed to Henderson." "The bridge at Henderson is safe. The rebels fired bridge after they left. The women of town put the fire out. All my available cavalry and two regiments of infantry are in pursuit." *O.R.*, I, xvii, part 2, 360. "Communication with Corinth is open by telegraph this morngs train from Corinth escaped the train that stalled from Corinth this P M is not yet in & cannot therefore report as state of road I do not think it is damaged Telegraph office at Henderson station destroyed" Telegram received, DNA, RG 393, Dept. of the Tenn., Telegrams Received. On the same day, Sullivan telegraphed to Lt. Col. John A. Rawlins. "Refugees from Tipton Co. give force of Rebels at 2000 engaged conscripting Dyson's springs theire Rendezvous crossing at Marshall Institute to go south" Telegram received, *ibid.*

Also on Nov. 25, USG telegraphed to Brig. Gen. Mason Brayman, Bolivar. "Gen'l Sullivan has sent Troops after guerrilles that took Henderson station. Troops from here are after those west from Bolivar." Telegram received, Brayman Papers, ICHi; copies, DLC-USG, V, 18, 30; DNA, RG 393, Dept. of the Tenn., Letters Sent. On the same day, Brayman telegraphed to USG. "Col Haynie sends two couriers from Bethel Henderson station was taken by large body of Rebel Cav. early this morng his communication with Jackson cut off He wants a Reg. sent down from Jackson says that Gen Dodge will send up a Reg from Corinth he has sent a Co. to McNary station & will send the forty eighth when Gen Dodges Reg arrives I think the Rebels will try to strike this road near Medon tonight I will strengthen our guards on Rail Road & be ready here" Telegram received, *ibid.*, Telegrams Received. On Nov. 26, Brayman telegraphed three times to USG. "The wire is cut between here and Jackson." "I can Send up a party with hand-car to repair the line. The break is five miles this side of Medon" "Lt. Col. McCullough with 300 4th Illinois Cavalry just arrived from Jackson, to stay to-night." ALS, Brayman Papers, ICHi. On the same day, Brayman reported his strength to Rawlins as under 800 effectives. ALS, *ibid.* On Nov. 27, Brayman telegraphed to USG. "Your dispatch received. I will have a force on the road north of here before they can arrive. It When, and where did they cross." ALS, *ibid.*

1. Henderson, Tenn., on the Mobile and Ohio Railroad, about fifteen miles southeast of Jackson. A report of Lt. Col. Phineas Pease, 49th Ill., Nov. 29, concerning the capture of Co. B, 49th Ill., at Henderson's Station on Nov. 25 is in *O.R.*, I, xvii, part 1, 525–26. On Dec. 1, Capt. Theodore S. Bowers issued Special Orders No. 35 thanking certain ladies who lived near Henderson's Station for extinguishing a fire set to destroy a railroad bridge. DS, DNA, RG 94, Dept. of the Tenn., Special Orders; DLC-USG, V, 16, 26, 27. Printed as Special Orders No. 31, Nov. 27, signed by Rawlins, in *O.R.*, I, xvii, part 1, 526.

On Jan. 16, 1863, Sullivan telegraphed to USG. "I have recd today the Sum eight thousand dollars or about that as an assessment levied on Secessionists living near the scene of the Henderson raid   what shall be done with the money   I need secret service money"   Telegram received, DNA, RG 94, War Records Office, Dept. of the Tenn. On Jan. 19, Sullivan telegraphed to Rawlins. "After the Rebel Raid by which Henderson station depot buildings &c were destroyed I assessed the secession sympathizers living near the place a sum sufficient to pay all damages   I have in my possession about eight thousand 8000 dollars   what shall be done with it   I need money as secret service fund having employed several citizens as scouts"   Telegram received, *ibid. O.R.*, I, xvii, part 2, 574–75. On Jan. 20, USG telegraphed to Sullivan. "Turn over to the District Provost Marshall the funds you have and give orders on him for the payment of scouts." Copies, DLC-USG, V, 18, 30; DNA, RG 393, Dept. of the Tenn., Letters Sent. On Jan. 23, USG telegraphed to the provost marshal, Jackson, Tenn. "The funds turned over to you by Genl Sullivan will be accounted for by the Provost Marshall General"   Copies, *ibid.*; *ibid.*, RG 94, Letters Received. Civilians assessed after the raid on Henderson attempted later to recover their money. Considerable correspondence on this subject is consolidated *ibid.*, 1623H 1864. See *HRC*, 44-2-184.

To Maj. Gen. Henry W. Halleck

La grange Ten.
Nov. 26th 1862

Gen. Halleck,

Having come across a pair of unmentionables in a deserted rebel house entirely unsuited in dimentions for any member of this Army, and thinking that so much material should not be lost in these times when the raw material from which they are manufactured is in such demand, I naturally cast around to think who of my acquainta[nces] they might be of service to.

I can think of no one but Col. Thom of your Staff. They are therefore to him respectfully donated, with such remarks in the presentation as you may choose to make.

Very respectfully
your obt. svt.
U. S. Grant

ALS, Bohemian Club Library, San Francisco, Calif.

To Brig. Gen. Charles S. Hamilton

———

Head Quarters 13th Army Corps
Department of the Tennessee
LaGrange Tenn Nov 26 1862

Brig Gen C S Hamilton
Comm'dg Left Wing Army in Field
General.

You will be prepared to move with your entire command except one Regiment of McArthur's Division now in charge of contrabands Southwards making Coldwater the first day by the most easterly roads found practicable for Artillery. Ross's and McArthur's Divisions are only embraced in the troops to march by this route. Quinby will march directly from that place taking everything clean from that place leaving no garrison[1]   He will encamp the first night to the right of Right Wing. Second day from the rear and come up and take his position with the Left Wing where he encamps in the evening. Three days rations will be taken in Haversacks and five in wagons. Two hundred thousand rations will be taken down the Railroad on Monday morning next as far as the road may then be practicable from which point your teams will have to haul further supplies. No provision will be made for a reserve for the entire command, but each Wing Commander will provide for and have charge of his own reserves. The order of march of each Wing will provided for by Wing Commanders.

Sherman leaves Memphis to-day and is instructed to reach water to the Southwest of Holly Springs on Sunday next. Our march must be so arranged as to reach water to the South, Southeast and South-west of Holly Springs on the same day. Each Commander will have with two hundred rounds of ammunition per man for the Infantry, and Cavalry and all the Artillery ammunition their means of transportation will allow. Further supplies will be provided by the Ordnance Officer under instructions which he will receive direct from these Hd-Qrs

Wing Commanders will require all men to keep in rank. At least one Field Officer should march in the rear of their Regiment and Company Officers should at all times be directly with their Companies. On the first halt Regimental commanders under supervision of Division and Brigade Staff Officers, should make inspection of their entire commands, and take from every Officer and Soldier who is not entitled to forage from the United States that may be found mounted his horse and horse equipments and send them back to the Quartermaster at this place

U. S. Grant

Maj Gen

Copies, DLC-USG, V, 18, 30; DNA, RG 393, Dept. of the Tenn., Letters Sent. *O.R.*, I, xvii, part 2, 362–63.

On Nov. 26, 1862, USG telegraphed to Brig. Gen. Charles S. Hamilton. "Special Order No 30 will go into effect immediately so far as Officers transferred reporting to new Commanders is concerned, but the object you ask will be obtained in another way" Copies, DLC-USG, V, 18, 30; DNA, RG 393, Dept. of the Tenn., Letters Sent. On the same day, Hamilton telegraphed to USG. "The following dispatch has been rec'd from Genl Ross   Capt Ryan bearer of flag of truce   he has returned having gone six (6) miles below Holly Springs   He saw no troops this side of Holly Springs.   a few soldiers are the first regular pickets they was a mile below town—delivered papers to Col Jackson—No news of Bragg & no information as to the movement of troops"   Telegram received, *ibid.*, Telegrams Received.

On Nov. 25, Brig. Gen. Leonard F. Ross, Davis' Mill, twice telegraphed to Lt. Col. John A. Rawlins. "Gen Hamilton informs me that he has recd no instructions about flag of truce that when recd he will transmit &c—The papers are not yet rec'd here   they must have miscarried—"   "The answer to flag of truce communication just recd   will send it fwd. by Capt Ryan at 3 Oclock tomorrow a m unless you wish it sent forward sooner"   Telegrams received, *ibid.* On the same day, USG telegraphed to Ross. "In the morning will answer for the flag of Truce dispatch"   Copies, DLC-USG, V, 18, 30; DNA, RG 393, Dept. of the Tenn., Letters Sent.

On Nov. 26, USG telegraphed to Hamilton. "I have just made an order for twelve non-commissioned officers or privates to be selected six from each wing, who have sufficient knowledge of medecine and surgery to act as Hospital Stewards to report to Dr Palmer at Grand Junction   Please make the detail, they will receive thirty dollars per month"   Copies, DLC-USG, V, 18, 30; DNA, RG 393, District of Corinth, Telegrams Received; *ibid.*, Dept. of the Tenn., Letters Sent. On the same day, Hamilton telegraphed to USG. "Where shall I send the sick who cannot be taken along—"   Telegram received, *ibid.*, Telegrams Received. On the same day, USG telegraphed to Hamilton. "A General Hospital is Established here at La-Grange." Copy, *ibid.*, District of Corinth, Telegrams Received.

On Nov. 27, USG twice telegraphed to Hamilton. "Sends the sick to Grand Junction & take the hote[l.] I will direct Medical Director to make suitable preperation for them" Copy, *ibid.* "Such sick as cannot be transported leave in Camp Hospital at Davis Mills with a suitable Regimental Surgeon in charge" Copies, *ibid.*; *ibid.*, Dept. of the Tenn., Letters Sent; DLC-USG, V, 18, 30.

On Nov. 27, Rawlins issued Special Field Orders No. 7. "Upon the forming of a Junction between the forces now moving from here under Major General McPherson and Brig Genl Hamilton with those from Memphis under Major General Sherman the Army in the Field will be known and designated as follows. *Right Wing.* Major General W T. Sherman commanding and will be composed of the troops now under his command and such as are transfered to it by Special Orders No. 30. *Centre* Commanded by Major General J B. McPherson *Left Wing* Commanded by Brig Genl C S. Hamilton" DS, DNA, RG 94, Dept. of the Tenn., General Orders; copies, *ibid.*, RG 393, Dept. of the Tenn., Special Orders; DLC-USG, V, 26, 27. *O.R.*, I, xvii, part 2, 364. On Nov. 27, Rawlins issued Special Orders No. 31 providing garrison forces for La Grange, Grand Junction, and Davis's Bridge. DS, DNA, RG 94, Dept. of the Tenn., Special Orders; copies, *ibid.*, RG 393, Dept. of the Tenn., General and Special Orders; DLC-USG, V, 16, 26, 27, 87. *O.R.*, I, xvii, part 2, 365. On Nov. 28, USG telegraphed to Brig. Gen. Mason Brayman, Bolivar. "Send the one hundred twenty sixth (126) Regiment to Coldwater on Monday next" Telegram received, Brayman Papers, ICHi. On the same day, Brayman replied to USG. "The 126th Ills. is on the way and will arrive at LaGrange tomorrow afternoon. Their waggons have not yet arrived, but will go forward when they come. I will send down to Col. Richmond to wait at LaGrange till Monday, unless you otherwise order." ALS, *ibid.*

On Nov. 23, Brig. Gen. Thomas A. Davies, Columbus, Ky., telegraphed to USG. "The one twenty sixth (126) Ills has arrived will start for Jackson between 5 & 6 this P M—" Telegram received, DNA, RG 393, Dept. of the Tenn., Telegrams Received; copy, *ibid.*, Hd. Qrs. District of Columbus, Telegrams Sent. On Dec. 5, USG telegraphed to Capt. Theodore S. Bowers, La Grange. "Have no arms for the 126th, nor dont know where they can be got. Must get along with the arms they have the best way they can. Send the worst ones to Jackson, Tenn., for repairs of the locks." Copies, DLC-USG, V, 18, 30; DNA, RG 393, Dept. of the Tenn., Letters Sent. Another copy, in DLC-USG, V, 91, is entered as sent by Rawlins.

1. On Nov. 26, USG telegraphed to Brig. Gen. Isaac F. Quinby, Moscow, Tenn. "Notify the telegraph operator at Moscow to pull up stakes and come in here as soon as you can dispense with him." Copies, *ibid.*, V, 18, 30; DNA, RG 393, Dept. of the Tenn., Letters Sent. On Nov. 27, Quinby telegraphed twice to Rawlins. "When will there be a train here from LaGrange there are large No of contrabands here whom I wish to send to the rear" "Your dispatches are recd the Contrabands and prisoners will be sent in tomorrow morning the ninth Ills Cav has been ordered in & on its arrival will be sent at once to Lagrange what do you mean by saying that the 28th Ills infy Col Johnson is at Lagrange In with J B McPherson" Telegrams received, *ibid.*, Telegrams Received.

To Brig. Gen. Charles S. Hamilton

———

La Grange Tenn
Nov 26th 1862

Brig Gen C S Hamilton
Com'dg Left Wing

The present organization of Cavalry will stand until a junction is formed with Sherman. I want you to establish a line of couriers with the post at Davis' Mills and the rear as we advance up as far as Holly Springs. The road will probably be in running order to Coldwater within twenty-four hours after we start and telegraph established. This will render courier posts north of Coldwater to move forward

U S Grant
Maj Gen

Copies, DLC-USG, V, 18, 30; (dated Nov. 27, 1862) DNA, RG 393, District of Corinth, Telegrams Received; (misdated Dec. 26) *ibid.*, Dept. of the Tenn., Letters Sent. On Nov. 26, Brig. Gen. Charles S. Hamilton had telegraphed to USG. "Rather than have the 2d second Iowa & 7th seventh Kansas Regts. of cavalry reported as col Dickey proposes Let me suggest the organization of all cavalry ~~with~~ into 2 divisions one (1) under Lee to embrace all well armed & tried regts for field duty & hold the others to be used for pickets & scouts—I believe the effectiveness of the cavalry arm will be greatly impaired by dividing it up on col Dickey's plan   to make it truly efficient it must have an active brave head.   the commander is the soul of the arm   a tried force kept together under Lee will by setting an example to others be of more benefit than it can possibly be by dividing it up—col Lee & myself will come over after dinner today—" Telegram received, *ibid.*, Telegrams Received.

To Brig. Gen. Leonard F. Ross

———

LaGrange Tenn
Nov 26th 1862

Brig Gen L F. Ross
Davis Mills Tenn

Mrs Rhinehardt living about two miles from your Head

Quarters immediately on the Railroad is represented as being Union in sentiment very old and with a number of young negroes to take care of while her place is stripped of everything her mules and fences all gone. Send out an Officer to investigate and if she is entitled to protection or the return of any thing have the best done you can

U S GRANT
Maj Gen

Copies, DLC-USG, V, 18, 30; DNA, RG 393, Dept. of the Tenn., Letters Sent.

To Col. Josiah W. Bissell

———

La Grange Tenn Nov 26th 1862

COL BISSELL
COMM'DG ENGINEER REG'T

Move your Regiment foward tomorrow by rail with camp and garrison equipage tools and everything as far as you find troops to the South. I want the road repaired to Holly Springs as soon as possible

U S GRANT
Maj Gen   .

Telegram, copies, DLC-USG, V, 18, 30; DNA, RG 393, Dept. of the Tenn., Letters Sent. On Nov. 26, 1862, USG again telegraphed to Col. Josiah W. Bissell. "Do not advance with your Regiment today than you can do with perfect security. Your train should return to night to Davis' Mills" Copies, *ibid.*

On Nov. 26, Col. Joseph D. Webster, Jackson, telegraphed to Lt. Col. John A. Rawlins. "It appears probable that we shall have work for the whole of the Engr regt with all the tools they can bring if they know of a pile driver let them bring it as I intend to substitute pile bridges for trusses where the latter are destroyed will send particulars as soon as Recd" Telegram received, *ibid.*, Telegrams Received. On the same day, USG wrote to Capt. Frederick E. Prime. "The Engineer Company passed by here without reporting and went on to Jackson last night If you will come over here immediately you can see Col Bissell and some of the men belonging to the Company that are to work on the Pontoon bridge and give such directions as you may wish" Copies, DLC-USG, V, 18, 30; DNA, RG 393, Dept. of the Tenn., Letters Sent.

On Nov. 18, USG had telegraphed to Maj. Gen. Stephen A. Hurlbut. "Order to rejoin their Regiment Company "E" Engineer Regiment relieving them from ther present duty by some of the Garrison. Lieut. Edinger of the Company may remain at Jackson for the present" Copies, *ibid*. On Nov. 25, USG telegraphed to Brig. Gen. Isaac F. Quinby. "Ther will be no train from here to Moscow today. You will send one Company of Col. Bissell's Engineer Regiment to Jackson Tenn to repair a Pontoon bridge. Instruct the Officer to report to Capt Prime at this place as he passes through." Copies, *ibid*. On Nov. 25, USG again telegraphed to Quinby. "Come up today" Copies, *ibid*.

On Dec. 3, USG telegraphed to Col. Robert Allen. "Have a pontoon bridge at Jackson in charge of Capt Randolph for repairs. Any lumber he may require is needed." Copies, DLC-USG, V, 18, 30, 91; DNA, RG 393, Dept. of the Tenn., Letters Sent. On Dec. 9, USG telegraphed to Bissell. "You will immediately send to Holly Springs the men detailed by Special Orders of 18th Nov from Hd Qrs, 13th Army Corps, Dept. Tenn. for duty in Ordnance repairing Dept." Copies, *ibid*.

To Elihu B. Washburne

Lagrange Tennessee
November 26th 1862

HON. E. B. WASHBURN,
DEAR SIR:

Our mutual friend, Surgeon Kittoe from Galena, who was recently before the Medical Board in St. Louis for examination for the position of Brigade Surgeon has just received the appointment of Assistant Surgeon of Volunteers from the President. The Dr. is now a full Surgeon of the 45th Ill. having passed his examination for the position. This then is a promotion downwards which of course he cannot accept.

What I want to state is that in tendering Dr. Kittoe the position of Assistant Surgeon, with the rank of Captain, when he is a full Surgeon already, with the rank of Major, there must be some mistake. I also want to add my testimony to the Dr.s great merit and do it through you as his letter declining this intended honor will take that channel.

Dr. Kittoe as Surgeon in charge of Hospital and in the field has won the confidance of officers of the line, and of his own department, to an extent rarely equaled. This has not been from his kind disposition alone but from his administrative ability and professional skill.

There are many persons who never knew Surgeon Kittoe until this War brought them together who, if brought low, either from wounds or sickness, would feel a greatful sense of relief if they avail themselves of his services.

You know his qualifications and like me will not believe that any Board that has been called to examine Surgeons for promotion are capable of giving such an examination as to place Dr. Kittoe down for a second position. His appointment for the Presidency of any of these Boards would not be out of place.

Yours Truly

U. S. Grant

ALS, DNA, RG 94, Personal Papers, Medical Officers and Physicians, Edward D. Kittoe. Kittoe, born in Woolwich, Kent, England, in 1814, served as apprentice to a surgeon and apothecary before emigrating to the U.S. at the age of 18. After graduating from Pennsylvania Medical College, he practiced medicine at Muncy, Pa., for ten years, then moved to Galena in 1851. *Memorials of Deceased Companions of the Commandery of the State of Illinois, Military Order of the Loyal Legion of the United States* (Chicago, 1901), pp. 38–39. He was appointed surgeon, 45th Ill., as of Aug. 30, 1861. On Jan. 19, 1863, the U.S. Senate received nominations of Kittoe as asst. surgeon as of Nov. 7, 1862, and surgeon as of Dec. 4. Both were confirmed.

To Edwin M. Stanton

Head Quarters, 13th Army Corps,
Dept. of the Tennessee,
Lagrange, Nov. 27th 1862

Hon. E. M. Stanton,
Sec. of War,
Washington D. C.
Sir:

I would respectfully recommend the appointment of Capt. T. S. Bowers,[1] now Aid–de–Camp on my Staff, to the position of Judge Advocate with the rank of Maj.

Also the appointment of 2d Lieut. Orlando H. Ross,[2] 20th
Ill. Vols. and Peter Hudson[3] of Burlington Iowa as Aides-de-
Camp, with the rank of Captain to fill vacancies.

> I have the honor very respectfully
> to be your obt. svt.
> U. S. GRANT
> Maj. Gen. Com

ALS, DNA, RG 94, Letters Received. On Dec. 11, 1862, Secretary of War Edwin
M. Stanton recommended all three appointments to President Abraham Lincoln,
and Lincoln transmitted this letter to the U.S. Senate as a nomination. *Senate
Executive Journal*, XIII, 45. On Jan. 24, 1863, USG wrote to Brig. Gen. Lorenzo
Thomas. "Whilst commanding the 13th Army Corps I named Capt. T. S. Bowers,
now Aid-de-Camp on my staff, for the position of Judge Advocate, and 2nd Lieut.
Orlando H. Ross, 20th Ill. Volunteers, and Peter Hudson of Burlington, Iowa, as
Aides-de-Camp with the rank of Capt. As nothing has been heard from these
appointments I would respectfully renew the recommendation and ask that the
commissions issued be dated back to the time when the 13th Army Corps was
named by the President." Copies, DLC-USG, V, 5, 8, 24, 88; DNA, RG 393,
Dept. of the Tenn., Hd. Qrs. Correspondence; (typescript) Atwood Collection,
InU. On Feb. 9, Col. James B. Fry, AGO, wrote to USG. "In reply to your letter
of the 24th ulto. I have to inform you that Capt. Bowers, 2d Lt. Ross, & Peter
Hudson have all been nominated for the positions which you have requested for
them on your Staff, and that their commissions will be forwarded to them as soon
as the Senate shall have confirmed these nominations" Copy, DNA, RG 94,
Letters Sent Concerning Commissions.

1. Theodore S. Bowers was confirmed as judge advocate with the rank of
maj. on Feb. 19, 1863.
2. The nomination of Orlando H. Ross as aide-de-camp with the rank of capt.
was not reported back by the Committee on Military Affairs and the Militia, but
was resubmitted by Lincoln on March 10, and confirmed the next day. The military status of Ross, USG's cousin, in fall, 1862, is unclear. On Sept. 2, Ross,
Columbus, telegraphed to USG. "By the request of Gen Quinby & with your
permission & authority I will remain a few days longer & take take charge of
the mails   answer at Columbus   I can get your reply in the mornig" Telegram
received, *ibid.*, RG 393, Dept. of the Tenn., Miscellaneous Letters Received.
On Sept. 5, Bowers issued Special Orders No. 185. "O. H. Ross, Special Military
Mail Agent, will hereafter have entire charge, control and direction of all mails
passing over the United States Military Railroad, from Corinth to Columbus,
and he alone is responsible for their proper transmission." Copy, *ibid.*, District
of West Tenn., Special Orders. This section, however, does not appear in other
copies of this document in DLC-USG. On Nov. 1, Lt. Col. John A. Rawlins wrote
to Lt. Col. Charles A. Reynolds. "You will place the name of O. H Ross, special
Military Mail Agent, on your report of persons and articles hired for the month
of September, and pay him at the rate of one hundred and five dollars per month,
and continue his name on said report, and pay him at the rate aforesaid until

further orders" Copies, *ibid.*, V, 18, 30; DNA, RG 393, Dept. of the Tenn.,
Letters Sent. Copies of this letter in the latter source and in DLC-USG, V, 18
are dated Sept. 1, and more than a slip of the pen was involved, since the heading
was "Dist. West Tennessee" and "Corinth" instead of "Dept. of the Tenn."
and "Jackson." Placement of the letter in the books, however, indicates that it
was written on Nov. 1 and deliberately predated. Also on Nov. 1, Rawlins issued
Special Orders No. 5. "Capt C A. Reynolds, Chief Qr Master of the Dept will
place the name of O H. Ross. Special Military Mail agent on his roll of his Extra
Duty men for the months of September and October and pay him at the rate of
One hundred & five dollars per month, and continue his name on said roll and pay
him at the rate aforesaid, while he remains on duty or until further orders."
Copies, *ibid.*, V, 16, 26, 27, 87; DNA, RG 393, Dept. of the Tenn., Special Orders.
On the "Report of Persons & Articles Hired" for Sept., signed by USG, Ross was
entered at the end, and the total expense was altered to reflect his salary. DS,
ibid., RG 92, Q. M. Reports.

On Oct. 6, Col. C. Carroll Marsh, 20th Ill., Jackson, wrote to Ill. AG Allen
C. Fuller recommending Ross for appointment as 2nd lt., Co. D, 20th Ill. ALS,
Records of 20th Ill., I-ar. This letter was endorsed by USG. "I approve of above
reccommendation" ES, *ibid.* Ross was appointed on Nov. 7, and mustered in by
Maj. William R. Rowley on Nov. 26. DS, *ibid.* On Nov. 26, Rawlins issued Special
Orders No. 30. "2nd Lieut. Orlando H. Ross, 20th Regt, Illinois Infy Vols, is
hereby appointed and announced as Agent and General Superintendent of Mili-
tary Mails for this Department and he will be respected and obeyed accordingly.
All Military Mail Messengers will be detailed from the ranks and be subject to
his orders." DS, DNA, RG 94, Dept. of the Tenn., Special Orders; copies, *ibid.*,
RG 393, Dept. of the Tenn., Special Orders; DLC-USG, V, 16, 26, 27. *O.R.*, I,
xvii, part 2, 363. On July 17, 1863, USG endorsed a copy of the section of Special
Orders No. 30 relating to Ross. "The within is a true copy of Order appointing
Lt. Ross Aid de Camp on my Staff. During all the time he served as such he was
one of my regular aides, allowed by law, and to the date of his acceptance of his
promotion to a Captaincy he is clearly entitled to the additional compensation
allowed aides by the regulations." AES, DNA, RG 94, Vol. Service Division,
Letters Received, 126 VS 1872. The copy of Special Orders No. 30 endorsed dif-
fered markedly from other copies. "2nd Lieutenant O H. Ross, Co "D" 20th
Illinois Infantry Volunteers, is hereby detached from his company and Regiment
and appointed and announced as aid-de-camp on the staff of the major General
commanding the Department, and will be respected and obeyed accordingly"
DS, *ibid.* A newspaper correspondent noted that "Mr. O. H. Ross, so long Gen-
eral Superintendent of Mails in this department, has been appointed an aid of
Gen. Grant's, with the rank of Lieutenant." Letter of "Entre Nous," Oxford,
Dec. 5, in *Chicago Times*, Dec. 12, 1862. The close connections of Ross with
USG's hd. qrs. apparently led to unusual and questionable efforts to arrange his
pay and status.

3. The nomination of Peter T. Hudson as aide-de-camp with the rank of
capt. followed precisely the same time pattern as that of Ross. See letter to Silas
A. Hudson, Nov. 15, 1862. On Dec. 11, Silas A. Hudson wrote to U.S. Representative Elihu B. Washburne. "Gen Grant wrote me from Lagrange Tenn—
Nov 27—he had on that day written the President asking him to appoint Capt
T. S. Bowers Major & Judge Advocate, and my brother, Peter T. Hudson, Aid-
de-Camp with the rank of Captain on his Staff. I wrote Gov Grimes, an old friend,

naming the appointments desired, and he assues me they shall be confirmed at once when sent in. But the General wishes they be made immediately, and writes me to have some friend of the parties call on the Pres- and make that request of him, and as I have reason to believe Gov Grimes is not the man to make that request, may I claim that you do so?" ALS, DLC-Elihu B. Washburne.

To Brig. Gen. Charles S. Hamilton

Head Quarters, Army in the Field
Old Lamar, Nov 28th 1862.

BRIG. GENL. C. S. HAMILTON
COMMDG LEFT WING.
GENL:

Move tomorrow at the earliest practical hour and reach the nearest water to the South or Southeast of Holly Springs. I have no information of water nearer than Lumpkin's Mills,[1] except directly east from Holly Springs. If I should not come up with you at Holly Springs tomorrow you can exercise your own judgment as to the expediency of sending McArthur's Division eastward to Chewalla Creek.[2]

Detail four good companies of Cavalry, well commanded to remain at Holly Springs until they receive orders from me. I want to send them to communicate with Sherman.

U. S. GRANT
Maj Gen.

P. S. Holly Springs will be my Head Quarters after tomorrow until further notice.[3]

U. S. G.

Copies, DLC-USG, V, 18, 30, 91; DNA, RG 393, Dept. of the Tenn., Letters Sent. *O.R.*, I, xvii, part 2, 365.

1. See telegram to Brig. Gen. Charles S. Hamilton, Nov. 12, 1862, note 1.
2. Chewalla Creek rises about five miles northeast of Holly Springs, then flows southward some ten miles before joining Tippah Creek.
3. In connection with this move, on Nov. 28, 1862, USG wrote a pass. "Pass Mrs. Grant servant & child to Columbus free." ADS, DLC-USG.

To Maj. Gen. Henry W. Halleck

———

Holly Springs [*Nov.*] 29th, [*1862*]

GEN H. W. HALLECK
GEN IN CHF
    Troops occupy Line six miles south of this   Cavalry four
miles from Tallahatchie, Considerable skirmishing today, Loss
slight,

U. S. GRANT, M.G.

Telegram received, DNA, RG 94, Generals' Papers and Books, Telegrams
Received by Gen. Halleck; *ibid.*, RG 107, Telegrams Collected (Bound); copies,
ibid., Telegrams Received in Cipher; *ibid.*, RG 393, USG Hd. Qrs. Correspondence; DLC-USG, V, 5, 8, 24, 88, 91. *O.R.*, I, xvii, part 1, 471.

To Maj. Gen. William T. Sherman

———

Head Quarters, Army in the Field
Holly Springs, Nov 29th 1862.
Saturday 11-30. A. M.

MAJ GEN. W. T. SHERMAN
COMMDG RIGHT WING.
GENL:
    Your note to Lee I have just read. Your calender is just one
day ahead of time, but by staying where you are to-day it just
brings you up to time.
    Two Divisions of Hamilton's column will encamp tonight at
Lumpkin's Mills, the third on Spring Creek[1] and not move from
there until his front is reconnoitred   The head of his column is
now there. There was a little skirmishing with rebel Cavalry at
this place. and some at Lumpkin's Mills.—[2] Reconnoitre your
front as you propose today and move tomorrow to a good position near Tchulahama[3] to morrow. Telegraphic communication
I hope will be open with thes rear tomorrow. The railroad will

also be open to Coldwater. I have directed that the Cars come up that far on Monday[4] with 200.000 rations. From that point they will have to be teamed. There is also 800.000 rations at Lagrange from which place they can be brought in case of accident. Two train loads of grain are also directed to be brought up on Monday and Tuesday or the earliest day thereafter practicable. You can make your calculations for rations and forage accordingly. It is not desirable that this forage should be used until it becomes necessary.

Your letter and Steele's were duly received.[5] Steele's is quite encouraging.

I have no reliable information from the enemy. A Contraband just in says he left the Tallahatchie on Tuesday and that they were then cooking rations to retreat. Opposed to this a Spy who was taken last night and who was pumped by one of Hamilton's scouts who was dressed in Secesh uniform and put in prison with him says that the enemy mean fight.

Yours &c

U. S. Grant
Major Genl.

P. S. Bragg's forces were anxiously looked for. The 3rd Michigan Cavalry will report to you tomorrow or the day following.

U. S. G.

Copies, DLC-USG, V, 18, 30, 91; DNA, RG 393, Dept. of the Tenn., Letters Sent. *O.R.*, I, xvii, part 2, 366–67.

1. Big Spring Creek rises two or three miles southeast of Holly Springs, then flows southward to the Tallahatchie River.
2. See following letter, note 1.
3. Chulahoma, Miss., about thirteen miles southwest of Holly Springs.
4. Dec. 1, 1862.
5. See letter to Maj. Gen. William T. Sherman, Nov. 14, 1862.

To Maj. Gen. William T. Sherman

Holly Springs, Nov 29th 1862
8 O'clock. P. M.

MAJOR GEN. W. T. SHERMAN.
COMMD.G RIGHT WING.
GENL:

Your two dispatches just received. I enclose with this one just received from Hamilton[1] which will give you the latest news from this front. I have directed Hamilton to move to his south and east so as to let McPherson, who is now here with one Division, in between him and you. Mc's second Division will be up by 10 A. M. tomorrow and could go on to Lumpkin's Mills but I will retain it until Monday. If you can find water to your south east or rather to the southeast of Tchullahoma I would like you to move in that direction. At Tchullahoma our front will be too extended. I will direct Hurlbut to send the Cavalry of which you speak, sent as you desire. I do not know positively of any ford on the Tallahatchie west of the railroad except at Wyatt.[2] To the east there are several but I cannot now send you a sketch showing them. The crossings between Coil's Ferry[3] and Wyatt I believe are all ferries. Between Wyatt and railroad I think there is no ford.

Yours Truly.
U. S. GRANT
Maj Genl.

Copies, DLC–USG, V, 18, 30, 91; DNA, RG 393, Dept. of the Tenn., Letters Sent. *O.R.*, I, xvii, part 2, 367.

1. On Nov. 29, 1862, Brig. Gen. Charles S. Hamilton, "Lumpkins—Sundown," wrote to USG. "Lee has pushed the enemy to within 4 miles of Tallo-hatchie, and will hold his position for the present, His advance was a continual skirmish. He sends in one prisoner, and finds 4 dead rebels on the road, The enemy will fight on the Tallohotchie, Country in front of us stripped of forage. Please notify me of the completion of telegraph, so that I can call in courier posts, My scout is in from *Grenada*, about (7 000,) seven thousand troops have come up to Van Dorn in last two weeks, Mouth of Tippoh creek strongly fortified, Enemy

has no idea of evacuating as yet, Scout heard nothing of movemt of Steele." ALS, DNA, RG 393, Dept. of the Tenn., Letters Received. *O.R.*, I, xvii, part 2, 367–68. See following letter.

2. Wyatt, Miss., about nine miles southeast of Chulahoma. On Nov. 17, Col. John V. D. Du Bois had telegraphed to USG. "One man from Holly Springs & one from Abbyville just in   The Tallahatchie is fordable at several places. The fords are deep. The Enemy are fortifying these fords   one more ford at Wyatt.   persons have just arrived to remount Texan Rangers   Rangers in command of Genl Whitfield" Telegram received, DNA, RG 393, Dept. of the Tenn., Telegrams Received.

3. Coit's Ferry, about twelve miles southwest of Wyatt.

To Brig. Gen. Charles S. Hamilton

——————

Head Quarters, Army in the Field
Holly Springs, Nov 29th 1862.

Brig. Gen. Hamilton
Commdg Left Wing.
Genl:

Telegraph complete and working to this point. Move a portion of your troops eastward from their present position if they can obtain water and be in supporting distance of each other. They should also move a few miles farther south. I want. to get McPherson in between you and Sherman to move southeast from his present position if water and proper ground can be found. I shall send him word very early in the morning to reconnoitre for these two conditions. Send back to Coldwater on Monday[1] all the teams you can spare with instructions to load up from the train and remain there until such time as you send for them or direct. A proper escort should accompany the train.[2] Your train is not yet through passing this point.—7-50.

Your teams will be nearer forage at Coldwater than here and be out of the way of operations.

One Division from your wing will be detailed, to be selected by you, to guard from Coldwater southward as far as it will hold. I have ordered up a Regiment from Bolivar for Coldwater which will be added to the Brigade sent back here so that the smallest

Brigade ~~sent back~~ here from the Division selected will be sufficient to send back here and Tuesday early enough to send it back.

> Respectfully &c
> U. S. GRANT
> Maj Genl.

Copies, DLC-USG, V, 18, 30, 91; DNA, RG 393, Dept. of the Tenn., Letters
Sent. *O.R.*, I, xvii, part 2, 366. On Nov. 29, 1862, 3:15 P.M., Brig. Gen. Charles
S. Hamilton, Lumpkin's Mills, wrote to USG. "Lee had quite a skirmish here, &
lost one man killed & 3 wounded, The rebel cavalry made a stand in force. He has
pushed the enemy some three miles beyond this point. Plenty of water here, but
country very broken & hilly. Divisions are going into camp. Forage is scarce, it
having been pretty well cleared out, Lee has used a section of Parrott guns for
the last two hours. I will report the result of Lees operations on his return, Quite
a number of rebels have been killed here   There is good camping ground here
for McPhersons whole force   We have captured 2 limbers from enemy" ALS,
DNA, RG 393, Dept. of the Tenn., Letters Received. *O.R.*, I, xvii, part 1, 491.
For a later letter from Hamilton of the same day, see preceding letter, note 1.

    1. Dec. 1.
    2. On Nov. 30, Lt. Col. John A. Rawlins wrote to Hamilton. "The wagons
directed in previous dispatch to be sent back on Monday to the train at Coldwater
will be started this evening so as not to interfere with Gen. Logan's march in the
morning. The 3rd Michigan Cavalry will remain where it is until you receive
further orders. Gen Grant will be down and see you tomorrow." Copies, DLC-
USG, V, 18, 30, 91; DNA, RG 393, Dept. of the Tenn., Letters Sent.

To Maj. Gen. William T. Sherman

Holly Springs, Nov 30th 1862

GEN W T. SHERMAN
COMMDG RIGHT WING.
GEN:

    At as early a day as practicable I want to have made a Cavalry
reconnoissance to the enemys right taking with them three days
rations. Tuesday[1] will probably be the day for starting this expedition and all the Cavalry except escort companies, and just sufficient for Cavalry picket duty, will be required.

    I will try to see you tomorrow and when relative positions

are fixed between the different Wings will establish telegraph offices to each.

If you are likely to have any important information within a few hours you can retain the messenger that takes this to bring it back. No new from Hamilton this mor[ning.]

> Yours Truly
> U. S. GRANT
> Maj Genl

Copies, DLC-USG, V, 18, 30, 91; DNA, RG 393, Dept. of the Tenn., Letters Sent. *O.R.*, I, xvii, part 2, 371.

1. Dec. 2, 1862.

To Brig. Gen. Charles S. Hamilton

> Hd Qrs, Army in the Field
> Holly Springs, Nov 30, 1862 5-40 P. M.

GEN. HAMILTON.
COMMDG LEFT WING
GEN.

Your dispatch just received. Watch the enemy closely as I know you are doing but instruct the advance not to attempt to carry any intrenchments until we are prepared. I will be up in the morning and we will prepare for a heavy reconnoisance to the southeast and to the enemy's rear if practicable.

A number of sick are being returned here without rations and without a Surgeon. Rations have been issued to the men and regimental Surgeons should attend to their own sick until preperations are made for them.

> Yours Truly
> U. S. GRANT
> Maj Genl.

Copies, DLC-USG, V, 18, 30, 91; DNA, RG 393, Dept. of the Tenn., Letters Sent. *O.R.*, I, xvii, part 2, 370. On Nov. 30, 1862, at 10:00 A.M., and again at

3:00 P.M., Brig. Gen. Charles S. Hamilton, Lumpkin's Mills, wrote to USG. "I send a little sketch of country in front. Lee camped with his cavalry at Ebenezer church last night. I have supported him with a battery and 4 regts Infanty this morning, and directed a reconnaissance to the river ~~that~~ The infantry is under Deitzler. They will avoid any engagement, ~~unless~~ except with Jacksons cavalry, & will make full report of country on main road. I shall send out a strong reconnassance under Quinby, taking a road from near Waterford to the south east, towards mouth of Tippah Creek, each reconnaissance will require two days— but in the mean time I shall move my camp to the south-east if I can find water, & go some miles. Lt Wibber 4' Ill Cav was seriously but not dangerously wounded in neck yesterday. I can make room for McPherson here—but from here to Tallohatchie there is no water on the road." "I have just heard from Lee. He has pushed the enemy to the river, & is himself within one mile of the river. He reports this side of river protected by two circular field-works, 4 to 6 embrasures each—and they are occupied in force. He will return this evening, leaving cavalry enough to mask our front. I have a negro, who left Abbieville last night at eleven o:c. He is servant to private in Gen Lovells force. Heard his master say that Price with his army had gone to Panola on Grenada & Memphis road. Says bulk of rebel army is at Tallahatchie, mouth of Tippah & at Rocky ford. He says orders were given yesterday morning to strike tents & put three days rations in havresacks, & *thinks* it is a preparation to leave, but knows nothing more to confirm it. Says the army ~~is~~ was in line of battle yesterday at Tallahatchie. Thinks Rail road bridge is not injured yet. Lee says quite a force will be necessary to carry works on this side. He has shelled them—but his fire was returned with interest. I suppose he is now falling back—but will keep force enough to mask the ground gained, & also to watch the enemy. The rebel pickets are within four miles of me on the South east—I will clean out things in that direction to-morrow morning" ALS, DNA, RG 393, Dept. of the Tenn., Letters Received. *O.R.*, I, xvii, part 2, 368–69. In another letter dated the same day at 3:00 P.M., Hamilton wrote to Col. Albert L. Lee acknowledging his second dispatch and approving his conduct in falling back. *Ibid.*, p. 369.

To Brig. Gen. Jeremiah C. Sullivan

BY TELEGRAPH FROM Holly Springs [*Nov.*] 30 *1862*

To GEN. SULLIVAN

Have you made arrangements to releive Col True[1] at Kenton   He is ignorant of even the means of supplying his regiment with clothing.[2] He should be brought at once under your own care

U. S. GRANT
Maj Genl

Telegram received, DNA, RG 393, 16th Army Corps, 4th Division, Telegrams Received; copies, *ibid.*, Dept. of the Tenn., Letters Sent; DLC-USG, V, 18, 30, 91. On Dec. 2, 1862, the 62nd Ill. left Kenton, Tenn., for Jackson.

On Nov. 26, Col. William S. Hillyer had written to Col. James M. True, 62nd Ill., Kenton. "Newspaper prohibitions are not permitted by Post Commanders. Such orders as your Order No 20 suppressing the Chicago Times can only be made by Department or District Commanders—the order is therefore rescinded" Copies, *ibid.*, V, 18, 30; DNA, RG 393, Dept. of the Tenn., Letters Sent. On Nov. 27, USG telegraphed to Brig. Gen. Jeremiah C. Sullivan. "Relieve the 54th Reg't Ills Vols from Kenton & exchange some regt from Jackson whose Comdg Officer knows his duty" Telegram received, *ibid.*, 16th Army Corps, 4th Division, Telegrams Received; copies (dated Nov. 24), *ibid.*, Dept. of the Tenn., Letters Sent; DLC-USG, V, 18, 30. In the telegram above, True was confused with Maj. John W. True, 54th Ill., who was not at Kenton. For the latter, see Lincoln, *Works*, V, 540; VI, 98.

1. James M. True of Mattoon was mustered in as col., 62nd Ill., on April 10, 1862, and served at that rank through the war.

2. On Nov. 30, Lt. Col. John A. Rawlins wrote to True. "There is plenty of clothing in the Department. Make out and send to Col Reynolds requisitions for such things as you need. He will attend to them at once. Cannot send Officers to St Louis." Copies, DLC-USG, V, 18, 30, 91; DNA, RG 393, Dept. of the Tenn., Letters Sent.

On Oct. 23, True telegraphed to USG. "What shall I do with the Guns that were collected under order some three months since shall I give them up to their owner or shall I turn them over to my successor when relieved" Telegram received, *ibid.*, Dept. of the Mo., Telegrams Received.

To Maj. Gen. Henry W. Halleck

Waterford Miss [*Dec.*] 1st 7 30 A M [*1862.*]

MAJ GEN H W HALLECK

Our Cavalry are now crossing Tallatchie. Infantry will follow immediately. The Rebels are evidently retreating   If so I will follow to Oxford   Our troops will be in Abbyville tomorrow or a battle will be fought   Sherman is up & will cross the Tallahatchie at Wyatt

U. S GRANT

Telegram received, DNA, RG 94, Generals' Papers and Books, Telegrams Received by Gen. Halleck; *ibid.*, RG 107, Telegrams Collected (Bound); copies, DLC-USG, V, 88, 91. *O.R.*, I, xvii, part 1, 471. Copies (misdated Nov. 29, 1862), DLC-USG, V, 5, 8, 24; DNA, RG 393, Dept. of the Tenn., Letters Sent.

To Maj. Gen. Henry W. Halleck

Head Qrs in Field
Near Abbeville Miss
Dec [2] 1862

MAJ GEN H W HALLECK
GEN IN CHIEF

The Enemy deserted their fortifications yesterday destroying all their stores they could not carry with them   The weather bad and stream somewhat swollen making it difficult to cross Some of the cavalry swam the River however and occupied this place[1] last night   Today pursuit was made to Oxford coming on Rear Guard of Enemy   Skirmishing lasted about two hours resulting in the capture of some sixty (60) Rebels   The pursuit will continue tomorrow but the roads are too impassible to get up supplies for a longer continuance of it. Genl Sherman crossing at Wyatt—

U S GRANT M G

Telegram received (dated Dec. 3, 1862), DNA, RG 94, Generals' Papers and Books, Telegrams Received by Gen. Halleck; *ibid.*, RG 107, Telegrams Collected (Bound); copy, *ibid.*, Telegrams Received in Cipher. *O.R.*, I, xvii, part 1, 472. Copies (dated Dec. 2), DLC-USG, V, 5, 8, 24, 88, 91; DNA, RG 393, Dept. of the Tenn., Hd. Qrs. Correspondence.

1. Before leaving Holly Springs on Dec. 1, USG wrote to Brig. Gen. Charles S. Hamilton. "You will make the 11th Ills. Vols. one of the 3 Regts to be selected by you to be left at this place as it is a small regt. numbering only about 200 men and I desire to leave the Col in command" Copies, DLC-USG, V, 18, 30, 91; DNA, RG 393, Dept. of the Tenn., Letters Sent. Col. Thomas E. G. Ransom, 11th Ill., although promoted to brig. gen. as of Nov. 29, was probably the officer intended. On Nov. 30, USG telegraphed to Brig. Gen. Thomas A. Davies, Columbus, Ky. "Send two Regiments from the first that arrived to La Grange." Telegram received (misdated 1863), *ibid.*, RG 94, War Records Office, Remount Station.

To Maj. Gen. William T. Sherman

Hd Qrs, In the Field
Abberville, Miss. Dec 2nd 1862.

MAJ GEN. SHERMAN.

McArthur's Division is here. Quinby with his Division and McPherson with Logan's Division[1] on the north side of the river with instructions to camp there for the night and repair bridges. Our Cavalry have gone to the front several hours since and are probably now at Oxford. Artillery has been heard to the south but as no messenger has returned I imagine it is nothing but an attempt on the part of the enemy to cover their retreat. I do not expect you to be able to cross to do anything tomorrow with your Arty or Infy. but with the Cavalry a reconnoissance can be made to your front and southwest.

If this rain continues the roads will become so impassable that the distance to haul supplies will have to be shortened all practicable. In that case you can move the forces with you to join those here and instruct the remaining Division to move up to their neighborhood of Lumpkin's Mills.

I cannot tell until news are received from the advance Cavalry whether I will pursue any further for the present or not with Infy and Arty.

Let me hear from you by the messenger that will deliver this.

Truly Yours
U. S. GRANT
Maj Genl.

Copies, DLC-USG, V, 18, 30, 91; DNA, RG 393, Dept. of the Tenn., Letters Sent. *O.R.*, I, xvii, part 2, 374. On Dec. 2, 1862, 2 P.M., Maj. Gen. William T. Sherman, Wyatt, wrote to USG. "I wrote you about two hours since but Grierson met your messenger at the Ferry & returned with it, & I send it with this—The roads here cut up terribly—Morgan Smith is hard at work on a Bridge   I have 4 boats in the River, and a kind of Raft made of the two halves of the Ferry boat which was a good large one cut in two. Grierson is now across with his Cavalry & my advance Regt. is across. I advise you let me hold this ground till you resolve what action to take. I can make a good bridge & clear out the obstructions in the Road. I will throw Morgan Smiths Division across as soon as the Bridge is done, and all my men & wagons will be up tonight. I will order Grierson tonight to look toward Oxford, cross to Abbeville, and come in tomorrow. I sent a train of 100 wagons to Cold water this morng for Rations & ordered it to come to Wyatt unless you ordered otherwise—there is a longer road nearer to Holly Springs and this is one of the main travelled Roads to Oxford. With a Bridge it will be as good a route as by Lumpkins Mills.

to Holly springs	20 miles
to Oxford.	14 miles
to Abbiville	6 miles.

This country is simply impracticable in rainy weather. Rumor among citizens is the Federals have Panola. Can it be possible that Steeles expedition did not reach Grenada & turnd to Panola.—This would account for the retreat.—But wont accomplish our purposes. I have a prisoner who says he went to Abbeville to get on the cars yesterday but they were so crowded that he could not get in, & was picked up this A M. by our men. From a high hill here at 11 A M I saw a high smoke at Oxford. I think the enemy has gone to Grenada & back up the Yallobusha. I will cross with two Divisions bring all transportation here, camp at the forks of the Road & report to you at Abbeville tomorrow Eving, unless you send me diffrnt orders by Grierson." ALS, DNA, RG 393, Dept. of the Tenn., Letters Received. *O.R.*, I, xvii, part 2, 374–75.

On Dec. 3, 1:00 P.M., Sherman wrote to USG. "Your messenger is just in bringing your note—Wyatt is a poor country for forage but there is plenty behind me. I will collect all I can, all my troops are up. We are building a good bridge. I have 100 wagons now at Holly Springs for provisions. I have plenty of meat & we find hogs & cattle which the commissaries take and accout for. I have sent out detachments in every direction to study the lay of the ground. Do you think it prudent to cut the road from Grenada to Panola? If so, I can do it. Grierson is still about & I have ~~his~~ a regiment reconnotering to College Hill, another on the bluff opposite. Balance in a long tongue or ridge down which this road descends. Now that the sun shines all are well and comfortable. I did intend to come on today but suppose it best to remain close with my Command. I did also intend to bring my troops across this afternoon but will finish my bridge good & strong & await orders. . . .My prepared map goes as far as Grenada and I find it very correct" Copy, DNA, RG 94, Generals' Papers and Books, William T. Sherman, Letters Sent. On the same day, Sherman wrote to Lt. Col. John A. Rawlins. "I am this moment in receipt of a letter of Col. Hyler [*Hillyer*] inviting me to meet Gen. Grant at Oxford tomorrow. I will leave here at 8. A. M. & reach there by 11 A. M. I have no Cavalry & must come without escort therefore I expect the Genl. to be there in advance of me. I enclose a sketch of a reconnoissiance to the front & will bring Mr. Frick my Topograpical Engineer along with his maps. The movement on the Mobile & Ohio Road is admirable" Copy, *ibid*.

1. On Dec. 2, Rawlins wrote to Maj. Gen. James B. McPherson. "If Brig Genl. Logan's Division has two days rations send it forward to Oxford early tomorrow morning." Copies, DLC-USG, V, 18, 30, 91; DNA, RG 393, Dept. of the Tenn., Letters Sent. *O.R.*, I, xvii, part 2, 376.

To Col. T. Lyle Dickey

————

~~Holly~~ ~~Springs~~ Abberville, Dec 2nd 1862.
COL. T. LYLE. DICKEY,
COMMDG CAVALRY DIVISION

In your pursuit tomorrow be cautious not to be led into ambush. Push them however as far as possible. When you discontinue the pursuit if practicable push off to the East and come back by some route off from the Rail Road living upon the enemy and examine their resources especially as to forage.

Grierson I presume has not been able to cross the river to day, and will not be able to join in the pursuit. I have instructed Sherman however to send him out to the Southwest from Wyatt.

I will send Infantry and Artillery to Oxford tomorrow

Respectfully,
U. S. GRANT
Maj Genl.

Copies, DLC-USG, V, 18, 30, 91; DNA, RG 393, Dept. of the Tenn., Letters Sent. *O.R.*, I, xvii, part 2, 376.

To Maj. Gen. Henry W. Halleck

————

Head Qrs Gen Grant
in the feald near Abbeville—
Dec 4th [Dec. 3] 12 20 P M 62

MAJ GEN H. W. HALLECK
GEN IN CHIEF.

How far south would you like me to go? We are now at Yocona[1] and can go as far as supplies can be taken.

I will cut the Mobile road south of Tupila. Would it not be well to hold the Enemy south of Yulebusha[2] & move a force from Memphis & Helena on Vicksburg with my present force it would not be safe to go beyond Granada & attempt to hold present lines of communication. I have heard nothing from Steele's Expedition but from the precipitate flight of the enemy I think it must have been successful[3]

U. S. GRANT
Maj Genl

Telegram received (dated Dec. 4, 1862), DNA, RG 94, Generals' Papers and Books, Telegrams Received by Gen. Halleck; *ibid.*, RG 107, Telegrams Collected (Bound); copy, *ibid.*, Telegrams Received in Cipher. *O.R.*, I, xvii, part 1, 472. Copies (dated Dec. 3), DLC-USG, V, 5, 8, 24, 88, 91; DNA, RG 393, Dept. of the Tenn., Hd. Qrs. Correspondence. On Dec. 5, Maj. Gen. Henry W. Halleck telegraphed to USG. "Destroy the Mobile road as you propose. It would also be well to disable the others if possible to Granada. But I think you should not attempt to hold the country south of the Tallahatchie. The troops for Vicksburg should be back to Memphis by the 20th. If possible collect at that place for that purpose as many as twenty-five thousand. *More* will be added from Helena, &c. Your main object will be to hold the line from Memphis to Corinth with as small a force as possible, while the largest number possible is thrown upon Vicksburg with the Gunboats. Keep me as fully advised as you can about Bragg's movements. He may cross at Decatur & attack Corinth." ALS (telegram sent), *ibid.*, RG 107, Telegrams Collected (Bound); copies, *ibid.*, RG 108, Telegrams Sent; *ibid.*, RG 393, Dept. of the Tenn., Hd. Qrs. Correspondence; DLC-USG, V, 5, 8, 24, 88 (2), 91. *O.R.*, I, xvii, part 1, 473. Context does not indicate whether Halleck was answering USG's telegram of Dec. 3, not received until 4:18 P.M., Dec. 4, or his telegram of Dec. 5, which may have reached Washington the same day. USG suggested the latter as more likely (*Memoirs*, I, 430), but was probably unaware of the delay in receipt of his Dec. 3 telegram.

1. The Yocona River, which flows from east to west in Miss., crosses the Mississippi Central Railroad tracks about seven miles south of Oxford.
2. The Yalobusha River flows from east to west in Miss., passing through Grenada, then joins the Yazoo about twenty-seven miles southwest of Grenada.
3. An undated telegram from Maj. Gen. William T. Sherman to USG was probably sent about this date. "If you have reason to believe Steele has taken Grenada a force of 10.000 men ought immediately to go by river to mouth of Yazoo & occupy the ground back of Vicksburg between the Yazoo & Black Rivers. Such a move would be final for the Mississippi valley" Copy, DNA, RG 94, Generals' Papers and Books, William T. Sherman, Letters Sent.

To Maj. Gen. Henry W. Halleck

Head qrs in Field
Abbeville Miss [*Dec.*] 3rd 6.30 P. M [*1862*]
MAJ GENL HALLECK

The following despatch from Genl Dodge received. "one of our most reliable Scouts has just arrived from Huntsville Ala. left that place last tuesday. Says Bragg was at Tullahoma[1] & along that Railroad but that a considerable force of his cavalry are on the road between Decatur Eddytown & Columbus[2] collecting large amount of forage & subsistence at points from ten to fifteen miles apart. gives the names of the persons the citizens & the soldiers say that a portion of Braggs army is ordered to Columbus by that Road & a portion to Chattanooga & that one other corps are ordered down to Columbus by a Road farther East he says that the cavalry are Scattered along the road in squads for Sixty miles as far as he went & very active in collecting supplies. he brought in with him Several refugees who live in that Section of country who all tell the Same Story up to tuesday no Infantry or artillery had passed Huntsville or Dcatur but Says the citizens at those places were looking for them Every day[3]

U. S. GRANT
Maj Genl

Telegram received, DNA, RG 94, Generals' Papers and Books, Telegrams Received by Gen. Halleck; *ibid.*, RG 107, Telegrams Collected (Bound); copies, *ibid.*, RG 393, Dept. of the Tenn., Hd. Qrs. Correspondence; DLC-USG, V, 5, 8, 24, 88, 91. *O.R.*, I, xvii, part 2, 377.

Brig. Gen. Grenville M. Dodge had already become active in USG's intelligence work. On Nov. 16, 1862, Dodge, Corinth, telegraphed to Lt. Col. John A. Rawlins. "I sent portion of my cavalry to big springs east of Guntown they returned to day captured 2 officers & several privates of the 26th Regt Miss Vols the Enemy have left Guntown & their advance now at Saltillo I have no doubt that a part of Braggs forces have crossed the Tennessee my scouts saw Cavalry in force & artillery but I am inclined to think in no very large force yet." Telegram received, DNA, RG 393, Dept. of the Tenn., Telegrams Received. On Nov. 18, USG telegraphed to Dodge. "Can you get information from the East, say as far as Florence? I want to hear from along the Tennessee from Tuscumbia eastward, to know if any rebel troops are crossing there" Copies, DLC-USG, V, 18, 30; DNA, RG 393, Dept. of the Tenn., Letters Sent; Dodge Papers, IaHA. *O.R.*, I, xvii, part 2, 353. On the same day, Dodge telegraphed to USG. "I have been watching that have 5 men now out on that direction up to this time nothing has crossed there is small div of infantry six pieces of artilley & some cavaly the 2 men returned from Atlanta Ga came down the Tenn. River from the noth west cor. of Georgia to Eastport but saw no troops as fast as new arrives will send it—with good Reg. of Cavaly I could force my way to Tuscumbia" Telegram received, DNA, RG 393, Dept. of the Tenn., Telegrams Received. On Nov. 19, Dodge telegraphed to Rawlins. "The scouts report five hundred (500) cavalry and infantry at the farm of Mr O'c May on muddy creek three (3) miles northwest of Jonesboro My cavalry are all out have none to send after them" Telegram received, *ibid.*

On Nov. 22, Rawlins wrote to Dodge. "A dispatch from Genl Rosecrans of date Nashville Tenn Nov 21 1862, just received, says there are some indications that the Rebels are attempting to cross the Tennessee from the east, that signs to that effect reached him that night You will send out spies and scouts, east and obtain all the information possible" Copies, DLC-USG, V, 18, 30; DNA, RG 393, Dept. of the Tenn., Letters Sent. On Nov. 21, Maj. Gen. William S. Rosecrans, Nashville, telegraphed to USG. "Look out for news towards the East. There may be some attempt to cross Rebel troops over the Tenne. River. No signs have reached me till to night. the indications as yet are but slight Notify Corinth to have spies East." Copy, *ibid.*, Dept. of the Cumberland, Telegrams Sent. *O.R.*, I, xx, part 2, 77. On Nov. 22, Dodge telegraphed to Rawlins. "Force of cav. Estimated at 500 have crossed the Tenn. above Eastport not Roddys men they were within 3 miles of Iuka I have a No. of scouts out in that direction but have not heard from there for four days the best spies for that country are with Genl Hamilton I would like one or 2 of them if you can do anything to hurry up the arms for Cavalry please do it the officers are in Jackson with the requisitons is there any force from Jackson or any other point on the Tenn River about 3 or 4 miles north of Pittsburg Landing the Cavy. Co. from Bethel report to me this morng that there were federal troops there it is also reported by scouts" Telegram received, DNA, RG 393, Dept. of the Tenn., Telegrams Received; copy, *ibid.*, District of Columbus, Telegrams Received.

On Nov. 24, Dodge telegraphed to USG. "Scouts in today from Decatur Florence and Tuscumbia & Dalton Ga. No troops of Braggs this side of Stevenson in force his troops reported at Tallahomia Decherd with a considerable force at Stevenison & Chattanooga his sick are being sent south towards Atlanta. The Infantry that was at Decatur have gone to Tupello Three (3) Regts but all the cavalry that was between Decatur & Stevinson has gone to Crains Creek just east of Cherokee this is all that is reliable Have one man yet at Dalton watching that R R—" Telegram received, *ibid.*, Dept. of the Tenn., Telegrams Received. On the same day, Dodge telegraphed to Rawlins. "There appears to be a concentration of troops at Tupello & Guntown about 3.000 with one battery have arrived there and conscripts are all being sent there the scouts say that they are cleaning out the wells & making large preparation at Tupello for troops The citizens say that they are going to winter there they have stretched a line of cavalry from Guntown to Cherokee & patrol the entire distance arresting every person who attempts to get through & let no one come this way they are very vigilant caught & hung two (2) of my spies saturday—" Telegram received, *ibid.* On Nov. 27, Dodge telegraphed to Rawlins. "A force of Cavalry reported at one thousand (1000) strong I Judge about five hundred (500) has crossed the Tenn below Savannah   they mean mischief some place north of this on on the Railroad   I have a small force of Cavalry following them up & have taken five of them prisoners   they say that they are ordered to cut the road between Jackson & Grand Junction" Telegram received, *ibid.* On Nov. 28, Dodge telegraphed to Rawlins. "There was about 30 deserters come in here from Tilghmans Division Pembertons army   they left Rocky ford sunday   they say his division consists of Exchanged Prisoners & numbers twenty thousand (20000) & is posted at Rocky ford" Telegram received, *ibid.* On Dec. 1, USG telegraphed to Dodge. "Keep me informed of appearances around you. Should you be advanced upon by any considerable force I will reinforce you" Copies, DLC-USG, V, 18, 30, 91; DNA, RG 393, Dept. of the Tenn., Letters Sent; Dodge Papers, IaHA.

Internal evidence suggests that an undated telegram from Dodge to USG was sent in late Nov. "Have had men come in today from Savannah clear round to Decatur   Nothing new except the cavalry north of Savannah has been massing for a week back for a raid somewhere. They probably crossed the river near Clifton   Did not cross this side of Saltillo which is below savannah—If possible order two hundred 200—cavalry horses to be sent me" Telegram received, DNA, RG 393, Dept. of the Tenn., Telegrams Received.

1. Tullahoma, Tenn., about fifty-five miles northwest of Chattanooga.
2. Decatur, Ala.; Elytown, Ala., about three miles west of the site of Birmingham; and Columbus, Ga., on the Ala. state line, about 175 miles south of Chattanooga, Tenn. Dodge's telegram as received and USG's retained copies of his telegram to Maj. Gen. Henry W. Halleck refer to Elytown rather than Eddytown; the latter is an error in transmission to Washington.
3. Telegram received, *ibid.*

To Maj. Gen. Henry W. Halleck

Head Quarters, Army in the Field
Abberville Miss. Dec. 3d 1862
The enclosed order is a sample of papers received daily from Hd Qrs. of the Dept. of the Mo. It is respectfully refered to Hd Qrs. of the Army with the request that Gen. Curtis may be notified to discontinue furloughing soldiers from this Dept. Granting leaves of absence to officers and making details from men.

U. S. GRANT
Maj. Gen

AES, DNA, RG 94, Vol. Service Division, Letters Received. Written on Special Orders No. 62, Dept. of the Mo., Nov. 27, 1862, detailing Private Samuel M.

McClurg, 10th Mo., as nurse. On Dec. 27, Maj. Gen. Henry W. Halleck endorsed this document. "Respectfully referred to Major Genl Curtis who should be fully aware that he can give no orders to officers or men on duty in another Dept. Complaints of this kind are much too frequent." AES, *ibid.* On Jan. 20, 1863, Maj. Gen. Samuel R. Curtis added his endorsement. "I hope Respectfully referred back through the Genl in chief with a request that Genl Grant will specify any instance when I have commanded troops in his Department except one which as I explained, occurred by mistake.—I suppose I can order the convalescent, as in this case, to take care of the sick which he sends to Hospitals *in my Department.* I had the honor to report to the Commanding General the removal of a force by orders from New Madrid in my Department by orders of General Grant, after I had informed the General that I could not spare it at that time.—General Grants officers and soldiers coming within my lines are subject to my orders, as the many thousands of my troops are under his, when they by my orders go to his relief as thousands have. If this be is not right I respectfully ask further instructions" AES, *ibid.*

On Nov. 22, 1862, Col. Joseph A. Mower, 11th Mo., asked instructions concerning a 2nd lt. of his regt. whose resignation had been accepted by Curtis. This letter was endorsed by Brig. Gen. Charles S. Hamilton. "The attention of the General Commanding Department is respectfully called to these enclosures. The action of Maj Genl's Curtis & Pope in accepting resignations of some officers, and granting leaves of absence to others, belonging to a command not in their Department, calls for serious reprehension, as affecting seriously the efficiency of this army." Copies, DLC-USG, V, 25; DNA, RG 393, Dept. of the Tenn., Endorsements. On Nov. 26, USG endorsed this letter. "Respectfully referred to Headquarters of the Army" Copies, *ibid.* The letter was forwarded to Washington along with an order of Curtis assigning a private in USG's command as orderly at Curtis's hd. qrs. DLC-USG, V, 21.

On Dec. 1, USG had endorsed two furloughs granted by Curtis to privates of the 59th Ill. and 16th Wis. "These furloughs are null and void under General Order No 78 War Dept. Washington D. C. which is still in force" Copy, *ibid.*, V, 91. On the same day, USG endorsed a section of Special Orders No. 62, Dept. of the Mo., mustering out an officer of the 10th Mo. "Respectfully referred to Hd Qrs of the Army Washington, D. C. to know by what authority Maj Gen. Curtis musters out of the service Officers belonging to Regts of this Dept" Copy, *ibid.* On Dec. 25, Curtis wrote to Maj. Thomas M. Vincent explaining the incident and forwarding relevant documents. "the whole matter was done in the hurry of business to accommodate the State authorities. Upon reflection and reexamination of the case, I believe what was done, although in itself right, should not have been done by me and will not be repeated hereafter. If Gen'l Grant desires it, I will rescind the orders, but suppose this would only postpone what has been done." Copy, Curtis Papers, IaHA. This letter was forwarded to USG. DLC-USG, V, 21.

On Dec. 6, Curtis wrote to USG. "Capt R McAllister was appointed as one of my Staff by the Secy of War. I am anxious to have him as Chief of my Commissary. If you can spare him from Cairo I will be obliged." Copy, Curtis Papers, IaHA. No answer was sent, but Curtis's letter was endorsed by Lt. Col. John P. Hawkins to Capt. Richard McAllister. "Capt. McAllister is needed at Cairo and his Services cannot be spared there." Copy, DNA, RG 94, Staff Papers, Richard McAllister. On Oct. 29, McAllister wrote to Curtis that he had complied with a request by Curtis to join his staff by forwarding the matter to USG. ALS, *ibid.*

Curtis eventually arranged to have McAllister ordered to his command through Col. Joseph P. Taylor, commissary gen. *Ibid.* USG relieved McAllister by Special Orders No. 20, Jan. 20, 1863. Copies, *ibid.*, RG 393, Dept. of the Tenn., Special Orders; DLC-USG, V, 26, 27.

On Dec. 10, 1862, Capt. James J. Palmer, 45th Ill., wrote that one of his men was on duty in a hospital in St. Louis. On Dec. 15, USG endorsed this letter to Curtis. "Respectfully forwarded to Gen'l S. R. Curtis, Comd'g Dept. of the Missouri who will please relieve Pvt. Ratzen and order him to return to his Regiment." Copy, *ibid.*, V, 25; DNA, RG 393, Dept. of the Tenn., Endorsements.

To Col. John C. Kelton

Head Quarters, Army in the Field
Abberville, Dec. 3d 1862

Col. J. C. Kelton
A. A. Gen. Washington, D. C.
Col.

I have been constrained to arrest and confine J. C. Van Duzer, Supt. of Telegraphs in this Dept.[1] I felt no disposition to restrain him of his liberty but I was afraid that if allowed to leave the Department, unrestrained, that he would so tamper with the operators along the line as seriously to interfere with the present working of the wires. In fast I was told that he made his boast that if discharged he would carry off the operators employed by him. I have ordered that he be sent out of the Department immediately, escorted to Cairo so as to prevent interferance on his part.

The difficulty with him has been as follows.—When I commenced the move from Corinth & Bolivar to Lagrange Mr. Van Duzer was in Cairo and I had to Superintend and direct the extension of telegraphs and establishment of offices, in person. After getting Mr. Van Duzer up to attend to his business he was very obstinate and seemed evidently inclined to the belief that he could only receive directions from Col. Stager.[2] Any directions that I would give were immediately dispatched to Washington and a wrong impression of the nature of the direction evidently conveyed.

On completing the line to Lagrange I was a whole day prevented from sending a dispatch because the wires were being
used from offices along the line sending *paying* dispatches. I
immediately ordered that no private dispatches should be sent.
This order was only continued in force one day however. I then
directed Col. Riggin A. D. C. to write an order, the very wording
of it dictated by myself, authorizing private dispatches to be sent
over the wires until 10 O'clock A. M. when they did not interfere
with the public service.[3] The following dispatch was the result
of this order.

Washington Nov. 14th 1862

To MAJ. GEN. U. S. GRANT,
 Some one signing himself John Riggin Supt. of Military
Telegraphs is interfering with the management of telegraphs
in Kentucky & Tennessee. This man is acting without the
authority of Col. Anson Stager, Gen. Supt. of Military tele-
graps. See Gen. Order No 38 Apl. 1862 and is an imposter.
Arrest him and send him North of your Dept. before he does
mischief by his interferance.

By Order of the Secretary of War
(Signed) P. H. Watson
Asst. Sec. of War[4]

The following was my reply.

Lagrange Nov. 14th 1862

P. H. WATSON, ASST. SEC. OF WAR, WASHINGTON D. C.
 John Riggin refered to in your dispatch is my Aid. He
has given but one order refering to telegraphing and that was
dictated by myself. It was that private dispatches might be
sent over the wires before 10 O'clock A. M. when they did
not interfere with Military dispatches.
 Col. Riggin is assigned the duty of Military Supt. of telegraphs within this Dept. a position which interferes with no
present arrangement but is intended solely for my relief.
Misrepresentations must have been made.

(Signed) U. S. GRANT
Maj. Gen.[5]

Asst. Sec. Watson replied to this as follows

"Col Anson Stager having been appointed by Sec.y of War Supt. of Military Telegraphs and of the construction and management of Military lines, Col. Riggin must not interfere. Col. Stager has appointed deputies believed to be competant, but if they fail in their duty a report of the facts to Col. Stager will bring a prompt removal.
(Signed)   P. H. Watson
Asst. Sec.y of War[6]

It was not intended that Col. Riggin should have any authority to interfere in any way with any arrangement made either by the Sec. of War or Col. Stager but simply that he should give my instructions to the Dept.y Supt. as to where wires should be run and where offices should be established, and see that it was done and report the fact.

After these dispatches I saw nothing to complain of until the 26th of Nov. On that date dispatches sent into the office in the morning were not sent off until 10 O'clock at night. The wires were down about three hours of that time but they were at work several hours in the morning and again in the evening several hours before they could be got off. The operator on being asked the reason for this replied that the wires were being used from other offices sending cotton dispatches.

I reminded Van Duzer that my order of the 14th was still in force, in this language.

Hd Qrs. 13th Army Corps
Lagrange 26th Nov. 1862

J. C. Van Duzer
Asst. Supt. Mil. Tel. Grand Junction
The order prohibiting the transmission of commercial or private dispatches over the telegraph lines between here and Cairo, except before the hour of 10 A. M. is still in force and must be enforced.
(Signed)   U. S. Grant
Maj. Gen. Com.[7]

Mr. Van Duzer replied that my orders should be obeyed,[8] but immediately removed the operator who had always been at my Hd Qrs. office and put in a new man, evidently because the first had done his duty in informing me why my dispatches had been detained. I sent for Mr. Van Duzer and warned him against changes at my Hd Qrs. for the future without consulting me. I permitted the change to take place however notifying Mr. Van Duzer that I would have no person about the office who would not let me know when dispatches could not be sent and the reasons why.

Some days after this I was astonished at receiving the following dispatch.

Washington Nov. 28th 1862

ALL OPERATORS IN DEPT. OF TEN.

Mr. J. C. Van Duzer has been assigned to the management of the U. S. Military Telegraph lines in the Dept. of the Tenn. You will obey instructions received from him. Orders from any other source will not be obeyed.

(Signed)   ANSON STAGER
Col. & Gen. Supt.
U. S. Mil. Tel.[9]

I was indignant at this interferance in my command and the implied charge of interferance on my part.[10] I have neither the time nor the inclination to take upon myself the duties of others and never proposed to curtail the prerogatives of either Col. Stager or Mr. Van Duzer, but as commander of the Dept. I see nothing in the order of the Sec. of War, refered to in one of these dispatches, that leaves the telegraphs in this Department a distinct institution that cannot be controlled or directed by the Dept. Comd.r.   Col. Stager sending this dispatch after my denial of any interferance on the part of Col. Riggin determined me to remove this man who I had no doubt was the cause of the whole controversy and who at any rate is entirely unfit for his position, at least in this Dept. There are some small matters not mentioned here against Van Duzer that convinces me of his unfitness for his place.

You will oblige me by laying this letter before the Sec. of War as embracing the charges I have against Mr. Van Duzer. I also have to request that some other person be appointed to fill his place. I have so little confidance in the man that unless ordered by some one whos orders I am bound to respect I cannot let him stay in this Dept.

Very respectfully
your obt. svt.
U. S. GRANT
Maj. Gen.

ALS, DNA, RG 107, Letters Received, Irregular Series. *O.R.*, I, xvii, part 2, 377–79. On Dec. 11, 1862, Maj. Gen. Henry W. Halleck endorsed this letter. "Respectfully referred to the Secty of War. I think that Genl Grant was fully justified in arresting Van Duser & sending him out of the Dept. He should not be permitted to return." AES, DNA, RG 107, Letters Received, Irregular Series. On Dec. 1, Col. Anson Stager wrote to Secretary of War Edwin M. Stanton. "I beg leave to submit the accompanying correspondence for your consideration, and to request that the position of the persons appointed from this Department may be more clearly defined—The usefulness of the Military Teleg. is in my opinion greatly impaired by the frequent interference of the Military authorities, (in the Western Departments,) with the practical details, & with the subordinates employed in this branch of service—The managers assigned to the charge of Telegraphs in the various Military Departments have always been specially instructed to comply with the wishes of the Commanding Generals, with promptness, and to the extent of all means at their disposal. A rule established by the War Department that all requirements of Commanding Officers relating to Military Telegraphs shall be made *through* the Officer placed in charge by this Department, would, I believe, remedy the evil. Complaints made to this Dep't by Commanding Generals of incompetency or neglect would secure the prompt dismissal of the offending parties. I only desire that the Military Telegraph may not fall into the hands of incompetent and unskilled persons, and that my authority may be commensurate with the responsibility attached to this branch of the public service—" ALS, *ibid*. On Nov. 13, John C. Van Duzer, Grand Junction, had telegraphed to Stager. "Have just seen a message to operators signed Col. Riggin Supt of Mil Telegraphs Dept of Mississippi—Have you any instructions for me in regard to it" Telegram received, *ibid*. On the same day, Van Duzer wrote to Stager, enclosing a copy of General Orders No. 6, Dept. of the Tenn. "Riggin knows nothing,—really & absolutely nothing—about the business of which he is made superintendent." Copy, *ibid*.

On Dec. 20, Van Duzer wrote to Stager. "A copy of the charges preferred against me by Maj Gen. U. S. Grant, with the endorsement of Maj Gen W. H. Halleck came to hand yesterday and I hasten to reply—You will please remember that I can not visit the persons to whom I refer as witnesses or hold Communication with them without exposing myself and them to arrest; I will however be as accurate as possible, and will state nothing that I can not substantiate by the evidence cited. To so much of Gen Grants letter of Charges as refers to to the Correspondence between himself and P. H. Watson, Assistant Secy of War and to so much thereof as refers to the Order issued by Col. A. Stager, Gen Supt. U. S. M. Tel. dated November 28, 1862 addressed to Telegraph Operators in the Department of Tennesee, I have no other reply to make than that I had nothing to do with either Correspondence or order, and Ought not to be held responsible for either. To the charge of remaining at Cairo I reply that my office was located at that place by Capt T. B. A. David, by whom I was appointed to the charge of the Telegraph in this district; that I had never received from his Successor Capt Sam. Bruch, any other orders, and that I obeyed promptly Gen Grants order to Come to the front, reporting in person to him at LaGrange within thirty-six hours after receiving it. To the charge of neglect of duty during the movement from Bolivar South the following Statement of facts is submitted as reply. Mr S. Palmer, Foreman, with a sufficient force of men and supply of materials to repair the lines to LaGrange was in Waiting at Bolivar two weeks before the advance of the forces; that he accompanied the advance and Opened an office at Grand Junction on the Same evening that Gen Grant arrived at LaGrange (three miles distant) And an office near Gen Grants Hd. Qrs. at LaGrange at 11 00 A M of the Succeding day; that all the Spare men and materiel were forwarded from other points on the line to Grand Junction as Soon as transportation could be had, and every exertion in my power made to establish and maintain lines and offices wherever Ordered by Gen Grant. To the charge of obstinacy and of Communicating to you erroneous impressions I aver in reply that I have promptly obeyed every order received by me either from Gen. Grant or Col Riggin, and have earnestly desired and endeavored to give Satisfaction by the discharge of my duties; that have held communication upon these subjects with Captain Bruch and yourself only and that I offered to submit my dispatches to Gen. Grants inspection: and that these communications were simple statements of facts without Suggestions as to what I desired, and that the two messages to you were in Answer to questions from you and not volunteered. The charge that Military messages were delayed to permit the transmission of Commercial or paying business rests upon the evidance of One Operator only, while the evidence of the Managers of the Offices at Cairo, Columbus, Jackson Grand Junction and the town office at LaGrange (which can be had at any time) Shows exactly the contrary. The delay of business upon the 26th ultimo, to which special reference is made, was owing entirely to the destruction of a portion of the line between Bolivar and Medon—which took place previous to 11 00 A. M. and was not fully repaired until midnight as can be shown by the evidence of W. M. Ingalls the person in charge of the Repairs, Chas. Bolivar, his assistant, and James W. Atwell, Operator at Medon (now at Bolivar) who was on the ground and assisting. The Substitution of J. C. Sullivan as manager of Gen. Grants Office, for I. G. Skinner, of which Complaint is made, was solely for the purpose of rendering the Service of that Office more efficient, and thus removing a cause of Complaint, and I was determined to the change at that time by the fact that on the evening of the 26th while repairs of the line were in progress, Mr. Skinner was unable to receive or get off his business, (as a better operator could have done) which had to be repeated for him by Grand Junction office, all which I explained to Gen Grant in person on the 27th and with which explanation he expressed himself Satisfied. To the charge of exciting the men in my employ to insubordination, I aver that the contrary is the truth, and that I can show by the evidence of the men themselves, that I used my entire authority and influence to prevent any action on their part which would in any way impair the efficiency of the Telegraph Service, and this I have done since as well as before my arrest. The general charges of unfitness for the position to which you, through Capt. David, appointed me, and in which Capt. Bruch continued me, I refer without comment to you and them, as a matter of which you and they can better judge, knowing me, than Gen. Grant, who certainly misapprehends my motives and I protest respectfully, misjudges my actions I have no desire to return to the management of the lines in Gen Grant's Command, but I desire to be removed therefrom by Capt. S. Bruch, and I further desire that I be permitted to return to the Department for the purpose of closing up my unfinished business therein; and that the Order prohibiting my return be rescinded so that I may pass through the Dept. without danger of arrest, should my duties at any time make it necessary or convenient to do so   Will you please submit this to the Secy of War, as my reply to the charges brought against me, and add such explanation as you can upon the matter of the Correspondence and Order, which in fact, are the grounds of my arrest and removal." ALS, *ibid.* An explanation for the entire controversy, offered much later and without substantiation, involved USG's deception by his former chief operator, Ira G. Skinner. William R. Plum, *The Military Telegraph During the Civil War in the United States* (Chicago, 1882), I, 267. See telegram to Maj. Gen. Henry W. Halleck, Dec. 5, 1862.

   There were other difficulties with telegraph operators. On Nov. 13, USG telegraphed to Maj. Gen. Stephen A. Hurlbut. "Please have the case of Redington Telegraph Operator investigated   If innocent his services are wanted"   Telegram received, DNA, RG 110, Records Relating to Telegraph Employees; copies (dated Nov. 16), *ibid.*, RG 393, Dept. of the Tenn., Letters Sent; DLC-USG, V, 18, 30. On Nov. 25, Brig. Gen. Mason Brayman, Bolivar, wrote at length to Lt. Col. John A. Rawlins accusing George P. Lenox, telegrapher at Bolivar, of disloyalty, collusion with cotton speculators, and delay in delivering telegrams. ADfS, Brayman Papers, ICHi. For both cases, see Plum, I, 258.

   1. Van Duzer, born in Erie County, N. Y., in 1827, after a brief career as printer and editor of country newspapers, took up telegraphy in 1848. Manager of a telegraph office in north Mo. at the outbreak of war, he was soon associated with Col. John J. S. Wilson in the establishment and maintenance of telegraph lines in USG's dept. On Nov. 7, 1862, William L. Gross of the telegraph office, Cairo, noted in his records: "Gen. Grant rather spicily telegraphed Van Duzer last night that if he didn't come down there immediately he would be obliged to appoint another man in his place." Gross Papers, OClWHi. On Nov. 30, Rawlins telegraphed to Col. Addison S. Norton, La Grange. "You will arrest at once Mr. J. C. Vandusen, Manager of the U.S. Military Telegraph in this Department for disobedience of orders and conduct prejudicial to the interest of the service. and keep him in close confinement prohibiting communication between him and all Telegraph Operators. He is perhaps at Grand Junction. If so send an Officer there for him"   Copies, DLC-USG, V, 18, 30, 91; DNA, RG 393, Dept. of the Tenn., Letters Sent. *O.R.*, I, xvii, part 2, 370. On the same day, USG telegraphed to Stager. "I have arrested Van Duzer   Will send charges by mail." Telegram received, DNA, RG 107, Letters Received, Irregular Series; copies, *ibid.*, RG 393, Dept. of the Tenn., Letters Sent; DLC-USG, V, 18, 30, 91. *O.R.*, I, xvii, part 2, 371. An undated telegram from USG to all operators in the Dept. of the Tenn. was probably sent on Nov. 30. "No orders from J. C. Van Duzer will

be obeyed—He being under arrest—" Telegram received, DNA, RG 107, Telegrams Collected (Unbound). On Nov. 30, Rawlins wrote to Capt. Theodore S. Bowers, La Grange. "Please send by the messenger sent from here today the dispatch of the Asst Secty of War to Genl Grant directing the arrest of Col. Riggin and Gen. Grant's ~~order~~ answer to the same. Also copy of the order signed by Col. Riggin that no commercial dispatches should be sent after 10 O'clock A. M. Also second dispatch from the Asst Secty of War on same subject. Also the one sent to Mr Vanduzen informing him that the order in regard to the time of transmitting commercial dispatches was still in force." Copies, DLC-USG, V, 18, 30, 91; DNA, RG 393, Dept. of the Tenn., Letters Sent. On Dec. 1, Asst. Secretary of War Peter H. Watson telegraphed to USG. "~~You will Report by telegraph the charges~~ Report to this Department by Telegraph the charges upon which ~~you~~ Van Duzer ~~is placed under~~ is arrested. ~~and sent out of your~~ Department—" ADfS, *ibid.*, RG 107, Telegrams Collected (Bound). *O.R.*, I, xvii, part 2, 371.

2. Stager, born in 1825 in Ontario County, N. Y., became a printer's apprentice at the age of sixteen, and a pioneer telegraph operator in 1846. Ten years later, he was appointed general superintendent, Western Union Telegraph Co. He was appointed capt., asst. q. m. of vols., on Nov. 11, 1861, and superintendent of the military telegraph with the rank of col. on Feb. 26, 1862.

3. On Nov. 11, USG telegraphed to the telegraph superintendent, Grand Junction. "Establish an Office at Genl Hamiltons Head Quarters   It is about two miles down the Rail Road from Junction   you will se a guard at the house" Copies, DLC-USG, V, 18, 30; DNA, RG 393, Dept. of the Tenn., Letters Sent. In an undated telegram, probably sent on Nov. 11, Van Duzer telegraphed to USG. "shall the office at Davis Mills ~~be ma~~ remain at that place or pushed ahead with an advance   we can open at Lamar this Evening if desired   Gen. Quinby has moved forward & no troops now in vicinity of office—" Telegram received, *ibid.*, Telegrams Received. On Nov. 12, USG telegraphed to Van Duzer. "Push the wires on and establish an office where Gen'l. Quinby may designate   the office at Davis' Mills will not be brocken up. Other troops will be sent there" Copies, DLC-USG, V, 18, 30; DNA, RG 393, Dept. of the Tenn., Letters Sent. On the same day, Van Duzer telegraphed to USG. "A quantity of commercial business which was received by connecting lines is at Cairo & can now be transmitted ~~once~~ over our lines without interfering with their military efficiency   will you modify your order relative to private busines so that it can be sent to its destination" Telegram received, *ibid.*, Telegrams Received. On the same day, Col. John Riggin, Jr., telegraphed to Van Duzer. "The telegraph lines within this Department may be used for conveying private dispatches daily before the hour of 10. A. M., except when public business will be thereby delayed." Copies, DLC-USG, V, 18, 30; DNA, RG 393, Dept. of the Tenn., Letters Sent.

4. ADfS (telegram sent), *ibid.*, RG 107, Letters Received, Irregular Series; telegrams received (2), *ibid.*, RG 109, Union Provost Marshals' File of Papers Relating to Individual Civilians. *O.R.*, I, xvii, part 2, 346.

5. Telegram received, DNA, RG 107, Telegrams Collected (Bound); *ibid.*, Letters Received, Irregular Series; copies, *ibid.*, RG 393, Dept. of the Tenn., Letters Sent; DLC-USG, V, 5, 8, 18, 24, 30; William L. Gross diary, OClWHi. *O.R.*, I, xvii, part 2, 347.

6. ALS (telegram sent), DNA, RG 107, Telegrams Collected (Bound); telegram received, *ibid.*, RG 107, Telegrams Collected (Unbound). *O.R.*, I, xvii, part 2, 347. On Nov. 14, USG telegraphed to Van Duzer. "You will report to

these Headquarters immediately." Copies, DLC-USG, V, 18, 30; DNA, RG 393, Dept. of the Tenn., Letters Sent.

7. Copies, *ibid.*

8. On Nov. 26, Van Duzer telegraphed to USG. "Your order shall be obeyed —allow me to explain that for several days previous to this date the lines have been not been fully occupied by the whole business offering and that the delay of today is in consequence of the wires being cut 5 miles south of Medon early in the day it is now Repaired" Telegram received, *ibid.*, Telegrams Received.

9. Copies, DLC-USG, V, 91; DNA, RG 107, Letters Received, Irregular Series. On Nov. 28, Van Duzer had telegraphed to Stager. "Col. Riggin again assumes control of lines. He does not sign as sup't, but by order of Gen'l Grant, who is very angry because of the messages from the War Department awhile ago—" Telegram received, *ibid.*

10. On Nov. 29, USG telegraphed to Stager. "Your insolent despatch to telegraph operators in this dept. just recd. My orders must be obeyed and Mr Van Duzer removed and some one else appointed to fill his place. I send Mr Van Duzer out immediately." Telegram received, *ibid.*; copies, *ibid.*, RG 393, Dept. of the Tenn., Letters Sent; DLC-USG, V, 18, 30, 91. *O.R.*, I, xvii, part 2, 368.

To Act. Rear Admiral David D. Porter

Abbeville, Dec 3rd 1862.

ADMIRAL PORTER,
CAIRO, ILLS.

Our move has been successful so far as compelling the evacuation of the Miss. Central road as as far as Grenada. A. Spy who left Corinth some weeks ago and just returned this evening reports that it is the intention of the rebels to evacuate Arkansas and concentrate their whole force East of the Miss.[1] In this event they will cross at Vicksburg. Please inform me of so much of your movements as you deem prudent to pass over the wires.

U. S. GRANT
Maj Genl.

Telegram, copies, DLC-USG, V, 18, 30, 91; DNA, RG 393, Dept. of the Tenn., Letters Sent. *O.R.*, I, xvii, part 2, 380. No response from Act. Rear Admiral David D. Porter to this telegram has been found, and this may explain why the next communication in USG's letterbooks to Porter, Dec. 8, 1862, was signed by Maj. Gen. William T. Sherman, who had previously corresponded with Porter. Copies, DLC-USG, V, 18, 30, 91; DNA, RG 393, Dept. of the Tenn., Letters Sent. *O.R.*, I, xvii, part 2, 392; *O.R.* (Navy), I, xxiii, 539–40.

1. On Dec. 3, USG telegraphed to Maj. Gen. Henry W. Halleck. "A volunteer sent south by Gen Rosecrans has just returned—reports that Arkansas forces are to cross the River. They will either make a stand at Vicksburg & Jackson or combine with forces against Rosecrans and abandon Mississippi" Telegram received, DNA, RG 94, Generals' Papers and Books, Telegrams Received by Gen. Halleck; *ibid.*, RG 107, Telegrams Collected (Bound); copy, *ibid.*, Telegrams Received in Cipher. *O.R.*, I, xvii, part 1, 472. Copies (dated Dec. 4), DLC-USG, V, 5, 8, 24, 88, 91; DNA, RG 393, Dept. of the Tenn., Hd. Qrs. Correspondence.

To Col. T. Lyle Dickey

Hd Qrs, Army in the Field
Abberville, Dec 3rd 1862.

COL. T. LYLE DICKEY
COMMDG CAVALRY DIVISION

Dispatch of 11 O'clock A. M to day received. It was my intention to send the expedition east to strike the Mobile and Ohio Rail Road as you propose, but thought first to give the Cavalry one days rest. You will however send them, if you deem it practicable immediately after driving the enemy beyond the Yokna river,[1] moving slow so as not to tire out the Cavalry. And after reaching the Rail Road and accomplishing the object of the expedition they will return to the main body of our forces at or near this place.

U. S. GRANT
Maj Genl.

Copies, DLC-USG, V, 18, 30, 91; DNA, RG 393, Dept. of the Tenn., Letters Sent. *O.R.*, I, xvii, part 2, 379–80.

1. The Yokna River, now named Yocona, then often referred to as Yaknapatapha (with great variation in spelling), flowed westward across Miss., crossing the Mississippi Central Railroad about seven miles south of Oxford.

To George G. Pride

Abberville, Miss. Dec 3rd 1862.

COL. G. G. PRIDE
CHIEF ENGR &c M. R. R.
HUDSONVILLE,[1] MISS.

Am glad to hear you are progressing so well with your works. Push on the repairs to the Tallahatchie. It is the intention to rebuild the Tallahatchie bridge, and Quinby has been directed to commence getting out timbers to that end.

U. S. GRANT
Major General.

Telegram, copies, DLC-USG, V, 18, 30, 91; DNA, RG 393, Dept. of the Tenn., Letters Sent. *O.R.*, I, xvii, part 2, 380. On Dec. 3, 1862, USG again telegraphed to George G. Pride. "Finish the railroad up to the Tallahatchie as speedily as possible." Copies, DLC-USG, V, 18, 30, 91; DNA, RG 393, Dept. of the Tenn., Letters Sent. On the same day, Lt. Col. John A. Rawlins telegraphed to Pride. "You will give the necessary instructions to the workman on the road where you are and come here to superintend the building of the Tallahatchie bridge." Copies, *ibid.* On the same day, Brig. Gen. Charles S. Hamilton wrote to USG. "The repairs on the bridge are likely to detain troops for three hours yet and Logan will have as much as he can do to get his Divisn. across to-day. Had I not better put Quinby in camp on the north side, and will it not be well to put a large force of soldiers at work getting out timbers for the rail-road bridge. With the assistance of the troops I think 10 days time may be saved in putting rail-road in order. Please send word by return courier" ALS, *ibid.*, Letters Received.

Also on Dec. 3, Rawlins wrote to the commanding officer, Holly Springs. "Col. Pride Chief Engr Military R. R. telegraphs that the three bridges between Holly Springs and Coldwater will be completed by tomorrow evening, that when the workmen leave there will be no guards. You will send a Regt. to guard the line of Rail Road from Coldwater to Holly Springs immediately. The strictest vigilance must be kept up in the protecting of our lines of communication. So instruct your guards." Copies, DLC-USG, V, 18, 30, 91; DNA, RG 393, Dept. of the Tenn., Letters Sent. On the same day, Rawlins wrote to Lt. Col. Charles A. Reynolds, Holly Springs. "You will make Holly Springs for the present our main Depot for supplies and get forward there all the supplies of every kind needed and issue from there as required. LaGrange will no longer be made a Depot. Any Artillery Horses that arrive send to the front." Copies, *ibid. O.R.*, I, xvii, part 2, 380. On the same day, USG wrote to Reynolds. "Leave thirty two (32) Artillery Horses at Lagrange subject to Gen. Logan's orders to bring up four Caissons from that place. Answer if it can be done and when." Copies, DLC-USG, V, 18, 30, 91; DNA, RG 393, Dept. of the Tenn., Letters Sent.

Also on Dec. 3, Rawlins wrote three times to Capt. Theodore S. Bowers.

"Cars will run through to Holly Springs by friday night or Sunday at farthest. Remain at LaGrange until you can come through on Rail Road. Lieut Dickey will wait and come with you." "Bring printing Office material &c with you to Holly Springs but dont start until you can come on the cars. Lieut Dickey will come with you. Send the 90th Ills. Vols. to report to Commdg Officer at Holly Springs for duty. Transportation can be furnished them at the latter place by the time they need it." "Send the 90th Ills. Vols. to Coldwater to relieve the 29th Ills. Vols. and order the 29th forward to Holly Springs." Copies, *ibid*.

On Dec. 4, Rawlins issued Special Field Orders No. 13. "Col J V. Du-Bois is hereby specially assigned to the command of the forces at Holly Springs and on the line of the Railroad from Coldwater to Waterford, and will so station his troops as to best guard that line of communication." DS, *ibid*., RG 94, Dept. of the Tenn., General Orders; copies, *ibid*., RG 393, Dept. of the Tenn., Special Orders; DLC-USG, V, 26, 27, 91.

1. Hudsonville, Miss., about seven miles north of Holly Springs.

To Col. T. Lyle Dickey

Hd Qrs, Army in the Field.
Oxford, Dec 4th 1862.

COL. T. LYLE. DICKEY
COMMDG CAVALRY DIVISION
COL:

Tilghman was left in command of troops at Rocky Ford[1] and must now be working his way south some distance east of the R. R. He will be easily confused and routed. Lookout for him and if a chance occurs attach him with your full force. In striking Eastward much will necessarily depend on the information you may be able to gather and your own discretion. If however you learn, as I think is the fact, Columbus is only defended by conscripts it would be a great strike to get in there and destroy the enemies Armories, Machine Shops &c. Hd Qrs. will be at Oxford at present and this the point for you to return to.

Your Truly
U. S. GRANT
Maj Genl

Copies, DLC-USG, V, 18, 30, 91; DNA, RG 393, Dept. of the Tenn., Letters Sent. *O.R.*, I, xvii, part 2, 385.

1. Rocky Ford, Miss., on the Tallahatchie River, about nineteen miles northeast of Oxford.

To Lt. Gen. John C. Pemberton

Head Quarters, 13th Army Corps
Dept. of the Tennessee
Oxford Dec. 5th 1862

LIEUT. GEN. PEMBERTON,
COMD.G CONFEDERATE FORCES,
GEN.

I have now several hundred Confederate prisoners who by the Hill Dix Cartel[1] will have to be sent to Vicksburg for exchange unless, by agreement, they will be received elswhere.

I propose to deliver them at such point in the Mississippi Centrail road as you may suggest and where an officer of your command may be to receive and receipt for them. Or I will parole and release them here sending rolls, certified to, for an officer of your Army to receipt if you prefer it.

Please inform me of your pleasure in this matter and I will conform to it.

I am Gen. very respectfully
your obt. svt.
U. S. GRANT
Maj. Gen. Com

ALS, CSmH. *O.R.*, II, v, 27. On Dec. 6, 1862, C. S. A. Lt. Gen. John C. Pemberton, Grenada, wrote to USG. "Your communication of 5th inst just received. The prisoners referred to I presume to be the sick who were necessarily left, and stragglers from this army. The former, if agreeable to you, I would prefer should be kept in hospital until they can be sent for; and proper receipts given—The latter —as the roads are in bad condition and railroad bridges destroyed—I would ask to be sent to Vicksburg Miss as is required by terms of the cartel. I have some

forty prisoners, taken in action, who will be sent to Vicksburg for exchange."
ALS, DNA, RG 393, Dept. of the Tenn., Letters Received. *O.R.*, II, v, 32.

1. The agreement between Maj. Gen. John A. Dix and C. S. A. Maj. Gen.
Daniel H. Hill, July 22, provided a formula for parole and exchange of all prisoners of war. *Ibid.*, II, iv, 266–68.

To Maj. Gen. Henry W. Halleck

Oxford Miss
Dec 5th 1. P. M 1862

MAJ. GEN H. W. HALLECK
GEN IN CHIEF

Roads have become too impassable to leave Railroad any great distance. Streams are high. The Railroad is now complete to Holly Springs & will be to Tallahatchie by Monday. From Tallahatchie to the Yockonia River the enemy were followed so closely that they could not destroy the Railroad or Telegraph. The Cavalry under Colonel Dickey are still out. If practicable will tap the Mobile Railroad before returning. If the Helena troops were at my command [I] think it practicable to send Sherman [to] take them & Memphis troops south [of] mouth of Black River[1] & thus secure Vicksburg & the state of Mississippi

U. S. GRANT

Telegram received, DNA, RG 107, Telegrams Collected (Bound); copies, *ibid.*, Telegrams Received in Cipher; *ibid.*, RG 393, Dept. of the Tenn., Hd. Qrs. Correspondence; DLC-USG, V, 5, 8, 24, 88, 91. *O.R.*, I, xvii, part 1, 472. On Dec. 5, 1862, USG sent two additional telegrams to Maj. Gen. Henry W. Halleck, the second at 4 P.M. "In my dispatch of this morning mouth of Yazoo instead Black river should have been said" "Cavalry are still in pursuit of retreating Enemy Have captured & killed many & forced them to destroy much property including cars. Cavalry will be near Coffeeville tonight" Telegrams received, DNA, RG 94, Generals' Papers and Books, Telegrams Received by Gen. Halleck; *ibid.*, RG 107, Telegrams Collected (Bound); copies, *ibid.*, Telegrams Received in Cipher; *ibid.*, RG 393, Dept. of the Tenn., Hd. Qrs. Correspondence; DLC-USG, V, 5, 8, 24, 88, 91. *O.R.*, I, xvii, part 1, 473. For the reply, see telegram to Maj. Gen. Henry W. Halleck, Dec. 3, 1862.

1. The Black River, into which the Cold Water, Tallahatchie, and Yocona rivers flow, joins the Yazoo River, and it is the latter that USG meant.

To Maj. Gen. Henry W. Halleck

Oxford Miss
Dec 5th 1862

MAJ GEN H. W. HALLECK
GEN IN CHIEF.

I have never ordered a purchase or the disbursement of a dollar for Telegraph purposes. Never interfered with the prerogatives of the Supt. Never ordered the establishment of an office or extension of a wire except through the asst Supt. When he could be reached. The asst Supt for this Dep't it is impossible for me to get along with. I arrested him & notified Operators of the fact & that his orders would not be obeyed. Col Stager was notified of the arrest

U. S. GRANT
Maj Genl

Telegram received, DNA, RG 94, Generals' Papers and Books, Telegrams Received by Gen. Halleck; *ibid.*, RG 107, Telegrams Collected (Bound); copies, *ibid.*, Telegrams Received in Cipher; *ibid.*, RG 393, Dept. of the Tenn., Hd. Qrs. Correspondence; DLC-USG, V, 5, 8, 24, 88, 91. *O.R.*, I, xvii, part 2, 386-87. On Dec. 5, 1862, Maj. Gen. Henry W. Halleck had telegraphed to USG. "The Secty of War has called my attention to your telegraphic despatches in regard to operators & offices. Col Stager was charged by the President, under a law of Congress, with the entire management of military telegraph operations. He directs all purchases, & appoints and removes all officers, under direction of the Secty of War. If any operator fails in his duty, report him for removal. In extreme cases he may be arrested, just as you can arrest an officer of the Navy or of the Treasury Dept. Col Stager directs all telegraphic purchases. In case of deficiencies report the fact, but do not order purchases. They cannot be paid for out of the Qr-Master's Dept. Any orders to that effect given by you will be immediately countermanded" ALS (telegram sent), DNA, RG 107, Telegrams Collected (Bound); telegram received, *ibid.*, RG 393, Dept. of the Tenn., Telegrams Received; DLC-Robert C. Clowry. *O.R.*, I, xvii, part 2, 386. See letter to Col. John C. Kelton, Dec. 3, 1862.

On Dec. 4, Capt. Samuel Bruch, Louisville, telegraphed to Col. Anson Stager. "The following order was rec'd this morning by W. L. Gross at Cairo. 'Keep the supplies required for use of officers on hand & order what you want from the East—By order Maj Gen Grant—signed JOHN RIGGIN JR Col & A.D.C.' Heard nothing from Van Duzer lately." Telegram received, DNA, RG 107, Telegrams Collected (Bound). On the same day, Edward Schermerhorn, Oxford, telegraphed to Stager. "By order of Genl Grant we have extended line to this place. Work does not go smoothly. Gen Grant gives operators choice of obeying his orders or working on fortifications. Men all dissatisfied & want to leave" Telegram received, *ibid. O.R.*, I, xvii, part 2, 385–86. On the same day, Col. John Riggin, Jr., telegraphed to the telegraph operator, Davis' Mill, Miss. "Will close his office and with his office and with his instrument &c proceed immediately to Abberville, Miss. and take charge of office there." Copies, DLC-USG, V, 18, 30, 91; DNA, RG 393, Dept. of the Tenn., Letters Sent.

Also on Dec. 4, Lt. Col. John McDermott, Grand Junction, telegraphed to USG. "I have the honor to report to you the following dispatch   Washington D C   Dec 4 6 45 P M   to Comdg officer Grand Junction   you will immediately take the parole of J C Vanduzer supt of Teleg & release him if he is in confinmt and report to this Dept   signed E M STANTON Secy of War   The officer in charge refuses to give him up   what shall I do in the premises" Telegram received, *ibid.*, Telegrams Received. See *O.R.*, I, xvii, part 2, 382. On the same day, USG telegraphed to McDermott. "Release Mr. J. C. VanDuzer on Parole as directed by the Secretary of War." Copies, DLC-USG, V, 18, 30, 91; DNA, RG 393, Dept. of the Tenn., Letters Sent. Misdated Dec. 3 in *O.R.*, I, xvii, part 2, 379.

On Dec. 5, USG telegraphed to the commanding officer, Grand Junction. "The release of Van Duzen on parole does not entitle him to interfere with telegraph matter or to remain in this Dept. He must leave by first train." Copies, DLC-USG, V, 18, 30, 91; DNA, RG 393, Dept. of the Tenn., Letters Sent. *O.R.*, I, xvii, part 2, 386. On the same day, 5:50 P.M., McDermott telegraphed to Halleck. "I have the honor to report that J. C. Van Duzer is held here under guard with a written order signed by Gen'l Grant for his removal to Cairo   I did not feel that I had the responsibility of him & declined to liberate him as I receive my orders from Gen Grant & not from the War Department. I had good reason to suppose the despatch bogus for the purpose of having Van Duzer released" Telegram received, DNA, RG 107, Telegrams Collected (Bound). *O.R.*, I, xvii, part 2, 386. Also on Dec. 5, William L. Gross, Cairo, telegraphed to Bruch. "Van Duzer arrived Cairo under guard & was put on board train going north. He goes to St Louis from which place he will communicate with you" Telegram received, DNA, RG 107, Telegrams Collected (Bound). On Dec. 7, John C. Van Duzer telegraphed to Bruch. "I was sent out of Dept under guard and Genl Tuttle informed me that he is ordered to arrest and confine me if I return   I do not understand that Gen Grant intends to give me any chance to show by an investigation that I was right. I desire to return to the Dept in preference to any other position in the service, but to do it must have safe conduct of War Dept or Genl Grant will shoot me" Telegram received, *ibid. O.R.*, I, xvii, part 2, 394.

To Maj. Gen. William T. Sherman

Hd Qrs, 13th Army Corps.
Oxford, Miss. Dec 5, 1862.

Maj Gen. Sherman
Commdg Right Wing.
Genl:

This will be handed you by Mr. W. A. Cox[1] of Holly Springs. Mr. Cox resides in Holly Springs and his brother on their joint plantations twelve miles south[2] near Chulahoma.

Their horses, mules, hogs &c and 155 bales of Cotton have been seized by your command. The Cotton has been sold by your Quartermaster, Smith[3] to a Jew by the name of Haas and delivered at Holly Springs by Govt teams at 35 cents as you will see by the contract a copy of which has been shown me.

Under my orders Chief Q. M. Reynolds has fixed point for the sale of Cotton where competition can give the Govt full value for confiscated Cotton. It is for this reason chiefly that I have ordered all Cotton seized to be turned over by other Q. Ms. to him for sale, and that claims can be determined by some uniform principle.—Inasmuch as the policy of the authorities at Washington has been evinced in orders to permit these people to sell their cotton where they do not come so clearly under the confiscation Act as to leave no question or doubt, I have instructed the Provost Marshals at the different points in the rear of the Army to permit owners to sell their Cotton unless they are or have been in Arms against the Govt or unless they have abandoned their property and gone South thereby evincing consciousness of guilt, or unless the party being a Citizen had committed some treasonable offense which justified his arrest and detention or unless the buyer or seller had violated some Military Order.

The Cotton sold by Q. M., Smith was seized by the Provost Marshal at Holly Springs under his orders from these Hd Qrs. to seize all Cotton found in Govt teams and is now held awaiting my orders.

The Coxes who claim to be the owners aver that they do not come under any of the exceptions above stated disqualifying them from selling. If so they are entitled to their Cotton upon their paying a good price for hauling it to market.

You will therefore direct Q. M., Smith to refund to Maas the money paid by him for the Cotton and hereafter he will report to Col. Reynolds, Chief Q. M. all cotton seized and all Cotton hauled by Govt teams.

I will direct Col. Reynolds to collect from the Coxes a suitable amount for hauling the Cotton and then order its delivery to them unless you know of some reason why this should not be done.

You can take any Cotton on your line of march and send it to Holly Springs or any other point where Govt teams are returning for supplies and have it reported to Col Reynolds who will have it sold if properly confiscated at public auction or charge the owners for its hauling if not.

This Cotton sold by Q. M, Smith exceeds the weight estimated over ten thousand pounds which probably occurred from the want of facilities to determine the exact or approximate weight. The value of this Cotton is forty cents and upwards in Holly Springs.—All funds will be drawn from the Chief Q. M. Before leaving LaGrange orders were issued that no Cotton Buyers should accompany the Army but would be allowed to follow as the Army advanced and buy in the rear, but in consequence of the total disregard and evasion of orders by the Jews my policy is to exclude them so far as practicable from the Dept.

All parties from whom Horses, Mules, forage &c are taken should have receipts given them when practicable. No receipts were given the Coxes.—On Second thought I have concluded that Q. M, Smith may retain the funds he received from Maas, but he will send Chief Q. M. Reynolds proper receipts for the amount as being received from him, and I will order ~~him~~ Reynolds to pay that amount to the Coxes in case the Cotton is delivered to them.

There are several orders on this subject issued by me which

you have not yet received and which I cannot now forward you as
I have not copies with me.

Very Respectfully &c

U. S. Grant

Maj Gen

Copies, DLC-USG, V, 18, 30, 91; DNA, RG 393, Dept. of the Tenn., Letters
Sent. On Dec. 5, 1862, Maj. Gen. William T. Sherman, College Hill, Miss.,
wrote to USG. "Your letter of this date is received. I regret the matter of the
cotton of Mr Cox   On the morning I was starting from Tchulahoma I started a
train of one hundred empty wagons for Coldwater for provisions. Capt Smith
reported to me that a good deal of cotton lay at ~~abundant~~ abandonned plantations
and wanted to send it in to Holly Springs that he might realize some money.
Having none, and having failed to receive any on repeated requisitions, I gave
my consent that he should send in a limited quantity according to existing orders.
He is now here and insists that some of the cotton taken was not the property of
Mr Cox, but on the other hand, Mr Cox asserts that all the cotton sent in by our
train bears his mark. If that be the case he should have the proceeds   All accounts
represent him as a good Union Man. It is impossible to delegate the authority to
seize cotton to any body,   It will demoralize the whole army and the less we do
the better   I have never yet been able to seize cotton horses, cattle hogs or any
thing without a Union owner turning up. My orders are that none but Brigade
Qr Masters shall take any forage, horses, mules, wagons or anything and that in
all instances receipts should be given and the property taken up as by purchase   I
make all efforts to see this order executed but I blush to say that horses have been
taken, hogs turkeys & chickens stolen, and disgraceful plundering done. Nothing
will check this but prompt punishment—Colonels do not & will not restrain their
men   All my Brigadiers and some Colonels are laboring to check this evil and I
hope in time to appoint an remedy but I fear a Corupt press has sown the seed
too deep to be easily eradicated   Mr Cox place was close to Chulahoma and no
white man there,—The soldiers soon raised the story that the owner was absent
and in the Confederate Service and the consequence was disgraceful plunder. Genl
Lauman whose division was near did all a man could do to check it, but unsuc-
cesfully and I witnessed with shame the damage done. I think Mr Cox can yet
get full recipts for his corn fodder &c and by securing the proceeds of this sale of
cotton he will be whole or nearly so, as to his rails he must await the end of the
war   I will see that Capt Smith or other Quarter Masters of my Divisions does
not truck any cotton or its proceeds   There is a good deal here & hereabouts
but the owners will turn up and claim the proceeds. The best plan is to allow all
in our Route to carry it to market and receive in exchange goods not contraband"
Copy, *ibid.*, RG 94, Generals' Papers and Books, William T. Sherman, Letters
Sent.

On Dec. 6, Lt. Col. John A. Rawlins wrote to Lt. Col. Charles A. Reynolds.
"Enclosed please find duplicate receipts of Capt. J. Condit Smith, Asst Qr. Master
U. S. Vols. for $23056.25 the proceeds of a lot of Cotton sold by him to one Mr.
Haas but which is claimed by Mr. Wm Cox and brother both of whom are Union
men. You will therefore turn over to Mr. Haas the sum of money mentioned in
the said receipts if you have it, if not give him a receipt for the amount and take

it up on your returns. The Cotton or such portions of it as belong to the Messrs. Cox you will cause to be delivered to them charging them for the benefit of Govt. $5. per bale for hauling it in Govt teams to Holly Springs (where it now is in the hands of the Provost Marshal) and the remainder if any sell for the benefit of Government." Copies, DLC-USG, V, 18, 30, 91; DNA, RG 393, Dept. of the Tenn., Letters Sent. On Dec. 11, Reynolds wrote to USG. "I have ordered Capt T. C. Bru Q M to the front. he is at LaGrange & will be there in a day or two he will look after the cotton   I have recd the receipt of Capt Smith a Q M but ~~have~~ not being inform I forwarded them to him   I have sent a commication in regard to it to Hd Qrs" ALS, *ibid.*, Miscellaneous Letters Received. On the same day, Reynolds telegraphed to Rawlins. "Capt J C Smith A Q M is here having been ordered by Gen Sherman to Memphis   do you wish the order obeyed   please forward the Communcation sent to Hd. Qrs. for examination for Capt Smith to me at this place" Telegram received, *ibid.*, Telegrams Received. On Dec. 12, Rawlins telegraphed to Reynolds. "The Genl directs that Genl. Shermans order to Capt. Smith's shall be obeyed." Copies, DLC-USG, V, 18, 30, 91; DNA, RG 393, Dept. of the Tenn., Letters Sent.

1. While at Holly Springs, USG maintained hd. qrs. at the mansion of William H. Coxe. Ruth Watkins, "Reconstruction in Marshall County," *Publications of the Mississippi Historical Society*, XII (1912), 157; Federal Writers' Project, *Mississippi* (New York, 1943), pp. 205–6.

2. This plantation, named Galena, is discussed *ibid.*, p. 439.

3. John C. Smith served as 2nd lt. and regt. q. m., 42nd Ill., from Oct. 16, 1861. On April 1, 1862, he was confirmed as capt., asst. q. m. of vols.

To Brig. Gen. Charles S. Hamilton

Oxford, Miss. Dec 5th 1862.

GEN. HAMILTON
ABBERVILLE, MISS.

I ordered up the remainder of Logan's Division yesterday and one of yours to come to-day. Finding that Logan's supplies could not reach him to march yesterday, You was ordered to send a Division as soon as practicable. The rain of last night making the roads so bad you you were then directed not to move any farther from your supplies.[1] There has been system enough but some failure in my dispatches reaching you.

U. S. GRANT
Maj Genl.

Copies, DLC-USG, V, 18, 30, 91; DNA, RG 393, Dept. of the Tenn., Letters Sent. *O.R.*, I, xvii, part 2, 387.

On Dec. 6, 1862, Lt. Col. John A. Rawlins wrote to Brig. Gen. Charles S. Hamilton. "You will put the Divisions of your command (the one at Waterford and the one at Abbeville) in the best possible condition for defense and the comfort of the men and let each remain where it now is until further orders, instructing the Commdg Officers of the respective Divisions to collect as much forage and supplies from the surrounding country as possible and sending out as far as is practicable to obtain it." Copies, DLC-USG, V, 18, 30, 91; DNA, RG 393, Dept. of the Tenn., Letters Sent. *O.R.*, I, xvii, part 2, 389. On the same day, Rawlins wrote to Maj. Gen. James B. McPherson. "You will put the Division you have at Waterford in the best possible condition for defense and the comfort of the men and leave it where it is until further orders, instructing Commdg Officer to collect as much forage and supplies as possible from the surrounding country as far out as it is practicable to obtain it." Copies, DLC-USG, V, 18, 30, 91; DNA, RG 393, Dept. of the Tenn., Letters Sent. *O.R.*, I, xvii, part 2, 389.

1. On Dec. 4, USG telegraphed to Hamilton. "As soon as practicable let McArthur's Division move up here and one Brigade of Quinby's move up to Abberville. Ross and the remainder of Quinby's forces had better remain where they are until the R. R. is completed." Copies, DLC-USG, V, 18, 30, 91; DNA, RG 393, Dept. of the Tenn., Letters Sent. *O.R.*, I, xvii, part 2, 385. On Dec. 5, USG telegraphed to Hamilton. "Owing to the bad condition of the roads do not move McArthur's Division any farther from their supplies." Copies, DLC-USG, V, 18, 30, 91; DNA, RG 393, Dept. of the Tenn., Letters Sent. *O.R.*, I, xvii, part 2, 387.

To Edwin M. Stanton

Head Quarters, 13th Army Corps.
Dept of the Tennessee.
Oxford, Miss. Dec 6th 1862.

HON. E. M. STANTON
SECTY OF WAR, WASHINGTON, D. C.
SIR:

Herewith I have the honor to enclose you letter books containing the private and official correspondence of Ex. Secretary of the Interior, Jacob Thompson.

These letters show the treasonable character of at least a portion of the Cabinet of the late Administration if evidence of this kind is necessary to convict them.

Mr. Thompson now Col. Thompson of the Southern Army left this place as our troops entered. I have directed that his fine residence be used as a Hospital for our Soldiers. Should I succeed in finding personal property of his that can be made use of by the Army I will appropriate it for such purpose.

I am entirely subsisting our animals upon the country through which we pass and as far as practicable subsisting the troops also.

Very Respectfully,
Your Ob't. Servant.
U. S. GRANT
Maj Genl.

Copies, DLC–USG, V, 5, 8, 24, 88, 91; DNA, RG 393, Dept. of the Tenn., Hd. Qrs. Correspondence. On Dec. 20, 1862, Asst. Secretary of War Christopher P. Wolcott wrote to USG. "The Secretary of War directs me to say that he has duly received your letter of the 6th instant, and also two letter books containing copies of letters written by Jacob Thompson, late Secretary of the Interior, and also a small package of letters addressed to the same person—which were transmitted with your letter. These papers I am instructed to say, are deemed very important as showing that Thompson was plotting the overthrow of the Government, even while he was one of its very highest functionaries, and bound by every conceivable obligation to shield it to the utmost of his power against all danger and menace. The Secretary thanks you for the promptness and vigilance which have marked your action in this matter." LS, *ibid.*, Letters Received. Jacob Thompson, born in N. C. and an 1831 graduate of the University of N. C., moved to Pontotoc, Miss., in 1835, but settled permanently at Oxford. A U.S. Representative (1839–51), prominent in the Democratic conventions of 1852 and 1856, he served as secretary of the interior from 1857 until his resignation in 1861, provoked by efforts to reinforce Fort Sumter. A vol. aide to Gen. Pierre G. T. Beauregard at Shiloh, he was currently serving unofficially as inspector gen. for Lt. Gen. John C. Pemberton and, according to his own recollections, advocating a cav. raid by Maj. Gen. Earl Van Dorn to cut USG's supply line. J. F. H. Claiborne, *Mississippi as a Province, Territory and State* . . . (Jackson, Miss., 1880), I, 459.

On Dec. 16, 1862, USG telegraphed to Maj. Gen. Henry W. Halleck. "I have confiscated one hundred & ninety (190) bales of Cotton for Maj Thompson." Telegram received, DNA, RG 94, Generals' Papers and Books, Telegrams Received by Gen. Halleck; *ibid.*, RG 107, Telegrams Collected (Bound); copies, *ibid.*, RG 393, Dept. of the Tenn., Hd. Qrs. Correspondence; DLC–USG, V, 5, 8, 24, 88, 91. All copies retained by USG refer to "Jake Thompson."

To Col. T. Lyle Dickey

Hd Qrs, 13th Army Corps
Dept of the Tenn
Oxford, Miss. Dec 6th 1862

COL T LYLE. DICKEY
COMMD.G CAVALRY DIVISION
COL.

Rest your horses and men where you are and when sufficiently recruited strike to the east and dstroy the Mobolile and Ohio R. R. as much as possible. As stated by me in a previous dispatch[1] it would be a great strike to reach Columbus & dstroy Armories and Machine shops there.

The Cavalry force you will have with you can subsist on the country through which you pass. The plundering propensity exhibited by some of the Cavalry should be suppressed as far as practicable. This can be partially done by making a detail from each Regt. and charge them with procuring rations and forage for their Regts. and replacing broken down animals.

This is no depot of supplies here or I would forward some to you. Let me know how soon you can start and I will relieve you by making an Infantry and Artillery demonstration in the same directions

Yours Truly,
U. S. GRANT
Maj Genl.

Copies, DLC-USG, V, 18, 30, 91; DNA, RG 393, Dept. of the Tenn., Letters Sent. *O.R.*, I, xvii, part 2, 388. On Dec. 6, 1862, 9:00 A.M., Col. T. Lyle Dickey, "at Prophits Farm—near Porters Bridge on Otucalofa river—17 miles from Oxford—" wrote to USG. "My command is in camp on the North side of the Otucalofa river & are resting & feeding—I have not yet received reports of casualties—but our loss is much less than at first supposed—Lt Lyford was at Water valley at 8-Oclock this morning—Shall we come on at once to Oxford or lie here a day or two—We need rations—forage can be had here I think our killed & wounded will not exceed thirty—& perhaps as many more missing I will ride forward toward Oxford a few miles about noon—" ALS, DNA, RG 393, Dept. of the Tenn., Letters Received.

1. See letter to Col. T. Lyle Dickey, Dec. 4, 1862.

To George G. Pride

By Telegraph from Oxford [*Dec.*] 6 *1862*

To Col Pride

I dont think that road from Memphis will be constructed   the Engineer Co at Jackson will come down as soon as they finish the pontoon bridge[1]   If we can get along ~~Engine~~ with no more Locomotives I would like to do it but if they are absolutely necessary they may be ordered   there is some fine square timber here and some already framed between this and the Tallahatchie sufficient for this End of the bridge

U S Grant
Maj Gen

Telegram received, Pride Papers, MoSHi; copies, DLC-USG, V, 18, 30, 91; DNA, RG 393, Dept. of the Tenn., Letters Sent. On Dec. 6, 1862, USG again telegraphed to George G. Pride. "There will be very few Cars required south of Tallahatchie. The force here will be diminished." Copies, *ibid*. On Dec. 9, USG telegraphed to Col. Joseph D. Webster, Holly Springs. "Lagrange will be kept up as a way station, and Holly Springs for the present the main terminus. Hope soon to make this place such." Copies, *ibid*.

1. See telegram to Col. Josiah W. Bissell, Nov. 26, 1862.

To Maj. Gen. Henry W. Halleck

Oxford, Dec 7th *1862*

Maj Gen. H. W. Halleck
Washington, D. C.

The Cavalry pursuit under Col. Dickey have now drawn off having followed the enemy to Coffeeville.[1]—Our loss nine killed, fifty six wounded and fifty six missing. We have captured about seven hundred of the enemy but can make no estimate of their killed and wounded. The enemy were forced to burn many stores, some Cars and their camp equipage.[2]

I will send two Division to Memphis in a few days as soon as I can learn the designs of the enemy.

Do you want me to command the expedition on Vicksburg or shall I send Sherman?[3]

U. S. Grant
Maj. Genl.

Telegram received, DNA, RG 107, Telegrams Collected (Bound); copies (dated Dec. 8, 1862), *ibid.*, Telegrams Received in Cipher; (dated Dec. 7) *ibid.*, RG 393, Dept. of the Tenn., Hd. Qrs. Correspondence; DLC-USG, V, 5, 8, 24, 88, 91. Dated Dec. 8 in *O.R.*, I, xvii, part 1, 473–74. For the Dec. 7, noon, telegram of Maj. Gen. Henry W. Halleck to USG, see letter to Maj. Gen. William T. Sherman, Dec. 8, 1862.

1. Coffeeville, Miss., on the Mississippi Central Railroad, about twenty-seven miles south of Oxford.

2. Reports of the engagement at Coffeeville, Dec. 5, by Col. T. Lyle Dickey, Col. Edward Hatch, 2nd Iowa Cav., C. S. A. Maj. Gen. Earl Van Dorn, and C. S. A. Brig. Gen. Lloyd Tilghman, are in *O.R.*, I, xvii, part 1, 494–96, 501–7. In his report to Lt. Col. John A. Rawlins, Dec. 7, Dickey assessed U.S. losses at 10 killed, 63 wounded, 41 captured; C. S. A. losses were "at least" 70 killed, 250 wounded, 750 captured. LS, DNA, RG 94, War Records Office, Union Battle Reports. *O.R.*, I, xvii, part 1, 496. Apparently Dickey was reporting the results of five days of action.

On Dec. 7, Maj. Gen. William T. Sherman wrote to Rawlins. "Col Grierson is just back. He is tired and has had not time to make a Report but I give the substance of his remarks. he reached Panola at 2 P. M yesterday   no enemy there, all gone South and the country stampeded. Steels men had been there last Tuesday   a large Cavalry force having approached within two miles and a few gone in   Grierson heard of our forces being at the Yocknopatofa twelve miles south of Panola, and went there but they had left last Thursday morning for the Tallahatchie at the mouth of Cold Water   Grierson heard from very many persons that the Helena forces approached the Tallahatchie perfectly unexpected, capturing every picket and a Rebel cavalry picket on this side was suprised by a shell coming into their Camp when they fled in utter confusion. At Panola a Regiment fled south without waiting. It seems our troops crossed the Tallahatchie at the mouth of Cold water and moved to the point on the Yocknapatofa where a small Cavalry force of 110 men proceeded to Coffeeville cut the wires and ~~took~~ broke a small piece of trestle which the enemy repaired in three hours,   Col Grierson reports that the utmost alarm seized all the inhabitants and that our Cavalry might then have broke the road all to pieces. There was a small cavalry skirmish at Oakland 20 miles south of Panola. He says it was universally represented that the Railroad Bridges across the Tallahatchie, Yocana and all way places on *that* Road were destroyed by the enemy in retreating. The People give it up as lost and the story was the ~~enemy~~ Army would proceed to Jackson and there make a final desperate stand. Country represented as devoid of forage, but a good deal of cotton lying about loose   I enclose a Panola newspaper which contains some news. Tomorrow Col Grierson will report in full"   Copy, DNA,

RG 94, Generals' Papers and Books, William T. Sherman, Letters Sent. On Dec. 8, Col. Benjamin H. Grierson prepared a detailed report for Sherman, which Sherman forwarded to USG's hd. qrs. LS, *ibid.*, RG 393, Dept. of the Tenn., Letters Received. *O.R.*, I, xvii, part 1, 516–18.

3. On Dec. 9, Halleck telegraphed to USG. "As it is possible that Bragg may cross at Decatur & fall upon Corinth, the security of that place should be carefully attended to. Do not make the Mississippi expedition so large as to endanger West Tennessee. I think twenty five thousand men in addition to the forces to be added from Helena will be sufficient; but send more if you can spare them. The President may insist upon designating a separate commander; if not, assign such officers as you deem best. Sherman would be my choice as the chief, under you." ALS (telegram sent), DNA, RG 107, Telegrams Collected (Bound); copies, *ibid.*, RG 108, Telegrams Sent; *ibid.*, RG 393, Dept. of the Tenn., Hd. Qrs. Correspondence; DLC-USG, V, 5, 8, 24, 88, 91. *O.R.*, I, xvii, part 1, 474.

To Maj. Gen. Henry W. Halleck

Oxford Miss Dec 8, 1862. (1.0 A M.)

MAJ GEN HALLECK
GEN IN CHF

Up to yesterday no Infantry has crossed the Tennessee going south from Decatur. Rebel cavalry are busy collecting forage & provisions   On line of railroad from Cherokee[1] to Saltillo there are about two thousand (2.000) Cavalry. Great number of cars have come up from Mobile toward Jackson Enterprise[2] Columbus & Saltillo.

At Mobile & Columbus rebels are working night & day on fortifications

The enemy have gone South of Yallabusha river

I will try & learn soon if they intend to stand there.

Deserters come in daily from Rebel army

U S. GRANT
Maj Genl

Telegram received, DNA, RG 94, Generals' Papers and Books, Telegrams Received by Gen. Halleck; *ibid.*, RG 107, Telegrams Collected (Bound); copies, *ibid.*, Telegrams Received in Cipher; *ibid.*, RG 393, Dept. of the Tenn., Hd. Qrs. Correspondence; DLC-USG, V, 5, 8, 24, 88, 91. *O.R.*, I, xvii, part 1, 474.

1. Cherokee, Ala., on the Memphis and Charleston Railroad, about eight miles east of Miss. No railroad linked Cherokee to Saltillo, Miss.; the reference

to the railroad in this sentence belongs with the preceding sentence, and appears there in USG's letterbooks.

2. Enterprise, Miss., on the Mobile and Ohio Railroad, about twelve miles south of Meridian, Miss.

To Maj. Gen. Henry W. Halleck

Oxford Miss
Dec 8th 10 P M 1862

MAJ GEN H. W. HALLECK
GEN IN CHIEF.
GENERAL.

Gen'l Sherman will command the expedition down the Mississippi. He will have a force of about forty thousand (40.000) men—will land above Vicksburg—up the Yazoo if practicable and cut the Mississippi Central R. R. and the Rail Road running East from Vicksburg where they cross Black river. I will cooperate from here. My movements depending on those of the Enemy. With the large Cavalry force now at my command I will be able to have them show themselves at different points on the Tallahatchie & Yallabusha and where an opportunity occurs make a real attack. After cutting the two Rail Roads Gen Shermans movements to secure the end desired will necessarily be left to his judgement.

I will occupy this Rail Road to Coffeeville.

U. S. GRANT
Maj Gen Com'dg

Telegram received, DNA, RG 94, Generals' Papers and Books, Telegrams Received by Gen. Halleck; *ibid.*, RG 107, Telegrams Collected (Bound); copies, *ibid.*, Telegrams Received in Cipher; *ibid.*, RG 393, Dept. of the Tenn., Hd. Qrs. Correspondence; *ibid.*, 13th Army Corps, Letters Received; DLC-USG, V, 5, 8, 24, 88, 91; (2) DLC-William T. Sherman; (3) McClernand Papers, IHi. *O.R.*, I, xvii, part 1, 474.

To Maj. Gen. William T. Sherman

———

Oxford ~~Tennessee~~ Miss
Dec. 8th 1862

GEN. SHERMAN.
DEAR GEN.

The following is Copy of dispatch just received from Washington.

Washington Dec. 7th 12 M.

GEN. GRANT.

The capture of Grenada[1] may change our plans in regard to Vicksburg. You will move your troops as you may deem best to accomplish the great object in view. You will retain till further orders all troops of Gen. Curtis now in your Dept.[2] Telegraph to Gen. Allen in St. Louis for all steamboats you may require.[3] Ask Porter to co-operate.[4] Telegraph what are your present plans.[5]

H. W. HALLECK,
Gen in Chief[6]

I wish you would come over this evening and stay to-night or come in the morning. I would like to talk with you about this matter. My notion is to send two Divisions back to Memphis and fix upon a day when they should effect a landing and press from here with this command at the proper time to cooperate. If I do no[t] do this I will move our present force to Grenada, including Steeles, repairing road as we proceed, and establish a Depot of provision there. When a goo[d] ready is had move immediately upon Jackson, cuting loose from the road. Of the two plans I look most favorably upo[n] the former.

Come over and we will talk this matter over.

Yours Truly
U. S. GRANT
Maj. Gen.

ALS, DLC-William T. Sherman.

1. On Dec. 4, 1862, Maj. Gen. Samuel R. Curtis telegraphed to Maj. Gen. Henry W. Halleck that Brig. Gen. Frederick Steele "has moved on Grenada." *O.R.*, I, xvii, part 2, 382. Although Steele advanced nearly to Grenada, Miss., the town remained in C. S. A. possession. USG apparently based his belief in the fall of Grenada, shown in the next paragraph, on Halleck's telegram. A dispatch from Cairo, Dec. 6, which erroneously reported the capture of Grenada, appearing in the *Chicago Tribune* on Dec. 7 and widely copied, probably provided Halleck with this misinformation.

2. See letters to Brig. Gen. Frederick Steele and to Commanding Officer, Friar's Point, Miss., Dec. 8, 1862.

3. On Dec. 8, Maj. Gen. William T. Sherman telegraphed to Col. Robert Allen, St. Louis, for supplies of coal, wood, and provisions. Copies, DLC-USG, V, 18, 30, 91; DNA, RG 393, Dept. of the Tenn., Letters Sent. On Dec. 11, Allen telegraphed to USG. "Your dispatch received. We will furnish the transportation you require as rapidly as possible. It cannot be done within the time you mention. Coal is very scarce—must depend principally upon obtaining it from points on the Ohio. I have telegraphed to all points. The river is low. I cannot tell how fast coal can be brought down. Steamboatmen inform me that with little delay wood can be chopped when coal cannot be supplied. I had, previous to your dispatch, informed the General-in-Chief and the Quartermaster-General that coal must be sent from the Ohio, and am informed that prompt attention will be given." *O.R.*, I, xvii, part 2, 399. On Dec. 12, Allen wrote to USG. "Your dispatch of the 9th instant was not received until night before last; giving us practically but three days to procure forty or fifty boats, and have them at Memphis in the time you prescribe. Coal is extremely scarce—the river very low, and but comparatively few boats now in port. Consequently your order cannot be fully complied with as to time, but everything possible, is being done, and Col. Parsons informs me that but a very brief delay will occur. The Colonel will himself take the supervision of the Fleet from here and Cairo, and report to you at the earliest possible moment. Be assured that every assistance in our power shall be given to forward your movements and secure its success. I have taken every precaution to secure necessary coal, but I am assured by every good Steamboatman, that wood can be cut in from two to four hours, from place to place, sufficient to run the boats twenty four. Orders have been given to take a good supply of axes to use when necessary. All the coal that can be procured will be taken by the boats, and afterwards coal will be sent after the fleet as fast as it can be obtained. Before receiving your dispatch, I had telegraphed to every point where coal could likely be supplied, and further, I had advised, the Genl. in Chief—the Quarter-Master General, and the Secretary of War of the scarcity, and recommended that extraordinary measures to be taken to send coal down the Ohio. Abundance of Commissary Stores will be found at Memphis and at Helena, and I have plenty of forage at Memphis for that and other points" LS, DNA, RG 393, Dept. of the Tenn., Letters Received. On the same day, Col. Lewis B. Parsons wrote to USG. "Col. Allen has advised you of what we are doing to comply with your orders. I hope to leave here by rail for Cairo to morrow evening, and to be able to leave Cairo with a large number of boats by Monday or Tuesday. At least *no efforts* shall be wanting on my part to have everything ready *as soon as possible*. I shall bring several first rate Steamboatmen with me to superintend loading and unloading, and suggest that no boats should be loaded till most or all th[e] boats are at Memphis, so as to divide properly." ALS (press), Parsons Papers, IHi. On Dec. 17, Capt. Charles

Parsons, St. Louis, telegraphed to USG. "Col Parsons has gone South with a large fleet of boats   I Send two 2 Old Railroad Supts to Ohio tomorrow for Six Locomotives   They shall be got as soon as possible   I Shall send cars made here to Columbus this week"   Telegram received, DNA, RG 393, Dept. of the Tenn., Telegrams Received; *ibid.*, RG 107, Telegrams Collected (Unbound). On Dec. 10, Col. Thomas J. Haines, St. Louis, telegraphed to USG. "if the Stores at Memphis get below a million & a half of rations please order boats here for more stores   we have no boats to send   two millions of rations were at Helena at last advices from which the troops below can draw   I have plenty of Stores to send you but no transportation"   Telegram received, *ibid.*, RG 393, Dept. of the Tenn., Telegrams Received. On Dec. 11, Lt. Col. John P. Hawkins, Holly Springs, telegraphed to USG. "I have recd the following dispatch from Col Haines   Does Genl Grant desire boats for Memphis which are to transport his troops down the river to take Comsy stores   I think there are Enough at Memphis & Helena for his purposes"   Telegram received, *ibid.* On the same day, USG telegraphed to Hawkins. "They will need at Memphis for the purposes mentioned in your dispatch of yesterday, one and a half millions of rations. If they are not there, they should be sent at once." Copies, DLC-USG, V, 18, 30, 91; DNA, RG 393, Dept. of the Tenn., Letters Sent.

4. On Dec. 8, Sherman wrote to Act. Rear Admiral David D. Porter outlining his plans and asking cooperation. Copies, *ibid.* *O.R.*, I, xvii, part 2, 392. On Dec. 8, Brig. Gen. James M. Tuttle, Cairo, telegraphed to USG. "Porter is here but most of his fleet is below at mouth yazoo   Genl Morgan and A J Smith past ten days ago with their division   I suppose they are at Memphis   Troops are still going down at rate of one Regiment per day"   Telegram received, DNA, RG 393, Dept. of the Tenn., Telegrams Received.

5. See preceding telegram.

6. ALS (telegram sent), DNA, RG 107, Telegrams Collected (Bound); telegram received (certified by USG ES), *ibid.*, RG 94, War Records Office, Dept. of the Tenn. *O.R.*, I, xvii, part 1, 473.

To Maj. Gen. William T. Sherman

Head Quarters, 13th Army Corps,
Dept. of the Tennessee,
Oxford Miss, Dec. 8th 1862

MAJ. GEN. W. T. SHERMAN,
COMD.G RIGHT WING
ARMY IN THE FIELD.
GEN.

You will proceed with as little delay as practicable to Memphis, Ten. taking with you one Division of your present command. On your arrival at Memphis you will assume command of all the troops there, and that portion of Gen. Curtis' forces at present East of the Mississippi river and organize them into Brigades & Divisions in your own way. As soon as possible move with them down the river to the vicinity of Vicksburg and with the cooperation of the Gunboat fleet under command of Flag Officer Porter proceed to the reduction of that place in such manner as sircumstances and your own judgement may dictate.

The amount of rations, forage, land transportation &c. necessary to take will be left entirely to yourself.

The Quartermaster in St. Louis will be instructed to send you transportation for 30.000 men. Should you still find yourself deficient your Quartermaster will be authorized to make up the deficiency from such transports as may come into the port of Memphis.

On ariving in Memphis put yourself in communication with Admiral Porter and arrange with him for his cooperation. Inform me at the earlyest practicable day of the time when you will embark and such plans as may then be matured.

I will hold the forces here in readines[s] to cooperate with you in such manner as the movements of the enemy may make necessary.

Leave the District of Memphis in the command of an efficient officer and with a garrison of four regiments of Infantry, the siege guns and whatever Cavalry force may be there.

One regiment of Infantry and at least one section of Artillery will also be left at Friar's Point[1] or Delta[2] to protect the stores of the Cavalry post that will be left there.

Yours truly,

U. S. GRANT

Maj Genl.

ALS, DLC-William T. Sherman. *O.R.*, I, xvii, part 1, 601; *O.R.* (Navy), I, xxiii, 539. USG later discussed this letter in terms of "forestalling" the plans of Maj. Gen. John A. McClernand. *Memoirs*, I, 430–31.

1. Friar's Point, Miss., on the Mississippi River, about sixty-five miles west of Oxford.
2. Delta, Miss., on the Mississippi River, at the mouth of Yazoo Pass, about five miles above Friar's Point.

To Brig. Gen. Frederick Steele

———

Hd Qrs. 13th Army Corps
Dept of the Tennessee
Oxford, Miss., Dec 8th 1862

BRIG. GEN. F. STEELE
COMMDG U. S. FORCES
HELENA, ARK.
DEAR GEN:

I have just received authority to retain all Gen. Curtis' forces now within my Dept until further orders. This is from the Genl in chief and contemplates their being used in a cooperative movement to effect the capture of Vicksburg. If these troops have gone back to Helena I wish you would return them to Friar's point or the most suitable place to march them directly upon Grenada or embark them for Vicksburg as I may decide on.

Gen. Halleck's dispatch was only this moment received and my mind is not fully made up as to the best method of capturing Vicksburg. I can by the time our troops could reach there, have the railroad completed to Grenada and a supply of provisions thrown in there. From that point Jackson, Miss. could be reached without the use of the road, Jackson once in our possession would soon insure the capitulation of Vickburg.

I rather incline however to the plan of sending your forces and all I can spare from Memphis and here, say 25.000 in addition to yours, down the Miss. to effect a landing above Vicksburg., probably a short distance up the Yazoo and have them cooperate with the Gun Boats, whilst I move south with the remainder of my forces from here.

Please inform me by return Couriers all you know about the present position of our Gun Boats,   You having been so long on the Miss. river looking towards Vicksburg are possessed of much information as to the best method of attacking that point that I am not possessed of. I would be very glad to have your views.

I shall send Sherman if the Miss. route is determined upon and would be very glad if you could accompany him.

I have no definite news of the result of Hovey's expedition.[1] From the enemy evacuating Tallahatchie so suddenly I judged that it had proven very successful. We followed up the evacuation with all dispatch, our Cavalry pressing their rear all the way from the river to Coffeeville, killing and wounding many and capturing about 700. Besides this many deserted and are coming in every day. Word was sent me to-day by a Deserter who gave himself up that there was near 2000 southern soldiers East of this place, scattered through the country, desirous of coming in if we would send out Cavalry to drive out the Guerrillas that hover in that direction and make it unsafe for them to venture in this direction.

Yours Truly
U. S. GRANT
Major Genl.

P. S. Send me word what number of men you have river transportation for.

I shall adopt the plan of sending a force down the Mississippi.

I will send instructions to the Commd'g Officer of the Cavalry forces that will necessarily be left behind for their guidance.

Copies, DLC-USG, V, 18, 30, 91; DNA, RG 393, Dept. of the Tenn., Letters Sent. O.R., I, xvii, part 2, 392-93.

On Dec. 9, 1862, Maj. Gen. William T. Sherman, College Hill, Miss., wrote to USG. "Col Grierson is about to start for Helena with your dispatches and I also towards Memphis   When he returns he will report to you in person. Col Grierson has been with me all summer and I have repeatedly written to you and spoken in his praise. He is the best Cavalry officer I have yet had. I commend him specially to your consideration. He has already had assigned to him a Brigade but the Cavalry has been so busy that he has not yet had his command. I ask for him any thing you can do for his benefit and the good of the service. I know that you will soon appreciate his merits." ALS, DNA, RG 393, Dept. of the Tenn., Letters Received; copy, Graff Collection, ICN. O.R., I, xvii, part 2, 396. On Dec. 9, Col. Benjamin H. Grierson wrote to his wife. "Genl Sherman leaves here to-day, with a portion of his command—for Memphis—to prepare a movemt. down the Miss. River—I with my command will remain here—under the command of Genl Grant—for the present—I however leave to-day taking the effective force of my Regt—& move south west—to communicate with Genl Steel—John will remain here—also my Waggon Train—& Sick—&c—Genl Sherman—says

I will be with him again—in about three weeks—The Bragade first assigned me —was no go—as the Col of the 3d Michigan Cavalry—ranked me—but Genl Sherman tells me that Genl Grant told him to-day that I should have a Brigade— & that he will so arrange it—so the matter will turn out all O.K—"   ALS, Grierson Papers, IHi.

On Dec. 12, Brig. Gen. Thomas A. Davies, Columbus, Ky., telegraphed to USG. "The following dispatch just recd from Genl Steele   I forward it to you: Hd Qrs Dist East Ark Helena Ark   Dec 6th 1862:   Genl: I am informed by Genl Hovey Comdg Expedition into Miss that Prices army is retreating South would it not be well to send this message to Gen Grant   Our demonstration from here seems to have been entirely successful   signed Fred Steele   Brig Genl Comdg"   Telegram received, DNA, RG 393, Dept. of the Tenn., Telegrams Received; copy, *ibid.*, Hd. Qrs. District of Columbus, Telegrams Sent.

On Dec. 13, Brig. Gen. Willis A. Gorman, Helena, Ark., wrote to USG. "Yours dated at Oxford Miss. Decr 8th 1862 and addressed to Brig. Genl. F. Steele Comdg. U S. forces at Helena has been received; also another letter of the same date addressed to the Comdg. Officer of the U. S. Cavalry forces at Friars Point Miss. The expedition which left this point under the command of Brig. Genl. Hovey and which moved in the direction of Grenada Miss. has returned and his forces are now all on this side of the River. As the General in Chief, evidently intended these Troops to be used in cooperation with others in the capture of Vicksburg, I will return them and out of them Garrison Friars Point, as indicated by you. You ask Genl. Steele's opinion as to the best point to land Troops below here with a view of attacking Vicksburg. Genl. Steele says that the troops should be landed at the lower end of Millikins Bend, opposite an Island called My Wifes Island—say two or three miles above the Yazoo River. From that point operations could be directed as may be hereafter indicated by yourself and Genl. Sherman. The above point is about Twenty five miles by water above Vicksburg and some less by land. I enclose the reply of Naval officer Gwin to your inquiry as to the present position of our Gun Boats between this and Vicksburg, from which you will perceive there are six Iron Clads—four light Draft. wooden Boats & two Rams. The enemy have a Battery on the Yazoo about fifteen miles from the mouth of that River and about twelve miles by land from Vicksburg. I have only about 12.000 Infantry for duty and about 4.700 Cavalry, and five efficient Batteries. You can rely upon 5.000 Infantry 2.000 Cavalry and two Batteries to accompany Genl. Sherman, which is a little more than the force sent on the Hovey expedition, but if when I meet Genl. Sherman he desires me to send the whole force except enough to Garrison this post, as I may not have time to communicate with Genl. Curtis I will take the responsibility of sending all." ALS, *ibid.*, Dept. of the Tenn., Letters Received. *O.R.*, I, xvii, part 2, 406–7; *O.R.* (Navy), I, xxiii, 633. On the same day, Brig. Gen. Frederick Steele, Helena, wrote to USG. "Curtis sent Gorman, the only Brig. Genl. in the Dept. to supersed me. He rilieved me in the command here once before and sent me to Pilot Knob, for which he was severely rapped by Halleck and ordered to send me back. Halleck also mentioned this movement in his official report to the President, as being most unfortunate   Curtis will do everything in his power to injure me, because I have denounced his d—d rascality. I shall go in command of the troops to cöoperate with you, from this station; and shall have the satisfaction of knowing that with you and Sherman I shall be properly dealt with. It is my opinion that if the movement down the river could be properly timed, it would be best for the troops not to debark on the Miss. at all, but, in connection with the gun boats to take the battery on the bluff up Yazoo river, and land the troops at that point under cover of the gun boats. This battery is 15 or 20 miles up the Yazoo, and 12 miles from Vicksburg on the road between the latter place and Yazoo City. I am afraid Gorman will refuse to give me as large a force as I desire, as he may well imagine that I shall not come under his command again if I can avoid it. He is an old acquaintance of mine, and I like him socially, but would rather be commanded by a military man. There is a movement by the Army here as well as by the citizens to get me rëinstated in this command. Our troops under Militia rule, has torn this country all to pieces, and the citizens are allarmed at the change of commanders. I will write to Sherman tonight." ALS, DNA, RG 393, Dept. of the Tenn., Letters Received. *O.R.*, I, xvii, part 2, 410.

1. Reports by Brig. Gen. Alvin P. Hovey of his expedition in Miss. are *ibid.*, I, xvii, part 1, 530–32.

To Commanding Officer, Cav. Forces, Friar's Point

Hd Qrs. 13th Army Corps.
Dept of the Tenn
Oxford, Miss. Dec 8th 1862.

COMMDG OFFICER
U. S. CAVALRY FORCES,
FRIAR'S POINT, MISS.
SIR:

By authority from the Genl in chief of the Army I retain under my command until otherwise directed all the forces from Gen. Curtis' Command now East of the Miss. river, or those who recently crossed to cooperate with me on this side.

All the Cavalry, one Regt of Infantry to be designated by Brig Genl. Hovey and at least one section of Artillery will rendezvous at Friar's Point or Delta whichever may be the most defensible point and best landing. The Infantry and Artillery will form the permanent garrison of the Post and will protect the stores for the entire command. The Senior Officer will command the whole, and make all reports to these Hd. Qrs. All the forces except the Cavalry and garrison for Friar's Point will receive instructions from Maj Gen. Sherman.

It is desirable that the Cavalry should be recruited as much as possible until about the 18th inst, after which it is expected of them to make an active campaign, instructions for which will be sent in due time.

Supplies of provisions and forage will be obtained from the chiefs of subsistence and Qr Masters Depts in Saint. Louis. As far as practicable however we should live off of the enemy. For this purpose you will appoint, if you have not already got a Qr. Master and Commissary. All propety taken should pass through their hands, and be accounted for and go to the benefit of the Government. Receipts must be given for all property taken where proprietors are at home, and in no case should wanton destruction of property be tolerated.

No lincensed trading will be tolerated for the present and all passing of citizens to and fro should be prohibited. Where foraging parties are sent out they should always be under the direction of an efficient Commissioned Officer, who will be held responsible for the good conduct of his men.

No straggling should be allowed from camp nor parties whilst out.

All information of the movements of the enemy will be sent here via river to Columbus and by telegraph from there, When it is of sufficient importance a Cavalry force may be sent here direct

Respectfully &c
U. S. GRANT
Maj Genl.

P. S. The Cavalry with the exception of one squadron to be left at Friar's Point may be sent immediately to Polkville[1] at the mouth of Coldwater keeping on the west bank for security. All the ferries from Ponola as far as south as practicable should be collected and taken to Polkville without delay.

Maj Genl.

Copies, DLC-USG, V, 18, 30, 91; DNA, RG 393, Dept. of the Tenn., Letters Sent. *O.R.*, I, xvii, part 2, 393–94. Brig. Gen. Cadwallader C. Washburn had commanded the cav. forces on the expedition from Ark. into Miss.; by this time, he had returned to Ark.

1. Polkville, Miss., at the confluence of the Cold Water and Tallahatchie rivers, about twenty-seven miles southeast of Friar's Point and about forty miles southwest of Oxford.

Calendar

1862, SEPT. 1. Col. Josiah W. Bissell, Memphis, to USG. "I have the honor to state that since the date of my last report I have loaded from Island No 10 & New Madrid on steamer Crescent City & delivered at Memphis Three 8 in Columbiads 19 chassis & carriages about 500 tons shot & shell also on steamer Emilie one 10 in Columbiad about 100 tons shot There are yet at Fort Pillow two 10 in Colds and at No 10 about 50 heavy guns most of which I shall deliver at Columbus—At Pacific Landing I seized a quantity of commissary stores destined for a guerilla band & delivered to C.S. at Columbus & in Tipton Co from sympathizers with guerillas mules, cattle, arms &c which are duly delivered here—I left a Company of 52d Indiana to drive in about 200 head of cattle belonging to one of the band I have taken the enclosed bond from the principal inhabitants of Tipton County which will check all unlawful enterprises in that quarter— The day after the bound was signed cotton was for the first time delivered at Randolph & quantities are now being sent in for sale—I have visited every plantation of any size & every town between Hickman & this place & think I can safely assure you that there will be no further trouble through that country—Herewith please find map with remarks thereon I go 25 miles down the river to day to assess upon the relatives of the leaders of the band ravaging the Country opposite & below payment for 2 steam boats burned by them, one a Governmt boat—Genl Sherman is highly pleased with what I am doing—Capt Hill—Engineer Rgt. & 60 men have completed the wrecking of the floating battery near Point Pleasant & have been sent to the wreck of the Steamer John Simands near Island No 10—"—ALS, DNA, RG 393, District of West Tenn., Letters Received.

The work of one detachment of Bissell's Mo. Engineers in transferring abandoned C. S. A. ordnance from New Madrid and Island No. 10 to Memphis, while another detachment under Bissell patrolled and mapped the Mississippi River, is described in W. A. Neal, *An Illustrated History of the Missouri Engineers and 25th Infantry Regiments* . . . (Chicago, 1889), pp. 60–63. See also Maj. Gen. William T. Sherman to Maj. John A. Rawlins, Sept. 4, 1862, copy, DLC-William T. Sherman. *O.R.*, I, xvii, part 2, 201. On Sept. 24, Brig. Gen. Isaac F. Quinby wrote to USG that some C. S. A. ordnance remained at Fort Pillow.—*Ibid.*, pp. 236–37; *O.R.* (Navy), I, xxiii, 377. On Aug. 11, Rawlins had issued Special Orders No. 160 directing Bissell to proceed to Memphis on a reconnaissance.—DS, DNA,

RG 94, Special Orders, District of West Tenn.; copies, *ibid.*, RG 393, USG Special Orders; DLC-USG, V, 15, 16, 82, 87. On Aug. 22, Bissell telegraphed to USG. "Have been to within twenty four (24) miles of Memphis find 3 Bridges down which will take next week to build Cannot hear of any obstructions beyond"—Telegram received, DNA, RG 393, Dept. of the Mo., Telegrams Received. On Aug. 26, Sherman wrote to USG telling him that several bridges in the neighborhood of Memphis had been destroyed.—Copies, *ibid.*, RG 94, Generals' Papers and Books, William T. Sherman, Letters Sent; DLC-William T. Sherman. *O.R.*, I, xvii, part 2, 187.

On Sept. 8, 1st Lt. Theodore S. Bowers issued Special Orders No. 188. "Col. J. W. Bissell, of Engineer Regt of the West, is hereby ordered to return the troops now under his command to their respective Commands, discharge the Steamer under his control and rejoin his Regiment with as little delay as possible."—DS, DNA, RG 94, Special Orders, District of West Tenn.; copies, *ibid.*, RG 393, USG Special Orders; DLC-USG, V, 15, 16, 82, 87. Bissell submitted another report which Sherman received on Sept. 13, which USG "approved with the exception of sentences of military commiss[ions] convened on Board Steamer Emilie &c &c."—DNA, RG 94, Generals' Papers and Books, William T. Sherman, Register of Letters Received; *ibid.*, RG 393, 15th Army Corps, Register of Letters Received. On Sept. 14, Sherman referred to USG charges against Bissell of alleged improper confiscation of cotton.—*Ibid.*, Dept. of the Tenn., 5th Division, Endorsements Sent.

1862, SEPT. 1. Capt. John R. Cannon, Cairo, to USG. "I have rec'd the following dispatch from your Chief Q M—Make arrangements for transferring your property you are ordered to be releived by Genl Grant. Will you stay proceedings & order to report to you at once."— Telegram received, DNA, RG 393, Dept. of the Mo., Telegrams Received.

1862, SEPT. 1. Capt. Gilbert A. Pierce, q. m., Paducah, to USG. "Shall boats be permitted to go up the Tenn' A number are waiting to go up for cargoes of cotton—"—Telegram received, DNA, RG 393, Dept. of the Mo., Telegrams Received.

1862, SEPT. 3.   Ed Jones, Columbus, Ky., to USG. "I have a permit from Gen sherman to ship goods from Cairo to memphis   the marshall will not permit me to ship without your permit   *answer—*" —Telegram received, DNA, RG 393, Dept. of the Mo., Telegrams Received. On Sept. 4, Brig. Gen. Isaac F. Quinby telegraphed to USG. "The goods about which a man named Jones from Memphis telegraphed you yesterday were not stopped here but by the Provost Marshall at Cairo   There does not seem to be any settled rules about permits to ship goods from Cairo—Col Lagow left last night for Memphis   I will defer my visit to Corinth until he goes down—" —Telegram received, *ibid.*

1862, SEPT. 4.   Col. Jesse I. Alexander, 59th Ind., Rienzi, Miss., to USG. "I have rec'd (200) two hundred recruits for my regt today & have been informed by the officer in charge that Lt spillman is somewhere on the road with 60 more—will you do me the favor to have the annexed telegraph sent forward—To L Noble adjt Genl Indianpolis—maj sabin arrived with (200) recruits   Please send liut spillman balance as soon as possible   then answer—"—Telegram received, DNA, RG 393, Dept. of the Mo., Telegrams Received.

1862, SEPT. 5.   Brig. Gen. Isaac F. Quinby to USG. "Am I to consider the Thirteenth Wisconsin Volunteers, all of which, except the company at Hickman, part sent to Smithland and Fort Henry, and also Captain Stenbeck's battery of artillery, sent by sections to the same points, as out of my command? The Seventy-sixth Illinois is now armed with the captured Enfield rifles. Major Bigney, commanding at Smithland, telegraphs the guerrilla chief, Johnson, has taken Uniontown and Caseyville and now threatens Smithland. The major asks for cavalry to attack and pursue. I have directed him to mount his infantry as far as practicable. It is said that 600 horses are at Smithland intended for Buell's army. Ought they not to be removed to safer point, as they cannot be sent forward?"—*O.R.*, I, xvii, part 2, 203.

1862, SEPT. 5.   Iowa AG Nathaniel B. Baker to USG. "I commissioned Capt Wm H Kinsman of Fourth (4th) Iowa infantry as Lt Col of twenty third (23d) Iowa   the war dept has advised me that he may accept   will you please allow him to report here in person immediately answer by telegraph"—Telegram received, DNA, RG 393, Dept. of the Mo., Telegrams Received.

1862, SEPT. 6. USG endorsement. "Respectfully forwarded to Head Quarters of the Army at Washington D.C."—ES, DLC-Robert T. Lincoln. Written on a letter of Aug. 31 from Maj. Quincy McNeil, Island No. 10, to Capt. Montgomery Rochester requesting a leave of absence to serve as clerk of the circuit court at Rock Island, Ill.—ALS, *ibid.* Maj. Gen. Henry W. Halleck disapproved the application.—AES (by Col. John C. Kelton), *ibid.* On Oct. 31, McNeil, then lt. col., wrote to President Abraham Lincoln making a similar plea.—ALS, *ibid.* On Dec. 6, Maj. John A. Rawlins ordered McNeil to remain with his command at Holly Springs, Miss.—Copies, DLC-USG, V, 18, 30, 91; DNA, RG 393, Dept. of the Tenn., Letters Sent.

1862, SEPT. 6. USG endorsement. "This Communication was referred to the commanding officer at Cape Girardeau, Mo. a copy of whose report is respectfully herewith enclosed, the oringinal having been forwarded direct to Hon. R. E. Trowbridge."—ES, DNA, RG 94, Letters Received. Written on a letter of July 28 from U.S. Representative Roland E. Trowbridge of Mich. to Brig. Gen. Lorenzo Thomas inquiring as to the whereabouts of Sgt. Thomas Kelly, commander of the magazine at Cape Girardeau, Mo., whose wife had not heard from him.—ALS, *ibid.* Enclosed is a letter of Sept. 3 from Lt. Stephen V. Shipman, post adjt., to Trowbridge explaining that Kelly had been injured in an explosion.—Copy, *ibid.*

1862, SEPT. 6. Brig. Gen. Stephen A. Hurlbut to USG. "The Board of Officers Convened in Obedience to Special Order No 167 Dist of West Tennessee of August 18th 1862 have examined the Officers named within, and instructed me to Report their opinions and decisions in respect of each, as the same is indicated by the remarks opposite their names respectively."—ALS, DNA, RG 393, Dept. of the Tenn., Miscellaneous Letters Received. Hurlbut enclosed a list of seventeen officers dismissed from the service.—*Ibid.*

1862, SEPT. 7. Col. John C. Kelton to USG. "You will direct Co. C. 5th Regiment Mo. Cavalry to join its regiment by the first convenient opportunity."—ALS, DNA, RG 108, Letters Sent by Gen. Halleck

(Press). At the end of July, Co. C, 5th Mo. Cav., Capt. Albert Borcherdt commanding, was assigned to the 5th Division, Army of the Miss., under Brig. Gen. Gordon Granger. At the end of Sept., the co. was assigned to the cav. command, 3rd Division, District of West Tenn., Col. John K. Mizner commanding.

1862, SEPT. 7. Brig. Gen. Isaac F. Quinby, Trenton, Tenn., to USG. "Will be in corinth by evening train—Capt Mitchell is with me col Lagaw did not get back from Memphis—"—Telegram received, DNA, RG 393, Dept. of the Tenn., Miscellaneous Letters Received.

1862, SEPT. 7. Brig. Gen. William S. Rosecrans to USG. "We have 2 large barges at Eastport one containing 40 pontoons   I think the remainder of the pontoons is at Hamburg   it seems too bad to destroy these as they may be wanted but if we must drop them down to Hamburg at Last—Where are those Patrol Gunboats for the Tennessee   I confess I leave this now with reluctance—"—Telegram received, DNA, RG 393, Dept. of the Mo., Telegrams Received; copy, *ibid.*, Army of the Miss., Telegrams Sent. On Sept. 3, 1st Lt. Theodore S. Bowers had issued Special Orders No. 183. "The Chief Quartermaster of the District will without delay cause all stores of every description to be removed from Hamburg to Corinth. To facilitate his movements all transportation not absolutely necessary for ordinary Camp purposes, and belonging to the Command of Major Gen. Ord, will be put in requisition for this purpose. Each regimental train will be under the control of the Regimental Quartermaster responsible for it, and will in every instance be accompanied by a responsible Acting Wagon Master appointed by him."—DS, *ibid.*, RG 94, Special Orders, District of West Tenn.; copies, *ibid.*, RG 393, USG Special Orders; DLC-USG, V, 15, 16, 82, 87. On Sept. 11, Capt. Charles A. Reynolds telegraphed to USG. "The india rubber pontoon train wagons and appurtanaces has all been brought up from hamburg—the pontoon boats that came down from Eastport belongs to Genl Buells army—they are worthless—Capt Prime recommends that they with the barges be destroyed—"—Telegram received, DNA, RG 393, Dept. of the Mo., Telegrams Received. On the same day, Maj. Gen. Edward O. C. Ord telegraphed to USG. "What shall I do with the steamers—"—Telegram received, *ibid.* On Sept. 12, Lt. Col. Robert N. Adams, Hamburg, telegraphed to USG. "Col Morton is at Pittsburg Landing   will return this P M"—Telegram received, *ibid*. On Sept. 11, Col. Thomas Morton, Hamburg, telegraphed to USG and Ord. "Can leave with all gov't property so soon as you send twenty teams in addition to the 15 sent by Capt Klinck   there is in river below three (3) barges and four (4) flats and some pontoons worthless which I will sink—the steamer baton rouge is here   orders to remain—what shall I do with her—The Capt awaits answer tonight"—Telegram received, *ibid*. On Sept. 12, Morton telegraphed to USG. "I deem it entirely unsafe to attempt to run the Steamer Baton Rouge out of river with troops and if any number the more the worse as I am creditably informed there is a strong force of enemy near Duck river run   they have two 2 Guns taken off the Terry   I would rather undertake to run the boat & get along with a crew of marines than send a hundred infantry   still I will do your calling—I can leave here tomorrow morning with all govt property and stores except Boats three (3) moddle barges with a R R car in good order & the Steamer Baton Rouge   please say what I will do with steamer   She is not worth much—"—Telegram received, *ibid*.

1862, SEPT. 9.   Brig. Gen. Jefferson C. Davis, Louisville, to USG. "Where is the fourth 4th Division army of the miss   I desire to proceed to Join it   please answer"—Telegram received, DNA, RG 393, Dept. of the Mo., Telegrams Received. Davis then commanded the 4th Division, Army of the Miss. The telegram was endorsed, probably by Col. George P. Ihrie, aide-de-camp to USG. "Answered G. P. I." —AE, *ibid*.

1862, SEPT. 9.   Brig. Gen. John M. Schofield to USG. "Capt Hendershot U.S.A. requests that requsition be made on him for recruits for the Iowa regt"—Telegram received, DNA, RG 393, Dept. of the Mo., Telegrams Received. Capt. Henry B. Hendershott, USMA 1847, was superintendent of the vol. recruiting service, and mustering and disbursing officer for the state of Iowa.

1862, SEPT. 9.   Col. Jesse I. Alexander, Rienzi, to USG. "Before receiving [d]ispatch of the sending of a [tr]ain I had destroyed all [br]idges & torn up track to within [. .] miles of this point. Had I not better load the train with stores & send back—"—Telegram received, DNA, RG 393, Dept. of the Mo., Telegrams Received.

1862, SEPT. 10. To Brig. Gen. John A. Logan. "Complaints have reached me that recruits for the Engineer Regt. are discouraged from serving, & in one or two instances furloughs have been given the men on the ground that they are not recognized by any existing law. We must hold all men that come to us & let the legality of holding them be settled by higher authority."—Telegram, copy, DNA, RG 393, 17th Army Corps, 3rd Division, Telegrams Received.

1862, SEPT. 10. To Brig. Gen. John A. Logan. "Permit Lt. Thompson to visit me at this place."—Telegram, copy, DNA, RG 393, 17th Army Corps, 3rd Division, Telegrams Received. On Sept. 10, Lt. Thompson telegraphed to USG. "Respectfully ask permission to visit you on business—"—Telegram received, *ibid.*, Dept. of the Mo., Telegrams Received.

1862, SEPT. 11. Brig. Gen. James W. Ripley, chief of ordnance, to USG. "For the purpose of obtaining for the use of this office a complete list of all the Forts and Batteries, whether permanant or field, in the United States, I have to request that you will furnish this office at your early convenience, with a list of all such works as are under your command, and the post office address of their respective commanders." —LS, DNA, RG 393, District of West Tenn., Letters Received.

1862, SEPT. 12. Brig. Gen. William S. Rosecrans to USG. "am going to Genl ords   will be down soon—"—Telegram received, DNA, RG 393, Dept. of the Mo., Telegrams Received.

1862, SEPT. 12. Col. William W. Lowe, Fort Henry, to USG. "Capts Steinbeck & Flood are very anxious to have the other sections of their Battery with them & I should be pleased to get them if the public interests would not thereby impaired—I have just returned with my command much exhausted   I intend to go or send a command at once to hunt up Napier & Algie   Will at once relieve Col Ransom an excellent Officer   has a splendid set of men with some troops to relieve him with   can keep this section of country clear of rebels—Woodwards band was completely demoralized but there are others quite troublesome—"—Telegram received, DNA, RG 393, Dept. of the Mo., Telegrams Received. Capt. Andrew Stenbeck, Battery H, 2nd Ill. Art., was serving at Fort Heiman, and Capt. James P. Flood,

Battery C, 2nd Ill. Art., at Fort Donelson. Capt. T. Alonzo Napier
and Capt. James B. Algee had participated in the capture of the steamboat *Terry.*

1862, SEPT. 12.   Col. William W. Lowe, Fort Henry, to USG. "One
company of my Reg't is from Missouri—within a few days applications
to join have come in from persons living where it was made up—Can
I send an Officer to the point   he could bring back enough to fill the
Company—"—Telegram received, DNA, RG 393, Dept. of the Mo.,
Telegrams Received.

1862, SEPT. 12.   Col. C. Carroll Marsh, Jackson, Tenn., to USG. "I
respectfully request permission for Col J. E. Smith to visit to your
Hd Qrs on business"—Telegram received, DNA, RG 393, Dept. of
the Mo., Telegrams Received.

1862, SEPT. 13.   To Maj. Gen. Horatio G. Wright. "asks that cer-
tain enlisted men of 7 Ills Cav. be ordered to join their Regt. at Corinth
Miss."—DNA, RG 393, Dept. of the Ohio (Cincinnati), Register of
Letters Received.

1862, SEPT. 14.   To hd. qrs., Dept. of the Miss. "Transmits descrip-
tive rolls 14th 16th & 17th Wisconsin Vols. will forward others asked
for as soon as received."—DNA, RG 393, Dept. of the Miss. and Mo.,
Register of Letters Received. On Sept. 25, Capt. Simon M. Preston
forwarded the rolls to the AGO.—*Ibid.*

1862, SEPT. 15.   Col. Robert Allen, St. Louis, to USG. "I will send
you five hundred (500) horses as fast as rail roads will carry them—"
—Telegram received, DNA, RG 393, Dept. of the Mo., Telegrams
Received; copies, *ibid.*, USG Hd. Qrs. Correspondence; DLC-USG,
V, 7. On Sept. 17, Allen wrote to USG. "I am sending horses to
Columbus to be forwarded to Corinth   I am informed just now by a
despatch that you have forbidden any more horses being sent from
Columbus to Corinth"—ALS, DNA, RG 393, District of West Tenn.,
Letters Received.

1862, SEPT. 16.   Brig. Gen. Lorenzo Thomas to USG. "Respectfully
returned to Maj Genl Grant. This record is irregular in several essen-

tial particulars   1st   It should contain a copy of the order under which
the Board was organized.   (this however is not absolutely required
as reference may be had to the Dept orders usually on file in this
Office:)   2nd   The Board appointed in this case was composed of
four members, and all of them or at least a majority should sign the
record.   3rd   In some instances the determination of the Board does
not appear sufficiently definite. The decision of the Board as to an
Officers Qualifications for his position, is the basis of final action in
these cases and should be plainly stated.   4th   Cases proper for a
Court Martial should not be brought before a Board of this kind."—
Copy, DLC-USG, V, 93. Written on the proceedings of a military
board examining officers at Jackson, Tenn., July 6, forwarded to hd.
qrs., U.S. Army, on Aug. 30.—*Ibid.*

1862, SEPT. 16.   Maj. Gen. Edward O. C. Ord to USG. "Orders have
been sent to Genl Ross to move the 6th Division—Hospital in my
command is it ordered by you to be broken up. This is the same hospital which I stated was flourishing & you directed me to continue Notwithstanding any orders of Medical Directors to the contrary. I placed
a Reg't with a view to guard it yesterday & the negro camp with a
view to its medicines   it should be broken up but the Comdg officer
of the garrison ought to know of it & give directions as I started to do
today—"—Telegram received, DNA, RG 393, Dept. of the Mo.,
Telegrams Received.

1862, SEPT. 16.   Brig. Gen. Stephen A. Hurlbut, Bolivar, to USG.
"Capt Frank of Co A 11th Ills has an order from you for Rail Road
Transportation.   he is here   I do not need them   I think they had
better join their Reg't by land through Chewalla   with your permission I will send them. I have destroyed a high trestle below Middlebury as the bridge at Davis Mills is nearly finished—"—Telegram
received, DNA, RG 393, Dept. of the Mo., Telegrams Received.
Capt. Otto Funke commanded Co. A, 11th Ill. Cav.

1862, SEPT. 16.   Brig. Gen. William S. Rosecrans to USG. "Dispatch received   Orders have been given."—Telegram, copy, DNA,
RG 393, Army of the Miss., Telegrams Sent.

1862, SEPT. 17.   Maj. John A. Rawlins to Brig. Gen. John A. Logan. "You will at once arrest Capt Rigby Provost Marshal, at Jackson, for ordering the return of Slaves from the Hospital at Jackson, to their claimants in violation of law & in violation of Genl Orders No 72. & Special orders No 172 from these Head Quarters"—Telegram, copy, DNA, RG 393, 17th Army Corps, 3rd Division, Telegrams Received. On Sept. 11, Brigade Surgeon James D. Strawbridge, Jackson, Tenn., had written to Surgeon John G. F. Holston, medical director, District of West Tenn., complaining that Capt. John W. Rigby, provost marshal at Jackson, had attempted to return to their owners several escaped slaves employed at the hospital at Jackson. In his attempts to stop Rigby, Strawbridge had run afoul of both Logan and Maj. Gen. John A. McClernand, who considered the doctor a troublemaker. Strawbridge complained that the Negroes were being removed "without any regard to the necessities of the Hospital—"—ALS, *ibid.*, District of West Tenn., Letters Received. With the letter, Strawbridge enclosed a number of documents supporting his claims.

1862, SEPT. 18.   Col. William W. Lowe, Fort Henry, to USG. "Have Just returned from an Expedition up the Tenn River in search of Napier   Hunted for him 3 days on Both sides of the Tenn river but did not find him   visited Camden & Took some arms   also found at different points a small lot of commissary stores   went to Rockport landing but could get no further   it is useless to attempt to send supplies up the Tenn river at this time   there is not water enough   steamboat men say there will soon be a rize"—Telegrams received (2), DNA, RG 393, Dept. of the Mo., Telegrams Received.

1862, [SEPT. ?] 19.   Col. Isham N. Haynie, Bethel, Tenn., to USG. "The guerrilas who were at Hamburg have gone back south   there are 75 or 80 now in Savanna   may I take Capt Breckenridge with his company & other over those after them—"—Telegram received, DNA, RG 393, Dept. of the Tenn., Telegrams Received.

1862, SEPT. 22.   USG endorsement. "Respectfully forwarded to Head Quarters of the Army for the information of the Gen. in Chief."—AES, DNA, RG 108, Letters Received. Written on a letter of Sept. 13 from Maj. Gen. William T. Sherman to Maj. John A. Rawlins reporting a cav. skirmish at Coldwater, Miss., and the destruction of a railroad bridge.—ALS, *ibid. O.R.*, I, xvii, part 2, 217–18. See also *ibid.*, pp. 215–16; *ibid.*, I, xvii, part 1, 57–60.

1862, SEPT. 23. To Governor Richard Yates of Ill. "Respectfully forwarded to His Excellency Richard Yates, Governor of the State of Illinois."—ES, Records of 64th Ill., I-ar. Written on a petition of Sept. 14 of commissioned officers of the Yates Sharpshooters protesting the proposed appointment of Capt. George W. Stipp as maj. and urging the promotion of Capt. John Morrill.—DS, *ibid.* On Sept. 16, Brig. Gen. William S. Rosecrans added a favorable endorsement.—AES, *ibid.* On Sept. 30, Rosecrans telegraphed to USG. "Captain Morrill Comd.g the Yates Sharp Shooters is the senior officer. The Major, Matteson, died Aug. 8th. Lt. Col. Williams has been discharged by order of the War Dept. Sept. 12th 1862 Both places are vacant. Morrill ought without doubt to have the Lt Colonelcy. He is a good soldier and officer acceptable to any commissioned office in his command. I have endorsed a paper signed by them and forwarded to Gov. Yates but learn that Williams and Captain Stippe who has been absent since the last of June are working to prevent Morrills promotion. Will you please use your influence in his favor with Gov. Yates and get Col. Dickey to do the same for the good of the service"—Copy, DNA, RG 393, Army of the Miss., Telegrams Sent. Although Stipp was appointed maj. as of Aug. 8, he was discharged on Nov. 19. Morrill was appointed lt. col. as of Sept. 12.

On Oct. 15, Rosecrans endorsed to USG a petition of officers of the Yates Sharpshooters to Yates requesting Morrill's promotion to lt. col. "Respectfully forwarded through Maj. Gen. Grant, begging him to join in recommending Capt. Morrill for promotion to the Lieut. Colonelcy of Yates Sharp Shooters.—Since the death of Maj. Matteson the charge of this entire Battln. has fallen upon Capt. Morrill, and he had discharged his duties, not only creditably, but ably. The Command has improved under him and fought splendidly at the Battle of Corinth."—Copy, *ibid.*, Endorsements.

1862, SEPT. 23. Col. William W. Lowe, Fort Henry, to USG. "One of my scouting parties under Lieut Waters, 5th Iowa Cavly, on the 18th captured near Huntington ~~eight~~ 8 horses, ~~eight~~ 8 mules, ~~one~~ 1 wagon and harness, ~~four~~ 4 barrels salt, ~~one~~ 1 rifle, ~~one~~ 1 common pistol, and ~~four~~ 4 revolvers. Another party under Capt. Wilcox yesterday had a skirmish in which ~~one~~ 1 guerrilla Captain was killed, and ~~four~~ 4 of his men captured. I now have Col. Hardy out after Woodward with a fair prospect of overhauling him. I would like to get the remainder of Stenbeck's and Flood's Batteries, having but one section of each. If the 13th Wisconsin can be replaced by another regiment I would wish to have it returned—"—Telegram, copy, DNA, RG 94, War Records Office, Union Battle Reports. *O.R.*, I, xvii, part 1, 62. On the same day, Lowe again telegraphed to USG. "A scouting party sent from Fort Donelson, under command of Capt. Croft, 5th Iowa Cavly, yesterday had a fight with rebels, killing ~~two~~ 2 and capturing ~~one~~ 1. He burned their stores, and threw their ammunition into the river."— Copy, DNA, RG 94, War Records Office, Union Battle Reports. *O.R.*, I, xvii, part 1, 62. On the same day, Lowe telegraphed to Maj. John A. Rawlins. "Does Presidents Proclomation with reference to confication contemplate the taking the oath allegiance by all citizens"—Telegram received, DNA, RG 393, Dept. of the Mo., Telegrams Received.

1862, SEPT. 24.   Maj. Gen. William T. Sherman to USG. "Respectfully forwarded to Genl. Grant. These infamous slanders should be punished."—Copy, DNA, RG 393, Dept. of the Tenn., 5th Division, Endorsements. Written on "Letters & Statements Concerning the charges of Dr. Parks against Capt. Fitch"—*Ibid.*

1862, SEPT. 25.   Col. William W. Lowe, Fort Henry, to USG. "Can I send a Soldier to Alton who got drunk & remained behind at Clarkseville was captured & paroled by rebel citizens and now refuses to do duty—I now have him in Irons—Am prepared to send off about ten (10) prisoners some citizens others Napier's & Woodwards men—" —Telegram received, DNA, RG 393, Dept. of the Mo., Telegrams Received. On Sept. 18, Lowe had telegraphed to Maj. John A. Rawlins. "Can I send to Alton a Soldier who got drunk & was left behind at Clarkseville was taken & paroled—an example ought to be made—" —Telegram received, *ibid.*

1862, SEPT. 26.   To Maj. Gen. Stephen A. Hurlbut. "Transmits and refers communication of Louisa J. Pearl asking for the discharge of Joseph Pearl Co E. 46 Ills. Infy."—DNA, RG 393, 16th Army Corps, District of West Tenn., 2nd Division, Register of Letters Received.

1862, SEPT. 26.   Maj. Gen. William T. Sherman, Memphis, to Maj. John A. Rawlins. "Nothing of interest here. I hear that Breckenridge with his [Ken]tuckians some 3000 have started for Kentucky, via Jackson, [Cha]ttanooga and Braggs' Route. Also that about 10.000 of the enemy had started for Rienzi to reinforce ~~Price~~ Price after the fight at Iuka had been heard from. All these things, doubtless reach you direct. The Regular packet 'Eugene' from St. Louis, with passengers & Stores (not public) landed on Tuesday, at the town of Randolph, and came near falling into the possession of a Band of Guerillas, and was fired into by some 25 to 40 of the Band. I immediately sent a Regiment up with orders to destroy the place, leaving one house and such others only as might be excepted in case of Extraordinary forbearance on part of owner. The Regiment has returned and Randolph is gone. It is no use tolerating such acts as firing on Steamboats. Punishment must be speedy, sure and exemplary, and I feel assured this will meet your views. I would not do wanton mischief or destruction, but so exposed are our frail boats, that we must protect them by all the terrors, by which we can surround such acts of vandalism, as decoying them to the shore, and firing on them regardless of the parties on board. That boat was laden with stores for the very benefit of families, some of whose members are in arms against us; and it was an outrage of the greatest magnitude, that people there or in connivance with them, should fire on an unarmed boat. The town was of no importance, but the Example should be followed up on all similar occasions. I will send full reports as soon as Colonel Walcutt reports.   all well here"—Copies, DNA, RG 94, Generals' Papers and Books, William T. Sherman, Letters Sent; *ibid.,* War Records Office, Union Battle Reports. *O.R.,* I, xvii, part 1, 144–45.

Sherman also discussed the destruction of Randolph, Tenn., in the course of a lengthy letter of Oct. 4 to USG.—Copies (2), DLC-William T. Sherman; DNA, RG 94, Generals' Papers and Books, William T. Sherman, Letters Sent. *O.R.,* I, xvii, part 2, 259–62. The same is true of a letter of Oct. 9 from Sherman to USG.—Copies, DNA, RG 94, Generals' Papers and Books, William T. Sherman, Letters Sent; DLC-William T. Sherman. *O.R.,* I, xvii, part 2, 272–74. On Oct. 18, Sherman wrote to Rawlins discussing recent reports of C. S. A. movements and also outlining a new policy. "The Boats navigating the River are now assailed above & below. I have sent a force above to Island 21, and now comes a call to send some to a post below. We will have to do something more than merely repel these attacks. We must make the people feel that evy attack on a Boat here, will be resented by the destruction of some one of their towns or plantations *elsewhere*—all adherents of their cause must suffer for these cowardly acts. I propose to expel ten secession families for evy boat fired on, thereby lessening the necessity for freighting boats for their benefit, and will visit on the neighborhood summary punishment. It may sometimes fall on the wrong head but it would be folly to send parties of Infantry to chase these mounted Guerillas."—ALS, DNA, RG 108, Letters Received. *O.R.,* I, xvii, part 2, 279–80. On Oct. 24, USG endorsed this letter. "Respectfully forwarded to Head Quarters of the army for the information of the Gen.-in-Chief embodying as it does a policy which I approve but have given no order for in regard to treatment of rebel families as a punishment to prevent firing into boats. Also to show the condition of the Helena force and for the general information contained herein."—AES, DNA, RG 108, Letters Received. *O.R.,* I, xvii, part 2, 280. A letter of Oct. 29 from Sherman to Rawlins discussed, among other matters, a cav. expedition to Randolph.—Copy, DNA, RG 94, Generals' Papers and Books, William T. Sherman, Letters Sent. *O.R.,* I, xvii, part 2, 855.

1862, SEPT. 27. Maj. Gen. William T. Sherman to USG. "Respectfully refered to Gen. Grant . . . The Law is clear & positive. No Officer can persume to judge in these cases, if Col. Bissell made a mistake he should be made to answer All negroes are free to return to their masters but force cannot be used to this end. Mr. De Loach can take his negroes if willing to go not otherwise"—Copy, DNA, RG 393, Dept. of the Tenn., 5th Division, Endorsements. Written on a letter of E. De Loach. "Makes statement in regard to Negroes, Mules, Horses &c taken from his plantation by Col. Bissell. Col. Bissell sent out for the property of Mr. Cavashere a guerrilla Captain & regrets that Mr De Loach was disturbed. Enclose copy of Col. Bissells letter to Gen. Sherman also statement of Lt. A. Jones"—*Ibid.* On Oct. 14, Sherman received from USG a "Petition of Mr. & Mrs Deloach of Collerville for release of their son in Alton prison."—*Ibid.,* RG 94, Generals' Papers and Books, William T. Sherman, Register of Letters Received; *ibid.,* RG 393, 15th Army Corps, Register of Letters Received. While traveling from Corinth to Memphis in June, USG stopped at the house of Josiah De Loach, who discouraged him from staying for dinner because he knew C. S. A. cav. were nearby. USG believed that De Loach saved him from capture.—*Memoirs*, I, 388–90; DNA, RG 217, Southern Claims Commission, Claims Files, Tenn., Shelby County, File 28,309; Harry M. Hill, "General Grant's Close Call," *Metropolitan Magazine*, XXVII (Nov., 1907), 218–21.

1862, SEPT. 30.   Maj. Gen. William T. Sherman to USG. "The taking of goods from Ashport was done by Col. Bissell. The cotton at Memphis taken at Randolph will be answered for properly. All these merchants who are so loyal sell to disloyal people. The thruth is *all* commerce should absolutely cease during War & it is absurd to be trying to carry on War & trade at the same time. The possession of the Mississippi by us with present Regulations of Trade is a source of supply to our Enemy"—Copy, DNA, RG 393, Dept. of the Tenn., 5th Division, Endorsements. Written on a letter of H. G. Boudon. "Concerning the Rebel Raid on Ashport and the conduct of our troops afterwards."—*Ibid.*

1862, OCT. 1.   Maj. John A. Rawlins to Maj. Gen. William S. Rosecrans. "Major Raymond's Battalion cannot be spared from Columbus at the present time. He will detain all convalescents belonging to his Battalion. Captain Alden will proceed with the others to Louisville, Ky."—ES, DNA, RG 393, Army of the Miss., Letters Received. Written on a letter of Sept. 29 from Maj. Samuel B. Raymond, 51st Ill., Columbus, Ky., to USG. "On the 11th Sept you issued special Order #191 directing me to proceed with my Battalion to Louisville Ky and report to Maj. Gen'l. Wright. On arriving at Columbus I was stopped by a verbal order from Gen'l. Quinby and went into camp at this place. While here I received permission to go to Illinois and get some recruits belonging to my Regiment, the 51st Ills. and while there saw General Paine in whose Division these men belong and he was anxious they should get to the Division at once. *I brought back over 100 men and now have in my battalion over 300 besides 173 which were stopped at Jackson and who were in charge of Capt H. N. Alden.* General, I see by the despatches that Buels forces arrived at or near Louisville some days since, and I and my command are very anxious to join our respective Regiments. We are doing no good here and are much needed where we belong and fear our Regiments will move again before we can reach them. On the behalf of my command, I pray you to be released from this place, and be ordered to our Division. My Colonel has resigned from disability, and has not been with his Command for some five months. I am informed by Gen'l. Paine that the Lt. Col. has also resigned and I feel my presence is needed and pray you to be allowed to join my Regiment   General, I respectfully refer you to General McArthur."—ALS, *ibid*.

1862, OCT. 1.   Capt. Charles A. Reynolds, Corinth, to USG. "Capt Tighe has sufficient for three thousand (3000) or four thousand (4000) complete uniforms   Gen. Rosecrans want two thousand suits—Capt Tighe has ordered a further supply   expects it daily   I leave for Jackson tomorrow"—Telegram received, DNA, RG 393, Dept. of the Mo., Telegrams Received.

1862, OCT. 2.   USG endorsement. "Respectfully forwarded to Head-quarters of the Army. Washington. D. C."—ES, DNA, RG 156, Letters Received. Written on a letter of Sept. 26 from Maj. Edwin H. Smith, 2nd Ill. Light Art., Columbus, Ky., to Brig. Gen. Isaac F. Quinby reporting a fire in the ordnance building.—ALS, *ibid*.

1862, OCT. 2.   USG endorsement. "Respy referred to His Exclleny O. P. Morton, Gov. of State of Indiana."—ES, Morton Papers, Indiana State Library. Written on a letter of Sept. 26 from Col. William H. Morgan, 25th Ind., Bolivar, to Ind. AG Larz Noble recommending the promotion of 1st Sgt. Rufus F. Larkin, 25th Ind., to 2nd lt.—ALS, *ibid*.

1862, OCT. 3.   Col. William W. Lowe, Fort Henry, to USG. "Loyal citizens armed & organized for the purpose of assisting us are coming in   can I accept their services & ration them. We now have about one hundred   ans' at once"—Telegram received, DNA, RG 393, Dept. of the Mo., Telegrams Received.

1862, OCT. 4.   To [Maj. Gen. Horatio G. Wright]. "Has been told that Lieut W. H Hannah & Serg't Howard of 4th Ohio Indpt Cavy. Co. are at Camp Dennison with 70 Recruits—requests that they be ordered to join their Company without delay."—DNA, RG 393, Dept. of Ohio (Cincinnati), Register of Letters Received.

1862, OCT. 5. To Brig. Gen. Grenville M. Dodge. "Release the funds of Mr. Thos. Boyle to go North."—ALS, DNA, RG 109, Union Provost Marshals' File of Papers Relating to Individual Civilians. See letter of "W. L. F.," La Grange, Tenn., Nov. 23, in *Missouri Democrat*, Nov. 26, 1862; *O.R.*, I, xvii, part 2, 418.

1862, OCT. 5. Brig. Gen. Grenville M. Dodge to USG. "The expedition I sent from here to fort Pillow by genl Quilby has returned they crossed the Hatchie & went to Covington & back by Dunhamville heard of force of enemy in Bethal direction nothing but bands of guerillas."—Telegram received, DNA, RG 393, Dept. of the Mo., Telegrams Received.

1862, OCT. 5. Col. Isham N. Haynie, 10:00 A.M., to USG. "I have just this instant learned that the Engineer Regiment is now in Corinth my Messenger by Hand car cant get to them. shall I send your orders by carrier to Corinth the most of their tools are here in charge of a sergeant with orders to remain until further orders"—Telegram received, DNA, RG 393, Dept. of the Tenn., Telegrams Received. Earlier on Oct. 5, Haynie telegraphed to USG. "The Engineer reg't went down yesterday at 7 oclock A M with Genl McPherson—Have not heard from them since will send Hand car down to R R to them with your order at once—"—Telegram received, *ibid.*

1862, OCT. 5. Col. William W. Lowe, Fort Henry, to USG. "A scouting party from my command under Maj Brackett 5th Iowa Cavly, when beyond Lafayette during the night of the 3rd inst. were fired upon by rebels and ~~one~~ 1 man killed; the fire was returned and ~~one~~ 1 rebel Lt. named Maddern, killed. The rebels fled in confusion, but could not be followed owing to dense fog."—Copy, DNA, RG 94, War Records Office, Union Battle Reports. *O.R.*, I, xvii, part 1, 150.

1862, OCT. 6. Maj. Gen. William T. Sherman to USG. "The board of Officers appointed to examine incompetent Officers having closed his business & a court martial being a tribunal for punishing specific acts & not general negligence & inefficiency, I recommend that Lieuts Vaughn & Tarpley 6th Ills Cav. be mustered out of U. S. service on the ground that they are not worthy their positions"—Copy, DNA, RG 393, Dept. of the Tenn., 5th Division, Endorsements. Written on a letter of Col. Benjamin H. Grierson, 6th Ill. Cav., submitting charges against 2nd Lt. Jacob E. Vaughn and 2nd Lt. Elijah G. Tarpley of his regt.—*Ibid.*

1862, OCT. 7.   To Maj. Gen. William T. Sherman. "The Co. spoken of cannot be spared at present from duty at Bird's Pt. The Guns will be sent you as soon as their whereabouts Can be ascertained"—Copy, DNA, RG 94, Generals' Papers and Books, William T. Sherman, Register of Letters Received. Written on a letter of Col. Benjamin H. Grierson, 6th Ill. Cav., concerning troops and guns of his regt.—*Ibid.*

1862, OCT. 7.   USG endorsement. "Capt Anneke is a Capt. of one of the Compys, of the 2d Ill Artillery, but has been acting on Gen McClernand's Staff, (with the uniform of Col of Artillery) as Chief of Artillery. When Gen McClernand left here, he took with him Capt Anneke, and all his Staff, besides Col Brayman, and one or two other officers without my knowledge"—Copy, McClernand Papers, IHi. Written on a letter of Oct. 3 from Capt. Fritz Anneke to Lt. Col. William L. Duff. "To day I received a letter addressed to me by your order under date of Sept 24th. That letter says. 'You will without delay rejoin your company and assume command.' Now you are aware that I am Aid de Camp to Maj General McClernand, and that as such, I have to receive orders only from him. I therefore decline to obey your order. As soon as Maj Gen McClernand will return from Washington, I shall submit that order of yours to him."—Copy, *ibid.* Anneke was mustered out of the 2nd Ill. Light Art. for promotion on Dec. 18, and later served as col., 34th Wis.

1862, OCT. 8.   USG endorsement. "Respectfully forwarded to Headquarters of the Army Washington, D. C."—ES, DNA, RG 94, Letters Received. Written on a petition of Sept. 22 from several officers at Fort Henry and Fort Donelson to President Abraham Lincoln recommending 2nd Lt. Shepard S. Rockwood, 13th Wis., for appointment as commissary of subsistence.—DS, *ibid.* Rockwood was appointed as of Nov. 26.

1862, OCT. 8.   Maj. Gen. William T. Sherman to USG. "This complicated duty of regulating & collecting the Rents of houses has been managed with consummate skill by Capt. Fitch & as a War measure will produce much good."—Copy, DNA, RG 393, Dept. of the Tenn., 5th Division, Endorsements. Written on a report for Sept. of the rental dept.—*Ibid.*

1862, OCT. 9.   Capt. J. Morris Young, 5th Iowa Cav., Humboldt, Tenn., to USG. "One of my Tennessee Cavalry Captains & 11 Men out scouting were captured at Daybreak this morning at the House of old David Nuns 18 Miles West of here by a ~~paty~~ Party of Rebel Soldiers. Reports also agree as to their being a considerable force of Rebels at Brownsville about 900 and that they are arranging to attack this place also to concentrate some force at McClellans tonight at 11 oclock & destroy the R R connection. Who am I to report to now"—Telegram received, DNA, RG 107, Telegrams Collected (Unbound). *O.R.*, I, xvii, part 1, 459.

1862, OCT. 10.   Brig. Gen. James M. Tuttle, Cairo, to USG. "The captain of Steamer City of Alton refuses to report to master of transportation   when ordered says He is in your employ & will do as He pleases   He ran into Naval Wharf Boat last night & damaged it very bad   is He in your employ"—Telegram received, DNA, RG 393, Dept. of the Mo., Telegrams Received. On Oct. 12, Tuttle telegraphed to Maj. John A. Rawlins. "Good news from Ky   Buels renewed the attack Thursday morning and after short engagement routed Braggs forces & drove them Eight (8) miles that day   Buel has heavy force thrown in ahead of him and is pushing Him hard in the rear   Rebels reported very much demoralized. Stewarts Cavalry made a Raid into Pennsylvania & took ~~Ca~~ Chambersburg   no troops there   I sent Mail forward as soon as I found that Capt Mitchell did not intend to obey orders but it did not get down in time for train. Gen Dodge has put another Boat into carry mail. The Capt Still refuses to report to master of transportation   He is in guard House"—Telegram received, *ibid.* For the *City of Alton* controversy, see dispatch from Cairo, Oct. 12, in *Chicago Tribune*, Oct. 13, 1862. On Oct. 28, Treasury agent David G. Barnitz, Cairo, wrote to William P. Mellen that the provost marshal at Columbus, Ky., had given the *City of Alton* a monopoly on carrying cotton to Cairo.—ALS, DNA, RG 366, Correspondence of the General Agent.

1862, OCT. 11.   USG endorsement. "Respectfully forwarded to Head quarters of the Army, Washington D. C."—ES, DNA, RG 393, Dept. of the Tenn., Letters Received. Written on a letter of Oct. 2 of Maj. Melanchthon Smith, provost marshal, Jackson, Tenn., concerning the seizure of money in the branch of the Union Bank of Tenn., Jackson, by Col. C. Carroll Marsh.—ALS, *ibid.* On Nov. 2, Lt. Col. John A. Rawlins endorsed papers in this matter to Smith. "Referred to Maj. Smith Provost Marshal of Jackson, who will at once take testimony in writing of the loyalty or disloyalty of the persons claiming the money, and return the same to these Head quarters, togither with these papers."—ES, *ibid.* This generated a quantity of statements, oaths, and a report of Nov. 21 addressed to USG by Lt. Col. George H. Campbell, provost marshal, Jackson, listing the loyal and disloyal depositors.—ALS, *ibid.*

1862, OCT. 11.   Maj. Gen. Horatio G. Wright, Cincinnati, to USG. "Maj. Gen. Cox is very desirous of obtaining the services of Lt. Col. J. N. McElroy, 20th Ohio as Inspector Genl.   Can you let me have him to assign to Genl. Cox."—Telegram, copies (2), DNA, RG 393, Dept. of the Ohio (Cincinnati), Telegrams Sent.

1862, OCT. 11.   Capt. John Hoey, New York, to USG. "The map goes forward this day"—Telegram received, DNA, RG 393, Dept. of the Mo., Telegrams Received.

1862, OCT. 12.   Maj. Gen. William S. Rosecrans to USG. "A large number of offices more or less severely wounded so as to be unable for duty applying for leaves of absence   shall I grant them"—Telegram received, DNA, RG 393, Dept. of the Mo., Telegrams Received; copy, *ibid.*, Army of the Miss., Telegrams Sent. On Oct. 12, Maj. John A. Rawlins telegraphed to Rosecrans. "You will grant leave of absence to wounded Officers in all merritorius cases on a Surgeons certificate." —Copy, *ibid.*, Telegrams Received.

1862, OCT. 14.   Brig. Gen. George W. Cullum to USG. "Capt Hoappner sick at St. Louis is relieved from your command & ordered to report to Genl Curtis.—Notify Genl Sherman & Capt Prime"— ALS (telegram sent), DNA, RG 107, Telegrams Collected (Bound);

telegram received, *ibid.*, RG 94, Staff Papers. Capt. Arnold Hoeppner, born in Prussia, was appointed aide de camp on Aug. 19, 1861.

1862, OCT. 14. Maj. Gen. William S. Rosecrans to USG. "On the within letter I have to make the following observations   1st. Col. Knobelsdorff got into a row with Capt. Barnett about his punishing a soldier, and was charged with calling on his men to interfere in what was considered a riotous manner. For this interference, it appears in evidence on his trial, he was arrested, and that, on that occasion, he was guilty of gross and wilful disobedience of orders. 2nd. He was ordered to report at my camp distant nine miles, to keep him from interfering with the discipline of the camp which Gen. Granger thought he would do. After his trial, he was ordered to Corinth for a similar reason. 3rd. He states an untruth when he says he was thereby prevented from getting up his defense, for, at his request, I gave him full liberty to return to Rienzi, whenever he wished. 4th. He states an untruth when he says, the charges made against him by Capt. Barnett were examined by the Court and found frivolous or without foundation. They were considered grave enough; but the Judge Advocate did not think it necessary to try him on them, as the others would be enough to dismiss him. 5th. He preferred a long list of untenable and foolish countercharges against Gen. Granger which satisfied me he had not judgement enough to command a company, they were submitted to the Court at the trial. Having received some favorable impression of his sprightliness and supposed instruction, I sent for him and had a long and kindly conversation with him, the issue of which was to leave the impression on my mind, that Col. Knobelsdorff is not a man of truth or justice, nor has he the principles of a soldier. The Court was composed of able and unbiased officers—they sentenced him to be cashiered. I approved the proceedings. I am satisfied that he is a selfish, mischief-making man and untruthful—without the true spirit of a soldier, whose influence would be dangerous, to discipline and demoralizing to the troops. The service has gained by his dismissal, and his return to it would be a misfortune—"—Copy, DNA, RG 393, Army of the Miss., Endorsements. Written on a letter of Aug. 26 of Col. Charles Knobelsdorff, 44th Ill., Corinth, "complaining of alledged injustice and oppression on the part of his superiors, &c."—*Ibid.*

1862, OCT. 15. Brig. Gen. Grenville M. Dodge to USG. "The Steam Boat Admiral was set on fire this morning The fire communicated to the Philadelphia used as a Store Boat by capt Lyman both Boats burnte We had taken most of Q M Stores off of Both yesterday so that our loss is small mostly in clothing and ordnance stores We saved all our store houses"—Telegram received, DNA, RG 393, Dept. of the Mo., Telegrams Received.

1862, OCT. 16. To Governor Oliver P. Morton of Ind.—Stan. V. Henkels Sale No. 988, Jan. 29, 1909, No. 506.

1862, OCT. 16. USG endorsement. "The within promotions recommended and respcty fowarded to His Excellency Gov Yates of Illinois"—ES, Records of 14th Ill., I-ar. Written on a letter of Oct. 12 from Col. Cyrus Hall, 14th Ill., Bolivar, Tenn., to Ill. AG Allen C. Fuller recommending nine officers and men of his regt. for promotion.—ALS, *ibid.*

1862, OCT. 16. USG endorsement. "The within promotions recommended and respectfully fowarded to His Excellency Gov Yates of Illinois."—ES, Records of 41st Ill., I-ar. Written on a letter of Oct. 8 of Col. Isaac C. Pugh, 41st Ill., "Camp near Bolivar Tenn," recommending 2nd Lt. Leander Green, 41st Ill., for promotion to 1st lt.—ALS, *ibid.*

1862, OCT. 18. To Maj. Gen. Horatio G. Wright. "Lt Col Foster of the 25th Ind has been detained at Henderson Ky. I particularly request that he may be ordered to his Regt at Bolivar Tenn"—Copies, DLC-USG, V, 1, 2, 3, 88; DNA, RG 393, USG Letters Sent.

1862, OCT. 19. USG endorsement. "Respectfully forwarded to Headquarters of the Army Washington D. C."—ES, DNA, RG 94, Letters Received. Written on a letter of Oct. 14 from Capt. Thomas D. Maurice, 1st Mo. Light Art., Corinth, to Lt. Col. Warren L. Lothrop, 1st Mo. Light Art., recommending Sgt. Gustav Dey, 2nd U.S. Art., for promotion.—ALS, *ibid.* Dey was not appointed 2nd lt., 2nd U.S. Art., until Oct. 31, 1863.

1862, OCT. 19.   USG endorsement. "Respectfully forwarded to Headquarters of the Army, Washington, D. C."—ES, DNA, RG 94, Letters
Received. Written on a letter of Oct. 13 from Sgt. Franklin L. McGinnis, 1st Mo. Light Art., to Lt. Col. Warren L. Lothrop requesting a
commission in the U.S. Army.—ALS, *ibid.* McGinnis was unsuccessful.

1862, OCT. 19.   L. M. Pettigrew, M. D., Cairo, to USG. "Can I have
permission to ship Drugs. medicines & goods to Bethel. Provost
Marshall at Bethel said there would be no difficulty. Am a Loyal man.
Please answer today"—Telegram received, DNA, RG 393, Dept. of
the Mo., Telegrams Received. The telegram is docketed "Secesh."

1862, OCT. 20.   Brig. Gen. Lorenzo Thomas to USG. "In view of
the numerous requests now being made by commanders in the field,
that Artillery Batteries in service may retain extra Lieutenants Sergts
and Corporals, I am directed by the Secty of War to inform you that
all Light Batteries having six guns and the requisite number of privates
will be allowed the additional Commissioned, and Non Commissioned
Officers as described in Genl Order No 126. Such Officers however in
batteries which have only four guns or are so reduced in strength as to
be equivalent to four gun batteries, will be mustered out of service
from the date of the receipt of said order if such has not already been
done. In all future inspections of the troops under your command the
above decision will apply, and the officers making such inspection will
be governed by the provisions of General—Order No 126 with the
lattitude expressed herein."—Copies, DNA, RG 94, Vol. Service
Division, Letters Sent; *ibid.*, RG 393, Dept. of the Tenn., Miscellaneous Letters Received; *ibid.*, 17th Army Corps, Letters Received; *ibid.*,
Military Division of the Miss., War Dept. Correspondence; DLC-
USG, V, 93. The same letter was also sent to a dozen other gen. officers.

1862, OCT. 21.   USG endorsement. "Respectfully forwarded to His
Excellency Richard Yates Governor of the State of Illinois"—ES,
Records of 53rd Ill., I-ar. Written on a letter of Oct. 14 from Maj.
Seth C. Earl, 53rd Ill., to Ill. AG Allen C. Fuller recommending seven
officers and men of his regt. for promotion.—ALS, *ibid.*

1862, OCT. 21.   Private Ira A. Batterton, 8th Ill., Rockford, Ill., to
USG. "Being desirous of rejoining the army, I write you requesting

the necessary orders. The circumstances are these: Through the request of Col. Rhoads, by Genl. Halleck's ~~order dated~~ July 25, 1862., I was ~~placed on the Regtl~~. Detailed for recruiting service from the 8th Ill Infy. of which I am a private of "K" company. ~~I~~ Was on detached Service a clerk at Genl Logans Hd. qrs. at that time,   Since ~~then~~ which ~~I~~ have been Stationed at Peoria Ill by ~~order of~~ Col. P. Morrison 8th U. S. A. & Supt. Genl. B. S. of Ill., attempting to console myself ~~with the idia~~ that I was *serving* my country in the best possible way and to recruit for the 8th. ~~Up to this I~~ Have been able to obtain only 14 recruits—a miserable farce on the recruiting service—and am fully satisfied that the 'old regts.' must be filled up in some other way than this. In the 'Universal Scramble' for Office' men prefer the New regiments. Having been for the past year, constantly on detached service in the Adjt Genls department, (Genl's MccLernad, Oglesby, and Logan,) as clerk ~~and~~ or a kind of Military Sec. I am desirous of returning to that position again somewhere in the army. Such a position will be more congenial to my (literary) habit of life, as affording me facilities for acquiring a knowledge of events and for constant practice of writing the Phonographic Short hand which I wrote with the fluency of speech during the last Prest campaign, as a Professional reporter. Hoping that I will be excused for the length of ~~my~~ letter and that you will *grant* my request, I am, Genl,"—ADfS, Mrs. John L. Probasco, Rockford, Ill.

1862, OCT. 22.   To Governor Oliver P. Morton of Ind. "Glad to have you furnish clothing for the regiments named, also for the twenty third (23) and fifty-second (52) Inda. if you can. Would also like to have more Indiana regiments to be clothed"—Telegram, copy, Morton Papers, In. On Oct. 21, Morton had telegraphed to USG. "I desire to furnish the 53d 48th & 25th Regts. with clothing   Have you any objections   answer!"—Telegram received, DNA, RG 393, Dept. of the Mo., Telegrams Received; copy, Morton Papers, In.

1862, OCT. 22.   Maj. Gen. William S. Rosecrans, Corinth, to USG. "There are seven men of the 21st Missouri Reg't who have been confined in the Guard House here for three (3) months waiting sentence having been tried by court Martial for Mutiny and seditious conduct—Whats to be done with them—Shall they be turned over to the Col and sent with their Reg't"—Telegram received, DNA,

RG 393, Dept. of the Mo., Telegrams Received; copy, *ibid.*, Army of the Miss., Telegrams Sent. On the same day, Maj. John A. Rawlins telegraphed to Rosecrans. "The men of the 21st Mo. Vols. mentioned in your dispatch will be turned over to Col. Moore to go with their Regiment."—Copy, *ibid.*, Telegrams Received.

1862, OCT. 24. To Brig. Gen. Lorenzo Thomas. "I respectfully transmit herewith abstract of Special Orders from Nos 214 to 229 inclusive, from these Head qrs, accepting Resignations   The original papers accompanying in each case."—Copies, DLC-USG, V, 4, 5, 7, 8, 88; DNA, RG 393, USG Hd. Qrs. Correspondence. On Nov. 5, USG drafted a similar letter to Thomas which was not sent.—Copy, DLC-USG, V, 88. Similar letters dated Nov. 22, Dec. 15, 1862, and Jan. 3, 16, 1863, were sent.—Copies, *ibid.*, V, 5, 8, 24, 88; DNA, RG 393, Dept. of the Tenn., Hd. Qrs. Correspondence.

1862, OCT. 24. USG endorsement approving the resignation of Capt. J. B. Cannon because of illness.—Kenneth W. Rendell, Inc., Catalogue 53 [1970], No. 72. Probably Capt. John R. Cannon of Ind., appointed asst. q.m. of vols. on June 9, 1862, who resigned on Nov. 6. See *Calendar*, Sept. 1, 1862.

1862, OCT. 24. Col. John A. Rogers, Trenton, Tenn., to USG. "E. J. White of Dresden Tennessee informs me that he has purchased a lot of dry goods in St Louis and caused them to be shipped to Hickman Kentucky where they have been stopped by some Military order   I presume the object of the order is to prevent such articles from passing into the hands of the enemy   I can safly recommend Mr White as a loyal man and am well confident that his intentions are to sell the goods in Dresden where the people are more loyal than they are perhaps in any other section of West Tennessee   please grant the Colonel E. J. White any privilege you can consistently with the public interest and confer a favor upon your unknown friend and obedient servant."—ALS, DNA, RG 109, Union Provost Marshals' File of Papers Relating to Individual Civilians.

1862, OCT. 25. To Brig. Gen. Grenville M. Dodge. "are the forty two 42 Bales bagging & 41 coils Rope seized at Ashport by Maj Strickland at Columbus mkd J A R, A M, H W C   If so send them to

Jackson   answer at once"—Telegram received, DNA, RG 393, Dept. of the Mo., Telegrams Received. On Nov. 1, USG telegraphed to Brig. Gen. Thomas A. Davies. "I ordered Gen Dodge to forward 41 coils of rope and a like number of bales of bagging belonging to Mr Rodgers and two other citizens of Brownsville. Gen Dodge replied that he would immediately   It has not yet arrived. Have it forwarded at once" —Copies, DLC-USG, V, 18, 30; DNA, RG 393, Dept. of the Tenn., Letters Sent.

1862, OCT. 25.   Capt. Embury D. Osband, Mattoon, Ill., to USG. "I shall condemn about five hundred & fifty (550) horses here and recommend that they ~~be~~ shuld be sold as soon as possible"—Telegram received, DNA, RG 393, Dept. of the Tenn., Telegrams Received. On Oct. 25, 1st Lt. Alonzo Eaton, Mattoon, telegraphed to USG. "Shall I advertise for sale the horses condemned by Capt Osband   answer immediately"—Telegram received, *ibid.*

1862, OCT. 26.   USG endorsement. "Respectfully forwarded to His Excllency Richard Yates, Governor of the State of Illinois, and recommended."—ES, Records of 50th Ill., I-ar. Written on a letter of Oct. 21 from Capt. Thomas W. Gaines, 50th Ill., Corinth, to USG threatening to resign if not promoted to maj.—ALS, *ibid.* Gaines was promoted to rank from Oct. 9.

1862, OCT. 28.   USG endorsement. "Respectfully forwarded to Hd Quarters of the Army, Washington, D. C."—ES, DNA, RG 393, Dept. of the Tenn., Letters Received. Written on a lengthy report of Oct. 17 from Col. Amory K. Johnson, 28th Ill., to Capt. Hiram Scofield concerning his delivery of 386 paroled prisoners to the C. S. A. following the battle of the Hatchie.—LS, *ibid.*

1862, OCT. 28.   To Col. Robert Allen. "Can you send two hundred (200) artillery Horses for the use of this Department? They are absolutely necessary."—Copies, DLC-USG, V, 18, 30; DNA, RG 393, Dept. of the Tenn., Letters Sent.

1862, OCT. 28.   To Capt. John C. Cox, commissary, Columbus, Ky. "I have ordered Capt. Lebo before a Board for examination. Send up a statement of his delinquencies."—Copies, DLC-USG, V, 18, 30; DNA,

RG 393, Dept. of the Tenn., Letters Sent. On the same day, Cox telegraphed to USG. "Order Per despatch rec'd immediate attention will be given to it—"—Telegram received, *ibid.*, Dept. of the Mo., Telegrams Received. William B. Lebo of Pa. was appointed commissary of subsistence with the rank of capt. as of Oct. 31, 1862; he resigned on April 5, 1864.

1862, OCT. 28. Petition to USG. "the undersigned Citizens of Hardin County would beg leave to Call your attention to James Amos a prisoner Confined at Alton Illinois whilst we are not advised upon what charges he was arrested and Confined we are of opinion that he occupies the Status of Citizen sympathysing with the southern Rebels and has not been Connected in any manner with the Southern Army as far as we are advised we therefore respectfuly solicit that he may be discharged upon bond or otherwise as you and the military authorities may deem proper"—DS (thirteen signatures), DNA, RG 109, Unfiled Papers, James Amos.

1862, OCT. 29. To Brig. Gen. Lorenzo Thomas. "I have the honor to acknowledge the receipt of Genl Orders of War Department of the Current Series from No 1 to No 159 inclusive, except No 138 which you will please foward."—Copy, DLC-USG, V, 88.

1862, OCT. 29. Brig. Gen. Thomas A. Davies to Maj. John A. Rawlins. "I have the honor to report an engagement near Waverly with Napiers Guerrillas by a detachment of the 83rd Regt Ills Vols and one Piece of Artillery and thirty (30) Cavalry under Maj E. C. Brott from Fort Donelson assisted by Lieut Col Patrick 5th Iowa Cavalry and Infantry from Fort Hieman our forces amounted to about 500 the enemy eight hundred (800) We killed twelve wounded several took 15 prisoners and destroyed 12 Barges and Row Boats of the Enemy who would make no further fight"—Telegram received, DNA, RG 94, War Records Office, Union Battle Reports; copy, *ibid.*, RG 393, Hd. Qrs. District of Columbus, Letters Sent. *O.R.*, I, xvii, part 1, 463. On Oct. 24, Brig. Gen. Grenville M. Dodge telegraphed to Rawlins. "Col Harding Comdg fort Donalson sends following 'Major E C Brott with one hundred seventy five (175) infty thirty five of fifth Iowa cavalry & one gun from Hoods Battery routed eight hundred (800) rebels yesterday morning near Waverly killing 24 wounded & taking pris-

oners alarge number   our loss two (2) killed and two (2) wounded' "
—Telegram received, DNA, RG *393*, Dept. of the Mo., Telegrams
Received. For a detailed report, see *O.R.*, I, xvii, part 1, 463–64.

1862, OCT. 30.   Chaplain Joel Grant, 12th Ill., Corinth, to Maj.
John A. Rawlins. "During the recent visit of Gen. Grant to this place
he was visited by Rev. Mr. Alexander, (Chaplain 14th. Mo., and now
in charge of the Camp of contrabands), who left with him a paper asking
that some person might be sent to Illinois to secure clothing for the
women and children under his care. He understood the General to
approve of his request, and to promise a detail accordingly, but as yet
has heard nothing. Will you be so good as to seek out the paper, and,
on finding, call the General's attention to the same."—ALS, DNA,
RG *393*, Dept. of the Tenn., Miscellaneous Letters Received. On
Nov. 6, Brig. Gen. Grenville M. Dodge, Corinth, telegraphed to USG.
"I request permission to send Rev Joel Grant north to obtain Clothing
for the contrabands   they are suffering for want of it—"—Telegram
received, *ibid.*, Telegrams Received. On the same day, Rawlins telegraphed to Dodge. "You can send Rev'd Joel Grant north for the
purpose of obtaining clothing for contrabands"—Copies, DLC-USG,
V, 18, *30*; DNA, RG *393*, Dept. of the Tenn., Letters Sent; Dodge
Papers, IaHA.

1862, OCT. 31.   To Col. John K. Mizner. "With Genl Hamiltons
permission you can visit Jackson. I have not got authority to purchase
arms but will let you have a portion of the 2700 Carbines, obtained by
Col. Dickey, when they arrive"—Copies, DLC-USG, V, 18, *30*; DNA,
RG *393*, Dept. of the Tenn., Letters Sent. On Oct. 31, Mizner, Corinth,
telegraphed to USG. "My scouts west of Pocahontas & Ripley report
no force of the Enemy this side of Holly Springs—Have you rec'd
authority to purchase arms & can I visit Jackson on Sunday—"—
Telegram received, *ibid.*, Telegrams Received.

1862, OCT. 31.   Maj. Thomas M. Vincent, AGO, Washington, to
USG. "I have respectfully to invite your attention to Par 1647. Revised
Regulations, and to request you to accept the resignations of all Volunteer officers who may tender them in accordance therewith. You will
please forward to this office, in each case, a copy of the Special Order of
acceptance, that the Governors of the respective States may be notified

and the vacancies filled as soon as possible."—LS, DNA, RG 393, Dept. of the Tenn., Letters Received.

1862, [OCT.]. To Maj. Gen. William T. Sherman. "This matter will be left entirely to the action of Maj Genl. Sherman Comdg at Memphis, Surg'n Derby's statement, if sustained by evidence, would show that this building is one that should by all means be retained without Compensation"—DNA, RG 393, 15th Army Corps, Register of Letters Received. Written on an "application of C. Collins concerning 'State Female College.' "—*Ibid.* On Oct. 31, Sherman endorsed this letter. "Surgeon Derby's statement is fully sustained, but the buildings have been restored to Collins, because in my judgement it was too far out for a hospital"—Copy, *ibid.*

1862, Nov. 1. To Brig. Gen. James M. Tuttle, Cairo. "Call Surgeon Franklin's attention to Genl. Orders No. 78 Adgt Generals Office Washington"—Copies, DLC-USG, V, 18, 30; DNA, RG 393, Dept. of the Tenn., Letters Sent.

1862, Nov. 1. Maj. Gen. James B. McPherson, Bolivar, to USG. "Can an Exchange be made for E. D. Butler Telegh Opr & rail road A[gt] at Tuscumbia who was captured near Burnsville just before the battle of Iuka Paroled by the Rebels & sent north from Vicksburg. Genl Rosecrans—promised to have him exchanged but probably forgot it—Butler has come down to see me & as I am going to send six (6) confederate prisoners south under a flag of truce tomorrow morning I thought it might be arraged to have the Exchanged for one of them—"—Telegram received, DNA, RG 109, Union Provost Marshals' File of Papers Relating to Individual Civilians. On the same day, Col. Joseph D. Webster telegraphed to McPherson. "One of the Confederate prisoners may be exchanged for E D Butler. You may make the necessary arrangements"—Copies, DLC-USG, V, 18, 30; DNA, RG 393, Dept. of the Tenn., Letters Sent.

1862, Nov. 1. Col. Isham N. Haynie, Bethel, Tenn., to USG. "I have authorized Thos Maxwell of savannah to procure from a sunken flat boat below Pittsburg muskets to be put in hands of union citizens of Harden county for their own protection & held subject to U S authority the number & kind to be reported here & receipted for   will you indicate your approval or disapproval"—Telegram received, DNA, RG 393, Dept. of the Mo., Telegrams Received. On Nov. 1, Lt. Col. John A. Rawlins drafted a reply on the reverse of Haynie's telegram. "Your action in ~~putting~~ giving arms to the Union men, on the conditions named is approved"—ADfS, *ibid.*; copies, DLC-USG, V, 18, 30; DNA, RG 393, Dept. of the Tenn., Letters Sent. See telegram to Maj. Gen. Henry W. Halleck, Aug. 29, 1862.

1862, Nov. 1.   Capt. George W. Haynie, Bethel, Tenn., to Lt. Col. John A. Rawlins. "Please inform me the shortest way to dispose of confisticated property   I have a considerable amount on hand & would like it disposed of—"—Telegram received, DNA, RG 393, Dept. of the Mo., Telegrams Received. On Nov. 1, USG telegraphed to Col. Isham N. Haynie. "Send your confiscated property to Chief Q Mr here" —Copies, DLC-USG, V, 18, 30; DNA, RG 393, Dept. of the Tenn., Letters Sent.

1862, Nov. 2.   To Maj. Gen. William S. Rosecrans. "Capt Wales left here several days since"—Telegram received, DNA, RG 393, Dept. of the Cumberland, Telegrams Received. On Nov. 1, Rosecrans, Bowling Green, Ky., telegraphed to USG. "Reported here bragg's force divided   some stay at Gap some go to Richmond some come to take Nashville   Capt Wills belongs to Mitchells division   if your let him come he will probably be maj of his rgt   if not he may lose it   let me hear from you"—Telegram received, *ibid.*, RG 94, War Records Office, Dept. of the Tenn.; copy, *ibid.*, RG 393, Dept. of the Cumberland, Telegrams Sent.

1862, Nov. 2.   Brig. Gen. Grenville M. Dodge, Corinth, to USG. "Co. F u s artillery has gone"—Telegram received, DNA, RG 393, Dept. of the Tenn., Telegrams Received. On Nov. 2, Lt. Col. John A. Rawlins issued Special Orders No. 6 assigning Capt. Albert J. S. Molinard to take command of Co. F., 2nd U.S. Art., at Grand Junction.—DS, *ibid.*, RG 94, Dept. of the Tenn., Special Orders; copies, *ibid.*, RG 393, Dept. of the Tenn., Special Orders; DLC-USG, V, 16, 26, 27, 87.

1862, Nov. 2.   Absalom H. Markland, special agent, U.S. Post Office Dept., Cairo, to USG. "For the purpose of facilitating the speedy transmission and accurate delivery of the mails for the officers and Soldiers of the Army, I have to request that the Post-Masters at Cairo, Ills., and Louisville, Ky, may be advised, when not incompatible with the public service, of the changes in location of the Divisions, Brigades, Regiments &c, of the Army under your command."—Copy, DLC-Absalom H. Markland. Copies of this letter were sent to three other gens. in the area.

1862, Nov. 3.   To Brig. Gen. Lorenzo Thomas concerning the case of Dr. W. R. Burke who held an irregular appointment as surgeon, Ill. Vols., recommending he be paid for services rendered.—DLC-USG, V, 25; DNA, RG 393, Dept. of the Tenn., Endorsements. This letter was returned with an endorsement by Secretary of War Edwin M. Stanton. "Respectfully returned to Maj. Gen. Grant. The decision has been made in the case of this officer in a letter to him of which the following is an extract. 'There is no evidence on file in this office of your muster into or of having rendered the service claimed. You cannot therefore be recognized as having been in the service of the United States.' "—Copies, *ibid.*

1862, Nov. 3.   USG endorsement. "Respectfully referred to Maj. Genl. Wright. The 59th Ill. Vols not being in this command."—ES, DNA, RG 109, Union Provost Marshals' File of Papers Relating to Two or More Civilians. Written on a letter of Oct. 5 from Lt. Col. Alfred W. Ellet, steam ram *Switzerland,* Mound City, Ill., to Capt. Joseph W. Paddock relating to charges of improper dealings in cotton brought against 1st Lt. George E. Currie, 59th Ill.—ALS, *ibid.* Additional material relating to the charges is *ibid.*

1862, Nov. 6.   Maj. Thomas M. Vincent, AGO, to USG. "Respectfully returned to Maj. Gen. U. S. Grant. It is not necessary to alter the date of acceptance in this case. An officer who remains on duty after rendering his resignation is entitled to receive pay to the date of which notice of its acceptance reached the regiment."—Copies, DLC-USG, V, 25; DNA, RG 393, Dept. of the Tenn., Endorsements. Written on a certificate of Oct. 25 of Maj. Charles S. Hayes, 5th Ohio Cav., concerning the pay of 1st Lt. Elijah J. Penn.—*Ibid.*

1862, Nov. 6.   Surgeon Horace R. Wirtz, Jackson, to USG. "Cannot the Genl comdg Districts discharge soldiers on certificates of disability & the medical Director of the District sign instead of me   I so understand orders No 36   please ans—"—Telegram received, DNA, RG 393, Dept. of the Tenn., Telegrams Received.

1862, Nov. 7.   Maj. Thomas M. Vincent, AGO, to USG. "Respectfully returned to Maj Genl Grant for a more specific report. None of these officers were absent sixty days and do not therefore come under the Provisions of Par 3 of Genl Orders No 100. It further appears that charges have been preferred against some of the Officers, and are to be against the others when they return, in which case the action by this Dept might be anticipated. As there is no certainty of their being absent without leave, their dismissal from the service will not be recommended until a further and more explicit report is received."—Copy, DLC-USG, V, 93. Written on a letter of Oct. 18 from Maj. William T. Strickland, 52nd Ind., Columbus, Ky., to Brig. Gen. Grenville M. Dodge concerning absent officers.—*Ibid.*

1862, Nov. 8.   Maj. Gen. Henry W. Halleck to USG. "Lieuts Philip Howell & Isaac Newell, Co. A. 7th Regt Ill vols, and Lieut Theodore Gildermeister, Co. F. same regiment, will be ordered to report for duty at Cairo, to Brig Genl Ellett, as early as they can be spared from the field."—ALS, DNA, RG 108, Letters Sent by Gen. Halleck (Press). On Nov. 18, Lt. Col. John A. Rawlins issued Special Orders No. 22 embodying these assignments.—DS, *ibid.*, RG 94, Dept. of the Tenn., Special Orders; DLC-USG, V, 16, 26, 27, 87.

1862, Nov. 9.   To Brig. Gen. Mason Brayman. "Let Mr Menl telegraph his Business"—Telegram received, Brayman Papers, ICHi.

1862, Nov. 9.   Col. Edward D. Townsend, AGO, to USG. "General Rosecrans states that Lieutenant Greenwood fifty first Illinois was left in Corinth. The General-in-Chief directs that he be ordered to join his Corps."—Telegram received, DNA, RG 107, Telegrams Collected (Unbound); copy, *ibid.*, RG 94, Letters Sent. On Nov. 4, Maj. Gen. William S. Rosecrans, Bowling Green, Ky., telegraphed to Brig. Gen. Lorenzo Thomas. "Lt Greenwood of the 51st Ill vols Infy Regt was left in Corinth through mistake   he belongs to this Corps. Please have him ordered here."—Telegram received, *ibid.*, RG 107, Telegrams Collected (Bound).

1862, Nov. 9. W. J. Stevens, railroad agent, Columbus, Ky., to USG. "your box of books arrived today   will send them to you tomorrow morning"—Telegram received, DNA, RG 94, War Records Office, Dept. of the Tenn. On Nov. 12, Lt. Col. John A. Rawlins telegraphed to Stevens. "What about those books? They have not yet arrived at Jackson. Please inquire into the matter and answer to night." —Copies, DLC-USG, V, 18, 30; DNA, RG 393, Dept. of the Tenn., Letters Sent. On the same day, Capt. Julius Lovell, asst. adjt. gen. for Brig. Gen. Thomas A. Davies, Columbus, telegraphed to Rawlins. "There is no box of books in the Express office here for Gen Grant there is no acct of any passing through this office for him   can gain no information in regard to it   the 31st Iowa just left this post for Helena Ark ~~under orders~~ under orders from curtiss"—Telegram received (dated Nov. 13), *ibid.*, Telegrams Received; copy (dated Nov. 12), *ibid.*, Hd. Qrs. District of Columbus, Telegrams Sent.

1862, Nov. 10. Brig. Gen. Thomas A. Davies, Columbus, Ky., to USG. "Can H. Rossman 14th Mo. Vols 2nd Div be detailed on duty as Secret detective in this district   Answer."—Copy, DNA, RG 393, Hd. Qrs. District of Columbus, Telegrams Sent.

1862, Nov. 12. USG endorsement. "The appointment of Lieut. Hibbard is respectfully forwarded with the recommendation that he receive the promotion asked. This Dept. is scarse of Quartermasters making it necessary to appoint Lieutenants who have not given bonds to act as such. Lieut. Hubbard is one who has given abundant satisfaction as such."—AES, DNA, RG 94, ACP, H787 CB 1863. Written on a letter of Nov. 9 from Brig. Gen. John McArthur to President Abraham Lincoln. "I would respectfully request the appointment of Lieut. Isaac J. Hibbard of the 16th Regiment Wis. Vol. Infantry as an Ass't Quarter Master of Vols. with the rank of Captain. For the past six months Lieut. Hibbard has been under my command,—lately as Acting Quartermaster on my staff. I cordially recommend him as an active, able officer and one who by his bravery on the battlefields of Shiloh and Corinth has deserved promotion."—ALS, *ibid.* No such appointment was made.

1862, Nov. 13. To Brig. Gen. Charles S. Hamilton. "Second Leiut Clayton 1st Minn Battery to report to me tomorrow morning"—Telegram, copy, DNA, RG 393, District of Corinth, Telegrams Received.

1862, Nov. 14. To Lt. Col. William McCullough. "Send Frank Foley, of Co "H" 4th Illinois Cavalry, with horse and equipments, to this place to report to Col. C. C. Marsh as permanent Orderly."— Copies, DLC-USG, V, 18, 30; DNA, RG 393, Dept. of the Tenn., Letters Sent.

1862, Nov. 15. To Brig. Gen. Thomas A. Davies, Columbus, Ky. "Permit Hospital Stores to pass over the road for all the posts in the Department. Instruct the Ass't. Sup't. to this effect."—Copies, DLC-USG, V, 18, 30; DNA, RG 393, Dept. of the Tenn., Letters Sent. On Nov. 15, Surgeon Hugo M. Starkloff, 43rd Ill., Bolivar, had telegraphed to USG. "My hospital steward telegraphs from Columbus that he cannot ship the hospital supplies for this post—your orders only permitting commissary goods. I respectfully request you to order the Agt at Columbus to ship them there are (300) sick here who are suffering for want of it—"—Telegram received, *ibid.*, RG 94, War Records Office, Dept. of the Tenn.

On Nov. 16, Brig. Gen. Mason Brayman, Bolivar, telegraphed to Lt. Col. John A. Rawlins. "Will Gen Grant direct Capt Lyman at Columbus to send forward medical supplies now there for this post & detained by him, they are needed"—Telegram received, *ibid.*, RG 393, Dept. of the Tenn., Telegrams Received. On Nov. 19, Brayman wrote to Rawlins. "Our Hospital supplies and medicines are detained at Columbus—being pushed back by other freights. We are suffering for them. Will Genl Grant instruct Capt. Lyman on the subject."—Copy, Brayman Papers, ICHi. On Nov. 20, Rawlins wrote to Davies. "Medical Director complains that Medical supplies are detained at Columbus Ky. Direct the Quartermaster there to send forward at once all Medical supplies, turned over to him for transportation to this place, and report reason for non compliance with previous orders for transportation of Medical supplies"—Copies, DLC-USG, V, 18, 30; DNA, RG 393, Dept. of the Tenn., Letters Sent. On Nov. 21, Capt. Charles W. Lyman wrote to USG's hd. qrs. explaining that the delay in sending medical supplies had been "occasioned by want of transportation."—*Ibid.*, Register of Letters Received; DLC-USG, V, 21.

1862, Nov. 16.   To Capt. Charles W. Lyman, Columbus, Ky. "Send on Monday and Tuesday, or as soon thereafter as possible, two train loads of short of forage."—Copies, DLC-USG, V, 18, 30; DNA, RG 393, Dept. of the Tenn., Letters Sent.

1862, Nov. 17.   To Brig. Gen. Grenville M. Dodge, Corinth. "Permit Lt. J T Bell to visit Iuka and return"—Copies, DLC-USG, V, 18, 30; DNA, RG 393, Dept. of the Tenn., Letters Sent; Dodge Papers, IaHA.

1862, Nov. 17.   To Lt. Goodrich, Davis' Mill, Miss. "Take such Ox Teams as are absolutely necessary for you work from £ Secessionists" —Copies, DLC-USG, V, 18, 30; DNA, RG 393, Dept. of the Tenn., Letters Sent.

1862, Nov. 17.   To agent, Adams Express Co., Cairo. "Send package for Dr Martin 3rd Regt. Iowa Vols, to your Agent at Jackson Tenn, so that he may get it"—Copies, DLC-USG, V, 18, 30; DNA, RG 393, Dept. of the Tenn., Letters Sent.

1862, Nov. 17.   Maj. Gen. Stephen A. Hurlbut, Jackson, Tenn., to USG. "says that among the Union men he found at La Grange last summer were J D Perry an outspoken Union man, Frank Cosselt, owing to his large am't of property not so much so. Thompson is not reliable. Sends this to aid in estimating these men"—DLC-USG, V, 21.

1862, Nov. 17.   Capt. Robert P. Sealy, 45th Ill., Grand Junction, to USG. "I Cannot find Musoad or his agent here"—Telegram received, DNA, RG 94, War Records Office, Dept. of the Tenn.

1862, Nov. 18.   USG endorsement. "Forwarded to Hd. Qrs. of the Army, Washington, D. C. and approved."—Copies, DLC-USG, V, 25; DNA, RG 393, Dept. of the Tenn., Endorsements. Written on an application of Nov. 16 of Maj. Edwin A. Bowen, 52nd Ill., for leave to attend to business.—*Ibid.*

1862, Nov. 18.   USG endorsement. "Respectfully forwarded to Headquarters of the Army, Washington, D. C."—ES, DNA, RG 192, Letters Received by Referral. Written on a letter of Oct. 25 from Capt.

John C. Cox to Maj. John A. Rawlins recommending 1st Lt. John
H. W. Mills, 1st Kans., and 2nd Lt. Jasper Johnson, 31st Ill., for
appointment as capt., commissary dept.—LS, *ibid.* Both appointments
were confirmed on Feb. 19, 1863.

1862, Nov. 18. USG endorsement. "Approved and respectfully forwarded to his Excellency, Richard Yates, Governor of the State of
Illinois. Lieut. Col. Rodgers was promoted for meritorious conduct at
the battle of Pittsburg Landing and has been the greater portion of the
time since, in command of his regiment, and under his command at the
battle of the Hatchie the regiment maintained its well known distinction for bravery discipline and efficiency and he the position his gal-
lantry had given him"—Copies, DLC-USG, V, 25; DNA, RG 393,
Dept. of the Tenn., Endorsements. Written on a petition of Nov. 14
of commissioned officers, 2nd Brigade, 4th Division, requesting the
promotion of Lt. Col. George C. Rogers, 15th Ill.—*Ibid.* On Dec. 17,
Rogers was promoted to col., 15th Ill., replacing Thomas J. Turner.

1862, Nov. 19. To Capt. James P. Harper, ordnance officer, Jackson,
Tenn. "Send 10 000 rounds ammunition for Smiths Carbines to the
7th Reg't Illinois Cavalry"—Telegram, copies, DLC-USG, V, 18, 30;
DNA, RG 393, Dept. of the Tenn., Letters Sent. On Nov. 19, Harper
telegraphed to USG. "Despatch recd   have no ammunition for Smiths
Carbines   made requisition on St Louis arsenal for it in August   Telegraphed again for it on the 12th October stating that if not on hand it
could be had from Mass. arms Co. Chicopee Mass & sent requisition
again for 100 000 rounds on Novr 7th but no answer"—Telegram
received, *ibid.*, Telegrams Received.

1862, Nov. 19. Brig. Gen. Charles S. Hamilton to USG requesting
permission to disband a disorganized and incompetently led cav. co.,
the Hatchie Scouts.—Copy, DNA, RG 393, District of Corinth, Letters
Sent. On Nov. 22, Lt. Col. John A. Rawlins endorsed this letter to
Hamilton granting his request.—Copy, *ibid.*, Dept. of the Tenn.,
Endorsements; DLC-USG, V, 25.

1862, Nov. 20. USG endorsement. "Military occupation now extending into Miss South of Bolivar orders have been made and will be
circulated immediately taking off Military restrictions from the intro-

duction of all articles necessary for family use, Salt & clothing included."—AES, DNA, RG 109, Union Provost Marshals' File of Papers Relating to Individual Civilians. Written on a statement of Nov. 20 of Maj. Gen. Stephen A. Hurlbut. "Mr Peter Casey a loyal citizen of Kentucky has permission to bring to Bolivar such goods as are permitted by the Regulations of the Treasury Department to be sold at said Post of Bolivar under such restrictions as may be imposed by Military orders. The amount permitted not to exceed Twenty Thousand Dollars"—ALS, *ibid.* On Feb. 7, 1863, Peter Casey, Memphis, wrote to USG. "Enclosed find the Permit you gave Novr 28th 1862 to my brother James for me. sickness prevented either of us, using it at the time. I could have sold the permit but not conscientiously & would not Mr Hough the Surveyor of Memphis will not let me take any thing out on this permit and says before he could do that he must have an *order* to pass the goods. I am now here almost ruined in a pecuniary point by the burning of my house and effects by the Guerrillas. If you could without interfering too much with the regulations or the welfare of the Government, give me a permit with the necessary *order* to trade in the surrounding country, or on the Memphis and Charleston railRoad I think I could in a manner make up my losses, probably more. If you give me a permit let it extend as much as you can Address me at Memphis Care of J. P. Turner . . . Col Lagow offered to take this down but after reading, I could not find him so send by mail. If there is any part obscure he ~~will~~ has kindly promised to explain"—ALS, *ibid.* On Feb. 14, USG endorsed this letter. "Respectfully refered to Maj. Gen. Hurlbut Comd.g Dist. of West Ten and 16th Army Corps. I do not propose to interfere with the subject of trade, beyond the order already published, but do not understand why Mr Yateman has undertaken to controll Military authority to such an extent."—AES, *ibid.*

1862, Nov. 20. Maj. Gen. Stephen A. Hurlbut, Jackson, to USG. "A deserter from Braggs army at Bethel reports that Andersons and Withers divisions ha[d] reinforced Price. and that Bragg is receiving reinforcements from Virginia. He says he left Murfreesboro a week ago I send it for what it is worth."—Copy, DNA, RG 393, District of West Tenn., 4th Division, Letters Sent.

1862, Nov. 22. To Brig. Gen. Lorenzo Thomas transmitting the proceedings of a court of inquiry held at Fort Pickering, Tenn., to consider cases of officers missing at the special muster of Aug. 18.— LS, DNA, RG 94, Vol. Service Division, Letters Received. On Nov. 23, USG sent a similar letter to Thomas.—LS, *ibid.* On Nov. 26, USG wrote three letters to Thomas transmitting results of courts of inquiry concerning officers absent on Aug. 18.—LS (2), *ibid.* One of these letters is represented only by a copy, *ibid.*, RG 393, Dept. of the Tenn., Hd. Qrs. Correspondence. On Dec. 27, USG wrote four similar letters to Thomas.—Copies, *ibid.*; DLC-USG, V, 5, 8, 24, 88. On Dec. 28, USG again wrote to Thomas on the same subject.—Copies, *ibid.* One case forwarded by USG, that of 1st Lt. Isaac L. Tice, 48th Ohio, was returned with an endorsement of Dec. 5 of Maj. Gen. Henry W. Halleck. "This officer left his command after a leave was refused & was absent a month, Dismissal recommended"—Copy, *ibid.*, RG 108, Endorsements.

1862, Nov. 23. To Brig. Gen. Lorenzo Thomas. "I have the honor to transmit herewith, communication of Lieut Col. C. J. Dobbs, 13th Regiment Indiana Volunteers, referred to me, for investigation by order of the Secretary of War, of date Oct. 24, 1862 and to invite attention to the endorsement of Brig. Gen. J. C. Sullivan, thereon."— LS, DNA, RG 94, Vol. Service Division, Letters Received. Written on a letter referred to USG's hd. qrs. by Maj. Thomas M. Vincent on Oct. 24, referred by Lt. Col. John A. Rawlins to Brig. Gen. Jeremiah C. Sullivan on Nov. 4, then endorsed by Sullivan. "Respectfully returned —Sergt. B. A. May was ordered to report to his regt. on the 13th day of October—I acted on what I thought was general custom in keeping faithful clerks and ordered his return as soon as I found that it was against Depart. Orders"—AES, *ibid.*

1862, Nov. 23. To Brig. Gen. Isaac F. Quinby, Moscow, Tenn. "Arrest Privates McElroy and Downer of Company I 7th Illinois Cavalry, and send them to the Provost Marshall here Also send George Steadman Company C same Regiment."—Copies, DLC-USG, V, 18, 30; DNA, RG 393, Dept. of the Tenn., Letters Sent. On Nov. 24, Quinby telegraphed to USG. "The members of the 7th Ills Cavalry whom you directed to be arrested with some other prisoners will start for Lagrange in a few minutes—"—Telegram received, *ibid.*, Telegrams Received.

1862, Nov. 23. Lt. Col. Greenville M. Mitchell, 54th Ill., Union City, Tenn., to USG. "Mr Bradford talked with you on train yesterday about his Co   shall I subsist them at this post   I have thirty contraband horses & a lot of saddles here   Bradford wishes them for his Co.   shall I let him have them   they will be useful for scouts"—Telegram received, DNA, RG 393, Dept. of the Tenn., Telegrams Received.

1862, Nov. 24. To Brig. Gen. Jeremiah C. Sullivan, Jackson. "Some of the stations north of Jackson in your District have prohibited Harde & Hough from selling papers & at Kenton arrested the boy engaged in this business. These parties pay the R R 1000 dollars per month for this privilege & so long as they have this contract post commanders have no right to molest them in this traffic. If there is any thing wrong let them report the matter to the Supt of the road & he will have it corrected"—Telegram received, DNA, RG 393, 16th Army Corps, 4th Division, Telegrams Received; copies (dated Nov. 26), *ibid.*, Dept. of the Tenn., Letters Sent; DLC-USG, V, 18, 30. On Oct. 30, George E. Hutchinson, agent for Harde & Hough, newsdealers, applied to Maj. Gen. Stephen A. Hurlbut for permission to sell newspapers within his district.—ALS, DNA, RG 109, Union Provost Marshals' File of Papers Relating to Two or More Civilians.

1862, Nov. 24. Brig. Gen. Charles S. Hamilton to USG. "The accused is one of the most worthless officers of the service and if he can be mustered out on 'general worthlessness,' and thus avoid the labor and expense of a Court Martial, I will most cordially endorse and recommend such a course of action. Resply. referred."—Copy, DNA, RG 393, Army of the Tenn., Left Wing, Endorsements. Written on charges against Col. John L. Doran, 17th Wis.—*Ibid.* On the same day, Lt. Col. Adam G. Malloy sent to USG's hd. qrs. a statement that Doran had improperly retained the post fund of $93; this was also endorsed by Hamilton. "I do not hesitate on saying that the mustering out of service of Col. Doran will be of greatest benefit to the service. He is a man who maintains no discipline, is at constant fraud with his Officers and whose personal and moral character is such as to render him entirely unworthy the position he holds."—Copies, DLC–USG, V, 25; DNA, RG 393, Dept. of the Tenn., Endorsements. On Nov. 25, Hamilton endorsed Doran's resignation. "This resignation is just received. I trust the Genl Comdg. will see the importance of accepting it immediately. The service and the good of the Regiment demands it —as also the services of the General and Field Officers who are on the Court to try Col. Doran. I send this by special messenger and beg to urge that the order of acceptance may be issued by return courier, as well as an order dissolving the Court."—Copy, *ibid.*, Army of the Tenn., Left Wing, Endorsements. See Benjamin P. Thomas, ed., *Three Years with Grant as Recalled by War Correspondent Sylvanus Cadwallader* (New York, 1955), pp. 30–31.

1862, Nov. 26. USG General Orders No. 10 concerning the duties of provost marshals.—Copies, DLC–USG, V, 13, 14, 95; (2) DNA, RG 393, Dept. of the Tenn., General and Special Orders; (printed) Oglesby Papers, IHi. *O.R.*, I, xvii, part 2, 363.

1862, Nov. 26. To Brig. Gen. Grenville M. Dodge, Corinth. "Make your own disposition of troops in your District. So Corinth and the Railroad north of it is held all required is accomplished"—Telegram, copies, DLC–USG, V, 18, 30; Dodge Papers, IaHA; DNA, RG 393, Dept. of the Tenn., Letters Sent. On Nov. 26, Dodge had telegraphed to USG. "with the present force do you consider it important to hold Reinzi would it not be better to draw that out post into this in side of tuscumbia which would give my outposts as follows—Glendale on East Tucumbia river on south & south west & Chewalla on west & north west—"—Telegram received, *ibid.*, Telegrams Received.

1862, Nov. 26. To Chaplain John Eaton, Jr., superintendent of contrabands, Grand Junction. "Send down the ox teams directed by the Provost Marshall on the 25 inst   The Provost Marshall has no one to send for them conveniently and a detail can be made from the contrabands to drive it down."—Copies, DLC–USG, V, 18, 30; DNA, RG 393, Dept. of the Tenn., Letters Sent.

1862, Nov. 26. Col. John V. D. Du Bois to USG. "Lt Col McDermott Comdg at Grand Junction reports following 'I have just recd information supposed to be reliable that there is a band of Guerrllas in & about

Salisbury five hundred strong they were with a man named Lowe who lives 2 miles this side of Salisbury' "—Telegram received, DNA, RG 393, Dept. of the Tenn., Telegrams Received. On the same day, Lt. Col. John McDermott, Grand Junction, telegraphed to Lt. Col. John A. Rawlins. "A citizen has arrived whom I have good reason to beleive to be loyal & reports five hundred (500) Rebel cavalry near salisbury—"—Telegram received, *ibid.*

1862, Nov. 27.   Petition to USG asking the release of Allen Harwell and James A. Jumper of Tishomingo County, Miss., arrested Aug. 26 and confined at Johnson's Island, Ohio.—DS, DNA, RG 109, Union Provost Marshals' File of Papers Relating to Two or More Civilians. Attached papers indicate that the two prisoners had been sent to Vicksburg for exchange on Nov. 22.—*Ibid.*

1862, Nov. 28.   To Brig. Gen. Jeremiah C. Sullivan, Jackson. "Send the money to sub treasurer in St Louis in charge of a trusty officer taking receipts for same send prisoner to Alton with charges send copy of charges & reciept for the money to Secretary Chase"—Telegram received, DNA, RG 393, 16th Army Corps, 4th Division, Telegrams Received; copies (dated Nov. 25), *ibid.*, Dept. of the Tenn., Letters Sent; DLC-USG, V, 18, 30.

1862, Nov. 28.   Brig. Gen. Grenville M. Dodge, Corinth, to USG. "Says Capt. Prime informs him he can get 150 or 200 Contrabands at Bolivar and Jackson. Sends Capt. Horn to bring them and asks for the order and instructions to obtain them."—DLC-USG, V, 21; DNA, RG 393, Dept. of the Tenn., Register of Letters Received. On Nov. 30, Lt. Col. John A. Rawlins telegraphed to Brig. Gen. Jeremiah C. Sullivan, Jackson. "How many contrabands can you furnish for work on fortifications at Corinth answer at once . . . P S Gen Sullivan will please report by telegraph his compliance with the above order"— Telegram received, *ibid.*, 16th Army Corps, 4th Division, Telegrams Received. *O.R.*, I, xvii, part 2, 371.

1862, Nov. 28.   2nd Lt. David B. Halderman, 122nd Ill., Trenton, Tenn., to USG. "I have forwarded 15 cases tried by the Military Commission for your revision—Your early attention to them is respectfully solicited—"—ALS, DNA, RG 109, Union Provost Marshals' File of

Papers Relating to Two or More Civilians. Halderman enclosed a list of cases considered.—AD, *ibid.* On March 2, 1863, Halderman telegraphed to USG. "No further business being before the military commission convened by your special order No 2 Jackson Tenn it adjourned *sin die*"—Telegram received, *ibid.*, RG 393, Dept. of the Tenn., Telegrams Received.

1862, Nov. 30. USG endorsement. "Respectfully forwarded to Headquarters of the Army Washington D C. and reccommend that 1st Lieut. Wallbridge 18th Wisconsin Volunteers be honorably discharged the service"—Copies, DLC-USG, V, 25; DNA, RG 393, Dept. of the Tenn., Endorsements. Written on a letter of Nov. 22 of Col. Gabriel Bouck, 18th Wis., requesting the discharge of 1st Lt. George R. Walbridge, absent from the 18th Wis. since wounded at Shiloh.— *Ibid.* On Nov. 30, Walbridge tendered his resignation "on account of wound on foot recd. at Shiloh, Tenn.," and on Dec. 5, Brig. Gen. Charles S. Hamilton endorsed this letter favorably to USG.—Copy, *ibid.*, District of Corinth, Endorsements.

1862, Nov. 30. To Capt. Christopher H. McNally, 3rd U.S. Cav., Detroit. "Cannot mount you here. Make requisition for Horses and equipments required on Gen. Robert Allen of Quartermaster's Department, Saint Louis, Mo."—Copies, DLC-USG, V, 18, 30, 91; DNA, RG 393, Dept. of the Tenn., Letters Sent.

1862, [Nov.]. USG endorsement. "Permission is granted to use the brick in the old walls of the burned Depot at Grand Junction for public use."—AES, Atwater Collection, ICHi. Written on a letter of Nov. 25 from Maj. Thomas E. Morris, 15th Mich., Grand Junction, to USG. "Application having been made here for permission to get brick for the purpose of putting up furnaces to heat camp hospitals &c I would ask permission to pull down and use the brick in the ruins of the burned depot at this place the walls of which are standing. Genl McArthur who I consulted upon the subject said he could see no objection whatever if the Commdg Genl would be pleased to grant such permission." —ALS, *ibid.*

1862, Dec. 1. To Brig. Gen. Jeremiah C. Sullivan, Jackson, Tenn. "Has the 29th Ills. yet started for Coldwater. If not hurry it forward."

—Telegram, copies, DLC-USG, V, 18, 30, 91; DNA, RG 393, Dept. of the Tenn., Letters Sent. Earlier on Dec. 1, Lt. Col. John A. Rawlins had telegraphed to Sullivan. "Send the 29th Ills. forward to Coldwater."—Copies, *ibid.* On the same day, Capt. Theodore S. Bowers issued Special Orders No. 35. "The District of Jackson, Commanded by Brig. Genl J C. Sullivan, will here after extend to Cold Water, Miss, and will include the Posts of Grand Junction and La Grange"—DS, *ibid.*, RG 94, Dept. of the Tenn., Special Orders; copies, *ibid.*, RG 393, Dept. of the Tenn., Special Orders; DLC-USG, V, 16, 26, 27.

1862, DEC. 1. Maj. Gen. John A. McClernand to USG. "Surgeon Hezekiah Williams has shown me an order made by your command, requiring him to report to his Regiment the 2nd. Ills. Light Artillery With every disposition to his duty Dr. Williams feels himself embarrassed. The reason of his embarrassment may be briefly stated as follows He was detached from his Regiment by order of Maj Genl. Halleck under instruction to report forthwith to Surgeon Simmons for special duty—again he was ordered by Surgeon Simmons to report to me for duty on my staff in which capacity he has been dilligently engaged ever since I reported here for duty in organizing the medical Department of the new Regiments in superintending hospitals & in inspecting recruits. He now finds your order What shall he do? Although I could illy part with him, yet if under the circumstances stated duty calls him elsewhere of course I acquiesce"—DfS, McClernand Papers, IHi. McClernand's request was granted on Dec. 13 by Special Orders No. 22, 13th Army Corps, Dept. of the Tenn.—DS, DNA, RG 94, Dept. of the Tenn., Special Orders; copies, *ibid.*, RG 393, Dept. of the Tenn., Special Orders; DLC-USG, V, 26, 27, 91; (designated Special Field Orders No. 16), McClernand Papers, IHi.

1862, DEC. 3. To Governor David Tod of Ohio. "Respectfully referred to Governor Tod. The 19th Regt. Ohio Vols. is not in this Department"—Copies, DLC-USG, V, 25; DNA, RG 393, Dept. of the Tenn., Endorsements. Written on a letter of Nov. 11 of 2nd Lt. Russell Case, 19th Ohio, tendering his resignation in order to accept an appointment as recruiting officer of the 125th Ohio.—*Ibid.*

1862, DEC. 8. To Maj. Samuel Breck, AGO, Washington. "Send books & blanks direct to Jackson-Tenn by Express We are out of every kind"—Telegram received, DNA, RG 107, Telegrams Collected (Bound). On Dec. 8, Breck telegraphed to USG. "The books and blanks you require are put up. How shall I direct them in order that they may go direct?"—LS (telegram sent), *ibid.*, Telegrams Collected (Unbound); telegram received, *ibid.*, RG 393, Dept. of the Tenn., Telegrams Received; copies (misdated Nov. 8), *ibid.*, Hd. Qrs. Correspondence; DLC-USG, V, 5, 8, 24, 88. On Jan. 21, 1863, USG telegraphed to Brig. Gen. Lorenzo Thomas. "The two hundred & seven boxes of blanks forwarded to this Dept reached Holly Springs on the night of nineteenth of December & were burned in Rebel raid on that place on twentieth The command is entirely out of blanks please duplicate former order"—Telegram received, DNA, RG 107, Telegrams Collected (Bound); copies, *ibid.*, RG 393, Dept. of the Tenn., Hd. Qrs. Correspondence; DLC-USG, V, 5, 8, 24, 88. On Jan. 23, Breck telegraphed to USG. "One Hundred and sixty three boxes of Books & blanks have been sent you to day, the remaind[er] will be sent as soon as possible"—LS (telegram sent), DNA, RG 107, Telegrams Collected (Unbound); telegram received, *ibid.*; *ibid.*, RG 393, Dept. of the Tenn., Telegrams Received. On Jan. 24, Breck sent to USG an itemized list of the books and blanks sent.—DS, *ibid.*, Letters Received.

Index

All letters written by USG of which the text was available for use in this volume are indexed under the names of the recipients. The dates of these letters are included in the index as an indication of the existence of text. Abbreviations used in the index are explained on pp. xvi–xx. Individual regts. are indexed under the names of the states in which they originated.

Abbeville, Miss.: C.S.A. at, 29n, 285n, 291, 312n, 313n, 334, 335n, 341, 342n, 343n, 363n, 366n; located, 293n; occupied by U.S., 367, 368, 369, 370n, 386, 392n, 397n

Abraham Lincoln Book Shop, Chicago, Ill.: document owned by, 120–21

Adams, Robert N. (Ohio Vols.), 421–22

Adams, Rufus (prisoner), 78n, 108, 109n

Adams, Wirt (C.S. Army), 40n

Adams Express Company, 451

Admiral (steamboat), 438

Alabama: corn from, 5n, 132n, 150n; C.S.A. troops from, 49n, 97n, 109n, 129n, 160n, 179 and n, 213n, 227n; citizens in U.S. Army, 97n

Alden, Henry N. (Ill. Vols.), 431

Alexander, James M. (Ill. Vols.), 444

Alexander, Jesse I. (Ind. Vols.), 419, 422

Algee, James B. (C.S. Army), 423, 424

Alger, Russell A. (Mich. Vols.), 17n

Allen, Benjamin (Wis. Vols.), 216, 217n

Allen, L. D., 21n

Allen, Robert (U.S. Army): telegram to, Oct. 31, 1862, 198n; sends troops, 198n; asked for forage, 213, 215n, 242; telegram to, Oct. 29, 1862, 215n; telegram to, Nov. 5, 1862, 260; sends q.m., 260n; supplies lumber, 260n, 355n; approves Cairo contracts, 274; sends blankets, 309, 309n–10n; telegram to, Nov. 13, 1862, 309n; telegram to, Nov. 14, 1862, 309n; telegram to, Nov. 18, 1862, 328n–29n; asked whereabouts of q.m., 328n–29n; telegram to, Dec. 3, 1862, 355n; supplies Vicksburg expedition, 404, 405n, 407; sends horses, 424, 442, 458; letter to, Oct. 28, 1862, 442

Alton, Ill.: prisoners sent to, 6n, 37 and n, 90n, 141n, 159n, 181, 204 and n, 336n, 428, 457; prisoners released from, 78 and n, 108–9, 109n, 153, 228, 229n, 240, 337, 430, 443

Ambulances, 100n, 214n, 270, 336n, 342 and n

Ammon's Bridge, Tenn., 96n

Amos, James (prisoner), 443

Anderson, George M. (citizen), 90n

Anderson, J. Patton (C.S. Army), 453

Anderson, Joseph M. (Ohio Vols.), 90n

Anderson's Mill, Tenn., 88n

Anneke, Fritz (Ill. Vols.), 434

Antietam, Md., battle of, 66n

Arkansas (gunboat), 255n

Arkansas: C.S.A. troops from, 40n, 76n, 97n, 126n, 129n, 195n, 197; illegal trade in, 135n; C.S.A. movements in, 385, 386n;

mentioned, 264n

Armstrong, Frank C. (C.S. Army): attacks Medon, 4 and n; raids Tenn., 5n, 6n, 7n, 8n, 34n, 35n; skirmishes at Britton's Lane, 9n, 336n; near Iuka, 39n, 41n, 58n, 64, 171; at Davis' Mills, 160n; at Salem, 208n

Arnold, Isaac N. (U.S. Representative), 265n

Ashport, Tenn., 135n, 136n, 431, 441

Atlanta, Ga., 374n

Atwell, James W. (telegraph operator), 382n

Aurora College, Aurora, Ill.: document in, 268n

Bacon, Pvt., 167n

Bailey, Jeremiah B. (Ill. Vols.), 321

Bailey, Mahlon G. (Ohio Vols), 323, 324

Baker, Nathaniel B. (Iowa AG), 419–20

Baker, Samuel R. (Ill. Vols), 228n

Baldwin, Silas D. (Ill. Vols.), 141n, 225n

Baldwyn, Miss.: C.S.A. at, 27n, 28n, 32n, 36n, 57n, 76n, 77n, 92n; C.S.A. movement from, 39n, 42n, 47n, 168, 177n; prisoners sent to, 49n, 214n; expedition to, 74n, 194n; located, 177n

Ballard County, Ky., 86n

Ballentine, John G. (C.S. Army), 141n

Bancroft Library, University of California, Berkeley, Calif.: documents in, 41n, 47n, 68–69, 82, 88, 88n, 91, 115n

Banks, 436

Barnett Knob, Miss.: U.S. troops at, 32n, 35n, 69n, 73n, 170, 172, 173, 177n; C.S.A. at, 38, 39n, 42n, 43n; located, 43n; reconnaissance near, 57n, 58n, 65n

Barnitz, David G. (U.S. Treasury Dept.), 202n, 435

Barrett, Wallace W. (Ill. Vols.), 437

Barry, William F. (U.S. Army), 327n

Bass, N. A. (of Jackson, Tenn.), 321

Bates, Edward (U.S. Attorney General), 87n

Baton Rouge (steamboat), 21n, 422

Batterton, Ira A. (Ill. Vols.), 439–40

Battery Rock, Ill., 151n

Bawdin, Mr. (merchant), 136n

Baxter, George L. (C.S. Army), 227n, 269

Bayou Manchac (La.), 255n

Bay Springs, Miss.: U.S. cav. near, 32n, 35n; C.S.A. near, 39n, 40n, 46, 47n, 168, 171, 212; located, 47n; reconnaissances toward, 64, 65n, 66n, 373n; C.S.A. retreat to, 73n, 76n, 77n; mentioned, 28n, 52n, 341

Bear Creek (Ala.), 5, 36*n*, 46, 57*n*, 73*n*, 169, 174

Beauregard, Pierre G. T. (C.S. Army), 34*n*, 398*n*

Belknap, William W. (Iowa Vols.): telegram to, Sept. 16, 1862, 54*n*; ordered to Corinth, 54*n*

Bell, Francis M. (Mo. Vols.), 339, 340*n*

Bell, J. T., 451

Belle Memphis (steamboat), 135*n*

Benton Barracks, St. Louis, Mo., 146 and *n*, 165 and *n*

Berry, Benjamin F. (Ill. Vols.), 90*n*

Bethel, Tenn.: road guarded from, 24, 64*n*; telegraph at, 64*n*, 96*n*; command of, 82*n*, 83*n*, 318*n*, 319*n*; threatened, 88*n*, 89*n*, 97*n*, 101*n*, 222, 223, 348*n*; troop movements at, 99, 113*n*, 123, 125*n*, 212, 213, 214*n*, 217, 218*n*, 271*n*; prisoners at, 100, 128, 129*n*; intelligence from, 103*n*, 104*n*, 106, 111*n*, 374*n*; supplies at, 124*n*, 125*n*, 439, 446; pillaging at, 195–96, 196*n*; guerrillas near, 426, 433; mentioned, 259*n*, 445, 453

Bickham, William D. (newspaper correspondent), 167*n*

Big Muddy, Tenn., 125*n*

Bigney, Thomas O. (Wis. Vols.), 419

Big Spring Creek (Miss.), 360, 361*n*

Bird's Point, Mo., 294*n*, 434

Bissell, Josiah W. (Mo. Vols.): transports art., 94*n*, 417, 418; telegram to, Nov. 26, 1862, 354; repairs railroad, 354, 354*n*–55*n*; telegram to, Nov. 26, 1862, 354*n*; telegram to, Dec. 9, 1862, 355*n*; charges against, 418, 430, 431

Blackland, Miss., 32*n*, 35*n*, 77*n*

Black River (Miss.), 372*n*, 390 and *n*, 403

Blair, Francis P., Jr. (U.S. Representative), 87*n*, 265*n*

Blakemore, H. B. (C.S. Army), 158*n*

Blankets, 179*n*, 309, 309*n*–10*n*

Blow, Henry T. (of St. Louis), 87*n*

Bluntsville, Ala., 27*n*

Blythe, Green L. (C.S. Army), 179*n*

Bohemian Club Library, San Francisco, Calif.: document in, 349

Boles, Calvin (prisoner), 108, 109*n*

Bolivar, Charles (military telegraph), 382*n*

Bolivar, Tenn.: attacked, 4*n*, 7*n*, 8*n*; threatened, 5, 6*n*, 7*n*, 10, 11*n*, 12, 13*n*, 16*n*, 24, 34*n*, 47*n*, 58*n*, 79, 80, 80*n*–81*n*, 84, 87, 88*n*, 91*n*, 92*n*, 96, 101*n*, 107 and *n*, 108*n*, 110, 194, 208*n*, 210, 212 and *n*, 217, 218*n*, 221–22, 224, 236 and *n*, 237 and *n*, 238*n*, 239, 243, 343*n*; troop movements at, 9*n*,

26, 28, 38, 41*n*, 46, 59–60, 60*n*, 67, 75 and *n*, 81 and *n*, 91*n*, 92*n*, 93, 99, 104, 104*n*–5*n*, 106, 107*n*, 111, 113*n*, 114, 117, 119*n*, 123, 133, 137*n*, 139, 150 and *n*, 169–70, 176, 196*n*, 206*n*, 223, 224, 231, 234 and *n*, 235, 243, 245–46, 246*n*, 247, 248*n*, 250 and *n*, 253, 254, 256 and *n*, 257*n*, 266, 270*n*, 271*n*, 348*n*, 352*n*, 363, 432; command of, 16*n*, 82 and *n*, 120*n*, 124*n*, 127, 131 and *n*, 148 and *n*, 251, 301*n*; garrisoned, 28, 29*n*, 30*n*, 31*n*, 98, 194, 200, 213, 214*n*, 235, 237 and *n*, 238*n*, 259*n*, 278 and *n*, 298*n*, 438; arrests at, 37 and *n*, 59 and *n*, 78 and *n*; intelligence from, 96*n*, 105; prisoners at, 104*n*, 108, 109*n*, 159*n*, 289, 290*n*, 445; USG at, 231 and *n*, 377, 382*n*; stores at, 233*n*, 249 and *n*, 250 and *n*, 272*n*, 450; trade at, 304*n*, 452, 453; telegraph at, 377, 382*n*, 383*n*; mentioned, 22, 152*n*, 160*n*, 166*n*, 283*n*, 302*n*, 425, 457

Bonneville, Benjamin L. E. (U.S. Army), 339*n*

Booneville, Miss.: railroad at, 27*n*, 49*n*; C.S.A. near, 31*n*, 32*n*, 34*n*, 35*n*, 36*n*, 39*n*, 40*n*, 42*n*, 47*n*, 49*n*, 77*n*; mentioned, 17*n*, 238*n*

Borcherdt, Albert (Mo. Vols.), 421

Borup, Lt. Col. (C.S. Army), 19*n*

Bouck, Gabriel (Wis. Vols.), 318*n*, 458

Boudon, H. G., 431

Bouton, Edward (Ill. Vols.), 293*n*

Bowen, Edwin A. (Ill. Vols.), 451

Bowen, John S. (C.S. Army), 75*n*, 80*n*, 180*n*, 211, 291, 312*n*

Bowers, Theodore S. (staff officer of USG): issues orders for USG, 3*n*, 44*n*, 85*n*, 348*n*, 357*n*, 418, 421, 459; writes for USG, 77*n*, 199*n*; promotion of, 203, 295, 356, 357*n*, 358*n*; duties of, 256*n*–57*n*, 352*n*, 384*n*, 387*n*–88*n*; telegram to, Dec. 5, 1862, 352*n*

Bowling Green, Ky., 261*n*, 446, 448

Boyle, Jeremiah T. (U.S. Army), 17, 18*n*, 19*n*, 190*n*

Boyle, Thomas (prisoner), 433

Brackett, Alfred B. (Iowa Vols.), 433

Bradford, Mr., 455

Bradstreet, Mrs. E. P. (of Cincinnati): pass for, Nov. 1, 1862, 332*n*; obtains cotton, 332*n*–33*n*

Braffitt, Charles (Ohio Vols.), 204 and *n*

Bragg, Braxton (C.S. Army): campaigns of, 6*n*, 13*n*, 34*n*, 36*n*, 82*n*, 184, 255*n*, 429, 435; intentions of, 31*n*, 132*n*, 179 and *n*, 280*n*, 310, 312*n*, 351*n*, 361, 372*n*, 373 and *n*, 374*n*, 402*n*, 446, 453; reinforcements for, 47*n*, 48*n*, 103*n*, 104*n*, 150*n*, 212

Brand (scout), 8*n*

Brayman, Mason (Ill. Vols.): and prisoners, 109*n*, 289*n*–90*n*; commands Bolivar, 245*n*, 249*n*, 450; telegrams to, Nov. 7, 1862 (2), 271*n*; sends teams, 271*n*; telegram to, Nov. 9, 1862, 281*n*; reports troop dispositions, 281*n*–82*n*, 343*n*, 348*n*, 352*n*; deals with citizens, 283*n*, 383*n*, 448; telegram to, Nov. 11, 1862, 290*n*; telegram to, Nov. 23, 1862, 343*n*; telegram to, Nov. 25, 1862, 348*n*; telegram to, Nov. 28, 1862, 352*n*; leaves dept., 434; telegram to, Nov. 9, 1862, 448

Breck, Samuel (U.S. Army): telegram to, Dec. 8, 1862, 459–60; sends forms, 459–60

Breckinridge, Capt. (scout), 426

Breckinridge, John C. (C.S. Army): intentions of, 27*n*, 32*n*, 34*n*, 46, 60*n*, 76*n*, 77*n*, 79, 101*n*, 170, 171, 429; movements of, 57*n*, 58*n*, 64, 65*n*, 80*n*, 82*n*, 87, 94*n*, 96–97, 96*n*, 97*n*, 150*n*

Britton's Lane, Tenn., skirmish of, 9 and *n*, 11*n*, 322*n*, 335, 336*n*

Brott, Elijah C. (Ill. Vols.), 443

Brown, Hugh G. (Iowa Vols.), 119*n*

Brown, Isaac N. (C.S. Navy), 255*n*

Browning, Orville H. (U.S. Senator), 289*n*

Brownsville, Tenn.: threatened, 4*n*, 6*n*, 10, 11*n*, 96*n*, 137*n*, 160*n*, 211, 212*n*, 213, 216, 435; located, 11*n*; occupied, 12, 24, 29*n*–30*n*, 31*n*; skirmish near, 181 and *n*; mentioned, 136*n*, 442

Brown University, Providence, R.I.: document in, 143*n*

Bru, T. C. (U.S. Army), 396*n*

Bruch, Samuel (U.S. Army), 382*n*, 383*n*, 391*n*, 392*n*

Bryant, George E. (Wis. Vols.), 20*n*, 137*n*

Bryant, Robert E. (U.S. Army), 333*n*

Buckland, Ralph P. (Ohio Vols.), 255*n*, 264*n*, 292, 293*n*, 294*n*

Buell, Don Carlos (U.S. Army): campaigns of, 6*n*, 27*n*, 31, 34*n*, 85*n*, 87, 122*n*, 179*n*, 431, 435; troops of, 33*n*, 147*n*; relieved, 182*n*, 184; investigated, 184*n*, 287*n*; supplies for, 419, 421

Buford, Napoleon B. (U.S. Army), 17*n*, 103*n*, 183*n*

Burgher's Ferry, Tenn., 225*n*

Burke, Patrick E. (Mo. Vols.), 41*n*, 144*n*

Burke, W. R. (Ill. Vols.), 447

Burlington, Iowa, 186 and *n*, 357 and *n*

Burnside, Ambrose E. (U.S. Army), 66*n*

Burnsville, Miss.: U.S. troops at, 32*n*, 35*n*, 36*n*, 41*n*, 69*n*, 76*n*; C.S.A. near, 39*n*, 47*n*, 61, 69*n*; and battle of Iuka, 48*n*, 52*n*, 56,

57*n*, 58*n*, 61, 63, 64, 65*n*, 168, 169, 170, 171, 177*n*, 178*n*; located, 58*n*; USG at, 67, 178*n*; prisoners from, 109, 445

Burrows, Jerome B. (Ohio Vols.), 298*n*

Butler, Benjamin F. (U.S. Army), 68*n*

Butler, E. D. (telegraph operator), 445

Byhalia, Miss., 141*n*, 312*n*

Cabell, William L. (C.S. Army), 28*n*

Cadwallader, Sylvanus (newspaper correspondent), 333*n*

Cairo, Ill.: reinforcements sent from, 11*n*, 12*n*, 33*n*, 54*n*, 125*n*, 198*n*, 226*n*, 279*n*, 297*n*; telegraph at, 20 and *n*, 377, 379, 382*n*, 384*n*, 391*n*, 392*n*; arrests at, 21, 22*n*, 86*n*; prisoners sent to, 55–56, 141*n*, 198*n*, 219, 289, 290*n*, 336*n*, 337; trade at, 85*n*, 102*n*, 135*n*, 136*n*, 333*n*, 334*n*, 419, 435, 439; signal corps at, 183*n*–84*n*; command of, 186, 218, 301*n*; Negroes at, 198*n*, 317*n*; liquor at, 201*n*, 202*n*; supplies at, 220*n*, 242, 329*n*, 405*n*, 406*n*; inspected, 241*n*; package tampering at, 265, 266*n*; contracts at, 273–75; mentioned, 66*n*, 89*n*, 122*n*, 156*n*, 185*n*, 286*n*, 287*n*, 340*n*–41*n*, 376*n*, 418, 445, 446–47, 448, 451

California, 179*n*, 296*n*

Callender, Byron M. (Mo. Vols.), 54, 55*n*

Callender, Franklin D. (U.S. Army), 12*n*, 165*n*

Callie (steamboat), 21

Camden, Tenn., 426

Campbell, Archibald B. (U.S. Army), 230

Campbell, Charles C. (Ill. Vols.), 230

Campbell, George H. (Ill. Vols.), 436

Campbell (steamboat), 151*n*

Campbell's Mill, Miss., 35*n*

Camp Dennison, Cincinnati, Ohio, 432

Canby, Edward R. S. (U.S. Army), 232*n*

Cannon, John R. (U.S. Army), 418, 441

Cape Girardeau, Mo., 420

Carlisle, Pa., 120*n*, 184*n*

Carpenter, Peter A. (Iowa Vols.), 98*n*

Carr, Eugene A. (U.S. Army), 125*n*

Carter, Julian (Ill. Vols.), 258, 259*n*

Cartersville, Miss., 69*n*

Case, Russell (Ohio Vols.), 459

Casey, James F. (brother-in-law of USG), 453

Casey, Peter (merchant), 453

Caseyville, Ky., 151 and *n*, 419

Cattle, 179*n*, 233*n*, 266, 370*n*

Cavashere, Mr. (guerrilla), 430

Chambers, Alexander (Iowa Vols.), 52*n*, 57*n*

Chambersburg, Pa., 435

Charleston, Miss., 312*n*

Chase, Salmon P. (U.S. Secretary of the Treasury), 23*n*, 201*n*, 332*n*, 457

Chattanooga, Tenn.: C.S.A. base at, 6*n*, 13*n*, 373, 374*n*; John C. Breckinridge at, 80*n*, 87, 94*n*, 97, 150*n*, 429; spies from, 313*n*

Cheek, Elijah (citizen), 90*n*

Cheney, John T. (Ill. Vols.), 19*n*

Cherokee, Ala., 374*n*, 402 and *n*

Chetlain, Augustus L. (Ill. Vols.), 149*n*

Chewalla, Tenn.: threatened, 5*n*, 27*n*, 97*n*, 98*n*, 101*n*, 103*n*, 113*n*, 115*n*, 206*n*, 223; defended, 35*n*, 41*n*, 53, 83*n*, 118, 126, 128 and *n*, 169, 250*n*, 251 and *n*, 456; skirmish near, 91*n*, 105, 106, 107*n*, 108*n*, 111*n*–12*n*, 123*n*, 124*n*; flag of truce at, 208*n*, 214*n*; mentioned, 231, 237, 242 and *n*, 425

Chewalla Creek (Miss.), 140*n*, 359 and *n*

Chicago, Ill., 20*n*, 281*n*, 305*n*, 317*n*, 326*n*, 329*n*

Chicago Historical Society, Chicago, Ill.: documents in, 249*n*, 271*n* (2), 281*n*, 281*n*–82*n*, 283*n*, 289*n*, 290*n* (2), 334*n*, 348*n* (4), 352*n* (2), 383*n*, 448, 450, 458

Chicago Public Library, Chicago, Ill.: document in, 48–49

Chicago Times (newspaper), 367*n*

Chicago Tribune (newspaper), 86*n*

Chicopee, Mass., 452

Chulahoma, Miss., 312*n*, 360, 361*n*, 362, 393, 395*n*

Church, Lawrence S. (Ill. Vols.), 220*n*

Cincinnati, Ohio: troop movements at, 13*n*, 18*n*, 33*n*, 94*n*; trade at, 22*n*, 332*n*, 334*n*; feeling toward USG at, 62; officers ordered to, 82*n*, 180*n*, 182 and *n*, 184 and *n*, 286*n*, 287*n*, 436; mentioned, 232*n*, 246, 305*n*

Cincinnati Commercial (newspaper), 167*n*

Cincinnati Gazette (newspaper), 20*n*

City of Alton (steamboat), 435

Clancy, Joseph (Wis. Vols.), 90*n*

Clark, Henry E. (C.S. Army), 205 and *n*

Clark, John (Wis. Vols.), 44*n*

Clark, Temple (U.S. Army), 217*n*

Clark, William (C.S. Army), 335*n*

Clark, William T. (U.S. Army): reports skirmish, 181*n*; telegram to, Nov. 2, 1862, 302*n*; as adjt., 302*n*

Clarkston, Mo., 205 and *n*

Clarksville, Tenn., 145, 146*n*, 428

Clayton, William Z. (Minn. Vols.), 450

Clayton Station, Tenn., 196*n*

Clear Creek (Miss.), 6*n*, 35*n*–36*n*, 39*n*, 49*n*, 97*n*

Clifton, Tenn., 375*n*

Clinton, Col. (C.S. Army), 40*n*

Clinton, Tenn., 100*n*

Clover Creek (Tenn.), 113*n*

Coal, 21*n*, 405*n*

Coffee, 150*n*, 316*n*

Coffeeville, Miss., 390*n*, 400, 401*n*, 403, 409

Cold Water, Miss.: C.S.A. at, 264*n*, 277*n*, 284*n*, 285*n*, 286*n*, 291, 426; U.S. troops at, 306*n*, 308*n*, 363, 364*n*, 370*n*, 395*n*, 458–59; railroad to, 353, 361, 387*n*, 388*n*

Cold Water River (Miss.): C.S.A. troops on, 82*n*, 179*n*, 291, 293*n*; bridge at, 299*n*, 303*n*, 306*n*, 308*n*, 315*n*; U.S. troops at, 350, 352*n*, 363, 401*n*, 412

College Hill, Miss., 370*n*, 395*n*, 409*n*

Collierville, Tenn., 347*n*, 430

Collins, C. (of Memphis), 445

Collins, James (prisoner), 108, 109*n*, 240

Colorado State Historical Society, Denver, Colo.: documents in, 186, 319–20

Colt's Ferry, Miss., 362, 363*n*

Columbus, Ga., 373, 375*n*

Columbus, Ky.: U.S. troops at, 33*n*, 156*n*, 157 and *n*, 158*n*, 195*n*, 197*n*, 198*n*, 205, 220*n*, 225 and *n*, 279*n*, 281*n*, 294*n*, 309*n*, 352*n*, 412, 431–32, 448; railroad at, 40*n*, 81*n*, 200, 305*n*, 328*n*, 329*n*, 406*n*; supplies at, 55*n*, 83*n*, 124*n*, 125*n*, 127*n*–28*n*, 142*n*, 165*n*, 213, 214*n*–15*n*, 232*n*, 247*n*, 249*n*, 281*n*, 282*n*, 304*n*, 417, 424, 432, 442, 449, 450, 451; USG visits, 84, 85 and *n*, 91, 163*n*, 312*n*, 338 and *n*; command of, 85*n*–86*n*, 187*n*, 193*n*; trade at, 102*n*, 136*n*, 333*n*, 334*n*, 419, 435, 441; troops sent from, 124*n*, 125*n*, 131, 151, 246, 247 and *n*, 248*n*, 297, 297*n*–98*n*, 344*n*, 368*n*; prisoners at, 141*n*, 146, 214*n*, 290*n*; mail at, 265*n*, 357*n*; Julia Dent Grant at, 359*n*; mentioned, 6*n*, 17*n*, 18, 30*n*, 60, 115*n*, 140*n*, 149*n*, 186, 250*n*, 263 and *n*, 296, 315*n*, 326*n*, 382*n*, 410*n*

Columbus, Miss., 212, 238*n*, 313*n*, 388, 399, 402

Columbus, Ohio, 264*n*, 265*n*

Connor, Thomas P. (citizen), 90*n*

Considine, John (Mich. Vols.), 90*n*

Cooke, Isaac N. (U.S. Army), 309*n*

Corinth, Miss.: threatened, 5*n*, 6*n*, 10, 13, 26, 27*n*, 28, 30*n*, 31, 32*n*, 34, 35*n*, 38, 39*n*, 40*n*, 41*n*, 42*n*, 43, 46, 48*n*, 50, 75*n*, 88*n*, 95 and *n*, 96–97, 99, 101*n*, 134, 168, 175, 176, 179*n*, 194, 195*n*, 197, 198*n*, 210, 212 and *n*, 213, 215–16, 216*n*, 217, 218*n*, 375*n*,

402*n*; railroad at, 7*n*, 13*n*, 17*n*, 33*n*, 200, 272*n*, 348*n*; siege of, 8*n*, 11*n*; prisoners at, 22, 23*n*, 37*n*, 143, 144*n*, 165*n*, 214*n*; garrisoned, 24, 53–54, 54*n*–55*n*, 59 and *n*, 67, 74, 79, 84, 132*n*, 155, 157*n*, 169, 202, 238, 276, 346*n*, 372*n*, 456; telegraph at, 31*n*–32*n*; expeditions from, 48*n*, 56, 57*n*, 58*n*, 64, 76, 77*n*, 192–93, 237, 237*n*–38*n*, 243, 250*n*, 254, 256, 257*n*, 266, 444; troop movements at, 61, 63, 80, 81 and *n*, 148 and *n*, 149, 150 and *n*, 170, 191 and *n*, 198*n*, 200, 231, 239, 253, 254, 269, 286*n*, 324, 348*n*, 419, 424, 433, 437, 438, 440, 442, 446; USG leaves, 67, 377, 430; command of, 83*n*, 91*n*, 92*n*, 138*n*, 142 and *n*, 187*n*, 192, 216, 217*n*, 250*n*; battle of, 97*n*, 103 and *n*, 104, 104*n*–5*n*, 106, 107, 107*n*–8*n*, 110, 111, 111*n*–12*n*, 112–13, 113*n*, 114, 114*n*–15*n*, 116–17, 117*n*, 118, 118*n*–20*n*, 122*n*, 123*n*–25*n*, 126, 127*n*, 130 and *n*, 131, 131*n*–32*n*, 140*n*, 143, 144*n*, 145*n*, 149*n*, 166*n*, 179*n*, 182 and *n*, 183*n*, 217*n*, 221–24, 229–30, 230*n*, 241, 291, 309, 345, 427, 449; wounded at, 124*n*, 156*n*; supplies at, 136*n*, 164*n*, 213, 213*n*–15*n*, 232*n*, 233*n*, 242, 260*n*, 261*n*, 270*n*, 271*n*, 281*n*, 284*n*, 304*n*, 309*n*, 421, 424; fortified, 157*n*, 160*n*, 231 and *n*; spies at, 310, 313*n*, 373*n*–75*n*, 385; Negroes at, 444, 457; mentioned, 22*n*, 61*n*, 156*n*, 167*n*, 171, 180*n*, 196*n*, 199*n*, 201*n*, 204*n*, 208*n*, 241*n*, 357*n*, 448
Cornell University, Ithaca, N.Y.: document in, 87*n*
Cosselt, Frank (of La Grange), 451
Cotton: purchased, 7*n*, 264*n*, 304*n*, 312*n*, 379, 383*n*, 417, 447; seized, 22*n*, 343*n*, 393–95, 395*n*–96*n*, 398*n*, 401*n*, 418, 431; shipped, 55*n*, 418, 435; burned, 191*n*, 225*n*, 348*n*; picked, 315 and *n*, 316*n*, 317*n*; regulated, 331, 332*n*–34*n*, 393–95, 395*n*–96*n*
Courtland, Ala., 34*n*
Courts-Martial: USG involvement with, 89, 89*n*–91*n*, 425; of officers, 177*n*, 196*n*, 217*n*, 322*n*, 433, 437; of soldiers, 204 and *n*, 440; dissolved, 258; for vandalism, 267; avoided, 455, 456
Covington, Mr. (of Miss.), 42*n*
Covington, Ky., 43–44, 62*n*, 155 and *n*, 344, 433
Cox, Jacob D. (U.S. Army), 436
Cox, John C. (U.S. Army): telegram to, Oct. 24, 1862, 232*n*; telegram to, Nov. 1, 1862, 232*n*; as commissary, 232*n*–33*n*, 249*n*, 282*n*, 442–43, 452; telegram to,

Nov. 2, 1862, 249*n*; letter to, Oct. 28, 1862, 442
Coxe, William H. (of Holly Springs), 393–94, 395*n*–96*n*
Crain's Creek (Ala.), 374*n*
Crawford, R. G. (prisoner), 108, 109*n*
Crescent City (steamboat), 417
Crocker, Marcellus M. (Iowa Vols.): at Bolivar, 11*n*, 16*n*; at Corinth, 38, 41*n*, 42*n*, 97*n*; promotion recommended, 157*n*, 161, 162*n*, 318, 320
Crockett, 32*n*, 35*n*, 36*n*, 40*n*
Croft, John T. (Iowa Vols.), 428
Cromwell, John N. (Ill. Vols.), 147*n*
Cullum, George W. (U.S. Army), 436
Cumberland Gap (Tenn.), 13*n*, 446
Cumberland River, 7*n*, 145, 146*n*, 447
Curtis, Samuel R. (U.S. Army): to aid USG, 68*n*, 84, 125*n*, 243*n*, 291, 404, 405*n*, 407, 408, 410*n*, 411; requests troops, 156*n*, 197*n*; telegram to, Oct. 20, 1862, 167*n*; deals with prisoners, 167*n*, 229*n*; quarrels with USG, 180*n*, 189, 190*n*, 200–201, 201*n*, 202*n*, 210, 210*n*–11*n*, 375, 375*n*–77*n*; telegram to, Oct. 25, 1862, 189; telegram to, Oct. 25, 1862, 190*n*; telegram to, Oct. 25, 1862, 201*n*; endorsement to, Dec. 15, 1862, 377*n*; mentioned, 436, 449
Cypress, Tenn., 131*n*

*D*acotah (steamboat), 141*n*
Dallam, Francis A. (U.S. Army), 124*n*
Dalton, Ga., 374*n*
Daly, John N. (C.S. Army), 126*n*
Dancer, James P. (prisoner), 37*n*
Daniel Able and Company (Cairo), 201*n*
Danville, Miss.: C.S.A. forces at, 5*n*, 42*n*; U.S. forces at, 8*n*, 17*n*, 24, 27*n*, 53, 57*n*, 97*n*
Davenport's Mills, Miss., 57*n*, 58*n*, 65*n*, 76*n*, 172
David, Thomas B. A. (U.S. Army), 382*n*, 383*n*
Davies, Thomas A. (U.S. Army): at Corinth, 3*n*, 24, 83*n*, 97*n*; and battle of Iuka, 64, 171; in battle of Corinth, 108*n*, 115*n*, 123*n*–24*n*, 230; commands Columbus, 187*n*, 192, 193*n*; consolidates forces, 190*n*, 279*n*, 297, 297*n*–98*n*, 352*n*; reports expeditions, 205 and *n*, 225 and *n*, 226, 296–97, 297*n*, 443; telegram to, Oct. 30, 1862, 225; telegram to, Oct. 30, 1862, 226; telegram to, Nov. 2, 1862, 247; sends troops, 247 and *n*, 248*n*, 253, 293*n*–94*n*, 368*n*; telegram to, Nov. 1, 1862, 248*n*; telegram to,

Davies, Thomas A. *(cont.)*
Nov. 2, 1862, 248*n*; investigates mail, 265*n*, 266*n*; telegram to, Nov. 9, 1862, 279*n*; telegram to, Nov. 8, 1862, 281*n*; sends art., 281*n*; letter to, Nov. 11, 1862, 297; telegram to, Nov. 30, 1862, 368*n*; telegram to, Nov. 1, 1862, 442; letter to, Nov. 15, 1862, 450; mentioned, 204*n*, 410*n*, 449

Davis, Charles H. (U.S. Navy), 340*n*

Davis, David (Ill. judge), 317*n*

Davis, Jefferson C. (U.S. Army), 422

Davis, Samuel B. (Iowa Vols.), 119*n*, 120*n*

Davis Bridge, Tenn.: skirmish at, 91*n*; repaired, 102*n*; C.S.A. cross, 104*n*; expedition to, 104*n*, 105 and *n*, 113*n*; located, 105*n*; battle at, 118*n*–19*n*, 129*n*; guarded, 217, 237*n*, 251*n*, 352*n*

Davis Creek (Tenn.), 257*n*

Davis' Mills, Miss.: bridge at, 60*n*, 191*n*, 425; C.S.A. at, 75*n*, 79, 80*n*, 81 and *n*, 82*n*, 87, 92*n*, 95*n*, 160*n*, 179*n*, 206*n*, 224, 249, 299*n*; located, 80*n*; prisoners at, 104*n*; expedition to, 136, 137*n*, 138*n*; supplies at, 246*n*, 451; railroad to, 268, 292, 315*n*, 425; occupied, 268*n*, 270*n*, 282*n*, 285*n*, 286*n*, 302, 303*n*, 307*n*, 308*n*, 335*n*, 351*n*, 353, 354*n*; hospital at, 352*n*; citizen of, 353–54; telegraph at, 384*n*, 392*n*

Dayton, Ohio, 314, 315*n*, 328*n*

Decatur, Ala.: U.S. troops at, 5, 16*n*, 57*n*; Braxton Bragg near, 372*n*, 373, 374*n*, 375*n*, 402 and *n*; located, 375*n*

Decherd, Tenn., 374*n*

De Ford, John W. (U.S. Signal Corps), 183*n*–84*n*

De Golyer, Samuel (Mich. Vols.), 281*n*, 298*n*

Deitzler, George W. (Kan. Vols.), 366*n*

De Loach, Josiah (of Tenn.), 430–31

Delta, Miss., 407 and *n*, 411

Denmark, Tenn., 9*n*

Dennis, Elias S. (Ill. Vols.), 9, 9*n*–10*n*, 11*n*, 336*n*

Denver, James W. (U.S. Army), 255*n*, 293*n*, 312*n*

Derby, Nelson R. (U.S. Army), 445

Deserters: provide information, 57*n*, 58*n*, 80*n*, 82*n*, 92*n*, 132*n*, 195*n*, 264*n*, 270*n*, 291, 293*n*, 375*n*, 402, 409, 453; as prisoners, 141*n*, 307*n*; pillage, 196*n*; improperly received, 197*n*, 198, 198*n*–99*n*; guarded against, 263, 307*n*

Des Moines City (steamboat), 12*n*

Detroit, Mich., 43, 50, 62, 458

Dey, Gustav (U.S. Army), 438

Dick, Franklin A. (of St. Louis), 87*n*

Dickerson, John H. (U.S. Army), 22*n*

Dickey, T. Lyle (Ill. Vols.): at battle of Iuka, 69*n*, 174, 177*n*–78*n*; accompanies USG, 87*n*, 257*n*; procures arms, 162, 163*n*, 164 and *n*, 165*n*, 444; writes to wife, 177*n*, 257*n*; organizes cav., 196*n*, 257*n*, 294, 353*n*; promotion recommended, 244, 318; letter to, Dec. 2, 1862, 371; expeditions of, 371, 386, 388 and *n*, 390, 399 and *n*, 400, 401*n*; letter to, Dec. 3, 1862, 386; letter to, Dec. 4, 1862, 388; letter to, Dec. 6, 1862, 399; mentioned, 427

Dix, John A. (U.S. Army), 389, 390*n*

Dobbs, Cyrus J. (Ind. Vols.), 454

Dodge, Grenville M. (U.S. Army): prepares for attack, 4*n*, 6*n*, 7*n*; reports C.S.A. movements, 34*n*, 82*n*, 140*n*, 190*n*, 225*n*, 312, 313*n*, 373, 373*n*–75*n*; commands Columbus, 85*n*, 149*n*; telegram to, Oct. 2, 1862, 102; regulates trade, 102 and *n*, 135*n*–36*n*, 441–42; telegram to, Oct. 4, 1862, 124*n*; telegrams to, Oct. 5, 1862 (3), 124*n*; sends supplies, 124*n*, 125*n*, 128*n*, 142*n*, 281*n*; sends troops, 124*n*, 125*n*, 140*n*, 348*n*; telegram to, Oct. 8, 1862, 125*n*; telegram to, Oct. 9, 1862, 125*n*; relays message, 139, 140*n*; telegram to, Oct. 8, 1862, 140*n*; telegram to, Oct. 9, 1862, 141*n*; deals with prisoners, 141*n*, 336*n*; telegram to, Oct. 11, 1862, 142*n*; telegram to, Oct. 15, 1862, 151; reports expeditions, 151 and *n*, 158*n*, 159*n*, 298*n*, 433, 443–44; telegram to, Oct. 18, 1862, 157; troop dispositions of, 157 and *n*, 158*n*, 195*n*, 254 and *n*, 269*n*, 271*n*, 373*n*–75*n*, 446, 448, 456; telegram to, Oct. 19, 1862, 157*n*; telegram to, Oct. 25, 1862, 157*n*; telegram to, Oct. 21, 1862, 159*n*; letter to, Oct. 24, 1862, 186; meets USG cousin, 186; telegram to, Oct. 23, 1862, 190*n*; commands Corinth, 192, 193*n*, 216, 217*n*, 250*n*, 286, 287*n*–88*n*; telegram to, Oct. 24, 1862, 193*n*; telegram to, Oct. 25, 1862, 195*n*; letter to, Nov. 3, 1862, 254*n*; letter to, Nov. 7, 1862, 269; letter to, Nov. 8, 1862, 287*n*; telegram to, Nov. 14, 1862, 288*n*; telegram to, Nov. 18, 1862, 373*n*–74*n*; telegram to, Dec. 1, 1862, 375*n*; letter to, Oct. 5, 1862, 433; sends mail, 435; reports fire, 438; telegram to, Oct. 25, 1862, 441–42; and Negroes, 444, 457; letter to, Nov. 17, 1862, 451; telegram to, Nov. 26, 1862, 456

Dollins, James J. (Ill. Vols.): at Corinth, 55*n*; at Humboldt, 137*n*, 195*n*, 240*n*,

282n; telegram to, Oct. 25, 1862, 195n; telegram to, Nov. 10, 1862, 282n

Doner, William H. (Ill. Vols.), 454

Doolittle, James R. (U.S. Senator), 203n

Doran, John L. (Wis. Vols.), 455–56

Dougherty, Henry (Ill. Vols.), 301n

Dresden, Tenn., 331n, 441

Druner (prisoner), 101n

Du Barry, Beekman (U.S. Army), 232 and n

Du Bois, John V. D. (U.S. Army): at Rienzi, 27n, 31n, 32n, 34n–35n, 36n, 39n, 40n; reports C.S.A. movements, 39n, 40n, 47n, 49n, 52n, 53n, 74, 74n–75n, 76 and n, 77n, 160n, 363n, 456–57; at Jacinto, 57n, 60–61, 176; telegram to, Sept. 17, 1862, 60–61; background, 61n; telegram to, Sept. 20, 1862, 74; expeditions of, 74n–75n, 97n, 227n, 299n, 363n; telegram to, Sept. 21, 1862, 76; promotion recommended, 157n, 185n; commands Holly Springs, 388n; mentioned, 316n

Ducat, Arthur C. (Ill. Vols.), 156n, 335n

Duck River (Tenn.), 21n, 422

Duff, L. N. (Columbus, Ky.), 17n

Duff, William L. (Ill. Vols.): returns slave, 86n; letter to, Nov. 1, 1862, 242; forage for, 242; background, 242n; chief of art., 242n, 295, 434

Duncan's Mill, Miss., 100n

Durhamville, Tenn., 433

Dyson's Springs, Tenn., 348n

Earl, Seth C. (Ill. Vols.), 439

Eastport, Ala., 8n, 58n, 170, 374n, 421

Eaton, Alonzo (Iowa Vols.), 442

Eaton, John, Jr. (Ohio Vols.): supervises Negroes, 315n–17n, 329, 330n, 456; background, 316n; letter to, Nov. 26, 1862, 456

Eaton, Mr. (of Columbus, Ky.), 265 and n

Ebenezer Church, Miss., 366n

Eddy, Asher R. (U.S. Army): ordered to Memphis, 260 and n; telegram to, Oct. 29, 1862, 260n

Eddyville, Ky., 226n

Edie, John R. (U.S. Army), 207n

Edinger, Milton D. (Mo. Vols.), 355n

Edmiston, John A. (Ill. Vols.), 321

Ellet, Alfred W. (U.S. Army), 447, 448

Elytown, Ala., 373, 375n

Emilie (steamboat), 417, 418

Engelmann, Adolph (Ill. Vols.), 101n

Enterprise, Miss., 402, 403n

Estanaula, Tenn., 4n, 7n, 9n, 11n, 206n

Eugene (steamboat), 429

Evans, Rowland N. (Ill. Vols.), 321

Evans' Bridge, Tenn., 103n

Evansville, Ind., 151n

Exchange (steamboat), 151n

Fairchild, D. W. (cotton buyer): telegram to, Nov. 18, 1862, 333n

Falkner, William C. (C.S. Army): movements of, 5n, 39n, 40n, 77n, 103n, 231n; organization of, 69n, 159n, 298n, 307n

Farmington, Miss., 32n, 38, 39n, 41n, 111n, 177n, 223

Farrand, Charles E. (U.S. Army), 123n

Farrington, Madison J. (of Memphis), 200, 202n

Farr's Mills, Tenn., 111n

Faulkner, W. W. (C.S. Army), 158, 158n–59n, 269n, 338n, 342n

Fentress, John R. (prisoner), 37 and n, 78

Ferrell, Charles M. (Ill. Vols.), 152n

Fitch, Henry S. (U.S. Army), 428, 434–35

Fleming, James C. (prisoner), 108, 109n

Flood, James P. (Ill. Vols.), 423–24, 428, 443

Florence, Ala., 373n, 374n

Flour, 150n

Foley, Frank (Ill. Vols.), 450

Fond du Lac, Wis., 72n, 265, 266n

Ford, William (Ill. Vols.), 91n, 97n

Forest Queen (steamboat), 225n

Forked Deer River (Tenn.), 6n

Fort, Greenbury L. (U.S. Army), 258, 259n

Fort Donelson, Tenn.: battle of, 10n, 162n, 181n, 301n, 322n; attacked, 11n, 12n; command of, 83n, 186; troops sent from, 145, 226n, 428, 443; mentioned, 241n, 424, 434

Fort Heiman, Tenn., 423, 443

Fort Henry, Tenn.: troops sent from, 11n, 12n, 145, 146n, 226n, 423, 426, 427–28, 433; command of, 83n, 186; prisoners at, 336n, 428; gunboat at, 340n; troops at, 419, 424; citizens at, 432; mentioned, 180n, 241n, 434

Fort Pickering, Memphis, Tenn., 255n, 454

Fort Pillow, Tenn., 11n, 31n, 136n, 141n, 417, 433

Foster, John S. (Ohio Vols.), 159n, 234 and n, 259n

Foster, John W. (Ind. Vols.), 438

Fowler, Jacob A. (citizen), 90n

Fox, George (Wis. Vols.), 217n

Franklin, Edward C. (U.S. Army): telegram to, Nov. 9, 1862, 282n; as surgeon, 282n, 445

Fredericktown, Mo., 322*n*
Freedley, Henry W. (U.S. Army), 229*n*
Friar's Point, Miss.: expedition from, 293*n*, 312*n*; garrisoned, 407, 408, 410*n*, 411–12; located, 407*n*
Frick, Kilian (U.S. Army), 370*n*
Fries, Peter (Ohio Vols.), 44*n*
Frisbie, Orton (Ill. Vols.), 321, 322, 322*n*–23*n*
Fry, James B. (U.S. Army), 357*n*
Fuller, Allen C. (Ill. AG): organizes regts., 157*n*, 158*n*, 296*n*; sends troops, 180*n*, 197*n*–98*n*, 220*n*, 280*n*, 281*n*; telegram to, Oct. 28, 1862, 197*n*; letter to, Oct. 29, 1862, 219; arms troops, 219, 220*n*, 281*n*, 298*n*; appointments recommended to, 358*n*, 438, 439
Fulton, Miss.: feint toward, 8*n*, 32*n*; and battle of Iuka, 52*n*, 65*n*, 69*n*, 72*n*, 73*n*, 76*n*, 170–71, 174–75; located, 177*n*
Funke, Otto (Ill. Vols.), 425

Gaines, Thomas W. (Ill. Vols.), 442
Gaines' Landing, Miss., 94*n*
Galena, Ill., 110, 221*n*, 355, 356*n*
Gallagher, W. D. (U.S. Treasury Dept.), 201*n*
Gambill, William C. (C.S. Army), 269*n*
Gamble, Hamilton R. (Gov. of Mo.), 339 and *n*, 340*n*
Garrettsburg, Ky., 296–97, 297*n*
Gay, Norman (U.S. Army), 144*n*
Gayosa, Tenn., 135*n*
Germantown, Tenn., 293*n*, 312*n*
Gilbert, Alfred W. (Ohio Vols.), 52*n*, 115*n*
Gildermeister, Theodore (Ill. Vols.), 448
Gillespie, William G. B. (Ill. Vols.), 271*n*
Gladiator (steamboat), 179*n*
Glendale, Miss., 35*n*, 41*n*, 51, 52*n*, 53*n*, 56, 456
Goodrich, Lt.: letter to, Nov. 17, 1862, 451
Gorman, Willis A. (U.S. Army), 410*n*, 411*n*
Graham, George W. (steamboat superintendent), 321
Graham, Nimrod P. (prisoner), 153
Grand Junction, Tenn.: C.S.A. near, 7*n*, 47*n*, 79, 88*n*, 92*n*, 94*n*, 96*n*, 100*n*, 160*n*, 191*n*, 194, 206*n*, 208*n*, 224, 236*n*, 249 and *n*, 375*n*, 456–57; reconnaissance toward, 59, 60*n*, 75 and *n*, 80*n*–81*n*, 82*n*, 113*n*, 191*n*; occupied, 133, 137*n*, 138*n*, 256, 257, 261, 290*n*, 330*n*, 352*n*, 446, 451, 459; railroad at, 138 and *n*, 304*n*, 375*n*; expedition to, 200, 235, 237 and *n*, 238*n*,

243 and *n*, 244–45, 245*n*, 245–46, 246*n*, 247, 249 and *n*, 251 and *n*, 254; supplies at, 233*n*, 270*n*–71*n*, 282*n*, 284*n*, 304*n*, 456; movement from, 270*n*–71*n*, 276*n*–77*n*; Negroes at, 316*n*, 329, 330*n*, 347*n*; USG returns to, 338*n*; hospital at, 351*n*–52*n*, 458; telegraph at, 381*n*, 382*n*, 383*n*, 384*n*, 392*n*
Granger, Gordon (U.S. Army): reports C.S.A. movements, 5*n*, 6*n*, 8*n*, 27*n*; ordered to Louisville, 7*n*, 8*n*, 12, 13*n*, 17 and *n*, 18, 18*n*–19*n*, 33 and *n*, 39*n*, 40*n*; charges against, 437; mentioned, 421
Grant, Frederick Dent (son of USG), 344–45
Grant, Jesse Root (father of USG): letter to, Sept. 17, 1862, 61–62; USG criticizes, 61–62, 344–45; USG writes to, 63; sister of, 186*n*; letter to, Nov. 23, 1862, 344–45
Grant, Joel (Ill. Vols.), 444
Grant, Julia Dent (wife of USG): advised to visit Detroit, 43, 50, 62; told about USG staff, 43, 51; letter to, Sept. 14, 1862, 43–44; USG wants to see, 44, 154–55; finances of, 50; informed of Corinth situation, 50, 110; letter to, Sept. 15, 1862, 50–51; letter to, Oct. 3, 1862, 110; travel plans of, 110; telegram to, Nov. 3, 1862, 256*n*; joins USG, 256*n*, 345; relations with father-in-law, 344; pass for, Nov. 28, 1862, 359*n*; leaves USG, 359*n*
Grant, Mary (sister of USG): and family matters, 50, 63, 154–55; corresponds with USG, 61, 345; requests appointment, 62; letter to, Sept. 17, 1862, 63; told about war, 63, 154–55; letter to, Oct. 16, 1862, 154–55
Grant, Susan A. (aunt of USG), 186*n*
Grant, Ulysses S.: commands at Corinth, 3–80 passim, 417–26 passim; rebuked, 20 and *n*, 162, 163*n*; prepared for battle at Corinth, 43, 50, 61, 63, 191 and *n*, 194, 195*n*, 197, 210, 212 and *n*, 213, 215*n*, 238; suggests wife go to Detroit, 43, 50, 62; health of, 44, 63, 84, 88*n*; finances of, 50; writes own orders, 51; and battle of Iuka, 56, 63, 64–65, 65*n*–66*n*, 68–69, 69*n*–70*n*, 70–71, 71–72, 73*n*–74*n*, 87*n*, 154, 168–76, 176*n*, 188–89, 275; criticizes father, 61–62, 344–45; comments on newspapers, 62, 455; releases citizen prisoners, 78 and *n*, 153–54, 228, 228*n*–29*n*, 240; at Jackson, 79–255 passim, 427–47 passim; visits St. Louis, 82, 84, 87, 87*n*–88*n*; at Columbus, 85 and *n*, 91, 163*n*; accused of drunkenness, 87*n*, 242*n*; and battle of Corinth, 95–143

passim, 221–24, 229–30, 230*n*; praises James B. McPherson, 121 and *n*, 130*n*, 131; Henry W. Halleck praises, 122*n*; quarrels with William S. Rosecrans, 131, 133, 134, 136, 137*n*–38*n*, 138, 139*n*, 142, 163–64, 164*n*–65*n*, 165, 165*n*–67*n*, 180*n*, 182*n*–83*n*, 275; regulates trade, 135, 135*n*–36*n*, 160–61, 290, 331, 332*n*–34*n*, 393–95, 398*n*, 452–53; deals with prisoners, 140 and *n*, 141*n*, 143, 146 and *n*, 198, 198*n*–99*n*, 239, 334–35, 335*n*–36*n*, 337, 389; Abraham Lincoln congratulates, 143*n*; recommends promotions, 145*n*, 161, 185, 202, 203 and *n*, 217*n*, 241, 244, 275, 317–18, 318*n*–19*n*, 320; wants visit from wife, 154–55, 256*n*; praises William T. Sherman, 180*n*; commands Dept. of the Tenn., 186–87, 187*n*; quarrels with Samuel R. Curtis, 189, 190*n*, 200–201, 210, 210*n*–11*n*, 375, 375*n*–76*n*; campaigns in Miss., 192–413 passim, 447–60 passim; plans operations against Vicksburg, 199–200, 262–63, 291–92, 310–12, 312*n*, 345–46, 346*n*, 350–51, 351*n*–52*n*, 353, 371–72, 390, 401, 403, 404, 405*n*–6*n*, 406–7, 408–9, 411–12; appoints staff, 220–21, 294–95, 295*n*–96*n*, 356–57, 357*n*–59*n*; punishes plundering, 266–67; advances to Holly Springs, 268 and *n*, 269–70, 272 and *n*, 275, 276, 278, 280*n*, 281, 281*n*–83*n*, 284, 284*n*–85*n*, 285–86, 292, 302, 304–5, 308 and *n*, 320, 359, 360–61, 362, 363–64, 364–65, 368*n*, 396*n*; discusses Cairo contracts, 273–75; excludes Jews, 283 and *n*, 394; develops Negro policy, 315, 315*n*–17*n*; advances to Oxford, 371, 396, 397*n*, 400, 402; difficulties with telegraph operators, 377–81, 381*n*–85*n*, 391, 391*n*–92*n*; saved from capture, 430–31

Grant, Ulysses S., 3rd (grandson of USG): document owned by, 288*n*–89*n*

Grant, William (Iowa Vols.), 90*n*

Gray, W. C. (prisoner), 109*n*

Green, Leander (Ill. Vols.), 438

Greenwood, Theodore E. (U.S. Army), 98*n*

Greenwood, William H. (Ill. Vols.), 448–49

Grenada, Miss.: demonstration toward, 59, 60*n*, 67, 93 and *n*; expedition to, 95, 243 and *n*, 254–55, 263, 264*n*, 275, 286, 291, 293*n*, 299, 312 and *n*, 313*n*, 340, 346, 353, 362*n*, 370*n*, 372 and *n*, 404, 405*n*, 408, 410*n*; C.S.A. movements at, 257, 362*n*, 366*n*, 385, 389*n*

Grider, S. E. (prisoner), 240

Grierson, Benjamin H. (Ill. Vols.): as messenger, 263*n*, 290, 293*n*, 310, 369*n*, 370*n*, 409*n*; regt. of, 294*n*, 434; advances from Memphis, 312*n*, 313*n*; on reconnaissance, 369*n*–70*n*, 371, 401*n*, 402*n*; William T. Sherman praises, 409*n*, 410*n*; writes to wife, 409*n*–10*n*

Grimes, James W. (U.S. Senator), 320 and *n*, 358*n*–59*n*

Grimes, S. F. (scout), 103*n*, 129*n*

Gross, William L. (telegraph operator), 383*n*, 391*n*, 392*n*

Gunter's Landing, Ala., 27*n*

Guntown, Miss.: C.S.A. at, 5*n*, 7*n*, 28*n*, 36*n*, 76*n*, 269*n*; C.S.A. leave, 35*n*, 39*n*, 42*n*, 47*n*, 373*n*, 374*n*; expedition to, 193, 287*n*

Gwin, William (U.S. Navy), 93*n*, 410*n*

Haas, Mr. (merchant), 393, 394, 395*n*

Hackleman, Pleasant A. (U.S. Army), 108*n*, 115*n*, 116, 117*n*, 143*n*

Haines, Thomas J. (U.S. Army): telegram to, Oct. 24, 1862, 232*n*; as commissary, 232*n*, 406*n*

Halderman, David B. (Ill. Vols.), 457–58

Hale's Landing, Tenn., 225 and *n*

Hall, Cyrus (Ill. Vols.), 438

Hall, Willard P. (Gov. of Mo.), 339*n*, 340*n*

Halleck, Henry W. (U.S. Army): rules on personnel matters, 3*n*, 45, 85*n*, 91*n*, 182, 210, 210*n*–11*n*, 232 and *n*, 260*n*, 275, 286*n*, 287*n*, 296*n*, 349, 420, 440, 448, 454, 459; informed of Armstrong raid, 4, 5, 9, 12–13; sends Gordon Granger to Louisville, 7*n*, 12, 17, 18*n*, 33 and *n*; rebukes USG, 20 and *n*, 163*n*, 391 and *n*; and arrests, 21, 22, 23*n*, 381*n*, 392*n*; informed of threat to Corinth, 23–24, 26, 31, 34, 46, 96–97, 197*n*, 210, 372*n*, 402*n*; orders attack on Iuka, 47*n*, 67, 71–72, 73*n*–74*n*; orders Yazoo River expedition, 68 and *n*, 93; informed of threat to Bolivar, 79, 84, 87, 210; sends troops to USG, 79, 125*n*, 130*n*, 131, 133, 158*n*, 197 and *n*, 210*n*, 243*n*, 261 and *n*, 262, 279*n*, 285, 286, 310; asks USG for information, 85*n*, 145, 145*n*–46*n*, 156*n*; informed of C.S.A. movements, 87, 95, 150*n*, 178–79, 181, 257, 373, 386*n*, 402, 430; receives charge against USG, 87*n*; informed of battle of Corinth, 111, 116–17, 118, 122*n*, 126, 130*n*, 133, 134; involved in promotions, 120–21, 130*n*, 131, 145*n*, 161, 185*n*, 244, 280*n*, 317–18; sends supplies, 121*n*, 165*n*, 298*n*, 299–300,

Halleck, Henry W. *(cont.)*
305*n*, 328 and *n*, 405*n*; deals with prisoners, 130*n*, 146, 158 and *n*, 159*n*, 198; regulates trade, 135 and *n*, 398*n*; and Vicksburg campaign, 199–200, 279*n*, 310, 345–46, 346*n*, 371–72, 372*n*, 386*n*, 390, 401, 402*n*, 403, 404, 405*n*, 408, 410*n*, 411; and conflict with Samuel R. Curtis, 200–201, 375, 376*n*, 410*n*; informed of expeditions, 205, 296–97; approves Mississippi Central campaign, 243 and *n*, 256, 268, 278, 280*n*, 288*n*, 304–5, 305*n*, 360, 367, 368, 372*n*, 390 and *n*, 400; informs USG of troop movements, 263, 291, 404, 405*n*; Negro policy of, 315*n*; mentioned, 51, 55*n*, 61*n*, 108*n*
—Correspondence from USG : telegram to, Sept. 1, 1862, 4; telegram to, Sept. 1, 1862, 5; telegram to, Sept. 2, 1862, 9; telegram to, Sept. 3, 1862, 12–13; telegram to, Sept. 4, 1862, 17; telegram to, Sept. 5, 1862, 21; letter to, Sept. 7, 1862, 22–23; telegram to, Sept. 9, 1862, 26; telegram to, Sept. 10, 1862, 31; telegram to, Sept. 11, 1862, 33; telegram to, Sept. 11, 1862, 34; telegram to, Sept. 15, 1862, 46; telegram to, Sept. 19, 1862, 67; telegram to, Sept. 19, 1862, 67–68; telegram to, Sept. 22, 1862, 68*n*; telegram to, Sept. 20, 1862, 71–72; telegram to, Sept. 22, 1862, 73*n*–74*n*; telegrams to, Sept. 22, 1862 (2), 79; letter to, Sept. 24, 1862, 84; telegram to, Sept. 24, 1862, 85; endorsement to, Nov. 20, 1862, 86*n*; telegram to, Sept. 25, 1862, 87; telegram to, Sept. 28, 1862, 93; telegram to, Sept. 30, 1862, 95; telegram to, Oct. 1, 1862, 96–97; telegram to, Oct. 4, 1862, 111; telegram to, Oct. 5, 1862, 116–17; telegram to, Oct. 5, 1862, 118; letter to, Oct. 5, 1862, 120–21; telegram to, Oct. 6, 1862, 126; telegram to, Oct. 7, 1862, 130; telegram to, Oct. 7, 1862, 130*n*; telegrams to, Oct. 8, 1862 (2), 133; telegram to, Oct. 8, 1862, 134; endorsement to, Oct. 8, 1862, 135; telegram to, Oct. 10, 1862, 145; telegram to, Nov. 1, 1862, 145*n*; telegram to, Oct. 13, 1862, 150*n*; telegram to, Oct. 17, 1862, 155; telegram to, Oct. 19, 1862, 158; telegram to, Oct. 21, 1862, 158*n*; telegram to, Oct. 21, 1862, 161; telegram to, Oct. 23, 1862, 178–79; telegram to, Oct. 23, 1862, 181; telegram to, Oct. 26, 1862, 185*n*; telegram to, Oct. 26, 1862, 197; telegram to, Oct. 26, 1862, 198; letter to, Oct. 26, 1862, 199–201; telegram to, Oct. 28, 1862, 205; telegrams to, Oct. 29,

1862 (2), 210; telegram to, Oct. 25, 1862, 211*n*; telegram to, Nov. 1, 1862, 232; telegram to, Nov. 5, 1862, 232*n*; telegram to, Nov. 2, 1862, 243; letter to, Nov. 2, 1862, 244; telegram to, Nov. 4, 1862, 256; telegram to, Nov. 6, 1862, 261; telegram to, Nov. 7, 1862, 268; telegram to, Nov. 9, 1862, 278–79; telegram to, Nov. 8, 1862, 279*n*; telegram to, Nov. 11, 1862, 280*n*; telegram to, Nov. 10, 1862, 288; telegram to, Nov. 11, 1862, 296–97; letter to, Nov. 12, 1862, 299–300; telegram to, Nov. 13, 1862, 304–5; telegram to, Nov. 15, 1862, 315; letter to, Nov. 15, 1862, 317–18; telegram to, Nov. 24, 1862, 345–46; letter to, Nov. 26, 1862, 349; telegram to, Nov. 29, 1862, 360; telegram to, Dec. 1, 1862, 367; telegram to, Dec. 2, 1862, 368; telegram to, Dec. 3, 1862, 371–72; telegram to, Dec. 3, 1862, 373; endorsement to, Dec. 3, 1862, 375; telegram to, Dec. 3, 1862, 386*n*; telegram to, Dec. 5, 1862, 390; telegrams to, Dec. 5, 1862 (2), 390*n*; telegram to, Dec. 5, 1862, 391; telegram to, Dec. 16, 1862, 398*n*; telegram to, Dec. 7, 1862, 400–401; telegram to, Dec. 8, 1862, 402; telegram to, Dec. 8, 1862, 403; endorsement to, Oct. 24, 1862, 430
Hamburg, Tenn., 21*n*, 58*n*, 136*n*, 421–22, 426
Hamilton, Charles S. (U.S. Army): troop dispositions of, 8*n*, 95*n*, 96*n*, 97*n*, 139*n*, 144*n*, 217, 218*n*, 231 and *n*, 236, 239, 287*n*, 307*n*, 325 and *n*, 329, 330*n*, 331*n*, 342, 344*n*, 452; watches C.S.A. movements, 17*n*, 26*n*, 27*n*, 32*n*, 35*n*–36*n*, 38, 39*n*, 40*n*, 42*n*–43*n*, 47*n*, 48*n*, 52*n*, 53*n*, 57*n*, 58*n*; at battle of Iuka, 65*n*, 69*n*, 71, 72*n*, 73*n*, 76 and *n*, 170, 172, 174, 175–76, 188; background, 72*n*; at battle of Corinth, 108*n*, 115*n*, 123*n*, 129*n*, 132*n*, 230; and personnel matters, 152*n*, 204*n*, 207, 216*n*–17*n*, 218*n*, 241*n*, 261*n*, 272*n*, 280*n*, 316*n*, 376*n*, 450, 455–56, 458; promotion of, 161, 162*n*, 202, 203*n*, 318; replaces William S. Rosecrans, 182, 183*n*, 185, 187*n*; defends Corinth, 191, 194, 195*n*, 212, 213 and *n*, 218*n*, 231 and *n*, 444; to destroy railroad, 192–94, 194*n*; reports C.S.A. movements, 195*n*, 206 and *n*, 208*n*, 212, 213*n*, 214*n*, 215–16, 216*n*, 227*n*, 238 and *n*, 347*n*, 351*n*, 362*n*–63*n*, 374*n*; and prisoners, 208 and *n*, 214*n*, 239, 351*n*; needs supplies, 213, 213*n*–15*n*, 227, 277*n*, 309 and *n*, 384*n*; in Mississippi Central campaign, 235, 237, 237*n*–38*n*, 244, 245*n*,

249 and *n*, 250, 251, 256, 257–58, 257*n*, 267*n*, 268*n*, 269, 270*n*–71*n*, 277*n*, 284, 284*n*–85*n*, 285–86, 286*n*, 298, 298*n*–99*n*, 302, 302*n*–3*n*, 306*n*, 307*n*, 308 and *n*, 342*n*–43*n*, 346, 347*n*, 350–51, 351*n*–52*n*, 353 and *n*, 359, 360, 361, 362, 362*n*–63*n*, 363–64, 364*n*, 365, 366*n*, 368*n*, 387*n*, 396, 397*n*; USG praises, 320; mentioned, 265, 266*n*, 332*n*

—Correspondence from USG: telegram to, Oct. 25, 1862, 192–93; telegram to, Oct. 25, 1862, 193–94; telegram to, Oct. 25, 1862, 194; telegram to, Oct. 25, 1862, 194*n*; letter to, Oct. 26, 1862, 202; telegram to, Oct. 28, 1862, 207; telegram to, Oct. 28, 1862, 208; telegram to, Oct. 29, 1862, 213; telegram to, Oct. 28, 1862, 214*n*; telegram to, Oct. 29, 1862, 215–16; telegram to, Oct. 29, 1862, 216; telegram to, Oct. 29, 1862, 217; telegram to, Oct. 29, 1862, 218*n*; telegram to, Oct. 30, 1862, 218*n*; telegram to, Oct. 30, 1862, 227; telegram to, Oct. 31, 1862, 231; telegram to, Nov. 1, 1862, 237; telegrams to, Nov. 1, 1862 (2), 237*n*; telegram to, Nov. 1, 1862, 238; telegram to, Nov. 1, 1862, 238*n*; telegrams to, Nov. 1, 1862 (2), 239; telegram to, Nov. 2, 1862, 249; telegram to, Nov. 2, 1862, 250; telegram to, Nov. 2, 1862, 250*n*; telegram to, Nov. 2, 1862, 251; letter to, Nov. 4, 1862, 257–58; letter to, Nov. 6, 1862, 267*n*; letter to, Nov. 7, 1862, 269–70; telegram to, Nov. 11, 1862, 280*n*; letter to, Nov. 9, 1862, 284; letter to, Nov. 9, 1862, 285–86; telegram to, Nov. 11, 1862, 298; telegram to, Nov. 11, 1862, 298*n*; telegrams to, Nov. 11, 1862 (3), 299*n*; telegram to, Nov. 12, 1862, 302; telegram to, Nov. 18, 1862, 307*n*; telegram to, Nov. 13, 1862, 308; telegram to, Nov. 13, 1862, 308*n*; telegram to, Nov. 13, 1862, 309*n*; telegram to, Nov. 14, 1862, 309*n*; telegram to, Nov. 16, 1862, 325; telegram to, Nov. 16, 1862, 325*n*; letter to, Nov. 18, 1862, 329; telegram to, Nov. 23, 1862, 342; telegram to, Nov. 24, 1862, 346; telegram to, Nov. 25, 1862, 347*n*; letter to, Nov. 26, 1862, 350–51; telegrams to, Nov. 26, 1862 (3), 351*n*; telegrams to, Nov. 27, 1862 (2), 351*n*–52*n*; letter to, Nov. 26, 1862, 353; letter to, Nov. 28, 1862, 359; letter to, Nov. 29, 1862, 363–64; letter to, Nov. 30, 1862, 365; letter to, Dec. 1, 1862, 368*n*; letter to, Dec. 5, 1862, 396; telegram to, Dec. 4, 1862, 397*n*; telegram to, Dec. 5, 1862, 397*n*; telegram to, Nov. 13, 1862, 450

Hammond, William A. (U.S. Army), 25*n*–26*n*, 120*n*

Hancock, Thomas H. (prisoner), 78 and *n*

Handy, Mr. (of Cincinnati), 334*n*

Hannah, William H. (Ohio Vols.), 432

Harde & Hough (newsdealers), 455

Hardin County, Tenn., 443, 445

Harding, Abner C. (Ill. Vols.), 428, 443–44

Harding, R. N. (prisoner), 55

Harlan, James (U.S. Senator), 320 and *n*

Harney, William S. (U.S. Army), 26*n*

Harper, James P. (Ill. Vols.): telegram to, Nov. 11, 1862, 259*n*; as ordnance officer, 259*n*, 452; telegram to, Nov. 19, 1862, 452

Harpers Ferry, Va., 66*n*

Harris, Thomas (prisoner), 108

Harris, Thomas H. (U.S. Army), 109*n*, 335*n*

Harvey, Charles E. (Mich. Vols.), 89 and *n*

Harvey's Mill, Miss., 52*n*

Harwell, Allen (prisoner), 457

Haskins, Alexander L. (Ohio Vols.), 209 and *n*

Hatch, Edward (Iowa Vols.), 27*n*, 49*n*, 69*n*, 401*n*

Hatchie River: C.S.A. near, 4*n*, 6*n*, 7*n*, 9*n*, 10, 11*n*, 27*n*, 36*n*, 48*n*, 76*n*, 77*n*, 88*n*, 91*n*, 96*n*, 104*n*, 105*n*, 180*n*, 206*n*, 216; guarded, 24, 82*n*, 139*n*, 231, 251*n*; expedition to, 32*n*, 97*n*, 99*n*–100*n*, 100, 101*n*, 102*n*, 105*n*, 113*n*, 211, 212*n*, 433; battle of, 117, 118, 118*n*–20*n*, 123, 123*n*–26*n*, 126, 127, 127*n*–28*n*, 128*n*–29*n*, 130 and *n*, 131, 131*n*–32*n*, 137*n*, 143, 144*n*, 166*n*, 221–24, 229–30, 240*n*, 335*n*, 345, 442, 452

Hatchie Scouts (cav. co.), 452

Hawkins, John P. (U.S. Army): promoted, 203; as commissary, 232 and *n*, 233*n*, 282*n*, 295, 376*n*, 406*n*; telegram to, Nov. 6, 1862, 233*n*; telegram to, Nov. 7 or 8, 1862, 233*n*; telegram to, Nov. 9, 1862, 282*n*; telegram to, Dec. 11, 1862, 406*n*

Hawkins, W. H. (C.S. Army), 229*n*

Hayes, Charles S. (Ohio Vols.), 191*n*, 230, 447

Haynie, George W. (Ill. Vols.), 446

Haynie, Isham N. (Ill. Vols.): telegram to, Sept. 25, 1862, 89*n*; reports from Bethel, 89*n*, 101*n*, 103*n*, 104*n*, 111*n*–12*n*, 125*n*, 128, 129*n*, 271*n*, 348*n*, 426, 433, 446; telegram to, Nov. 9, 1862, 271*n*; promotion of, 318*n*–19*n*; arms citizens, 445; telegram to, Nov. 1, 1862, 446

Hays, Lt., 101*n*

Hay's Bridge, Tenn., 343*n*

Haywood, Robert W. (C.S. Army): as raider, 181 and n, 240n; identified, 181n; regt. captured, 334, 335n, 336n, 337

Hazel Dell (steamboat), 151n

Hébert, Louis (C.S. Army), 74n

Helena, Ark.: trade at, 50; expeditions from, 59, 68n, 94n, 95, 180n, 257, 263, 264n, 279, 286, 291, 292, 312n, 313n, 340, 341n, 371, 372n, 390, 401n, 402n, 408, 410n; garrisoned, 141n, 197 and n, 243n, 309n, 405n, 406n, 430, 449

Helm, Ben Hardin (C.S. Army), 80n, 297n

Hendershott, Henry B. (U.S. Army), 422

Henderson, Ky., 438

Henderson, Tenn., 112n, 347, 348n–49n

Hernando, Miss., 179n, 293n, 312n

Hibbard, Isaac J. (Wis. Vols.), 449

Hickenlooper, Andrew (Ohio Vols.), 296n

Hickman, Ky., 6n, 417, 419, 441

Hildebrand, Jesse (Ohio Vols.): letter to, Sept. 11, 1862, 37; releases prisoners, 37 and n, 78 and n, 108–9, 109n, 153–54, 228, 228n–29n, 240, 337; identified, 37n; letter to, Sept. 21, 1862, 78; letter to, Sept. 22, 1862, 78n; letter to, Sept. 24, 1862, 78n; letter to, Oct. 3, 1862, 108–9; letter to, Oct. 16, 1862, 153–54; letter to, Oct. 30, 1862, 228; letter to, Nov. 1, 1862, 240; letter to, Nov. 20, 1862, 337

Hill, Daniel H. (C.S. Army), 389, 390n

Hill, Eben M. (Mo. Vols.), 417

Hill, Jerome B. (prisoner), 78n, 108, 109n, 154

Hillyer, Robert C. W., San José, Costa Rica: document owned by, 93n

Hillyer, William S. (staff officer of USG): on leave, 43, 44n; wife of, 44n; writes for USG, 51, 66n, 180n, 249n, 367n; orders for, Sept. 26, 1862, 93n; liaison with William T. Sherman, 93n, 256n, 264n, 370n; at Corinth, 144n; reports Iuka battle, 174; issues liquor permits, 201n; releases prisoner, 229n; reassigned, 294

Hindman, Thomas C. (C.S. Army), 94n, 310, 313n

Hock's Crossing, Miss., 129n

Hoeppner, Arnold (U.S. Army), 436–37

Hoey, John, 436

Hoffman, William (U.S. Army), 229n

Hoge, George B. (Ill. Vols.), 281n, 293n

Holcomb, Benjamin F. (Ill. Vols.), 259n

Holcombe, Philip (C.S. Army), 269n

Holloway, William R. (secretary to Gov. of Ind.), 287n

Holly Springs, Miss.: C.S.A. forces at, 7n, 16n, 47n–48n, 58n, 60n, 88n, 92n, 101n, 129n, 138n, 139n, 160n, 178–79, 179n, 180n, 206n, 208n, 215, 224, 238 and n, 249, 250n, 251n, 255n, 262, 263, 264n, 269n, 278, 280n, 284n, 291, 444; expeditions to, 76n, 131n, 132n, 176, 238 and n, 243, 250n, 254, 257, 268 and n, 269, 270n–71n, 276, 276n–77n, 278, 280n, 284, 284n–85n, 285–86, 286n, 290–91, 292, 293n, 298, 298n–99n, 302, 302n–3n, 304, 306n–7n, 308 and n, 311, 320, 340, 353, 359; prisoners sent to, 141n, 180n, 214n, 240n; occupation of, 302, 302n–3n, 304, 306n–7n, 311, 346, 350, 351n, 360, 363–64, 363n, 364n, 365, 368n, 370n, 396n, 420; railroad at, 315n, 354, 355n, 390, 400n; raid on, 317n, 460; cotton at, 333n, 393, 394, 395n, 396n; prisoners at, 335n, 341; supplies sent to, 341, 370n, 387n–88n, 406n; mentioned, 237n, 332n, 347n

Holmes, Theophilus (C.S. Army), 94n, 310, 312n, 313n

Holmes, Thomas (C.S. Army), 147n

Holston, John G. F. (U.S. Army): at battle of Corinth, 144n, 230; relieved, 145n; at battle of Iuka, 176, 189; background, 178n; and slaves, 426

Holt, Joseph (U.S. Judge Advocate), 86n, 90n

Hooker, Joseph (U.S. Army), 66n

Hopkinsville, Ky., 226 and n, 227n

Horn, Capt., 457

Hospitals: at Iuka, 8n, 73n, 76n, 146n, 176, 214n, 341, 342n; for insane soldiers, 44n; at Corinth, 58n, 115n, 144n; supplies for, 66n, 233n, 241n, 450, 458; Negroes at, 86n, 426; near Holly Springs, 306n; at Grand Junction, 330n; at La Grange, 351n; at Davis' Mills, 352n; administered, 355, 425, 459; in Mo., 376n, 377n; prisoners in, 389n; at Oxford, 398; at Memphis, 445

Hotaling, John R. (Ill. Vols.), 119n

Hough, Ruel (surveyor of Memphis), 453

House, Capt. (scout), 103n

Houston, Capt., 111n–12n

Hovey, Alvin P. (U.S. Army): penetrates Miss., 264n, 293n, 312n, 313n, 409, 410n, 411 and n; pay for, 309n

Howard, Ocran H. (U.S. Signal Corps), 183n–84n

Howard, Sgt. (Ohio Vols.), 432

Howe, James H. (Wis. Vols.), 263n, 293n

Howe, William W. (Kan. Vols.), 74n–75n

Howell, Philip (Ill. Vols.), 448

Hudson, Bailey W. (uncle of USG), 186n

Hudson, John B. (Ohio Vols.), 320n

Hudson, Peter T. (staff officer of USG),

319, 320n, 357 and n, 358n–59n
Hudson, Silas A. (cousin of USG): visits Columbus, 186; identified, 186n; writes to USG, 218; requests appointments, 319, 358n–59n; letter to, Nov. 15, 1862, 319–20
Hudsonville, Miss., 277n, 307n, 308n, 387, 388n
Hughes, Charles M. (Ohio Vols.), 323, 324
Humboldt, Tenn.: threatened, 5, 6n, 435; skirmish near, 19n–20n; road guarded to, 24, 200; garrisoned, 125n, 207n, 259n, 331n; troops leave, 137n, 141n, 195n, 211, 281 and n, 282n, 283n; prisoners at, 240n
Humphrey, Wesley (Ill. Vols.), 45, 45n–46n
Huntingdon, Tenn., 34n, 427
Huntington, W. W., 149n
Huntington Library, Henry E., San Marino, Calif.: documents in, 217n, 389
Huntsville, Ala., 27n, 195n, 373
Hurlbut, Stephen A. (U.S. Army): moves to Bolivar, 28, 29n–30n, 31n, 41n, 46, 127, 127n–28n, 129n, 131 and n, 132n, 137n; telegram to, Sept. 13, 1862, 30n; telegrams to, Sept. 14, 1862 (2), 30n; sends troops to Corinth, 30n, 41n; prepares demonstration, 48n, 59–60, 60n, 67, 75 and n, 136, 137n, 138n; telegram to, Sept. 17, 1862, 59–60; deals with prisoners, 59n, 140, 140n–41n, 289, 290n, 336n; telegram to, Sept. 18, 1862, 60n; telegram to, Sept. 21, 1862, 75; telegram to, Sept. 21, 1862, 75n; threatened at Bolivar, 79, 80, 80n–81n, 81, 81n–82n, 88, 88n–89n, 95n–96n, 97n, 98, 99, 100n–101n, 191n, 206n, 234 and n; telegram to, Sept. 22, 1862, 80; telegram to, Sept. 23, 1862, 81; telegram to, Sept. 22, 1862, 81n; promoted, 82n; telegram to, Sept. 25, 1862, 88n; reports C.S.A. movements, 88n, 89n, 92n, 95n–96n, 159n, 453; telegram to, Oct. 1, 1862, 98; telegram to, Oct. 1, 1862, 98n; telegram to, Oct. 1, 1862, 99; at battle of the Hatchie, 100, 103, 104, 105 and n, 106, 107 and n, 111, 112–13, 113n, 114, 117, 118, 118n–19n, 120n, 123 and n, 125n–26n, 126, 127n, 129 and n, 140, 221–23, 230; and railroads, 101n, 272n, 283 and n, 425; telegram to, Oct. 3, 1862, 103; telegram to, Oct. 3, 1862, 104; telegram to, Oct. 3, 1862, 105; telegrams to, Oct. 3, 1862 (2), 106; reinforced, 106, 107n, 141n, 148n, 247; telegram to, Oct. 3, 1862, 106n–7n; telegram to, Oct. 4, 1862, 112–13; telegram to, Oct. 4, 1862, 114; telegram to, Oct. 6, 1862, 127; telegram to, Oct. 6,

1862, 127n; telegram to, Oct. 8, 1862, 136; telegram to, Oct. 8, 1862, 137n–38n; ordered to Grand Junction, 138, 139–40; telegram to, Oct. 9, 1862, 140; telegram to, Oct. 9, 1862, 140n; USG wants, 180n; commands District of Jackson, 187n, 243n, 253–54, 254n, 283n; informed of C.S.A. movements, 191n, 206n; disciplines command, 196n, 207n, 322n, 355n, 383n, 420; telegram to, Nov. 17, 1862, 207n; letter to, Oct. 29, 1862, 211; prepares expedition to Hatchie River, 211, 212n, 218n; letter to, Nov. 1, 1862, 234; letter to, Nov. 3, 1862, 253–54; on Davis Creek, 257n; telegram to, Nov. 5, 1862, 258; sends troops to USG, 258, 258n–59n, 281, 281n–83n, 330n–31n, 362; telegrams to, Nov. 6, 1862 (2), 259n; telegram to, Nov. 7, 1862, 259n; telegram to, Nov. 8, 1862, 259n; telegram to, Nov. 9, 1862, 281; deals with civilians, 282n–83n, 451, 453, 455; telegram to, Nov. 9, 1862, 283; telegram to, Nov. 10, 1862, 289; telegram to, Nov. 12, 1862, 300; ordered to Memphis, 300, 301n, 302n, 312 and n; telegram to, Nov. 19, 1862, 330n; telegram to, Nov. 18, 1862, 355n; telegram to, Nov. 13, 1862, 383n; endorsement to, Feb. 14, 1863, 453; mentioned, 221n, 287n, 343n, 428
Hurricane Creek (Miss.), 35n
Hurst, Fielding (Tenn. Vols.), 195–96, 196n, 245n
Hutchinson, George E. (newsdealer), 455

Ihrie, George P. (staff officer of USG): staff duties of, 23n, 241 and n, 290n, 294; telegram to, Nov. 1, 1862, 241; telegram to, Nov. 1, 1862, 241n; writes for USG, 268n, 270n, 422
Illinois: troops from, 131, 155, 210n, 274n, 285, 293n; election in, 265n, 270n; bans Negroes, 317n
Illinois Central Railroad, 305n, 314
Illinois State Archives, Springfield, Ill.: documents in, 45, 45n–46n, 116, 228n, 358n, 427, 438 (2), 439, 442
Illinois State Historical Library, Springfield, Ill.: documents in, 3n, 84, 122n, 143n, 144n, 145n (2), 160–61, 162, 176n, 177n–78n, 186–87, 187n, 199–201, 220–21, 252–53, 257n, 273–75, 289n (2), 295n, 299–300, 316n, 326n, 327n, 328, 328n, 329n (2), 333n–34n, 403, 405n, 409n–10n, 434, 456, 459 (2)

Illinois Volunteers
—2nd Cav., 60*n*, 119*n*, 137*n*, 159*n*, 181*n*, 283*n*
—4th Cav., 47*n*, 159*n*, 330*n*, 348*n*, 366*n*, 399*n*
—6th Cav., 263*n*, 294*n*, 433, 434
—7th Cav.: assigned, 52*n*, 69*n*, 218*n*, 332*n*, 344*n*; personnel of, 90*n*, 269*n*, 424, 452, 454–55
—9th Cav., 352*n*
—11th Cav., 283*n*, 425
—12th Cav., 283*n*
—7th Inf., 448
—8th Inf., 89 and *n*, 90*n*, 253, 258, 259*n*, 439–40
—11th Inf., 90*n*, 91*n*, 282*n*, 318, 368*n*
—12th Inf., 444
—14th Inf., 438
—15th Inf., 452
—17th Inf., 152*n*, 271*n*, 282*n*
—18th Inf., 90*n*, 283*n*
—20th Inf.: promotions in, 161, 318, 357 and *n*, 358*n*; sent to La Grange, 258, 259*n*, 281*n*; offenses of, 321–22, 322*n*–23*n*
—22nd Inf., 301*n*
—25th Inf., 8*n*, 90*n*
—28th Inf., 352*n*, 442
—29th Inf., 90*n*, 152*n*, 283*n*, 388*n*, 458–59
—30th Inf., 10*n*, 336*n*
—31st Inf., 259*n*, 452
—41st Inf., 271*n*, 438
—43rd Inf., 450
—44th Inf., 90*n*, 437
—45th Inf., 109*n*, 161, 259*n*, 318, 355, 356*n*
—46th Inf., 248*n*, 428
—47th Inf., 124*n*, 147*n*, 227, 228*n*
—48th Inf., 318*n*–19*n*, 348*n*
—49th Inf., 348*n*
—50th Inf., 442
—51st Inf., 448–49
—52nd Inf., 45, 45*n*–46*n*, 141*n*, 185*n*, 451
—53rd Inf., 439
—54th Inf., 7*n*, 125*n*, 219*n*, 330*n*–31*n*, 367*n*, 455
—55th Inf., 264*n*, 294*n*
—56th Inf., 8*n*
—57th Inf., 141*n*, 198, 198*n*–99*n*
—59th Inf., 376*n*, 431–32, 447
—62nd Inf., 157 and *n*, 330*n*–31*n*, 366, 367*n*
—63rd Inf., 116 and *n*
—64th Inf., 230, 427
—71st Inf., 6*n*, 7*n*, 157, 157*n*–58*n*
—72nd Inf., 12*n*, 247, 248*n*, 253, 344*n*
—76th Inf.: needs arms, 6*n*, 7*n*, 419; and slave, 86*n*; at Bolivar, 124*n*, 125*n*, 128*n*, 137*n*, 141*n*

—81st Inf.: at Cairo, 12*n*; sent to USG, 54*n*, 125*n*, 282*n*–83*n*; at Humboldt, 137*n*, 195*n*, 240*n*
—83rd Inf., 12*n*, 443
—90th Inf., 388*n*
—93rd Inf., 279*n*, 280*n*, 298*n*
—95th Inf.: sent to USG, 180*n*, 197*n*, 220*n*, 279*n*, 280*n*; assigned, 283*n*, 298*n*, 330*n*, 331*n*, 344*n*
—103rd Inf., 180*n*, 197*n*, 198*n*, 280*n*
—106th Inf., 259*n*, 279*n*, 280*n*, 281*n*
—108th Inf., 298*n*
—109th Inf., 158*n*, 248*n*, 259*n*, 298*n*, 344*n*
—111th Inf., 180*n*, 197*n*, 248*n*, 280*n*
—113th Inf., 279*n*, 280*n*, 281*n*, 293*n*
—114th Inf., 279*n*, 280*n*, 298*n*
—116th Inf., 220*n*, 279*n*, 280*n*, 293*n*
—119th Inf., 259*n*, 280*n*, 283*n*, 298*n*
—120th Inf., 280*n*, 298*n*
—122nd Inf., 195*n*, 457–58
—124th Inf., 125*n*
—126th Inf., 352*n*
—127th Inf., 279*n*, 297*n*, 298*n*
—1st Light Art., 19*n*, 283*n*, 318
—2nd Light Art.: assigned, 41*n*, 280*n*, 294*n*, 419, 423–24, 428; on expedition, 205 and *n*; officers of, 242*n*, 248*n*, 259*n*, 432, 434, 459
—3rd Light Art., 220*n*, 280*n*, 281*n*
—Mercantile Battery, 279*n*, 298*n*
Indiana Historical Society, Indianapolis, Ind.: documents in, 286*n*, 287*n*
Indianapolis, Ind., 333*n*, 419
Indiana State Library, Indianapolis, Ind.: documents in, 287*n*, 432, 440
Indiana University, Bloomington, Ind.: document in, 357*n*
Indiana Volunteers
—14th Battery, 283*n*
—13th Inf., 348*n*, 454
—16th Inf., 117*n*
—22nd Inf., 124*n*
—23rd Inf., 440
—25th Inf., 432, 438, 440
—33rd Inf., 282*n*
—34th Inf., 135*n*
—48th Inf., 440
—52nd Inf., 7*n*, 31*n*, 417, 440, 448
—53rd Inf., 440
—59th Inf., 419
—83rd Inf., 279*n*, 293*n*, 298*n*
—93rd Inf., 297*n*, 298*n*
Ingalls, W. M. (military telegraph), 382*n*
Iowa State Department of History and Archives, Des Moines, Iowa: documents in, 41*n*, 54*n*–55*n*, 55–56, 63, 85*n* (2),

140n, 190n, 193n, 201n, 254n, 288n, 298n, 336n, 373n–74n, 375n, 376n (2), 444, 451, 456

Iowa Volunteers
—2nd Cav., 353n, 401n
—5th Cav., 427, 428, 433, 435, 443
—4th Inf., 419
—11th Inf., 90n
—13th Inf., 23n, 161, 318
—15th Inf., 120n, 318
—16th Inf., 52n
—23rd Inf., 419
—31st Inf., 449

Ironton, Mo., 125n

Island No. 10 (Mississippi River), 8n, 158n, 190n, 248n, 417, 420

Island No. 21 (Mississippi River), 429

Iuka, Miss.: U.S. troops at, 8n, 26n; captured, 31n, 34n–36n, 38–39, 39n–43n, 47n, 48n, 52n, 57n, 58n; battle of, 63, 64–65, 65n–66n, 68–69, 69n–70n, 70–71, 71–72, 72n–74n, 74, 76n, 77n, 87n, 143, 144n, 149n, 154, 166n, 168–76, 176n–78n, 184n, 188–89, 222, 275, 345, 429, 445; hospital at, 146n, 214n, 239, 341, 342n; mentioned, 374n, 451

Jacinto, Miss.: U.S. troops at, 17n, 24, 35n, 139n; located, 24n; threatened, 32n, 34n, 35n–36n, 38, 39n, 40n, 47n, 52n, 97n; and battle of Iuka, 57n, 58n, 60–61, 65n, 66n, 69n, 73n, 76 and n, 169, 170, 171, 173, 176

Jackson, Thomas J. (C.S. Army), 66n

Jackson, William H. (C.S. Army): movements of, 34n, 75n, 82n, 179n, 181n, 190n, 191n, 212n, 306n, 312n, 343n, 366n; exchanges prisoners, 335, 336n, 351n

Jackson, Miss.: C.S.A. movements at, 5n, 94n, 160n, 238, 250n, 264n, 312n, 386n, 401n, 402, 429; prisoners at, 82n; threatened by U.S., 132n, 403, 404, 408

Jackson, Tenn.: threatened, 4n, 7n, 9n, 10, 11n, 12, 88n, 99; troops sent to, 16, 54n–55n, 104n, 125n, 132n, 145n, 149, 157 and n, 198n, 247, 248n, 279n, 281n, 297, 298n, 352n, 367n; USG hd. qrs. at, 24, 43, 79, 80, 82 and n, 83n, 87, 110, 186, 202n, 243 and n, 256n, 273; troops sent from, 30n, 41n, 106, 107n, 111, 159n, 211, 236, 258, 258n–59n, 269n, 298n, 348n; intelligence from, 34n, 103, 453; railroad at, 101n, 122n, 169–70, 200, 222, 272, 283, 303–4, 314n, 354n, 355n, 375n; prisoners at, 109n, 159n, 239, 334n, 457; telegraph at, 112n, 113n, 382n; supplies for, 142n,

159, 159n–60n, 163n, 219, 232n, 233n, 242, 260 and n, 278n, 279, 282n, 352n, 400, 432, 442, 449, 452, 459; medicine at, 145n, 156n, 426, 448; garrisoned, 152n, 214n, 215n, 283 and n, 321, 322n, 349n, 425, 431, 458; citizens of, 153, 156n, 436; command of, 187n, 253, 300, 301n, 451, 458–59; cotton at, 333n; mentioned, 77n, 93n, 120n, 148n, 184n, 208n, 284n, 286n, 287n, 343n, 374n, 424, 444, 455

Jews, 283 and n, 393, 394

John Simonds (steamboat), 417

Johnson, Adam R. (C.S. Army), 151n, 419

Johnson, Amory K. (Ill. Vols.), 206n, 277n, 352n, 442

Johnson, Andrew (Gov. of Tenn.), 145n, 156n, 196n

Johnson, H. P. (C.S. Army), 126n

Johnson, Jasper (Ill. Vols.), 259n, 452

Johnson, L. H. (C.S. Army), 158n

Johnson's Island, Ohio, 229n, 457

Johnston, Joseph E. (C.S. Army), 150 and n, 160n, 212

Johnston's Mill, Miss., 52n

Jones, A., 430

Jones, Daniel W. (C.S. Army), 126n

Jones, Ed (Columbus, Ky.), 419

Jones, Robert B. (Ind. Vols.), 135n

Jonesborough, Miss., 95n, 96n, 130 and n, 131n, 374n

Jumper, James A. (prisoner), 457

Jumpertown, Miss., 31n, 160n

Kansas Volunteers
—7th Cav.: movements of, 35n, 55n, 57n, 74n–75n, 92n, 268n, 271n, 278, 280n, 311, 353n; recruiting for, 152n; promotion of col., 318
—1st Inf., 149, 452

Keefe, James, 90n

Kelly, Edward (Ill. Vols.), 90n

Kelly, Thomas (Mich. Vols.), 420

Kelton, John C. (U.S. Army): letter to, Sept. 7, 1862, 23–24; receives USG reports, 23–24, 87n, 168–76, 176n, 188–89, 221–24, 229–30, 230n, 377–81; forwards charges against USG, 87n; reports reinforcements, 122n; letter to, Oct. 21, 1862, 162; rebukes USG, 162, 163n; letter to, Oct. 22, 1862, 168–76; letter to, Oct. 25, 1862, 176n; letter to, Oct. 25, 1862, 188–89; letter to, Oct. 30, 1862, 221–24; letter to, Oct. 31, 1862, 229–30; letter to, Dec. 3, 1862, 377–81; transmits orders, 420

Kennard, George W. (Ill. Vols.), 321

Kent, R. B. (of Jackson, Tenn.), 321
Kenton, Tenn.: garrisoned, 157 and *n*, 247, 281, 297, 298*n*, 366, 367*n*; located, 158*n*; arrest at, 455
Kentucky: defended, 18*n*, 155, 186, 255*n*, 279*n*, 282*n*, 296–97, 300, 310, 435; threatened, 47*n*, 65*n*, 82*n*, 94*n*, 95*n*, 97, 169, 170, 175, 212, 264*n*; C.S.A. troops from, 82*n*, 227*n*, 270*n*, 297*n*
Ketchum, William S. (U.S. Army), 220*n*, 285
King, Henry (Ill. Vols.), 321
Kinney, Thomas J. (Ill. Vols.), 220*n*
Kinsell, Russell B. (Ohio Vols.), 323, 324
Kinsman, William H. (Iowa Vols.), 419
Kirkwood, Samuel (Gov. of Iowa), 11*n*, 12*n*, 125*n*
Kisner, Eliphas (Ohio Vols.), 90*n*
Kittoe, Edward D. (Ill. Vols.), 355–56, 356*n*
Klinck, John G. (U.S. Army), 21, 22*n*, 271*n*, 296*n*, 422
Klinck, Leonard G. (steamboat capt.), 21, 21*n*–22*n*
Knight, Thomas (citizen), 90*n*
Knobelsdorff, Charles (Ill. Vols.), 437
Kossuth, Miss.: C.S.A. at, 5*n*, 6*n*; occupied, 6*n*, 17*n*, 53, 55*n*, 92*n*, 95*n*, 96*n*, 97*n*, 139*n*, 169; reconnaissance near, 32*n*, 35*n*, 36*n*; located, 55*n*
Kusgrave, Mr. (of Hale's Landing), 225*n*

La Fayette, Ind., 43, 44*n*
La Fayette, Tenn., 344*n*, 433
Lagow, Clark B. (staff officer of USG): at Memphis, 29*n*, 264*n*, 419, 421; writes for USG, 65*n*–66*n*; at battle of Iuka, 69*n*, 174, 177*n*–78*n*; in St. Louis, 87*n*; duties of, 294; ill, 295*n*; mentioned, 453
Lagow, David (brother of staff officer): telegram to, Nov. 25, 1862, 295*n*
La Grange, Tenn.: C.S.A. at, 81*n*, 96*n*, 222, 246*n*, 249; expedition to, 81*n*, 137*n*, 138*n*, 179*n*, 206*n*; supplies at, 246*n*, 278 and *n*, 309*n*, 341, 361, 387*n*, 388*n*; occupation of, 256, 256*n*–57*n*, 257–58, 259*n*, 262, 266, 281, 281*n*–83*n*, 288, 290, 293*n*, 335*n*–36*n*, 352*n*, 368*n*, 459; movements from, 262–63, 263*n*, 264*n*, 268 and *n*, 270*n*–71*n*, 272, 276, 276*n*–77*n*, 325; prisoners at, 289, 289*n*–90*n*, 298*n*, 455; telegraph at, 303*n*, 377, 378, 382*n*; trade at, 304*n*; Negroes at, 315; railroad from, 326*n*, 352*n*, 400*n*; cotton at, 331, 332*n*, 333*n*, 394, 396*n*; hospital at, 351*n*; citizens of, 451; mentioned, 285*n*, 296*n*, 358*n*

Lake, A. T. (Ill. Vols.), 90*n*
Lamar, Miss.: James B. McPherson at, 276*n*, 277*n*, 284, 284*n*–85*n*, 286*n*; located, 285*n*; troops sent to, 299*n*, 306*n*, 307*n*, 308*n*; telegraph at, 384*n*
Lane, Henry S. (U.S. Senator), 287*n*
Larkin, Rufus F. (Ind. Vols.), 432
Larned, Charles T. (U.S. Army): as paymaster, 147*n*–48*n*, 309 and *n*; telegram to, Nov. 15, 1862, 309*n*; telegram to, Dec. 8, 1862, 309*n*
Latham's Mill, Miss., 308*n*
Lauman, Jacob G. (U.S. Army): on expedition to Grand Junction, 60*n*, 75 and *n*, 80*n*; at battle of the Hatchie, 119*n*, 230; commands movement toward Holly Springs, 176, 395*n*; at battle of Iuka, 189; sent to Memphis, 312 and *n*, 313*n*
Lawler, Michael K. (Ill. Vols.): expeditions of, 9*n*, 222, 223; and battle of Corinth, 101*n*, 102*n*, 103*n*, 111*n*, 112*n*; commands at Jackson, 148*n*, 149; regts. of, 253, 254, 258, 259*n*
Lazelle, Henry M. (U.S. Army), 141*n*
Lebo, William B. (U.S. Army), 442–43
Lee, Albert L. (Kan. Vols.): on reconnaissance, 32*n*, 35*n*, 40*n*, 47*n*, 77*n*, 97*n*, 99*n*, 342, 343*n*; praised, 75*n*, 353*n*; takes prisoners, 92*n*, 335, 336*n*; telegram to, Oct. 30, 1862, 152*n*; recruits, 152*n*; advances to Holly Springs, 268*n*, 270*n*, 276*n*, 277*n*, 278, 280*n*, 284*n*–85*n*, 298*n*–99*n*, 302*n*–3*n*, 304, 306*n*–7*n*, 308 and *n*, 311, 364*n*; background, 280*n*; captures Ripley, 280*n*, 307*n*; promotion of, 280*n*, 318; advances toward Tallahatchie River, 346, 347*n*, 360, 362*n*, 366*n*
Lee, Robert E. (C.S. Army), 66*n*
Leggett, Mortimer D. (Ohio Vols.): reports battle of Sharpsburg, 66*n*; promotion of, 161, 162*n*, 318; defends USG, 166*n*–67*n*; commands reconnaissance, 206*n*; warned, 236*n*
Lenox, George P. (telegraph operator), 383*n*
Leonard, J. M. (spy), 38, 42*n*
Lewis, Sely (spy), 91*n*
Lexington, Ky., 13*n*, 227*n*
Lightford, R. L. (prisoner), 37*n*
Lincoln, Abraham (U.S. President): and Negroes, 86*n*, 317*n*, 428; reviews courts-martial, 90*n*, 91*n*, 204; appointments by, 121, 355, 357*n*, 358*n*–59*n*, 391*n*, 434, 449; telegram to, Oct. 10, 1862, 143; and battle of Corinth, 143 and *n*; praises USG, 143*n*, 288*n*; endorsement to, Oct. 1, 1862, 162*n*;

asked for promotions, 162n, 203n, 217n, 244, 318n–19n; endorsement to, Oct. 22, 1862, 217n; associated with Leonard Swett, 273, 276n; and Vicksburg expedition, 289n, 402n; mentioned, 182n, 196n, 410n, 420

Liquor: trade in, 23n, 135n, 200, 201n–2n, 233n; abuse of, 25, 26n, 428; and USG, 87n, 242n

Little, Lewis H. (C.S. Army), 72, 73n, 74n

Little Rock, Ark., 94n, 243n, 263, 291

Logan, John A. (U.S. Army): expeditions of, 13n, 19, 20n, 81n; arrives at Jackson, 16 and n; telegram to, Sept. 4, 1862, 19; telegram to, Sept. 5, 1862, 19n; reports C.S.A. movements, 19n–20n, 31n, 34n; telegram to, Sept. 9, 1862, 28; telegrams to, Sept. 8, 1862 (4), 29n; reports U.S. movements, 29n; telegram to, Sept. 10, 1862, 30n; telegram to, Sept. 12, 1862, 30n; telegram to, Sept. 15, 1862, 31n; telegram to, Sept. 11, 1862, 41n; telegram to, Sept. 14, 1862, 41n; sends troops to Corinth, 41n, 54n–55n; telegram to, Sept. 16, 1862, 48n; instructed to attack, 48n; telegram to, Sept. 17, 1862, 54n; threatened at Jackson, 54n–55n; and battle of Corinth, 101n–2n, 104n; recommends promotions, 116, 162n; receives complaints, 196n, 423, 426; commands at Bolivar, 234n, 235; in Mississippi Central campaign, 245n, 258, 259n, 277n, 364n, 369, 370n, 387n, 396; telegrams to, Sept. 10, 1862 (2), 423; mentioned, 221n, 309n, 440

Longstreet, James (C.S. Army), 66n

Lothrop, Warren L. (Mo. Vols.), 188, 438, 439

Louisville, Ky.: Gordon Granger ordered to, 7n, 13n, 17, 18 and n, 33 and n; believed secure, 44; troops sent to, 156 and n, 431; William S. Rosecrans ordered to, 183n, 261n; mentioned, 309n, 336n, 391n, 422, 447

Love, Mrs. Walter, Flint, Mich.: documents owned by, 203, 244

Lovejoy, Owen (U.S. Representative), 265n

Lovell, Julius (U.S. Army), 248n, 449

Lovell, Mansfield (C.S. Army): movements of, 97n, 179n, 222, 291, 366n; at battle of Corinth, 115n, 116, 117n, 154; background, 117n

Lowe, Eager M. (Ill. Vols.), 199n

Lowe, Mr. (guerrilla), 457

Lowe, William W. (Iowa Vols.): attacked, 11n, 12n; supplies information, 146n; expeditions of, 226n, 426, 427–28, 433; asks about prisoners, 336n, 428; organizes command, 423, 424; asks about citizens, 432

Lumpkin's Mill, Miss.: C.S.A. evacuate, 298n, 299n, 302, 303n; located, 303n; skirmishes at, 306n, 307n, 364n; occupied, 359, 360, 362 and n, 366n, 369, 370n

Lyford, Stephen C. (U.S. Army): as chief of ordnance, 54, 55n, 97n, 220n, 245, 246n, 249, 250, 295, 296n, 399n; background, 55n; takes flag of truce, 156n, 159; telegram to, Oct. 30, 1862, 220n; recommended for col., 296n

Lyman, Charles W. (U.S. Army): as q.m., 142n, 213, 214n–15n, 242n, 282n, 438, 450, 451; telegram to, Oct. 28, 1862, 214n; letter to, Nov. 16, 1862, 451

McAllister, Richard (U.S. Army), 376n–77n

McAmon, William W. (Mo. Vols.), 90n

McArthur, John (U.S. Army): garrisons Corinth, 24, 35n, 41n; and battle of Iuka, 64, 70n, 73n, 171; assignments for, 83n, 284n; skirmishes, 91n; in battle of Corinth, 107n, 123n, 230; requests appointments, 120n, 449; at Ripley, 139n; inspected, 241n, 242n; guards Negroes, 316n, 329, 350; in Mississippi Central campaign, 350, 359, 369, 397n; mentioned, 309n, 432, 458

McClellan, George B. (U.S. Army), 66n, 72n, 204n, 265n, 328n

McClernand, John A. (U.S. Army): plans Vicksburg expedition, 180n, 288, 288n–89n, 310, 340n–41n, 407n; troops recruited for, 197n, 279n, 285, 286n; staff of, 295n, 434, 440, 459; mentioned, 24, 220n, 287n, 426

McClurg, Samuel M. (Mo. Vols.), 375n–76n

McCormick, Capt. (Ind. Vols.), 7n

McCown, Joseph B. (Ill. Vols.), 116n

McCown's Mill, Tenn., 282n

McCullough, William (Ill. Vols.): as cav. officer, 47n, 348n, 450; letter to, Nov. 14, 1862, 450

McDermott, John (Mich. Vols.): skirmishes, 91n; guards Grand Junction, 330n; telegram to, Dec. 4, 1862, 392n; holds telegrapher, 392n; reports guerrillas, 456–57

McDonald, John (Mo. Vols.), 91n

McDowell, John A. (Iowa Vols.), 264n

McElmurry, William L. (citizen), 90n

McElroy, James (Ill. Vols.), 454
McElroy, James N. (Ohio Vols.), 436
McGinnis, Franklin L. (Mo. Vols.), 439
McGrath, James (Ill. Vols.), 90n
Mack, Alonzo W. (Ill. Vols.), 137n
McKean, Thomas J. (U.S. Army): letter to, Sept. 16, 1862, 53–54; commands Corinth, 53–54, 59, 61, 64n, 92n, 176; letter to, Sept. 18, 1862, 64n; reassignment requested, 83n; in battle of Corinth, 97n, 107n, 108n, 123n, 124n, 129n, 144n, 230n; reinforced, 149; assigned to Jackson, 302n; mentioned, 309n
McLain, Robert (C.S. Army), 126n
McLean, Nathaniel H. (U.S. Army), 45n, 190n, 246n–47n
McMichael, William (U.S. Army), 46n
McNairy Station, Tenn., 348n
McNally, Christopher H. (U.S. Army): letter to, Nov. 30, 1862, 458
McNeil, Quincy (Ill. Vols.), 158n–59n, 420
McPherson, James B. (U.S. Army): as railroad superintendent, 13n, 17n, 30n, 33n, 38, 39n, 40n, 55n, 81n, 122n; and battle of Corinth, 103n, 111 and n, 112n, 115n, 116–17, 123n–24n, 126, 128n, 129n, 131n, 139n, 150n, 223, 224, 230, 433; command sought for, 121 and n, 131, 132n; promotion of, 130n, 320; commands at Bolivar, 148 and n, 160n, 177n, 191n, 206 and n, 212 and n, 218n, 235 and n, 236 and n, 282n; William T. Sherman wants, 180n; telegram to, Oct. 25, 1862, 191; defends Corinth, 191, 212 and n; telegram to, Oct. 25, 1862, 192; investigates pillaging, 192 and n; letter to, Oct. 28, 1862, 206; letter to, Oct. 29, 1862, 212; telegrams to, Oct. 29, 1862 (2), 212n; telegram to, Nov. 1, 1862, 235; telegram to, Nov. 1, 1862, 236; telegram to, Nov. 1, 1862, 236n; in Mississippi Central campaign, 237, 244–45, 245–46, 245n, 246n, 250n, 251 and n, 256, 257 and n, 259n, 268n, 270n–71n, 276, 276n–77n, 284, 284n–85n, 285, 286n, 290, 325, 338 and n, 342, 343n, 352n, 362, 363, 364n, 366n, 369, 370n, 397n; letter to, Nov. 2, 1862, 244–45; telegram to, Nov. 2, 1862, 245–46; letter to, Nov. 8, 1862, 276; telegram to, Nov. 8, 1862, 277n; letter to, Nov. 9, 1862, 285n; staff of, 296n; asks about prisoners, 336n, 445; telegram to, Nov. 21, 1862, 338; telegram to, Nov. 22, 1862, 338n; mentioned, 7n, 73n, 157n
Maddern, Lt. (C.S. Army), 433
Madison, Relly (Ill. Vols.), 48n
Magruder, John B. (C.S. Army), 64, 66n, 171

Maguire, J. P. (merchant), 202n
Major, James P. (C.S. Army), 208n
Malloy, Adam G. (Wis. Vols.), 455
Mann, P. A. (C.S. Army), 28n
Maps, 174, 229, 237n, 268n, 312n, 370n, 417, 436
Marietta, Miss., 32n, 47n, 65n, 77n
Marietta, Ohio, 209
Markland, Absalom H. (U.S. Post Office), 156n, 446–47
Marsh, C. Carroll (Ill. Vols.): promotion of, 161, 162n, 318; prepares expedition, 212n; telegram to, Oct. 27, 1862, 215n; sends tools, 215n; reports stealing, 322n–23n; recommends appointment, 358n; requests pass, 424; seizes money, 436; orderly for, 450
Marsh, Mrs. Theodore McCurdy, Springfield, N.J.: document owned by, 44n
Marshall Institute (Tenn.), 348n
Martin, Dr. (Iowa Vols.), 451
Martin, John D. (C.S. Army), 126 and n, 127n, 128
Martin, Thomas (Ohio Vols.), 324
Martin's Bridge, Tenn., 344n
Mason Station, Tenn., 343n
Matteson, Frederick W. (Ill. Vols.), 427
Mattoon, Ill., 442
Maurice, Thomas D. (Mo. Vols.), 438
Maury, Dabney H. (C.S. Army), 58n, 92n, 291, 293n
Maxey, John J. (Ill. Vols.), 137n
Maxwell, Thomas (of Savannah, Tenn.), 445
May, B. A. (Ind. Vols.), 454
Medicine: sickness, 8n, 33n, 39n, 44n, 58n, 73n, 94n, 124n, 156 and n, 248n, 270n, 282n, 312n, 316n, 344–45, 351n–52n, 365, 374n, 376n, 389n, 431; surgeons, 25, 25n–26n, 45, 45n–46n, 120n, 144n, 145n, 176, 295, 335, 336n, 355–56, 426, 436, 445, 447, 448; wounds, 73n, 98n, 115n, 118n, 119n, 120n, 124n, 127, 127n–28n, 137n, 143, 146n, 176, 184n, 189, 211n, 214n, 230, 239, 341, 342n; supplies, 334n, 439, 450. *See also* Hospitals
Medon, Tenn.: attacked, 4 and n, 9 and n, 12, 166n; located, 4n; threatened, 348n; telegraph at, 382n, 385n
Meigs, Montgomery C. (U.S. Army), 405n
Mellen, William P. (U.S. Treasury Dept.), 102 and n, 201n–2n, 435
Memphis, Tenn.: troops sent from, 12, 24, 26, 28, 29n–30n, 46; art. at, 19n, 282n, 417, 418; threatened, 27n, 77n, 82n, 92n,

95, 225*n*; expeditions from, 47*n*–48*n*, 59, 67, 68*n*, 429; troops sent to, 79, 93, 94*n*, 149, 158*n*, 200, 219, 247 and *n*, 248*n*, 254, 255 and *n*, 256*n*, 261 and *n*, 262, 279*n*, 291–92, 293*n*, 294*n*, 297, 297*n*–98*n*, 320, 401; command of, 82*n*, 84, 93 and *n*, 94*n*, 131 and *n*, 132*n*, 187*n*, 300, 301*n*; garrisoned, 91*n*, 130*n*, 155, 291–92, 293*n*, 294*n*, 310–11, 312*n*, 372*n*, 445; trade at, 135*n*, 264*n*, 331, 332*n*, 419, 431, 453; prisoners at, 141*n*, 142*n*, 146, 154, 159*n*, 219, 336*n*; liquor at, 200, 201*n*–2*n*; and Mississippi Central campaign, 250, 256, 262, 270*n*, 288, 291–92, 293*n*–94*n*, 305*n*, 340, 350, 352*n*; supplies at, 260 and *n*, 275, 279*n*, 280*n*, 299–300, 305 and *n*, 315*n*, 326 and *n*, 396*n*; railroad at, 305 and *n*, 315*n*, 326 and *n*, 328 and *n*, 329*n*, 400; and Vicksburg expedition, 310–12, 312*n*, 345, 371, 372*n*, 390, 401, 404, 405*n*, 406–7, 406*n*, 408, 409*n*; mentioned, 153, 218*n*, 309*n*, 338, 343*n*, 366*n*, 421, 430

Memphis and Charleston Railroad, 5, 8*n*, 30*n*, 58*n*, 332*n*, 402 and *n*

Memphis and Ohio Railroad, 28*n*

Menl, Mr., 448

Meridian, Miss., 94*n*, 250*n*, 255*n*, 263

Meriwether, R. M. (C.S. Army), 158*n*

Metcalf, Lyne S. (U.S. Army), 242*n*

Mexican War, 52*n*, 74*n*, 149*n*, 227*n*, 276*n*, 313*n*

Michigan Volunteers
—2nd Cav., 6*n*
—3rd Cav., 47*n*, 52*n*, 72*n*, 95*n*, 361, 364*n*
—12th Inf., 89 and *n*
—15th Inf., 90*n*, 318*n*, 330*n*, 458
—1st Light Art., 281*n*, 298*n*

Middleburg, Tenn.: threatened, 11*n*, 16*n*, 80*n*, 191*n*, 281*n*, 425; rations at, 233*n*, 271*n*

Middleton, Tenn., 41*n*

Miller, Madison (Mo. Vols.), 339*n*

Milliken's Bend, La., 410*n*

Mills, John H. W. (Kan. Vols.), 452

Minnesota, 210*n*, 243*n*, 285, 450

Mississippi: C.S.A. troops from, 5*n*, 126*n*, 129*n*, 147*n*, 373*n*; operations in, 88*n*, 186, 305*n*, 386*n*; citizens of, 97*n*, 150*n*

Mississippi and Tennessee Railroad, 299

Mississippi Central Railroad: attacked, 4 and *n*; cut, 93*n*, 94*n*, 403; controlled, 133, 200; derailment on, 170; engines for, 299–300; abandoned, 385; repaired, 387 and *n*, 388*n*, 390; mentioned, 11*n*, 388, 389

Mississippi Department of History and Archives, Jackson, Miss.: document in, 59

Mississippi River: operations on, 93*n*–94*n*, 95, 180*n*, 201, 255*n*, 263, 288*n*, 385, 386*n*, 403, 407, 408, 409 and *n*, 410*n*–11*n*, 411, 429–30; trade on, 135, 135*n*–36*n*, 431; mapped, 417; mentioned, 332*n*

Missouri Historical Society, St. Louis, Mo.: document in, 400

Missouri Volunteers
—Bissell's Engineers: personnel of, 182*n*, 423; sent to La Grange, 259*n*; repairs bridges, 278 and *n*, 400; repairs railroad, 354, 354*n*–55*n*; transports art., 417–18; at Corinth, 433
—5th Cav., 420–21
—5th Inf., 16
—7th Inf., 149*n*, 161, 223, 318
—8th Inf., 91*n*
—10th Inf., 376*n*
—11th Inf., 41*n*, 48*n*, 52*n*, 115*n*, 161, 376*n*
—14th Inf., 144*n*, 444, 449
—18th Inf., 338–39, 339*n*–40*n*
—21st Inf., 12*n*, 440–41
—24th Inf., 90*n*
—1st Light Art., 438, 439

Mitchell, Capt. 421

Mitchell, Capt. (steamboat capt.), 435

Mitchell, Greenville M. (Ill. Vols.), 455

Mitchell, Robert B. (U.S. Army), 446

Mitchell's Mill, Miss., 35*n*

Mizner, John K. (Mich. Vols.): at Iuka, 8*n*, 47*n*; and battle of Iuka, 53*n*, 57*n*, 65*n*, 71, 72*n*, 188; identified, 72*n*; on reconnaissances, 76*n*, 168*n*, 444; organizes cav., 196*n*, 410*n*, 421, 444; receives flag of truce, 208*n*; complaint about, 218*n*; and battle of Corinth, 230; letter to, Oct. 31, 1862, 444

Mobile, Ala.: newspapers of, 75*n*; troop movements at, 87, 97, 180*n*, 195*n*, 215, 227*n*, 250*n*, 251*n*, 263, 264*n*, 291, 402; threatened, 132*n*, 195*n*, 206, 238 and *n*, 255*n*; visit to, 312*n*

Mobile and Ohio Railroad: troops travel on, 106, 227*n*, 402, 403*n*; control of, 132*n*, 134, 168, 177*n*; cut, 348*n*, 371, 372*n*, 386, 390, 399; repaired, 370*n*; mentioned, 158*n*, 341

Molinard, Albert J. S. (U.S. Army), 446

Montezuma, Tenn., 92*n*

Montgomery, Ala., 238*n*

Moore, David (Mo. Vols.), 35*n*, 157*n*, 440, 441

Moore, John C. (C.S. Army), 129*n*

Moore, Mrs., 69*n*

Morgan, George H. (Mo. Vols.), 338–39, 339*n*–40*n*

Morgan, George W. (U.S. Army), 406*n*

Morgan, John H. (C.S. Army), 11n, 226, 226*n*–27*n*, 264*n*

Morgan, William H. (Ind. Vols.), 432

Morray, James B. (Ill. Vols.), 294*n*

Morrill, John (Ill. Vols.), 427

Morris, Thomas A. (U.S. Army), 287*n*

Morris, Thomas E. (Mich. Vols.): endorsement to, [Nov.], 1862, 458

Morrison, Pitcairn (U.S. Army), 440

Morrison, William R. (Ill. Vols.), 89*n*, 195–96, 196*n*, 318*n*–19*n*

Morton, Oliver P. (Gov. of Ind.): and Lewis Wallace, 287*n*; promotion recommended to, 432; endorsement to, Oct. 2, 1862, 432; USG writes to, 438; telegram to, Oct. 22, 1862, 440; furnishes clothing, 440

Morton, Thomas (Ohio Vols.), 21*n*, 22*n*, 41*n*, 421–22

Moscow, Tenn.: occupied, 7*n*, 282*n*, 286, 292, 293*n*, 325, 331*n*–32*n*, 343*n*, 352*n*; threatened, 96*n*, 277*n*, 308, 347*n*; arrests at, 454

Mound City, Ill., 282*n*, 447

Mount Pinson, Tenn., 348*n*

Mount Pleasant, Miss., 293*n*, 343*n*

Mower, Joseph A. (Mo. Vols.): on reconnaissance, 27*n*, 35*n*, 42*n*, 48*n*, 51, 52*n*, 53*n*, 58*n*, 66*n*; background, 52*n*; wounded, 115*n*; promotion of, 161, 162*n*; at battle of Iuka, 169; mentioned, 376*n*

Mudd, John J. (Ill. Vols.), 181 and *n*, 192 and *n*, 236*n*, 246*n*

Muddy Creek (Tenn.), 113*n*, 125*n*, 127*n*, 374*n*

Mumfordsville, Ky., 104*n*

Murfreesborough, Tenn., 453

Murphy, Robert C. (Wis. Vols.): abandons Iuka, 38–39, 40*n*, 41*n*, 48*n*, 168, 176*n*, 177*n*; court-martialed, 177*n*

Muscle Shoals (Tennessee River), 212, 213*n*

Musoad, 451

Myers, William (U.S. Army): telegram to, Nov. 9, 1862, 282*n*

My Wife's Island (Mississippi River), 410*n*

Nabers, R. D. (merchant), 202*n*

Napier, T. Alonzo (C.S. Army), 336*n*, 423, 424, 426, 428, 443

Naron, L. H. (scout), 76*n*, 77*n*

Nashville, Tenn., 6*n*, 36*n*, 48*n*, 85*n*, 374*n*, 446

Neely, R. P. (prisoner), 37 and *n*, 78, 109*n*

Negroes: at Iuka, 32*n*; returned, 32*n*, 86*n*, 354, 426, 430; bring information, 32*n*, 88*n*, 92*n*, 231*n*, 236*n*, 238*n*, 251*n*, 270*n*, 347*n*, 361, 366*n*; at Corinth, 54; captured, 151*n*; employed, 160*n*, 195*n*, 240*n*, 258, 331, 347*n*, 426, 456, 457; from Vicksburg, 198, 198*n*–99*n*; policy concerning, 315, 315*n*–17*n*; in camps, 329, 330*n*, 350, 352*n*, 425, 444; transport cotton, 332*n*

Neilson, Joseph H. (prisoner), 37*n*

Nelson, Horatio C. (Ill. Vols.), 332*n*

Nelson, William (U.S. Army), 13*n*

Newark, N.J., 44*n*

Newberry Library, Chicago, Ill.: document in, 409*n*

New Castle, Tenn., 206*n*

Newell, Cicero (Mich. Vols.), 263*n*

Newell, Isaac (Ill. Vols.), 448

New Madrid, Mo.: guerrillas near, 6*n*; trade near, 135*n*; expeditions from, 158*n*, 225*n*; troops removed from, 189, 190*n*, 200–201, 376*n*; art. at, 417; mentioned, 8*n*, 205

New Orleans, La.: threatened, 31, 250*n*, 257; intelligence from, 68*n*; expedition from, 243*n*, 263, 279, 286, 291; mentioned, 117*n*, 340*n*

Newspapers: publish news of USG, 20 and *n*, 275, 345; USG reads, 62; published in C.S.A., 75*n*, 264*n*, 312*n*, 401*n*; correspondents arrested, 86*n*; create dissension, 165, 166*n*, 167*n*; report U.S. movements, 180*n*, 238 and *n*, 287*n*; report liquor shipment, 200, 201*n*; report falsehoods, 238 and *n*, 273, 276*n*; report plundering, 267*n*; Charles S. Hamilton requests, 269, 270*n*; suppressed, 367*n*, 455

New York City, 121*n*–22*n*, 162, 163*n*, 265*n*, 270*n*, 436

New-York Historical Society, New York, N.Y.: document in, 285–86

Nixon, John S. (of Covington), 62 and *n*

Noble, Lazarus (Ind. AG), 419, 432

Noble, Silas (Ill. Vols.), 75*n*

Nolin's Cross-Roads, Miss., 139*n*

North, James M. (Ill. Vols.), 321

Norton, Addison S. (Ill. Vols.), 152*n*, 383*n*

Nunns, David (of Tenn.), 435

Oakland, Miss., 401*n*

Oaths: taken by prisoners, 78*n*, 108, 109*n*, 141*n*, 153–54, 167*n*, 228, 229*n*, 240*n*; taken by citizens, 333*n*, 428, 436

Obion River (Tenn.), 7*n*, 158*n*, 190*n*, 225*n*, 235*n*, 278*n*, 331*n*

O'Connor, Patrick (Wis. Vols.), 90*n*
Oglesby, Richard J. (U.S. Army): leave for, 3 and *n*; wounded, 112*n*, 115*n*, 116, 143 and *n*, 144*n*–45*n*; promoted, 145*n*; clerk for, 440
Ohio: troops from, 262, 264*n*, 265*n*, 279*n*, 293*n*, 300, 310; railroad equipment from, 329*n*, 406*n*
Ohio River, 18*n*, 155, 405*n*
Ohio Volunteers
—5th Cav.: on reconnaissance, 47*n*, 191*n*; court-martial in, 204 and *n*; at Bolivar, 245*n*; horse equipments for, 246, 247*n*; pay for, 447
—15th Cav., 230
—4th Independent Cav., 234 and *n*, 259*n*, 283*n*, 330*n*, 432
—3rd Inf., 41*n*
—22nd Inf., 90*n*–91*n*
—27th Inf., 115*n*, 315*n*–16*n*
—37th Inf., 72*n*
—39th Inf., 28*n*, 48*n*, 52*n*
—63rd Inf., 209 and *n*
—72nd Inf., 264*n*, 294*n*
—77th Inf., 37*n*, 94*n*
—78th Inf., 161, 162*n*, 318
—81st Inf., 41*n*, 323–24, 324*n*
—14th Light Art., 283*n*
Oliver, John M. (Mich. Vols.), 107*n*, 267*n*, 318*n*
Ord, Edward O. C. (U. S. Army): commands Jackson, 24; defends Corinth, 35*n*, 38, 39*n*, 41*n*, 42*n*, 53, 55*n*, 59, 76, 81*n*, 91, 91*n*–92*n*, 425; letter to, Sept. 13, 1862, 41*n*; telegram to, Sept. 15, 1862, 47*n*; and battle of Iuka, 47*n*, 48*n*, 51–52, 52*n*, 56, 63, 65*n*–66*n*, 67, 68–69, 69*n*–70*n*, 70, 71 and *n*, 72, 73*n*, 74, 76, 154, 169, 170, 172–74, 175, 178*n*, 184*n*, 189; letter to, Sept. 16, 1862, 51–52; letter to, Sept. 17, 1862, 56; letter to, Sept. 17, 1862, 59; telegram to, Sept. 20, 1862, 68–69; reinforces Bolivar, 81*n*, 88 and *n*, 89*n*, 101*n*; telegram to, Sept. 23, 1862, 82; assigned command, 82 and *n*, 83*n*, 202; telegram to, Sept. 25, 1862, 88; telegram to, Sept. 27, 1862, 91; and battle of Corinth, 113*n*, 115*n*, 117*n*, 118, 118*n*–20*n*, 123*n*, 124*n*, 126 and *n*, 140*n*, 143, 223, 230; telegram to, Oct. 4, 1862, 115*n*; wounded, 119*n*, 120*n*, 129, 184; recommends promotions, 162*n*; telegram to, Sept. 20, 1862, 173–74; letter to, Oct. 24, 1862, 184; investigates Don Carlos Buell, 184*n*; mentioned, 421, 422, 423
Orizaba, Miss., 39*n*, 40*n*

Osband, Embury D. (Ill. Vols.), 83*n*, 442
Osceola, Ark., 190*n*
Osterhaus, Peter J. (U.S. Army), 312*n*
Otuckalofa Creek (Miss.), 399*n*
Oxford, Miss.: threatened, 93*n*, 94*n*, 139, 292, 311; C.S.A. at, 150*n*, 398 and *n*; advance to, 367, 368, 369, 370*n*, 371, 396, 397*n*; occupied, 388, 399*n*; telegraph at, 391*n*–92*n*; hospital at, 398; railroad at, 400 and *n*; expedition from, 403, 404, 407, 408; mentioned, 104*n*, 147*n*, 410*n*

Pacific Landing, Mo., 417
Packard, Mr., 149*n*
Paddock, Joseph W. (U.S. Army), 447
Paden, Miss., 38, 43*n*
Paducah, Ky., 12*n*, 21*n*, 151, 226*n*, 282*n*, 294*n*, 418
Page, John (Ill. Vols.), 90*n*
Paige, Charles L. (Ill. Vols.), 321
Paine, Eleazer A. (U.S. Army), 431, 432
Palestine, Ill., 295*n*
Palmer, Dr., 351*n*
Palmer, James J. (Ill. Vols.), 377*n*
Palmer, Solomon (military telegraph), 382*n*
Panola, Miss., 93*n*, 313*n*, 366*n*, 370*n*, 401*n*, 412
Parkman, E. (of Jackson, Tenn.), 153
Parks, Dr. (of Memphis), 428
Parson, Burton (Ind. Vols.), 282*n*
Parsons, Charles (U.S. Army), 329*n*, 406*n*
Parsons, Lewis B. (U.S. Army): telegram to, Nov. 17, 1862, 328; procures railroad equipment, 328, 328*n*–29*n*; background, 328*n*; telegram to, Dec. 3, 1862, 329*n*; supplies Vicksburg expedition, 405*n*, 406*n*
Patrick, Matthewson T. (Iowa Vols.), 443
Pearce, E. T. (staff officer of Charles S. Hamilton), 284*n*
Pearl, Joseph (Ill. Vols.), 428
Pease, Phineas (Ill. Vols.), 348*n*
Peebles, R. A. (merchant), 201*n*
Pemberton, John C. (C.S.A. Army): replaces Earl Van Dorn, 160*n*; commands at Holly Springs, 178–79, 179*n*, 180*n*; background, 180*n*; exchanges prisoners, 214*n*, 389, 389*n*–90*n*; reinforces Mobile, 227*n*; evacuates Holly Springs, 278, 280*n*, 291; reoccupies Holly Springs, 284*n*, 285*n*; letter to, Nov. 23, 1862, 341–42; supplies prisoners, 341–42, 342*n*; at Abbeville, 343*n*; USG plans to attack, 346; deserters from, 375*n*; letter to, Dec. 5, 1862, 389; inspector gen. for, 398*n*
Penn, Elijah J. (Ohio Vols.), 447

Peoria, Ill., 440
Perry, J. D. (of La Grange), 451
Pettigrew, L. M. (of Cairo), 439
Peyton's Mills, Miss., 57*n*, 69*n*, 76*n*
Phelps, S. Ledyard (U.S. Navy), 93*n*, 141*n*
Philadelphia (store boat), 438
Piene's Mill, Miss., 32*n*
Pierce, Gilbert A. (U.S. Army), 418
Pigeon Roost Road (Tenn.), 293*n*, 312*n*
Piggott, Michael (Mo. Vols.), 41*n*
Pillow, Gideon J. (C.S. Army), 101*n*, 138*n*
Pilot Knob, Mo., 115*n*, 410*n*
Pinson, R. A. (C.S. Army), 181*n*
Pittsburg Landing, Tenn., 107*n*, 111, 374*n*, 421–22, 445
Platte Valley (steamboat), 135*n*, 190*n*
Pocahontas, Miss.: C.S.A. at, 36*n*, 97*n*, 98, 101*n*, 103*n*, 104*n*, 106, 113*n*; troops sent to, 41*n*, 104 and *n*, 105*n*; skirmish at, 95*n*, 96*n*, 123, 124*n*, 125*n*; occupation of, 150*n*, 217, 218*n*, 231 and *n*; expedition to, 195*n*, 223, 237*n*, 238*n*, 250*n*, 251, 444; mentioned, 118*n*, 128*n*, 138*n*, 153
Point Pleasant, Mo., 135*n*, 417
Polkville, Miss., 412, 413*n*
Pope, Charles A. (of St. Louis), 345
Pope, John (U.S. Army), 182*n*, 228*n*, 286*n*, 376*n*
Poplar Corners, Tenn., 6*n*
Porter, Capt. (C.S. Army), 269*n*
Porter, David D. (U.S. Navy): cooperates in Vicksburg expedition, 293*n*, 340, 341*n*, 346, 385, 404, 406*n*, 407; telegram to, Nov. 22, 1862, 340; background, 340*n*–41*n*; telegram to, Nov. 23, 1862, 341*n*; telegram to, Dec. 3, 1862, 385
Porter, Horace (U.S. Army), 247*n*
Porter's Bridge, Miss., 399*n*
Porter's Creek (Tenn.), 113*n*, 127*n*, 251*n*
Port Hudson, La., 255*n*, 291, 293*n*
Portis, John W. (C.S. Army), 49*n*
Powell, John W. (Ill. Vols.), 41*n*, 230
Preston, Simon M. (U.S. Army), 424
Price, Sterling (C.S. Army): movements reported, 5*n*, 6*n*, 7*n*, 11*n*, 13*n*, 16*n*, 19, 32*n*, 64*n*, 81*n*, 85*n*, 92*n*, 95 and *n*, 96*n*, 139*n*, 150*n*, 156*n*, 179*n*, 180*n*, 206 and *n*, 210, 216*n*, 251*n*, 264*n*, 270*n*, 285*n*, 291, 312*n*, 313*n*, 343*n*, 366*n*, 410*n*; threatens Corinth, 26, 26*n*–27*n*, 28*n*, 46, 47*n*, 48*n*, 191 and *n*, 194, 195*n*, 210, 212, 214*n*; strength of, 34, 35*n*, 36*n*, 47*n*, 92*n*, 142, 179*n*, 429, 453; at battle of Iuka, 34*n*, 35*n*, 36*n*, 39*n*–43*n*, 47*n*, 52*n*, 57*n*–58*n*, 64, 65*n*, 67, 69*n*, 71, 72, 74 and *n*, 76, 76*n*–77*n*, 87 and *n*, 154, 168–69, 171, 175; prisoners of,

48, 49*n*; at battle of Corinth, 96, 97*n*, 101*n*, 105*n*, 110, 112*n*, 115*n*, 116, 128, 129*n*, 222
Pride, George G. (staff officer of USG): supervises railroads, 121, 121*n*–22*n*, 295, 304*n*, 305*n*, 314, 314*n*–15*n*, 328*n*, 387 and *n*, 400 and *n*; and liquor shipment, 200; forwards intelligence, 212*n*, 278*n*, 302*n*; telegram to, Nov. 8, 1862, 278; telegrams to, Nov. 15, 1862 (2), 305*n*; telegram to, Nov. 15, 1862, 305*n*–6*n*; telegram to, Nov. 14, 1862, 314; telegrams to, Nov. 14, 1862 (2), 315*n*; telegram to, Nov. 16, 1862, 326; telegram to, Nov. 25, 1862, 326*n*; telegram to, Dec. 3, 1862, 387; telegram to, Dec. 3, 1862, 387*n*; telegram to, Dec. 6, 1862, 400; telegram to, Dec. 6, 1862, 400*n*
Prime, Frederick E. (U.S. Army): fortifies Corinth, 54, 55*n*, 108*n*, 213, 214*n*, 215*n*; employs Negroes, 160*n*, 457; telegram to, Nov. 2, 1862, 215*n*; promotion recommended, 241, 244, 318; as chief of engineers, 295, 436; letter to, Nov. 26, 1862, 354*n*; and pontoons, 354*n*, 355*n*, 421
Prince, Edward (Ill. Vols.), 39*n*, 52*n*, 296*n*, 344*n*
Princeton University, Princeton, N.J.: documents in, 53–54, 269–70
Pritchard, J. A. (C.S. Army), 126*n*
Probasco, Mrs. John L., Rockford, Ill.: document owned by, 439–40
Pugh, Isaac C. (Ill. Vols.), 438
Purdy, Tenn., 88*n*, 96*n*, 100*n*, 101*n*, 107*n*, 111*n*

Quinby, Isaac F. (U.S. Army): commands at Columbus, 6*n*–7*n*, 12*n*, 33*n*, 83*n*, 85*n*, 357*n*, 417, 419, 431, 432, 433; leave for, 85 and *n*; controversies about, 85*n*, 86*n*; disciplines troops, 90*n*, 454–55; goes to Corinth, 182, 183*n*, 192, 193*n*, 421; advances to Holly Springs, 270*n*, 277*n*, 284, 284*n*–85*n*, 286*n*, 299*n*, 302*n*, 303*n*, 306*n*, 307*n*; telegram to, Nov. 11, 1862, 303*n*; sent to Moscow, 325 and *n*, 331*n*–32*n*, 343*n*–44*n*, 347*n*, 350, 352*n*, 355*n*; letter to, Nov. 18, 1862, 331; handles cotton, 331, 332*n*, 333*n*; letter to, Nov. 20, 1862, 332*n*; telegram to, Nov. 23, 1862, 343*n*; telegram to, Nov. 24, 1862, 344*n*; in Mississippi Central campaign, 350, 352*n*, 366*n*, 369, 384*n*, 387 and *n*, 397*n*; telegram to, Nov. 26, 1862, 352*n*; telegrams to, Nov. 25, 1862 (2), 355*n*; letter to, Nov. 23, 1862, 454; mentioned, 132*n*, 242*n*, 309*n*

Ramer, Tenn., 101*n*, 102*n*, 103*n*, 111*n*
Randall, William H. F. (U.S. Army), 117*n*
Randolph, Mahlon (Mo. Vols.), 355*n*
Randolph, Tenn., 94*n*, 136*n*, 225*n*, 417, 429, 430, 431
Ransom, Thomas E. G. (Ill. Vols.), 226*n*, 282*n*, 296, 318, 368*n*, 423
Ratzen, Pvt. (Ill. Vols.), 377*n*
Rawlins, John A. (staff officer of USG): health of, 43; telegram to, Sept. 29, 1862, 85*n*; telegram to, Sept. 27, 1862, 163*n*; promotion of, 203, 275, 294; protests arrest, 220–21, 221*n*; mentioned passim
Ray, A. D. (C.S. Army), 109*n*
Raymond, Samuel B. (Ill. Vols.), 431–32
Reardon (of Miss.), 65*n*, 170
Reddington, William B. (telegraph operator), 383*n*
Reelfoot Lake (Tenn.), 158*n*
Reid, Hugh T. (Iowa Vols.), 318, 319*n*, 320
Religion, 100*n*, 109*n*, 195*n*, 252, 316*n*, 444. *See also* Jews
Reynolds, Charles A. (U.S. Army): as q.m., 52, 54, 136*n*, 260, 367*n*, 387*n*, 421, 432; procures funds, 162, 163*n*; promoted, 203, 295; reported dead, 260*n*; handles cotton, 332*n*, 393, 394, 395*n*–96*n*; pays Orlando H. Ross, 357*n*–58*n*; letter to, Dec. 3, 1862, 387*n*
Reynolds, Joseph J. (U.S. Army), 44*n*
Rhinehardt, Mrs. (of Davis' Mills), 353–54
Rhoads, Frank L. (Ill. Vols.), 89 and *n*, 440
Rice, Lafayette M. (Mo. Vols.), 90*n*
Richardson, Robert V. (C.S. Army), 343*n*, 344*n*
Richardson, William A. (U.S. Representative), 319*n*
Richmond, Jonathan (Ill. Vols.), 352*n*
Richmond, Ky., 13*n*, 446
Richmond, Va., 6*n*, 179*n*, 255*n*
Rienzi, Miss.: skirmish at, 5*n*; occupied, 8*n*, 17*n*, 24, 49*n*, 57*n*, 74, 74*n*–75*n*, 92*n*, 95*n*, 96*n*, 139*n*, 144*n*, 160*n*, 169, 176, 227*n*, 238*n*, 419, 437, 456; expeditions from, 26*n*–27*n*, 39*n*, 40*n*, 42*n*, 47*n*, 53*n*, 76*n*, 77*n*, 97*n*; threatened, 27*n*, 31*n*, 32*n*, 34*n*–35*n*, 36*n*, 97*n*, 134, 429; railroad at, 193, 194*n*, 422
Rigby, John W. (Ill. Vols.), 426
Riggin, John, Jr. (staff officer of USG): and prisoners, 55, 228, 228*n*–29*n*; as staff officer, 202*n*, 338 and *n*; supervises telegraph, 295, 378, 379, 380, 381*n*, 382*n*, 384*n*, 385*n*, 391*n*, 392*n*
Rinaker, John I. (Ill. Vols.), 195*n*
Ripley, James W. (U.S. Army), 163*n*, 423

Ripley, Miss.: skirmishes near, 5*n*, 6*n*, 224; expeditions to, 7*n*, 280*n*, 284, 307*n*, 444; C.S.A. movements near, 27*n*, 32*n*, 35*n*, 36*n*, 39*n*, 40*n*, 42*n*, 77*n*, 92*n*, 95 and *n*, 96*n*, 101*n*, 104*n*, 160*n*, 180*n*, 210, 215, 216*n*, 218*n*, 222, 224, 227*n*, 231*n*, 257, 269*n*; occupation of, 132*n*, 133, 137*n*, 138*n*–39*n*, 166*n*, 169, 196*n*, 238*n*
Robinson, Montgomery (citizen), 90*n*
Robinson, Mr. (of Grand Junction), 206*n*
Rochester, Montgomery (U.S. Army), 347*n*, 420
Rockford, Ill., 220*n*, 439
Rock Island, Ill., 420
Rockport Landing, Tenn., 21*n*, 426
Rockwood, Shepard S. (Wis. Vols.), 434
Rocky Ford, Miss., 366*n*, 375*n*, 388, 389*n*
Roddey, Philip D. (C.S. Army), 34*n*, 212, 213*n*, 374*n*
Rodgers, Benjamin F. (Ill. Vols.), 205 and *n*, 225*n*
Rodgers, Mr. (of Brownsville), 442
Rodgers, Mr. (of Tenn.), 192
Rogers, George C. (Ill. Vols.), 452
Rogers, J. E. (C.S. Army), 269*n*
Rogers, John A. (Tenn. Vols.), 441
Rogers, William P. (C.S. Army), 126*n*
Rorey's Mill, Miss., 35*n*
Rosecrans, William S. (U.S. Army): reports C.S.A. movements, 5*n*–6*n*, 31*n*, 32*n*, 34*n*, 35*n*, 36*n*, 39*n*, 179*n*, 374*n*, 446; informed of C.S.A. movements, 6*n*, 38–39, 40*n*, 66*n*, 88, 92*n*, 150 and *n*, 386*n*; wants to attack, 7*n*, 27*n*; reports troop positions, 8*n*, 17*n*, 96*n*, 148 and *n*, 184–85, 185*n*, 193*n*; defends Corinth, 24, 26*n*, 27*n*–28*n*, 34, 39*n*, 41*n*, 42*n*, 52*n*–53*n*, 55*n*, 56, 57*n*–58*n*, 61, 91*n*, 92*n*, 95*n*, 96*n*, 97*n*, 149, 150*n*, 157*n*, 159 and *n*, 160*n*, 421, 423, 431; and Negroes, 32*n*, 160*n*; deals with sick, 33*n*, 124*n*, 145*n*, 156*n*; in battle of Iuka, 36*n*, 38, 39*n*, 40*n*, 48*n*, 56, 57*n*–58*n*, 61, 63, 64–65, 65*n*, 66*n*, 67, 68, 69*n*, 70, 71 and *n*, 72, 72*n*–73*n*, 74, 76*n*–77*n*, 87*n*, 154, 169, 170–75, 177*n*–78*n*, 188, 275, 425; deals with prisoners, 37*n*–38*n*, 49*n*, 128, 146, 146*n*–47*n*, 156*n*, 160*n*, 165, 165*n*–66*n*, 167*n*, 208*n*, 335*n*, 445; promoted, 71*n*; assigned command, 82*n*–83*n*; disciplines troops, 90*n*, 177*n*, 196*n*, 217*n*, 265*n*, 436, 440–41; in battle of Corinth, 95*n*, 96*n*, 97*n*–98*n*, 98, 99, 100 and *n*, 103, 104*n*, 105*n*, 107, 107*n*–8*n*, 111 and *n*, 112–13, 112*n*, 114, 114*n*–15*n*, 117 and *n*, 119*n*, 123*n*–24*n*, 126*n*, 149*n*, 182 and *n*, 221–23, 229; pursues C.S.A. after Corinth,

Rosecrans, William S. *(cont.)*
118, 119*n*, 123, 123*n*–24*n*, 125*n*, 126 and *n*, 127*n*, 128*n*–29*n*, 129, 130*n*, 131, 131*n*–32*n*, 133, 136, 137*n*–38*n*, 138, 139 and *n*, 142 and *n*, 144*n*; wants reinforcements, 132*n*, 134; occupies Ripley, 133, 138, 138*n*–39*n*; needs supplies, 142*n*, 147*n*, 148*n*, 164*n*–65*n*, 432; spies of, 156 and *n*, 157*n*, 310, 312, 313*n*; ill, 156*n*, 157*n*, 159*n*–60*n*; recommends promotions, 157*n*, 185*n*, 427; quarrels with USG, 163–64, 164*n*–65*n*, 165, 165*n*–67*n*, 180*n*, 182*n*–83*n*; reassigned, 180*n*, 182, 182*n*–83*n*, 184, 185, 194*n*, 237*n*; and signal corps, 183 and *n*; staff of, 233*n*, 243*n*, 260*n*–61*n*, 261*n*–62*n*, 448–49; praised by Abraham Lincoln, 288*n*, 289*n*
—Correspondence from USG: letter to, Sept. 14, 1862, 38–39; letter to, Sept. 15, 1862, 48–49; telegram to, Sept. 18, 1862, 64–65; letter to [Sept. 18], 1862, 66*n*; telegram to, Sept. 28, 1862, 92*n*; telegram to, Oct. 2, 1862, 99; telegram to, Oct. 2, 1862, 100; telegram to, Oct. 3, 1862, 107; telegram to, Oct. 3, 1862, 107*n*; telegram to, Oct. 4, 1862, 114; telegram to, Oct. 5, 1862, 123; telegrams to, Oct. 5, 1862 (2), 123*n*; telegram to, Oct. 6, 1862, 128; telegrams to, Oct. 6, 1862 (2), 128*n*; telegram to, Oct. 6, 1862, 129; telegram to, Oct. 7, 1862, 131; telegram to, Oct. 8, 1862, 138; telegram to, Oct. 8, 1862, 138*n*; telegram to, Oct. 9, 1862, 142; telegram to, Oct. 11, 1862, 142*n*; telegram to, Oct. 11, 1862, 146; telegram to, Oct. 11, 1862, 146*n*; telegram to, Oct. 11, 1862, 148; telegram to, Oct. 11, 1862, 149; telegrams to, Oct. 11, 1862 (2), 149*n*; telegram to, Oct. 13, 1862, 150; telegram to, Oct. 18, 1862, 156; telegrams to, Oct. 18, 1862 (2), 157*n*; telegram to, Oct. 19, 1862, 159; telegram to, Oct. 21, 1862, 163–64; telegram to, Oct. 21, 1862, 164*n*; telegram to, Oct. 21, 1862, 165; telegram to, Sept. 18, 1862, 171–72; telegram to, Oct. 23, 1862, 182; telegram to, Oct. 23, 1862, 183; telegram to, Oct. 24, 1862, 184–85; telegram to, Oct. 24, 1862, 193*n*; telegram to, Oct. 20, 1862, 196*n*; telegram to, Oct. 30, 1862, 260*n*; telegram to, Nov. 1, 1862, 260*n*; telegram to, Nov. 2, 1862, 446
Rosenbach Foundation, Philip H. & A.S.W., Philadelphia, Pa.: documents in, 154–55, 344–45
Ross, Leonard F. (U.S. Army): reports Armstrong raid, 4*n*, 9*n*, 11*n*, 13*n*, 16*n*;

reinforced, 7*n*, 10, 11*n*, 16; letter to, Sept. 2, 1862, 10; reports C.S.A. movements, 10, 11*n*, 96*n*, 347*n*; telegram to, Sept. 3, 1862, 16; requests leave, 16*n*, 148*n*, 234*n*, 235; moves to Corinth, 30*n*, 38, 41*n*, 53, 59*n*, 425; arrests citizens, 37*n*, 109*n*; advances to Glendale, 51–52, 52*n*; and battle of Iuka, 57*n*, 60*n*, 63, 64, 65*n*, 66*n*, 169–70, 171, 172; letter to, Sept. 18, 1862, 63; sent to Bolivar, 80, 81*n*, 104*n*, 105*n*, 113*n*; guards railroad, 100*n*, 101*n*; and battle of the Hatchie, 106, 124*n*–25*n*, 126*n*, 128*n*; telegram to, Oct. 5, 1862, 124*n*; threatens Davis' Mills, 136, 137*n*, 138*n*, 141*n*; recommends promotion, 162*n*; in Mississippi Central campaign, 262*n*, 299*n*, 325*n*, 344*n*, 347*n*, 350, 397*n*; communicates with C.S.A., 335*n*–36*n*, 351*n*; telegram to, Nov. 25, 1862, 351*n*; letter to, Nov. 26, 1862, 353–54; protects citizen, 353–54; mentioned, 309*n*, 329
Ross, Orlando H. (cousin of USG), 357, 357*n*–58*n*
Rossman, H. (Mo. Vols.), 449
Rouse, James (Ill. Vols.), 109*n*
Rowley, William R. (staff officer of USG): writes for USG, 37*n*, 109*n*, 234*n*, 290*n*; health of, 43; escorts insane soldiers, 44*n*; promotion of, 203, 275; praises John A. Rawlins, 221*n*; as mustering officer, 295, 358*n*
Ruckersville, Miss.: threatened, 7*n*; U.S. reconnaissance near, 32*n*, 95*n*, 96*n*, 97*n*; C.S.A. near, 95*n*, 96*n*, 251*n*; expedition to, 100*n*, 127*n*, 132*n*
Russellville, Ala., 5*n*, 72*n*, 73*n*
Rust, Albert (C.S. Army), 80*n*, 96, 97*n*, 291
Rutgers University, New Brunswick, N.J.: documents in, 338, 338*n*
Ryan, Capt., 336*n*, 351*n*

Sabin, Elijah (Ind. Vols.), 419
Safford, Alfred B. (of Cairo), 274
St. Louis, Mo.: troops sent from, 11*n*, 12*n*; officers in, 25, 26*n*, 122*n*, 149*n*, 326 and *n*, 328*n*–29*n*, 355, 367*n*, 392*n*, 436; USG visits, 82, 84, 87, 87*n*–88*n*, 93*n*, 110; trade at, 102*n*, 135*n*, 200, 201*n*, 202*n*, 274, 441; prisoners in, 144*n*, 165 and *n*, 167*n*; supplies at, 213, 215*n*, 227*n*, 232*n*, 242, 282*n*, 309 and *n*, 404, 405*n*, 406*n*, 407, 412, 424, 452, 458; hospital at, 377*n*; mentioned, 20*n*, 44*n*, 68*n*, 109*n*, 179*n*, 198*n*, 228, 260*n*, 305 and *n*, 345, 429, 457

Salem, Miss., 7*n*, 95, 96*n*, 160*n*, 208*n*, 222
Salt, 135*n*–36*n*, 190*n*, 427, 453
Saltillo, Miss., 28*n*, 373*n*, 375*n*, 402
Sanders, Addison H. (Iowa Vols.), 308*n*
Sanderson, William L. (Ind. Vols.), 120*n*, 124*n*
Saulsbury, Tenn., 13*n*, 19, 20*n*, 95*n*, 191*n*, 206*n*, 208*n*, 457
Savannah, Tenn., 21*n*, 104*n*, 375*n*, 426, 445
Schermerhorn, Edward (telegraph operator), 391*n*–92*n*
Schoff, James S., New York, N.Y.: documents owned by, 55*n*, 61–62
Schofield, John M. (U.S. Army), 12*n*, 264*n*, 422
Scofield, Hiram (U.S. Army), 442
Scott, Joseph (prisoner), 165*n*, 167*n*
Scott, Mr. (guide), 270*n*
Scott Creek (Tenn.), 256, 257*n*, 270*n*
Sealy, Robert P. (Ill. Vols.), 451
Sears, William S. (Ill. Vols.), 321
Semple, Alexander C. (U.S. Army), 190*n*, 301*n*
Seward, William H. (U.S. Secretary of State), 332*n*
Sharp, Joshua W. (Pa. Vols.), 187–88, 188*n*
Sharpe, Alexander B. (U.S. Army), 119*n*
Sheean, David (partner of John A. Rawlins), 220–21, 221*n*
Sheridan, Philip H. (U.S. Army), 17*n*
Sherman, William T. (U.S. Army): counters Armstrong raid, 10, 19, 29*n*; commands Memphis, 24, 29*n*, 82*n*, 91*n*, 153, 187*n*, 255*n*–56*n*, 293*n*, 417, 418, 430, 433, 434–35, 436, 445; reports C.S.A. movements, 29*n*, 179*n*, 180*n*, 255*n*, 312*n*–13*n*, 429; sends force toward Miss., 47*n*, 131 and *n*, 138*n*, 139–40, 140*n*, 426–27; confers with USG, 84, 338 and *n*, 370*n*; plans Yazoo River expedition, 93, 93*n*–94*n*; telegram to, Oct. 8, 1862, 139–40; deals with prisoners, 141*n*, 146, 336*n*; sends spies, 150 and *n*; letter to, Oct. 16, 1862, 153; praised, 180*n*, 320; signal officers for, 183*n*–84*n*; permits liquor in Memphis, 201*n*, 202*n*; endorsement to, [Oct.], 1862, 202*n*; reinforced, 245, 248*n*, 257, 262, 263*n*, 264*n*, 265*n*, 279*n*, 293*n*, 300, 434; in Mississippi Central campaign, 250 and *n*, 254–55, 255*n*, 256, 257, 262–63, 263*n*, 264*n*, 285–86, 286*n*, 288, 290–92, 293*n*, 310–12, 312*n*–13*n*, 340, 341*n*, 350, 352*n*, 353, 359, 360–61, 362, 363, 364–65, 367, 368, 369, 369*n*–70*n*, 371, 401, 402*n*, 405*n*; letter to, Nov. 3, 1862, 254–55; letter to, Nov. 6, 1862, 262–63; regulates trade, 264*n*, 290, 419, 431; letter to, Nov. 10, 1862, 290–92; letter to, Nov. 14, 1862, 310–12; letter to, Nov. 15, 1862, 312*n*; letter to, Nov. 29, 1862, 360–61; letter to, Nov. 29, 1862, 362–63; letter to, Nov. 30, 1862, 364–65; letter to, Dec. 2, 1862, 369; on Vicksburg expedition, 372*n*, 385*n*, 390, 401, 402*n*, 403, 404, 405*n*, 406–7, 406*n*, 409 and *n*, 410*n*, 411 and *n*; letter to, Dec. 5, 1862, 393–95; cotton policy of, 393–95, 395*n*, 396*n*; letter to, Dec. 8, 1862, 404; letter to, Dec. 8, 1862, 406–7; praises Benjamin H. Grierson, 409*n*, 410*n*; destroys Randolph, 429, 430; endorsement to, [Oct.], 1862, 445
Shiloh, Tenn., battle of: officers at, 45*n*, 121, 319*n*, 398*n*, 449; charges against USG after, 166*n*; Iuka compared with, 178*n*; new regts. at, 275; mentioned, 58*n*, 322*n*, 458
Shipman, Stephen V. (Wis. Vols.), 420
Shirk, James W. (U.S. Navy), 250*n*
Silence, S. O. (Tenn. Vols.), 214*n*, 239, 240*n*, 334, 335*n*
Simmons, Samuel (U.S. Army), 66*n*, 189
Simons, James (U.S. Army), 459
Simpson's Ferry, Tenn., 88*n*, 89*n*
Skinner, Ira G. (telegraph operator), 382*n*, 383*n*
Skylark (steamboat), 21
Slaves. *See* Negroes
Slemons, W. F. (C.S. Army), 40*n*
Smith, Andrew J. (U.S. Army), 406*n*
Smith, Caleb B. (U.S. Secretary of the Interior), 332*n*
Smith, Dick (of Miss.), 35*n*
Smith, Edmund Kirby (C.S. Army), 13*n*, 155*n*, 264*n*
Smith, Edwin H. (Ill. Vols.), 432
Smith, Jason B. (Ill. Vols.), 294*n*
Smith, John Condit (U.S. Army), 393, 394, 395*n*, 396*n*
Smith, John E. (Ill. Vols.), 161, 162*n*, 318, 424
Smith, Joseph L. Kirby (Ohio Vols.), 115*n*
Smith, Martin L. (C.S. Army), 255*n*
Smith, Melanchthon (Ill. Vols.), 436
Smith, Morgan L. (U.S. Army), 24, 255*n*, 293*n*, 312*n*, 369*n*
Smith, Mrs. (of Grand Junction), 330*n*
Smith, W. A. (prisoner), 109
Smithland, Ky., 12*n*, 151*n*, 190*n*, 419
Snow, James A. (citizen), 90*n*
Somerville, Tenn.: expeditions to, 41*n*, 113*n*, 206*n*, 283*n*, 342, 343*n*–44*n*; C.S.A.

Somerville, Tenn. *(cont.)*
at, 82*n*, 88*n*, 95, 96*n*, 105*n*, 113*n*, 210, 212*n*, 222, 257, 313*n*; located, 96*n*
Southern Illinois University, Carbondale, Ill.: documents in, 56, 63, 64*n*, 334–35
Spain (of Miss.), 32*n*
Spaulding, Zeph S. (Ohio Vols.), 97*n*
Spencer & Wells (hotel proprietors), 23*n*
Sperry, Isaiah M. (Ill. Vols.), 294*n*
Spies: serve U.S., 5*n*, 31*n*, 39*n*, 40*n*, 65*n*, 76*n*, 150*n*, 156 and *n*, 170, 264*n*, 310, 312, 312*n*–13*n*, 343*n*, 361, 362*n*, 373, 373*n*–75*n*, 385, 386*n*, 449; of C.S.A., 6*n*; convicted, 91*n*; paid, 348*n*
Spilman, Cyrus C. (Ind. Vols.), 419
Spooner, Benjamin J. (Ind. Vols.), 293*n*
Sprague, John W. (Ohio Vols.), 209*n*
Spring Creek (Tenn.), 101*n*
Springfield, Ill., 281*n*, 289*n*
Stack, Herman (Ill. Vols.), 90*n*
Stager, Anson (U.S. Army): clashes with USG, 377–80, 381*n*–85*n*, 391, 391*n*–92*n*; telegram to, Nov. 30, 1862, 383*n*; background, 384*n*; telegram to, Nov. 29, 1862, 385*n*
Stanley, David S. (U.S. Army): on expeditions, 5, 8*n*; background, 8*n*; division of, 42*n*, 270*n*, 284*n*, 302*n*–3*n*, 309*n*; in battle of Iuka, 57*n*, 58*n*, 65*n*, 66*n*, 69*n*, 71, 72*n*, 73*n*, 76 and *n*, 77*n*, 170, 172, 174, 177*n*, 188; moves to Kossuth, 92*n*, 95*n*, 96*n*, 97*n*; in battle of Corinth, 108*n*, 123*n*–24*n*, 129*n*, 139*n*, 230; promotion of, 185*n*; recommends appointment, 228*n*; reassigned, 243*n*, 261, 262*n*
Stanton, Benjamin (Lt. Gov. of Ohio), 167*n*
Stanton, Col. (C.S. Army), 76*n*
Stanton, Edwin M. (U.S. Secretary of War): rules on personnel matters, 26*n*, 148*n*, 233*n*, 323, 324*n*, 339, 439, 447, 454; receives charges against USG, 87*n*; endorsement to, Nov. 15, 1862, 120*n*; recommends appointments, 121*n*, 122*n*, 356–57, 357*n*, 376*n*; asked for arms, 164*n*, 165*n*; sends troops to USG, 197*n*; letter to, Oct. 30, 1862, 220–21; arrest protested to, 220–21, 221*n*; and Vicksburg expedition, 289*n*, 405*n*; Negro policy of, 315*n*, 317*n*; letter to, Nov. 27, 1862, 356–57; manages telegraph, 378, 379, 380, 381 and *n*, 383*n*, 391*n*, 392*n*; letter to, Dec. 6, 1862, 397–98; informed of treason, 397–98, 398*n*; mentioned, 12*n*, 161*n*, 229*n*
Starkloff, Hugo M. (Ill. Vols.), 450
Starring, Frederick A. (Ill. Vols.), 12*n*, 247, 248*n*, 253

Steadman, George (Ill. Vols.), 454
Steele, Frederick (U.S. Army): and Yazoo River expedition, 68*n*, 93 and *n*, 94*n*; ordered to Pilot Knob, 115*n*, 125*n*, 410*n*; in Mississippi Central campaign, 264*n*, 312*n*, 340, 346, 361, 362*n*, 370*n*, 372 and *n*, 401*n*, 404, 405*n*, 410*n*; letter to, Dec. 8, 1862, 408–9; and Vicksburg expedition, 409–9, 409*n*, 410*n*–11*n*; mentioned, 50, 92*n*, 124*n*
Stenbeck, Andrew (Ill. Vols.), 419, 423, 428
Stephenson County Historical Society, Freeport, Ill.: document in, 290–92
Stevens, Victor H. (Ill. Vols.), 321
Stevens, W. J. (railroad agent), 329*n*, 449
Stevenson, John D. (Mo. Vols.): in Armstrong raid, 9*n*; in battle of Corinth, 111*n*, 149 and *n*, 223; background, 149*n*; promotion of, 161, 162*n*, 318; moves to La Grange, 253–54, 258, 259*n*, 283 and *n*
Stevenson, Ala., 374*n*
Stipp, George W. (Ill. Vols.), 427
Stone, Lyman H. (U.S. Army), 25, 25*n*–26*n*
Strahon, Mr. (prisoner), 109*n*
Strawbridge, James D. (U.S. Army), 426
Stricklain, Mrs. (of Miss.), 48*n*
Strickland, William T. (Ind. Vols.), 441, 448
Strickle, Abraham E. (U.S. Army), 233*n*–34*n*
Stuart, David (Ill. Vols.), 255*n*, 264*n*, 292, 293*n*, 294*n*
Stuart, James E. B. (C.S. Army), 264*n*, 435
Sulivane, E. Clement (C.S. Army), 239, 240*n*, 334, 335*n*
Sullivan, Jeremiah C. (U.S. Army): at battle of Corinth, 115*n*; commands at Jackson, 301*n*, 334*n*, 343*n*, 366, 454, 457, 458–59; moves to Holly Springs, 306*n*, 307*n*, 308*n*; telegram to, Nov. 23, 1862, 334*n*; telegram to, Nov. 23, 1862, 343*n*; telegram to, Nov. 25, 1862, 347; recaptures Henderson, 347, 348*n*–49*n*; background, 347*n*–48*n*; telegram to, Jan. 20, 1863, 349*n*; telegram to, Nov. 30, 1862, 366; telegram to, Nov. 27, 1862, 367*n*; telegram to, Nov. 24, 1862, 455; bans newspapers, 455; telegram to, Nov. 28, 1862, 457; telegram to, Dec. 1, 1862, 458; mentioned, 109*n*
Sullivan, John C. (telegraph operator), 382*n*
Swan, William S. (Ill. Vols.), 141*n*, 198, 198*n*–99*n*
Sweeney, Thomas W. (Ill. Vols.), 185*n*
Swett, Leonard (Ill. lawyer), 273–74, 276

Switzerland (steam ram), 447
Swords, Thomas (U.S. Army), 314*n*

Taggart, John P. (Ind. Vols.), 301*n*
Tallahatchie River (Miss.): C.S.A. movements near, 11*n*, 29*n*, 280*n*, 303*n*, 305, 306*n*, 311, 312*n*, 313*n*, 343*n*, 346, 347*n*, 360, 361, 371, 401*n*, 403, 409; railroad to, 94*n*, 387 and *n*, 390, 400 and *n*; U.S. movement toward, 276, 293*n*, 311, 312*n*, 313*n*, 346, 347*n*, 362*n*, 366*n*, 367, 368, 369, 369*n*–70*n*, 371, 372*n*; bridged, 343*n*, 369, 369*n*–70*n*, 387 and *n*; fords, 362
Tallaloosa, Miss., 311, 313*n*
Tannrath, Benjamin (Mo. Vols.), 227*n*
Tarpley, Elijah (Ill. Vols.), 433–34
Taylor, Charles (Ill. Vols.), 321
Taylor, Edward (prisoner), 240*n*
Taylor, John W. (U.S. Army), 189, 260*n*–61*n*
Taylor, Joseph C. (citizen), 90*n*
Taylor, Joseph P. (U.S. Army), 377*n*
Taylor, Mrs. (of Miss.), 35*n*
Taylor, R. R. (of Ballard County, Ky.), 86*n*
Taylor, Robert (prisoner), 240*n*
Taylor, William H. H. (Ohio Vols.), 246
Tecumseh (steamboat), 225*n*
Tennessee: threatened, 46, 47*n*, 65*n*, 67, 82*n*, 96*n*, 169, 170; U.S. troops from, 196*n*, 229*n*, 240*n*, 245*n*, 331*n*, 335*n*, 435; defended, 264*n*, 293*n*, 346*n*, 347, 402*n*; trade in, 332*n*, 333*n*–34*n*, 441; mentioned, 83*n*, 111*n*, 181*n*, 186, 378
Tennessee River: steamboats on, 21 and *n*, 418, 421–22; C.S.A. movements near, 34*n*, 47*n*, 57*n*, 58*n*, 87, 169, 174, 212, 343*n*, 373*n*, 374*n*, 375*n*, 402 and *n*, 426
Texas: C.S.A. troops from, 58*n*, 74*n*, 126*n*, 129*n*, 179, 195*n*, 197, 363*n*
Thielemann, Christian (Ill. Vols.), 293*n*, 312*n*
Thirds, William (Ill. Vols.), 86*n*
Thom, George (U.S. Army), 349
Thomas, Lorenzo (U.S. Army): telegram to, Sept. 1, 1862, 3; handles personnel matters, 3, 152, 187–88, 188*n*, 286*n*, 420, 439, 443, 448–49, 454; endorsement to, Oct. 28, 1862, 86*n*; letter to, Sept. 26, 1862, 89; administers military justice, 89, 89*n*–91*n*, 204 and *n*, 322*n*, 424–25, 454; letter to, Oct. 16, 1862, 152; telegram to, Oct. 24, 1862, 185*n*; USG reports to, 185*n*, 327, 460; letter to, Oct. 25, 1862, 187–88; letter to, Oct. 29, 1862, 187*n*; orders transmitted to, 187*n*, 441; letter to, Oct. 27,

1862, 203; receives recommendations, 203, 357*n*, 447; telegram to, Oct. 28, 1862, 204; letter to, Nov. 22, 1862, 322*n*; letter to, Nov. 16, 1862, 323–24; letter to, Nov. 17, 1862, 327; letter to, Nov. 22, 1862, 338–39; letter to, Jan. 24, 1863, 357*n*; letter to, Oct. 24, 1862, 441; letter to, Oct. 29, 1862, 443; letter to, Nov. 23, 1862, 454; telegram to, Jan. 21, 1863, 460
Thomas, R. H., 233*n*
Thomason, James (citizen), 90*n*
Thompson, Charles R. (Mo. Vols.), 182*n*
Thompson, Jacob (U.S. Secretary of the Interior), 397–98, 398*n*
Thompson, Lt., 423
Thompson, Mr. (of La Grange), 451
Thrush, William A. (Ill. Vols.), 147*n*
Thurston, William H. (Ind. Vols.), 59 and *n*
Tice, Isaac L. (Ohio Vols.), 454
Tighe, John H. (U.S. Army), 260 and *n*, 261*n*, 309*n*, 432
Tilghman, Lloyd (C.S. Army): movements of, 139*n*, 291, 312*n*, 375*n*, 388, 401*n*; commands prisoners, 179, 180*n*
Tippah Creek (Miss.), 359*n*, 362*n*, 366*n*
Tipton County, Tenn., 348*n*, 417
Tishomingo County, Miss., 457
Tobin, Thomas F. (C.S. Army), 165*n*–66*n*
Tod, David (Gov. of Ohio): telegram to, Oct. 28, 1862, 209; organizes regts., 209 and *n*, 323, 324, 459; endorsement to, Dec. 3, 1862, 459
Tonny's Bridge, Miss., 128*n*
Toone Station, Tenn., 9*n*, 113*n*
Townes, Robert R. (U.S. Army), 101*n*–2*n*
Townsend, Edward D. (U.S. Army), 86*n*, 90*n*, 188*n*, 207*n*, 232*n*, 233*n*, 448
Trade: improper, 85*n*, 135, 135*n*–36*n*, 343*n*, 439, 441, 447; regulated, 102 and *n*, 160–61, 161*n*, 264*n*, 290, 304*n*, 331, 332*n*–34*n*, 412, 431, 435, 452–53; in liquor, 200, 201*n*–2*n*
Trenton, Tenn.: threatened, 6*n*; troops sent from, 111, 195*n*; garrisoned, 125*n*, 281, 331*n*; mentioned, 82*n*, 85*n*, 113*n*, 229*n*, 421, 441, 457
Trowbridge, Roland E. (U.S. Representative), 420
True, James W. (Ill. Vols.), 157*n*, 366, 367*n*
True, John W. (Ill. Vols.), 219*n*, 367*n*
Truesdale, Mr. (postmaster), 156*n*–57*n*
Trumbull, Lyman (U.S. Senator), 288*n*–89*n*
Tullahoma, Tenn., 373, 374*n*, 375*n*
Tunison, John (Ill. Vols.), 321, 322

Tupelo, Miss.: C.S.A. movements at, 7*n*, 28*n*, 35*n*, 36*n*, 64, 76*n*, 92*n*, 101*n*, 132*n*, 150*n*, 171, 195*n*, 212, 215, 227*n*, 374*n*; threatened by U.S., 193, 194 and *n*, 371
Tupper, Nathan W. (Ill. Vols.), 293*n*
Turner, J. P. (of Memphis), 453
Turner, Justin G., Los Angeles, Calif.: documents owned by, 60–61, 66*n*, 74, 76
Turner, Thomas J. (Ill. Vols.), 452
Tuscaloosa, Ala., 150*n*
Tuscumbia, Ala., 5, 8*n*, 32*n*, 373*n*, 374*n*, 445, 456
Tuscumbia River (Miss.): troop movements near, 17*n*, 40*n*, 97*n*, 101*n*, 103*n*, 115*n*, 123*n*, 128*n*, 132*n*, 250*n*, 251*n*, 456; bridged, 40*n*, 101*n*, 103*n*, 113*n*
Tuttle, James M. (U.S. Army): sends troops southward, 10, 11*n*–12*n*, 54*n*, 125*n*, 198*n*, 226*n*, 246*n*, 248*n*, 279*n*, 286*n*, 406*n*; telegram to, Sept. 4, 1862, 20; investigates telegraph leak, 20 and *n*; makes arrests, 22*n*, 392*n*, 435; letter to, Sept. 17, 1862, 54*n*; letter to, Sept. 16, 1862, 55–56; deals with prisoners, 55–56, 198, 198*n*–99*n*, 290*n*, 336*n*; command of, 85*n*, 218, 301*n*; forwards information, 115*n*, 151*n*, 265*n*, 435; telegram to, Oct. 26, 1862, 198*n*; approves liquor shipment, 202*n*; letter to, Oct. 29, 1862, 218; telegram to, Nov. 1, 1862, 246*n*; telegram to, Nov. 6, 1862, 265; investigates package tampering, 265 and *n*; telegram to, Nov. 9, 1862, 279*n*; telegram to, Nov. 10, 1862, 286*n*; telegram to, Nov. 14, 1862, 301*n*; telegram to, Nov. 18, 1862, 301*n*; telegram to, Nov. 17, 1862, 301*n*; sick, 301*n*; asks about Negroes, 317*n*; telegram to, Oct. 31, 1862, 336*n*; letter to, Nov. 1, 1862, 445
Tweeddale, William (Mo. Vols.), 235*n*
Twenty Mile Creek (Miss.): C.S.A. near, 6*n*, 26*n*, 27*n*, 28, 77*n*; bridged, 6*n*, 32*n*, 194*n*; located, 31*n*; railroad at, 32*n*, 49*n*
Tyler, Peter A. (Ohio Vols.), 323, 324*n*

Union Bank of Tennessee, Jackson, Tenn., 436
Union City, Tenn.: garrisoned, 155, 247, 259*n*, 281 and *n*, 297, 297*n*–98*n*, 331*n*, 455; prisoners at, 219
Uniontown, Ky., 419
United States Army
—2nd Art., 438, 446
—3rd Cav., 285, 291, 458
—4th Cav., 182*n*
—1st Inf., 53
—13th Inf., 94*n*
—15th Inf., 207*n*
United States Congress, 71*n*, 161*n*, 185, 250*n*, 319*n*, 327
United States Post Office, 446–47
United States Treasury Department: agents suspected in steamboat capture, 21; regulates trade, 23 and *n*, 102 and *n*, 135*n*–36*n*, 160–61, 161*n*, 200, 201*n*–2*n*, 265, 290, 332*n*–34*n*, 453; short of money, 147*n*
University of California at Los Angeles, Los Angeles, Calif.: documents in, 99, 100, 107, 107*n*, 123, 123*n* (2), 128, 128*n* (2), 129, 131, 138, 142, 146, 148, 149*n*

Van Buren, Tenn.: C.S.A. threaten, 11*n*, 75*n*, 80*n*, 88*n*, 137*n*; occupied, 137*n*, 245, 251 and *n*; reconnaissance to, 206*n*, 236*n*; located, 245*n*
Van Buskirk, Mr. (railroad conductor), 101*n*
Van Derferd (of Miss.), 35*n*
Van Dorn, Earl (C.S. Army): movements of, 7*n*, 26, 26*n*–27*n*, 31, 36*n*, 46, 47*n*–48*n*, 57*n*–58*n*, 65*n*, 76*n*, 77*n*, 80*n*, 81*n*, 92*n*, 94*n*, 95, 95*n*–96*n*, 96–97, 98, 101*n*, 169, 170, 175, 179*n*, 180*n*, 214*n*, 280*n*, 312*n*–13*n*, 398*n*, 401*n*; strength of, 47*n*, 362; at battle of Corinth, 110, 112*n*, 115*n*, 116, 117*n*, 119*n*, 123*n*, 138*n*, 154, 222; aide captured, 118*n*, 239, 240*n*, 306*n*, 334, 335*n*; discontent with, 150*n*; exchanges prisoners, 160*n*, 208*n*, 214*n*, 239, 240*n*, 334–35, 335*n*–36*n*; letter to, Nov. 19, 1862, 334–35
Van Duzer, John C. (U.S. Army): as telegraph superintendent, 20*n*, 32*n*, 66*n*; arrest of, 377*n*–81*n*, 381*n*–85*n*, 391, 391*n*–92*n*; letter to, Nov. 26, 1862, 379; background, 383*n*; telegram to, Nov. 12, 1862, 384*n*; telegram to, Nov. 14, 1862, 384*n*–85*n*
Van Hosen, George M. (Iowa Vols.), 22, 23*n*, 37*n*
Vaughn, Jacob E. (Ill. Vols.), 433–34
Vaughn, Thomas F. (Ill. Vols.), 220*n*, 280*n*, 281*n*
Veatch, James C. (U.S. Army), 119*n*, 230, 255*n*
Vicksburg, Miss.: C.S.A. movements at, 5*n*, 27*n*, 31*n*, 65*n*, 93 and *n*, 94*n*, 170, 179*n*, 238*n*, 255*n*, 263, 347*n*, 385, 386*n*; prisoners exchanged at, 49*n*, 104*n*, 141*n*, 159*n*, 198 and *n*, 199*n*, 214*n*, 336*n*, 337, 389, 389*n*–90*n*, 445, 457; campaign against, 93 and *n*, 94*n*, 183*n*–84*n*, 200, 279*n*, 293*n*,

295*n*, 310–12, 312*n*–13*n*, 341*n*, 345–46, 346*n*, 350–51, 351*n*–52*n*, 371–72, 372*n*, 390, 401, 402*n*, 403, 404, 405*n*–6*n*, 406–7, 408–9, 409*n*–11*n*, 411–12; cotton at, 332*n*
Villepigue, John B. (C.S. Army): movements reported, 10, 11*n*, 29*n*, 34*n*, 75*n*, 79, 80*n*, 92*n*, 95, 96, 97*n*, 101*n*, 110, 222, 255*n*, 263, 291; background, 11*n*; dies, 291, 293*n*
Vincent, Thomas M. (U.S. Army): organizes regts., 262, 265*n*, 324*n*, 339*n*, 340*n*; AGO duties of, 376*n*, 444–45, 447, 448, 454
Virginia, 150*n*, 289*n*, 310, 453

W. B. Terry (steamboat), 21, 21*n*–22*n*, 422, 424
Waddell, Lloyd D. (Ill. Vols.), 282*n*
Wadsworth, David D. (Ill. Vols.), 321
Walbridge, George R. (Wis. Vols.), 458
Walcott, Christopher P. (U.S. Asst. Secretary of War), 398*n*
Walcutt, Charles C. (Ohio Vols.), 429
Walker, Mr. (railroad agent), 249*n*, 303–4
Wallace, Lewis (U.S. Army), 19*n*, 286, 286*n*–87*n*
Walsh, Stephen (Mich. Vols.), 90*n*
Ward, Guy C. (Ill. Vols.), 149*n*
Washburn, Cadwallader C. (U.S. Army), 279*n*, 412*n*–13*n*
Washburne, Elihu B. (U.S. Representative): visits USG, 11*n*, 273; knows John A. Rawlins, 220; reelected, 265*n*; letter to, Nov. 7, 1862, 273–75; informed of Cairo contracts, 273–75; assists in appointments, 275, 355–56, 358*n*–59*n*; letter to, Nov. 26, 1862, 355–56
Washington, D.C.: arms and funds procured at, 147*n*, 162, 163*n*, 164, 164*n*–65*n*; opinion of USG at, 288*n*–89*n*; mentioned, 20*n*, 21, 44*n*, 55*n*, 66*n*, 86*n*, 89, 89*n*–90*n*, 115*n*, 117*n*, 121*n*, 122*n*, 145*n*, 167*n*, 184, 185*n*, 190*n*, 199*n*, 209*n*, 220*n*, 275, 280*n*, 286*n*, 287*n*, 296*n*, 305*n*, 319*n*, 323*n*, 324, 326, 332*n*, 344*n*, 345, 372*n*, 375*n*, 376*n*, 377, 392*n*, 393, 404, 420, 432, 434, 436, 438, 439, 442, 444, 445, 451, 458, 459
Waterford, Miss., 307*n*, 366*n*, 367, 388*n*, 397*n*
Waters, David A. (Iowa Vols.), 427
Water Valley, Miss., 399*n*
Watson, Peter H. (U.S. Asst. Secretary of War): and military discipline, 86*n*, 87*n*; writes about arms, 164*n*, 220*n*; telegram to, Nov. 14, 1862, 378; instructs about telegraph, 378, 379, 382*n*, 384*n*

Watts (tugboat), 151*n*
Waverly, Tenn., 331*n*, 443–44
Webber, William W. (Ill. Vols.), 366*n*
Webster, Joseph D. (staff officer of USG): and troop movements, 6*n*, 177*n*; supervises railroads, 122*n*, 272, 283*n*, 294, 303–4, 347, 354*n*, 400*n*; telegram to, Nov. 7, 1862, 272; telegram to, Nov. 8, 1862, 272*n*; telegram to, Nov. 9, 1862, 272*n*; telegram to, Nov. 10, 1862, 272*n*; promotion of, 272*n*, 318; letter to, Nov. 10, 1862, 283*n*; letter to, Nov. 12, 1862, 303–4; telegrams to, Nov. 15, 1862 (2), 304*n*; telegram to, Nov. 17, 1862, 304*n*; telegram to, Nov. 18, 1862, 304*n*; telegram to, Dec. 9, 1862, 400*n*; exchanges prisoners, 445
Weldon, James (Ill. Vols.), 90*n*
Wells, Dr. (of Miss.), 32*n*, 36*n*
Western Reserve Historical Society, Cleveland, Ohio: documents in, 20, 383*n*, 384*n*
Wheaton, Loyd (Ill. Vols.), 116 and *n*
White, E. J. (merchant), 441
White, Joseph W. (of St. Louis), 50
Whitehurst, Eli, 212
Whitesburg, Ala., 57*n*
Whitfield, John W. (C.S. Army), 72, 73*n*, 74*n*, 363*n*
Wilcox, Jeremiah C. (Iowa Vols.), 42*n*, 427
Wiles, William M. (Ind. Vols.), 74*n*, 446
Wilkinson, F. (prisoner), 55
Williams, David E. (Ill. Vols.), 427
Williams, George A. (U.S. Army), 227, 228*n*, 230, 241, 244, 318
Williams, Hezekiah (Ill. Vols.), 459
Wilson, James H. (U.S. Army), 295, 295*n*–96*n*, 307*n*
Wilson, John J. S. (telegraph superintendent), 383*n*
Wirtz, Horace R. (U.S. Army), 144*n*, 145*n*, 295 and *n*, 448
Wisconsin, 210*n*, 243*n*, 270*n*, 279*n*, 286*n*
Wisconsin, State Historical Society of, Madison, Wis.: document in, 203*n*
Wisconsin Volunteers
—7th Battery, 207*n*
—8th Inf., 41*n*, 168
—12th Inf., 124*n*, 125*n*, 128*n*, 137*n*, 141*n*
—13th Inf., 6*n*, 419, 428, 434
—14th Inf., 90*n*, 424
—16th Inf., 44*n*, 216, 217*n*, 376*n*, 424, 449
—17th Inf., 90*n*, 103*n*, 424, 455–56
—29th Inf., 198*n*
—32nd Inf., 198*n*, 247*n*, 255*n*, 263*n*, 293*n*, 298*n*
Withers, Jones M. (C.S. Army), 453
Wolf River (Tenn.): C.S.A. at, 80*n*, 96*n*,

Wolf River (Tenn.) *(cont.)*
343*n*; expedition toward, 137*n*, 138*n*; U.S. troops at, 256, 257, 302, 303*n*; located, 256*n*
Wood, Fernando (U.S. Representative), 265*n*
Wood, Peter P. (Ill. Vols.), 19*n*
Wood, Robert C. (U.S. Army): letter to, Sept. 7, 1862, 25; background, 25*n*; as asst. surgeon gen., 25*n*–26*n*, 295*n*; telegram to, Dec. 18, 1862, 295*n*
Wood, William D. (act. Mo. AG), 339*n*–40*n*
Woodward (of Tenn.), 129*n*
Woodward, Thomas G. (C.S. Army), 296, 297*n*, 423, 428
Wright, Horatio G. (U.S. Army): reinforced, 13*n*, 18, 18*n*–19*n*, 31, 33*n*, 94*n*, 431; telegram to, Sept. 4, 1862, 18; background, 18*n*; telegram to, Sept. 5, 1862, 22*n*; handles personnel matters, 22*n*, 82*n*, 190*n*, 209, 302*n*, 436, 438; sends troops to USG, 125*n*, 130*n*, 131, 197*n*, 246, 424, 432; telegram to, Oct. 23, 1862, 209; telegram to, Nov. 2, 1862, 246; may be relieved, 287*n*; telegram to, Oct. 28, 1862, 302*n*; asked for railroad equipment, 305*n*, 314 and *n*, 315*n*; telegram to, Nov. 14, 1862, 314; telegram to, Nov. 26, 1862, 314*n*; letter to, Oct. 18, 1862, 438; endorsement to, Nov. 3, 1862, 447; and cotton, 447
Wyatt, Miss., 362, 363*n*, 367, 368, 369*n*, 370*n*, 371

Yaknapatapha River (Miss.). *See* Yocona River
Yalobusha River (Miss.), 370*n*, 371, 372*n*, 402, 403
Yates, Richard (Gov. of Ill.): sends troops to St. Louis, 11*n*, 12*n*; letter to, Sept. 14, 1862, 45; commissions surgeon, 45, 46*n*; letter to, Oct. 4, 1862, 116; promotions recommended to, 116, 228*n*, 296*n*, 427, 438, 439, 442, 452; sends troops to USG, 125*n*, 197*n*, 243*n*; endorsement to, Nov. 24, 1862, 228*n*; telegram to, Nov. 9, 1862, 296*n*; endorsement to, Sept. 23, 1862, 427; endorsements to, Oct. 16, 1862 (2), 438; endorsement to, Oct. 21, 1862, 439; endorsement to, Oct. 26, 1862, 442; endorsement to, Nov. 18, 1862, 452
Yazoo City, Miss., 411*n*
Yazoo River (Miss.): falsely reported threatened, 5*n*; planned expedition to, 59–60, 67, 68*n*, 93, 93*n*–94*n*, 95, 200, 264*n*, 341*n*, 346, 372*n*, 390 and *n*, 403, 406*n*, 408, 410*n*, 411*n*; located, 60*n*; fortifications on, 255*n*, 410*n*; cotton near, 312*n*
Yeatman, Thomas H. (U.S. Treasury Dept.), 453
Yocona River (Miss.), 371, 372*n*, 386 and *n*, 390, 401*n*
York, Thomas (citizen), 90*n*
Young, J. Morris (Iowa Vols.), 435
Young's Bridge, Miss., 97*n*, 100*n*, 101*n*